Frontier Regulars
1866-1891

Frontier Regulars

THE UNITED STATES ARMY
AND THE INDIAN

☆ 1866-1891 ☆

by ROBERT M. UTLEY

University of Nebraska Press
Lincoln and London

First Bison Book printing: September 1984
Most recent printing indicated by the first digit below:
5   6   7   8   9   10

Library of Congress Cataloging in Publication Data
Utley, Robert Marshall, 1929–
   Frontier regulars.
   Reprint. Originally published: New York : Macmillan,
c1973.
   Bibliography: p.
   Includes index.
   1. Indians of North America—Wars—1866–1895. 2. United
States. Army—History. 3. West (U.S.)—History—1848–
1950. 4. United States. Army—Military life—History—
19th century. I. Title.
[E83.866.U87 1984]   973.8   84-7484
ISBN 0-8032-9551-0 (pbk.)

∞

Reprinted by arrangement with Macmillan Publishing Company, Inc.

☆ CONTENTS ☆

☆ LIST OF MAPS ☆

ERRATA

p. 25, l. 28:	Merrit *should be* Merritt
p. 112, l. 31:	restored *should be* resorted
p. 116, l. 6:	eleven troops *should be* eight troops
p. 118, l. 29:	May 2 *should be* May 3
p. 120, l. 17:	August 22–23 *should be* August 21–22
p. 132, l. 23:	Department of Dakota, not *the* Dakota
p. 150, l. 9:	Kansas *should be* Kansans
p. 155, l. 33:	three chiefs *should be* four
p. 181, l. 2:	has *should be* had
p. 193, l. 37:	Freedman's *should be* Freedmen's
p. 296, l. 19:	Same
p. 194, l. 32:	Cohise's *should be* Cochise's
p. 205, l. 23:	June 3 *should be* June 1
p. 213, l. 27:	wtih *should be* with
p. 230, ll. 20, 24:	Henely *should be* Heneley
p. 241, l. 21:	Nabraska *should be* Nebraska
p. 246, l. 24:	Serman *should be* Sherman
pp. 253–54:	John S. Gray, Centennial Campaign, *makes a persuasive case for fewer Indians than given here.*
p. 260, l. 7:	trumpeter orderly *should be* orderly trumpeter
p. 268, l. 19:	Bonnett *should be* Bonnet
p. 303, l. 9:	on *should be* of
p. 315, l. 10:	Wallowa Valley
p. 323, l. 14:	subsitute *should be* substitute
p. 326, l. 10:	trial *should be* trail
p. 327, l. 11:	Piautes *should be* Paiutes
p. 335, l. 21:	Chief Douglas *should be* Chief Johnson
p. 351, l. 16:	Zargosa *should be* Zaragosa
p. 362, l. 14:	May 23 *should be* May 24
p. 364, l. 2:	1,000 *should be* 350
p. 364, ll. 13–18:	*should read* "trapped Victorio amid three peaks called Tres Castillos." *Dead Indians numbered 62. Who fired fatal bullet not known.*
p. 377, l. 29:	guage *should be* gauge
p. 380, l. 4:	Benito *should be* Bonito
p. 389, l. 14:	bed *should be* bend
p. 407, l. 28:	At *should be* as

Introduction

IN A PREVIOUS volume of this series, I sketched the story of the
handful of blue-clad frontiersmen who contended with the Indian tribes of the trans-Mississippi West in the years between the
Mexican War and the Civil War.[1] I also dealt with the Volunteers
who replaced the Regulars during the Civil War years and who
on almost every front stepped up the scale and effectiveness of
warfare against the Indians. In the present volume my subject is
the Regular Army that took up the task after Appomattox and
carried the Indian Wars to their tragic and bloody conclusion at
Wounded Knee Creek in 1890.

The frontier Regulars saw themselves as the advance guard of
civilization, sweeping aside the savage to make way for the stock-
man, the miner, the farmer, and the merchant. This stereotype is
evident in the writings of officers such as Nelson A. Miles, George
A. Custer, George A. Forsyth, John G. Bourke, George F. Price,
T. F. Rodenbough, James Parker, and William H. and Robert G.
Carter; of officers' wives such as Mrs. Custer, Mrs. Biddle, Mrs.
Summerhayes, and Mrs. Boyd; and of friendly newsmen such as
John F. Finerty. It is to be glimpsed in the art of Frederic Remington and Charles Schreyvogel. Above all, it is to be credited to Captain Charles King, who in dozens of novels reinforced the army's
view of itself. King summed it up years later in an address to Indian War veterans:

It is all a memory now, but what a memory, to cherish! . . . A more
thankless task, a more perilous service, a more exacting test of leadership, morale and discipline no army in Christendom has ever been

called upon to undertake than that which for eighty years was the lot of the little fighting force of Regulars who cleared the way across the continent for the emigrant and settler.[2]

Others saw the Regulars in a different light. Eastern humanitarians assailed them as butchers, rampaging around the West gleefully slaughtering peaceable Indians and taking special delight in shooting down women and children. Antislavery leaders such as Wendell Phillips and William Lloyd Garrison turned energies liberated by the Emancipation Proclamation to a crusade in behalf of the red men, and the army felt the sting of rhetoric sharpened in the long war against the slavocracy. "I only know the names of three savages upon the Plains," declared Phillips in 1870, "—Colonel Baker, General Custer, and at the head of all, General Sheridan." Baker's assault on a Piegan village in 1870 inspired a verse that typified the humanitarian stereotype of the army:

> Women and babes shrieking awoke
> To perish 'mid the battle smoke,
> Murdered, or turned out there to die
> Beneath the stern, gray, wintry sky.[3]

Until recent years, the heroic stereotype of the frontier army dominated the collective memory of Americans. It found its most vivid expression in the motion pictures of John Ford and the characterizations of John Wayne. Today, however, a nation increasingly troubled by its historic treatment of the Indians has substituted the ugly for the heroic stereotype. In great quantities of popular literature, in television productions, and in motion pictures such as *Little Big Man* and *Soldier Blue*, the frontier Regulars are depicted as the nineteenth-century humanitarians saw them.

Each of the stereotypes contains some small truths and some large untruths. Just as campaigning troopers sported both black hats and white hats—and any other hue that suited their fancy—so a fair appraisal of the Indian-fighting army must acknowledge a mix of wisdom and stupidity, humanity and barbarism, selfless dedication and mindless indifference, achievement and failure, triumph and tragedy; but above all, as in most human institutions, of contradictions and ambiguities. I hope that in the following pages the frontier Regulars emerge in a characterization that strikes a truthful balance between the two stereotypes.

An expression of gratitude is due the following people for reading all or part of the manuscript or for other helpful kindnesses: Louis Morton of Dartmouth College, editor of the series in which this volume appears; Francis Paul Prucha of Marquette University; Harry H. Anderson of the Milwaukee County Historical Society; Robert Murray, Gordon Chappell, and Verne Ray; Andrew Wallace of Northern Arizona University; Donald J. Berthrong of Purdue University; James S. Hutchins of the Smithsonian Institution; Sidney B. Brinckerhoff of the Arizona Historical Society; and my colleagues in the National Park Service, Franklin G. Smith, Merrill J. Mattes, Roy E. Appleman, Erwin N. Thompson, John D. McDermott, Edwin C. Bearss, and Albert H. Schroeder. Special thanks go to Walter T. Vitous of Olympia, Washington, for the maps.

ROBERT M. UTLEY

Washington, D.C.
December 1972

NOTES

1. *Frontiersmen in Blue: The United States Army and the Indian, 1848–1865* (New York, 1967).
2. Quoted in Robert G. Carter, *On the Border with Mackenzie* (1935; reprint, 1961), pp. 46–47.
3. Both quotations are in Robert Winston Mardock, *The Reformers and the American Indian* (Columbia, Mo., 1971), p. 69.

Frontier Regulars
1866-1891

ONE

Return to the Frontier

Maj. Gen. William Tecumseh Sherman passed the winter of 1865–66 in St. Louis, headquarters of his first postwar command. Seven years earlier the fortunes of the blunt eccentric had reached new depths in a shabby law office in Leavenworth, Kansas. Only four years earlier his sanity had been widely questioned. Now, at forty-six, he was the hero of Atlanta and the already legendary March to the Sea, the nation's second soldier, surpassed in popular esteem only by Ulysses S. Grant, and the ruler of a military domain sweeping west from the Mississippi River to the crest of the Rocky Mountains and north from Texas to the British possessions.

The physical and emotional toll of four years of war showed plainly in Sherman's face. Gray flecked his unruly red hair and beard. Seams furrowed his high forehead and cheekbones and pulled at eyes whose faintly wild cast betrayed his nervous temperament. An awesome command presence born of wartime triumphs prompted almost instant deference, even from those of the highest station. Even so, his stature did not insure universal admiration. Quick of mind, fiercely independent of thought, uninhibited and articulate in expressions of opinion, disdainful of political and social imperatives, he effortlessly offended anyone who annoyed or inconvenienced him. With his family he enjoyed a warm if occasionally strained relationship. With his wartime comrades he repaid veneration with affection. With the Regulars of his new plains command he showed his pride in their achievements, his solicitude for their comfort, and his sympathy for their distress over the frustrations of Indian duty. In return, they accorded him loyalty and respect.[1]

Sherman approached his postwar duties with a zeal born of a love of the West and a vision of its destiny. He had served as a lieutenant in California after the Mexican War and later tried his hand at banking in San Francisco and the law in Kansas. Failure in these enterprises had not weakened his conviction that Americans must meet the West's challenge, populate its vast reaches, develop its rich potential, and make it a viable part of the Republic.[2]

The Union's ordeal resolved by four years of bloodletting, the West once more exerted its magnetism on the American imagination. In none did the lure of the frontier kindle more enthusiasm than the restless Sherman. A St. Louis office could not contain him during a summer in which a hundred thousand countrymen, energized, emboldened, and freed from narrow concerns by the war, were expected to push up the Arkansas, the Smoky Hill, the Platte, and the Missouri in search of new opportunities in the West. Early in the season he made a swing along the eastern margin of the Great Plains. Late in the summer, accompanied by his brother John, U.S. Senator from Ohio, he journeyed up the Platte as far as Fort Laramie, visited Denver, and crossed the Rockies to Fort Garland, then returned down the Smoky Hill. Everywhere his observations reinforced his conviction that the army would have a large role to play in the postwar West.[3]

What Sherman saw were multitudes of emigrants pouring westward on the Oregon-California Trail, the Santa Fe Trail, and the Smoky Hill Trail. Their wagons mingled with freight trains laden with merchandise and with stagecoaches hurrying passengers and mail to the growing cities of the Rockies, the Southwest, the Great Basin, and the Pacific Slope. Many eagerly sought wealth in the new mineral districts opened during the war years in Montana, Idaho, and Arizona, or in the older ones of California, Nevada, and Colorado. Others sought the free land offered by the Homestead Act of 1862. Still others were attracted by the commercial or political opportunities of a growing country. The surge of migration would add a million citizens to the census rolls of the western states and territories between 1860 and 1870 and another two and one-half million by 1880.[4]

Equally portentous to one who had known the prewar West

were the twin bands of iron fingering westward from the Missouri River in Kansas and Nebraska. When Sherman began his late-summer trip in August, the Union Pacific's Eastern Division (later the Kansas Pacific) had reached Manhattan, Kansas, 115 miles from the Missouri, and would be at Fort Riley in another month. Farther north, the general and his brother rode the main line of the Union Pacific from Omaha almost to Fort Kearny, 194 miles, before taking to ambulances for the journey up the Platte to Fort Laramie.[5] Almost two thousand miles of plains, mountains, and deserts separated the Missouri from the Pacific. But Sherman's recent comrade-in-arms, Grenville Dodge, the Union Pacific's chief engineer, gave every evidence of narrowing the gap in record time, while at the California end of the route Central Pacific labor gangs tore at the summit of the Sierra Nevada.

Sherman clearly perceived the profound military implications of the railroads. Furthermore, he needed no gift of prophecy to foresee the enormous influence they would exert on the settlement and economic and political development of the West. Finally, no less clearly did he understand the meaning for the Indian, and thus for the army, of the scenes that unfolded before him in August and September 1866.

Twenty-five years of intermittent warfare had obliterated or crushed many of the tribes that stood athwart the westward movement. The unconquered tribes were nomadic or seminomadic. They needed a great deal of country, and the resources it contained, to sustain their way of life. Already, perhaps ten times as many whites as Indians peopled the West, and hundreds of thousands more were coming. Where they passed and where they settled, the Indians found no welcome. Buffalo and other game and food supplies diminished. The timber that served as firewood and the grass that furnished forage grew scarce along the white man's roads and vanished altogether around the white man's settlements. The territory in which the Indian could roam undisturbed contracted.

Sherman saw it happening to the Sioux and Northern Cheyennes in 1866. Formerly they had ranged the Great Plains from the Arkansas to the upper Missouri. Then the California and Oregon migrations of the 1840s and 1850s sliced across their domain and they were shouldered northward from the Platte. Next came pressures from Minnesota and Dakota that crowded them westward from the Missouri. Finally, the gold strikes in Colorado, Idaho, and Montana raised barriers to the west.

"The poor Indian finds himself hemmed in," declared Sherman.[6] In the Congress Senator Lot Morrill of Maine stated the same conclusion: "As population has approached the Indian we have removed him beyond population. But population now encounters him on both sides of the continent, and there is no place on the continent to which he can be removed beyond the progress of population."[7]

The story was the same everywhere—on the southern Plains, where the Texas frontier and the road up the Arkansas limited the range of Kiowas, Comanches, and Southern Cheyennes; in the Southwest, where Apaches eked out a bare subsistence from a desert land filling with gold-seekers; and in Montana, Idaho, and eastern Oregon, where miners overran the mountain-and-plateau homeland of Flatheads, Blackfeet, Nez Percés, Bannocks, and Paiutes. In Idaho and Arizona hostilities already proclaimed the Indian's determination to resist the invasion. On the Great Plains, scene of massive campaigns in the closing years of the Civil War, Sherman could find no Indian threat that did not vanish as he neared its reported source; yet he discerned "a general apprehension of danger." "There is a universal feeling of mistrust on both sides," he added, "and this will sooner or later result in a general outbreak."[8]

Sherman had witnessed the opening of the final act of the frontier drama. Back in St. Louis by late October, he looked to the future certain in the knowledge that for some time to come the destinies of the army and the Indian were to be interlocked in the American West.

By no means all the Indians inhabiting the American West in 1866 were prospective opponents of the frontier army. The government counted some 270,000 people in 125 distinct groups plus an assortment of "other Indians," "other bands," and "etceteras."[9] Some of these, such as the Pueblos of the Southwest and the Crows of Montana, had chosen to accommodate peacefully to the American presence. Others, such as the Navajos of Arizona and New Mexico and coastal groups of the Pacific Northwest, had fought the whites in earlier times and had lost. Still others, terrorized by more powerful tribes and decimated by the white man's diseases and vices, had never gathered the strength to fight. In 1866 only a handful of tribes retained the power and will to contest the westward movement. On the Great Plains they were the Sioux, Cheyenne, Arapaho, Kiowa, and Comanche. In the Rocky Mountains they were the Nez Percé, Ute, and Bannock. In the Northwest they were the Paiute and Modoc. And in the Southwest they were the Apache. Totaling less than one hundred thousand people, these "hostile" Indians engaged the United States in the final struggle for the American West.

Culturally, the tribes differed markedly from one another. They spoke different languages, were organized according to different political and social forms, and worshipped different deities. The Plains people were highly mobile, counting wealth in great pony herds that enabled them to range over vast distances in pursuit of the buffalo. They hunted other game, too, but from the buffalo they satisfied almost all their needs—food, shelter, clothing, utensils. By contrast, the desert and plateau dwellers were less mobile, lived in brush lodges, traveled largely on foot, subsisted on small game and nuts, and sometimes planted crops. The mountain tribes imbibed of influences from both the Plains and plateau groups and developed special characteristics of their own as well. Religion, though varying in content and form from tribe to tribe, was pervasive, controlling, and ordered almost entirely by the phenomena of nature.

Despite cultural diversity, the tribes shared certain characteristics that had important military implications. One was this very diversity. People accorded their allegiance to the family, band, and tribe, and only vaguely if at all to the race. They viewed themselves not as Indians but as Sioux or Nez Percé or Apache. They fought one another more often and more violently than they fought the whites. Alliances sometimes brought them together against an enemy, red or white, but not for long. Never did the perception of a fatal threat to the race overcome the traditional rivalry and particularism of tribes to inspire Indian resistance rather than simply tribal resistance.

Another common strand was a highly democratic political structure. Whatever the precise form of tribal organization, authority usually resided in many leaders instead of few. Decisions affecting a tribe had to be made by a tribal council or similar governing organ that brought together many representatives of the people.

Occasionally leaders of great personal stature emerged, but they almost always expressed their influence through the established system. With so many voices of authority, and those sharply limited, decisions came hard or not at all. On large questions of peace and war, tribes often fractionated, with bands and even families pursuing separate courses. Also, because it was never understood by white officialdom, this system created constant confusion and misunderstanding in dealings with the white world; government authorities invariably regarded a "chief" as an absolute ruler and his promises as binding on his people.

The tribes also shared a long history of warfare and, accordingly, well-developed military traditions and institutions. Above all else, society rewarded the successful warrior. He fought principally for the honors of war, both individual and group, for plunder and revenge, and for defense of home and family against the aggressions of enemy warriors similarly motivated. This war complex largely governed hostilities with whites as well as other Indians. Whites offered opportunities for plunder and honor and sometimes presented a threat to home and family that required defensive action or retaliation. Actually, in the two decades after 1866 the threat was far more grave. At stake were no less than homeland, subsistence, and way of life. Yet only dimly, if at all, did the Indians perceive their final wars with the whites in these apocalyptic terms rather than the traditional terms of glory, plunder, and revenge.

Exalting war, Indian culture produced a superb warrior. From childhood he received intensive training and indoctrination. Courage, physical strength and endurance, stealth, cunning, horsemanship, and mastery of bow and arrow, lance, and knife marked his fighting qualities. With firearms he attained less skill, but as growing numbers of breech-loading, metallic-cartridge weapons, including repeaters, fell into his hands, he achieved a firepower that made him much more formidable than his forebears. He excelled at guerrilla warfare—at hit-and-run raids, at harassment, at exploitation of the environment for his own advantage and the enemy's disadvantage. Except when surprised or his family endangered, he fought only on his own terms, when success seemed certain. Man for man, the Indian warrior far surpassed his blue-clad adversary in virtually every test of military proficiency.

The war complex, rewarding individual exploits, did not encourage teamwork. A war chief or leader of a war party did not "command." He led through personal influence. Warriors followed his direction only as it suited their inclination. Team discipline often collapsed when opportunities for personal distinction presented themselves. With superior discipline and organization, therefore, a military unit could usually win an open contest with an equal or larger force of warriors. Such contests were rare, however, because Indians rarely allowed themselves to be drawn into open combat.

By 1866, even though the United States continued to define its Indian relations in treaties, none of the tribes more than remotely resembled the independent sovereignties, masters of their own destiny, implied by the practice. Almost all had treaties with the United States government and agencies at which they drew such issues of goods, and perhaps rations, as were prescribed by treaty. Some tribes had fallen or been forced into virtually total dependence on the government and lived continuously near the agency. Others, not yet dependent, visited their agency periodically. A few broke into "friendly" and "hostile" factions, with the former embracing the agency and the latter, except for infrequent visits, holding aloof. Finally, a small handful of tribes or bands proudly disdained all association with whites. But even they had become accustomed to such useful items of white manufacture as firearms and metal implements and utensils, obtained through less isolationist intermediaries.

The government organization charged with the conduct of Indian relations was the Bureau of Indian Affairs, a component of the Department of the Interior. The bureau's field service manned the agencies. In 1866, in the trans-Mississippi West, there were sixty-one agencies grouped in fourteen superintendencies. Presenting attractive opportunities for profiteering at Indian expense, the bureau had become badly tainted by corruption and a victim, too, of patronage politics. Agents had the reputation, often deserved, of being party hacks in quest of a quick fortune in the West and retirement to a more congenial clime. Few, whatever their honesty, possessed qualifications for the difficult task of dealing with Indians.

"It has been the settled policy of the government," wrote the Secretary of the Interior in 1866, "to establish the various tribes upon suitable reservations and there protect and subsist them until

they can be taught to cultivate the soil and sustain themselves."[10]
This goal, of course, was actually only a means to a larger goal:
to remove the Indians from the paths of westward expansion and
—a consoling legalism—to extinguish Indian "title" to lands on
which whites wanted to settle.

The policy was not wholly cynical. Americans—at least those
comfortably distant from the frontier—felt genuine sympathy for
the Indian and demanded that government policy be grounded in
humanity. Policy makers correctly perceived that, whatever the
morality, westering emigrants would not be denied the Indians'
land if it held mineral or agricultural potential. The Indians' survival depended on moving them out of the way. How much better
if they could also be given the great gift of the white man's civilization and be transformed into self-sufficient citizens. This policy,
concluded the Secretary, "is no doubt the best, if not the only
policy that can be pursued to preserve them from extinction." So
far, it had proved highly successful in separating the Indian from
his homeland but not notably so in transforming him into a
white man.

Behind the Indian Bureau—indeed, sometimes in front of it—
stood the U.S. Army. The army had fought and counseled with
Indians since the beginning of the republic. It had followed the Indian frontier over the Appalachian Mountains, across the prairies
and woodlands of the continent's heartland, and finally to the
plains, mountains, and deserts of the trans-Mississippi West. Now,
as the Indian frontier found no further territory in which to recede,
the army prepared to play its part in the final extinction of the
Indian's freedom.

General Sherman's inspection tour gave him fresh understanding of the crisis confronting the western tribes in 1866. On occasion their plight moved him to sympathy. Far more engaging,
however, was the great work of tapping the resources of the West
and peopling it with white Americans. The excitement of advancing the frontier, of subduing the wilderness, of bringing civilization to virgin territories, gripped him no less than his countrymen.
Where the Indians interfered with the process, they had to be
crushed. With the fraud, deceit, injustice, and debauchery visited
on the submissive or the conquered, he had no patience; but this
could be blamed on Indian agents and traders. The soldier's task
lay with the unsubmissive, those who resisted the ordained open-

ing of the West. This task he approached with an enthusiasm
and a fixity of purpose uncomplicated by sentiment.

NOTES

1. There are many biographies of Sherman. The best is Lloyd Lewis, *Sherman: Fighting Prophet* (New York, 1932).
2. Robert G. Athearn, *Willian Tecumseh Sherman and the Settlement of the West* (Norman, Okla., 1956), pp. 4–5 and *passim*.
3. These travels are chronicled in *ibid.*, chaps. 1–6. Sherman's letters from the West are in House Ex. Docs., 39th Cong., 2d sess., No. 23.
4. Included are all states and territories west of the tier anchored by Minnesota on the north and Louisiana on the south. Population rose from 1.3 million in 1860 to 2.3 million in 1870 and to 4.9 million in 1880.
5. Athearn, p. 56.
6. House Ex. Docs., 39th Cong., 2d sess., No. 23, p. 10.
7. *Cong. Globe*, 40th Cong., 1st sess., p. 672 (July 16, 1867).
8. House Ex Docs., 39th Cong., 2d sess., No. 23, pp. 7, 11.
9. Commissioner of Indian Affairs (hereafter CIA), *Annual Report* (1866), pp. 370–72.
10. *Ibid.*, p. i.

TWO

The Postwar Army:
Command, Staff, and Line

DURING THE EARLY MONTHS OF 1866, as General Sherman
poured over his maps and impatiently plotted his summer's
tour, Congress debated long hours over the size and shape of the
postwar Regular Army. Radicals bent on harsh treatment of
the conquered South demanded a large army to further their plans
for Reconstruction. So did western representatives attuned to the
needs of the frontier. Supporters of the mild southern policies of
President Andrew Johnson joined with guardians of the federal
budget to resist a large peacetime army.[1] General Grant urged an
army of 80,000. Secretary of War Edwin M. Stanton was willing
to settle for one of 50,000.[2]

Members argued long hours over whether Negro soldiers, who
had performed well in the volunteer service during the war,
should be incorporated into the Regular Army. Sen. James A. Mc-
Dougall of California expressed a strong minority opinion when
he declared that "this undertaking to place a lower, inferior, different race upon a level with the white man's race, in arms, is against
the laws that lie at the foundation of true republicanism."[3] But
Sen. Henry Lane of Indiana touched a more responsive chord by
pointing out that a constitutional amendment had just made Ne-
groes American citizens. It was academic whether military service
was a burden or a privilege. "If it is either, the colored people are
equally bound to bear the burden or equally entitled to participate
in the privilege."[4]

The Senate passed its own version of a military bill early in the
session, but the House withheld agreement. A flurry of bills ema-

nating from the military committees of both houses recorded every
viewpoint and carried the debates through the spring and into the
summer.

The delay worried General Grant. Demobilization had begun
promptly after the Confederate surrender. By the late spring of
1866, almost a million volunteers had been mustered out of the
service. The Regular Army, last reorganized in 1861, had retained
its separate identity during the war; but by 1865, because of the
superior attractions of the volunteer regiments, it had dwindled to
a mere skeleton. Although recruited to more than 30,000 men by
mid-1866, the Regular Army hardly sufficed to meet the demands
deluging Grant from the West and South while Congress debated.[5]

Finally, on July 28, 1866, President Johnson signed the "Act
to increase and fix the Military Peace Establishment of the United
States."[6] In the army line, the law increased the cavalry from six
to ten regiments and the infantry from nineteen to forty-five regiments. The artillery remained at five regiments. Enlistments were
set at five years for the cavalry, three for the infantry. Up to one
thousand Indian scouts were authorized as needed on the frontier.
Two cavalry and four infantry regiments were to be composed of
black enlisted men and white officers, and wounded officers and
soldiers were to make up four infantry regiments known as the
Veteran Reserve Corps.[7]

Cavalry regiments numbered twelve companies (or troops)
each, artillery regiments twelve companies (or batteries) each,
and infantry regiments ten companies. Each regiment was commanded by a colonel, backed by a lieutenant colonel. To permit a
three-battalion (or squadron) employment, cavalry regiments
rated three majors. So did artillery. The smaller infantry regiments had only one major. Companies were commanded by a captain, assisted by a first lieutenant and a second lieutenant.[8]

The War Department staff, as defined by the act of 1866, consisted of ten administrative and technical bureaus, officially called
departments or corps: the Adjutant General's Department, the
medium of orders and commands and the custodian of records and
archives; the Inspector General's Department, charged with inspecting and reporting on the proficiency, discipline, and leadership of the Army, together with its arms, accouterments, clothing,
quarters, and other matériel; the Judge Advocate General's De-

partment (or Bureau of Military Justice), reviewing authority for
military courts and source of legal advice for the Secretary of
War; the Quartermaster's Department, responsible for barracks
and quarters, transportation of personnel and matériel, and procurement and distribution of most classes of supplies; the Subsistence Department, responsible for the content, procurement, and
distribution of rations; the Medical Department, custodian of the
health and hygiene of the army; the Pay Department, whose paymasters traveled endlessly to distribute the soldiers' wages; the
Corps of Engineers, charged with mapping and construction; the
Ordnance Department, responsible for testing, selecting, procur-
ing or manufacturing, and distributing arms, ammunition, and all
related accouterments and equipment; and the Signal Corps, the
infant service concerned with communication, particularly flags,
torches, and telegraph.[9]

The army line would be led in part by regular officers and in
part by former volunteer officers given regular army appointments.[10] A separate act had revived the grade of general, dormant
since George Washington's death.[11] Grant sewed on four stars,
while his three as lieutenant general fell to Sherman. The army
act provided, in addition, for five major generals and ten brigadier
generals of the line. The staff departments were to be headed by
brigadier generals, but the Inspector General and the Chief Signal
Officer were to be colonels.

The law did not specify a numerical strength for the army but
instead incorporated the principle of expansible units fathered by
Secretary of War John C. Calhoun nearly half a century earlier.
Companies could be varied from 50 to 100 privates at the President's discretion. When the War Department fixed company
strength at 64 privates, the total paper strength of the army, both
staff and line, thus became 54,302 officers and enlisted men.

An army of 54,000 seemed much more responsive to western
needs than the prewar army of 18,000. Now, however, the opening of new areas to settlement and the launching of the transcontinental railroad had dramatically enlarged western needs. Now,
too, Reconstruction duties would absorb up to one-third of available manpower. In 1867 the President offset some of the negative
consequences of these factors by authorizing one hundred privates
to companies on the frontier. This permitted a peak strength of
56,815 in September 1867.[12] But thereafter erosion set in.

In the officer corps, the problem was not to recruit but to sort out competing claims for the limited vacancies. Regular officers who had held high rank in the Volunteers reverted to their regular grades or scrambled for higher ones in the new regiments. Volunteers aspiring to a regular army career applied for the vacancies apportioned them by the army act. Generals became colonels, majors, and sometimes even captains, while colonels and majors found themselves lieutenants.

All contended for the brevet grades being generously doled out in recognition of wartime services. Rare was the veteran who could not boast brevets several levels above actual rank; most of the regimental commanders, colonel by actual rank, could be addressed as general, and not a few company commanders, captain by actual rank, cherished brevets of colonel or even general. Brevet appointments were not mere empty honors. Officers could be assigned to commands according to brevet rank. And in the first few years after the war they received such assignments with a frequency that amounted to abuse and that finally called forth reform.[13]

In the quest for preferment, whether regular or brevet, candidates marshalled support wherever it could be found, and appointments owed as much to influence of highly placed friends, military or political, as to the professional qualifications of the appointee.

Meanwhile, a new system of geographical commands, similar to the prewar system, was organized. The West fell into two military divisions, separated roughly by the continental divide. Sherman, now lieutenant general, headed the Division of the Missouri from his St. Louis headquarters, while Maj. Gen. Henry W. Halleck—"Old Brains"—commanded the Division of the Pacific from San Francisco.

The divisions in turn were divided into military departments. In the Division of the Missouri, General Sherman judged the huge plains department run by Gen. John Pope for almost a year to be too unwieldly and broke it into three departments. Maj. Gen. Winfield Scott Hancock took over the Department of the Missouri (Missouri, Kansas, Colorado, and New Mexico), Bvt. Maj. Gen. Philip St. George Cooke the Department of the Platte (Iowa, Nebraska, Utah, and part of Dakota and Montana), and Bvt. Maj. Gen. Alfred H. Terry the Department of Dakota (Minnesota and the rest of Dakota and Montana). Indian Territory also came within Sherman's division as part of the Department of Arkansas, commanded by Bvt. Maj. Gen. Edward O. C. Ord. Texas, where Reconstruction was to overshadow frontier defense for several years, fell within the Department of the Gulf, which was not part of Sherman's division. In Halleck's Pacific Division, Bvt. Maj. Gen. Irvin McDowell headed the Department of California (California, Nevada, and Arizona) and Bvt. Maj. Gen. Frederick Steele the Department of the Columbia (Oregon, Washington, and Idaho).[14]

By the end of 1866 the Regular Army authorized by the act of July 28 had been largely created and had been posted to the South and West to relieve the Volunteers. In a sense this new Regular Army became two armies, one serving the Congress in the Reconstruction South, the other serving the Executive in the frontier West. Although personnel and units moved easily between the two armies, only in Texas, where frontier and South merged, did they overlap. But for a decade the fortunes of each of these armies importantly influenced the fate of the other.

The act of 1866 laid the foundation for the postwar Regular Army. The forces assembled under this law fought the plains wars of 1866–69, fanned out to guard the Texas frontier, contended ineffectually with Apaches in the Southwest, and defeated the Paiutes of Oregon and Idaho. Then, in 1869, the accession of Ulysses S. Grant to the Presidency and still another army act gave the Regular Army a new leadership and a new and leaner shape.

For General Sherman, the election of Grant to the Presidency meant "the dreaded banishment to Washington."[15] Dutifully but unhappily he moved from St. Louis to his new residence and affixed to his uniform the four-starred shoulder straps shed by his friend. Sherman hated Washington politics and bureaucracy. Tactless, uncompromising, impatient, he never became accommodated to the terms of official life in the capital. His failure to adjust cost the army badly needed political support during a period of declining fortunes and made his term of office, 1869–83, a constant personal frustration. At the same time, as Russell Weigley has noted, Sherman was "one of the most cerebral and innovative" commanding generals in the army's history.[16] Through his dedi-

cation to professionalism, his fierce rejection of political entangle-
ments, his forceful personality, and his hold on the affections of
rank and file alike, he stamped the army with his character and
made it peculiarly his own. Even beyond his own time, through
Philip H. Sheridan (1883–88) and John Schofield (1888–95),
in spirit and tone the U.S. Army remained distinctively "Sherman's
Army."[17]

Sherman's arrival in Washington coincided with the first of a
succession of cutbacks that severely weakened the army line. The
reductions came as part of a broader attack in Congress on the
army that persisted for a decade and that was motivated by economy, political partisanship, and hostility to such domestic uses of
the Regulars as policing elections and quelling labor riots (see
Chapter Four).

The army appropriation act of March 3, 1869, cut the number
of infantry regiments from forty-five to twenty-five and limited the
line brigadiers to eight instead of ten. The act reduced the army
from the 54,000 maintained under the act of 1866 to 37,313.[18]
Again the following year, in July 1870, the army appropriation
act emerged from Congress laden with provisions of sweeping
scope. Included were abolition of the grades of general and lieutenant general when they were vacated by Sherman and Sheridan,
a reduction of major generals to three and brigadiers to six, and a
limit on enlisted men of 30,000.[19] Finally, beginning in 1874, the
annual army appropriation acts carried a proviso that prohibited
expenditure of funds to recruit the army beyond 25,000 enlisted
men—an army that with officers numbered just over 27,000.[20]

In five years Congress had cut the army by half. The enlisted
complement was reduced mainly by stopping enlistments until
attrition produced the result enjoined by law. But attrition could
not relieve the army of nearly 900 officers made surplus by the
series of laws. Although some officers resigned of their own voli-
tion, retiring boards and "Benzine Boards," the latter to identify
substandard officers, eliminated most of the surplus. For many
thus separated with a year's pay, the cuts worked great hardship
and sometimes injustice. But the Benzine Boards also rid the officer corps of many who were unfit to wear shoulder straps.[21]

The series of reductions imposed severe handicaps on the army
line. Engineers, ordnance, commissary, medical, quartermaster,
the Fort Leavenworth Prison guard, the West Point detachment,

and recruiting details absorbed three to four thousand men. Ten cavalry regiments, five artillery regiments, and twenty-five infantry regiments shared the balance. But because of the lag of casualties —discharge, death, desertion—behind replacement, actual strength always fell at least ten percent below authorized strength. Rarely, under the ceiling of 25,000, did the regimental rolls bear the names of more than 19,000 soldiers.[22]

The true measure of the cuts manifested itself at the company level. With 430 companies to man some 200 posts, the company and troop, rather than the regiment, was the basic tactical unit. Except for the reorganization of 1869, the reductions affected the number of men, not the number of units. Accordingly, with each reduction, the company shrank in numbers and efficiency. In the typical year of 1881, actual enlisted strength of the 120 cavalry troops averaged 58 (46 privates); of the 60 artillery companies and batteries, 40 (28 privates); and of the 250 infantry companies, 41 (29 privates). But the sick, imprisoned, detached, and detailed to daily and extra duty made further inroads. Fortunate was the company commander who could actually muster three-fourths of the men carried on his rolls.[23]

Such "companies are almost ridiculous," commented General Sherman, "compelling commanding officers to group two and even four companies together to perform the work of one."[24] An officer of the black Twenty-fourth Infantry, a perenially understrength regiment, testified in 1876 that the largest company in the regiment mustered seven soldiers fit for duty. "It is rather stupid work for an officer to go out and drill four men," he said, but he had done it often. Moreover, "I have seen a captain go on parade with only his sergeant, the captain forming the front line and the sergeant the rear."[25] Colonel John Gibbon fought the Battle of the Big Hole in 1877 with six companies of the Seventh Infantry numbering 15 officers and 146 enlisted men, or about 24 men per company, and sustained a costly reverse.[26]

The infantry suffered acutely. Infantry regiments were allowed but ten companies each, as compared with twelve for cavalry and artillery. In addition, authorized company strength was lower. To compound the inequity, in 1876, because of the Custer disaster and particularly troubled conditions on the Rio Grande frontier, Congress authorized an additional 2,500 enlisted men to bring cavalry troops to 100. The expansion was temporary, until the emergency subsided, but the return to 25,000 was not to be effected at the expense of the cavalry. As a result, a ceiling of 37 soldiers per company was imposed on the infantry, which usually meant less than 25 men for duty.[27]

Officers, too, despite the political rhetoric about a superabundance, were scarce in the field. Detached service and sick and ordinary leave kept the companies constantly under-officered. "I am captain of Company D," testified an officer of the Third Cavalry in 1876; "I am absent on sick-leave; my first lieutenant is absent on recruiting service; my second lieutenant is an aide-de-camp to General Crook, and there is not an officer on duty with the company."[28] The following year Col. Wesley Merritt counted only one of his twelve first lieutenants on duty with the Fifth Cavalry.[29] The Seventh Cavalry went into the Battle of the Little Bighorn with fifteen of its forty-three officers absent, including the colonel, two majors, and four captains.[30]

The Army had indeed become a skeleton. And the skeleton, as General Schofield pointed out, was "very expensive in proportion to its effective strength." When trouble occurred, companies on the scene were too weak to handle it and had to be speedily reinforced from elsewhere.[31] Personnel costs dropped, but transportation costs soared. Aside from expense, the system heightened the danger to troops on the scene while awaiting reinforcements, and weakened defenses in areas from which the reinforcements were drawn. "The unavoidable result," concluded Col. Philippe Régis De Trobriand, "is that finally an excessive reduction of the Army becomes more expensive than would be its maintenance to a normal strength, and that it costs the people more to stop evils and repair damages than it would cost to prevent them."[32]

Military leaders countered the congressional injunction in several ways. First, they sought to throw off the arbitrary ceiling altogether and return to the expansible principle embedded in the army act of 1866. Under this principle, the army would routinely exist at whatever level Congress desired, but the President would be empowered to increase companies serving on the frontier to 100 men when in his judgment conditions warranted.[33] Other efforts centered on removing the annual proviso that kept the maximum level at 25,000 men instead of 30,000[34] and on having the limit apply only to the line, with the noncombatant force provided for separately.[35] Finally, since Congress remained adamant on the size of the army, most officers were prepared to accept fewer regiments in exchange for larger companies.[36] The reduction bills reported by the House military committee provided for fewer regiments, but the legislative maneuverings by which these measures became attached to appropriations bills eliminated this feature.[37]

The Regular Army officer corps created by the army act of 1866 was a mixture of West Point graduates and veterans of Civil War volunteer service. After the vacancies reserved for former Volunteers by the 1866 act had been filled, however, reduction of the army, combined with the necessity to absorb the annual crop of academy graduates, limited appointments from civil life and gradually raised the ratio of West Pointers to civil appointees. The rising percentage of West Pointers did not imply a rising West Point dominance of the officer corps. Civil appointees under the 1866 act claimed at least two years of wartime service, often in high grades, and as a class they performed fully as well on the frontier as the West Pointers. By the turn of the century, in fact, the army's top leadership was heavy with generals who owed their regular army commissions to Civil War volunteer service, among them Nelson A. Miles, William R. Shafter, Adna R. Chaffee, and Henry W. Lawton.

Army policy formulated in 1867 called for one-fourth of the vacancies in the grade of second lieutenant to be filled from the enlisted ranks.[38] An act of 1878 established machinery to open commissions to more enlisted men. This produced only twenty promotions in two years and by 1890 was pronounced a failure because it left the initial judgment to the company commander rather than providing an examination system.[39]

Even so, officers elevated from the ranks were fairly common. Most, veterans of Indian service in the 1850s, had won their commissions in the Civil War. Many claimed foreign origins, especially Irish and German. In 1874, for example, the *Army Register* carried 193 officers commissioned from the ranks, or about thirteen percent of the line leadership. Eighty-seven of these were of foreign birth. They were a tough, experienced, hard-drinking lot. Few rose above captain, and few survived into the 1880s, but while they lasted they imparted a distinctive tone to the frontier companies.

Typifying this class of officer was Capt. Thomas Byrne of the Twelfth Infantry. "Tommy Byrne was a fine old soldier, one who loved his profession and felt a great pride in his position," recalled an officer who knew him. "His one failing was an over-indulgence in alcohol which he strictly contended he took only as 'medicine,' for the '*neuralgy.*' "

Pay and promotion obsessed the officer corps and profoundly affected its attitudes and state of mind. Postwar pay scales fixed in 1870 granted company and field grade officers annual salaries ranging from $3,500 for a colonel to $1,400 for an infantry second lieutenant,[40] sums considerably less than those earned by men in comparable civilian positions.[41] Furthermore, expenses incurred in frequent changes of station, the high cost of goods on the frontier, and losses (fluctuating between twelve and forty percent) in converting currency into coin, the circulating medium on the frontier, made the pay even more inadequate.[42] Yet almost yearly a movement gathered in Congress to effect further reductions. The most serious occurred in 1876. Championing this effort, which would have cut infantry second lieutenants to $1,300, Rep. H. B. Banning gratuitously explained that "small salaries are best for young officers who know little of the real value of money. It teaches them to avoid extravagance and practice economy."[43] Worse than the low pay, testified Gen. Christopher C. Augur, "more wearing and trying—is the *annual apprehension*, inevitable as fate, which comes upon all, that the meager provisions they have barely been able to make for the comfort of their families and the education of their children may all be broken up by a reduction of their pay."[44]

Even more than pay, the promotion system badly damaged the officer corps. Through captain, promotion occurred according to seniority in the regiment, through colonel in the arm (i.e., cavalry, infantry, artillery), and through major general by presidential appointment. The shrinking army and the rigidity of the seniority rule stagnated promotion for three decades. An analysis in 1877 showed that a new second lieutenant could look forward to reaching the grade of major in twenty-four to twenty-six years and colonel in thirty-three to thirty-seven years.[45] Moreover, regimental promotion of company officers capriciously favored some and penalized others. In some regiments fortune shone on lieutenants by removing their elders, while in others the oldsters hung on year after year. John W. Summerhayes, whose wife wrote one of the classic accounts of military life on the frontier, fought through four years of the Civil War only to endure twenty-two years as a lieutenant before President Grover Cleveland, seeking to unlock promotion in the Eighth Infantry, appointed him a quartermaster captain.[46] Among first lieutenants of artillery, reported General Schofield in 1887, the term of service as second lieutenant varied from nine months to eleven years. Of two officers commissioned the same year, one led the other in seniority by ten years.[47]

One result of sluggish promotion was an aging officer corps. Officers advanced in age much faster than in rank. In 1866, regular army grades from lieutenant to general were filled with comparatively youthful veterans of the war. By 1886 they were twenty years older but not much higher in rank. Despite laws in 1870 and 1882 liberalizing retirement,[48] the officer corps grew overage in grade. In another decade, predicted the *Army and Navy Journal* in 1877, "there will not be one-fourth part of the present field officers in the Army physically capable of supporting the hardships of an active campaign. They will be wornout old men."[49] By 1890 Gen. O. O. Howard could declare that "almost all the captains of infantry and artillery are too old for duty involving marching on foot or even drill requiring continuous quick movements."[50]

"Nothing else does so much to dampen military ardor as the sense of hopeless justice in respect to promotion," declared General Schofield in 1887.[51] For years he and other thoughtful officers had advocated reform. Promotions should be by seniority in arm, they contended. Officers should be assigned to rather than commissioned in particular regiments—e.g., Anson Mills would be major, cavalry, rather than major, Ninth Cavalry. And at least in the lower grades, examinations for physical and professional fitness should precede promotion.[52] At last, in 1890, Congress enacted these reforms by decreeing promotion by arm and examinations for promotions through major.[53]

Frustrated in substantive advancement, officers exalted the honorary commissions they had won for Civil War services. But the liberal bestowal of brevet promotions at the close of the war, especially for meritorious staff duty far from the battlefields, cheapened the distinction. More than a thousand officers in 1869 boasted one or more brevets, and 138 of them claimed the brevet of major general.[54] Officers wore the uniform of their brevet grade, and in certain circumstances their brevet rank prevailed, even over an officer of superior regular rank. Confusion, uncertainty, and embarrassment resulted.[55] In 1869 and 1870 Congress moved to deflate the system by requiring officers to wear the uniform and insignia of their regular rather than brevet rank and to be addressed in orders and communications by their regular rank. All circumstances in which brevet took precedence over regular rank were eliminated except that of special presidential assignment, and even in this circumstance pay was to be according to regular rank. Another act specified that in the future brevets could be awarded only for distinguished conduct in the presence of the enemy.[56] Despite the law, military courtesy continued to demand the use of brevet distinctions in social and official intercourse and even in official documents.[57]

Although many high officers believed that the brevet system should be abolished altogether,[58] it was virtually the only means of recognizing battlefield heroism. Efforts to extend the brevet system to Indian warfare, however, encountered the opposition of Sen. John A. Logan, powerful chairman of the Senate Committee on Military Affairs. President Grant sent nominations to the Senate for confirmation, but Logan refused to report them from his committee. "I have opposed all the time brevetting men for making assaults on the Indians," he explained in 1876, "on the ground that the law recognizes brevets only in time of war for gallant conduct in the face of the enemy." Congress had not declared war on the Indians. "If the Senate will not recognize glory in Indian warfare," he asserted, "there will not be any glory in Indian warfare."[59] Finally, in 1890, Congress invited brevet nominations for Indian engagements since 1867, and the War Department, after careful study of the records, submitted 144 names for recognition.[60]

As officers aged without advancement, their initiative, energy, and impulse for self-improvement diminished. Their concerns narrowed. They fragmented into hostile factions—staff and line, infantry and cavalry, young and old, West Point and Volunteer, Civil War veteran and peacetime newcomer. They bickered incessantly over petty issues of precedence, real or imagined insults, and old wartime controversies. They preferred charges on the slightest provocation and consequently had to spend a preposterous share of their time on court-martial duty.[61] They exploited every possible political connection in the quest for preferment. It is true that the origins of military professionalism are found in this period. But it is also true that the parade ground of a two- or three-company post in the West defined the intellectual and professional horizons of most line officers in the postwar decades.

Nor did the enlisted complement rise above mediocrity. The army offered few incentives to attract recruits of high caliber. Pay ranged from $13 a month for privates to $22 for line sergeants.[62] On the frontier the paymaster arrived infrequently, and then paid in currency that had to be converted to specie at a discount.[63] Superior performance brought few rewards.[64] Most civilians looked upon soldiers with condescension if not contempt. Execrable living conditions and harsh discipline scarcely enhanced the attraction of the ranks. Not until the 1890s, after the Indian Wars, did reforms make military life more agreeable.

Gone, therefore, were the legions of fresh young men fired by a sense of mission to save the Union. The postwar regular ranks filled with recruits of a lower order of intelligence, physical fitness, and motivation. The *New York Sun*'s charge that "the Regular Army is composed of bummers, loafers, and foreign paupers"[65] was only partially accurate; there were other undesirables as well: criminals, brutes, perverts, and drunkards, to name a few. But there were also active youths seeking adventure, men of varying ability fleeing misfortune, and "foreign paupers" who turned out to be excellent soldiers. Moreover, in times of national depression such as followed the Panic of 1873, the quality of recruits rose notably if only temporarily. Nevertheless, as General Ord observed in 1872, while the government had developed a greatly improved rifle, "I rather think we have a much less intelligent soldier to handle it."[66]

The enlisted force represented widely varying social and economic backgrounds. Reflecting the location of the recruiting depots, however, it drew heavily on the urban poor. A scattering of skilled tradesmen could be found in most units, but unskilled laborers predominated. Of 7,734 enlistees in 1882, for example, 2,373 identified themselves as laborers, 838 as soldiers, and 668 as farmers. There were also substantial numbers of teamsters, clerks, bakers, and blacksmiths, but few claiming such occupations as architect, butcher, cabinetmaker, musician, or schoolteacher.[67] The average age of recruits ranged in the middle twenties.

THE POSTWAR ARMY: COMMAND, STAFF, AND LINE

Foreigners formed a conspicuous part of the Regular Army. A table compiled by the Adjutant General covering the years 1865 through 1874 showed half of all recruits to have been born in a foreign country. Ireland led, with more than twenty percent of the total. Germany followed, with twelve percent. Much opinion held that the American Army should contain more Americans; the Inspector General, for example, in 1888 labeled the percentage of foreigners a "mortifying spectacle."[68] But many of the foreign recruits had seen military service in their homeland, quickly adapted to their new life, and often rose to noncommissioned rank in a short time. "Of the foreigners," observed a Fourth Cavalry officer, "I preferred the Irish—they were more intelligent and resourceful as a rule. However, if a German was fit to be a noncommissioned officer he usually made a good one—he was feared by the men, did not curry favor, but was rigid in carrying out orders."[69]

Because the army held so little appeal, it suffered from an extraordinary turnover. Each year death, desertion, and discharge claimed from twenty-five to forty percent of the enlisted force.[70] Desertion ate at the ranks with cancerous voracity. The desertion rate fluctuated between a high of 32.6 percent in 1871, when the pay reduction of 1870 took effect, and a low of 6.2 percent in 1891. In 1891 the Adjutant General calculated that, of the 255,712 men signed up since 1867, fully 88,475, or about one-third, had deserted. Such defections were incredibly wasteful as well as hurtful to morale, discipline, and efficiency. Many studies probed for causes and remedies, but not until after the Indian Wars was the affliction eased.[71] Reenlistments scarcely offset the loss of experienced men. About one thousand reenlisted each year; they made up a cadre of some six to seven thousand veterans of one or more five-year terms. Combined with the almost total absence of formal training, the high loss rate and low reenlistment rate kept the ranks heavy with inexperienced men.

The noncommissioned officers formed the backbone of the enlisted force. The tough but paternalistic Irish or German first sergeant, his sleeve bright with hash marks, became almost a stereotype in his own time, as a veteran cavalry officer recalled:

It was a fine sight to see one of these old men on muster or monthly inspection. Erect and soldierly, with his red face glistening, his white hair cut close, his arms and accouterments shining, not a wrinkle in his neat-fitting uniform, nor a speck of dust about him, his corps badge, and it may be a medal, on his breast, he stood in the ranks among the others like an oak tree in a grove of cottonwood saplings.[72]

Although many corporals and sergeants personified this stereotype, the noncommissioned corps as a whole inspired continuing criticism for brutality and neglect of duty. Officers often attributed the high desertion rate to tyrannical NCOs and believed that the need to attract better men to these posts justified significantly higher pay, even as much as $50 to $75 a month.[73]

Much thought and discussion centered on how to improve the quality of the rank and file. One way was to improve the quality of recruits. Better pay and living conditions might have brought in better men. Tighter mental and physical requirements might have screened out many of the bad prospects. Recruiting rendezvous located in rural areas instead of the big cities might have lured more of the healthy young farm boys that officers judged to make the best soldiers. One proposal was to "localize" regiments on the Prussian pattern. Regiments would obtain their own recruits from assigned home localities, thus attracting better men and fostering a solidarity born of common origins and community pride.[74] No such innovations were attempted, however, and it may be doubted that, even with the dramatic drop in desertions that probably would have resulted, enough men of the desired character could have been persuaded to enlist.

Another approach to the problem, stressed repeatedly by military leaders, was to provide better training of recruits. They received only rudimentary instruction at the recruit depots—Jefferson Barracks, Missouri, for cavalry; David's Island, New York, and Columbus Barracks, Ohio, for infantry and artillery—before being forwarded to their units. Here, theoretically, company officers and NCOs trained them in their duties. But in practice fatigue, guard, and other daily levies on the undermanned companies rarely left men enough time for training, and rarely, in fact, was there any training. Deficiencies were most glaring in horsemanship and marksmanship—the latter aggravated by economy strictures that allowed no more than a handful of cartridges a year for target practice. Experience, especially in field operations, helped some. But most companies contained a high proportion of men unversed in the basic military skills.[75]

The army's dismal showing in the Sioux and Nez Percé operations of 1876–77, especially at the Little Bighorn and Big Hole, stirred tentative beginnings at reform. In 1881 "companies of in-struction" were organized at the recruit depots to give enlistees four months of basic training before their assignment to a unit.[76] In 1878 post schools for the education of soldiers, optional since they were authorized in 1866, were made mandatory.[77] New in-terest awakened in target practice as ammunition restrictions were relaxed and competition was encouraged.[78] Even so, throughout the 1880s, while units remained understrength and widely dis-persed on frontier duty, meaningful training continued to be more a hope than a reality. The Seventh Cavalrymen who fought at Wounded Knee in 1890 were almost as green as those who had fought at the Little Bighorn in 1876.[79]

Unit pride and esprit de corps did not sink to lows implied by the rapid turnover and marginal quality of the enlisted comple-ment. Scattered widely, companies rarely, if ever, came together to serve as a regiment or even a significant portion of it. Com-panies provided the familiar associations, common experiences, and distinctive characteristics and traditions with which men iden-tified. The company, therefore, rather than the regiment, com-manded loyalties and fostered solidarity.

Some of the regiments succeeded in establishing their individu-ality and inspiring pride in their members. Custer's Seventh Cav-alry reflected the flamboyance of its commander from 1867 to 1876 and thereafter found a powerful bond in memory of the Little Bighorn. Miles' Fifth Infantry drew inspiration from its superior record in the Red River and Sioux wars and from its cam-paigns mounted on Indian ponies. Of the cavalry, Mackenzie's Fourth, Merrit's Fifth, and Carr's Sixth enjoyed notable traditions, while infantry regiments of special character included Floyd-Jones' Third, Hazen's Sixth, Gibbon's Seventh, Kautz' Eighth, and Ruger's Eighteenth.[80]

The Ninth and Tenth Cavalry and Twenty-fourth and Twenty-fifth Infantry were especially distinctive because they were com-posed of black enlisted men and white officers. "Buffalo soldiers," the Indians labeled the Tenth Cavalry troopers, who proudly made the buffalo the central figure of the regimental crest. Soon the term came to signify all the black soldiers. Throughout the closing decades of Indian conflict, the "blacks in blue" formed a conspicu-ous and controversial part of the Regular Army.[81]

The blacks brought to the army certain strengths and weaknesses that in large measure reflected their heritage of slavery and subordination. Almost all were illiterate, throwing on their officers the burden of paperwork. Few possessed the mechanical skills necessary for the daily functioning of a military unit. Lack of resourcefulness, initiative, and a sense of responsibility made them more dependent upon good leaders than white soldiers and less effective when acting individually. At the same time, the blacks excelled in discipline, morale, patience and good humor in adversity, physical endurance, and sobriety. Above all, they performed well on campaign and in combat. Even their severest critics testified to their exceptional record of field service. General Sherman, for example, conceding his preference for white troops, declared of the blacks in 1874: "They are good troops, they make first-rate sentinels, are faithful to their trust, and are as brave as the occasion calls for."[82]

None captured the special character of the buffalo soldiers, both in paint and prose, better than artist Frederic Remington. Campaigning with them in Arizona, he wrote:

The Negro troopers sat about, their black skins shining with perspiration, and took no interest in the matter at hand. They occupied such time in joking and in merriment as seemed fitted for growling. They may be tired and they may be hungry, but they do not see fit to augment their misery by finding fault with everybody and everything. In this particular they are charming men with whom to serve. Officers have often confessed to me that when they are on long and monotonous field service and are troubled with a depression of spirits, they have only to go about the campfires of the Negro soldier in order to be amused and cheered by the clever absurdities of the men. . . . As to their bravery: "Will they fight?" That is easily answered. They have fought many, many times. The old sergeant sitting near me, as calm of feature as a bronze statue, once deliberately walked over a Cheyenne rifle pit and killed his man. One little fellow near him once took charge of a lot of stampeded cavalry horses when Apache bullets were flying loose and no one knew from what point to expect them next.[83]

As the years passed, the black regiments came to contain an unusually large percentage of veterans. To the white man, explained Secretary of War Redfield Proctor in 1889, the army too often offered merely a refuge, while to the black man it offered a career.[84] Black regiments consistently enjoyed high reenlistment and low desertion rates. The leadership, too, demonstrated unusual continuity. Col. Edward Hatch commanded the Ninth Cavalry from 1866 to 1889, Col. Benjamin H. Grierson the Tenth from 1866 to 1890. Col. Joseph H. Potter headed the Twenty-fourth Infantry for thirteen years and Col. George Andrews the Twenty-fifth for twenty-one years. Similar instances of longevity existed among field and company officers. Moreover, unit pride and esprit de corps ran high in the black regiments, the product, in part, of this personnel continuity, but also of increasing professionalism, superior performance, a solidarity born of prejudice, and a determination to demonstrate the potential of the black race. As the Tenth Cavalry chaplain astutely observed, black soldiers "are possessed of the notion that the colored people of the whole country are more or less affected by their conduct in the Army."[85]

Despite their proven worth, the black regiments were the target of searing racial prejudice. In 1873 an officer's wife at Camp Supply, Indian Territory, recorded a typical sentiment in praising a new commander for abolishing racially mixed guards: "It was outrageous to put white and black in the same little guard room, and colored sergeants over white corporals and privates."[86] A memorable and well-publicized incident occurred at Fort Leavenworth in 1867. The post commander, Col. William Hoffman, ordered the "nigger troops" of the Tenth Cavalry not to form on parade so close to his men of the Third Infantry. Colonel Grierson sprang to the Tenth's defense, and the two colonels engaged in a heated dispute in front of the assembled command.[87] Although most officers of black regiments took great pride in their units, they suffered social condescension, if not ostracism, from the rest of the officer corps.[88] Worse yet, the black regiments endured discrimination in both the quantity and quality of supplies, equipment, and horses, and for twenty-five years they remained without relief in the most disagreeable sectors of the frontier.

Not surprisingly, therefore, sentiment flourished for abolition of the black regiments. They were branded inefficient and costly in comparison with white regiments. Quartermaster officers produced figures purporting to show that black regiments used up more horses and lost or damaged more equipment than the white regiments. Blacks were said to be careless, irresponsible, lazy, dishonest, and immoral. Moreover, black and white units supposedly did not mix well in the same garrison.[89] While citing all these ar-

guments, proponents of abolishing the black regiments presented
their efforts as motivated by a desire to eradicate the racial discrimination that barred blacks from all but four regiments and
thus denied them constitutional rights so recently won. In Congress the movement expressed itself in attempts to repeal the
"class legislation" that provided for these regiments. Opponents
exposed this hypocrisy by pointing out that repeal would place
enlistment of blacks wholly at the discretion of recruiting officers
and would therefore result in eliminating them from the army altogether.[90] Paradoxically, the failure of the attempts in the 1870s
to abolish racial segregation in the army insured blacks the continuing source of racial pride provided by the Ninth and Tenth
Cavalry and Twenty-fourth and Twenty-fifth Infantry.

Although Sherman held the post of commanding general of the
army and profoundly influenced its character, he did not actually
command it. The army staff—more exactly, the War Department
staff—remained resolutely outside Sherman's army. And the complications that the staff's independence created for the commanding
general in turn made his authority over the line more nominal
than real.

The staff bureaus not only serviced the army line and provided
staff officers for the division and department commanders. Several
had important nonmilitary responsibilities, usually specifically assigned by act of Congress. The Corps of Engineers, for example,
found greater employment in river and harbor work and lake
and coast surveys than in military construction projects. The burgeoning weather forecasting responsibilities of the Signal Corps
dominated this bureau until they were finally transferred to the
Department of Agriculture in 1890. Moreover, the procurement
and distribution functions of the supply bureaus were carried out
in an environment more civilian than military.

These considerations were cited to justify a distinction between
the business of the War Department and the business of the army,
and in turn to justify a direct reporting relationship of the staff
heads to the Secretary of War. This was a feature of the coordinate system by which the War Department had been organized
since the presidency of Andrew Jackson. Theoretically, the President exercised his constitutional authority as commander in chief
directly through the commanding general. The civilian Secretary

of War was presumed not to possess the military competence to participate in command functions. Instead, working through the staff chiefs, he concerned himself with the political, administrative, and fiscal affairs of the department. Ever since 1836, army regulations had reflected this division of authority by reserving fiscal powers to the Secretary and "discipline and military control" to the commanding general.

The coordinate system pleased neither the Secretary nor the commanding general. From the Secretary's viewpoint, the hallowed tradition of civilian control of the military was compromised by an arrangement that gave him access to the army line only through a general not of his choosing and beyond his power to remove; moreover, such access as this afforded was confused by the general's direct channel to the President. From the general's viewpoint, on the other hand, the privileged position of the staff wrought havoc with the principle that the operational commander should control his logistics. The staff chiefs, independent of the commanding general, presided over virtually autonomous bureaucratic domains, reported directly to the Secretary, and through detailed knowledge of their departments brought decisive influence to bear on him.

In theory, the coordinate system favored the commanding general because it gave him a direct relationship with the President. But a strong Secretary, coupled with a weak or indifferent President, placed the general at a serious disadvantage. In the War Department staff bureaus, which had counterparts in the headquarters of the territorial divisions and departments, the Secretary possessed an apparatus by which he might reach the army without recourse to the commanding general. Winfield Scott had confronted such a Secretary in Jefferson Davis during the 1850s. Sherman confronted such a Secretary in William W. Belknap during the 1870s. Both generals lost, and both served virtually as commanding generals without a command.[91]

Grant had seemingly resolved the issue the day after taking office as President. The order of March 5, 1869, naming Sherman to the top command also specified that the chiefs of the staff bureaus would report to and serve under the commanding general and that all orders of the President and Secretary of War to the army, line and staff alike, would be transmitted through the commanding general. But Grant's Secretary, his wartime comrade

and chief of staff, John A. Rawlins, insisted that the order be rescinded. He was sick and soon to die. Grant yielded. On March 26
another order restored the direct relationship of the staff chiefs
with the Secretary. Stunned and badly hurt, Sherman accepted
the defeat, but he never forgave Grant.[92]

Rawlins allowed Sherman in practice what was withheld in
theory. But Rawlins lived to hold the office only six months. His
successor, William W. Belknap, proved less charitable. Belknap
and the staff denied Sherman even the vaguely defined "discipline
and military control" of the army. They consulted him occasionally,
but for the most part left him to learn from the newspapers of
developments in the War Department. Belknap made personnel
assignments and ordered troop movements through Adj. Gen. Edward D. Townsend or simply left Townsend to attend to such
matters in the Secretary's name. So frustrated and humiliated did
Sherman become that in 1874, following the example of Winfield
Scott two decades earlier, he abdicated all pretense at command
and moved his headquarters to St. Louis.[93]

In the spring of 1876, a scandal broke over Belknap. Ironically,
it sprang from one of the issues over which he and Sherman had
clashed—the power to appoint post traders (or sutlers). Belknap
gained this power by statute in 1870. He or his wife, or both, used
it improperly for profit. Their exposure in 1876 prompted Belknap's hasty resignation and protracted impeachment proceedings
in Congress.[94] The new Secretary, Alfonso Taft, lured Sherman
back to Washington by promising that all orders to the army
would go through him, and by placing him over the Adjutant
General and Inspector General, the staff chiefs most intimately
concerned with "discipline and military control." The others, more
fiscal, administrative, and civil in character, continued to report
to the Secretary.[95] This arrangement still denied Sherman control
of the supply, ordnance, and medical services so vital to line operations, but, together with a series of considerate Secretaries, it
made his last years of active service personally tolerable and officially productive.

The relationship between the commanding general and the Secretary of War was but part of the larger and more fundamental
problem of the relationship between staff and line. As Col. John
Gibbon stated it, the staff was "completely separated in sympathy
from the Army proper, and with the single exception of the Medi-

cal Corps, almost completely so in fact."[96] For four decades after
the Civil War, the resulting hostility between staff and line deeply
troubled the army.

Life tenure and the near autonomy of their bureaus gave staff
officers in Washington great power. Few Secretaries of War possessed the background or interest or stayed long enough in office
to gain more than nominal control of these potentates. Moreover,
long residence in Washington and the favors at their command
encouraged staff chiefs to cultivate key members of Congress and
thus to influence legislation favorable to the staff while diverting
the impact of congressional economy moves from staff to line.
"The result," noted a disgruntled field officer, "is that nearly every
chief of bureau in the War Department has a little army of his
own, apparently independent of all superior authority except
Congress."[97]

The independence reached even into the divisions and departments, where staff officers theoretically served the generals to
whom they were assigned. But these officers usually owed their
appointments to Washington, and they looked as much for guidance and support to their bureau heads as to the general on whose
staff they served.[98] Backed by their chiefs in Washington and a
mammoth complexity of regulations, the division and department
staffs crippled the ability of operational commanders to control
their own logistics. The staff decided what was needed where, and
how and when to get it there. If the responsible commander had
different ideas, he might persuade, but not compel, the staff to
modify the decision.[99]

Stationed almost entirely in the cities, staff officers enjoyed
privileges and comforts unknown to officers at remote border posts.
Compared with the line, moreover, the staff seemed swollen with
personnel and high rank. It claimed almost half the army's colonels and lieutenant colonels and more than half its brigadier generals and majors. For the line, a bitter truth lurked in a capital
correspondent's quip that "there are generals enough to officer the
Turkish Army playing billiard every afternoon at Geary's opposite Military headquarters. . . . Like good soldiers, they are found
where the balls fly thickest."[100]

If for all these reasons the line resented the staff, so, for the
same reasons, the line envied the staff. Line officers competed so
strenuously for appointments to the staff that they demeaned their

arms and widened the gulf between line and staff all the more. Maj. William R. Price lamented the tendency of the line officer "to look to the staff as the highest object of his ambition, . . . the only outlet whereby he can ever come in contact with his countrymen, relatives, and friends."[101] This greatly disturbed Sherman, who declared in 1876: "It is now too much the *fashion* for officers of the line themselves to belittle their military calling, and to exalt 'into staff duty' the commonest duties outside their regiment and company, such as Centennial, fancy boards, wig-wag, etc., and to seek details through their sisters, mothers, friends, and members of Congress; a cause that has and will continue to degrade us as a profession, and finally result in ruin unless checked."[102]

Successive congressional committees investigated the staff system to exhaustion.[103] Line officers repeatedly advanced standard remedies: subordinate the staff bureaus to the commanding general; reduce them and deprive them of their top-heavy superstructure; consolidate similar bureaus, such as Adjutant General with Inspector General and Quartermaster with Commissary and Pay; abolish permanent appointments and interchange officers between staff and line, thus promoting understanding and harmony. The staff met these proposals with vague legalisms about the prerogatives and responsibilities of the President, the Secretary of War, and the Congress, and with ridicule of the notion of tinkering with machinery that had performed so splendidly in the greatest war of all time. Indeed, so politically well connected were the bureaus that public defense was rarely necessary. Legislation to curb them usually failed in Congress. As Sherman noted, they "will not be brought into the Army for discipline if human cunning and lobbying can prevent it."[104]

None of the line generals brought greater clarity and objectivity of analysis to the question than John M. Schofield. He did not think the staff ought to be reduced, he testified in 1878. Staff needs depended less on the size of the army than on the extent of territory it occupied. An army that manned some two hundred posts scattered across the continent needed the same staff whether fifteen or fifty thousand strong. Nor was organization the true issue; organization of the bureaus was good enough. "Any possible question of their consolidation or reorganization anyway is utterly insignificant as compared with that of their union with the line as part of one whole under one head."[105] "Here is the whole

question in a nut shell," he wrote Sherman. "Shall due subordination be enforced throughout the Army? or, shall every chief of
staff in Washington have a separate command, and that extending
even within the limits of Division and Departments?"[106] As early
as the 1870s General Schofield advocated the solution ultimately
adopted after the Spanish-American War dramatized the urgency
of reform: a general staff united under a chief of staff and wedded
to the line by a system of rotation. And this organization, Schofield
came to recognize, left no place for a commanding general.[107]

Theoretically, the commanding general commanded the division
and department commanders, and through them the army line.
Actually, beneath the line generals so many communications chan-
nels, formal and informal, ran to the ten staff chiefs in Washington that, as Sherman often complained, he commanded nothing
more than his personal staff of six colonels. Nevertheless, he enjoyed a close and influential relationship with the line generals.
He supported, counseled, and encouraged them and, most importantly in his view, defended their prerogatives against the aggressions of the staff.[108] In the management of field operations, however, he played little part. This responsibility fell mainly on the
department commanders, sometimes closely directed by the division commander, but more often with only nominal oversight
from above.

This handful of officers—the lieutenant general, three major
generals, and six brigadiers—formed an exclusive club whose
composition underwent few changes throughout Sherman's regime. They owed their rank to wartime services rather than seniority and were comparatively young when Sherman went to
Washington. They served long enough to become highly experienced, if not always inspired, department or division commanders.
When they transferred, they simply exchanged places with a colleague doing similar service.

Philip H. Sheridan inherited Sherman's three stars and succeeded to the command of the Military Division of the Missouri.
His fourteen-year tenure spanned the period of the most intense Indian conflicts on the Great Plains. From his Chicago headquarters
Sheridan monitored and gave direction to operations from Dakota
and Montana to Texas and New Mexico. Veteran brigadiers
headed his four departments. Verbose and contentious John Pope
commanded the Department of the Missouri for thirteen years.

The wealthy bachelor, Alfred H. Terry, whose cultural and professional attainments earned him wide respect, presided over the Department of Dakota from 1866 to 1868 and 1873 to 1886. Quietly competent Christopher C. Augur managed the Department of the Platte for four years and Texas for three. Honest, impulsive Edward O. C. Ord—"a rough diamond," said Sherman, "always at work on the most distant frontier"[109]—followed Augur at both headquarters. George Crook commanded the Platte for seven years, from 1875 to 1882.

Sheridan proved less able than Sherman to hold the loyalty and affection of subordinates. His relations with some department commanders—notably Pope, Crook, and Ord—fluctuated between frigidity and hostility. His preferential treatment of favored young colonels such as Custer, Mackenzie, and Miles angered many. Those who had incurred his displeasure, such as Colonels Grierson and Hazen, suffered petty indignities and prolonged discrimination. Shortly after Sheridan's death, Crook pronounced a stinging judgment that, while reflecting no credit on its author, reveals the extreme antipathy Sheridan could arouse in associates: "The adulations heaped on him by a grateful nation for his supposed genius turned his head, which, added to his natural disposition, caused him to bloat his little carcass with debauchery and dissipation, which carried him off prematurely."[110]

The Military Division of the Pacific fell to one of the three major generals. George H. Thomas, Halleck's successor, commanded it for only a year, 1869–70, before a fatal heart attack passed it to scholarly John M. Schofield. Portly, bald yet magnificently whiskered, Schofield occupied the division's San Francisco headquarters from 1870 to 1876 and again in 1882–83. Irvin McDowell held the post from 1876 to 1882. Stiff, formal, tactless, and often querulous in official intercourse, McDowell was still well known for sumptuous hospitality, financed from a personal fortune, and for wide-ranging cultural interests.[111]

Neither Schofield nor McDowell managed his department commanders as closely as Sheridan. Since the division commander also commanded the Department of California, there were but two. Oliver O. Howard, the one-armed "praying general," commanded the Department of the Columbia from 1874 to 1881. He replaced Edward R. S. Canby, slain by Modocs in the Lava Beds in 1873 (see Chapter Twelve). George Crook gained fame for his Apache campaigns while head of the Department of Arizona, 1871 to 1875 and 1882 to 1886.

The department commander—situated high enough to gain perspective without losing a focus on local conditions—was the key link in the frontier army's chain of command. He kept in touch with post commanders, set standards and guidelines, and usually provided positive leadership. Some department commanders, such as Crook, Terry, and Howard, exercised personal command of major expeditions. Others, such as Augur, Pope, and Ord, worked through subordinates.

The large measure of autonomy permitted department commanders was a source of strength in localized Indian troubles. When hostilities flowed across department boundaries, however, division commanders experienced great difficulty in enforcing cooperation and coordination; and when two divisions became involved, the commanding general in Washington encountered even greater difficulty. The pursuit of the Nez Percés in 1877 and the Ute campaign of 1879 afford notable examples. Occasionally boundaries were redrawn to avoid such problems. The addition of Indian territory to Texas in 1871 placed both the source and the objective of Kiowa-Comanche raids under a single commander. The advantages of embracing such persistently troublesome tribes as the Sioux and the Apaches under single commands might have seemed equally obvious. Yet the former remained the responsibility of the commanders of two departments and the latter the commanders of two divisions, three departments, and a district.

From commanding general to post commander, the frontier army hung from a loose chain of command. In part this weakness was inherent in the continental dimensions of the army's task, the inadequacy of manpower and other resources allocated to it, the unclear division of responsibility within the Indian Bureau, and the ambiguous character of Indian relations. But also in part the weakness stemmed from a military system that reduced the commanding general to a figurehead, pitted line and staff against each other, and limited a commander's control of his logistics.

Beyond these deficiencies, however, lay a more fundamental question. Throughout the debates over size, composition, and command of the peacetime army, apparently no one thought to ask whether traditional organization truly fitted the special conditions of the army's mission in the West. This question in turn formed part of a larger question that received barely any attention from military leaders: how most effectively to constitute and employ the nation's military resources to subjugate and control the Indians? This was the army's primary employment for a century. Yet never did its leaders face up to the problem of doctrine.

NOTES

1. The debates are in *Cong. Globe*, 39th Cong., 1st sess., under listings for H.R. 361 and S. 138.
2. C. Joseph Bernardo and Eugene H. Bacon, *American Military Policy: Its Development Since 1775* (Harrisburg, Pa., 1957), p. 236.
3. *Cong. Globe*, 39th Cong., 1st sess., p. 1380 (March 14, 1866).
4. *Ibid.*, p. 3669 (July 9, 1866).
5. Russell F. Weigley, *History of the United States Army* (New York, 1967), p. 262. Bernardo and Bacon, pp. 235–36.
6. 14 Stat. 332–38 (July 28, 1866).
7. The act was not as generous to the infantry as it appears. Actually, only the four black regiments and the four Veteran Reserve Corps regiments were new. The wartime regular infantry had consisted of ten regiments of ten companies each and nine regiments of twenty-four companies each divided into three eight-company battalions. By the addition of two companies, each of these battalions became one of the new regiments, and twenty-seven regiments were formed from nine at a cost of fifty-four instead of two hundred seventy companies. These became the Eleventh through Thirty-seventh Regiments. The colored regiments were the Thirty-eighth through Forty-first, and the VRC regiments were the Forty-second through Forty-fifth.
8. Cavalry companies officially became *troops* in 1883, and battalions became *squadrons* in 1889. Since the new terms enjoyed wide unofficial usage before being officially adopted, and to avoid changing nomenclature in mid-volume, I have used troop and squadron throughout. Squadron refers to any grouping of two or more troops of less than regimental strength. Only two of the twelve components of the artillery regiments were equipped with artillery. These were called light batteries. The rest were in all but name infantry companies. A good discussion of army organization in this period is Don Russell, "The Army of the Frontier, 1865–1891," *The Westerners Brand Book* (Chicago), 6 (July 1949), 33–35, 38–40. See also H. R. Hikok, "Our Cavalry Organization as Viewed in the Light of Its History and of Legislation," *Journal of the U.S. Cavalry Association*, 22 (1912), 995–1009.
9. L. D. Ingersoll, *A History of the War Department of the United States* (Washington, D.C., 1879). Raphael P. Thian, comp., *Legislative History of the General Staff of the Army of the United States . . . from 1775 to 1901* (Washington, D.C., 1901). The titles of the department chiefs were: Adjutant General, Inspector General, Judge Advocate General, Quartermaster General, Commissary General, Surgeon General, Paymaster General, Chief of Engineers, Chief of Ordnance, and Chief Signal Officer.
10. All original vacancies in the grades of first and second lieutenant were to be filled by volunteer officers who had served creditably for at least two years in the war. In grades above first lieutenant, two-thirds of the original vacancies in the cavalry and half of those in the infantry were to be filled in the same way. The volunteer appointments were to be distributed

among the states and territories (excepting California, Oregon, and Nevada) in proportion to the troops they furnished during the war, a stipulation that provided members of Congress with a large patronage reservoir.

11. 14 Stat. 223 (July 25, 1866).

12. Secretary of War (hereafter SW), *Annual Report* (1867), p. 416.

13. Regarding the award of brevet rank in the closing years of the war and immediately thereafter, the army's authority on brevets wrote: "The government appeared not to know where to stop in the bestowal of these military honors, and no one who had earned reward, even in the smallest degree, was knowingly overlooked. Brevet shoulder straps were showered down 'as thick as leaves in Vallambrosa!' " James B. Fry, *The History and Legal Effect of Brevets in the Armies of Great Britain and the United States* (New York, 1877), p. 224.

Three boards of officers were convened in March 1866 to make recommendations based on more reliable authority than the urgings of members of Congress, but this by no means eliminated the political element. Although combat officers bitterly resented it, brevets were also liberally dispensed for meritorious staff service; since staff officers served close to the sources of power, most were able to win generous brevet recognition. As one of the examining boards foresaw, the Civil War veteran who lacked a brevet came to be regarded as having failed in his duty. General Fry listed some 2,200 Regular Army officers who received approximately 4,000 brevets for Civil War service.

There is no really satisfactory way to handle brevets in a work such as this. In general, I have tried, in a fashion I hope not excessively obtrusive, to give an officer the rank, regular or brevet, in which he was serving, while mentioning his other rank too where it seems important. Thus Bvt. Maj. Gen. A. J. Smith, colonel of the Seventh Cavalry, is General Smith because of serving as a district commander in his brevet grade; but Bvt. Maj. Gen. George A. Custer, lieutenant colonel of the Seventh Cavalry, is Colonel Custer because of serving in his regular rank as regimental commander. It should be noted, however, that socially and often officially both were addressed as general regardless of whether they were serving as such.

14. SW, *Annual Report* (1866), pp. 1–2. All the brevets but Steele, who was colonel of the Twentieth Infantry, were regular brigadiers.

15. In a letter to brother John quoted in Athearn, *William Tecumseh Sherman and the Settlement of the West*, p. 233.

16. Weigley, p. 273.

17. Cf. Samuel P. Huntington, *The Soldier and the State: The Theory and Politics of Civil-Military Relations* (Cambridge, Mass., 1957), pp. 230–31.

18. 15 Stat. 315–18 (March 3, 1869). The act also stopped appointments and promotions in the staff bureaus until Congress could agree on their proper peacetime size. In the next five years, lobbying by staff officers gained six laws making exceptions to this injunction. Finally, in 1874, Congress acted to fix the composition of the bureaus. 18 Stat. 244–45 (June 23, 1874). Under the 1869 act, the staff numbered 633 officers and 1,861 enlisted men. Under the 1874 act it numbered 521 officers and 679 enlisted men.

19. 16 Stat. 315–21 (July 15, 1870). Sheridan remained lieutenant general when he replaced Sherman in 1883 but was given four stars by act of Congress in June 1888, two months before his death. Thereafter, until the grade of lieutenant general was revived in 1900, the senior major general commanded the army.

20. 18 Stat. 72 (June 16, 1874). For organization of the army following each of these laws, see F. B. Heitman, *Historical Register and Dictionary of the United States Army* (2 vols., Washington, D.C., 1903), 2, 606–13.

21. *Ibid.*, SW, *Annual Report* (1869), pp. 26–28, 235; (1870), pp. iii–xv; (1871), pp. 1, 22–23.

22. SW, *Annual Report* (1879), p. iii; (1880), p. 3; (1881), pp. 133–34.
23. *Ibid.* (1873), p. 24; (1874), p. 3; (1881), pp. 4, 32.
24. *Ibid.* (1881), p. 32.
25. Capt. Henry C. Corbin before House Committee on Military Affairs, March 2, 1876, House Reports, 44th Cong., 1st sess., No. 354, p. 210.
26. SW, *Annual Report* (1877), pp. 47–49. See below, pp. 306–307.
27. 19 Stat. 98 (July 24, 1876) and 19 Stat. 204 (Aug. 15, 1876). SW, *Annual Report* (1876), p. 24; (1877), pp. iii–iv. See also James D. Richardson, comp., *A Compilation of the Messages and Papers of the Presidents, 1789–1897* (10 vols., Washington, D.C., 1897), 7, 473.
28. Capt. Guy V. Henry before House Committee on Military Affairs, Feb. 14, 1876, House Reports, 44th Cong., 1st sess., No. 354, p. 191.
29. To Rep. Levi Maish et al, Fort D. A. Russell, Wyo., Dec. 29, 1877, House Misc. Docs., 45th Cong., 2d sess., No. 56, pp. 85–87.
30. See the listing of field and staff of the Seventh Cavalry in Robert M. Utley, *Custer Battlefield National Monument* (National Park Service, Washington, D.C., 1969), p. 49.
31. To Rep. H. B. Banning, San Francisco, Feb. 15, 1876, House Reports, 44th Cong., 1st sess., No. 354, p. 27.
32. To Rep. Levi Maish et al, Jackson Barracks, La., Jan. 12, 1878, House Misc. Docs., 45th Cong., 2d sess., No. 56, p. 134.
33. House Reports, 44th Cong., 1st sess., No. 354, p. 27. SW, *Annual Report* (1874), pp. iv–v; (1877), pp. 47–49; (1878), p. 436. Richardson, 7, 473. House Misc. Docs., 45th Cong., 2d sess., No. 56, pp. 122, 125.
34. House Misc. Docs., 45th Cong., 2d sess., No. 56, p. 45. Richardson, 7, 617. SW, *Annual Report* (1881), p. 32; (1882), pp. iv, 4.
35. SW, *Annual Report* (1873), p. 24; (1877), p. 6; (1879), pp. iii, 4.
36. Sherman to Sen. John A. Logan, June 27, 1874, in Sherman Papers, vol. 90, pp. 339–41, LC. Sherman to J. D. Cameron, Sept. 1876, in James A. Garfield, "The Army of the United States," *North American Review, 136* (1878), 202. House Reports, 44th Cong., 1st sess., No. 354, p. 226.
37. House Reports, 43d Cong., 1st sess., No. 384, p. 1. *Cong. Rec.*, 44th Cong., 1st sess., p. 3357 (May 27, 1876).
38. GO 93, Hq. of the Army, Oct. 31, 1867, in House Reports, 44th Cong., 1st sess., No. 354, pp. 136–37.
39. 20 Stat. 150 (June 28, 1878). SW, *Annual Report* (1880), p. 36; (1890), pp. 10–11.
40. 16 Stat. 320 (July 15, 1870). Other rates: lieutenant colonel, $3,000; major, $2,500; mounted captain, $2,000; unmounted captain, $1,800; mounted first lieutenant, $1,600; unmounted first lieutenant, $1,500; mounted second lieutenant, $1,500. Major generals received $7,500, brigadiers $5,500. Sherman and Sheridan received $13,500 and $11,000, respectively. These sums, exceedingly generous in relation to other high government officials' salaries, were in recognition of Civil War services.
41. Maj. Samuel Breck to Schofield, Feb. 10, 1876, House Reports, 44th Cong., 1st sess., No. 354, p. 139. Garfield, "Army of the United States," p. 465.
42. C. C. C. Carr, " 'The Days of the Empire'—Arizona, 1866–1869," *Journal of the U.S. Cavalry Association,* 2 (1869), 5. Col. I. V. D. Reeve to Rep. John Coburn, Minneapolis, March 20, 1872, House Reports, 42d Cong., 3d sess., No. 74, p. 159. Col. Alfred Sully to Rep. H. B. Banning, Fort Vancouver, Wash., Feb. 24, 1876, *ibid.*, 44th Cong., 1st sess., No. 354, p. 108. Brig. Gen. O. O Howard to Banning, Portland, Oreg., Feb. 25, 1876, *ibid.*, p. 39.
43. House Reports, 44th Cong., 1st sess., No. 354, p. 2. *Cong. Rec.*, 44th Cong., 1st sess., p. 2038 (March 29, 1876).
44. To Rep. H. B. Banning, New Orleans, Feb. 16, 1876, House Reports, 44th Cong., 1st sess., No. 354, p. 47.
45. *Army and Navy Journal, 15* (Oct. 6, 1877), 138–39.

46. Martha Summerhayes, *Vanished Arizona· Recollections of My Army Life* (1908; Lippincott ed., Philadelphia, 1963), pp. 236–37. An officer complained in 1885 that he had seen fifty of his juniors in his arm pass him on the seniority list. *Army and Navy Journal*, 22 (Jan. 3, 1885), 451.

47. SW, *Annual Report* (1887), pp. 121–22.

48. 16 Stat. 317 (July 15, 1870), which cut the army to 30,000 men, provided for retirement after 30 years' service. 22 Stat. 118 (June 28, 1882) raised the figure to 40 years, but made retirement mandatory at age 64. Officers retired under this provision were placed on the unlimited retired list. Those retired by a retiring board for disability were placed on the limited list. Because the latter could not exceed 400, the regular rolls were usually burdened with from 60 to 80 incapacitated officers drawing pay and blocking promotion but performing no service. SW, *Annual Report* (1890), pp. 12–13.

49. *Army and Navy Journal*, *15* (Dec. 22, 1877), 313.

50. SW, *Annual Report* (1890), pp. 153–54.

51. *Ibid.* (1887), pp. 121–22.

52. House Reports, 44th Cong., 1st sess., No. 354, p. 30. House Misc. Docs., 45th Cong., 2d sess., No. 56, pp. 24–25. SW, *Annual Report* (1885), pp. 63, 75; (1886), pp. 17–19. Richardson, *8*, 514.

53. 26 Stat. 562 (Oct. 1, 1890).

54. Senate Ex. Docs., 39th Cong., 1st sess., No. 41. In regular rank 10 of the 138 were major generals, 23 brigadiers, 56 colonels, 34 lieutenant colonels, 12 majors, and 3 captains. *Ibid.*, 40th Cong., 3d sess., No. 27.

55. An officer at Fort Lyon, Colo., pointed up the absurdity of the system in an 1869 diary entry: "Brevet Colonel and Captain [Richard C.] Lay inspected and mustered the whole command at this post this afternoon. It was interesting to see him require General [William H.] Penrose to march his company past him in review, he (Penrose) wearing the uniform of a Brigadier-General and Colonel Lay only the straps of a Captain." George A. Armes, *Ups and Downs of an Army Officer* (Washington, D.C., 1900), pp. 286–87.

56. 15 Stat. 281 (March 1, 1869). 15 Stat. 318 (March 3, 1869). 16 Stat. 319 (July 15, 1870). Fry, *History and Legal Effects of Brevets*, pp. 230–31.

57. The Adjutant General ruled that the law did not prohibit an officer from affixing his brevet rank to his signature in official reports. Fry, p. 231. Since the newspapers customarily used an officer's brevet grade, the public, observed Colonel Gibbon, believed the army composed mainly of colonels and generals. House Misc. Docs., 45th Cong., 2d sess., No. 56, p. 270.

58. Among them Sherman, Thomas, Hancock, McDowell, and Schofield. Senate Ex. Docs., 39th Cong., 1st sess., No. 41. House Reports, 40th Cong., 3d sess., No. 33, pp. 94, 110, 128.

59. *Cong. Rec.*, 44th Cong., 1st sess., p. 3951 (June 21, 1876). See also Sherman to SW McCrary, March 20, 1878, Sherman Papers, vol. 90, pp. 545–48, LC.

60. 26 Stat. 13 (Feb. 27, 1890). SW, *Annual Report* (1890), pp. 52–53.

61. "The charges and counter-charges made by our officers of late . . . have done more to damage us in public estimation than any other single cause," declared Sherman in scolding Colonel Gibbon for preferring charges against General Pope. "The Army today has plenty of honorable employment to occupy the time and talents of all, without resolving itself into a General Court to investigate allegations of fraud, prying, scandal and gossip dating back ten and fifteen years." Sherman to Gibbon, May 31, 1879, Sherman Papers, vol. 91, pp. 190–91, LC.

62. 16 Stat. 21 (July 15, 1870) lowered pay rates that had been temporarily increased in 1864. 17 Stat. 116–17 (May 15, 1872) did not restore the cuts but provided graduated pay for longevity. Under this law the highest paid enlisted men were sergeant majors and quartermaster sergeants of Engi-

neers, at $36 a month. For the third, fourth, and fifth years of the first
enlistment, monthly pay rose by one dollar, but the increase was retained
until discharge. After the first enlistment, this longevity pay ceased to increase, but thenceforth only one of the three dollars was retained.

63. Col. I. V. D. Reeve declared that the Thirteenth Infantry was paid only
twice during its service in Dakota and Montana from 1866 to 1868. To
Rep. John Coburn, March 20, 1872, House Reports, 42d Cong., 3d sess.,
No. 74, p. 159. Jack D. Foner, *The United States Soldier Between Two
Wars, 1865–1898* (New York, 1970), p. 17.

64. The Certificate of Merit, authorized in 1847, rewarded distinguished service involving peril of life and carried a compensation of an additional two
dollars a month pay. Between 1874 and 1891, only fifty-nine of these were
issued. Medals of Honor, authorized in 1863, were for distinguished service
in action. Four hundred and nineteen of these were awarded for Indian
War service, but many came belatedly, years after the deed for which they
were presented. SW, *Annual Report* (1891), p. 313. James R. Moriarity
III, "The Congressional Medal of Honor in the Indian Wars," in Ray
Brandes, ed., *Troopers West: Military and Indian Affairs on the American
Frontier* (San Diego, 1970), pp. 149–69.

65. Quoted in *Army and Navy Journal*, 15 (Oct. 20, 1877), 170.

66. SW, *Annual Report* (1872), p. 53. For the composition of the enlisted
complement, see Don Rickey, Jr., *Forty Miles a Day on Beans and Hay:
The Enlisted Soldier Fighting the Indian Wars* (Norman, Okla., 1963),
chap. 2.

67. SW, *Annual Report* (1882), pp. 60–63. The reports of the Adjutant General in the annual reports of the Secretary of War present recruiting
statistics.

68. *Ibid.* (1888), p. 101.

69. James Parker, *The Old Army Memories, 1872–1918* (Philadelphia, 1929),
p. 18.

70. Cf. SW, *Annual Report* (1879), p. 35; (1881), p. 72; (1882), p. 52;
(1883), p. 80. House Reports, 43d Cong., 1st sess., p. 384.

71. Foner, *passim*, and tables on pp. 222–24. Rickey, pp. 143 *passim*. SW, *Annual Report* (1891), pp. 9, 63. The literature concerning desertion is
abundant, especially in the annual reports of the Secretary of War and the
files of the *Army and Navy Journal*.

72. George A. Forsyth, *The Story of the Soldier* (New York, 1900), pp.
131–32.

73. Rickey, pp. 58–62. Foner, pp. 61–62. See remarks of General Ord in SW,
Annual Report (1874), p. 34; Paymaster General Alvord in *ibid.* (1879),
p. 416; and Capt. Guy V. Henry in House Reports, 44th Cong., 1st sess.,
No. 354, pp. 189–90.

74. See, for example, Maj. William R. Price, April 2, 1872, in House Reports,
42d Cong., 3d sess., No. 74, pp. 133–37; Cols. J. I. Gregg and Edward
Hatch, Jan. 7 and 8, 1878, in House Misc. Docs., 45th Cong., 2d sess., No.
56, pp. 87–90; and Insp. Gen. R. P. Hughes in SW, *Annual Report* (1888),
p. 101.

75. Rickey, pp. 86–87, 99–102. James S. Hutchins, "Mounted Riflemen: The
Real Role of Cavalry in the Indian Wars," in K. Ross Toole et al, eds.,
Probing the American West: Papers from the Santa Fe Conference (Santa
Fe, N.M., 1962), pp. 79–85. Frank D. Reeve, ed., "Frederick E. Phelps:
A Soldier's Memoirs," *New Mexico Historical Review*, 25 (1950), 113.
W. P. Hall, "The Use of Arms, Mounted," *Journal of the United States
Cavalry Association*, 1 (1888), 34–37. Parker, pp. 22–23. SW, *Annual
Report* (1871), pp. 71–73; (1878), p. 31; (1879), pp. 67–68, 135–36.

76. SW, *Annual Report* (1881), p. 46; (1885), p. 76. Rickey, pp. 33–34.

77. SW, *Annual Report* (1878), p. v. Foner, pp. 25–28. Arlen L. Fowler, *The
Black Infantry in the West, 1869–1891* (Westport, Conn., 1971), chap. 5.

Army educational programs originated principally in the black regiments, each of which was provided with a chaplain, among whose duties were those of schoolteacher.

78. Largely as a result of editorial promptings by the *Army and Navy Journal*, the National Rifle Association was formed in 1871 and annual rifle matches were inaugurated at Creedmoor, New York. In 1875 the Regular Army began to participate with militia units in the Creedmoor competitions. The NRA and Creedmoor helped kindle intense interest and activity in target shooting throughout the army in the 1880s. Donald N. Bigelow, *William Conant Church and the Army and Navy Journal* (New York, 1952), pp. 184–86.

79. Robert M. Utley, *The Last Days of the Sioux Nation* (New Haven, Conn., 1963), p. 202. But see also Edward S. Godfrey, "Cavalry Fire Discipline," *Journal of the Military Service Institution of the United States, 19* (1896), 259, for indications that the men at Wounded Knee knew how to use their weapons.

80. Rickey, chap. 5. Histories of each regiment are in Theo. F. Rodenbough and William F. Haskin, *The Army of the United States: Historical Sketches of Staff and Line* (New York, 1896). See especially Charles King's essay on esprit de corps, pp. ix–xii.

81. For the history of these units see William H. Leckie, *The Buffalo Soldiers: A Narrative of Negro Cavalry in the West* (Norman, Okla., 1967); Fowler, Rodenbough, pp. 280–97; Foner, chap. 7.

82. House Reports, 43d Cong., 1st sess., No. 384, p. 8. For characteristics of black soldiers, in addition to sources cited in note 71 above, see especially Maj. Guy V. Henry in *Army and Navy Journal, 21* (Jan. 26, 1884), 525; and Parker, pp. 92–93, 104–05.

83. Quoted in Harold McCracken, ed., *Frederic Remington's Own West* (New York, 1960), p. 69.

84. SW, *Annual Report* (1889), p. 9.

85. *Army and Navy Journal, 14* (Jan. 27, 1877), 395.

86. Frances M. A. Roe, *Army Letters from an Officer's Wife* (New York, 1909), pp. 103–4.

87. Leckie, p. 14. Armes, p. 230.

88. Charles J. Crane, *Experiences of a Colonel of Infantry* (New York, 1922), pp. 254–55.

89. For sample testimony see House Reports, 44th Cong., 1st sess., No. 354, pp. 46, 61, 93, 94, 117; House Misc. Docs., 45th Cong., 2d sess., No. 56, pp. 150–53; *ibid.*, No. 64, pp. 120–21; Garfield, "The Army of the United States," p. 206. Among those quoted in behalf of abolition are Generals Sherman, Sheridan, and Ord and Cols. James Oaks, John H. King, H. B. Clitz, and, surprisingly, George Andrews of the Twenty-fifth Infantry. Quartermaster cost estimates, which ignore a host of variables, are in *Cong. Rec.*, 44th Cong., 1st sess., p. 3838 (June 16, 1876).

90. *Cong. Globe*, 42d Cong., 3d sess., pp. 1763–64 (Feb. 25, 1873). *Cong. Rec.*, 44th Cong., 1st sess., p. 3357 (May 27, 1876); pp. 3457–69 (June 1, 1876); p. 3838 (June 16, 1876).

91. The history of this problem is perceptively and incisively treated in Huntington, pp. 230–31. See also Weigley, *History of the United States Army*, pp. 285–89, and *Towards an American Army: Military Thought from Washington to Marshall* (New York and London, 1962), *passim*, but especially chap. 10; Bernardo and Bacon, pp. 251–56; Leonard D. White, *The Republican Era, 1869–1901: A Study in Administrative History* (New York, 1963), pp. 140–46; and John M. Schofield, *Forty-Six Years in the Army* (New York, 1897), chap. 22. I have treated Scott's feud with Davis in *Frontiersmen in Blue*, pp. 48–50.

92. The two orders are in Richardson, 7, 20–21. Sherman's bitterness is a recurring theme in his correspondence in the Library of Congress.

93. The exchange of letters with Belknap, May 8 and 11, 1874, is in vol. 90, pp. 323–24, of the Sherman Papers, LC. Sheridan berated his chief for shaking the confidence of the army and the people in "the stability and steadiness which they have always attached to your character" and for setting a precedent that "places the General in Chief in retirement for all time to come." Sheridan to Sherman, May 31, 1874, Sherman Papers, vol. 37, LC.

94. The charges centered on the sale of the lucrative Fort Sill tradership to a New York entrepreneur, who in turn permitted the regular trader to retain the monopoly in return for regular kickbacks which were shared with the Secretary or his wife. See Robert C. Prickett, "The Malfeasance of William Worth Belknap," *North Dakota History, 17* (1950), 5–52, 97–134. For the impeachment proceedings, see *Cong. Rec.,* 44th Cong., 1st sess., vol. 4, pt. 7 (March 2–Aug. 1, 1876).

95. Sherman to Sheridan, April 1, 1876, Sherman-Sheridan Letters, Sheridan Papers, LC.

96. To Sherman, Fort Shaw, Mont., March 15, 1877, House Misc. Docs., 45th Cong., 2d sess., No. 56, p. 125.

97. Lt. Col. W. P. Carlin to Rep. Levi Maish et al, Standing Rock Agency, Dak., Jan. 6, 1878, House Misc. Docs., 45th Cong., 2d sess., No. 56, p. 146.

98. "Instead of generals selecting their adjutant generals," complained General Hancock in 1869, "the adjutant generals select their generals." House Reports, 40th Cong., 3d sess., No. 33, p. 188. In furtherance of his fiscal accountability, the Secretary of War retained the right to select and assign disbursing officers. Sherman to Sheridan, Oct. 20, 1878, Sherman-Sheridan Letters, Sheridan Papers, LC.

99. With his usual exaggeration, General Pope protested that the staff controlled supplies and transportation, "but they are absolutely without any responsibility for results at all. Any disaster, dishonor, or suffering occasioned by the failure to furnish any article needed for the soldier is charged, and naturally charged, upon the military commander, though he has no more power over such matters than the coroner in Cincinnati." Pope to Judge M. F. Force, Fort Leavenworth, Kan., March 13, 1876, quoted in Garfield, p. 445. Although Pope was not without his sources of power over the staff, his operations in the Red River War of 1874–75 had been badly compromised by supply problems on which he was not consulted.

100. Quoted in *Army and Navy Journal, 15* (Nov. 3, 1877), 199. He was referring not only to regular but brevet generals, who were another source of resentment. At the close of the Civil War the staff had insured itself a generous bestowal of brevets for "faithful and meritorious service." In 1869, in the Quartermaster Department alone, of the 88 officers 10 boasted brevets of major general and 22 of brigadier general. House Reports, 40th Cong., 3d sess., No. 33, pp. 1–2. In 1876 the staff claimed 7 of the 13 brigadiers, 31 of the 75 colonels, 37 of the 80 lieutenant colonels, and 172 of the 242 majors; yet the staff conceded the line all but 100 of the 590 first lieutenants and all but 10 of the 445 second lieutenants. House Reports, 44th Cong., 1st sess., No. 354, p. 88.

101. To Rep. John Coburn, April 2, 1872, House Reports, 42d Cong., 3d sess., No. 74, p. 134. See also comments of Col. J. J. Reynolds in *ibid.,* p. 209.

102. Sherman to Pope, April 24, 1876, Sherman Papers, vol. 90, pp. 417–19, LC. Officers were detailed to the Centennial Exposition in Philadelphia in 1876. Wig-wag refers to the Signal Corps.

103. See especially House Reports, 40th Cong., 3d sess., No. 33; House Reports, 42d Cong., 3d sess., No. 74; House Reports, 44th Cong., 1st sess., No. 354; and House Misc. Docs., 45th Cong., 2d sess., No. 56.

104. Sherman to Sheridan, Dec. 30, 1878, Sherman-Sheridan Letters, Sheridan

Papers, LC. In a letter to Sheridan of Jan. 10, 1879 (*ibid.*), Sherman observed that "the young Staff officers have been busy as bees—running around of nights—saying that I and the Generals want to usurp the powers of the President, Secretary of War—Congress and of the Government itself."

105. Schofield to Rep. Levi Maish et al, West Point, Jan. 3, 1878, House Misc. Docs., 45th Cong., 2d sess., No. 56, pp. 25–26.
106. Schofield to Sherman, Dec. 24, 1878, Sherman Papers, vol. 49, LC.
107. Schofield had proposed a chief of staff under the commanding general in 1876. House Reports, 44th Cong., 1st sess., No. 354, p. 28. Schofield's views are set forth in his autobiography, chaps. 22 and 26. See also Weigley, *Towards an American Army*, chap. 10. Huntington, pp. 163, 190, discusses the origins of the principle of civilian control.
108. Sherman to Sheridan, Dec. 20, 1869, and Sept. 26, 1872, Sherman-Sheridan Letters, Sheridan Papers, LC.
109. To Terry, Dec. 5, 1880, Sherman Papers, vol. 91, pp. 541–44, LC.
110. *General George Crook: His Autobiography*, ed. Martin F. Schmitt (Norman, Okla., 1946), p. 134 n.
111. He dabbled in music, painting, architecture, and landscape architecture. A perceptive and candid obituary appeared in the *Army and Navy Journal*, 22 (May 9, 1885), 827.

☆ THREE ☆

The Problem of Doctrine

PARADOXICALLY, the postwar decades brought to the army, besides stagnation, an awakening professionalism. The example of Prussia, dramatized by the Franco-Prussian War of 1870–71, provided one stimulus, the restless, innovative Sherman another. Strengthening the infant Artillery School and the Engineering School of Application during the 1870s, founding the School of Application for Infantry and Cavalry at Fort Leavenworth in 1881, Sherman laid the foundations of a system of advanced military education. He created opportunities for officers to observe foreign armies and report on their practices. Under his patronage, Lt. Col. Emory Upton traveled around the world and set forth his findings in *The Armies of Asia and Europe*. Although not published until 1904, the contents of Upton's enormously influential *The Military Policy of the United States* reached a wide audience in other forms almost immediately after his tragic suicide in 1884. From its founding in 1863, the *Army and Navy Journal* provided a forum for exchange of opinion. Professional journals began to appear in the 1880s, organs of newly created associations for promoting the study and discussion of military theory, such as the Military Service Institution of the United States and the U.S. Cavalry Association. By the 1890s, when the Indian Wars finally dragged to a close, professionalism flourished in the army.[1]

The gathering currents of military professionalism, centering on conventional wars of the future, left almost wholly untouched the unconventional wars of the present. Neither West Point nor the postgraduate schools addressed themselves more than incidentally to the special conditions and requirements of Indian warfare. Indian campaigns found their way into professional literature as interesting history rather than as case studies from which lessons of immediate relevance might be drawn. Sherman's belief that the British experience in India might suggest techniques applicable to the American West partly motivated Upton's world travels. But *The Armies of Asia and Europe*, reflecting the author's enchantment with the Prussian war machine, contained no prescriptions for unconventional warfare. Military thought continued to focus on the next foreign war, as General Hancock made clear when he advised a congressional committee in 1876 that the Indian service of the Army was "entitled to no weight" in determining the proper strength, composition, and organization of the army.[2] Yet for a full century, with brief interludes of foreign and civil war, Indian service was the primary mission of the army.

Three special conditions set this mission apart from more orthodox military assignments. First, it pitted the army against an enemy who usually could not be clearly identified and differentiated from kinsmen not disposed at the moment to be enemies. Indians could change with bewildering rapidity from friend to foe to neutral, and rarely could one be confidently distinguished from another.

Second, Indian service placed the army in opposition to a people that aroused conflicting emotions. Soldiers who had witnessed the plunder, rape, torture, and mutilation of Indian hostilities had no difficulty viewing the adversary as a savage beast. Yet between conflicts troops and Indians mingled with enough familiarity to reveal dimensions of Indian character that a white man could find fascinating and even admirable, and to disclose something of the injustice, deceit, fraud, and cruelty the Indian endured from government officials and frontier citizens. Ambivalence, therefore, marked military attitudes toward the Indians—fear, distrust, loathing, contempt, and condescension, on the one hand; curiosity, admiration, sympathy, and even friendship, on the other.

And third, the Indian mission gave the army a foe unconventional both in the techniques and aims of warfare. Cunning, stealth, horsemanship, agility and endurance, skill with weapons, mobility, and exploitation of the natural habitat for military advantage marked his techniques. He fought on his own terms and, except when cornered or when his family was endangered, declined to fight at all unless he enjoyed overwhelming odds. Rituals and taboos decreed by religion ordered his conduct of war. A distinctive value system made plunder and combat honors as much the motivation and goal of war as defense of home and family.

These special conditions of the Indian mission made the U.S. Army not so much a little army as a big police force. Scattered in tiny contingents through the frontier regions, it was charged with watching over the Indians and punishing those who declined to do the Great Father's bidding. Long experience might have suggested that the realities of its chief employment be acknowledged in an organization and doctrine adapted to the police function. Instead, for a century the army tried to perform its unconventional mission with conventional organization and methods. The result was an Indian record that contained more failures than successes and a lack of preparedness for conventional war that became painfully evident in 1812, 1846, 1861, and 1898.

That military leaders failed to develop a formal doctrine of Indian relations—for in fact this service entailed much more than merely Indian fighting—is primarily an indictment of their prescience. They simply did not forsee that Indian resistance would engage the army for a hundred years. The current or at most the next war would be the last, and then they could get on with their main business. To devise a special system for so seemingly transitory a purpose did not occur to them. Therefore, the Indian troubles that occupied the army year after year called forth a body of essentially orthodox strategies only slightly modified by the special conditions of the police function.

The basic strategy, as the chairman of the Board of Indian Commissioners explained it to Red Cloud in 1871, was for "the Great Father to put war-houses all through the Indian country."[3] As General Ord observed, "building posts in their country . . . demoralizes them more than anything else except money and whiskey."[4] Such garrisons made bluecoats visible to the Indians and placed them close enough to help prevent trouble and to react to it promptly when it broke. Both Sherman and Sheridan favored this approach, and they could point to Montana and Texas as examples of systematic pacification and settlement of frontier areas by advancing lines of forts.[5]

The flaws in this system arose mainly from the small size of the army. To be truly effective, the network of forts needed to be comprehensive enough to cover all potential trouble spots and strongly enough held to permit the prompt application of force sufficient to meet probable contingencies. An army of 25,000, with other responsibilities as well, could meet neither requirement. It could not man a hundred posts with effective garrisons, much less the larger number the effort implied.

An alternative approach held that troops should be concentrated at a few strategically located posts from which they could operate in strength wherever needed. General Pope and others who urged concentration were actually less concerned with Indian strategy than with the injury to regimental drill, discipline, and administration caused by dispersion. Almost everyone, even Sherman and Sheridan, conceded the benefits that would flow from concentration, but until the middle 1880s it was both practically and politically impossible. Settlers demanded protection in visible proximity, sometimes justifiably, sometimes not, and they never relinquished a nearby fort without a political struggle. Nor did they quietly acquiesce in the removal of a military market. (Testified one well-traveled observer: "There is a fort at Salt Lake City, which is there for the purpose, as I believe, of eating up Brigham Young's provisions—his surplus food."[6]) Also, since large permanent posts required specific congressional authorization, which was exceedingly difficult to obtain, the small temporary posts had to be maintained simply for the shelter they afforded the troops. Finally, the generals seem to have sensed, if they did not clearly perceive, that concentration could not work well until the Indians themselves had been concentrated on reservations and until railroad construction had progressed so far as to insure rapid movement in most directions.[7]

In 1880 Sherman judged the railroads sufficiently advanced to begin recasting the western military system, and the Secretary of War announced concentration as an official policy. Against congressional parsimony and the resistance of local constituents to abandonment of posts, however, the program proceeded slowly. Between 1880 and 1889 the number of western posts dropped from 111 to 82. In the next two years, with the prospect of Indian hostilities manifestly receding, the number fell to 62 in 1891.[8]

Torn between dispersion and concentration, the army pursued an Indian strategy that combined dispersion for defense with temporary concentration for offense. It was not a satisfactory strategy.

The dispersed garrisons were too few and too weak to present an effective defense. The offensive expeditions, formed only by further weakening the defenses, took too long to assemble and proceeded under handicaps that too often negated their effectiveness for offense.

The principal handicap was lack of mobility. In fact, the offensive expedition represented a wager of strength against mobility. Such a column could not begin to match the Indian's mobility, and reasonably alert tribesmen could almost always evade one. But if the quarry could be brought to bay, the army's superiority in numbers, firepower, organization, and discipline prevailed. One officer likened a typical expedition to a dog fastened by a chain— "within the length of chain irresistible, beyond it powerless. The chain was its wagon train and supplies."⁹

A column operating almost anywhere in the West devoted enormous effort to logistics. Supply depots had to be spotted at strategic points and guarded. Wagon trains or river steamers, usually owned by civilian firms under military contract, stockpiled supplies at the depots. Other trains shuttled between depot and field forces and accompanied the field forces. Each infantry company required at least one six-mule wagon, each cavalry troop three.¹⁰ Forage for mules and horses had to be hauled because "American" stock, unlike Indian ponies, could not subsist solely on grass, which often was not to be had anyway. Oxen did not require grain but were even slower than mules. Thus encumbered, a large command faced formidable odds indeed in trying to run down Indians who lived off the land, traveled lightly and swiftly, and when pressed scattered to reunite later at an appointed rendezvous. The Terry-Crook campaign of August 1876 against the Sioux furnishes an example of how decisive logistics could be; it ended with the troops expending virtually all their energy and resources simply keeping themselves supplied (see Chapter Fifteen).

Gen. George Crook met the challenge of mobility by making his forces dependent upon mule rather than wagon transportation. Other commanders at times experimented with mule trains, with indifferent to intolerable results depending on how badly they managed the enterprise. But Crook refined the science of organizing, equipping, and operating mule trains into perhaps the highest state of perfection in the history of the U.S. Army. He lavished unceasing study and care on the selection of both mules and attendants—civilians preferred—and on the proper design, mounting, and packing of pack saddles. Efficiently managed, therefore, his trains gave him mobility, as is eloquently attested in the recollections of one of Geronimo's warriors: "Troops generally carry their ammunition and supplies in wagons, therefore they follow the flat country. It was only when Gen. George Crook chased the Indians with a column supplied by mule pack trains that the Apaches had a hard time staying out of reach."[11]

Another aspect of mobility was the endurance of cavalry horses. Even when not deprived of regular grain allowances, horses quickly deteriorated under extended exertion, and rare was the campaign that afforded either grain or nutritious grasses in sufficient abundance. Transportation limited the former, drouth, winter, or prairie fire the latter. In 1882 the Assistant Quartermaster General of the army stated as a military principle that "Unless cavalry operate in a country well supplied with forage a large amount of wagon carriage must be furnished for forage, and in such cases cavalry is of little value except to guard its own train, and to do that in the presence of an enterprising enemy it will need the addition of infantry."[12]

Experience in the West, most notably against the Sioux and Nez Percés in 1876–77, tended to confirm this principle. Indeed, the poor performance of the cavalry in these campaigns led to an extended debate over the comparative efficiency of infantry and cavalry in Indian warfare. Infantry officers, incensed over the shrinkage the foot regiments suffered in order to permit the expansion of the mounted regiments in 1876 (see pp. 16–17), proclaimed the superiority of their arm. As the Sixth Infantry's Col. William B. Hazen stated the case: "After the fourth day's march of a mixed command, the horse does not march faster than the foot soldier, and after the seventh day, the foot soldier begins to outmarch the horse, and from that time on the foot soldier has to end his march earlier and earlier each day, to enable the cavalry to reach the camp the same day at all."[13] Critics also asserted that cavalry as it had developed in America was essentially mounted infantry. Cavalrymen rode to the battlefield and then dismounted to fight. They made indifferent infantry because they were armed with lighter weapons and were distracted by their horses. The trooper, even cavalry officers conceded, fought on foot because he had not been trained to fight on horseback.[14]

No substantive changes of organization or method resulted from the debate. In fact, while articulating some truths not wholly appreciated in earlier years, infantrymen somewhat overstated their case. Despite its deficiencies of staying power and mounted performance, cavalry remained the arm most likely to close with Indians in combat. Under favorable circumstances foot troops might get into a village of Indians, conceded Col. John Gibbon, as his own Seventh Infantry had at the Big Hole; "but, as a general rule, and especially when they are on the alert, cavalry is the only arm of the service with which that can be done."[15] General Sherman remained convinced that "cavalry is the most efficient arm of the service for the present existing condition of things in the Indian country."[16] The controversy damaged the cavalrymen's ego but not their preeminence in Indian warfare.

Lacking mobility, heavy offensive columns brought the enemy to battle only when he could be surprised, usually in his village encumbered with his family. The surprise attack on a village produced casualties and panic and ended with the destruction of food, shelter, stock, and other possessions. The psychological effect on the Indian survivors as well as on allied groups often led to surrender.

To achieve surprise required not only a careless enemy but also excellent intelligence and reconnaissance services. White frontiersmen and friendly Indians, wise in wilderness and Indian lore, were hired or enlisted to provide these services. "California Joe" Milner, "Buffalo Bill" Cody, "Lonesome Charlie" Reynolds, "Yellowstone" Kelly, Frank Grouard, Al Sieber, and Crow, Arikara, Osage, Shoshoni, and Apache scouts proved indispensable in locating the objective and easing a command into striking position. In employing auxiliaries so well adapted to both enemy and terrain, the army made a modest departure from conventional methods, but then failed to carry it to a logical conclusion.

Two other strategies improved prospects for a successful surprise attack. First was the winter campaign. Indians tended to neglect ordinary precautions in the winter. With game and grass scarce, they were also less mobile. Regular army forces ran great risks in winter operations, but the returns could be correspondingly rewarding. The second strategy involved converging columns. Several forces moving on an area of operations from different directions were more likely than one to fall on an Indian camp.

Converging columns could also harry an enemy into submission simply by keeping him constantly on the move and fearful of a surprise attack. Converging columns worked well in the Red River War of 1874–75, but failed spectacularly in the Sioux War of 1876.

The surprise attack on the village was total war. In such encounters women and children were nearly always present. They mingled with the fighting men, often participated in the fighting, and in the confusion and excitement of battle were difficult to identify as noncombatants. In engagement after engagement women and children fell victim to army bullets or were cast upon a hostile country, often in winter, without food or shelter.

Total war raised disturbing moral questions, not only for the eastern humanitarians who shrilly protested military butchery, but for the army as well. Some officers openly acknowledged the intent of the surprise attack to be indiscriminate killing. "The confessed aim is to exterminate everyone," concluded Colonel de Trobriand, "for this is the only advantage of making the expedition; if extermination were not achieved, just another burden would be added —prisoners."[17] Other officers went to great lengths to distinguish between combatants and noncombatants. General Crook, for example, constantly emphasized this policy.[18] Even Wounded Knee, which took the lives of at least sixty-two women and children, discloses extraordinary efforts to avoid harming them.[19]

A generalization that acknowledges the varying attitudes of commanders toward this issue is difficult. However, conceding instances of purposeful slaughter, conceding instances of deliberate or careless killing of noncombatants by individual soldiers, and conceding instances in which commanders failed to take proper precautions, it seems clear that most officers tried hard to spare women and children. The officer corps subscribed to a Sir Walter Scott code of chivalry that exalted womanhood. Although perhaps not embracing Indian womanhood, it nevertheless held in contempt the mistreatment of women. In the majority of actions, the army shot noncombatants incidentally and accidentally, not purposefully.

But what of the morality of a strategy aimed at finding and destroying Indian villages where women and children would unquestionably be present and suffer death or injury? This is a question not to be asked of the Indian Wars alone but of all conflicts in which war has been waged on whole populations. Whether, as General Sherman contended, such warfare is in the end more humane because it is more speedily and definitively ended may be argued. The significant point is that Sherman's strategy for the conquest of the Indians was as moral, or immoral, as his march across Georgia in the Civil War or as more recent military actions involving civilian populations. The ethical questions implicit in the style of war against the Indians are appropriate not solely to a characterization of the frontier army but rather to a discussion of the whole sweep of American military history and tradition.

Humanitarians, appalled by the killing of women and children, scored the army for practicing extermination. Some pronouncements of Sherman, Sheridan, and others sound like exterminationism. But closer examination reveals most such assertions to have been addressed not to the Indian race as a whole but only to those portions of it that defied the government's will. Extermination—a later generation would call it genocide—is the systematic obliteration of a whole people. Many officers believed that extinction was the Indian's ordained fate, but few advocated or attempted to bring it about by war. Rather it was an impulse to civilize the Indian that dominated military attitudes as it dominated public sentiment and government policy—and that belies the charge that the United States pursued a policy of genocide. Nor was genocide the result; in less than a century following the end of warfare, the Indian population doubled.

Though frequently criticized, the standard offensive method was never seriously threatened. Heavy columns of infantry and cavalry, locked to slow-moving supply trains, continued to crawl about the vast western distances in search of an enemy who could scatter and vanish almost instantly. Such expeditions ran up an impressive record of failure, but they also scored enough successes to discourage serious analysis of their validity or of possible alternatives. Most experienced officers knew their foe as a master of guerrilla warfare. Some even spoke of using his own techniques against him. But few ever went beyond this recognition to elaborate a doctrine combining the advantages of the two kinds of warfare.

One who came close was the erudite Frenchman, Col. Philippe Régis de Trobriand. He believed that the enemy's advantages could be largely offset, first, "by forming auxiliary squadrons composed of frontiersmen who know the Indians and who are able to fight them their own way"; and, second, "by enrolling in volunteer companies the Indians themselves who are allies of the United States and who are at war with the hostile tribes, the line officers being taken exclusively from among the men of the plains who are familiar with the habits, ideas, and languages of the tribes."[20]

Use of experienced frontiersmen against the Indians was hardly original with de Trobriand. Western governors and congressional representatives regularly advocated the muster of state or territorial Volunteers into federal service for Indian duty. Army leaders usually opposed these efforts because Volunteers lacked discipline, resisted federal authority, and were given to excessive plundering of both the enemy and the federal treasury. De Trobriand's scheme would have considerably lessened these disadvantages by incorporating special units of frontiersmen directly into the Regular Army. The one notable test of such a plan, Maj. George A. Forsyth's scout company in Kansas in 1868 (see pp. 147–48), yielded encouraging results. After the Battle of Beecher's Island, however, it was disbanded, and if a comparable unit was ever proposed, it failed to surmount barriers of convention and economy.

Nor was the use of Indians against Indians an original idea. Throughout the Indian Wars, the army employed Indian scouts. The army act of 1866 authorized 1,000 scouts, although after Congress imposed a ceiling of 25,000 on enlisted strength the number was administratively limited to 300 except on special occasions. Commanders testified emphatically to their worth.[21] In de Trobriand's view, however, they were valuable not solely as scouts, guides, and trailers but as fighters as well. Organized in military units under white officers, they would function roughly as regular troops in all situations except combat, when they would throw aside the white man's trappings and fight as Indians. Even as de Trobriand wrote, Frank and Luther North were validating this thesis on the central plains. From 1866 to 1870 their famous battalion of Pawnee scouts showed conclusively that Indians could be organized into military units and employed with good effect against other Indians.[22]

Another who viewed Indian warfare with rare insight was George Crook. Like de Trobriand, he saw the advantages of friendly tribesmen as auxiliaries in campaigns against hostiles. He used Shoshonis against Paiutes in Oregon in 1866–68, Pimas and Maricopas against Apaches in Arizona in 1872–73, and Shoshonis and Crows against Sioux in Wyoming and Montana in 1876. In these operations Crook did not organize his allies as formally as suggested by de Trobriand or practiced by the North brothers, or as he himself did in Arizona in later years. Usually they fought under their own leaders and followed their own inclinations as often as the instructions of the officers or white scouts assigned to accompany them.

Crook gave this approach a significant variation. Rather than seek allies in one tribe to fight another, he turned to the very tribe against which his operations were directed. The efficacy of this method lay not only in matching the enemy's special skills but also in the psychological impact on the enemy of finding his own people arrayed against him. "To polish a diamond there is nothing like its own dust," Crook explained to a reporter in 1886:

It is the same with these fellows. Nothing breaks them up like turning their own people against them. They don't fear the white soldiers, whom they easily surpass in the peculiar style of warfare which they force upon us, but put upon their trail an enemy of their own blood, an enemy as tireless, as foxy, and as stealthy and familiar with the country as they themselves, and it breaks them all up. It is not merely a question of catching them better with Indians, but of a broader and more enduring aim—their disintegration.[23]

Applied successfully by both Crook and Col. Nelson A. Miles in the closing stages of the Sioux War of 1876 (see Chapter Fifteen), the practice received its most intensive test under Crook's supervision in the Apache conflicts of the 1880s (see Chapter Nineteen).

Exclusive or even major use of Indians as combat forces entailed grave risks. They were kinsmen, racial if not tribal, of the people being hunted, and one could never be fully certain of their reliability. Good leadership offset much of the gamble. Crook chose his scout officers with great care. Young men of ambition, dedication, sensitivity, and above all rapport with their men offered the best prospects. These officers, remarked one perceptive observer, were less "Indian-fighters" than "Indian-thinkers."[24] Whether scouts or fighting auxiliaries, Indians compiled an almost uniform record of faithfulness—the mutiny at Cibicu was a rare exception (see p. 372)—but this record failed to allay widespread suspicions. General Sheridan's distrust of Apache scouts led to the greatest disappointment of Crook's career (see p. 386).

Finally, Crook recognized that successful Indian strategy involved far more than simply fighting Indians. He framed four precepts to guide him in dealing with them: first, to make no promises that could not be kept; second, to tell the truth always; third, to provide remunerated labor; and fourth, "to be patient, to be just, and to fear not."[25] Unfortunately, few officers of either the army or the Indian Bureau possessed the intellectual and human qualities to follow such a code. And even Crook, sharing authority with civilian officials and reporting to superiors who could overrule him, found adherence discouragingly difficult and sometimes impossible.

The nation's leaders failed to heed the lessons of Crook's experience. With a conventional military force they tried to control, by conventional military methods, a people that did not behave like conventional enemies and, indeed, quite often were not enemies at all. Usually, the situation did not call for warfare, merely for policing. That is, offending individuals or groups needed to be separated from the innocent and punished. But this the conventional force could rarely do. As a result, punishment often fell, when it fell at all, on guilty and innocent alike. Instead of a conventional army, a force was needed endowed with the capability of differentiating between guilty and innocent and, employing the Indian's own fighting style, of effectively contending with the guilty.

The Indian scout companies evolved in the 1870s and 1880s by Crook and others suggested what might be achieved by Indian auxiliaries given a scale and continuity sufficient to permit the full effect to be demonstrated. A brief experiment in the early 1890s of creating an Indian company in every regiment stationed in the West represented misdirected effort; it aimed less at exploiting the Indian's peculiar abilities than transforming him into a conventional soldier, and anyway the Indian Wars had ended by the time the program got fully under way.[26] Nor did the reservation police forces organized by the Indian Bureau beginning in 1878 meet the need, although they did remarkably well considering their limitations. They were small, badly equipped, underpaid, without overall direction or coordination, and buffeted by the partisan and patronage politics that afflicted the Indian Bureau.[27]

Some thought the Northwest Mounted Police developed by the British to bring law and order to the Canadian West offered an ideal model. But as Sheridan and others pointed out, the 300 red-coated constables succeeded mainly because the sparsity of settlement prevented serious competition between whites and Indians for the lands and resources of the Northwest Territories.[28]

Ironically, the only serious proposal for an Indian auxiliary force of meaningful composition and magnitude came from none other than a Commissioner of Indian Affairs. In this annual report for 1878 Commissioner Ezra A. Hayt proposed the formation of a corps of 3,000 Indians, "enlisted from the young men of the most warlike tribes, and placed under the command of Army officers of experience." Held in large bodies, fully controlled by the War Department, this auxiliary force would stand ready to rush to the scene of actual or threatened hostilities.[29]

In size, composition, leadership, and control, Hayt's reasoning seems sound. In employment, however, he might have given further thought to dispersing the force sufficiently to allow it to perform a police as well as a military function. A force of 3,000 would have yielded 15 four-company battalions of 200 Indians each. Recruited from and distributed among the potentially most troublesome tribes, properly trained and officered, such battalions might have prevented or contained many an outbreak and, brigaded with other Indian battalions and bolstered by regular units, could have rapidly quelled uprisings that could not be averted.

Commisioner Hayt's proposal seems not to have sparked any interest in the War Department, and he himself soon lost his post in one of the scandals that periodically rocked the Indian Bureau. The Regular Army continued to grapple cumbersomely with a mission for which it was badly organized and trained. How different might have been the history of the westward movement had a paramilitary force such as Hayt advocated been created and employed as a prominent adjunct to the army line.

NOTES

1. Weigley, *History of the United States Army*, pp. 272–81. Stephen E. Ambrose, *Upton and the Army* (Baton Rouge, La., 1964). Bigelow, *William Conant Church and the Army and Navy Journal.*
2. House Misc. Docs., 45th Cong., 2d sess., No. 56, p. 5.

3. CIA, *Annual Report* (1871), p. 24
4. March 5, 1867, in Senate Ex. Docs., 40th Cong., 1st sess., No. 13, p. 83.
5. SW, *Annual Report* (1879), pp. 4–6.
6. Felix Brunot, chairman of the Board of Indian Commissioners, Jan. 15, 1874, in House Reports, 43d Cong., 1st sess., No. 354, p. 157.
7. Considerable debate and discussion focused on this issue. See especially Sherman to Sheridan, Jan. 16, 1873, Sherman-Sheridan Letters, Sheridan Papers, LC; SW, *Annual Report* (1871), pp. 24, 40–47; (1872), p. 69; (1875), p. 77; (1876), p. 452; (1877), pp. 58–59, 63; (1880), pp. 53, 209–10; House Reports, 43d Cong., 1st sess., No. 384, pp. 159–62, 177–78, 189, 218–19, 223; House Reports, 44th Cong., 1st sess., No. 354, pp. 60, 61; House Misc. Docs., 45th Cong., 2d sess., No. 56, pp. 84, 123, 133, 270; House Misc. Docs., 45th Cong., 2d sess., No. 64, p. 69.
8. Figures are from tables in SW, *Annual Report* (1880), pp. 10–33; (1889), pp. 96–114; (1891), pp. 104–22. See also *ibid.* (1880), pp. iv, 4–5; (1881), pp. 35–36; (1882), pp. 5, 10–20, 69, 80, 96, 101; (1883), pp. 9, 105; (1884), pp. 48, 84, 103; *Army and Navy Journal*, 20 (Sept. 30, 1882), 195.
9. G. W. Baird, "General Miles's Indian Campaigns," *Century Magazine*, 42 (July 1891), 351.
10. S. B. Holabird, "Army Wagon Transportation," *Ordnance Notes—No. 189* (Ordnance Department, Washington, D.C., April 15, 1882), pp. 1–3.
11. Jason Betzinez, with Wilbur S. Nye, *I Fought with Geronimo* (Harrisburg, Pa., 1959), p. 37. For Crook and his mule trains, see John G. Bourke, "Mackenzie's Last Fight with the Cheyennes: A Winter Campaign in Wyoming and Montana," *Journal of the Military Service Institution of the United States*, 11 (1890), (reprint ed., Bellevue, Neb., 1970), pp. 14–16; Bourke, *On the Border with Crook* (New York, 1891), pp. 138–39, 150–56; A. A. Cabannis, "Troop and Company Pack-Trains," *Journal of the U.S. Cavalry Association*, 3 (1890), 248–52; W. E. Shipp, "Captain Crawford's Last Expedition," *ibid.*, 5 (1892), 348–49; and Emmett M. Essin, III, "Mules, Packs, and Packtrains," *Southwestern Historical Quarterly*, 74 (1970), 52–63.
12. Holabird, p. 3.
13. To House Military Committee, April 11, 1878, House Misc. Docs., 45th Cong., 2d sess., No. 56, p. 454. See also pp. 44 (Marcy), 123 (Hazen again), 138 (Sully), and 237 (Miles).
14. *Army and Navy Journal*, 15 (May 4, 1878), 630–31; (May 11, 1878), 647. Hutchins, "Mounted Riflemen: The Real Role of Cavalry in the Indian Wars." W. E. Shipp, "Mounted Infantry," *Journal of the U.S. Cavalry Association*, 5 (1892), 76–80. Schofield in SW, *Annual Report* (1888), p. 104.
15. Testimony before the House Military Committee, April 26, 1878, House Misc. Docs., 45th Cong., 2d sess., No. 56, pp. 269–70.
16. House Reports, 43d Cong., 1st sess., No. 384, p. 283.
17. Philippe Régis de Trobriand, *Military Life in Dakota: The Journal of Philippe Régis de Trobriand*, trans. Lucille M. Kane (St. Paul, 1951), p. 64.
18. Bourke, *On the Border with Crook*, p. 182. Bourke, *An Apache Campaign in the Sierra Madre* (New York, 1958), p. 85.
19. Utley, *The Last Days of the Sioux Nation*, chap. 12.
20. De Trobriand, *Military Life in Dakota*, p. 65.
21. See, for example, SW, *Annual Report* (1867), pp. 59–60 (Augur), 79 (Steele), 73–74 (Halleck), 126–27 (McDowell).
22. George Bird Grinnell, *Two Great Scouts and Their Pawnee Battalion* (Cleveland, Ohio, 1928). Robert Bruce, *The Fighting Norths and Pawnee Scouts* (New York, 1932). Donald F. Danker, ed., *Man of the Plains: Recollections of Luther North, 1856–1882* (Lincoln, Neb., 1961).
23. Charles F. Lummis, *General Crook and the Apache Wars* (Flagstaff, Ariz.,

1966), p. 17. This is a series of articles correspondent Lummis wrote for the *Los Angeles Times* during the Geronimo campaign of 1886. See also Crook's similar thoughts regarding the Sioux operations in "The Apache Problem," *Journal of the Military Service Institution of the United States,* 27 (1886), 260. Crook set forth his views at considerable length in his annual report for 1883 in SW, *Annual Report* (1883), pp. 164–69.

24. Frederic Remington, "How an Apache War Was Won," in McCracken, ed., *Frederic Remington's Own West*, p. 49.

25. Crook, "The Apache Problem," p. 267.

26. Foner, *The United States Soldier Between Two Wars*, pp. 129–31.

27. For a history of reservation police, see William T. Hagan, *Indian Police and Judges* (New Haven, Conn., 1966).

28. SW, *Annual Report* (1878), p. 37. House Misc. Docs., 45th Cong., 2d sess., No. 64, p. 24. *Army and Navy Journal, 14* (July 14, 1877), 784. For the Canadian experience, see C. P. Stacey, "The Military Aspect of Canada's Winning of the West, 1870–1885," *Canadian Historical Review, 21* (1940), 1–24; Douglas Hill, *The Opening of the Canadian West* (New York, 1967); and John Peter Turner, *The North-West Mounted Police, 1873–1893* (2 vols., Ottawa, 1950). A comparative study of Canadian and American Indian policy and experience is badly needed.

29. CIA, *Annual Report* (1878), pp. x–xii.

FOUR

The Army, Congress, and the People

SHERMAN'S FRONTIER REGULARS endured not only the physical isolation of service at remote border posts; increasingly in the postwar years they found themselves isolated in attitudes, interests, and spirit from other institutions of government and society and, indeed, from the American people themselves. The Civil War had cemented powerful bonds between the people and their army. Postwar developments loosened, then almost entirely severed these bonds. Reconstruction plunged the army into tempestuous partisan politics. Then frontier service removed it largely from physical proximity to population and, except for an occasional Indian conflict, from public awareness and interest. Besides public and congressional indifference and even hostility, the army found its Indian attitudes and policies condemned and opposed by the civilian officials concerned with Indian affairs and by the nation's humanitarian community. One author has called the postwar decades "the Army's Dark Ages."[1] Truly did the Regulars feel that they contended with a host of enemies in the rear.

Although the army counted many staunch defenders among the national legislators, the Congress as an institution seemed chronically hostile. The hostility sprang from motives both old and new. Economy, ever a special concern of legislators, remained as vital an imperative as before the war. "If we continue to make these appropriations of the people's money to keep up this great army," warned a House member in 1869, "our constituents will run every one of us into the Potomac."[2] The familiar argument that standing armies menace democratic institutions continued to find its way into debates. The army, declared New York's veteran congressman Fernando Wood in 1876, "performs none of the legitimate functions of our Government in time of peace. It is inappropriate to such a period, having no uses, no duties, no affinity, or sympathy with the workings of a political institution founded on free opinion." Wood favored abolishing the War Department altogether and vesting its peacetime functions in the Interior Department.[3]

To these traditional sources of congressional antimilitarism the postwar years added fresh cause for hostility as Reconstruction drew the army increasingly into partisan politics. "The employment of the army in a service so closely related to political action," wrote Congressman James A. Garfield in 1878, "produced not a little prejudice against the entire military establishment."[4] Given the extreme passions Reconstruction engendered, the army's actions were bound to be too harsh for some and too mild for others.

The intimate relations with Congress fostered by Reconstruction in turn encouraged officers to participate rather freely in political campaigns and to lobby with members of Congress in behalf of both institutional and personal interests. Sherman deprecated such activity and studiously avoided it himself—too much so, in Sheridan's opinion.[5] Sherman viewed the army as "sheriffs of the nation." Sheriffs execute the law, he pointed out. They neither make nor interpret it and should not go into court to discuss it with judge or jury.[6] Few subordinates followed Sherman's example, and one irate House Democrat pointed out that some day the opposition party might gain control of the White House and conclude that officers doing double duty as soldier and politician deserved a rest—"that it will be but just to permit them to retire temporarily, at least, to some cool and invigorating climate like that of Alaska."[7] A War Department order of 1873 prohibited officers from coming to Washington without permission of the Secretary of War,[8] but this had little effect, especially since Washington-based staff officers were the worst offenders.

During the years of Republican domination, before southern Democrats began returning in strength, the principal threat in Congress came from economizers determined to abolish regiments no longer needed for Reconstruction rather than permit their employment on the frontier. This motive largely dictated the army reductions of 1869, 1870, and 1874. Also constantly menacing was the personal antipathy of Sen. John A. Logan, sometime chairman of the Senate Committee on Military Affairs, former volunteer general, and founder of the Grand Army of the Republic. Contemptuous of military professionalism, spokesman for the militia tradition, and embittered at Sherman for a fancied wartime injury,[9] Logan caused the army acute discomfort for two decades.

A combination of developments intensified the army's congressional troubles in the middle 1870s. In 1875 the Democrats captured the House of Representatives and held control, with one two-year interlude, until 1889. In the chaotic and bitterly contested presidential election of 1876, the Grant administration stationed troops at southern polling places and, especially in Louisiana, roused the fury of southern Democrats. The following year the Hayes administration used troops to suppress labor disorders in the big manufacturing centers of the East, thereby antagonizing northern Democrats representing these urban constituencies. For four years, 1875–79, House Democrats went after the army with a vengeance. Only by the most diligent effort did the Republican-controlled Senate save the army from emasculation.

Strategists for the campaign were the Democrats of the House Committee on Military Affairs, especially Chairman Henry B. Banning of Ohio and his energetic lieutenant, Edward S. Bragg of Wisconsin. Although northerners and former Union volunteer generals, they drew their support in the committee from southern congressmen who had but recently worn gray uniforms. Sherman regarded Banning and Bragg as tools of these southerners, and he discerned in their efforts nothing less than a plot to destroy the army altogether or to reconstitute it under former Confederate generals such as P. G. T. Beauregard and Cadmus Wilcox. "The Rebs whom we beat in the War will conquer us in politics," he predicted gloomily.[10]

Banning opened his offensive in February 1876 with an exhaustive investigation of military affairs, and by June the House had passsed two measures reducing and reorganizing the army and cutting officers' pay. Senator Logan bottled up both bills in the Senate military committee. The House built the reductions into the army appropriation bill, and the Senate appropriations committee as promptly cut them out. By July, when the conference committee met to resolve the differences between the House and Senate bills, word of the Custer disaster had broken, and the

House conferees receded in exchange for a provision authorizing a joint commission to consider reform and reorganization and to report to the next session of Congress. Indeed, instead of a decrease the army received a 2,500-man increase to meet the emergency dramatized by Custer's death.[11]

The joint commission called for by the army appropriation act drew members from the House, the Senate, and the army, including Banning and Sherman. Secretary of War Don Cameron presided. Despite frequent meetings during the autumn and winter of 1876, the Cameron Commission failed to report to Congress as directed. According to Sherman, Banning frustrated its deliberations by rarely attending meetings and studiously avoiding a position on any issue. Since no bill lacking his endorsement could clear the House military committee, none emerged from the commission.[12]

Angry Democrats, now further incensed by the use of troops in the South during the election of 1876, assailed the army again in the second session of the forty-fourth Congress. Charging that the Republican administration had trumped up an Indian scare to win an increase in the cavalry so that the infantry could be used for political purposes in the South, they loaded down the army appropriation bill with provisions for reducing enlisted strength (to 17,000) and the pay of generals. They also included a section enjoining the army from supporting the claim of either of the state governments contending for legitimacy in Louisiana. This last provision proved fatal to the bill, for Republicans viewed it as an unconstitutional invasion of the President's powers as commander in chief. Throughout the final day of the session, March 3, 1877, House and Senate conferees strove desperately to find a compromise. A last-minute effort to appropriate temporary funding aborted when midnight interrupted a roll-call vote and automatically ended the forty-fourth Congress.[13]

The failure of the appropriation bill did not seriously interfere with the army's supply services because suppliers could look forward to recompense when a bill was eventually enacted. But with the close of the fiscal year on June 30, 1877, the army ceased to receive pay. Issue of rations, clothing, and other provisions to enlisted men was not affected, but officers, dependent upon their pay for these necessities, endured severe hardship. Most of them had to resort to credit or loans, frequently at usurious rates. Finally, in October 1877, President Hayes called a special session of Congress. Although the familiar controversies threatened for a time to produce still another stalemate, Congress at length heeded the President's plea to defer debate on these questions to the regular session and on November 17 gave the army an appropriation act.[14]

Having sabotaged the Cameron commission, Banning in January 1878 brought forth his own bill. Besides reducing the size of the army, it called for automatic abolition of the army upon the failure of Congress, as in 1877, to pass an appropriation bill. Even his own committee balked at this. Another bill in this session aimed at abolishing West Point Military Academy and another at dramatizing the size of the officer corps by requiring officers in Washington to wear their uniforms at all times. Although these proposals failed, a measure for cutting enlisted and commissioned strength, and for barring use of the army in civil disturbances, gained House approval on May 28—again as part of the army appropriation bill rather than as substantive legislation. Again Senate Republicans pronounced the bill unacceptable. Again the issue was resolved by adopting the Senate version and setting up still another joint committee to consider the whole question of army reform.[15]

The new joint committee mounted the most ambitious effort of all to settle the vexing questions of size, organization, and administration of the army. Chaired by Sen. Ambrose E. Burnside of Rhode Island, ill-starred but nonetheless highly respected Civil War general, the committee drew its members from the two houses of the Congress. Their report, unveiled on December 12, 1878, recommended a comprehensive bill of 724 sections, including one containing the Articles of War and another updating the 1863 Army Regulations. The bill provided for a 25,000-man army, reduction of infantry regiments to eighteen and cavalry regiments to eight, consolidation of the Adjutant General's and Inspector General's departments into a general staff, and a limited mobility between line and staff. The grades of general and lieutenant general were to be abolished when vacated by Sherman and Sheridan.[16]

The Burnside bill offered the first really well-reasoned plan since the Civil War for giving the Regular Army a stable, politically acceptable organization. Sherman, Schofield, Hancock,

and other generals extended warm endorsements. Banning supported it. But staff officers, their privileges threatened, lobbied
furiously against it. So did economizers and foes of a regular
army of any size or composition, who sponsored amendments to
lower the ceiling to twenty, seventeen, and even fifteen thousand.
Nor did the bill contain the so-called *posse comitatus* clause, the
restraint on executive use of the army against citizens that Democrats viewed as beyond compromise. Finally, as Sherman noted,
"the bill is so infernal long that it offers a vast surface for attack."[17] Despite vigorous support, the legislation failed in both
House and Senate. Predictably, parts of it became attached to the
annual appropriation bill. Tests showed that all differences between House and Senate could be reconciled save one—the *posse
comitatus* issue. Again, as with its predecessor in 1877, the final
session of the forty-fifth Congress expired on March 3, 1879,
without an appropriation of funds for the army.[18]

With the angry debates on the Burnside measures, congressional concern with the army reached a climax. A special session
in the spring of 1879 quietly enacted an appropriation bill.[19]
Thereafter, as sectional passions cooled and, for one term at least,
Republicans captured both Houses, congressional efforts to destroy or weaken the army diminished, as did efforts at needed
reform. Not until the Spanish-American War reawakened some
of the old controversies was the army again given intense congressional scrutiny.

The army's congressional problems in the 1870s sprang chiefly
from its employment in the South. Frontier concerns became involved, however, when Democrats charged the Grant and Hayes
administrations with exploiting the Indian menace as an excuse
for maintaining a large army which could be loosed on the people
when the interests of the reigning party dictated. The Indians, in
this view, should be dealt with as had earlier generations—by
calling out militia in time of war and keeping only so many
Regulars as needed to guard the forts in time of peace.[20] Frontier
concerns also intruded, more fortunately for the army, in the tendency of Texas' powerful Democratic delegation to vote on military
issues as westerners rather than as southerners. Sherman regarded their defection from Democratic ranks as crucial to the
army's interests on more than one occasion.[21] Finally, the antago-
nisms expressed in the Congress and the threat of adverse legis-

lation kept the frontier Regulars constantly unsettled. As General Sheridan put it to a House committee in 1874: "Almost all of you have commanded troops, and know what a panic is. The Army is kept in a condition of constant panic all the time."[22]

Congressional attitudes toward the army reflected attitudes increasingly prevalent among the overwhelming portion of the population that did not reside near Indian country. Now and then the people saw their army employed in such controversial causes as Reconstruction, overseeing elections, and labor disorders. Most of the time it remained effectively hidden from view on the remote frontier. No very strong constituency or interest group in the East depended on it or spoke for its welfare. More fundamental, the burgeoning industrialization of the postwar decades gave rise to a widespread conviction that war had become a thing of the past. Articulated by Herbert Spencer and John Fiske, this "business pacifism," as Samuel P. Huntington has labeled it, held war so irrational and destructive of economic productivity and material well-being as to be unthinkable in the new industrial age. In such an intellectual climate, military institutions of any kind became anachronistic.[23] Physically, politically, socially, and intellectually, these factors separated the army from the people. Although less vocal in their antipathy, the people constituted the most dangerous of the army's critics.

This isolation from the people did not pass unrecognized by the Regulars. For most, it was simply an acute awareness of the ignorance, disinterest, or hostility of civilians. As an officer's wife wrote upon returning to a Montana post after furlough: "The winter East was enjoyable and refreshing from first to last, but citizens and army people have so little in common, and this one feels after being with them a while, no matter how near and dear the relationship may be."[24] In less personal terms, the *Army and Navy Journal* constantly drew attention to the problem, as in an 1877 editorial: "The present trouble with the Army is that it is separated from the knowledge and affections of the people who pay the taxes, and is only seen from year to year in the form of heavy appropriations."[25] Sherman and his generals, most notably John Pope, perceived the problem. "It is essential," Pope told a congressional committee in 1878, that the army's "relation to the people and to the government should be made closer and more harmonious. Unless this can be done it always invites and will always provoke criticism and unfriendly action."[26]

Proposed remedies were few and vague. Deploring the American tendency to copy from the French, Sherman declared that a nation's institutions should "harmonize with the genius and tone of the mass of the people. Our people are not French but American and our army should be organized and maintained upon a model of our own, and not copied after that of the French, who differ from us so essentially."[27] Pope held similar views, and he urged Congress to give the United States a military system "in harmony with the spirit of our government and the feelings and habits of our people." But other than advocating merit promotion as a means of ending the undemocratic exclusiveness of the officer corps—a cause the *Army and Navy Journal* also espoused—Pope provided no more specific description of such a system than Sherman.[28] Most responsive to the need, although designed for other needs as well, were proposals to localize unit recruiting by tying each regiment to a particular area of the nation. In the roots regiments and brigades traced to home communities, Asst. Insp. Gen. James A. Hardie pointed out in 1874, lay much of the strength of the Civil War volunteer armies.[29] Neither this nor any other remedy, however, gained acceptance.

In the long view, Huntington argues persuasively, the army profited from its separation from the people. Turning inward, it laid the groundwork for a professionalism that was to prove indispensable in the great world wars of the twentieth century. The postgraduate military school system, original thought about the nature and theory of warfare, and professional associations and publications trace their origins to this time of rejection by the people. In parsimonious appropriations and the low esteem of their countrymen, however, the frontier Regulars paid heavily for a future gain that few could then foresee.[30]

If the public's view of the army began to soften as the frontier period drew to a close, a large share of the credit is due to one man. Capt. Charles King turned to the pen after an Apache bullet ended his career in the Regular Army. For four decades, beginning in 1880, he told Americans about their soldiers out on the frontier. In almost seventy novels and other books, he portrayed his characters in warm and appreciative terms. A frontier veteran, viewing King's record as early as 1894, marveled at "the load of indifference, ignorance, suspicion and malice regarding the regulars which has been cleared away from American homes through the instrumentality of his versatile pen."[31] For all their romanticism, King's novels did indeed give countless readers a new sympathy for their border defenders and help arrest the drift of the army away from the people.[32]

NOTES

1. William A. Ganoe, *The History of the United States Army* (New York, 1924), chap. 9.
2. *Cong. Globe*, 40th Cong., 3d sess., p. 950 (Feb. 6, 1869).
3. *Cong. Rec.*, 44th Cong., 1st sess., p. 3780 (June 13, 1876).
4. "The Army of the United States," p. 195. See also Bigelow, *William Conant Church and the Army and Navy Journal*, pp. 176–77.
5. "It would be well to be a little conservative on the subject of requests made by Congressmen, and to yield as far as you can consistently with the public service and justice to officers. They do not understand our standard, get angry, and the [staff] Bureaus at Washington know how to fan the flame to limit your legitimate rights by law." Sheridan to Sherman, April 3, 1876, Sherman Papers, vol. 43, LC.
6. *Army and Navy Journal*, 14 (Oct. 14, 1876), 155.
7. *Cong. Globe*, 42d Cong., 2d sess., p. 1875 (March 21, 1872).
8. SW, *Annual Report* (1873), pp. 5–6. House Ex. Docs., 43d Cong., 1st sess., No. 275.
9. During the Battle of Atlanta, Sherman bypassed Logan, heir apparent, and named Howard to command the Army of the Tennessee after the death of Gen. James B. McPherson. Logan erroneously attributed the decision to West Point prejudice against Volunteers. Lewis, *Sherman: Fighting Prophet*, pp. 388–89, 603–06.
10. Sherman to Sheridan, Jan. 10, 1879, Sherman-Sheridan Letters, Vol. 2, Sheridan Papers, LC. See also Sherman to Rep. J. D. Cox, Feb. 25, 1878, Sherman Papers, vol. 90, pp. 537–40, LC.
11. House Reports, 44th Cong., 1st sess., No. 354 [Banning Committee Report]. *Cong. Rec.*, 44th Cong., 1st sess., pp. 3356–64 (May 27, 1876); pp. 3457–69 (June 1, 1876); p. 3780 (June 13, 1876); pp. 3837–51 (June 16, 1876); pp. 3874–75 (June 17, 1876); pp. 4720–21, 4743 (July 19, 1876); pp. 5674–75, 5694–96 (Aug. 15, 1876). 19 Stat. 97–101 (July 24, 1876). 19 Stat. 204 (Aug. 15, 1876).
    The increase originated in a measure sponsored by the Texas delegation in both House and Senate requiring each cavalry troop stationed on the frontier to be increased to 100 enlisted men and a "sufficient force" of cavalry to be stationed on the Texas frontier. This provision, inserted by amendment in the House on June 17 and the Senate on June 26, preceded the Custer battle and grew wholly out of conditions in Texas. It was contained in the appropriations act as passed on July 24. Subsequently, however, on August 15, Congress responded to the Sioux crisis by temporarily lifting the 25,000-man ceiling by 2,500 in order that the cavalry could be increased to 100 men as required by the Texans' amendment without reducing the infantry.
12. Sherman to Sen. J. D. Cameron, Jan. 31, 1878, Sherman Papers, vol. 90, pp. 511–12, LC. (Cameron had left the War Department and won a Senate

seat.) Sherman to Rep. J. D. Cox, Feb. 25, 1878, *ibid.*, pp. 537–40. *Army and Navy Journal*, *15* (March 9, 1878), 489.

13. *Cong. Rec.*, 44th Cong., 2d sess., pp. 2111–20, 2151–52, 2171, 2230, 2178, 2193, 2241–42, 2214, 2246, 2248–52 (March 2–3, 1877).

14. Richardson, *Messages and Papers of the President*, 7, 452–54. *Cong. Rec.*, 45th Cong., 1st sess., pp. 222, 285–302, 306–26, 328–39, 345–52 (Nov. 8–12, 1877); pp. 415–23 (Nov. 15, 1877); pp. 510–14 (Nov. 17, 1877). 20 Stat. 1–4 (Nov. 21, 1877).

15. Garfield, "The Army of the United States," pp. 463–65. *Cong. Rec.*, 45th Cong., 2d sess., pp. 3534–55, 3579–89, 3615–25, 3631–46, 3669–84, 3715–30, 3731–36, 3760–71, 3793–3813, 3836–55, 3873–78, 3907, 4016, 4021, 4059, 4073, 4180–4200, 4234–48, 4295–4307, 4386, 4358, 4400, 4647, 4648, 4684–86, 4719, 4258, 4876 (May 18–June 21, 1878). House Misc. Docs., 45th Cong., 2d sess., No. 56. 20 Stat. 145–52 (June 18, 1878).

16. Senate Ex. Docs., 45th Cong., 3d sess., No. 555. Bernard L. Boylan, "The Forty-Fifth Congress and Army Reform," *Mid-America*, *61* (1959), 173–86.

17. Sherman to Sheridan, Dec. 30, 1878, Sherman-Sheridan Letters, Sheridan Papers, LC.

18. Boylan. *Cong. Rec.*, 45th Cong., 3d sess., pp. 125, 297–300, 849–50, 689, 896, 897–926, 963–76, 1034–41, 1059–69, 1132–45, 1707–14, 1755–67, 1809–25 (Dec. 18, 1878–March 3, 1879). Sherman to Sheridan, Dec. 18, 1878, Sherman-Sheridan Letters, Sheridan Papers, LC. Schofield to Sherman, Dec. 20, 1878, Sherman Papers, vol. 49, LC.

19. 21 Stat. 30–35 (June 23, 1879).

20. Cf. *Cong. Rec.*, 45th Cong., 2d sess., p. 3585 (May 20, 1879). Sherman to Sheridan, Jan. 10, 1879, Sherman-Sheridan Letters, Sheridan Papers, LC.

21. Sherman to Sheridan, Nov. 20, 1877, Sherman-Sheridan Letters, Sheridan Papers, LC. See also pp. 353–54.

22. House Reports, 43d Cong., 1st sess., No. 384, p. 229.

23. Huntington, *The Soldier and the State*, pp. 222–30. See also Weigley, *History of the United States Army*, pp. 270–72.

24. Roe, *Army Letters from an Officer's Wife*, p. 333.

25. *Army and Navy Journal*, *15* (Sept. 8, 1877), 72–73. See also *ibid.* (Dec. 1, 1877), 265; and Bigelow, pp. 187–88.

26. House Misc. Docs., 45th Cong., 2d sess., No. 56, p. 34. See also the speech to a veteran's group quoted by Weigley, pp. 270, 272.

27. Sherman to Rep. S. A. Hurlbut, May 26, 1874, Sherman Papers, vol. 90, pp. 326–35, LC.

28. House Misc. Docs., 45th Cong., 2d sess., No. 56, pp. 33–34.

29. House Reports, 43d Cong., 1st sess., No. 384, p. 245. The most detailed exposition of this scheme was by Maj. William R. Price in a letter to Rep. John Coburn, April 2, 1872, *ibid.*, 42d Cong., 3d sess., No. 74, pp. 135–36.

30. Huntington, chap. 9.

31. W. H. Carter in *Journal of the U.S. Cavalry Association*, 7 (1894), 323–24.

32. For a sketch of King, see Don Russell's introduction to King's *Campaigning with Crook* (Western Frontier Library ed., Norman, Okla., 1964), pp. vii–xxii. See also Russell's "Captain Charles King, Chronicler of the Frontier," *Westerners Brand Book* (Chicago), *9* (March 1952), 1–3, 7–8, which lists all sixty-nine of King's books.

FIVE

Weapons, Uniforms, and Equipment

IN ARMAMENT, CLOTHING, AND ACCOUTERMENTS, the postwar Regular Army regressed to the conservatism of prewar years. Warehouses bulged with stocks accumulated during the Civil War. Depletion of these stocks, by issue, condemnation, and sale, consumed fifteen years or more for some categories. Innovation thus came slowly and modestly. Even after the approval of new uniforms and weapons in the early 1870s wartime items continued to be issued. The new patterns, scarcely major departures from the old, endured for twenty years with only minor and infrequent improvements.

The most significant advances were in weapons technology. Breech-loading arms and metallic cartridges, employed on a limited scale but with dramatic effect in the Civil War, reached the hands of all Regulars soon after the war's end. The Civil War musket had to be loaded at the muzzle with powder and ball contained in a paper cartridge and a percussion cap for ignition placed in a receptacle under the hammer. Fixed ammunition combined ignition, propellant, and projectile in a single metal cylinder inserted at the breech. Besides ease of loading and rapidity of fire, the metallic cartridge permitted greater velocity and accuracy.

The standard infantry arm for seven years following the Civil War was a modification of the famed Springfield rifle-musket. By August 1867 about 50,000 of these, left over from the war, had been altered to fire a metallic cartridge loaded at the breech. Most of these were the so-called "Allin Conversion" effected at the U.S. Armory at Springfield, Massachusetts, although some were modified by private contractors. Most, too, featured a reduction in caliber from .58 to .50. An 1868 improvement substituted a wholly new barrel rather than brazing a .50-caliber tube in the original .58-caliber barrel. "Almost unanimous opinion," wrote General Grant in 1867, "pronounces the weapon simple, strong, accurate, and not apt to get out of order."[1]

Cavalry carbines attained no such easy standardization. Some regiments carried the Spencer, others the Sharps, and all from time to time used a scattering of experimental models. Most troopers preferred the Spencer, a .50-caliber repeater fed from a tube in the stock containing seven rounds. The Spencer had proved itself in the Civil War. A unit armed with it could deliver devastating sustained fire, as Custer's Seventh Cavalry demonstrated at the Washita in 1868. Also popular, and preferred by many even though a single-shot, was the Sharps carbine. A sturdy and powerful veteran of frontier service since the 1850s, the Sharps was originally a breech-loading percussion arm using a paper cartridge. By 1869, however, the Ordnance Department had altered some 30,000 to receive a .50-caliber metallic cartridge.[2]

In 1872 an arms board was convened under the presidency of General Terry to select a single breech-loading system of rifles and carbines. After testing more than one hundred types, the board settled on the tried and popular Springfield Allin system. The model 1873 Springfield rifle and carbine resulted. Single-shot, caliber .45, these weapons served the army, with periodic improvements, for the next twenty years.[3] The infantry version Colonel Gibbon pronounced "a first-rate rifle, and probably the best that was ever placed in the hands of troops."[4] The cavalry carbine impressed some as too light, and at the Little Bighorn enough of them jammed to stir considerable criticism. It quickly subsided, however, and the Springfield carbine seems to have performed satisfactorily for the balance of the army's Indian service.[5]

Metallic-cartridge pistols began to appear in the early 1870s, gradually replacing the cap-and-ball six-shooters of Colt and Remington popularized in the Civil War. Colt's 1872 army revolver, the famed "Peacemaker," emerged the overwhelming favorite. The Army bought almost 13,000 of these single-action, .45-caliber six-shooters in 1873–74 and about 1,000 each year thereafter until 1891. A Remington .44-caliber and a Smith and Wesson .45-caliber, the latter with an automatic ejector perfected by Maj. George W. Schofield of the Tenth Cavalry, gave the Colt its principal but never very serious competition.[6]

In addition to carbine and pistol, cavalrymen also received a saber. It was heavy, cumbersome, and noisy, and its owner rarely got close enough to an Indian to use it. Few officers required their men to carry it in the field. Even so, proposals to abandon the saber altogether drew opposition from such champions of "cold steel" as old Gen. Philip St. George Cooke. Somehow the saber seems to have reassured them that the cavalry had not degenerated into mere mounted infantry, as many charged. "Give our troopers the saber. Sharpen it and teach them to use it," implored an anonymous correspondent of the *Army and Navy Journal* who signed himself "Sabre of the Regulars." "It never misses fire, and who does not believe that the gallant Custer would not have given millions for an hundred sabres when he made the last stand?"[7] The saber figured in a few engagements with Indians, but for most units it remained almost exclusively an ornament for inspection and parade.

The improved firearms that suddenly appeared in the hands of the bluecoats at the close of the Civil War took the Indians by surprise. The Sioux, for example, suffered bloody repulses at the Wagon Box and Hayfield fights of 1867 because of the deadly fire of the Allin-converted Springfields recently issued to the Twenty-seventh Infantry (see Chapter Eight). But as the soldiers obtained better arms, so too did the Indians. Indeed, while the army moved toward a single-shot system, warriors came increasingly into possession of repeaters. Favored over all others was the almost legendary Winchester, a weapon particularly well designed for mounted use. The number of warriors who boasted such weapons was greatly exaggerated. Most, if they owned a gun at all, had to content themselves with old trade muskets of doubtful utility or captured military arms. Too, ammunition was difficult to obtain, and few Indians became any better marksmen than their soldier opponents. Nevertheless, enough repeaters found their way into Indian hands, largely through traders, to prompt speculation on the changing nature of Indian warfare. "As long as the muzzle-loading arms were in use we had the advantage of them," declared General Crook in 1878, "and twenty men could whip a hundred, but since the breech-loaders came into use it is entirely different; these they can load on horseback, and now they are a match for any man."[8]

The anomaly depicted by survivors of the Little Bighorn (not without considerable exaggeration) of Sioux warriors armed with Winchester repeaters gunning down troopers armed with single-shot Springfields dramatized the need for a military repeater. Shortly after the Custer disaster, Colonel Mackenzie formally applied to have his regiment's Springfields replaced with Winchesters, but the Ordnance Department replied that the Winchester attained less range by 100 yards than the Springfield as well as less penetrating power by one-half.[9] Throughout the 1870s and 1880s, the Ordnance Department tested one magazine system after another, only to reaffirm each time its preference for the Springfield. Not until 1892 did the long reign of the 1873 Springfield draw to a close with the adoption of the Krag-Jorgensen magazine rifle.[10]

The army boasted one weapon that, when it could be employed, invariably dispersed, repulsed, and demoralized Indian concentrations. Although some commanders regarded artillery as useless in Indian warfare,[11] cannon accompanied many offensive expeditions and figured importantly in numerous engagements. The rough western terrain demanded light, easily transported types. One such, the twelve-pounder mountain howitzer, had been a familiar fixture on the frontier since the 1840s. In the postwar years, breech-loading, rifled steel cannon and Gatling guns became increasingly conspicuous.

The Hotchkiss "mountain gun" provided the most popular and effective artillery piece for western service. A 1.65-inch, 2-pounder steel rifle, it could be fired rapidly and accurately at ranges up to 4,000 yards. Above all, it was light and compact enough to be taken almost anywhere on a wheeled carriage. General Miles declared in 1890 that he had campaigned with the mountain gun all over the northern plains and had found only one area, the timbered country around Yellowstone National Park, where it could not follow the cavalry.[12]

The Gatling gun gave less satisfaction. Forerunner of the machine gun, the Gatling fired 350 rounds of rifle ammunition per minute from a bank of ten revolving barrels turned by a crank and fed from a hopper. Gatlings "are worthless for Indian fighting," Miles declared. "The range is no longer than the rifle and the bullets so small that you cannot tell where they strike."[13] Moreover, the Gatling easily fouled with the refuse of black powder cartridges and jammed with overheating. It was also cumbersome; rather than have his march slowed, Custer refused to take a Gatling platoon up the Rosebud to the Little Bighorn.[14]

Whether Gatlings, rifles, or howitzers, artillery contingents almost never came from the artillery regiments. Instead, details from infantry or cavalry manned the weapons and condemned cavalry horses drew them. Col. Henry J. Hunt of the Fifth Artillery, who had been the Army of the Potomac's chief of artillery in the Civil War, thought this outrageous, especially since half of the ten light batteries authorized for the regular artillery regiments were not mounted and equipped. Hunt believed Gatlings would be found highly effective in Indian warfare if served by trained artillerists and strong animals.[15] Lending support to his belief was an experiment conducted in Texas by General Ord. In 1878 he added a Gatling platoon formed from detailed men of the Twenty-fourth Infantry to Battery F, Second Artillery, and gave it extensive training. The unit impressed both Ord and Colonel Mackenzie with its accuracy of fire as well as its mobility. In 1881, equipped with Gatlings and field artillery, the battery took station at Fort Leavenworth as part of the new Cavalry and Infantry School.[16]

The Regulars went west in 1866 attired in the familiar blue of the Union armies—dark blue blouse and light blue trousers trimmed in the distinctive colors of the wearer's arm of service. To the vast annoyance of Quartermaster General Meigs, this uniform drew widespread and chronic complaint. No one liked the cumbersome and fragile "Kossuth" hat with its high crown, turned-up brim on one side, and decorative ostrich feathers. Less objectionable was the kepi or forage cap, but it too looked unsightly when compared with the trim French model from which it had been copied. More fundamental were defects of cut, sizing, and quality, largely the result of contract profiteering during the war. Soldiers had to bear the cost of tailoring issue clothing to acceptable standards of comfort and appearance, and then sustained additional expense when, because the cheap cloth swiftly wore out in hard frontier service, they overdrew their clothing allowance. Moreover, the single weight of the uniform roasted the wearer in hot weather and chilled him in cold.[17]

Although the Civil War uniform stocks were not finally exhausted until about 1880, a shortage in certain sizes led, in 1872, to a revision of uniform regulations. The new uniform, according to General Sherman, was the creation of Insp. Gen. Randolph B. Marcy, who designed it and secured its adoption by Secretary of War Belknap during Sherman's absence in Europe in 1871–72.[18] The most notable changes, reflecting Prussian influence, were in the dress uniform. Cavalry and artillery sported a spiked helmet bearing a large metal eagle and supporting a horsehair plume, yellow for cavalry, red for artillery. Infantry received a handsome shako with a light blue plume for officers and pompon for enlisted men. A subsequent change, in 1881, gave the infantry spiked helmets, too, with white instead of blue plumes.[19] Blouses and trousers, trimly cut, better fitting, and ornamented with piping and facings identifying the arm of service, gave soldiers a smarter appearance than previously. Officers presented a dazzling array of gold cords, tassles, epaulettes, and a double row of brass buttons. Undress uniforms, after a brief and unfortunate experiment with plaited blouses for infantry, were also made more acceptable. Both cavalry and infantry rated a simple five-button blouse with falling collar, although the old cavalry shell jacket with yellow trim and the nine-button infantry frock coat, both with standup collars, continued to be issued until the wartime stocks were depleted.

Even though the new regulations substituted a cut-down *chasseur* kepi presenting the rakish French appearance absent in the earlier model, undress headgear continued to present problems. Soldiers complained that the kepi gave no protection to the head and indeed could only be kept there with great difficulty. "A clam-shell would be as good," remarked a soldier in 1876.[20] The black 1872 campaign hat, featuring an unusually wide brim that could be hooked to the crown to produce a Napoleonic effect, offered a completely unsatisfactory alternative to the kepi. It lost its sizing after the first wetting and quickly went to pieces. Col. David S. Stanley called this hat "the most useless, uncouth rag ever put on a man's head."[21] A more orthodox hat, with narrower brim, adopted in 1876, gave scarcely greater satisfaction either for comfort or durability. "Hence in the field," summed up a campaigner in 1877, "we see no forage caps, but in their stead hats—white hats, brown hats, black hats, all kinds of hats except the Service hat, for that, too, is unsuitable."[22]

Besides a variety of hats in a still greater variety of shapes, a typical column on campaign displayed blue, gray, or even checked shirts and faded regulation trousers. Horsemen often lined the seat with canvas or wore trousers made entirely of canvas. More stylish types affected white corduroy breeches, while "the true dandy," as a New York correspondent reported from the Yellowstone in 1876, "dons a buckskin shirt with an immense quantity of fringe dangling about in the wind."[23] Cavalrymen stuffed their trousers into troop boots, infantrymen into socks tied up over the cuffs. Canvas leggings replaced the latter method in the infantry in the late 1880s. Leather gauntlets appeared in 1884. Although an occasional shoulder strap identified an officer, evidence of rank was scarce in the field.

Equally casual and expedient were methods of carrying ammunition, equipment, and utensils. Soldiers disliked the regulation black leather cartridge boxes, originally designed for paper cartridges but adapted to metallic ammunition by adding sheepskin lining or banks of loops. McKeever, Dyer, Hagner, and King were the principal models tested in the 1860s and 1870s. As early as 1866, Capt. Anson Mills sewed leather loops to a standard belt and thus distributed the weight evenly around the waist, and in 1867 Col. William B. Hazen invented a looped leather device that slid on and off the belt. Rather than use the boxes, soldiers improvised their own looped belts until the Ordnance Department at last, in late 1876, bowed to the demand and began manufacturing "prairie belts" of canvas loops sewed on a leather backing. By devising a means of weaving loops and body in a single fabric, Mills vastly improved the prairie belt. His 1881 woven cartridge belt, adopted by the army, was the forerunner of an elaborate system of webbed equipment that spread around the world and made its inventor a wealthy man.[24]

The mounted trooper stowed mess gear and other possessions into saddle bags behind his McClellan saddle. He tied his blanket in a roll in front of the saddle and his blouse or overcoat in the rear. The saddle also supported lariat, picket-pin, canteen, and other utensils. The carbine, attached to a broad leather sling across his left shoulder, fitted awkwardly into a socket on the right side of the saddle. A sheath knife hung from the waist belt on his left hip, a black leather holster containing his revolver, butt forward, on his right hip. The foot soldier rarely bothered with the regulation knapsack, preferring instead to distribute the weight of his gear in a blanket roll slung over the shoulder. His bayonet, like the cavalryman's saber, usually remained behind. A good sheath knife proved as essential as in the cavalry. Rifle and canteen completed the "web-foot" outfit.

The absence of satisfactory summer and winter garb inflicted continuing hardship. Troops in the desert Southwest appealed for lighter, better ventilated clothing. Farther north, even with the heavy, light-blue overcoat, the regulation wool uniform gave scant protection against the winter blasts of the Great Plains and Rocky Mountains. The Quartermaster General's Clothing Bureau tested innovations, but the line as often simply improvised to meet the need.

In the 1870s the Clothing Bureau experimented with a variety of Arctic overcoats, caps, gauntlets, and boots. Buffalo, beaver, bear, seal, and muskrat furs were tried, along with canvas lined with sheepskin or blanket material. The buffalo garments proved the most effective and in fact gained wide use before winning official sanction. By the late 1870s, special winter clothing had become standard for northern posts. An officer's wife described the typical soldier thus attired setting forth "in the blackness and bitter cold of a winter night in Dakota": "Clad in buffalo skins, trousers and overocat with the fur inside, mufflers over his ears, hands incased in fur mittens, his face in a mask, leaving space sufficient only to see his way, he presents an appearance rivaling his Eskimo brother."[25]

Concessions to hot weather came more slowly. In 1875 Quartermaster General Meigs obtained from the British Minister in Washington some white cork helmets such as the Queen's troops used in India and elsewhere. Tested for five years and slightly modified, the sun helmet won approval in 1880. In 1886 white cotton duck blouses, trousers, and overalls were issued experimentally in Texas and proved so popular that the following year they, too, won approval. Even so, straw hats from the post trader's store enjoyed greater favor than cork helmets, and cotton uniforms never replaced the more informal apparel frontier soldiers had always worn. As an ultimate in expedient response to hot weather, Captain Lawton's troops combed Mexico's Sierra Madre in 1886 attired in moccasins, battered campaign hats, and long underwear (see Chapter Twenty).[26]

America's frontier soldiers, a perceptive English observer summed up, looked like *banditti* but boasted a "practical adaptability" for their service that would surprise the well-turned-out "barrack-yard" soldiers of Europe.[27] More graphically, if also more verbosely, a *New York Times* reporter said almost the same thing in describing the arrival of the Fifth Cavalry at Fort Fetterman en route to join Crook in July 1876:

... They came along in thorough fighting trim, flanking parties out, and videttes too; and the wagon train of forty wagons following with a strong cavalry guard. To a fastidious eye, ... there was something quite shocking in the disregard of regulation uniform, and the mud-bespattered appearance of the men; but it was a pleasure to see how full of vim, of spirit, and emphatically of fight, the fellows looked. ... About the only things in their dress which marked them as soldiers were their striped pants and knee boots, both well bespattered with mud. Their blue Navy shirts, broad brimmed hats, belts stuffed with cartridges, and loose handkerchiefs knotted about the neck, gave them a wild, bushwhacker appearance, which was in amusing contrast with their polished and gentlemanly manners.[28]

With only slight changes of detail, the journalist might have been describing almost any frontier column on the march between 1866 and 1890.

NOTES

1. SW, *Annual Report* (1867), pp. 17–18. Arcadi Gluckman, *United States Muskets, Rifles, and Carbines* (Buffalo, N.Y., 1948), pp. 273–89. See also SW, *Annual Report* (1866), p. 5; (1869), pp. 442–43.
2. Gluckman, pp. 395–98, 421–22, 438–40. SW, *Annual Report* (1866), p. 5; (1869), p. 442; (1871), p. 250.
3. Gluckman, pp. 289–93, 406–9.
4. Testimony before House Military Committee, April 26, 1878, House Misc. Docs., 45th Cong., 2d sess., No. 56, p. 264.
5. *Army and Navy Journal*, *14* (Aug. 26, 1876), 78; *15* (April 27, 1878), 610. SW, *Annual Report* (1877), p. 52. Colonel N. A. Miles before House Military Committee, Dec. 13, 1877, House Misc. Docs., 45th Cong., 2d sess., No. 56, p. 240. Kenneth M. Hammer, *The Springfield Carbine on the Western Frontier* (Bellevue, Neb., 1970). John E. Parsons and John S. du Mont, *Firearms in the Custer Battle* (Harrisburg, Pa., 1953).
6. Arcadi Gluckman, *United States Martial Pistols and Revolvers* (Buffalo, N.Y., 1939), pp. 213–17, 230, 233–36. James S. Hutchins, "Boots and Saddles on the Frontier," *Westerners Brand Book* (Chicago), *12* (March

1966), 6–7. Parsons and du Mont. Exhaustive tests of these three pistols at the Springfield Armory in 1876 produced this conclusion: "The record of this trial shows the Colt revolver to be the most serviceable of the three arms under consideration, and the one best adapted to the military service. It is simple in its mechanism, stable in its structure, and will endure the most severe tests to which it may be subjected in the hands of the cavalry soldier." *Army and Navy Journal, 14* (Feb. 10, 1877), 435–39.

7. *Army and Navy Journal, 14* (Oct. 14, 1876). 154. For Cooke see *ibid., 15* (May 25, 1878), 678. For other opinions see *ibid., 15* (April 27, 1878), 610 (Carr); (May 4, 1878), 628 (Merritt); (July 6, 1878), 778 (Brackett).

8. *Army and Navy Journal, 15* (June 29, 1878), 758. See also Crook's "The Apache Problem," pp. 259–60, for further discussion. For Indian arms at the Little Bighorn, see Parsons and du Mont, chap. 3.

9. *Army and Navy Journal, 14* (Aug. 26, 1878), 48.

10. Gluckman, pp. 330–32. Sidney B. Brinckerhoff and Pierce Chamberlain, "The Army's Search for a Repeating Rifle, 1873–1903," *Military Affairs, 32* (1968), 20–30.

11. E.g., General Crook (*Autobiography*, p. 146) and Colonel Merritt (*Army and Navy Journal, 15* [May 4, 1878], 628).

12. Miles to Ruger, Dec. 7, 1890, Military Division of the Missouri Letters Sent 1890–91, National Archives. I have described this weapon and its fearful work at Wounded Knee in *The Last Days of the Sioux Nation*, chap. 12. See also S. E. Whitman, *The Trooper: An Informal History of the Plains Cavalry* (New York, 1962), pp. 186–87. A sheaf of reports from 1877 to 1880 filed as #1716, Office of the Chief of Ordnance Letters Received 1880, RG 156, National Archives, contains excellent data on the Hotchkiss gun, as well as an endorsement of May 6, 1880, by General Crook declaring artillery of any kind useless in Indian warfare.

13. Miles to Sherman, July 8, 1876, Sherman Papers, vol. 44, LC. See also the account of Gatling performance in Miles' Sioux operations of October 1876, *Army and Navy Journal, 14* (Feb. 10, 1877), 431.

14. Rickey, p. 219. Whitman, pp. 185–86.

15. Hunt to Rep. Levi Maish, Feb. 11, 1878, House Misc. Docs., 45th Cong., 2d sess., No. 56, pp. 94–96.

16. E. B. Williston, "Machine Guns in War," *Army and Navy Journal, 23* May 29, 1886), 890–91.

17. This discussion rests importantly on Gordon Chappell, *The Search for the Well-Dressed Soldier, 1865–1890* (Museum Monograph No. 5, Arizona Historical Society, Tucson, 1972); James S. Hutchins, "The Cavalry Campaign Outfit at the Little Big Horn," *Military Collector and Historian, 7* (1956), 91–101; and Hutchins' introduction to a reprint of *Ordnance Memoranda No. 29: Horse Equipment and Cavalry Accoutrements as Prescribed by G.O. 73, A.G.O., 1885* (Pasadena, Calif., 1970). See also Donald E. Kloster, "Uniforms of the Army Prior and Subsequent to 1872," *Military Collector and Historian, 14* (1962), 103–12; M. I. Luddington, comp., *Uniform of the Army of the United States from 1774–1889* (Washington, D.C., 1889); Rickey, *Forty Miles a Day on Beans and Hay*, chap. 11; and Whitman, *The Trooper*, chap. 13; Erna Risch, *Quartermaster Support of the Army: A History of the Corps, 1775–1939* (Washington, D.C., 1962), pp. 500–5.

18. Sherman to Sheridan, March 11, 1873, Sherman-Sheridan Letters, Sheridan Papers, LC.

19. Gordon Chappell, *Brass Spikes and Horsehair Plumes: A Study of U.S. Army Dress Helmets, 1872–1903* (Museum Monograph No. 4, Arizona Pioneers Historical Society, Tucson, 1966).

20. *Army and Navy Journal, 14* (Sept 2, 1876), 58.

21. Quoted in James S. Hutchins, "The Army Campaign Hat of 1872," *Military Collector and Historian, 16* (1964), 65–73.
22. *Army and Navy Journal, 15* (Sept. 15, 1877), 90.
23. *Ibid., 14* (Aug. 12, 1876), 4.
24. Chappell, *The Search for the Well-Dressed Soldier*, pp. 21–27. Anson Mills, *My Story* (Washington, D.C., 1918), pp. 314–31.
25. Alice Blackwood Baldwin, *Memoirs of the Late Frank D. Baldwin, Major General, U.S.A.* (Los Angeles, 1929), p. 32. Evolution of winter clothing is described by Chappell, *Search for the Well-Dressed Soldier*, pp. 27–32. See also Risch, p. 503.
26. Gordon Chappell, *Summer Helmets of the U.S. Army, 1875–1910* (Wyoming State Museum Monograph No. 1, Cheyenne, 1967). Risch, pp. 503–5. SW, *Annual Report* (1888), p. 307.
27. Archibald Forbes, "The United States Army," *North American Review, 135* (1882), 145.
28. *Army and Navy Journal, 14* (Aug. 12, 1876), 4.

SIX

Army Life on the Border

Young Min! I conghratulate yiz on bein assigned to moi thrupe, becos praviously to dis toime, I vinture to say that moi thrupe had had more villins, loyars, teeves, scoundhrils and, I moight say, dam murdhrers than enny udder thrupe in de United States Ormy. I want yiz to pay sthrict attintion to jooty—and not become dhrunken vaga-bonds, wandhrin all over the face of Gods Creashun, spindin ivry cint ov yur pay with low bum-mers. Avoide all timptashuns, loikewoise all discipashuns, so that in toime yiz kin become non-commissioned offizurs; yez'll foind yer captin a very laynent man and very much given to laynency, fur oi niver duz toi no man up bee der tumbs unless he duz bee late for roll-call. Sarjint, dismiss de detachmint.[1]

THUS DID CAPT. GERALD RUSSELL greet a contingent of re-cruits to his troop of the Third Cavalry at Fort Selden, New Mexico, in 1869, and thus might any recruit have been welcomed to his new life on the frontier between 1866 and 1890. For the next five years he would live in dark, dirty, overcrowded, vermin-infested barracks, sharing a straw-filled mattress with a "bunkie." He would eat bad food, badly prepared. He would labor long hours at menial tasks that neither required nor helped to inculcate military skills. He would endure strict discipline fortified by se-vere, often brutal penalties for transgressions. Occasionally he would go out on scout or patrol or even campaign. Probably he would never see combat. His comrades would come from almost every walk of life and stratum of society. Except for those for-mally clothed with rank and authority, the army wiped out such distinctions, and anyway one did not inquire into the origins of his fellows. He would find them profane, contentious, and addicted to gambling and whiskey. With them he would brave danger, discomfort, hardship, boredom, and loneliness. With them he would develop bonds, if not of friendship, at least of the solidarity formed of shared adventure.

Officers fared better, of course. They enjoyed privileges, comforts, and social relationships that made life more bearable. They brought their families with them. They found relief in an occasional furlough. They could afford servants—detailed enlisted men, called "dog robbers," or girls brought from the East and often promptly lost in marriage to a soldier. Even so, officers could only ameliorate, not escape, the conditions of army life on the border. Reporting at his first frontier station in 1871, Lt. Frederick E. Phelps could not have felt much more elation over the prospects of commissioned life at Fort Bayard, New Mexico, than filled the recruit experiencing his first taste of enlisted life at Fort Selden two years earlier:

The locality was all that could be desired; the Post everything undesirable. Huts of logs and round stones, with flat dirt roofs that in summer leaked and brought down rivulets of liquid mud: in winter the hiding place of the tarantula and the centipede, with ceilings of "condemned" canvas; windows of four and six panes, swinging, doorlike, on hinges (the walls were not high enough to allow them to slide upward): low, dark and uncomfortable. Six hundred miles from the railroad . . . with nothing to eat but the government rations— beef, bacon, coffee, sugar, rice, pepper, salt, and vinegar,—together with a few cans of vegetables divided pro rata, old Fort Bayard was the "final jumping off place" sure enough, I thought, as I rode into it in the summer of 1871.[2]

Whether blessed with a tolerable climate and attractive surroundings, like Fort Bayard, or less favorably endowed, like Fort Selden, most forts resembled one another in the appearance they presented and the quality and style of life they sustained. The typical fort looked more like a village than a fort. Only a handful, thrust into hostile Indian country, displayed stockades or other defenses, such as Forts Phil Kearny and C. F. Smith on the Bozeman Trail, or Fort Cummings in New Mexico. Indians occasionally tried to run off a fort's grazing stock or harried outlying facilities, but the chances of a direct attack, such as occurred at

Fort Apache, Arizona, in 1881 were so remote that defensive works of any kind were rarely erected. A frontier post, therefore, was simply a distinctively grouped collection of buildings made of lumber, stone, or adobe, depending upon local building materials. Barracks faced officers' quarters across a parade ground. At either end and elsewhere in the vicinity stood administrative offices, warehouses, workshops, corrals, the post trader's store, and "suds row," home of NCOs married to laundresses. An impressively structured flagpole lifted the national colors high above the parade ground.

"Some of what are called military posts," declared General Sherman in 1874, "are mere collections of huts made of logs, adobes, or mere holes in the ground, and are about as much *forts* as prairie dog villages might be called *forts*."[3] This condition resulted from laws and regulations decreeing that virtually all frontier posts be erected by the troops themselves from whatever materials could be obtained in the vicinity.[4] Since the Indian frontier shifted so frequently and was expected to disappear so soon, ran the argument, the expense of more substantial installations could not be justified. As it turned out, the Indians held out longer than expected, and the "temporary" posts continued to be used year after year, even after strategically obsolete, simply because there was nowhere else to shelter the troops. Sherman constantly lamented the abominable habitations in which his men had to live, but not until the 1880s, as the concentration program gathered momentum (see p. 47), did conditions begin to improve. As late as 1884, soldiers quipped that if they wanted to be well cared for, they must become inmates of either the military prison or a national cemetery.[5]

To the perceptive journalist DeB. Randolph Keim, the frontier fort suggested "the peculiar inspiration of a ship at sea; isolation within and desolation without."

The same rigid enforcement of discipline unremittingly exacted, as if in the face of the enemy. The commandant, a sort of supreme authority, executive, legislative, and judicial. All the forms of military etiquette observed. The flag hoisted every morning at sunrise and dropped at sunset, attended by the same roll of the drum, and the same reverberations of the evening gun. A furlough or brief "leave" was one of those pleasures in anticipation, which seemed to compensate for the lack of other mental relief. If there be any who deserve the sympathies of those who enjoy comfortable and secure homes in the settlements, they are the officers and soldiers condemned to the isolation of duty on the plains.[6]

Rigid stratification, both official and social, and precise definition of roles characterized the military community. Rank ordered privilege, authority, and social standing. Under the post commander, each officer and enlisted man had his part to play. The post adjutant and sergeant major were the administrative voices of the commanding officer, with whom they shared offices at post headquarters. Most of the commander's orders were transmitted through these men. The post quartermaster officer and sergeant were responsible for clothing, housing, and supplying the garrison, the post commissary officer and sergeant for feeding it. They occupied offices in the quartermaster and commissary warehouses. The post surgeon, aided by a noncommissioned hospital steward, presided over the hospital and looked after the sanitary conditions of the fort. Company officers could be found supervising their units in the field or occupied with paper work in the company orderly room in the barracks. Sergeants and corporals of the line usually stayed with the troops. Numerous enlisted specialists— blacksmith, farrier, saddler, wagoner, wheelwright—worked in shops that formed part of the quartermaster and cavalry corrals. An infantry bugler or cavalry trumpeter regulated the daily routine of the military community.[7]

The principal pastime was "fatigue," a military euphemism for manual labor. "This 'labor of the troops' was a great thing," observed Capt. John G. Bourke. "It made the poor wretch who enlisted under the vague notion that his admiring country needed his services to quell hostile Indians, suddenly find himself a brevet architect, carrying a hod and doing odd jobs of plastering and kalsomining."[8] A petition to Congress drawn up by a group of disenchanted soldiers in 1878 set forth the complaint in detail:

We first enlisted with the usual ideas of the life of a soldier; . . . but we find in service that we are obliged to perform all kinds of labor, such as all the operations of building quarters, stables, storehouses, bridges, roads, and telegraph lines; involving logging, lumbering, quarrying, adobe and brick making, lime-burning, mason-work, plastering, carpentering, painting, &c. We are also put at teaming, repairing wagons, harness, &c., blacksmithing, and sometimes wood-chopping and hay-making. This in addition to guard duty, care of horses, arms, and equipments, cooking, baking, police of quarters and stables, moving stores, &c., as well as drilling, and frequently to the exclusion of the latter.[9]

General Pope complained that his posts were "garrisoned by enlisted laborers rather than soldiers."[10] They made poor laborers, and labor prevented them from being made into good soldiers. It also helped sustain the high desertion rate. Most officers saw the answer to the problem in hired civilian labor, but this solution found little favor with War Department and congressional economizers.[11] Throughout the frontier period, drudge labor occupied most of the time and energy of the troops.

Discipline varied from regiment to regiment and post to post, but rarely could be called lax. As suggested by Captain Russell's welcoming speech at Fort Selden, the slightest infractions might bring swift and harsh retribution. "Drastic measures had to be used in those days," recalled an officer's wife. "The men, both foreign and domestic, were a hard set." Her husband brought two bullies to heel by physically throwing them out of a squadroom in which they had provoked a riot, then marching them about the post in a barrel with the top and bottom knocked out and a heavy log on their shoulders.[12] Among punishments prohibited by regulation but commonly meted out by officers and NCOs were bucking and gagging, spread-eagling, confinement in a sweatbox, repeated dunking in a stream, marching to exhaustion carrying a log or a knapsack full of bricks, and suspension by thumbs, wrists, or arms. More acceptable penalties were extra duty, restriction of liberty or privilege, and for NCOs reduction in rank.[13]

Courts-martial fortified the disciplinary practices of officers and NCOs. General courts-martial, convened by department commanders, tried enlisted men accused of serious crime and officers charged with any offense. Regimental and garrison courts dealt with minor transgressions. The most common offenses, defined in the Articles of War, were desertion, drunkenness, insubordination, disobedience, malingering, neglect of duty, and the "Devil's Article"—"disorders and neglects . . . to the prejudice of good order and military discipline." Typical sentences awarded officers were suspension from rank and pay for a specified period or dismissal from the service. Before the U.S. military prison opened at Fort Leavenworth in 1874, soldiers convicted for major crimes were confined in state or territorial penitentiaries. For minor offenses, hard labor and forfeiture of pay were the only punishments authorized. Although branding and tattooing had been proscribed along with flogging, desertion still might earn the traditional drumming-out ceremony to the strains of the "Rogue's March":

> Poor old soldiers! Poor old soldiers!
> Tarred and feathered and sent to hell,
> because they wouldn't soldier well.[14]

Critics both in and out of the army pointed to serious flaws in the system of military justice. The Articles of War, dating from 1806, were ambiguous, vague, and badly outdated. They left most punishments to the discretion of the courts, which resulted in widely varying sentences for the same offense. Also, they required the confinement of the accused until a verdict had been reached and approved by the reviewing authority, which often kept innocent men in the guardhouse and at hard labor for months even after they had been found innocent. Aggravating the inherent defects were faults of administration—unconscionable delays in bringing an accused to trial, excessive use of courts-martial as an instrument of discipline and misuse as a means of pursuing personal controversies,[15] political interference with judicial findings,[16] promiscuous mixing in confinement of first offenders with hardened criminals, and frequently uninformed, arbitrary, and capricious conduct of court members. Truly did many a soldier look on the machinery of military justice as a dispenser merely of punishment rather than of justice. Not until the late 1880s, however, did a reform movement get underway.[17]

The soldier's ration left much to be desired. Mainstays were range beef of dubious quality served sliced and in hash and stew, salt pork, beans, rice, bread or hardtack, and coffee. Dried vegetables and fruit occasionally appeared on the mess tables but were not well received.[18] These rations, drab enough to begin with, invariably suffered in preparation. Each company handled its own mess. Under army regulations, company commanders detailed men for ten-day tours as cooks and bakers, with the result, declared an investigating board in 1878, that "the food is, as a general rule, miserably cooked, while the man is in the kitchen long enough to ruin his clothing, without extra pay to replace it."[19] This board produced a cooking manual and endorsed a movement, already underway, to have cooks and bakers specially enlisted and trained. Although repeatedly urged by leading officers, this sensible reform did not win approval until after the frontier period.[20]

Both officers and enlisted men constantly sought ways to add variety to the diet. The post trader sold tinned delicacies and, at times, fresh foods at prices that customers eagerly paid, even though exorbitant. In some localities hunting and fishing provided keen sport as well as opportunities for enriching the menu; buffalo, deer, elk, and antelope, grouse, pheasant, and wild turkey, trout and bass could go far toward easing the perennial discontent over rations. Officers' families frequently kept chickens, pigs, or even a cow, usually to the irritation of neighbors and the indignation of the post surgeon, who was charged with maintaining standards of sanitation. Finally, most garrisons attempted to cultivate vegetable gardens, but more often than not drouth, hail, frost, or locusts wrought disaster. An inventive old officer explained what happened to his garden at Fort Rice, Dakota, in the summer of 1873: "The damn hoppers came along, by God, and ate my garden, by God, then the birds ate the hoppers, by God, and we killed and ate the birds, by God, so that we were even in the long run, by God."[21]

Sanitary conditions at the typical frontier post rarely fostered good health. Water, frequently of doubtful purity, came from the nearest spring or stream or was caught and stored in cisterns. Pit toilets and "honey wagons" received human waste, often in disconcerting proximity to the water supply. Improper storage and preparation of food invited disorders of stomach and bowels. Notions of personal hygiene were primitive and facilities for satisfying them equally so. Some post surgeons struggled manfully to improve conditions and enforce standards, but without notable effect until the late 1880s, when the larger posts began to receive water and sewage systems, modern kitchens, and other amenities of civilization.[22]

Not surprisingly, disease produced many more casualties than Indian arrows and bullets. Medical records disclose that each year, for every 1,000 men, surgeons treated about 1,800 cases, of which about 1,550 were for disease and 250 for wounds, accidents, and injuries. About 13 of each 1,000 died, 8 from disease and 5 from wounds, accidents, or injuries. And approximately 30 of each 1,000 received disability discharges.[23] Venereal diseases led all others in incidence, with malarial, respiratory, and digestive following closely.[24] Cholera swept the West in 1867.[25] Isolated garrisons suffered severe consequences from improper diet. At Fort McDowell in 1866 dysentery sent fifteen men to their graves wrapped in blankets or nailed in improvised coffins bearing such inscriptions as "40 Pairs Cavalry Trousers."[26] At Fort Phil Kearny a soldier recorded: "The Spring of 1867 was the time the effects of the spoiled flour and bacon showed up. All of the men that were at the fort at the time it was established got the scurvy. Some lost their teeth and some the use of their legs. In the spring when the grass was up there were lots of wild onions and the scurvy gang was ordered out to eat them."[27]

The Medical Department never attained a strength or competence commensurate with the need. Every post and fixed detachment rated a surgeon or assistant surgeon. The army acts of 1866 and 1869 provided for 222 medical officers, a figure roughly comparable to the need. But the section of the latter act stopping staff appointments and promotions, combined with the perennial difficulty of attracting qualified doctors, drove vacancies to a high of 64 in 1873. In 1874 Congress removed the ban on staff appointments and promotions, but in 1876 cut the medical staff to 192. To close the gap between the need and the supply, the Surgeon General contracted with as many as 175 civilian doctors. Unless seeking a regular commission, however, contract surgeons were not very reliable, and to make matters worse, in 1874 Congress limited their number to 75. Whether regular or contract, moreover, most army surgeons lacked the competence of their brethren in civil life. Low pay and frontier discomforts discouraged able doctors from seeking a military career.[28]

For diversion, officers and enlisted men alike turned heavily to drinking and gambling. Both pastimes were constant scourges for which the army never found a remedy. Until 1881 the post trader dealt in spirits, but on February 2 of that year President Hayes, an ardent temperance advocate, banned such sales on military reservations. "Hog ranches," offering whiskey of scandalous content, card tables, and often feminine pleasures, had always spotted the fringes of every reservation. Throughout the 1880s, thanks to Hayes' prohibition, they flourished as never before. The rise of the post canteen, a recreation center offering beer and light wines as well as wholesome amusements, gradually put the hog ranches out of business in the early 1890s.[29]

Ingenuity and labor, of course, produced other diversions. Although the army act of 1869 abolished regimental bands, almost every regiment maintained one, consisting of detailed men and paid for from the regimental fund or by subscription.[30] At posts with a regimental headquarters, the band presented concerts, lent distinction to dress parades, and inspired frequent balls and hops. At posts not so favored, ensembles were improvised, and dances occurred with scarcely less regularity.[31] Minstrels, charades, and theatricals were carefully planned and rehearsed and proudly presented, sometimes to the citizens of nearby communities.[32] Horse- and foot-racing, baseball, and other athletic competitions were frequent.[33] Hunting and fishing found enthusiasts. Newspapers and magazines, rare and always out of date, traveled through the garrison until read to shreds. Post libraries of varying quality offered other fare.[34] Temperance societies and church groups occupied some men.[35] Along officers' row, formal dinners, with fine silver, china, and linen assembled from several households, and with champagne and tinned delicacies purchased from the post trader, were common occurrences.[36]

Special occasions such as weddings, holidays, courts-martial, and visits of generals prompted detailed planning, lavish decoration, and elaborate ceremony. Christmas dinner was a splendid feast, the culmination of months of preparation. Independence Day featured strenuous celebration, exemplified in the journal entry for July 4, 1882, of an officer at Fort Stockton, Texas:

I got up a big affair today. Invited ranchmen and cowboys to take an active part in the performances. My company put up a greased pole, and we had a pig shaved and greased. Got up a wheelbarrow race and sack race, Major McClellan excusing his whole command in order that they might enjoy the fun. Had several splendid horseraces. . . . I treated the cowboys to plenty of beer, made a short speech and invited them to vote for Hon. John Hancock as the best man they could send to Congress. He was duly elected.[37]

A garrison's ladies played a special role in the life of the military community. Regulations made no provision for officers' wives, but almost every post contained at least a few, and the larger and more accessible often boasted a full complement. Also, each company rated four laundresses who received rations and compensation. In 1875 there were 1,316, mostly the wives of enlisted men.

In 1878 Congress, reflecting a growing but not unchallenged opinion in the army that laundresses caused more bother than justified, struck them from the rolls.[38]

Of the laundresses, one distinguished veteran recalled, with perhaps a touch more sentiment than warranted, "They were good, honest, industrious wives, usually well on in years, minutely familiar with their rights, . . . which they dared to maintain with acrimonious volubility, . . . and they were ever ready for a fight, yet they were kind at heart if rough in manners, always ready to assist in times of distress."[39] Another observer, scanning officers' row, identified these types: the "female C.O.," who "organized her staff, openly criticized the position of officers at dress parade, received reports and marvelled at the magnanimity that allowed a soldier 'seven nights in bed' "; the "picturesque little lady" with "plenty to wear but nothing to do"; the "late sergeant's wife," her husband now an officer thanks to the war, "who displayed a better development of muscle than brain"; the "beauty in laces and jewels"; the "aristocratic dame"; and of course "the charming conversationalist and delightful hostess and 'good Army woman.' "[40]

Greatly outnumbered by the men, revered, protected, and exalted as mandated by Victorian mores, army women enjoyed a prominence in the frontier milieu unintended by the authors of army law and regulation. Women introduced an element of grace, refinement, and comfort to garrison life conspicuously lacking at the few especially primitive posts to which none would go. They took the lead in planning, promoting, and staging entertainments. They brought to them the indispensable element of feminine participation. They formed an extremely close-knit society cemented by common hardship, sacrifice, and adventure. At the same time, all too many of them indulged in petty gossip, contention, and jealousy, whose harmful effects were magnified by their isolation from outside relationships. "The most discordant garrisons are those comprising the greatest number of ladies," remarked a disgruntled officer, who entitled the first chapter of his book "Ladies in the United States Army to the Prejudice of Good Order and Discipline."[41] Finally, to a handful of the ladies posterity is indebted for its record of life at the frontier army post.[42]

If this record exhibits a less than appealing life style, it is notable that almost all veterans of the frontier army—ladies and officers, that is, not enlisted men—looked back on it with not only a vast relief that it lay in the past but also with strong feelings of nostalgia. It was a nostalgia evoked by images of the harsh beauty and sweeping vistas of desert and plains, of dazzling sunsets, of pine-clad high country and snowy peaks, of the ever-changing moods of a land repulsive yet also strangely inviting. It was a nostalgia, too, born of hardships endured, of obstacles overcome, and of human bonds forged by shared privation, danger, and tragedy. All who served on the frontier could appreciate the sentiments of Maj. Anson Mills and his associates as the steamer bearing them to a new station cast off from Fort Yuma: "We took off our shoes and beat the dust of Arizona over the rail, at the same time cursing the land."[43] But they could also unite with Martha Summerhayes in a softer judgment: "With the strange contradictoriness of the human mind, I felt sorry that the old days had come to an end. For, somehow, the hardships and deprivations we have endured, lose their bitterness when they have become a memory."[44]

NOTES

1. Lansing B. Bloom, "Bourke on the Southwest," *New Mexico Historical Review*, 9 (1934), 52.
2. Reeve, "Frederick E. Phelps: A Soldier's Memoirs," pp. 50–51.
3. House Reports, 43d Cong., 1st sess., No. 384, p. 3.
4. A War Department order of 1868 specified that no permanent buildings could be erected except on authority of the Secretary of War. Temporary buildings were permitted, but no contracts could be concluded or materials purchased except on War Department authority. The 1872 appropriations act carried a rider that no permanent post costing more than $20,000 could be built without congressional authorization. SW, *Annual Report* (1869), p. 231; (1872), p. 36.
5. *Ibid.* (1884), p. 89.
6. *Sheridan's Troopers on the Borders: A Winter Campaign on the Plains* (Philadelphia, 1891), p. 59.
7. Rickey, *Forty Miles a Day on Beans and Hay*, chap. 6, describes the daily routines in detail.
8. Bourke, *On the Border with Crook*, p. 7.
9. Senate Reports, 45th Cong., 3d sess., No. 555, pp. 487–88. See also *Army and Navy Journal*, 5 (March 14, 1868), 474.
10. SW, *Annual Report* (1877), p. 67.
11. *Ibid.* (1870), p. 5; (1879), pp. 67, 84; (1881), pp. 76–77. House Misc. Docs., 45th Cong., 2d sess., No. 56., pp. 36, 87–88.
12. Ellen McG. Biddle, *Reminiscences of a Soldier's Wife* (Philadelphia, 1907), pp. 28–29.
13. Discipline and military justice are well treated in Rickey, chaps. 8 and 9; and Foner, *The United States Soldier between Two Wars*, pp. 8–10, and chaps. 2, 4, 5.
14. Such a drumming-out, at Fort Wingate, New Mexico, in 1868, is described in Baldwin, *Memoirs of the Late Frank D. Baldwin*, pp. 154–55.

15. Calling for reform, President Grover Cleveland in 1885 counted 2,328 general and 11,851 regimental and garrison court cases. More than half the army had thus been tried in one year, and all too often, he noted, for frivolous offenses. Richardson, *Messages and Papers of the Presidents, 8,* 348.

16. "Every worthless man in the Army," declared the writer of a letter to the editor, "appears to have his political protector standing by him with shield broad enough to ward off the just sentence of the most solemnly constituted tribunal." *Army and Navy Journal, 15* (Jan. 12, 1878), 362.

17. Foner, *passim,* traces the reform movement in detail. See also SW, *Annual Report* (1867), p. 416; (1868), p. 24; (1886), p. 317; (1890), pp. 4–5; and House Misc. Docs., 45th Cong., 2d sess., No. 56, p. 22.

18. Rickey, pp. 116–20. Foner, pp. 21–22.

19. Senate Ex. Docs., 45th Cong., 2d sess., No. 47.

20. SW, *Annual Report* (1876), p. 75; (1878), p. 418; (1887), pp. 82–83. *Army and Navy Journal, 12* (Feb. 20, 1875), 443.

21. Charles Braden, "The Yellowstone Expedition of 1873," *Journal of the U.S. Cavalry Association, 16* (1905), 240–41. See also SW, *Annual Report* (1868), p. 23.

22. An excellent view of sanitary conditions at a typical post is David A. Clary, "The Role of the Army Surgeon in the West: Daniel Weisel at Fort Davis, 1868–1872," *Western Historical Quarterly, 3* (1972), 53–66.

23. Based on analysis of statistics presented in the annual reports of the Surgeon General in annual reports of the Secretary of War.

24. SW, *Annual Report* (1889), pp. 621–870, contains an unusually detailed analysis of the health of the army. See also Rickey, pp. 130–34.

25. SW, *Annual Report* (1867), p. 12.

26. Carr, "The Days of the Empire," pp. 13–14.

27. Merrill J. Mattes, *Indians, Infants and Infantry: Andrew and Elizabeth Burt on the Frontier* (Denver, Colo., 1960), p. 148.

28. The Army's medical history in this period is treated in P. M. Ashburn, *A History of the Medical Department of the United States Army* (Boston, 1929). See also the published annual reports of the Surgeon General. For the organization of the Medical Department after each pertinent army act, see Heitman, *Historical Register and Dictionary of the United States Army,* 2, 602–15. Surgeons ranked as major, assistant surgeons as first lieutenant for three years and captain thereafter.

29. Foner, pp. 28–30, 70–80. Rickey, pp. 200–4. Forsyth, *The Story of the Soldier,* pp. 140–41. Carter, *On the Border with Mackenzie,* p. 420. SW, *Annual Report* (1870), p. 35; (1881), pp. 45, 79; (1884), p. 83. Bigelow, *William Conant Church and the Army and Navy Journal,* p. 193. For Hayes' executive order, see Richardson, 7, 640.

30. SW, *Annual Report* (1875), pp. 4–5. House Misc. Docs., 45th Cong., 2d sess., No. 56, p. 272.

31. Rickey, pp. 198–99. Roe, *Army Letters from an Officer's Wife,* pp. 142–45, 185–90. Elizabeth B. Custer, *Boots and Saddles, or Life in Dakota with General Custer,* ed. Jane R. Stewart (Norman, Okla., 1961), pp. 83–84. Mrs. M. A. Cochran, *Posey; or From Reveille to Retreat, An Army Story* (Cincinnati, 1896), pp. 160–62. *Army and Navy Journal, 8* (Jan. 7, 1871), 330.

32. Rickey, pp. 197–98. *Army and Navy Journal, 8* (March 8, 1871), 490; (Jan. 14, 1871), 347; *20* (June 2, 1883), 992.

33. Parker, *The Old Army Memories,* p. 26. *Army and Navy Journal, 14* (Aug. 19, 1876), 22; (May 19, 1877), 652. Duane N. Greene, *Ladies and Officers of the United States Army; or, American Aristocracy, A Sketch of the Social Life and Character of the Army* (Chicago, 1880), p. 183.

34. Post libraries were usually paid for from the post fund, which came mostly

from money saved on the soldier's bread ration. Secretary of War McCrary believed that Congress should authorize subscriptions to newspapers and magazines. General Pope waged an unsuccessful campaign for years to get part of the fines levied on soldiers as punishments diverted from the Soldiers' Home in Washington, D.C., to the enrichment of post libraries. SW, *Annual Report* (1872), p. 49; (1876), pp. 453–54; (1877), pp. vii–viii, 64–66.

35. Rickey, pp. 161–63. Foner, pp. 29, 79–80. *Army and Navy Journal, 8* (March 18, 1871), 491; *21* (Nov. 17, 1883), 309. The army contained thirty post chaplains and a regimental chaplain for each of the four black regiments. They attracted much criticism as a "useless and worthless set of drones and idlers," as Col. Innis Palmer phrased it. House Reports, 44th Cong., 1st sess., No. 354, p. 52. General Sherman thought so too. House Reports, 43d Cong., 1st sess., No. 384, p. 283.

36. Roe, p. 216.

37. Armes, *Ups and Downs of an Army Officer*, p. 505.

38. Whitman, *The Troopers*, chap. 10, is an excellent statement of the role of women. For laundresses, see SW, *Annual Report* (1874), p. 96; (1875), pp. 5, 175; (1879), p. 33; House Reports, 44th Cong., 1st sess., No. 354, pp. 198, 204; Senate Reports, 45th Cong., 3d sess., No. 555, Pt. 2, pp. 450–51; 20 Stat. 150 (June 18, 1878); *Army and Navy Journal, 12* (Feb. 27, 1875), p. 459.

39. Forsyth, pp. 133–34.

40. *Army and Navy Journal, 15* (June 15, 1878), 721.

41. Greene, p. 31.

42. Notably: Elizabeth B. Custer, *Boots and Saddles; Following the Guidon* (New York, 1890); and *Tenting on the Plains, or Gen'l Custer in Kansas and Texas* (New York, 1893). Biddle, *Reminiscences of a Soldier's Wife.* Summerhayes, *Vanished Arizona*. Mrs. Orsemus B. Boyd, *Cavalry Life in Tent and Field* (New York, 1894). Lydia Spencer Lane, *I Married a Soldier* (Philadelphia, 1893).

43. Mills, *My Story*, p. 152.

44. *Vanished Arizona*, p. 206.

SEVEN

Fort Phil Kearny, 1866

GENERAL SHERMAN'S summer tour of the Plains in 1866 gave him direct knowledge of his new command. It extended from Canada to Texas and from the Mississippi to the summits of the Rocky Mountains. The largest portion was the Great Plains— a vast expanse of rolling, treeless grasslands, drained by the great river systems of the Missouri and Arkansas, seared by summer heat and swept by awesome winter storms, home of powerful horse-mounted tribes that hunted the buffalo from the Canadian prairies to the West Texas deserts.

With the wartime Volunteers dissipating before the Regular Army could be recruited and posted, Sherman needed a year or two of peace on the Great Plains. His strategy for 1866 was therefore frankly defensive, aimed only at holding the lines of communication, shepherding the season's emigration safely to the mountains, and averting incidents likely to trigger into open hostility the "universal feeling of mistrust on both sides" so evident during his western tour. "All I ask is comparative quiet this year," he wrote Grant's chief of staff, "for by next year we can have the new cavalry enlisted, equipped, and mounted, ready to go and visit these Indians where they live."[1]

Time favored Sherman in another way, perceived by none more clearly than he. Every mile the railroads penetrated the Plains simplified the military problem. Troops could be moved more rapidly. Forts could be provisioned more efficiently and cheaply. Supplies adequate to support large-scale offensive operations could be stockpiled at advanced bases in a fraction of the time consumed by slow-moving wagon trains. "I hope the President and Secretary of War will continue, as hitherto, to befriend these roads as far as the law allows," he wrote to Grant in the spring of 1866.[2] For his own part: "It is our duty, and it shall be my study, to make the progress of construction of the great Pacific railways . . . as safe as possible."[3]

Meanwhile, there were emigrant and freight trains and stage-coaches to protect as well as railroad builders. Sherman applied himself during 1866 to this task and to recruiting and distributing the Regular Army units assigned to the Division of the Missouri. Detailed instructions were published regulating the season's travel. Trains were to assemble at designated rendezvous points, and military commanders along the roads were to insure compliance with stipulated requirements of strength, organization, and armament.[4] Regulars marched forth to replace Volunteers as guardians of the Plains travel routes.

In the Department of the Missouri (commanded by General Pope until General Hancock took over in August) lay the Smoky Hill Trail and the older Arkansas River route, formerly known as the Santa Fe Trail. Denver-bound travelers used both routes. Branches of the latter led to Santa Fe and other destinations in the Southwest. A string of forts guarded both roads. Tracing the Smoky Hill Trail were Forts Riley, Harker, Hays, and Wallace. Forts Zarah, Larned, Dodge, and Lyon watched over the Arkansas Road as far as eastern Colorado. In New Mexico Fort Union drew together the Mountain and Cimarron branches of the road to Santa Fe.[5]

The other major routes lay in General Terry's Department of Dakota and General Cooke's Department of the Platte. From his headquarters in St. Paul, Minnesota, Terry concerned himself chiefly with the Missouri River pathway to the Montana mines. This was both a land and a water route. Steamboats carried travelers from St. Louis, Leavenworth, Omaha, and Sioux City as far as the old trading station of Fort Benton, the head of navigation. Overland emigrants made their way from Minnesota along the upper reaches of the Missouri to the mountains. To guard the river and watch the Sioux, Terry had garrisons at Forts Randall, Sully, Rice, Berthold, and Union in Dakota and at Camp Cooke in Montana.

General Cooke, headquartered at Omaha, was responsible for the most heavily used of the Plains thoroughfares—the Platte Road (the old Oregon-California Trail). Guarding its main stem, now teeming with Union Pacific work crews, were Forts Kearny, McPherson, and Sedgwick. At Fort Sedgwick the road forked, one branch running up the South Platte by Fort Morgan to Denver, the other up the North Platte by Fort Mitchell to Fort Laramie, thence by Forts Casper and Bridger to Utah, Oregon, and California.

Also falling within Cooke's department was a new road connecting the Platte route with Montana. The Bozeman Trail, angling northwest from Fort Laramie along the eastern base of the Bighorn Mountains to Bozeman and Virginia City, offered travelers the shortest route to the Montana gold fields. At the forks of the Powder River stood Fort Reno, a reminder of the army's failure to crush Sioux opposition to the road and a platform for future attempts to extend military protection to it.

Only a handful of the outposts on the Plains highways dated from before the Civil War. The rest had been called into being by the bloody Indian war of 1864–65, the legacy of which still hung forebodingly over both the northern and southern Plains. A series of treaties with all the warring tribes in the autumn of 1865 had restored peace. In the south, Kiowas, Comanches, Kiowa-Apaches, Cheyennes, and Arapahoes had agreed to withdraw to the territory south of Kansas and east of New Mexico. In the north, all seven tribes of Teton Sioux—Oglala, Hunkpapa, Miniconjou, Brulé, Two Kettle, Blackfeet, and Sans Arc—together with the Upper and Lower Yanktonai Sioux tribes, had agreed to leave the warpath and "withdraw from the routes overland already established, or hereafter to be established through their country."[6]

Officials of the Indian Bureau were sure that this comprehensive set of treaties would bring lasting peace to the Great Plains. But the chiefs who signed treaties did not always fully represent all bands of the tribes thus bound. Nor did the chiefs always understand everything they agreed to. Nor, in the highly democratic and individualistic tribal society, were they always able to make their people comply with the engagements they did understand, especially when the customs of generations were surrendered. Nor did they always see good reason for keeping promises while the

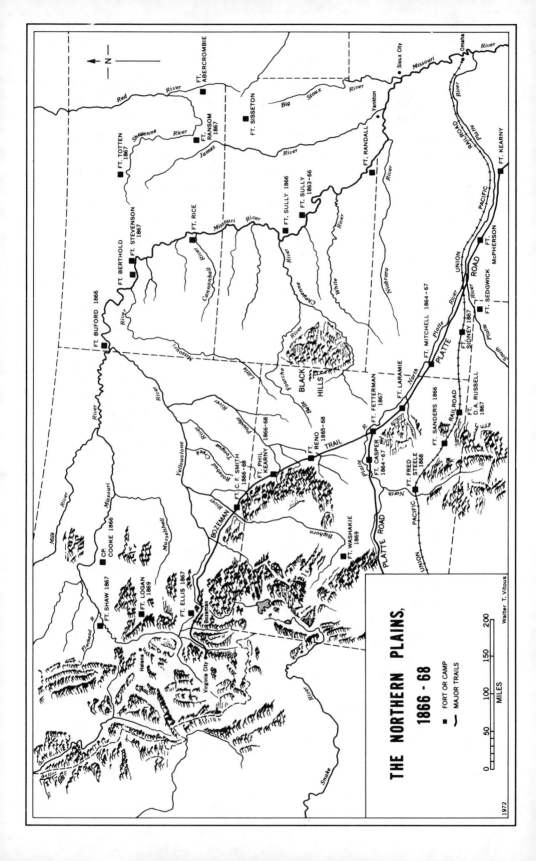

THE NORTHERN PLAINS, 1866-68

■ FORT OR CAMP
⌐ MAJOR TRAILS

MILES
0   50   100   150   200

Walter T. Vitous

1972

other party to the agreement so often broke promises. No less than earlier treaties did those of 1865 paper over such obstacles to genuine agreement.

On the southern Plains, although signed by an impressive array of chiefs, the Little Arkansas treaties seemed to military observers unlikely to keep the Indians in their newly designated homeland. Kiowas and Comanches had raided the Texas frontier—Spanish, Mexican, then Anglo-American—for more than a century. Cheyennes and Arapahoes had hunted for generations in the buffalo ranges now bisected by the Smoky Hill Trail in western Kansas and eastern Colorado. From the first years of the Santa Fe Trail, nearly half a century earlier, all the tribes had been irresistibly drawn to the white man's roads. And the bitterness engendered by the recent hostilities still burned deeply—Sand Creek in particular. Even though the treaty with the Cheyennes expressly repudiated Sand Creek and provided indemnification, Cheyennes would never forget or forgive the wanton butchery of Black Kettle's band by Col. John M. Chivington's Colorado Volunteers on November 29, 1864. Even so, the summer of 1866 passed with only minor incidents, attributed chiefly to the warlike Cheyenne Dog Soldiers.

On the northern Plains, the chiefs who signed could claim to represent no more than a few friendly bands along the Missouri River, a fact the peace commissioners concealed, if indeed they even knew. Farther west, in the Powder River country, the warriors who had confounded Gen. Patrick E. Connor's heavy columns the previous summer subscribed to no such sweeping concession as withdrawal from any road "hereafter to be established"; they had just fought a war to prevent the opening of the Bozeman Trail. Moreover, like their friends in the south, the Southern Oglalas and Southern Brulés were accustomed to hunt on the south side of the great Platte Road. Finally, again like their southern friends, many Indians in the northern tribes had succumbed to the lure of the treasure to be obtained through barter or theft along the white man's roads. Tacitly acknowledging the softness of their 1865 treaties, the peace commissioners went back up the Missouri in 1866 to find some more chiefs to sign. Other commissioners journeyed to Fort Laramie on the same mission.

A veteran of many years' frontier duty and also an outspoken critic of the treaty system, General Pope had no illusions about lasting peace. "I do not consider the treaties lately made with the

Sioux, Cheyennes, Arapahoes, and Comanches worth the paper they are written on," he informed Sherman on August 11, 1866. "I have myself no doubt that hostilities will again break out on the Platte, the Smoky Hill, and the Arkansas rivers before the beginning of winter."[7] At this very time, as Sherman was traveling up the Platte, hostilities had already broken out with the Sioux north of the Platte. Even at Fort Laramie, however, the edge of the zone of hostilities, the full magnitude of the war did not register with Sherman. In truth, the Teton Sioux not only had no intention of withdrawing from the Bozeman Trail to Montana, they had no intention of allowing the whites to use it at all.

Among the travelers on the Platte Road in 1866 were two battalions of the Eighteenth Infantry. One of the three-battalion regiments, soon to be broken into three regiments by the army act of July 28 (see Chapter Two), the Eighteenth had fought well under Sherman in Georgia. Attrition had wasted it, but an infusion of recruits in April 1866 filled the Second and Third Battalions to authorized strength. They marched from Fort Kearny on May 13, the Third Battalion to garrison posts along the Platte Road to Utah, the Second to protect the Bozeman Trail. Seven hundred strong, the Second Battalion included a contingent of 200 men mounted on the horses of discharged Volunteers and the superb regimental band armed both with musical instruments and seven-shot Spencer repeating carbines. Standard armament for the rest of the battalion, however, was the now-obsolete Springfield muzzle-loading rifle-musket.

No one expected the Bozeman Trail assignment to involve combat. Peace commissioners were already at Fort Laramie persuading the Powder River chiefs to put their marks on a treaty similar to those concluded the previous autumn on the Missouri. At Sherman's suggestion, some of the officers had even brought their wives and children along; Sherman, visiting Fort Kearny on May 16, urged the ladies to record their experiences in a diary.[8] For his part, the regimental commander, Col. Henry B. Carrington, expected to overcome any opposition from the Sioux and Cheyennes by "patience, forebearance, and common sense."[9]

Carrington managed his regiment by the same principles. Well educated in the humanities, self-educated in all branches of military science, he was an organizer and planner of proven merit. He was also a political appointee to the Regular Army and a veteran of five years of desk duty. Only extraordinary qualities of leadership could have bridged the gulf that the colonel's comfortable wartime billet opened between him and the battle-hardened officers of his regiment. But as a leader Carrington proved inept, tolerant of insubordination, lenient toward offenders against discipline, hesitant when opposed, excitable under pressure, and defensive about his lack of command and combat experience.[10]

At Fort Laramie the peace commissioners had succeeded in gathering an authoritative representation of chiefs, including even the Oglala and Miniconjou Sioux leaders who had successfully fought off General Connor's columns in 1865 and who still expressed the temper of the warriors in the Powder River country. That Man-Afraid-of-His-Horse, Red Cloud, and others had come in at all was viewed as a favorable omen. That their people had passed a winter of near starvation was another, convincing the commissioners that presents and the promise of $70,000 a year in annuity issues would win assent to any agreement. On these rewards the chief negotiator, Indian Superintendent E. B. Taylor, dwelled at length while deliberately obscuring the *quid pro quo*—acquiescence in the Bozeman Trail and military stations to guard it.[11]

Approaching Fort Laramie on June 16, Colonel Carrington got a more accurate reading of peace prospects from Chief Standing Elk of the Brulé Sioux. When informed of Carrington's mission, he replied: "The fighting men in that country have not come to Laramie, and you will have to fight them."[12] And so it proved. Bound for the Powder River country, Carrington's arrival at Fort Laramie exposed Superintendent Taylor's deceit. "The Great Father sends us presents and wants us to sell him the road," stormed Red Cloud in council, "but White Chief goes with soldiers to steal the road before Indians say Yes or No."[13] Wrathfully the Powder River chiefs broke off the talks and led their people northward, vowing to fight any whites who tried to use the route. But other chiefs, whose game resources were not imperiled by the road, had no compunctions about giving it away, and they signed.[14] "Satisfactory treaty concluded with the Sioux and Cheyennes," Taylor wired the Commissioner of Indian Affairs. "Most cordial feeling prevails."[15]

Guided by the mountain-wise old frontiersman Jim Bridger,

the Second Battalion, Eighteenth Infantry, marched out of Fort
Laramie on June 17. At the forks of Powder River, 169 miles
from Laramie, Carrington dropped off one of his eight companies
to garrison Fort Reno, a relic of General Connor's campaign the
previous summer.[16] From the sterile, wind-swept valley of the
Powder, the Bozeman Trail climbed to the foothills of the Bighorn Mountains. On July 13, sixty-seven miles northwest of Reno,
the command camped at the forks of Piney Creek in a pleasant
glade shadowed by snow-capped Cloud Peak. Here Carrington
marked the site of his headquarters post, Fort Phil Kearny. On
August 3, his stockade already taking shape, the colonel detached
two companies under Capt. Nathaniel C. Kinney to follow the
Bozeman Trail along the base of the mountains to the Bighorn
River and there, ninety-one miles from Fort Phil Kearny, plant the
third post. On August 12 Kinney founded Fort C. F. Smith.

Within less than a week after Carrington's arrival on Piney
Creek, Red Cloud struck. From swelling camps in the Tongue
River Valley some fifty miles to the north, Oglalas, Miniconjous,
Sans Arcs, Brulés, and even Cheyennes and Arapahoes sought to
throw back the soldiers and close the road to Montana. Nearly
every train, military and civilian, lost stock to the raiders, and
many had to fight off attackers as well. The warriors also closed
in on Fort Phil Kearny, harassing trains bringing logs from the
nearby "pinery" for construction of the post, running off stock,
and killing anyone who strayed from the fort without proper precautions.[17]

Carrington had come to the Powder River country equipped for
one task and had found himself confronted by quite another. He
had the men, arms, and supplies to build and garrison forts but
not to contest an active enemy. Almost all his resources went into
the construction of Forts Phil Kearny and C. F. Smith; the former,
nearing completion by December, stood as a monument to his engineering and organizing skills. Beyond an elaborate set of rules
for travelers, therefore, he provided little protection to the trains
between the three forts. Although western newspapers proclaimed
Powder River in the grip of full-scale war, in official circles the
spirit of Superintendent Taylor's "most cordial feeling" continued
to prevail, lulling travelers with a sense of security that prompted
them to string out in small, inadequately armed groups and to
neglect elementary security precautions.

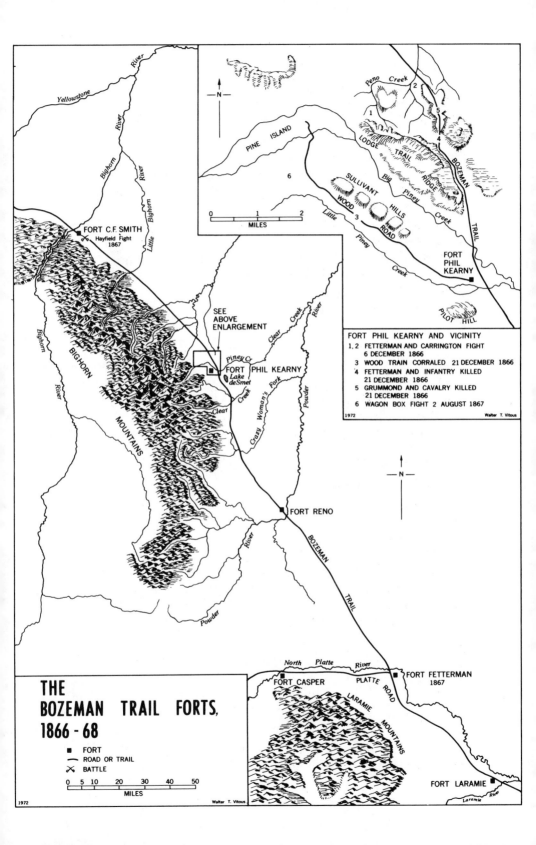

FORT PHIL KEARNY AND VICINITY

1, 2 FETTERMAN AND CARRINGTON FIGHT
6 DECEMBER 1866
3 WOOD TRAIN CORRALED 21 DECEMBER 1866
4 FETTERMAN AND INFANTRY KILLED
21 DECEMBER 1866
5 GRUMMOND AND CAVALRY KILLED
21 DECEMBER 1866
6 WAGON BOX FIGHT 2 AUGUST 1867

1972   Walter T. Vitous

THE
BOZEMAN TRAIL FORTS,
1866-68

■ FORT
— ROAD OR TRAIL
✕ BATTLE

0 5 10   20   30   40   50
MILES

1972   Walter T. Vitous

Carrington's most urgent task was to whip his command into fighting shape—two-thirds of the men were untrained recruits. Instead, he employed them all in building a more elaborate and formidable fort than the nature of Indian warfare required. He scheduled no drill or training for six months. Under the strain of continued Sioux harassment, the race to finish the fort before winter, and the tension among the officers, discipline and morale deteriorated.

So did relations between Carrington and the officer corps. The more hostile officers—Capt. Frederick H. Brown, Adj. William H. Bisbee, Lt. George W. Grummond—scarcely concealed their contempt and often violated the spirit, if not the letter, of Carrington's policies. Unable to enforce his will on the rebels, he reacted with tolerance and took more and more of their responsibilities on himself.[18]

The most serious contention centered on strategy. Carrington thought almost exclusively in defensive terms, a frame of mind symbolized by his stockaded and bastioned fort. His subordinates, humiliated by Sioux aggressions and no more versed in Indian warfare than he, bitterly resented his refusal to let them use part of the troops for offensive operations. The Indian forays in the vicinity of Fort Phil Kearny, mostly against grazing stock herds, afforded the officers the opportunities they craved. They responded with erratic, unorganized, and often unauthorized pursuits.[19]

Carrington achieved scarcely greater rapport with the department commander, General Cooke. Reports of his inspector general following a visit to Fort Phil Kearny in August and private letters reaching his headquarters from some of Carrington's disaffected subordinates reinforced Cooke's natural suspicion of a politically appointed officer.[20] Moreover, reflecting the growing stress of his situation, Carrington's reports displayed a confusing inconsistency, at times bristling with alarm, at other times soothing with assurance. Cooke probably despaired of satisfactory military performance as long as Carrington commanded and simply procrastinated until time produced another commander. This could be expected by the end of the year, when the reorganization of the Eighteenth Infantry was to take effect. The Second Battalion, at Fort Phil Kearny, was to become the Twenty-seventh Regiment, and Carrington had already asked to stay with the Eighteenth, whose headquarters would be at Fort Casper. So his appeals for more officers and men, for cavalry, for breech-loading rifles, and for greater ammunition reserves stirred only routine activity in department headquarters. In return Carrington earned fussy reprimands for the irregularity of his reports (delayed by the hazards of the trail) and pointed suggestions that more aggressive action against the Indians might be in order.[21]

During November Carrington finally received some reinforcements—forty-five infantrymen and a troop of sixty men of the Second Cavalry. All were straight from the recruiting rendezvous. The cavalrymen, armed with muzzle-loading muskets and Starr carbines, could scarcely mount their horses without help.[22] This paltry addition of manpower brought the garrison of Fort Phil Kearny to 10 officers, 3 surgeons, and 389 enlisted men.[23] At this same time Fort Laramie, remote from the hostile zone, boasted a complement of 12 companies, more than 700 men.[24]

Also in November, Carrington received several fresh officers to replace some who had been reassigned. The new arrivals raised the quotient of disaffection in the officer corps. The most troublesome were Capts. William J. Fetterman and James Powell. Fetterman, a superb combat officer and veteran of the regiment's Georgia campaigns, promptly joined with Captain Brown and Lieutenant Grummond in promoting an expedition to clean out the Sioux villages on Tongue River. Powell, a steady old Regular with thirteen years' enlisted service in the West before the war, had a better sense of reality but nonetheless became one of Carrington's most outspoken critics. Of his senior officers, Carrington could count as properly loyal only Capt. Tenodor Ten Eyck, and he was an alcohol-numbed mediocrity.[25]

By early December, with most of the work on the fort completed, Carrington had been brought to a commitment to some form of offensive operation. On November 12, displaying an abysmal ignorance of conditions in the Powder River country, General Cooke had given explicit instructions to strike the Indians in their winter camps, and two weeks later Carrington had promised "to make the winter one of active operations in different directions, as best affords chance of punishment."[26]

A "chance of punishment" seemed to present itself on December 6, when Indians attacked the wood train on the road to the pinery west of the fort. Carrington sent Captain Fetterman with about thirty horsemen under Lt. Horatio S. Bingham to lift the siege and

drive off the assailants, pressing them along their usual withdrawal route around the west end of the Sullivant Hills, across Big
Piney, and over Lodge Trail Ridge to Peno Creek (see map).
Carrington would lead twenty-five mounted infantrymen under
Lieutenant Grummond up the Bozeman Trail and drop into
Peno Valley behind the Indians. Fetterman got to Peno Creek before Carrington. The warriors, about one hundred in number,
turned on their pursuers. The green cavalrymen panicked and
stampeded. Trying to rally them, Lieutenant Bingham got cut off
and shot with arrows. Carrington tarried on Lodge Trail Ridge,
then became engaged separately from Fetterman. Only the fortunes of conflict spared the command from greater loss than Bingham and a sergeant killed and five men wounded.[27]

The Sioux doubtless drew their own lessons from the fight.
Since early autumn they had been plotting "two big fights with
the whites, one at Pine Woods [Fort Phil Kearny] and one at Big
Horn [Fort C. F. Smith]."[28] To accomplish this, they looked to the
timeworn decoy tactic, which rarely worked because it required a
discipline and coordination foreign to Indian character. The action
of December 6 may have been such an attempt, and almost surely
it convinced the Indians that a decoy could be made to succeed
against the soldiers. They tried again on December 19 but failed
because Captain Powell, commanding the relief detachment, declined to pursue.

On the morning of December 21 the Indians once more set the
stage. Between 1,500 and 2,000 warriors gathered at the scene of
the fight of December 6 and concealed themselves in the ravines
on both sides of a long narrow ridge, covered with snow and ice,
by which the Bozeman Trail descended from Lodge Trail Ridge.
High-Back-Bone of the Miniconjous organized the operation, and
a young Oglala named Crazy Horse led the decoy party. Whether
Red Cloud took part is a matter of dispute.[29]

When the wood train came under attack, Carrington again selected Captain Powell to head the relief column. Pleading seniority,
however, Captain Fetterman demanded the assignment, and the
colonel yielded. (Fetterman was a brevet lieutenant colonel, Powell
a brevet major.) Carrington gave Fetterman the same explicit and
emphatic orders he had given Powell two days earlier: relieve
the wood train and under no circumstances pursue the Indians
beyond Lodge Trail Ridge. The near-disaster of December 6 had

shown Carrington the perils of the broken terrain on the other side of the precipitous elevation that divided Big Piney from Peno Creek. Fetterman assembled a picked force of forty-nine infantrymen and marched out of the stockade. Lieutenant Grummond and twenty-seven cavalrymen, armed with the band's Spencer carbines, followed as soon as their horses had been saddled. Captain Brown, who never missed a fight, went along, as did two civilians, James Wheatley and Isaac Fisher, who carried Henry repeating rifles. In all, the relief force numbered three officers, seventy-six soldiers, and two civilians.

Instead of following the wood road, Fetterman at once turned north toward the Bozeman Trail and disappeared beyond the shoulder of the Sullivant Hills. This was not necessarily cause for alarm; by marching up Big Piney north of the Sullivant Hills he might take the Indians in the rear. But he did not do this. He forded Big Piney on the ice and followed the Bozeman Trail up Lodge Trail Ridge. The command was briefly seen from the fort ascending the slope in skirmish formation, exchanging desultory fire with a scattering of Indians. Then it vanished. The sound of heavy firing from beyond Lodge Trail Ridge moved Carrington to dispatch Captain Ten Eyck and forty infantry and dismounted cavalry to Fetterman's support. They reached the summit of the ridge, three miles from the fort, in time to see hundreds of warriors swarming on the slopes and withdrawing to the north. Scattered along the narrow ridge that carried the road down to Peno Valley, the troops discovered the bodies of Fetterman and his men, stripped of clothing and barbarously mutilated.[30]

Since no man of Fetterman's command escaped, how the battle had progressed can only be surmised. It seems likely that, after the decoy party had drawn the troops to the Lodge Trail crest, Grummond's cavalry charged ahead of the infantry down the long narrow slope, since known as Massacre Ridge. They had almost reached Peno Valley when the warriors burst from concealment on either side of the ridge. A handful of troopers and the two civilians dismounted and took cover among some rocks, but most of the cavalry retreated part way back toward the infantry and dismounted to fight on a rise of ground. Farther up the ridge Fetterman and the infantry made their stand at the site of the present monument. Some of the cavalry succeeded in getting back to the infantry, as did Captain Brown. Thus, in three separate groups, none within support or view of the others, Fetterman's troops were wiped out in less than an hour. Estimates of Indian casualties range from a mere handful up to a hundred in killed and wounded.[31]

The next day, after the last of the bodies had been brought in by a detachment under Carrington himself, a fierce blizzard swept in, piling snow to the height of the stockade and deepening the fear of an assault on the fort itself. Already, on the night of the twenty-first, Carrington had launched John "Portugee" Phillips on an epic four-day ride through bitter cold and drifting snow to take the news of the disaster and an appeal for help to the outside world. This first dispatch reached General Cooke on the day after Christmas. Carrington's official report, an almost incoherent self-justification betraying a state of mind bordering on panic, arrived early in the new year.

No long search was required to find a scapegoat. General Cooke left no doubt of his choice for the distinction. "Colonel Carrington is very plausible," he advised army headquarters, "an energetic, industrious man in garrison; but it is too evident that he has not maintained discipline, and that his officers have no confidence in him."[32] Also, Cooke's orders for a relief column enjoined its commander, Lt. Col. Henry W. Wessels, to replace Carrington in command of Fort Phil Kearny, a move long planned as part of the regimental reorganization but by its timing broadcasting the department commander's assessment of culpability.[33] General Sherman shared Cooke's view. "I know enough of Carrington to believe that he is better qualified for a safe place than one of danger," he wrote privately to a colleague.[34] For his part, General Grant was not inclined to place the blame solely on Carrington. Without even consulting Sherman, he caused orders to be issued on January 9, 1867, replacing Cooke with Bvt. Maj. Gen. Christopher C. Augur.[35]

Two official investigations were promptly launched, one an army court of inquiry, the other part of the mission of a presidentially appointed peace commission reporting to the Secretary of the Interior. Both took voluminous testimony. The army inquiry came to nothing, despite General Grant's opinion that the evidence warranted formal charges against Carrington.[36] The Interior Department's commissioners never subscribed to a joint report, but the conclusions of its spokesman, John B. Sanborn, exonerated Carrington: "The difficulty 'in a nutshell' was, that the commanding officer of the district was furnished no more troops or supplies for this state of war than had been provided and furnished him for a state of profound peace."[37]

This was indeed a large difficulty. But there was another large difficulty, clearly revealed by the testimony taken by both investigating bodies: the army had selected a suitable commanding officer for a state of profound peace but a most unsuitable one for a state of war. This view prevailed in the close-knit army community, and Carrington contended with it for only three years.[38] Suffering from a hip injury, he left the service in 1870 and devoted the remaining forty-two years of his life to vindicating his management of the Bozeman Trail defenses. With his contemporaries he achieved indifferent success. With historians of later generations he largely succeeded, for it is his version that until recent years has colored most accounts of the events culminating on Massacre Ridge on December 21, 1866.[39]

NOTES

1. From Fort McPherson, Nebraska Territory, Aug. 21, 1866, House Ex. Docs., 39th Cong., 2d sess., No. 23, p. 6.
2. From Omaha, May 14, 1866, *ibid.*, p. 2.
3. Annual report, Nov. 5, 1866, in SW, *Annual Report* (1866), pp. 21–22.
4. The regulations, which provoked considerable protest from travelers delayed or inconvenienced, were drawn up and issued by General Pope on February 28, 1866, while he still commanded a Department of the Missouri that embraced most of the Great Plains. Sherman confirmed the orders on March 26. Senate Ex. Docs., 40th Cong., 1st sess., No. 2.
5. The best reference work on military installations, used throughout this volume, is Francis Paul Prucha, *Guide to the Military Posts of the United States* (Madison, Wis., 1964). Also useful to supplement Prucha is Robert W. Frazer, *Forts of the West* (Norman, Okla., 1965).
6. I have dealt with these wars and treaties in *Frontiersmen in Blue*, chaps. 14 and 15. The treaties are printed in Charles J. Kappler, comp., *Indian Affairs: Laws and Treaties* (2 vols., Washington, D.C., 1904), 2, 883–908.
7. From Fort Union, N.M., Aug. 11, 1866, in SW, *Annual Report* (1866), p. 30.
8. Margaret I. Carrington, *Absaraka, Home of the Crows*, ed. Milo M. Quaife (Chicago, 1950), pp. xli–xlix, 39–40. Frances C. Carrington, *Army Life on the Plains* (Philadelphia, Pa., 1910), p. 61. In 1866 Margaret was Carrington's wife. She took Sherman's advice, and her book is the result. First published by Lippincott in 1868, it went through at least eight editions. I have used the Lakeside Classics edition. After Margaret's death in 1870, Carrington married Frances Grummond, widow of a lieutenant killed in the Fetterman disaster. With help from her husband, she wrote the second book cited.
9. Senate Ex. Docs., 50th Cong., 1st sess., No. 33, p. 6. This is Carrington's

official history of his Bozeman Trail operations and includes most of his official communications. Although submitted to a special commission investigating the Fetterman debacle in 1867, it went unpublished until 1887, when Carrington, fighting for vindication, got the Senate to call for its publication. (Hereafter cited as "Carrington History.")

10. This is my own assessment, adduced from study of the voluminous documentation of Carrington's Bozeman Trail record, but cf. Robert A. Murray, "Commentaries on the Col. Henry B. Carrington Image," *Denver Westerners Roundup*, 24 (March 1968), 3–12, and Michael Straight, "Carrington: The Valor of Defeat," *Corral Dust* (Potomac Westerners, Washington, D.C.), 4 (December 1959), 25–27. Straight's *Carrington* (New York, 1960) is an excellent novel that gives further characterization of Carrington. My account is based on the following sources: the "Carrington History" cited in n. 9 above; official records of the War and Interior departments, including the report of the Sanborn investigation, published in Senate Ex. Docs., 40th Cong., 1st sess., No. 13; and Carrington's report of the Fetterman disaster in Senate Ex. Docs., 49th Cong., 2d sess., No. 97. The books by Margaret and Frances Carrington cited in n. 8 above are also important. Excellent secondary accounts are Dee Brown, *Fort Phil Kearny, An American Saga* (New York, 1962); J. W. Vaughn, *Indian Fights: New Facts on Seven Encounters* (Norman, Okla., 1966), chap. 2; and Roy E. Appleman, "The Fetterman Fight," in Potomac Westerners, *Great Western Indian Fights* (New York, 1960), chap. 10. Rich in detail and careful analysis is Robert A. Murray, *Military Posts in the Powder River Country of Wyoming, 1865–1894* (Lincoln, Neb., 1968), Part I. For the Indian side, see James C. Olson, *Red Cloud and the Sioux Problem* (Lincoln, Neb., 1965), chaps. 3 and 4; George E. Hyde, *Red Cloud's Folk: A History of the Oglala Sioux Indians* (Norman, Okla., 1937); and George Bird Grinnell, *The Fighting Cheyennes* (2d ed., Norman, Okla., 1956). Badly outdated but still helpful if used with caution is Grace R. Hebard and E. A. Brininstool, *The Bozeman Trail* (2 vols., Cleveland, Ohio, 1922).

11. Sources for the council and its background are Senate Ex. Docs., 40th Cong., 1st sess., No. 13; CIA *Annual Report* (1866), pp. 204–13. Olson, chap. 3, has an excellent analysis of this and other, unpublished, evidence.

12. "Carrington History," p. 5.

13. Frances Carrington, pp. 46–47.

14. George E. Hyde, *Spotted Tail's Folk: A History of the Brulé Sioux* (Norman, Okla., 1961), pp. 115–17.

15. Olson, p. 38. In November 1866 Secretary of the Interior Orville H. Browning removed Taylor. "Some of the rogues in partnership with Taylor in robbing the Indians had made the President believe that Taylor was his friend and ought not to be removed," Browning wrote in his dairy. "I undeceived him—satisfied him that Taylor was a political hypocrite and a faithless officer, . . ." James G. Randall, ed., *The Diary of Orville Hickman Browning* (2 vols., Springfield, Ill., 1933), 2, 107.

16. See Utley, *Frontiersmen in Blue*, pp. 325–30. General Connor established the post in August 1865 as Fort Connor, but its name was changed in November to Fort Reno. Two companies of the Fifth U.S. Volunteers— "Galvanized Yankees"—held it during the winter. Verging on mutiny over their delayed discharge, they were relieved by Carrington and sent east to be mustered out.

17. According to the Sanborn investigation, between July 26 and December 21 the Sioux on the Bozeman Trail and in the vicinity of Fort Phil Kearny killed 5 officers and 91 enlisted men, killed 58 civilians and wounded 20, and stole 306 oxen and cows, 304 mules, and 161 horses. They made 51 separate hostile demonstrations against Fort Phil Kearny. These figures include losses in the battles of December 6 and 21. Senate Ex. Docs., 40th Cong., 1st sess., No. 13, p. 62.

18. The unpublished testimony taken by the Sanborn investigation and the army court of inquiry portrays these conditions clearly. See Murray, "Commentaries on the Col. Henry B. Carrington Image"; and Vaughn, pp. 24–28.

19. Testified Adjutant Bisbee: "Troops were in the habit of dashing helter-skelter over the stockade whenever an Indian appeared, without regard to orders, and generally before the Commanding Officer knew there were Indians about." Vaughn, p. 28.

20. Murray, p. 9. Vaughn, p. 25.

21. Correspondence between Carrington and Cooke is in the "Carrington History."

22. *Ibid.*, pp. 31, 37.

23. Murray, pp. 165–66. The infantry were in Companies A, C, E, and H of the Eighteenth and Company K of the new Twenty-seventh, the last being the forty-five recruits. The cavalry were in Troop C of the Second. In reckoning the strength of Fort Phil Kearny, the civilian quartermaster and contractor employees should not be overlooked; there were more than 150, many better armed than the soldiers. Murray, pp. 83–84.

24. Senate Ex. Docs., 40th Cong., 1st sess., No. 13, p. 66.

25. The other officers, besides Carrington, were Lts. Wilbur F. Arnold (adjutant), Winfield S. Matson (quartermaster), Alexander H. Wands, and Horatio S. Bingham (cavalry commander). Surgeon Samuel M. Morton was assisted by two civilian contract surgeons, C. M. Hinds and a Dr. Ould.

26. "Carrington History," pp. 34–36.

27. This action is carefully reconstructed in Vaughn, pp. 32–43. Carrington's official report is in the "Carrington History," pp. 36–38; Fetterman's in Senate Ex. Docs., 40th Cong., 1st sess., No. 13, pp. 37–38.

28. "Carrington History," pp. 20–21, 29–30. This word reached Carrington from some friendly Cheyennes and also by way of the Crow Indians near Fort C. F. Smith. See also the report of N. B. Buford, member of the investigating commission, of an interview with some Indian participants in Senate Ex. Docs., 40th Cong., 1st sess., No. 13, p. 59.

29. Hyde, *Red Cloud's Folk*, pp. 146–49.

30. In his official report Carrington chronicled the mutilation in candid detail: "Eyes torn out and laid on the rocks; noses cut off; ears cut off; chins hewn off; teeth chopped out; joints of fingers; brains taken out and placed on rocks with other members of the body; entrails taken out and exposed; hands cut off; feet cut off; arms taken out from sockets; private parts severed and indecently placed on the persons; eyes, ears, mouth, and arms penetrated with spearheads, sticks, and arrows; ribs slashed to separation with knives; skulls severed in every form, from chin to crown; muscles of calves, thighs, stomach, breast, back, arms, and cheek taken out." "Carrington History," p. 41.

31. All the sources cited in n. 3, contain important material bearing on the Fetterman disaster. The most authoritative reconstructions of the action and the main reliance for my account are those of Vaughn and Appleman, who have carefully studied the evidence on the battlefield itself.

It has been customary to place sole blame on Fetterman for flagrantly disobeying orders and leading his men into an ambush. The weight of the evidence still supports that conclusion. As Vaughn has pointed out, however, by the time Fetterman was observed ascending Lodge Trail Ridge the attack on the wood train had been broken off and Carrington had ample time to recall him if he regarded the movement as improper. Also, Fetterman may have intended to go no farther than the Lodge Trail crest, but found himself drawn beyond it when the cavalry made an unauthorized charge.

32. Dec. 27, 1866, Senate Ex. Docs., 40th Cong., 1st sess., No. 13, p. 29. Also, Cooke's endorsement on Carrington's official report pictured the troops rushing "helter-skelter" in pursuit of the Indians and even "leaping over the

stockade" in their eagerness to join battle. This was published with Carrington's report in 1887, Senate Ex. Docs., 49th Cong., 2d sess., No. 97. Years later, Cooke apologized to Carrington for this hasty and ill-considered language with the explanation that it had been framed by a staff officer—almost certainly Captain Bisbee, who had just joined Cooke's staff. Hebard and Brininstool, *1*, 340. Straight.

33. Dec. 26, 1866, Senate Ex. Docs., 40th Cong., 1st sess., No. 13, p. 28. That the orders were more than routine is indicated by Cooke's telegram of the same date to Grant's chief of staff requesting that if this transfer were disapproved Wessels be kept at Fort Reno and assigned to command the district in his brevet grade of brigadier general, which would have placed Carrington under an officer his junior in lineal rank. *Ibid.*, p. 27.

34. To Gen. C. C. Augur, Feb. 28, 1867, quoted in Athearn, p. 99.

35. Athearn, p. 100. Olson, p. 53, n. 56. Augur, colonel of the Twelfth Infantry, was assigned in his brevet grade.

36. Murray, "Commentaries on the Col. Henry B. Carrington Image," p. 11.

37. Senate Ex. Docs., 40th Cong., 1st sess., No. 13, p. 66.

38. For evidence of this attitude see particularly General Augur's views in Olson, p. 55, n. 67; and the account of Maj. Alfred E. Bates in T. F. Rodenbough, *From Everglade to Cañon with the Second Dragoons* (New York, 1875), pp. 376–77.

39. For recent scholarship based on the unpublished testimony before the two investigating bodies, see Murray, Vaughn, and Straight.

Hancock's War, 1867

THE FETTERMAN DISASTER shocked and outraged the army. "We must act with vindicative earnestness against the Sioux," Sherman telegraphed Grant, "even to their extermination, men, women, and children."[1] At the frontier posts attitudes hardened into undiscriminating hostility toward all Indians.[2] Westerners shared the army's militancy and went still further in demanding retaliation. Their newspapers called for extermination of the Indians; some even scored the army for timidity. Railroad and stagecoach interests reinforced Sherman's aggressive designs.[3] Military contractors and freighters joined in the clamor, although army officers recognized their motives as hardly disinterested.[4]

Such sentiments sprang from the same climate of opinion that had made possible the Sand Creek butchery in 1864, and Sherman's utterances made him appear no more inclined than the discredited Colonel Chivington to distinguish between hostile and peaceful or combatant and noncombatant. The Regular Army had taken great pains to dissociate itself from the excesses of the Colorado militia. Now the army itself helped blur the distinction.

Sand Creek had dramatized the Indian problem to the nation's humanitarian community, mobilizing religious and reform groups and stirring Abolitionists in search of a new cause. Sand Creek and the expensive war it ignited on the Plains gave rise to a peace policy that flowered in the profusion of treaties concluded in the autumn of 1865. Even after the Fetterman disaster, the spirit of conciliation glowed warmly in Washington offices and eastern parlors. An influential body of opinion held that negotiations in good faith offered a surer means than naked force of bringing peace to the West. Both Secretary of the Interior Orville H. Browning and Commissioner of Indian Affairs Lewis V. Bogy favored sending out peace emissaries to restore harmonious relations and gather data to support a comprehensive program for assembling all western tribes on reservations.[5]

On this and other issues the army and the Indian Bureau feuded openly during the winter of 1866–67. Much of the contention centered on whether licensed traders should be allowed to sell arms and ammunition to peaceful Indians. Secretary Browning and Commissioner Bogy contended that they were necessary for hunting purposes. The army, aware that the Indians had got along fairly well with bows and arrows for generations, vigorously condemned such sales. General Cooke had banned arms sales in the Department of the Platte in July 1866. General Hancock, sustained by Sherman and Grant, followed in January 1867.[6]

Both Browning and Bogy regarded this prohibition as the chief cause of Indian hostility and the army's intervention not only uncalled for but unlawful. Bogy complained that his greatest burden was "the constant interference on the part of the military with all Indian affairs." It was "unwarranted" and "imperious," and unless checked it would lead to "nothing less than the destruction of our entire western settlements, and the entire column of western emigration." Bogy went so far as to attribute the Fetterman disaster to the army's inhuman denial to Red Cloud's people of the arms necessary for laying in their winter's meat. "Almost in a state of starving," he explained, "having made repeated attempts at a conference [with Carrington], that they might make peace and obtain supplies for their families, and the rescinding of the order prohibiting them from obtaining arms and ammunition, [the Sioux] were rendered desperate, and restored to the stratagem which proved too successful."[7]

Such fantasy lent color to charges of army officers and westerners that the peace proponents were impractical visionaries. Far better to return responsibility for Indian management to the War Department and do away with the ambiguous and demoralizing division of authority between civil agents and army officers. General Pope, the army's wordy, self-appointed expert on Indian policy, had publicly championed this move for three years. Both Sherman and Grant officially recommended it in their annual re-

ports in November 1866. In the wake of Fetterman's annihilation
the time seemed propitious for bringing about such a change.
Pope wrote an elaborate justification. So did Col. Ely S. Parker,
Grant's Seneca Indian aide, who also drafted a bill that was introduced in the Senate on February 9, 1867.[8]

But the peace proponents commanded considerable political
strength, and they ticked off an impressive list of Indian outbreaks
they credited to army blunders. Powerful support of their position
came on January 25, 1867, with publication of the report of a
special joint committee of Congress chaired by Sen. James R.
Doolittle of Wisconsin. The committee had been formed almost
two years earlier as a result of the furore over Sand Creek and
had conducted an exhaustive investigation into "the condition of
the Indian tribes and their treatment by the civil and military
authorities of the United States." The Doolittle Report piled up a
mountain of authoritative testimony showing the fate overtaking
the Indian at the hands of the white man, tracing most Indian
wars to white aggressions, and favoring policies of moderation
and conciliation.[9]

Although the transfer measure carried in the House of Representatives, buttressed by the Doolittle Report, the peace elements
blocked it in the Senate, where Sherman's words about crushing
the Sioux with vindictive earnestness were quoted to show that the
army, in its present frame of mind, could not be trusted with Indian management.[10] At the same time, Secretary Browning persuaded President Johnson and most of the Cabinet to approve a
conciliatory approach to the hostiles rather than the "crude" policies urged by Stanton and Grant. The result was another peace
commission, appointed by the President and reporting to Browning. The commissioners were not only to look into the causes of
the Fetterman affair but also to hold friendly talks with the Plains
tribes, test their temper and disposition to settle on a reservation,
and find out whether they really had to have arms and ammunition to hold off starvation.[11] Angry and discouraged over the turn
of events, Sherman drew small comfort from the fact that four of
the six commissioners, including chairman Alfred Sully, were
military men; their character as peace emissaries could not help
but seriously complicate his plans.[12]

By March 1867 these plans had been developed. In the Department of the Platte General Augur was to organize a striking force

of 2,000 cavalry and infantry under Col. John Gibbon to punish the Sioux and Cheyennes in the Powder River country. "No mercy should be shown these Indians," Sherman declared, "for they grant no quarter nor ask for it." In the Department of the Missouri General Hancock was also to form an expedition to show the flag to the Cheyennes and Kiowas south of the Arkansas River. Reports reaching Hancock suggested that these tribes planned to take the warpath in the spring, and his assignment was "to confer with them to ascertain if they want to fight, in which case he will indulge them."[13]

Even as he reported his plans, Sherman conceded that Colonel Gibbon's expedition would have to be postponed. General Sully and his fellow commissioners were already in Omaha on their way to talk with the Sioux. Sherman could hardly avoid instructing Augur not to launch Gibbon until the commission had demonstrated its inability to negotiate the Sioux into submission. No such obstacle blocked Hancock. He set forth to bully the southern Plains tribes. Instead he touched off a bloody and perhaps needless war, portrayed the army to the public even more sharply in the image of Colonel Chivington, and insured that the legacy of Sand Creek rather than of the Fetterman disaster would shape Indian policy in 1867.

Tall, handsome, robust, immaculately uniformed, Hancock "presented an appearance," recalled General Grant, "that would attract the attention of an army as he passed."[14] Not alone for holding the Union center at Gettysburg against Pickett's charge did newsmen label him "Hancock the Superb." He fought superbly in almost every major battle of the Army of the Potomac. But his military career had given him little knowledge of Indians.

The attitudes of the southern Plains tribes in 1866–67 presented Hancock with the classic dilemma in which the army so often found itself. The principal leaders of the Cheyennes, Arapahoes, Kiowas, and Comanches wanted to avoid trouble with the whites, even if it meant abandoning some of their historic haunts. The chiefs always had great difficulty restraining their warlike young men. Now the postwar spurt of travel and the advance of the railroad added deeply felt grievances to the natural raiding impulse, making the warriors even less amenable to tribal leadership. Edward W. Wynkoop, agent for the Cheyennes and Arapahoes, and Jesse H. Leavenworth, agent for the Kiowas and Comanches, labored to reinforce the chiefs in their pacific efforts. Both agents exaggerated only slightly in asserting that their tribes were at peace.

But every tribe contained elements whose behavior weakened the assertion. By their menacing attitude the Cheyenne Dog Soldiers belied the protestations of the peace chiefs Black Kettle and Little Robe that the Cheyennes would leave the Smoky Hill Road alone. Their Arapaho allies under Little Raven displayed similar ambivalence.[15] From newly reactivated Fort Arbuckle, in Indian Territory, came reports that showed the Comanches still raiding in Texas.[16] The commanders at Forts Larned and Dodge, edgy after the Fetterman slaughter, passed on alarmist reports of tribal combinations forming for a general war in the spring. The Kiowas in this neighborhood were badly fragmented. Lone Wolf and Kicking Bird spoke for peace, but what the officers on the Arkansas heard more loudly were the blustery threats of Satanta to drive out the whites altogether if they did not stop running off his buffalo and burning his timber.[17] Although Kiowa raiders continued to plague Texas settlements, with one or two exceptions the specific charges against them turned out to rest on groundless rumors.[18] Complicating the situation still further, bands of Southern Brulé and Oglala Sioux of uncertain disposition had dropped down from the Platte and Republican to mingle with the Cheyennes and Arapahoes.

If the insolent threats and scattering of minor depredations were allowed to pass unnoticed, they could well escalate into trouble of more serious proportions. As Sherman advised Hancock: "This cannot be tolerated for a moment. If not a state of war, it is the next thing to it, and will result in war unless checked."[19] But, as always, how to single out the few to be checked without alarming the many needing no check posed a thorny problem. In effect, Sherman and Hancock resolved on some insolent threats of their own. On March 11, 1867, Hancock advised Agents Wynkoop and Leavenworth that he intended to lead an army to the Plains to show the Indians that he could whip them if they tormented the travel routes. He planned to talk with the chiefs. If they wanted war, he would oblige them. If not, they must stay clear of the roads.²⁰ "We go prepared for war," the general proclaimed to his troops, "and will make it if a proper occasion presents. . . . No insolence will be tolerated."²¹

The command Hancock placed in camp at Fort Larned on April 7 was of suitably impressive dimensions—fourteen hundred soldiers in eleven troops of the Seventh Cavalry, seven companies of the Thirty-seventh Infantry, and a battery of the Fourth Artillery. The colonel of the Seventh was Bvt. Maj. Gen. Andrew Jackson Smith, a blunt, irascible old dragoon of almost thirty years' service. Since Smith commanded the District of the Upper Arkansas, the regiment fell to his youthful and flamboyant lieutenant colonel, George Armstrong Custer. Slight of build, with long blond hair and a walrus mustache, Custer had rocketed to fame as a hard-hitting—some said reckless—cavalry leader in the Civil War. A major general with his own division at twenty-five, he now had to content himself with a regiment. Hancock's expedition gave Custer his first experience with Indians. By the time of his last, on the Little Bighorn nine years later, he would be, depending on one's point of view, either famous or infamous, idolized or abominated.²²

For the first of Hancock's meetings, Agent Wynkoop promised to bring in a delegation of chiefs from a village of Cheyenne Dog Soldiers and Oglala Sioux reposing on Pawnee Fork, thirty-five miles upstream from Fort Larned. A snow storm and a buffalo herd delayed the meeting five days, and then only two chiefs and a dozen warriors appeared. They were important chiefs—Tall Bull and White Horse—and despite his irritation at the poor showing, Hancock arrayed his officers in dress uniform and held a council. He lectured the Cheyennes sternly, gave them their choice of war or peace, and announced that on the morrow he would march up Pawnee Fork to the village and deliver his message to the rest of the chiefs.²³

Predictably, the approach of so many soldiers badly frightened the Indians, and the women and children stampeded to the hills. Camping half a mile from the village, Hancock directed the chiefs to round them up and bring them back. That night, alerted that the men might be getting ready to leave too, he had Custer throw a cordon of cavalry around the village. But the lodges were deserted; the Indians had already taken flight. "This looks like the commencement of war," concluded Hancock.

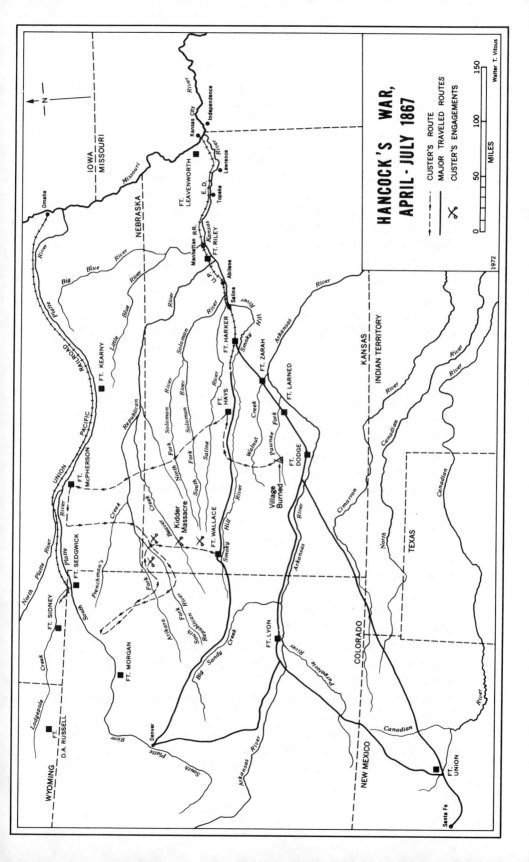

HANCOCK'S WAR,
APRIL - JULY 1867

- - - CUSTER'S ROUTE
——— MAJOR TRAVELED ROUTES
✗ CUSTER'S ENGAGEMENTS

MILES
0   50   100   150

Walter T. Vitous

1972

N

IOWA

MISSOURI

Missouri River

Kansas City

Independence

Lawrence

Topeka

FT. LEAVENWORTH

E. D.

Manhattan RR.

FT. RILEY

Abilene

Salina

Kansas River

FT. HARKER

Smoky Hill River

Smoky Hill

FT. ZARAH

Arkansas River

FT. LARNED

KANSAS

INDIAN TERRITORY

Canadian River

Canadian River

NEBRASKA

Omaha

Platte River

Big Blue River

Little Blue River

Blue River

FT. KEARNY

Republican River

Solomon River

North Fork Solomon River

South Fork Solomon River

Saline River

FT. HAYS

Smoky Hill River

Walnut Creek

Pawnee Fork

FT. DODGE

Village Burned

Arkansas River

Cimarron

North Canadian

TEXAS

UNION PACIFIC RAILROAD

FT. McPHERSON

Platte River

North Platte River

Beaver Creek

Kidder Massacre

FT. WALLACE

Smoky Hill River

Arkansas River

FT. LYON

COLORADO

FT. SEDGWICK

Frenchman's Fork

Republican River

Arikara Fork

South Republican River

Big Sandy Creek

Purgatoire River

FT. SIDNEY

South Platte River

FT. MORGAN

Denver

South Platte River

Arkansas River

NEW MEXICO

Lodgepole Creek

FT. D.A. RUSSELL

WYOMING

Canadian River

FT. UNION

Santa Fe

The Sioux and Cheyennes hurried north, Custer in close pursuit with eight troops of the Seventh Cavalry. The Indians, by scattering into small parties, left the cavalry with no trail large enough to follow. When Custer reached the Smoky Hill Road he found it a shambles—stage stations burned, stock run off, and citizens butchered. Putting in at Fort Hays before continuing the pursuit, Custer found himself suddenly immobilized. Forage thought to have been stockpiled had been delayed by high water.

Back on Pawnee Fork, Hancock agonized for three days over whether to destroy the abandoned village. He thought the Indians guilty of "bad faith" in not acceding to his wishes and tried hard to convince himself that their flight was sufficient provocation. Wynkoop and Leavenworth argued insistently that the Indians were innocent of any offense and had run solely because they feared another Chivington massacre. To burn the village would compound the injury already done and make war certain. General Smith agreed. A courier from Custer decided the question, even though some doubt arose that the Pawnee Fork fugitives had indeed committed the Smoky Hill outrages. It made no difference anyway, Hancock concluded, "for I am satisfied that the Indian village was a nest of conspirators." On April 19, over Wynkoop's forceful protest, he put to the torch 111 Cheyenne lodges, 140 Sioux lodges, and immense quantities of camp equipage.

At Forts Dodge and Larned, Hancock delivered his familiar war-or-peace ultimatum to Arapaho and Kiowa chiefs from camps south of the Arkansas. Satanta, the unpredictable Kiowa war leader, seemed so sincerely devoted to peace that Hancock presented him with a major general's dress uniform. Reaching Fort Hays on May 2, he found Custer still paralyzed by want of forage. As soon as the grass grew greener, Hancock directed, Custer was to take the field. "War is to be waged against the Sioux and Cheyenne Indians between the Arkansas and the Platte." With that, the department commander repaired to Fort Leavenworth.[24]

During May and June the Sioux and Cheyennes waged their own war between the Arkansas and the Platte. They struck repeatedly at mail stations, stagecoaches, wagon trains, and railroad workers on the Platte, the Smoky Hill, and the Arkansas. The progress of rail construction slowed, and for a time stagecoaches on the Smoky Hill quit running altogether. Satanta repaid Hancock's generosity by flaunting his new uniform while running off the stock herd at Fort Dodge. In remote western Kansas, Fort Wallace endured constant harassment, and its garrison skirmished several times with Cheyenne war parties.[25]

With six troops of the Seventh Cavalry, about 300 men, Custer set forth on June 1 to search out the hostiles along a thousand-mile swath to the Platte, the Republican, and back to the Smoky Hill. Inconclusive clashes with Sioux warriors marked his progress. He pushed the command to exhaustion, and troopers deserted by the score. The column dragged into Fort Wallace on July 13 with horses unfit for further campaigning.[26]

For the rest of the summer Indian warriors ran wild on the Arkansas, Smoky Hill, and Platte. Agents Leavenworth and Wynkoop protested that their tribes had sought peaceful refuge south of the Arkansas, and each ascribed the continuing hostilities to the other's Indians.[27] In truth the peace elements of all the tribes had gone south of the Arkansas, but the war factions had stayed north of the river to enjoy a raiding season as exciting and profitable as that of 1864.

The inability of the troops to prevent headline-making raids on stage stations and coaches and railroad workers aggravated another problem that plagued Sherman. The governors of Kansas, Colorado, Montana, and even Minnesota bombarded him and his superiors with appeals for authority to call out Volunteers to help the Regulars. Nothing so complicated an Indian war as undisciplined Volunteers riding about the countryside in search of Indians, and Sherman wanted no part of them. "I think I comprehend the motives of some of the Governors," he advised Grant, "whom I would not entrust with a picket post of fifty men, much less with the discretionary power to call out troops at national cost."[28] Denial of such petitions exposed Sherman to scathing newspaper criticism and risked disasters that might be charged to his intransigence. But to all he gave the same answer: they could organize Volunteers if they wanted but must provide the financing themselves and hope that Congress would later pick up the bill. Under this condition, he knew, merchants would not advance credit and Volunteers would not volunteer.

It was a delicate business, however, because of the chance that Volunteers might really be needed. The acting governor of Montana Territory, a volatile Irishman named Thomas Francis Meagher, played on this factor adroitly enough to bring Sherman to an ambiguous sanction of the muster of 800 Volunteers. John M. Bozeman, well-known pathfinder, had been murdered by Blackfeet Indians on his own Bozeman Trail, and settlers in the Gallatin Valley persuaded themselves that it portended a massive assault on their homes by Red Cloud's Sioux. It did not, but Meagher's rank-heavy battalion, commanded by a brigadier general, managed to run up a claim of more than a million dollars in June and July, half of which Congress finally paid.[29]

A. C. Hunt and Samuel J. Crawford, governors of Colorado and Kansas, pressed their case with fervor. Sherman succeeded in fending off Hunt, but Crawford, with powerful aid from Senator Edmund G. Ross in Congress and the Sioux and Cheyennes on the Smoky Hill, at last won the general's reluctant consent. In mid-July the Eighteenth Kansas Volunteer Cavalry, a 353-man battalion, was mustered into federal service.[30] It performed creditable work in helping the Regulars patrol the travel routes, and on August 22-23 two troops participated with a troop of the Tenth Cavalry in a major action on Beaver Creek with several hundred Sioux and Cheyennes.[31]

Except for this initiative and Custer's abortive expedition, Hancock's forces spent the summer in strictly defensive duties. For Kansas, Colorado, and Indian Territory, Hancock counted the equivalent of two and one-half regiments of infantry (elements of Third, Sixth, Thirty-seventh, and Thirty-eighth) plus the Seventh and Tenth Cavalry, the last not yet fully organized. Little more than 4,000 officers and men held eighteen forts and camps and guarded more than 1,500 miles of major travel arteries. All the regiments struggled under a heavy burden of untrained recruits, and to make matters worse, all were continuously decimated that summer by desertion and cholera, both of epidemic proportions. Not surprisingly, they failed to secure every target the hostiles might elect to hit.[32]

North of Hancock's department Generals Terry and Augur, both concerned mainly with the Sioux, also remained on the defensive that summer. Plans for the expedition against Red Cloud's Sioux fell quietly in the wastebasket. Even though the Sully Commission succeeded in holding friendly talks only with the friendly bands along the Missouri and the Platte, Sherman could not risk an offensive against the hostile Sioux as long as peace emissaries were anywhere near them. Besides, raids on the Union Pacific tied down troops that would have formed the expedition. And the bad publicity provoked by "Hancock's War" made another offensive politically hard to justify. Sherman keenly felt the need to have the Powder River Sioux "taken down a good many notches," but after three months of indecision he finally gave up the idea.[33]

Generals Terry and Augur continued to devote themselves to strengthening the rudimentary defenses they had inherited. Terry, charged with protecting steamboat and overland traffic to Montana, bolstered and extended the defense system laid out by General Sully during the campaigns of 1864 and 1865. Forts Ransom and Totten joined the older Forts Abercrombie and Sisseton (Wadsworth) as way stations on the land routes by which travelers from Minnesota reached the Missouri River corridor to the mountains. Along the Missouri itself, the detachments occasionally at the trading posts of Forts Union and Berthold since 1864 were given permanent stations with the establishment nearby of Forts Buford and Stevenson. Added to Forts Randall, Sully, and Rice down river, the new posts brought the Missouri under military surveillance all the way to the mouth of the Yellowstone. Farther west, where misplaced Camp Cooke had proved of marginal value, Terry gave Montana two new forts—Shaw on Sun River and Ellis in the strategic pass by which the Powder River Sioux threatened the settlers in the Gallatin Valley.[34]

In the Department of the Platte, as the Union Pacific left the emigrant roads at the forks of the Platte and advanced directly westward up Lodgepole Creek, General Augur established new posts to provide protection to survey and labor crews. To Forts Kearny, McPherson, and Sedgwick he added Forts Sidney, D. A. Russell, Sanders, and Fred Steele. On the road up the North Platte, while keeping venerable Fort Laramie, he abandoned Forts Mitchell and Casper. At the same time, he established Fort Fetterman at the point where the Bozeman Trail veered northward from the Platte to Forts Reno, Phil Kearny, and C. F. Smith.[35]

Terry and Augur had the Sioux country ringed with forts— Terry seven along the line of the Missouri from Randall to Ellis, backed by four between Minnesota and the Missouri River; Augur seven along the line of the Platte and the Bozeman Trail and a string of another six along the Union Pacific between the

North and South Platte. To hold these lines, as well as posts in Minnesota and Utah, Terry commanded four regiments of infantry (Tenth, Thirteenth, Twenty-second, Thirty-first) and Augur five (Fourth, Eighteenth, Twenty-seventh, Thirtieth, and Thirty-sixth). In addition, Augur had the Second Cavalry and a highly effective battalion of Pawnee Indian Scouts.[36]

The Sioux and their Northern Cheyenne allies were surrounded —by some 5,000 officers and enlisted men, chiefly infantry, strung in tiny clusters around a perimeter 2,500 miles in extent. Because of weakness in numbers, lack of mobility, and the restraints imposed by successive waves of peace commissioners, they had no choice but to remain on the defensive. No such inhibitions held back the Indians. The very presence of soldiers aroused their fury. So did the swelling parade of steamboats on the Missouri, the voracious demands of their boilers on the lightly timbered river bottoms, the rapid progress of the railroad up the Platte, and above all the continuing shrinkage of the buffalo herds caused by all this activity along the rim of the Indian homeland. On the Missouri, the Platte, and the Powder, the Sioux and Northern Cheyennes demonstrated that peace depended on more than the soothing words of peace commissioners.

In Dakota, camps of hostile Hunkpapa, Blackfeet, Miniconjou, Sans Arc, and Yanktonai Sioux ranged from the lower Yellowstone and Little Missouri to the Heart and Cannonball. Increasingly they gave allegiance to a chief destined to become the most powerful and implacably hostile of all the Sioux leaders—Sitting Bull. War parties from these camps held the upper Missouri in a state of chronic insecurity. They fired on steamboats, sniped at express riders, and knocked off camps of woodchoppers who supplied the boats with fuel. They continued to war on their hereditary enemies, the Arikaras, Mandans, and Gros Ventres, who resided in helpless dependence on the government at the Fort Berthold agency. Fort Stevenson endured occasional harassment. Fort Buford, from the day of its founding in 1866, was a special target of Sioux aggression. Warriors repeatedly ran off its cattle and mules, collided with herd guards, and fell on parties of soldiers that strayed beyond the limits of safety.[37]

Along the line of the Union Pacific, raiding parties from south of the Platte followed end-of-track across western Nebraska while, farther west, others from the Powder River camps fell on surveyors marking the line across Wyoming. Although General Augur kept two infantry regiments and half a cavalry regiment employed in guard and escort duty, they proved insufficient to insure workers and surveyors against Indian attack.[38]

The Bozeman Trail remained Augur's most worrisome problem. The Fetterman disaster had awakened the army to the weakness of Forts Reno, Phil Kearny, and C. F. Smith. By July 1867 more than 900 officers and soldiers of the Eighteenth and Twenty-seventh Infantry and Second Cavalry held the three forts, and another 500 men were building Fort Fetterman as the southern anchor of the road. Even so, the defenders defended little more than their own stations. Throughout 1867 the Powder River chiefs closed the road to all but heavily armed military trains. Almost no civilian parties reached Montana by this route during the year. The Indians also subjected Forts Phil Kearny and C. F. Smith to the same kind of harassing pressures that had so plagued Carrington the previous year. And once more they laid plans to wipe out the hated forts altogether.[39]

In July 1867, after the annual sun dance, the Powder River bands came together in a great enclave on the Little Bighorn River. They were mainly Oglala Sioux and Northern Cheyennes, but embraced also some Miniconjou and Sans Arc Sioux and Northern Arapahoes. The leaders resolved to destroy Forts Phil Kearny and C. F. Smith but could not agree on which one to strike first. Settling the dispute in typically democratic fashion, some 500 to 800 warriors, mostly Cheyennes, headed for Fort C. F. Smith, while another 1,000, accompanied by Red Cloud himself, set forth for Fort Phil Kearny.[40]

During July both forts had received reinforcements and new commanders. Col. John E. Smith, Twenty-seventh Infantry, commanded Fort Phil Kearny, while his lieutenant colonel, Luther P. Bradley, took over Fort C. F. Smith. Although the post on the Bighorn now sheltered almost 400 defenders, Fort Phil Kearny, with less than 300, was actually weaker than it had been under Carrington. Of large significance in the coming contests, Smith and Bradley had brought new breech-loading Springfield rifles and metallic cartridges to substitute for the old muzzle-loaders. Neither fort stood in much jeopardy from the forces descending on them. But each had an exposed outpost. At Fort C. F. Smith it was a hay-mowing camp in a creek bottom two and one-half miles to the northeast. A corral of logs and willow boughs woven on pole stringers, about 100 feet on each side, had been erected as a refuge in case of attack. At Fort Phil Kearny woodcutters still worked at the old pinery of Carrington's time. About five miles west of the post, fourteen wagon boxes had been removed from their running gear and formed into a corral in which to pen mules at night. On these two outposts the Sioux and Cheyenne assaults fell.

The warriors who chose Fort C. F. Smith as the objective had only twenty miles to ride from the Little Bighorn and they reached their destination early on August 1. Twelve civilians worked the mowing machines that morning, while Lt. Sigismund Sternberg and nineteen soldiers stood guard. The Indians gave ample warning of their presence, and their concerted rush on the corral found the whites well posted behind its foundation logs—all but Lieutenant Sternberg, whose notions of proper combat behavior did not include officers in the prone position. A withering fire from the new Springfields threw back the assailants, but not before a bullet punched into the lieutenant's brain. Al Colvin, one of the civilians, took charge. His leadership proved of high order, and his Henry repeater swelled the firepower of the defenders. Until late in the day the warriors kept the corral under continuous fire, mostly showers of arrows. Three more times they tried to overrun it, twice mounted and once on foot. Each time firepower shattered the assault short of the objective. The battle site could not be seen from the fort, and not until late in the afternoon did Colonel Bradley send out a relief force. By that time the Indians had all but given up; exploding case shot from a howitzer hastened their withdrawal. Outnumbered at least twenty to one, Colvin and his men had held their position for more than six hours, sustaining casualties of three killed and two wounded.[41]

The Wagon Box Fight at Fort Phil Kearny the next day bore remarkable similarity to the Hayfield Fight. Veteran Capt. James W. Powell, a contemporary of Fetterman, and his company of the Twenty-seventh Infantry guarded the woodcutters. The Sioux attack, which began with seizure of a mule herd, caught the whites dispersed in several parties. Some made it to the fort, while others took refuge in the wagon-box corral. Powell counted thirty-two defenders—Lt. John C. Jenness, twenty-six soldiers, four civilians, and himself. The tribesmen used the same tactics as at

Fort C. F. Smith, alternating sniping fire with massed charges that carried almost to the wagon boxes before collapsing. Again the breech-loading rifles did heavy execution and saved the day. Lieutenant Jenness caught a bullet in the head and died. Five privates were killed and two were wounded. Powell, a cool observer, estimated Indian casualties at no less than 60 killed and 120 wounded. The battle lasted for four and one-half hours before a relief force from Fort Phil Kearny reached the scene and sent the Indians scampering with howitzer fire.[42]

The Wagon Box and Hayfield Fights seemed to have no unsettling effect on the Indians. Even though they had suffered greater casualties than customary, they had gained much stock and felt no sense of defeat. For the morale of the Bozeman Trail's defenders, on the other hand, the engagements worked wonders. They showed that the Sioux and Cheyennes were not invincible and that Fetterman's fate did not necessarily await men surrounded by many times their number of Indians if they were properly armed and resolute. On the strategic level, however, a cogent question increasingly nagged policy makers: how could so large a commitment of manpower and expense to the Bozeman Trail defenses be justified if the Indians were still powerful enough to deny the route to all but military traffic? Red Cloud and his fellow chiefs gave no sign of relenting in their demand for abandonment of the Bozeman Trail forts as the price of a peace treaty. On the other side, there were signs that the government, if not the army, might indeed be brought to pay Red Cloud's price.

NOTES

1. Senate Ex. Docs., 40th Cong., 1st sess., No. 13, p. 27.
2. John B. Sanborn, late brigadier general of Volunteers, one of the commissioners investigating the Fetterman affair, found that "Army officers of high grade openly proclaim their intentions to shoot down any Indian they see, and say that they instruct their men to do likewise." In time of war military posts used to afford refuge to neutral or friendly tribesmen. Now "Indians flee from them as from a pestilence." From Fort Laramie, May 18, 1867, *ibid.*, pp. 111–14.
3. See Athearn, *Sherman and the Settlement of the West*, chaps. 7 and 8.
4. Reported an inspecting officer, Lt. Col. Orville E. Babcock, from Denver in May 1866: "Speculators and men wishing the presence of troops are greater enemies and need more watching than the Indians." House Ex. Docs., 39th Cong., 2d sess., No. 20, p. 5.
5. House Ex. Docs., 39th Cong., 2d sess., No. 88.

6. Senate Ex. Docs., 40th Cong., 1st sess., No. 13, pp. 7–11, 18–20, 23–24, 40–42, 52–55. *Ibid.*, 39th Cong., 2d sess., No. 16, p. 8. House Ex. Docs., 41st Cong., 2d sess., No. 240, pp. 41–43, 46–48. *The Diary of Orville Hickman Browning*, 2, 137–38.

7. To Browning, Feb. 4, 1867. He voiced similar views on Jan. 23 and 31. See House Ex. Docs., 39th Cong., 2d sess., No. 71, pp. 3, 11. Curiously, Cooke's order of July 31 purported simply to extend to army officers a policy already communicated by the Commissioner of Indian Affairs—Bogy's predecessor—to western Indian agents.

8. *Cong. Globe*, 39th Cong., 2d sess., p. 1108 (Feb. 9, 1867). Pope had delivered himself of detailed policy recommendations in the 1850s, but the latest round began with a long letter to Secretary of War Stanton on Feb. 6, 1864, when Pope commanded the Department of the Northwest. It was published in the *Army and Navy Journal*, April 26, 1864, and later in his report to the Joint Committee on the Conduct of the War. A succession of policy declarations followed. For his and Parker's justifications, see Senate Ex. Docs., 40th Cong., 1st sess., No. 13, pp. 45–52. For the recommendations of Grant and Sherman see SW, *Annual Report* (1866), pp. 18, 20; Senate Ex. Docs., 40th Cong., 1st sess., No. 13, pp. 40–41; and Athearn, pp. 110–11. Sen. James F. Wilson stated that Parker drafted the transfer bill. *Cong Globe*, 39th Cong., 2d sess., p. 1677 (Feb. 21, 1867). For Pope's frontier career see Richard N. Ellis, *General Pope and U.S. Indian Policy* (Albuquerque, N.M., 1970.)

9. Senate Reports, 39th Cong., 2d sess., No. 156. For the travels of this committee in 1865, see Utley, *Frontiersmen in Blue*, pp. 312–15.

10. Debates on the transfer issue centered not on the bill drafted by Colonel Parker nor on a similar one that had been introduced in the House on January 9, but rather on an amendment to a bill the Senate had passed in the first session of the 39th Congress providing for a system of inspections of the Indian Service recommended by the Doolittle Committee. An amendment in the House substituted the transfer measure for the body of the original bill as passed by the Senate. The House passed the amended bill, the Senate rejected the House amendment, and the conferees could not agree before the session ended on March 3. For these debates, see *Cong. Globe*, 39th Cong., 2d sess., pp. 843–44 (Jan. 29, 1867), 878–82 (Jan. 30), 891–99 (Jan. 31), 1623–24 (Feb. 20), 1679–84 (Feb. 21), 1712–20 (Feb. 22), 1790 (March 2), 1923–24 (March 1), 1988 (March 2). Sherman's words were quoted by Sen. Samuel C. Pomeroy of Kansas, p. 1624.

11. For Browning's arguments in Cabinet meetings, see *The Diary of Orville Hickman Browning*, 2, 126 (Jan. 25, 1867), 128 (Feb. 5), 135 (March 8). Browning's instructions to the commissioners, Feb. 18, 1867, are in Senate Ex. Docs., 40th Cong., 1st sess., No. 13, pp. 55–56.

12. Sully had led campaigns against the Sioux of Dakota in 1863, 1864, and 1865. See Utley, *Frontiersmen in Blue*, chaps. 13–15. He was now lieutenant colonel of the Third Infantry but was serving in his brevet grade of brigadier general. Other commission members were John B. Sanborn and Napoleon B. Buford (both wartime volunteer generals, recently mustered out), Col. Ely S. Parker, Judge J. F. Kinney, and G. P. Beauvais.

13. Sherman to Asst. Adj. Gen. Hq. of the Army, March 13, 1867, Senate Ex. Docs., 40th Cong., 1st sess., No. 7, pp. 1–3.

14. *Personal Memoirs of U. S. Grant*, ed. E. B. Long (Cleveland and New York, 1952), p. 582.

15. Donald J. Berthrong, *The Southern Cheyennes* (Norman, Okla., 1963), pp. 259–65. Wilbur S. Nye, *Plains Indian Raiders: The Final Phases of Warfare from the Arkansas to the Red River* (Norman, Okla., 1968), pp. 47–51, 66–67. The Dog Soldiers originated as one of the soldier societies common to the Plains tribes. Warrior societies filled social and military pur-

poses and also acted as camp police. The Dog Soldiers formed the most militant and elite of the Cheyenne soldier societies. Beginning about 1837 it transformed itself into a separate Cheyenne band that became the nucleus for the most courageous and skilled warriors and that won renown for its warlike deeds. In the Plains wars of 1864–69, the Dog Soldiers consistently resisted the efforts of the peace chiefs to reach an accommodation with the whites. See George E. Hyde, *Life of George Bent, Written from His Letters*, ed. Savoie Lottinville (Norman, Okla., 1967), pp. 337–38.

16. Feb. 16, 1867, Senate Ex. Docs., 40th Cong., 1st sess., No. 13, pp. 81–82.

17. *Ibid.*, pp. 50–54, 79, 101–2. House Ex. Docs., 41st Cong., 2d sess., No. 240, pp. 41–42, 48–49. Nye, pp. 64–67. For the situation among the Kiowas at this time, see James Mooney, *Calendar History of the Kiowa Indians*, 17th Annual Report of the Bureau of American Ethnology (Washington, D.C., 1898), pp. 180–81, 313–20.

18. The principal documented charge was the Box atrocity. In August 1866 a war party under Satanta had murdered James Box in Montague County, Texas, and carried his wife and four children into captivity. An infant died, but the mother and three children were ransomed by officers at Fort Dodge in October. Senate Ex. Docs., 40th Cong., 1st sess., No. 13, pp. 99–100. The Peace Commission of 1867, which included three generals, later exonerated the Kiowas of other depredation charges on which Hancock's campaign had been premised. House Ex. Docs., 40th Cong., 2d sess., No. 97, p. 13. But in truth both Kiowas and Comanches had been raiding extensively in Texas.

19. March 14, 1867, reducing to writing the conclusions of a conference between Sherman and Hancock in St. Louis on March 8. House Ex. Docs., 41st Cong., 2d sess., No. 240, pp. 98–99.

20. *Ibid.*, pp. 16–17, 92–94.

21. Hancock's General Field Order No. 1, Fort Riley, March 26, 1867, *ibid.*, pp. 12–13.

22. Biographical treatments of Custer range from the adulation of Frederick Whittaker's *Complete Life of Gen. George A. Custer* (New York, 1876) to the almost pathological hostility of Frederick F. Van de Water's *Glory Hunter: A Life of General Custer* (Indianapolis, Ind., 1934). The most balanced is Jay Monaghan's *Custer: Life of General George Armstrong Custer* (Boston, 1959).

23. Hancock's expedition is voluminously documented by official records published in House Ex. Docs., 41st Cong., 2d sess., No. 240; Senate Ex. Docs., 40th Cong., 1st sess., No. 13; and CIA, *Annual Report* (1867), pp. 310–14. Accounts of participants are Henry M. Stanley, *My Early Travels and Adventures in America and Asia* (2 vols., New York, 1905), *I*, 11–60 [Stanley, who later found Livingston in Africa, reported the expedition for the *Missouri Democrat*]; Theodore Davis, "A Summer on the Plains," *Harper's New Monthly Magazine*, *36* (February 1868), 292–307; and George A. Custer, *My Life on the Plains*, ed. Milo M. Quaife (Lakeside Classics edition, Chicago, 1952), chap. 2. Reliable secondary accounts are Berthrong, pp. 271–82; William H. Leckie, *The Military Conquest of the Southern Plains* (Norman, Okla., 1963), pp. 39–47; Nye, chap. 8; Hyde, *Life of George Bent*, chap. 9; Minnie Dubbs Millbrook, "The West Breaks in General Custer," *Kansas Historical Quarterly*, *36* (1970), 113–48.

24. Hancock's final report, May 22, 1867, House Ex. Docs., 41st Cong., 2d sess., No. 240, pp. 78–92.

25. For Indian raids see Marvin H. Garfield, "Defense of the Kansas Frontier, 1866–67," *Kansas Historical Quarterly*, *I* (1931–32), pp. 330–32; sources cited in n. 23 above; and Mrs. Frank C. Montgomery, "Fort Wallace and Its Relation to the Frontier," *Kansas Historical Collections*, *17* (1926–28), 189–282.

26. Custer describes the campaign in graphic detail in *My Life on the Plains*, chaps. 5–7, as does Davis, "A Summer on the Plains," pp. 299–307. See especially, however, the careful reconstruction in Lawrence A. Frost, *The Court-Martial of General George Armstrong Custer* (Norman, Okla., 1968), chaps. 3–8. From Fort Wallace Custer and a small detachment hastened to Fort Hays for supplies. Then Custer went on to Fort Harker, saw General Smith briefly, and took the train to Fort Riley, where his wife was staying. For this trip and for harsh punitive measures against deserters, he was court-martialed and sentenced to a year's suspension from rank and pay. The court-martial proceedings form chaps. 9–11 of Frost's book.

27. House Ex. Docs., 41st Cong., 2d sess., No. 240, pp. 25–26, 35, 111–18.

28. Athearn, p. 147. Sherman's difficulties with the governors are detailed on pp. 144–48, 155–58, 163–66, 169–70.

29. James L. Thane, Jr., "The Montana 'Indian War' of 1867," *Arizona and the West, 10* (1968), 153–70. Athearn, pp. 133–43 ff.

30. Athearn, pp. 169–70. Garfield, pp. 338–40. Samuel J. Crawford, *Kansas in the Sixties* (Chicago, 1911), pp. 251–62.

31. Armes, *Ups and Downs of an Army Officer*, pp. 231–56. George B. Jenness, "The Battle of Beaver Creek," *Transactions of the Kansas State Historical Society, 9* (1905–06), 443–52. Jenness commanded the Kansas cavalry. Nye, chap. 11.

32. See troop distribution tables in SW, *Annual Report* (1867), pp. 39–42. All the contemporary literature deals with the terror and death wrought by the cholera at all the Plains posts. Desertions from the army between Oct. 1, 1866, and Sept. 20, 1867, totaled 13,608. The Seventh Cavalry alone sustained 512. *Ibid.*, p. 475.

33. Athearn, pp. 129–31, 149–52. SW, *Annual Report* (1867), pp. 32, 65–66. House Ex. Docs., 40th Cong., 1st sess., No. 240, pp. 58–60.

34. SW, *Annual Report* (1867), pp. 49–52. Frazer, *Forts of the West*, pp. 80, 83–84, 110–11, 113–15. Ray H. Mattison, "The Military Frontier on the Upper Missouri," *Nebraska History, 37* (1956), pp. 168–72.

35. Frazer, pp. 90, 181, 184–86.

36. SW, *Annual Report* (1867), pp. 38–42, 59.

37. Robert G. Athearn, *Forts of the Upper Missouri* (Englewood Cliffs, N.J., 1967), chaps. 13 and 14. SW, *Annual Report* (1869), pp. 58–59. *Army and Navy Journal*, 7 (April 23, 1870), 563. A graphic and literate view of army life on the upper Missouri at this time is De Trobriand, *Military Life in Dakota*. The author, colonel of the Thirty-first Infantry, commanded the military district, with headquarters at Fort Stevenson.

38. SW, *Annual Report* (1867), p. 59. See also Edwin L. Sabin, *Building the Pacific Railway* (Philadelphia and London, 1919), pp. 236–40; George B. Grinnell, *The Fighting Cheyennes* (2d ed., Norman, Okla., 1956), pp. 263–68; and Danker, *Man of the Plains*, pp. 58–61. Luther North, subject of the last work, was a captain in the Pawnee Scout battalion commanded by his brother, Frank.

39. SW, *Annual Report* (1867), pp. 58–59, 436–39. Conditions at Fort C. F. Smith are well set forth in Mattes, *Indians, Infants, and Infantry*, chaps. 6–8; at Fort Phil Kearny in Murray, *Military Posts in the Powder River Country*, pp. 86–101.

40. Hyde, *Red Cloud's Folk*, pp. 158–59. Mattes, pp. 132–34, citing official reports from Fort C. F. Smith. Officers here got their information about the Sioux from the friendly Crows, who lived nearby.

41. Roy E. Appleman, "The Hayfield Fight," in Potomac Westerners, *Great Western Indian Fights*, chap. 11. Mattes, pp. 134–38. Vaughn, *Indian Fights*, chap. 3. Internal evidence in contemporary sources suggests that this estimate of Indian losses is too low, but other firsthand estimates are wildly high. Whether Colonel Bradley knew of the peril to the hay party

and elected to sacrifice it rather than risk a relief column is a matter of dispute. Bradley's record is otherwise highly creditable.

42. Appleman, "The Wagon Box Fight," in Potomac Westerners, *Great Western Indian Fights*, chap. 12. Robert A. Murray, "The Wagon Box Fight: A Centennial Appraisal," in *The War on Powder River* (Bellevue, Neb., 1969), pp. 27–30. Again, estimates of the number of Indians and their losses vary widely. Most contemporary white estimates of the total force range from 1,500 to 4,000. Powell is the only white to place casualties lower than 400, and some go as high as 1,000. By contrast, Indian estimates, as recorded by Hyde (*Red Cloud's Folk*, p. 159) are 1,000 participants, of whom six were killed and six wounded. Hyde's first figure seems the more probable, while his second is as absurdly low as white estimates are high. Powell's estimate of Indian loss seems most credible.

NINE

The Peace Commission of 1867

GENERAL HANCOCK HAD PRESENTED the peace advocates with a powerful weapon. In "Hancock's War," with all of its overtones of what Sherman labeled "the Chivington process,"[1] they found dramatic confirmation of their contention that heavy-handed military policies provoked most Indian wars. Even Generals Sully, Buford, and Sanborn condemned Hancock's actions; shock waves from the Kansas hostilities had rolled northward and disrupted their "friendly talks" with the Sioux.[2] Had Hancock not bullied the Cheyennes and burned the Pawnee Fork village, they may well have embarked on a summer of bloodletting anyway. The lid was off the powder keg and other incidents could easily have produced sparks. But it was Hancock who ignited the powder and thereby so weakened the army's arguments, despite vociferous western support, that cooperation in a peace venture became politically necessary.

By the summer of 1867 a policy proposal of fairly definite outline had taken shape in the thinking of Indian administrators and their political supporters. It held forth the short-term promise of restoring peace to the Plains and the long-term promise of a solution to the Indian problem. In its latest version the "concentration policy" contemplated the establishment of two vast reservations, one north of Nebraska, the other south of Kansas, on which all the roving tribes would be persuaded to gather. Except for government administrators, no whites would be permitted. Here the tribes would no longer threaten the travel routes and settlements. Here they could be insulated from the kind of interracial contact that in the past had infected them with so many of the white man's vices and that had produced so many incidents leading to hostilities. And here, ultimately, they could be "educated," "civilized," and endowed with the privileges and obligations of United States citizenship.[3]

Ironically, the pacific concentration policy owed a large debt to a militant proposal espoused by General Sherman in his annual report for 1866 and urged vigorously thereafter. He wanted to restrict the southern Plains tribes south of the Arkansas and the northern Plains tribes north of the Platte. Any Indians found out of bounds without a military pass would be treated as hostiles. Secretary Browning and Commissioner of Indian Affairs Bogy agreed with Sherman's goal of clearing the belt of country that contained the travel routes and settlements of all Indians, but they emphatically dissented from his desire to accomplish it by forceful methods that ignored the treaty rights of the Indians—especially the rights of the Cheyennes to hunt on the Smoky Hill.[4]

Bogy's successor as Commissioner of Indian Affairs (Bogy failed of confirmation in the Senate) also embraced the creed of negotiated peace leading to concentration. A former Tennessee congressman of large girth and conspicuous piety, Nathaniel G. Taylor gave further refinement to the idea.[5] So did the peace commissioners Buford and Sanborn.[6] Although dubious about negotiation, Sherman saw that the objectives of concentration coincided with his own military objectives. With reservations defined, he could assume that any Indians found off them were hostile and act accordingly. This would alleviate the "unnatural attitude" into which his soldiers had been thrust, "when the people of the frontier universally declare the Indians to be at war, and the Indian commissioners and agents pronounce them at peace, leaving us in the gap to be abused by both parties."[7]

Commissioner Taylor laid out the proposal in a letter of July 12, 1867, transmitted to the Senate.[8] The scholarly, soft-spoken chairman of the Committee on Indian Affairs, Sen. John B. Henderson of Missouri, at once introduced legislation. After heated debate and considerable amendment, the bill passed both houses of Congress on July 20.[9] General Sherman aided its progress by sending Secretary Stanton a telegram that was read on the Senate floor. As long as 50 Indians remained between the Platte and the Arkansas, he said, they would tie down 3,000 soldiers. "Rather get them out as soon as possible, and it makes little difference whether they be coaxed out by Indian commissioners or killed."[10] The act created a peace commission to try to coax them out. The commissioners were to go west and talk with the hostile tribes, learn the causes of hostility, and negotiate treaties removing the causes. They were also to examine the territory east of the Rockies for suitable reservations on which the tribes could be concentrated and begin supporting themselves. As a concession to western belligerence, the act carried an amendment by Kansas Sen. Edmund G. Ross authorizing the Secretary of War, in the event the commission failed, to accept up to 4,000 Volunteers "to conquer a peace."

The act of July 20 named four of the peace commission members—Taylor, Sanborn, Senator Henderson, and Samuel F. Tappan, the last a long-time crusader for humanitarian causes whose investigation of Colonel Chivington had earned him some notoriety as a friend of the Indian. In addition, the President was to appoint three army generals. In another stroke of irony, he named General Sherman to head the army delegation. The other military appointments went to old Gen. William S. Harney, retired veteran of conflicts with the Seminoles and Sioux before the Civil War,"[11] and Alfred H. Terry, the lawyer-general who headed the Department of the Dakota.[12]

The peace commission organized at St. Louis early in August 1867 and headed up the Missouri River, its first object to deal with the troublesome Sioux. Determined to give the peace offensive a fair trial, Sherman instructed his department commanders to place all troops on the defensive and subordinate their movements to the plans of the commission. ("If entirely in order," grumped an Omaha editor in response, "we should like to enquire when they have been on the offensive."[13]) Runners set forth to invite Red Cloud and his fellow chiefs to gather at Fort Laramie in mid-September. Other emissaries arranged for a mid-October meeting with the southern Plains Indians. Meanwhile, the commissioners talked with friendly Sioux bands on the upper Missouri and, in September, with Spotted Tail's technically peaceable Brulés at North Platte, Nebraska. Word from Fort Laramie offered little hope that Red Cloud would come in. The commissioners postponed the Fort Laramie conference, therefore, and turned to the October appointment. General Augur substituted for Sherman, who had been called suddenly to Washington by the President.[14]

The tribesmen of the southern Plains proved more willing than Red Cloud to meet with the Great Father's emissaries. Some 5,000 Indians gathered at a popular sun-dance ground at Medicine Lodge Creek, Kansas, seventy miles south of Fort Larned. This site had been chosen because the Cheyennes refused to come any closer to the Arkansas River forts. Even so, while the commissioners negotiated with the Kiowas, Comanches, and Kiowa-Apaches, most of the Cheyennes remained sullenly on the Cimarron River, forty miles distant. Hancock's destruction of the Pawnee Fork village still rankled, and a summer of successful warfare had done much to dim the attractions of the peace table. Several days of feasting, oratory, and distribution of presents put the Kiowas, Comanches, and Kiowa-Apaches in a cooperative frame of mind. Only after their chiefs had fixed their marks on a treaty on October 21, however, did the Cheyennes begin to drift in to pick up their share of the presents. On October 28 the Cheyenne and Arapaho chiefs also signed a treaty.[15]

The Medicine Lodge treaties embodied the principles of the concentration policy. They defined two large reservations in western Indian Territory. The Kiowas, Comanches, and Kiowa-Apaches were to be concentrated on one, the Cheyennes and Arapahoes on the other. No unauthorized whites would be admitted. Government teachers would educate the young. Seeds and agricultural implements would be furnished the adults, together with instructors to teach them how to farm. Each year for thirty years, under the watchful eyes of an army officer, the government would issue specified amounts of clothing and other presents. In return the Indians relinquished all rights to territory outside the reservations—although reserving the right to hunt anywhere south of the Arkansas so long as enough buffalo survived to justify the chase. In addition, they promised to withdraw all opposition to railroads and military posts and to refrain from harming white people or their property. In short, nomadic warrior-huntsmen were to be transformed into sedentary agriculturalists and inculcated with Anglo-Saxon values.[16]

The peace commission report, submitted to the President on January 7, 1868, elaborated the tenets of concentration as applied in the Medicine Lodge treaties and urged them as the foundation of future U.S. Indian policy. Conquest by kindness rather than armed force would be the guiding principle. Through wise and benevolent administration the Indian would not only be removed from the paths of expansion but also taught how to live like his white brothers, and ultimately be lifted to the grace of U.S. citizenship. The report neatly disposed of the thorny transfer question by advocating a separate, cabinet-level Department of Indian Affairs. It pointed to the need for thorough revision of the Indian Intercourse Laws. And it framed an eloquent appeal for mutual trust and understanding in interracial relations.

The evangelical and antimilitary tone of the report stamps it as the product of Commissioner Taylor's pen. With what misgivings and suppressed irritation Generals Sherman, Terry, Augur, and Harney affixed their signatures may be surmised. But Hancock's War and the image in which it had cast the army left them little practical choice but to let the theoreticians try their way. If it worked, the army's frontier mission would be much simplified. If not, the army would surely regain its lost stature.

While the proponents of concentration could draw satisfaction from the creation of a great southern reservation, they had to confess failure in the north. They had gone to Fort Laramie in November, after the Medicine Lodge council, to meet with Red Cloud. Instead, they found only a few Crows, long one of the friendliest of the Plains tribes. Red Cloud had sent a message: he would call off the war only after the army abandoned Forts Phil Kearny and C. F. Smith. When spring came, the commission's report suggested, another attempt could be made to bring him to the council table and complete the grand design of concentration.

Early in April 1868 the peace commissioners set forth for Fort Laramie. (Henderson remained behind for the Johnson impeachment trial; Sherman, recalled from Omaha for the same purpose, got to Fort Laramie the first week in May.) With them the officials carried a treaty draft that conceded all of Red Cloud's demands. The Bozeman Trail would be yielded. Its guardian forts would be abandoned. Already, on March 2, General Grant had issued orders for the garrisons to withdraw when summer dried the road.[17]

For the army, it was an unpalatable but not indigestible prescription. The forts had cost a great deal of blood, toil, and treasure, and to hand them over to Red Cloud's torch-bearing warriors was deeply humiliating. Such abject surrender, furthermore, could not help but inspire them—and by example their brethren of the southern Plains—to further resistance. Besides, strategists contended, the forts were needed to keep the Indians off the railroad and to serve as offensive bases when the time of reckoning came. Yet top officers had to admit that with available resources the road could not be made safe for travelers, and the withdrawal would free a full regiment of infantry for more mobile use along the railroad. And they conceded the obvious truth that every mile the Union Pacific advanced toward the shorter Salt Lake City–Virginia City route made the Bozeman Trail that much more obsolete.[18]

The treaty laid before the Indians at Fort Laramie also defined a reservation on which to concentrate the Sioux and other northern tribes—nearly all of present South Dakota west of the Missouri River. It granted hunting rights on the Republican River and in Nebraska and Wyoming north of the Platte. And, a further necessary concession to the Red Cloud people, it reserved the Powder River country as "unceded Indian territory" on which no white might trespass without Indian consent. In its other provisions the Fort Laramie Treaty closely paralleled the Medicine Lodge treaties.[19]

Agents of the peace commission had been laboring all winter to round up key Sioux leaders for the April meeting, but none was on hand to greet the commissioners. For almost a month they waited. Spotted Tail and his Brulés came up from the Republican River country and signed on April 29, but still Red Cloud held back. "When we see the soldiers moving away and the forts abandoned," was the message received early in May, "then I will come down and talk." Most of the commissioners departed, but Harney and Sanborn persisted, and on May 25 and 26 they managed to sign up an encouraging array of Oglala, Miniconjou, and Yanktonai leaders. Meanwhile, the veteran Jesuit missionary Pierre Jean DeSmet once more stepped into his familiar role as peacemaker for the Indian Bureau and journeyed to the upper Missouri to collect other needed signatures. During a dramatic visit to camps at the mouth of the Powder, he failed to soften the rocklike resistance of Sitting Bull, but did succeed in mellowing some of his militant followers. On July 2, at Fort Rice, they joined with other Hunkpapa, Blackfeet, Sans Arc, Two Kettle, and Santee leaders in signing the treaty. It now bore almost 200 signatures—but still not that of Red Cloud.[20]

By early August the Twenty-seventh Infantry had packed up and moved out of the Bozeman Trail posts. Red Cloud's warriors promptly burned Forts Phil Kearny and C. F. Smith. Although the Indians knew of the decision to abandon the forts, they had not relaxed the pressure on them, and even after the troops left depredations continued around Forts Fetterman, Sanders, and Laramie until late September. Then the hostiles passed October laying in their winter's meat. Finally, early in November, Red Cloud and most of the hostile chiefs showed up at Fort Laramie. On the sixth, Red Cloud placed his mark on the copy of the treaty left behind by the peace commission the previous May.[21]

Congress, preoccupied with the impeachment of President Johnson, proved almost as dilatory as the Sioux. Senator Henderson's bills to create a separate Indian Department and organize territorial governments for the two great Plains reservations died in committee, together with bills introduced by friends of the army to transfer the Indian Bureau to the War Department. On July 25 the Senate finally consented to the ratification of the Medicine Lodge treaties. Not until February 24, 1869, two months after Red Cloud's grudging acquiescence, did the Fort Laramie Treaty gain like approval. Repeated warnings from the Indian Bureau that the Plains tribes faced starvation failed to hasten the slow progress of the regular Indian appropriation bill.[22] Senator Henderson managed to insert provisions for the first installment of clothing and other annuity goods for the Medicine Lodge signatories, but his amendments to appropriate funds for concentrating and feeding the tribes covered by both the Medicine Lodge and Fort Laramie treaties ran into trouble in the conference committee charged with reconciling the House and Senate versions of the bill. As finally approved on July 27, 1868, the bill appropriated half a million dollars for this purpose. But the Indian Bureau, as always struggling under allegations of corruption, was not to be entrusted with the money. The law specified that it be spent under the direction of General Sherman.[23]

In the context of the feud over transfer of the Indian Bureau, here indeed was an irony. Without disturbing the formal organization of Indian administration, Congress in effect handed the Plains tribes over to the army. Lacking control of the rations, the regular agents could not expect to concentrate the Indians or to exercise much authority over them once concentrated. The Plains Indians were subordinated to the very influences from which Taylor, Henderson, and Tappan had sought to liberate them.

Sherman lost no time in seizing the initiative. On August 11, 1868, he issued orders creating two new military districts, one to coincide with the northern reservation, the other with the southern. General Harney would command one, Bvt. Maj. Gen. William B. Hazen (colonel of the Thirty-eight Infantry) the other.[24] Controlling "all issues and disbursements," these officers would be certain to rule the reservations in fact, if not in name.

Shepherding the Platte and Powder River Sioux to General Harney's reservation turned out to be an undertaking of several years' duration. But from most appearances the Fort Laramie Treaty could be counted a success. It ended the Red Cloud War. Red Cloud submitted himself to Indian Bureau paternalism, and although he remained a maddeningly disruptive influence for the next forty-one years, he never again took the warpath. Many of his people chose the same course, and a state of comparative tranquility settled on the northern Plains. But not all Indians followed. Some stayed in the unceded territory, a nucleus for people disenchanted with reservation life. This small cloud increasingly darkened the Powder and Yellowstone. In 1876 it burst. In that costly and dramatic war Forts Phil Kearny and C. F. Smith would have been priceless; indeed, one may well doubt that the war would have occurred at all had the treaty of 1868 not denied the army its hard-won positions on the Powder and Bighorn.

The Medicine Lodge treaties, so very much easier to negotiate, proved less enduring than the Fort Laramie Treaty. The Senate had scarcely approved them, in fact, before war came once more to the southern Plains.

The tribes party to the Medicine Lodge treaties passed the winter of 1867–68 south of the Arkansas. The Kiowas and Comanches continued to raid the Texas frontier and also played havoc with Chickasaw horse herds near Fort Arbuckle. The Cheyennes and Arapahoes impressed the perennially optimistic

Agent Wynkoop as tranquil and contented. They had but one grievance. At Medicine Lodge the peace commission had promised them arms and ammunition, and impatience for their delivery was fast turning to discontent. In June 1868 a Cheyenne war party seeking revenge for a past humiliation assailed a Kaw Indian settlement near Council Grove, Kansas. At once, Indian Superintendent Thomas Murphy ordered the arms withheld from the Cheyennes. Wynkoop thought this action unjust and provocative. So did the Cheyennes, and they refused to accept any of their annuities until the ban was lifted. Wynkoop finally prevailed. On July 23 the Indian Bureau authorized the issue if the agent judged it necessary to keep the peace. On August 9 most of the tribe gathered at Fort Larned to receive a modest shipment of 160 pistols, 80 Lancaster rifles, and kegs of powder and lead.[25]

Several days earlier a party of about 200 Cheyenne warriors, unaware of the government's decision to give in, had ridden north to raid the Pawnees. En route they picked up twenty Sioux and four Arapahoes. Only a handful actually went to the Pawnee country. The rest rode among the new settlements on the Saline and Solomon Rivers. There appears to have been no concerted intent to start trouble, and just how it began is a matter of conflicting evidence. Whiskey, ill temper stemming from the arms ban, misunderstandings between the Indians and suspicious settlers, and perhaps some white provocation all played a part. Even after the first collisions had occurred, the majority of the warriors wanted to avoid more, but at last they all united in a savage raid. Between August 10 and 12 they robbed and burned cabins, ran off stock, ravished five women, and killed fifteen men. "War is surely upon us," conceded Superintendent Murphy.[26]

The war had been in progress for two months when the peace commission convened in Chicago on October 7, 1868. All were present except Senator Henderson, and General Grant, now Republican candidate for President, sat in on the meeting. For a time the seeming success of the commission had softened Sherman's opinion of the "peace doctrine." Now the Cheyenne outbreak stiffened his attitude and also made it politically more marketable. The two-day meeting was a heated struggle between Sherman on the one hand and Taylor and Tappan on the other. Sherman, commanding the votes of Harney, Terry, and Augur, won on every issue. The resolutions, made public on October 9, called for abrogating the provision of the Medicine Lodge treaties permitting the Indians to hunt outside the reservation boundaries and for using military force to compel them to move to their new homes. On larger policy matters, the resolutions urged that the government no longer recognize Indian tribes as "domestic dependent nations" and that, consistent with existing treaties, all Indians be held individually subject to U.S. laws. And finally, the Indian Bureau ought to be transferred to the War Department.[27]

With this resounding affirmation of a forceful Indian policy, the peace commission adjourned, never to meet again. The Red Cloud problem had not been finally mastered at this time, and the southern Plains tribes with which peace had been concluded were now once more at war. The peace commission was, therefore, widely viewed as a failure. Yet it left a legacy of large consequence. Some of the fundamental principles of its January report persisted in the thinking of policy makers and formed the bedrock of President Grant's celebrated Peace Policy. Concentration, education, "civilization," and agricultural self-support would all be major features of that policy. But the principle of force planted in the October record of the peace commission by Sherman and his colleagues would also emerge as a feature of Grant's policy. As stated by Sherman in his annual report for 1868, the true concentration policy involved a "double process of peace *within* their reservations and war *without*."[28] Whether Commissioner Taylor and his associates in Washington liked it or not, this was the policy Sherman's columns were even then applying in the war that had flared on the Saline and Solomon in August.

NOTES

1. Athearn, *William Tecumseh Sherman and the Settlement of the West*, p. 160.
2. Senate Ex. Docs., 40th Cong., 1st sess., No. 13, pp. 57–60, 87–88, 111–14.
3. For analyses of the concentration policy, see Loring B. Priest, *Uncle Sam's Stepchildren: The Reformation of United States Indian Policy, 1865–1887* (New Brunswick, N.J., 1942), chap. 1; and Henry E. Fritz, *The Movement for Indian Assimilation, 1860–1890* (Philadelphia, 1963), chap. 3.
4. SW, *Annual Report* (1866), p. 20. Senate Ex. Docs., 40th Cong., 1st sess., No. 13, pp. 17–18. House Ex. Docs., 39th Cong., 2d sess., No. 71, pp. 12–13.
5. The Senate apparently withheld confirmation of Bogy as part of the conflict building between Congress and President Johnson. Secretary Browning regarded it as a calamity. He urged Henry H. Sibley of Minnesota as Bogy's successor but had to defer to the President's insistence on Taylor, whom he viewed as unqualified. "I now have a Methodist preacher at the

head of the Bureau," he wrote. "I will do the best I can with him." *The Diary of Orville Hickman Browning*, 2, 136 (March 12, 1867), 141 (April 1).

6. Sanborn, May 18, 1867, and Buford, June 6, Senate Ex. Docs., 40th Cong., 1st sess., No. 13, pp. 57–60, 111–14.

7. In a lengthy policy analysis, July 1, 1867, replying to General Buford's letter of June 6, SW, *Annual Report* (1867), p. 67.

8. Senate Ex. Docs., 40th Cong., 1st sess., No. 13, pp. 1–6.

9. 15 Stat. 17–18 (July 20, 1867). For the debates on S. 136, see *Cong. Globe*, 40th Cong., 1st sess., pp. 655 (July 15, 1867), 667–73 (July 16), 678–90 (July 17), 702–15 (July 18), 753–57 (July 20).

10. From Fort McPherson, July 17, Senate Ex. Docs., 40th Cong., 1st sess., No. 13, p. 121.

11. Harney had been brought out of retirement to help negotiate the Little Arkansas treaties of 1865 and now was again tapped for a peace mission. The Sioux had three names for Harney that summarize his prewar reputation as an Indian-fighter: "The Butcher," "The Hornet," and "The Big Chief Who Swears." Utley, *Frontiersmen in Blue*, p. 119.

12. For excellent character sketches of the commissioners see *Army and Navy Journal*, 5 (Dec. 7, 1867), 251.

13. *Omaha Weekly Herald*, Aug. 22, 1867, quoted in Olson, *Red Cloud and the Sioux Problem*, p. 63 n.

14. The peace commission report, Jan. 7, 1868, is in House Ex. Docs., 40th Cong., 2d sess., No. 97, and is also printed in CIA, *Annual Report* (1868), pp. 26–50. For a detailed account of the commission's activities, see Douglas C. Jones, *The Treaty of Medicine Lodge: The Story of the Great Treaty Council as Told by Eyewitnesses* (Norman, Okla., 1966). Sherman was brought to Washington as a move in President Johnson's battle with Congressional Radicals over Reconstruction policy. The War Department had become a battleground of the conflict, and Johnson, unable to win Grant to his cause, hoped to make Sherman Secretary of War. Sherman declined to take sides or in any way compromise his relations with Grant. Athearn, p. 183. Rachel Sherman Thorndike, ed., *The Sherman Letters: Correspondence between General and Senator Sherman from 1837 to 1891* (New York, 1894), pp. 296–300.

15. In addition to sources cited in n. 14, see Berthrong, *The Southern Cheyennes*, pp. 289–300; Mooney, *Calendar History of the Kiowa*, pp. 183–86; Nye, *Plains Indian Raiders*, pp. 105–12; and Hyde, *Life of George Bent*, pp. 281–85.

16. The treaties are in Kappler, *Indian Affairs: Laws and Treaties*, 2, 977–89. These treaties were signed by a more representative group of chiefs than most. Among the Kiowas were Satank, Satanta, Kicking Bird, Woman's Heart, and Stumbling Bear. Comanches included Ten Bears, Tosawi (Silver Brooch), Horse's Back, and Iron Mountain. Important Cheyennes included Bull Bear, Black Kettle, Spotted Elk, Gray Beard, and Tall Bull. Little Raven and Storm were among the Arapahoes.

17. The full text of Grant's order is in Olson, pp. 71–72.

18. *Ibid.*, pp. 62, 70–72. Athearn, p. 198. SW, *Annual Report* (1867), pp. 58–59, 65–66; (1868), pp. 3, 23.

19. The text is in Kappler, 2, 998–1007. The unceded territory was defined as "north of the North Platte River and east of the summits of the Big Horn Mountains." The eastern boundary, of course, coincided with the western boundary of the reservation, but no northern limits were set.

20. For the activities at Fort Laramie, see Olson, pp. 71–78. For DeSmet's activities, see Stanley Vestal, *Sitting Bull, Champion of the Sioux* (2d ed., Norman, Okla., 1957), chap. 15. There is confusion in the records over whether Man-Afraid-of-His-Horse signed on May 25 or later, when Red Cloud finally signed. See Olson, p. 75 n., 79 n.

21. Olson, pp. 75–82. SW, *Annual Report* (1868), pp. 22–23, 30–31. For a first-hand account of the withdrawal from the Bozeman Trail forts, see Mattes, *Indians, Infants, and Infantry*, pp. 163–71.
22. CIA, *Annual Report* (1868), pp. 52–62.
23. 15 Stat. 222 (July 27, 1868). For the debates see *Cong. Globe*, 40th Cong., 2d sess., pp. 2614–21, 2637–43, 2682–86, 2707–12 (May 27–30, 1868), 4271–75, 4303–6 (July 21, 1868). Rep. Benjamin Butler of Massachusetts, chairman of the House Appropriations Committee, led the opposition to turning the funds over to the Indian Bureau and, as senior House manager on the conference committee, substituted the provision for its expenditure by Sherman. See debates above cited and Athearn, pp. 209–10. The United States Indian Commission of New York, a citizens' pressure group boasting a galaxy of big-name philanthropists, took credit for originating the formula and inducing Butler to promote it. CIA, *Annual Report* (1869), pp. 70, 95–96. Mardock, *The Reformers and the American Indian*, pp. 34–35.
24. SW, *Annual Report* (1868), pp. 8–9.
25. House Misc. Docs., 41st Cong., 2d sess., No. 139, pp. 1–8. Senate Ex. Docs., 40th Cong., 3d sess., No. 13, pp. 2–9, 16–17, 30. CIA, *Annual Report* (1868), pp. 64–66. Berthrong, pp. 299–305.
26. Senate Ex. Docs., 40th Cong., 3d sess., No. 13, pp. 18–20. SW, *Annual Report* (1868), pp. 10–16. Berthrong, pp. 305–6. Leckie, *Military Conquest of the Southern Plains*, pp. 71–72. Nye, pp. 119–20. P. H. Sheridan, *Record of Engagements with Hostile Indians within the Military Division of the Missouri from 1868 to 1882* (Washington, D.C., 1882), pp. 7–8, in Joseph P. Peters, comp., *Indian Battles and Skirmishes on the American Frontier, 1790–1898* (New York, 1966).
27. The resolutions are in CIA, *Annual Report* (1868), pp. 271–72. See also Athearn, pp. 226–28.
28. SW, *Annual Report* (1868), p. 1.

☆ TEN ☆

Operations on the Southern Plains, 1868-69

GENERAL HANCOCK WAS NOT THE ONLY OFFICER whose actions in 1867 embarrassed the Johnson Administration. Harshly applying the new Reconstruction Laws in Louisiana, the commanding general of the Fifth Military District had gratified Congressional Radicals, but infuriated President Johnson. In August 1867 orders originated with the President for the two generals to exchange commands.[1]

Maj. Gen. Philip Henry Sheridan lacked the gentlemanly polish of Hancock. A short, stout Irishman with piercing eyes and black mustache, thirty-six and a bachelor, he combined pugnacity in official intercourse with reserve in all but intimate social intercourse. In the latter he could be witty and fun-loving. An English nobleman found him "a delightful man, with the one peculiarity of using the most astounding swear words quite calmly and dispassionately in ordinary conversation."[2] Scarcely less revered by his troops than Sherman, "Little Phil" was a brilliant combat leader, attentive to the wants of his men and in a fight always in the front. He gloried in a Civil War record that left him excelled in popular affection only by Grant and Sherman. Alert, observant, and energetic, he owed his repeated battlefield triumphs, thought a West Point classmate, to audacity coupled with "a perfect indifference as to how many of his men were killed if he only carried his point."[3] He identified the objective and went for it by the most direct means and without much respect for the conventions of "civilized" warfare. With Sherman, he subscribed to the doc-

William Tecumseh Sherman headed the army from 1869 to 1883. A public posture of heroic proportions and a powerful personality overcame the limitations on the commanding general's authority and gave him an influence that made the army distinctively "Sherman's Own" even after his term of office. (National Archives)

Lt. Gen. Philip H. Sheridan commanded the Division of the Missouri from headquarters in Chicago from 1869 to 1883, then succeeded Sherman as commanding general of the army. A tough-minded realist with emphatic opinions and elastic ethics, he administered the vast Great Plains region during the final years of warfare with the buffalo-hunting tribes. He is shown here with some of his favorite officers at Topeka, Kansas, in 1872. *Seated left to right:* Lt. Col. George Armstrong Custer, Seventh Cavalry; Sheridan; Maj. Nelson B. Sweitzer, Second Cavalry; Lt. Col. James W. Forsyth, aide-de-camp. *Standing left to right:* Lt. Col. George A. Forsyth, military secretary; Maj. Morris J. Asch, surgeon; Lt. Col. Michael V. Sheridan, aide-de-camp and brother of General Sheridan. (National Park Service, Custer Battlefield National Monument)

While the cavalry sought out the enemy, the "web-feet" of the infantry had to content themselves with such unglamorous tasks as guarding supply bases and escorting wagon trains, as depicted here by Frederic Remington. (Denver Public Library Western Collection)

Frederic Remington's
The Trooper

Prussian influence replaced French in dress uniforms adopted in 1871. On the left, H. Charles McBarron represents a signal sergeant, cavalry officer, and enlisted troopers of one of the black regiments. (Department of the Army) Below, in undress and fatigue uniforms, the kepi headgear still reflected the French model. This is a company of the Third Infantry at Fort Meade, South Dakota, in 1890. (Library of Congress) On the opposite page, campaign attire remained serviceable and highly individual, as Frederic Remington suggests in these two drawings from *Century Magazine*.

On the plains, where Indians rarely attacked a military installation, the typical fort was not the log stockade usually depicted in motion pictures. It consisted instead of barracks, officers' quarters, and utility buildings grouped around a parade ground. Above is Fort Custer, Montana, and left is Fort Davis, Texas, both shown in the middle 1880s. (National Archives and National Park Service)

Leaders of the Kiowa war faction, Satanta (above), Satank (top right), and Big Tree (bottom right) were arrested at Fort Sill in 1871 after a dramatic confrontation with General Sherman. Satank was shot down while trying to escape, but Satanta and Big Tree served time in the Texas penitentiary. Released, they resumed old habits and, after the Red River War of 1874–75, were again sent to prison. All three were photographed at Fort Sill in 1870 by William S. Soule. (Smithsonian Institution, Bureau of American Ethnology)

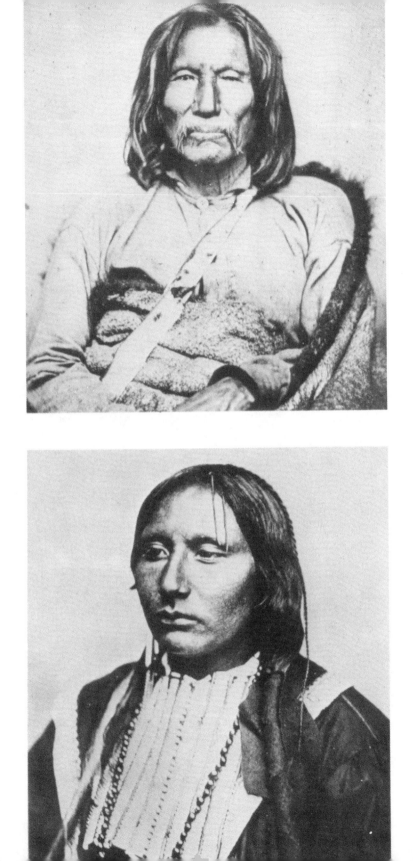

Capt. William J. Fetterman discovered that eighty men could not, as he had boasted, ride through the entire Sioux nation. Montana artist Charles M. Russell depicts the annihilation of Fetterman's command near Fort Phil Kearny on December 21, 1866. (Whitney Gallery of Western Art, Cody, Wyoming)

Group of Oglala Sioux warriors at Pine Ridge Agency, 1892. (Smithsonian Institution)

Typical village of the Plains tribes. This is Sitting Bull's camp on the Missouri River near Fort Yates, Dakota, about 1883. (Denver Public Library Western Collection)

From "Captain Jack's Stronghold" in the heart of northern California's rugged lava beds, a handful of Indians held off a besieging army in the Modoc War of 1872–73. Here pickets watch for enemy movements. (National Archives)

Edward R. S. Canby. His assassination during a peace conference with Modocs in 1873 made him the only regular general killed by Indians in U.S. history. (Library of Congress)

In these scenes Frederic Remington portrayed closing episodes of the Nez Percé flight from Idaho across Montana to within fifty miles of sanctuary in Canada. *Fighting Over the Captured Herd* (above) represents one phase of the Battle of Bear Paw Mountain, September 30, 1877. *The Surrender of Chief Joseph* (below) depicts the dramatic moment when, facing Colonel Miles, the Nez Percé leader uttered the memorable words, "From where the sun now stands, I will fight no more, forever." (National Archives)

With unostentatious but superior competence, Brig. Gen. Christopher C. Augur commanded the Department of the Platte (1867–71), Department of Texas (1872–75), and Department of the Missouri (1881–83). (National Archives)

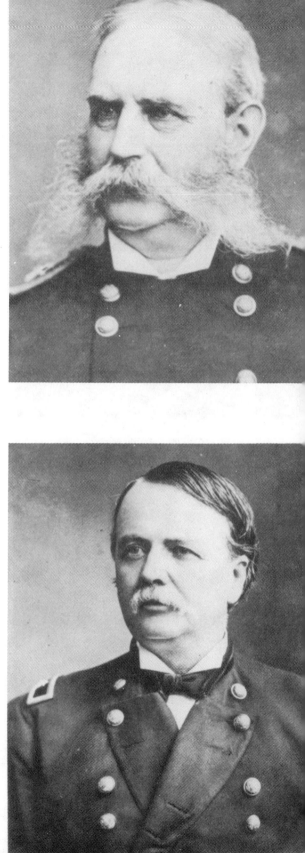

John Pope was a controversialist and never used one word where ten would do, but he proved to be a capable administrator as commander of the Department of the Missouri from 1870 to 1883. (National Archives)

Alfred H. Terry. Long-time commander of the Department of Dakota, Terry is best remembered as Custer's superior in the Little Bighorn campaign of 1876. He spoke several languages, appreciated art and literature, studied for the law but did so well as a volunteer general that he earned a star in the postwar Regular Army. Wealthy, a bachelor, he enjoyed wide respect and affection in the Army. (National Park Service, Custer Battlefield National Monument)

Oliver Otis Howard. The one-armed "praying general" inflicted sermons and hymns on garrisons he inspected, but the Indian's religion eluded his comprehension. He made peace with Cochise in 1872 and pursued Chief Joseph across Idaho and Montana in 1877. (Oregon Historical Society) trine of total war—of subjecting a whole enemy population to the horrors of war and thereby undermining the will to resist.[4]

Sheridan and his military colleagues viewed the Cheyenne raids of August 1868 as the basest kind of perfidy.[5] Top officials of the Indian Bureau, usually quick to explain an outbreak in terms of military provocation, conceded that the government had met its commitments under the Medicine Lodge treaties and had given no just cause for offense.[6] Only Agent Wynkoop excused the Cheyennes, stoutly maintaining that the war found its origins in the failure of Congress to appropriate funds for liberal food issues and in the decision to withhold arms and ammunition.[7]

The truth is that, despite the sincere professions of peace chiefs such as Black Kettle, most Cheyennes were not ready to abide by the white man's rules. They had only the dimmest understanding of the contents of the Medicine Lodge treaties—in fact were concerned with treaties and treaty councils mainly as a means of getting presents, especially arms and ammunition. Although not averse to receiving annuity issues on the reservation, or even to living there during the hard winter months, few were prepared to settle permanently within arbitrary lines marked out by the white man.[8] Also, they were no less reconciled in 1868 than in 1867 to yielding the buffalo ranges of western Kansas. Further aggravating this resentment, the railroad now approached the Colorado boundary, drawing fingers of settlement up the Smoky Hill, Solomon, Saline, and Republican valleys into the heart of the buffalo country.[9] And finally, the innate raiding impulse of the Plains warrior had yet to be checked either by events or by the influence of the peace chiefs.

Thus, while the peace elements of the Cheyennes and Arapahoes crossed the Arkansas and headed south to escape the predictable military reaction to the August raids, many of their young men joined the war factions in the haunts of the perennially hostile Dog Soldiers to the north and west. In this country, too, roamed large numbers of Southern Brulés and Oglalas and Northern Cheyennes and Arapahoes, many from as far distant as the Powder River country. Perhaps numbering a thousand lodges, they drew supplies at Fort Laramie and at the Upper Platte Agency at North Platte, Nebraska.[10] Besides helping their brethren fight the whites, they fueled the aggressive propensities of the southerners by pointing out that the whites might be made to give up the Smoky Hill by the same means that had brought them to abandon the Bozeman Trail.[11] From August through October, raiders from these bands struck repeatedly at farms, ranches, way stations, and travelers in a broad swath extending from the Saline and Solomon settlements almost to Denver and Fort Lyon. Besides stealing countless heads of stock and other plunder, they killed seventy-nine settlers and wounded nine more.[12]

The intentions of the Kiowas and Comanches remained unclear. In February 1868 Agent Leavenworth had gone to the new Kiowa-Comanche Reservation in Indian Territory and established his agency in Eureka Valley, near old Fort Cobb. Several thousand of his charges drifted in seeking food. None had been promised in the Medicine Lodge treaties, and he had none to give. Between raids into Texas, therefore, they terrorized the agent and the peaceful Wichitas whose agency stood nearby. When they burned the Wichita agency in May, Leavenworth took fright and headed east, soon afterward submitting his resignation. Most of the Kiowas and the Yamparika Comanches, about 2,000 in number, then went north to the Arkansas. The balance of the Comanches who had been at Eureka Valley—mainly Nakoni, Penateka, and Kotsoteka—camped on the Canadian River to the north and west.[13] Although all continued to raid in Texas, this had never counted against them in Kansas, and how to handle them in the war against the Cheyennes and Arapahoes was one of the many vexing questions that troubled General Sheridan as the summer of 1868 drew to a close.

Sherman and Sheridan were of a single mind on strategy. Atlanta and the Shenandoah Valley furnished the precedents. Like Georgians and Virginians four years earlier, the Cheyennes and Arapahoes would suffer total war. "These Indians require to be soundly whipped," said Sherman on September 26, "and the ringleaders in the present trouble hung, their ponies killed, and such destruction of their property as will make them very poor."[14] With the reservations now clearly defined, for the first time there seemed some hope of separating the innocent from the guilty. General Hazen, charged by Sherman with military responsibility for the southern reservations, would go to abandoned Fort Cobb, on the new Kiowa-Comanche Reservation, and provide food and protection for the innocent. Sheridan would war relentlessly against the guilty. With this approach, thought Sherman, the government could "hold out the olive branch with one hand and the sword in the other." But Cobb was not to be a refuge for the guilty, and if they sought safety there Sheridan was to follow and mete out "just punishment."[15]

Nor was total war to be the only innovative feature of the strategy. Past experience showed that little success could be gained while the season favored Indian movements. During September and October, Sheridan would field as many columns as possible in Kansas. But this would be only a holding operation, aimed at diverting the hostiles from raids on the settlements and nudging them south of the Arkansas. The real offensive would begin when the snow fell. Winter inhibited the Indian's mobility by weakening his ponies and diminishing his food supply. It dampened his war ardor, dulled his watchfulness, and accordingly made him more vulnerable to surprise attack. Pessimists warned Sheridan that the blizzards and subzero temperatures of a plains winter held perils for an offensive column, too. Actually, Kit Carson had shown in the Navajo campaign of 1863–64 that winter operations were possible and could bring impressive results. Sheridan seems not to have known of this precedent. He regarded his projected undertaking as an experiment to test whether troops could endure and the supply services support a winter campaign. If he succeeded, the enemy at best would be struck a destructive blow and driven to the new reservations; at worst shown that no longer did winter afford respite and security. As early as mid-September Sherman and Sheridan had agreed on a winter offensive, but not until October 9, following Sherman's victory over Taylor and Tappan at the Chicago meeting of the peace commission (see pp. 138–39), did he authorize Sheridan to proceed.[16]

Go ahead in your own way [Sherman instructed his subordinate] and I will back you with my whole authority. If it results in the utter annihilation of these Indians, it is but the result of what they have been warned again and again. . . . I will say nothing and do nothing to restrain our troops from doing what they deem proper on the spot, and will allow no mere vague general charges of cruelty and inhumanity to tie their hands, but will use all the powers confided to me to the end that these Indians, the enemies of our race and of our civilization, shall not again be able to begin and carry out their barbarous warfare on any kind of pretext they may choose to allege. I believe that this

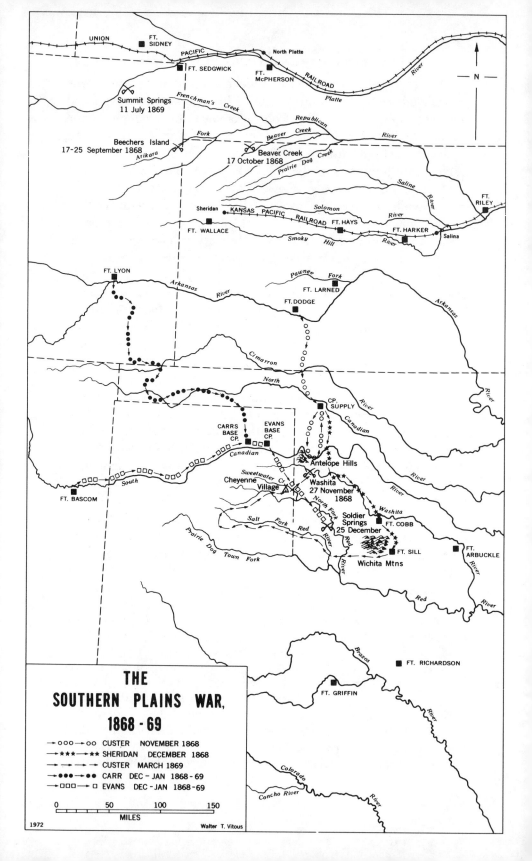

UNION
FT.
SIDNEY
PACIFIC
North Platte
FT. SEDGWICK
FT.
McPHERSON
RAILROAD
River
Summit Springs
11 July 1869
Frenchman's
Creek
Platte
— N —

Republican
Beaver   Creek
Beechers Island
17-25 September 1868
Fork
Arikara
Beaver Creek
17 October 1868
River
Prairie Dog   Creek
Saline
River
FT.
RILEY

Sheridan   KANSAS   PACIFIC   RAILROAD
FT. HAYS
Solomon
River
FT. WALLACE
Smoky   Hill   River
FT. HARKER
Salina

FT. LYON
Arkansas   River
Pawnee   Fork
FT. LARNED
Arkansas
FT. DODGE
River

Cimarron
North
River
CP.
SUPPLY
Canadian
CARRS
BASE
CP.
EVANS
BASE
CP.
Canadian
Antelope Hills
River
FT. BASCOM
South
Sweetwater   Cr.
Cheyenne
Village
Washita
27 November
1868
Washita
Soldier
Springs
25 December
FT. COBB
FT.
ARBUCKLE
Prairie   Dog
Town   Fork
Salt   Fork
Red
North Fork
Red   River
FT. SILL
Wichita Mtns
Red   River
Red   River

FT. RICHARDSON
Brazos
FT. GRIFFIN
River

THE
SOUTHERN PLAINS WAR,
1868-69

→∘∘∘→∘∘ CUSTER   NOVEMBER 1868
→★★★→★★ SHERIDAN DECEMBER 1868
→ - →- → CUSTER   MARCH 1869
→●●●→●● CARR   DEC - JAN 1868-69
→□□□→□ EVANS   DEC - JAN 1868-69

0   50   100   150
MILES
1972   Walter T. Vitous

Colorado
River
Concho River

winter will afford us the opportunity, and that before the snow falls, these Indians will seek some sort of peace, to be broken next year at their option; but we will not accept their peace, or cease our efforts till all the past acts are both punished and avenged.[17]

While the generals formulated their plans for a winter campaign, Sheridan's troops had not been idle. In late August he concentrated the Seventh Cavalry on the Arkansas and dispatched the Tenth Cavalry to the Republican and Smoky Hill. He commissioned his aide, Maj. George A. Forsyth, to enlist a company of fifty frontiersmen and cover the railroad toward Fort Wallace. Appeals for more cavalry won a prompt response. Early in September a seven-troop squadron of the Fifth Cavalry, assembled from Reconstruction stations in the South, reached Kansas and went to the Republican to support the Tenth. Early in October Sherman bowed to Sheridan's request and secured authority to call out a regiment of Volunteers. Governor Crawford promptly donned a colonel's uniform and readied the Nineteenth Kansas Cavalry to participate in the winter offensive.[18]

Also late in August, Sheridan turned his attention to the Cheyennes and Arapahoes already south of the Arkansas. Agent Wynkoop protested their peaceable disposition, but Sheridan believed that the scattering of depredations on the Arkansas and along the Cimarron Cutoff of the Santa Fe Trail could be laid squarely on these innocents. He assembled some five to six hundred men in eight troops of the Seventh Cavalry and one company of the Third Infantry and sent them south under Bvt. Brig. Gen. Alfred Sully, lieutenant colonel of the Third Infantry and commander of the District of the Upper Arkansas. Sully enjoyed a bright and well-merited reputation as an Indian-fighter, the result of aggressive campaigns against the Sioux in 1863–65. Now, unaccountably, he turned into a cautious, slow-moving general who set the pace in an ambulance rather than on horseback. The column left Fort Dodge on September 7, skirmished halfheartedly with Cheyennes on the Cimarron and the North and South Canadian, and on September 14 turned back to Fort Dodge. Asked why by a lieutenant, Sully replied, "Oh, these sand hills are interminable."[19]

Meanwhile, at Fort Hays, Major Forsyth recruited and organized his fifty "first class hardy frontiersmen," signing them up as quartermaster employees in the absence of other authorization. Many were veterans of the Union or Confederate army, seasoned plainsmen, and average to excellent marksmen. Lightly equipped for rapid movement, by mid-September the company found itself on a warm trail leading up the Arikara fork of the Republican River north of Fort Wallace.

At dawn on September 17 Indians jumped the scouts' camp. Forsyth hastily disposed his men in a perimeter on a small brushy island in the middle of the dry stream bed. Soon he was surrounded by six to seven hundred warriors—Pawnee Killer's Oglalas and Cheyenne Dog Soldiers of Bull Bear, Tall Bull, and White Horse. The scouts alternately dug rifle pits and fired at circling Indians. Three times during the day masses of horsemen bore down on the island in frontal charges—a rarity in Indian warfare—only to split at the last moment under the impact of disciplined volley fire from Spencer repeating carbines. But the defenders suffered severely—almost half their number killed or wounded and most of their horses slain. Lt. Frederick Beecher was dead, Surgeon John H. Mooers fatally wounded, and Forsyth himself immobilized with bullets in his leg and thigh. For the next seven days the Indians held the company under close siege. Two pairs of scouts succeeded in slipping through to Fort Wallace, 85 miles away, and on September 25 a column of Tenth Cavalry "Buffalo Soldiers" under Capt. Louis H. Carpenter finally lifted the siege.

In the Battle of Beecher's Island Forsyth had lost six killed and fifteen wounded. He reported Indian casualties of thirty-five killed and a hundred wounded; Indian sources later conceded but six dead. It had been an action of little consequence, but one that would be long remembered and glorified in the annals of the Indian-fighting army.[20]

Hoping to relieve the pressure on the settlements until winter, Sheridan kept columns in the field throughout October. South of the Arkansas the Seventh Cavalry scouted Medicine Lodge Creek and the Big Bend of the Arkansas. (Once more the Seventh followed the energetic Custer, happily freed, by petition of Sully, Sheridan, and Sherman, from the idleness enforced by court-martial in 1867.) But the most actively hostile Indians were still north of the railroad. A column from General Augur's department under Lt. Col. Luther P. Bradley swept up the Republican. The newly arrived squadron of the Fifth Cavalry scouted the same area and exchanged fire with Tall Bull's Dog Soldiers on October

14 and 25–26. The most severe encounter of the month occurred on Beaver Creek on the seventeenth, when several hundred Cheyennes fell on a squadron of the Tenth Cavalry escorting Maj. Eugene A. Carr in search of his Fifth Cavalry command. Capt. Louis H. Carpenter kept his black troopers well in hand and held off the attackers for eight hours.[21]

While his troops fought the Cheyennes, Arapahoes, and Sioux, Sheridan had sought to keep the Kiowas and Comanches neutral. On September 20 he and General Hazen met with tribal leaders at Fort Larned and made arrangements to escort their people to Fort Cobb. Sheridan would provide rations en route. To give him time to haul in the necessary food, the Kiowas and Comanches went on a buffalo hunt, promising to return in ten days. During this time the hostilities with the Cheyennes and Arapahoes intensified. The Kiowas and Comanches grew suspicious of the army's intentions and decided to continue to Fort Cobb without benefit of military companionship. When they failed to keep their rendezvous with Hazen at Fort Larned, Sheridan concluded that they had joined the hostiles, and this belief prompted his request for authority to muster the Nineteenth Kansas. While Sheridan made final arrangements to thrust south with the sword, Hazen repaired to Fort Cobb to hold forth the olive branch.[22]

Actually, Sheridan planned to swing with *three* swords at the winter camps of the Indians, known to be in the Canadian and Washita valleys. From the District of New Mexico, Bvt. Maj. Gen. George W. Getty was to launch a column eastward down the South Canadian. Composed of six troops of the Third Cavalry, two companies of the Thirty-seventh Infantry, and four mountain howitzers, it numbered 563 men. Maj. Andrew W. "Beans" Evans (whom one observer swore had "registered a vow never to smile") led it out of Fort Bascom, New Mexico, on November 18. Major Carr (a brevet major general) was to command a second column —his own seven troops of the Fifth Cavalry and another force of four troops of the Tenth Cavalry and one of the Seventh already out under Capt. William H. Penrose of the Third Infantry (a brigadier general by brevet). This represented a combined force of about 650. Carr's command, which was to operate southward toward Antelope Hills and the head of Red River, left Fort Lyon, Colorado, on December 2 guided by a daredevil young plainsman who had captured Sheridan's fancy and one day would capture the world's fancy—"Buffalo Bill" Cody. Not much was expected of Evans and Carr. They were to act as "beaters in" for the third and strongest column. Commanded by Sully and accompanied by Sheridan himself, this force was to consist of eleven troops of Custer's Seventh Cavalry, five infantry companies, and Colonel Crawford's Nineteenth Kansas Volunteer Cavalry. Sully and Custer established a supply depot, Camp Supply, on the North Canadian a hundred miles south of Fort Dodge and were anxiously awaiting the arrival of Crawford's Kansas when Sheridan appeared on November 21 in the midst of a snow storm.[23]

On the way in he had crossed a fresh trail, undoubtedly made by a war party heading north toward the Kansas settlements. Although anxious to take advantage of the discovery, first he had to mediate a dispute over rank. Fearful lest Colonel Crawford claim seniority, Lieutenant Colonel Sully had issued an order assuming command in his brevet grade of brigadier general. Lieutenant Colonel Custer had promptly countered with an order assuming command in his brevet grade of major general. Sheridan confirmed Custer and ordered Sully back to his district headquarters. Then, to compound the irony, Sheridan announced that he had decided not to wait any longer for Crawford's Kansans. Custer would take the trail at once with the Seventh Cavalry.[24]

More than 800 strong and leading a long string of supply wagons, the regiment marched from Camp Supply early on November 23. Twelve inches of wet snow covered the ground, and a heavy fall piled up more throughout the day. It hid the trail Custer was to follow, but after four cheerless, comfortless days he found the quarry anyway, nestled in their teepees in the Washita River Valley. At dawn on November 27, with no knowledge of enemy strength, he hastened to the attack. Buglers sounded the charge, the band blared "Garryowen"—or as much of it as the musicians could master before their instruments froze—and in four attack groups the cavalry swept into the valley from as many directions.[25]

The objective turned out to be fifty-one Cheyenne lodges belonging to Black Kettle, champion of peace and hapless victim of a similar dawn attack four years earlier at Sand Creek. Only a week earlier Black Kettle and Little Robe had ridden down to Fort Cobb to grasp General Hazen's olive branch. But Hazen could not very well make peace with people against whom Sheridan had declared war, and he turned them away with advice to deal with the "big war chief," Sheridan. In the course of this interview Black Kettle confessed himself powerless to keep his young men from raiding in Kansas. Many of his followers rejoiced at Hazen's rebuff.[26] In fact, it was the trail of a returning war party of one hundred, made after the snow storm, that led Custer to the peace chief's village, which was found to contain four white captives (two of whom were killed by the Indians at the first attack) and abundant evidence of the romps of his young warriors through the Kansas settlements.

Flushed from their lodges by the dawn attack, Black Kettle's startled people scattered in a frantic search for cover. The warriors, posting themselves behind trees, fallen logs, and the stream bank, fought desperately to shield the flight of their families. Black Kettle and his wife, mounted on a single pony, were cut down early in the fight. So was Chief Little Rock. Within ten minutes the troops had possession of the village, but throughout the morning, fighting on foot, they labored to wipe out pockets of resistance. Some of the Cheyennes succeeded in escaping down the valley. One such group brought Maj. Joel H. Elliott and about fifteen men in pursuit. A warrior force converged to the rescue, cut off Elliott, and wiped out the detachment to a man. No one knew where Elliott had gone or what had happened to him.

Custer had achieved his triumph by finding the enemy and striking at once, without losing any time in reconnaissance. Now came the penalty. In the middle of the morning fresh warriors, well armed and painted for battle, began to appear on the hillsides. Questioning captive women, Custer learned that the valley for ten miles downstream harbored the winter camps of other Cheyenne bands, as well as Arapaho, Kiowa, and Comanche. By noon hundreds of horsemen from these camps ringed Black Kettle's village. Custer established a perimeter defense and met the sorties of warrior groups against his lines with limited counterattacks. At the same time, he destroyed the tepees and all their contents of food, robes, weapons, and utensils, and also—a grievous blow to the Cheyennes—slaughtered most of the 875 ponies captured in the first assault.

The reinforcements from down river probably did not badly outnumber the cavalry and therefore did not raise the deadly peril later dramatized by Custer and Sheridan.[27] But they did promise

to make the victory considerably more costly to the victors. Custer
was encumbered by his wounded and by fifty-three captive women
and children. His supply train was back on the trail and exposed
to enemy attack. His overcoats and haversacks had been left at the
previous night's camp site. He was ignorant of Elliott's whereabouts and was prevented by the fighting from conducting a serious search. Hoping to extricate himself without further loss, as
dusk gathered Custer mounted the regiment and, with colors flying and band playing, advanced boldly down river as if to attack
the other villages. The Indians quickly drew off to defend their
homes. As night fell, he suddenly turned and slipped out of the
valley. To Sheridan's acclaim, he proudly led the regiment into
Camp Supply on December 2.

The Battle of the Washita was a ringing affirmation of Sheridan's strategy. Custer had lost Major Elliott, Capt. Louis M.
Hamilton, and nineteen men killed, and three officers and eleven
soldiers wounded. But he had dealt the Cheyennes a devastating
blow. He reported 103 warriors slain. Even if exaggerated, as
claimed by Indian sources,[28] the real impact on the Indians lay in
the destruction of their food, shelter, transportation, and other
possessions and in the demonstration that troops could seek them
out in winter. The triumph was not without its tinge of sour-
ness, however. Humanitarians castigated Custer for slaughtering
women and children. In a widely published letter full of tributes
to Black Kettle and denunciations of the army, Agent Wynkoop
resigned his post.[29] Even though it could be shown that Black
Kettle's people were not as pacific as he himself, and that most
of the slain noncombatants had been honestly mistaken for warriors, or indeed were themselves fighting as warriors, Custer found
himself compared with Chivington and the Washita with Sand
Creek. Moreover, his decision to abandon the battlefield without
searching for Elliott and his men, of honestly debatable military
necessity, clouded his reputation in army circles and opened a
wound in the Seventh Cavalry that would not heal as long as he
commanded it.

Sheridan regarded the Battle of the Washita only as the opening gun. He intended to march to the Washita, pick up the Indian
trail, and try for another fight. He lost a few days refitting the
Kansas troops, who had finally been found struggling blindly in
the snow-choked gorges of the Cimarron. The ordeal had ruined

their horses and converted them for the most part into infantry. On December 7, fifteen hundred strong, the column took up the march in subzero temperatures, followed two days later by another blizzard sweeping down from the north. On the Washita a detachment examined Custer's battleground and found and buried the butchered corpses of Major Elliott and his party. On the twelfth the command resumed the march, following an Indian trail that led down the Washita toward Fort Cobb.[30]

Five days and seventy-six miles later the pursuit reached its objective. But here the Sherman-Sheridan strategy of sword and olive branch, so appealingly simple and sensible in prospect, fouled on the old dilemma of how to distinguish a friendly Indian from a hostile. The Indians were Kiowas led by Lone Wolf and Satanta, and they presented Sheridan with a document signed by General Hazen attesting to their peaceful character. Sheridan thought this "a pretty good joke." He had just followed their trail from the Washita battlefield and was certain that, after the battle of November 27, they had rushed into Fort Cobb and duped Hazen into certifying their good conduct.

Actually, Hazen was substantially right. Since his arrival at Fort Cobb on November 8, some 6,000 Comanches, Kiowas, and Kiowa-Apaches had assembled in the Washita and Canadian Valleys within 20 to 100 miles of the fort and had begun to draw rations. That the blandishments of the Cheyennes failed to induce them to join in the war is amply revealed by evidence gathered by Hazen's efficient intelligence network. After the Washita fight, in which some of them unquestionably had participated, the Comanches and about half the Kiowas fled with the Cheyennes and Arapahoes southward to the North Fork of Red River, just west of the Wichita Mountains. Here, in a grand council early in December, the Cheyenne persuasions were rejected in favor of rations at Fort Cobb. By December 10 the runaway Kiowa and Comanche bands had begun to return hesitantly to the Washita Valley. Hazen gave them his protection.[31]

Sheridan's appearance on December 17 badly frightened the Kiowas, and they prepared for instant flight should the soldier chief disregard Hazen's testament to their character. Although convinced that the Kiowas richly deserved punishment, Sheridan had to be content with ordering Lone Wolf and Satanta to move their village at once to Fort Cobb. When they gave evidence of duplicity in responding to the order, Sheridan had them seized as hostages. Still, even after the column reached Cobb the next day, the village failed to appear. He then "put on the screws." The chiefs would be hanged if the village had not surrendered within forty-eight hours. The threat produced enough of a compliance to allow Sheridan to lift the ultimatum, although by no means all the Kiowas came in.[32]

Nor did all the Kiowas and Comanches who had been on the Washita at the time of the Custer battle return after the Red River convocation. Horse Back's Nakoni Comanches and Woman's Heart's Kiowas stayed on the North Fork of Red River, the Comanche village of sixty lodges at Soldier Spring and the Kiowa village a short distance downstream. Carr and Evans had been wandering around the wintry plains to the north and west for several weeks performing their assigned mission as "beaters in" for Custer. On Christmas Day Evans discovered the Comanches, cleared out their village with howitzer fire, and quickly seized it. He had about 300 Third Cavalrymen; the rest guarded the supply train and the base camp he had planted back on the Canadian. The Comanches, reinforced by the Kiowas, brought some 200 warriors to the counterattack. All day the two sides skirmished while the troops burned the village and its stores, including several tons of dried buffalo meat. Finally the Indians drew off, and Evans, hampered by broken-down horses, declined to pursue. He had but one casualty and estimated that the enemy had lost twenty-five to thirty. Like the Washita battle, however, the chief significance of the Battle of Soldier Spring lay in the destruction of the camp and the further notice to the Indians that winter no longer was a time of security. Part of these bands went to Fort Cobb. The rest sought succor with the Kwahadi Comanches on the Staked Plains and almost at once surrendered at Fort Bascom.[33]

Except for the perennially isolationist Kwahadis, most of the Kiowas and Comanches had come in by the end of December. With thousands of Indians and soldiers camped around Fort Cobb, the sparse winter grass all but vanished. Rain fell constantly and turned the ground to deep mud. Early in January Sheridan moved troops, Indians, and agency thirty miles to the south and established them on a pleasant grassy site at the eastern base of the Wichita Mountains, selected earlier by Bvt. Maj. Gen. Benjamin H. Grierson, colonel of the Tenth Cavalry and commander of the district. Grierson's black troopers began erecting substantial stone buildings for a post that Sheridan soon named Fort Sill, in honor of a West Point classmate slain in the Civil War.[34]

The Cheyennes and Arapahoes remained west of the Wichita Mountains. Using Black Kettle's captive sister as an emissary, Custer coaxed some of the chiefs in for a parley and learned that the fugitives were hungry, destitute, and in large part favorable to surrendering. Late in January Custer and fifty-seven cavalrymen circled the Wichita Mountains and started Little Raven's Arapahoes, sixty-five lodges, toward Fort Sill. The Cheyennes, however, had withdrawn farther west, toward the Staked Plains. Sheridan determined to temporize with them no longer but to run them down and compel them either to surrender or to fight.[35]

On March 2 Custer led the Seventh Cavalry and the Nineteenth Kansas west from Fort Sill. Sheridan had gone to Camp Supply to arrange for the logistical support of the expedition from there instead of Fort Sill. He intended to meet Custer on the North Fork of Red River. But on the very day that Custer left Fort Sill Sheridan received orders at Camp Supply to hasten to Washington. On March 6, as he neared Fort Hays, a courier handed him another dispatch. Two days earlier, Ulysses S. Grant had been inaugurated President of the United States. He had promptly appointed Sherman General of the Army and Sheridan Lieutenant General. It fell to Custer, therefore, to wrap up the winter campaign.[36]

The Cheyennes had scattered over the rolling plains at the eastern edge of the Staked Plains escarpment, leaving Custer almost no promising trails to follow. Sending part of the command to rest on the Washita, he took 800 men and the strongest horses and got on the trail of a single lodge. On March 15 he found a large Cheyenne village under Little Robe and Medicine Arrow strung along Sweetwater Creek just west of the present Texas-Oklahoma boundary. With two white women held captive in the camp, Custer forebore to attack but in a parley seized three chiefs as hostages. After three days of tense negotiation, the Cheyennes gave in, surrendered the prisoners, and promised to follow him to Camp Supply as soon as their ponies grew stronger.

Custer could not wait to escort the Cheyennes because his horses were dying from want of forage and his men were beginning to subsist on mule meat. As an encouragement to the Indians to keep their word, however, he retained the three hostages and promised to release them and the prisoners taken at the Battle of the

Washita, now held at Fort Hays, when the Cheyennes surrendered at Camp Supply. Ragged and exhausted, his troopers reached Camp Supply on March 28.[37]

The other columns had long since returned to their stations. After the fight at Soldier Spring on December 25, Evans had marched almost to Fort Cobb, reprovisioned, and returned to his supply base on the Canadian. This he abandoned on January 26 and was back at Fort Bascom by February 7.[38] Carr and Penrose had passed December and January scouting the two branches of the Canadian and their tributaries. They found no Indians and dissipated all their energies in an unequal contest with winter storms and uncertain supply lines before returning, badly used up, to Fort Lyon on February 19.[39] With the arrival of Custer's column at Fort Hays on April 6, Sheridan's winter campaign officially closed, and the Nineteenth Kansas was disbanded.

Although the winter campaign had ended, it had yet to produce clear results. The Kiowas and Comanches had been consolidated at Fort Sill and the Arapahoes cowed. The Cheyennes procrastinated. Most of them declared for peace, but they could not bring themselves to report at Camp Supply, even after the Fort Hays prisoners were liberated in June. And the Dog Soldiers, refusing to accept the peace decision, headed north to join the Sioux. By early May they were once more in their old haunts on the upper Republican. The summer offered every prospect of duplicating the previous two summers.[40]

From Omaha General Augur appealed for more cavalry to help meet the threat. Orders went out for Major Carr and the Fifth Cavalry, recuperating at Fort Lyon from their winter's ordeal, to march to Fort McPherson, on the Platte. To the full-bearded cavalryman, it was a welcome summons. Although rare command qualities studded his career with combat achievements, a generously proportioned and highly sensitive ego also made it a tedious chronicle of invidious comparison and petty contention. At the moment, the honors heaped on Custer and the Seventh Cavalry for the Washita rankled, the more so because his own winter campaign, so full of hardship and bereft of spectacle, had gone largely unnoticed. Tall Bull offered an opportunity to even the score with the Seventh.[41]

The "Republican River Expedition" marched out of Fort McPherson on June 9. It consisted of eight troops of the Fifth Cavalry and a three-company battalion of Pawnee Indian scouts, nearly 500 men in all. Frank North commanded the Pawnees, and Bill Cody, by now a fixture with the regiment, went along as chief scout and guide. Early in July, far up on the Arikara Fork, near Forsyth's battlefield, Carr found a large, warm trail. It had been made by Tall Bull's main camp, augmented by some Sioux and Arapahoes, eighty-four lodges altogether. The Indians had decided to abandon their traditional range and join the Sioux north of the Platte. They had halted at Summit Springs, in a narrow valley bordered by sand hills, some sixty miles up the south Platte from Fort Sedgwick. They were waiting for high water to subside before crossing when Carr spotted them on July 11.

With some 250 troopers and 50 Pawnees, Carr swept through the tepees. Not until the command was within fifty yards did the victims discover its approach. Indians poured from the village. Most fled, but some took cover in ravines and depressions and held out to the last. The Pawnees fought with memorable ferocity. Tall Bull was cut down—by Bill Cody, some say, by Frank North, according to others. Carr, who had but one soldier wounded, reported fifty-two Indians killed, sex unspecified, and prisoners totaling seventeen women and children. In the village when the cavalry attacked were Mrs. Susanna Alderdice and Mrs. Maria Weichell, captured on the Saline on May 30. Mrs. Alderdice had been slain at the opening shot, but Mrs. Weichell, though badly wounded, survived. Carr destroyed the camp and its contents and with a pony and mule herd of more than 400 head marched to Fort Sedgwick.

Although destined not to command the public interest of the Washita, Summit Springs proved of more lasting consequence. Together with some further pressure from the Fifth Cavalry, it broke the grip of the Dog Soldiers on the upper Republican and Smoky Hill for all time. It also shattered the cohesiveness of the Dog Soldiers, ending their days of effective resistance as a group. Some of them, under White Horse, went north to join the Northern Cheyennes. Most, under Bull Bear, drifted south during the fall months and, with their less belligerent brethren, surrendered piecemeal at Camp Supply.

The operations of 1868–69 went far toward attaining Sherman's goal of clearing the belt of territory between the Arkansas and the

Platte of Indians. The southern Plains tribes had been permanently shifted southward, concentrated in Indian Territory, and locked to the institutions of control and acculturation envisioned by the peace commission of 1867. They had not acquiesced in these institutions or lost their spirit of independence, but a large step had been taken toward their ultimate conquest.

How much of this result may be ascribed to Sheridan's winter campaign is difficult to say, since not until after Carr's summer victory did it become clearly apparent. One may fairly conclude, however, that the winter campaign deserves the larger credit. The damage it wrought was less material than psychological. On the Washita and Sweetwater and at Soldier Spring, the army demonstrated that it could seek out the Indians during their most vulnerable season. The constant fear of waking one morning to the blare of bugles and crash of carbines came to seem even more intolerable than accommodating to the government's demands. Yet for the Cheyennes, even after this admission, fear of treachery and reluctance to give up their freedom caused delay. Thus, it remained for Summit Springs to bring the Dog Soldiers belatedly to this conclusion and to catalyze the rest of the Cheyennes into acting on it.

The army had learned some lessons from the experience, too. It had learned that winter operations could be hazardous and costly. Snow, mud, and cold inhibited movement and caused suffering and exhaustion to man and beast. The logistical implications were also serious. Sheridan's large force camped at the site of Fort Sill depended on a 200-mile supply line back to Fort Gibson by way of Fort Arbuckle, and muddy roads kept his command constantly at the brink of a supply crisis. The diminishing flow of supplies from Fort Bascom to the Canadian River depot contributed to Major Evans' decision to close out his campaign, and the impossibility of keeping Carr supplied from Fort Lyon was the crucial factor in his premature withdrawal from the field.[42]

More consequential, however, was the effect on the stock, both cavalry horses and draft mules. None of the columns could stockpile sufficient forage to sustain the animals, and winter grass and cottonwood boughs provided an expedient that made up almost none of the deficiency. Forced to unusual exertions by snowy or muddy footing and unsheltered from the elements, they succumbed by the hundreds to starvation, exhaustion, and exposure.

The Nineteenth Kansas was all but unhorsed even before reaching Camp Supply to begin the campaign. At Sill Custer endured a month's delay in launching his final movement against the Cheyennes because his horses had to recuperate at Fort Arbuckle, where Sheridan had bought some cornfields from the Chickasaws and Choctaws.[43] In March a New York visitor to Fort Sill noted at Custer's abandoned camp site that "the dead carcasses of dozens of horses . . . lay scattered about, tainting the fresh spring air with their disgusting stench."[44] Even after reducing his command to weed out the weak horses, Custer reached the Sweetwater with two-thirds of his remaining 800 men dismounted. During the march from there to Camp Supply his mules perished in such numbers that he had to burn nearly all his wagons. The three-day trek from Supply to Dodge cost the column 276 horses.[45] Evans and Carr suffered similar losses—Evans 172 horses and 64 mules in a ten-day march from the Washita back to his depot early in January.[46] Time and again worn-out animals forced Custer, Carr, and Evans to modify their plans or forego opportunities.

Despite the staggering logistical obstacles, the hardships, and the ever-present danger of a norther of such proportions as to bring disaster to an isolated command, the winter campaign of 1868–69 had largely confirmed Sheridan's assumptions. Sustained, large-scale winter operations were possible, and they offered opportunities for high returns that justified the higher risks. Neither Sheridan nor Sherman would forget this precedent as the army faced future Indian troubles.

NOTES

1. *Personal Memoirs of P. H. Sheridan* (2 vols., New York, 1888), 2, chap. 11.
2. The Earl of Dunraven, quoted in Marshall Sprague, "The Dude from Limerick," *The American West*, 3 (Fall 1966), 54.
3. *Personal Memoirs of Major General D. S. Stanley, U.S.A.* (Cambridge, Mass., 1917), p. 23.
4. Sheridan's postwar career is dealt with in C. C. Rister, *Border Command* (Norman, Okla., 1944).
5. Sheridan, 2, 290–95. Sherman in Senate Ex. Docs., 40th Cong., 3d sess., No. 13, pp. 24–25.
6. CIA, *Annual Report* (1868), pp. 2, 257–58. Senate Ex. Docs., 40th Cong., 3d sess., No. 13, pp. 11, 16.
7. Senate Ex. Docs., 40th Cong., 3d sess., No. 13, pp. 16–17, 26–27.
8. CIA, *Annual Report* (1869), pp. 82, 58, 391. SW, *Annual Report* (1868), pp. 10–12.
9. Cf. Hyde, *Life of George Bent*, pp. 286–87.

10. CIA, *Annual Report* (1868), pp. 249–54. There were about 350 lodges of Brulés, 350 of Oglalas, 150 of Northern Cheyennes, and 150 of Northern Arapahoes. Both Indian and white evidence clearly establishes that a substantial portion of these Indians fought with the Cheyennes against the army columns that campaigned on the Republican in September and October, for which see below (pp. 147–49).

11. Or at least so charged the army, with compelling logic. SW, *Annual Report* (1868), pp. 3–4, 10–12.

12. Sheridan's annual report, Oct. 15, 1868, SW, *Annual Report* (1868), p. 20. For a tabulation of depredations from August 10 to October 21, see *ibid.*, pp. 13–16. See also Sheridan, *Record of Engagements*, p. 8 and *passim*, in Peters, *Indian Battles and Skirmishes*.

13. House Misc. Docs., 41st Cong., 2d sess., No. 139, pp. 5–8. CIA, *Annual Report* (1868), pp. 287–88. Senate Ex. Docs., 40th Cong., 3d sess., No. 18, Pt. 1, pp. 18–21. W. S. Nye, *Carbine and Lance: The Story of Old Fort Sill* (Norman, Okla, 1937), pp. 46–48. Rupert N. Richardson, *The Comanche Barrier to South Plains Settlement* (Glendale, Calif., 1933), pp. 312–17. In November General Hazen gave the following estimate of Kiowas and Comanches of whom he had knowledge: Comanches, 5,000 (500 Penatekas, 500 Nakonis, 750 Yamparikas, 600 Kotsotekas, 2,000 Kwahadis, 650 in small scattered bands); Kiowas, 1,500; Kiowa-Apaches, 500. The Kiowas and Yamparikas had come down from the Arkansas, bringing with them the Kiowa-Apaches. The rest had remained in Indian Territory during the summer. Few of the Kwahadis had ever been to an agency. They ranged westward to the Staked Plains of the Texas Panhandle and into eastern New Mexico.

14. SW, *Annual Report* (1868), p. 12.

15. The quotation is from Sherman to Sheridan, Oct. 15, 1868, Senate Ex. Docs., 40th Cong., 3d sess., No. 18, Pt. 1, pp. 3–5. See also Sherman to Schofield, Sept. 17, 1868, in Senate Ex. Docs., 40th Cong., 3d sess., No. 13, pp. 24–25. A relic of the prewar military frontier, Fort Cobb offered no more facilities than a pair of rundown barracks and a warehouse.

16. Thorndyke, *Sherman Letters*, p. 322. Senate Ex. Docs., 40th Cong., 3d sess., No. 18, Pt. 1, p. 203. Senate Ex. Docs., 40th Cong., 3d sess., No. 13, pp. 22–23. SW, *Annual Report* (1869), p. 44. Sheridan, 2, 297, 307, 310. Sheridan, *Record of Engagements*, p. 14. For the Navajo campaign, see Utley, *Frontiersmen in Blue*, pp. 241–45.

17. Oct. 15, 1868, Senate Ex. Docs., 40th Cong., 3d sess., No. 18, Pt. 1, pp. 3–5.

18. SW, *Annual Report* (1868), p. 17. George F. Price, *Across the Continent with the Fifth Cavalry* (2d ed., New York, 1959), pp. 128–32. Crawford, *Kansas in the Sixties*, pp. 317–21. Sheridan, 2, 299.

19. SW, *Annual Report* (1868), pp. 17–18. E. S. Godfrey, "Some Reminiscences, Including an Account of General Sully's Expedition against the Southern Plains Indians, 1868," *Cavalry Journal, 36* (1927), 417–25. Lonnie J. White, "General Sully's Expedition to the North Canadian, 1868," *Journal of the West, 11* (1972), 75–98. Berthrong, *Southern Cheyennes*, pp. 318–20. Nye, *Plains Indian Raiders*, pp. 123–24. Sheridan, *Record of Engagements*, pp. 8, 11, in Peters. This source erroneously lists the Sully fights in August.

20. SW, *Annual Report* (1869), p. 18. Berthrong, pp. 310–14. George A. Forsyth, "A Frontier Fight," *Harper's New Monthly Magazine, 91* (1895), 42–62. L. H. Carpenter, "The Story of a Rescue," *Journal of the Military Service Institution of the United States, 17* (1895), 267–76. Hyde, *Life of George Bent*, pp. 297–308. Considerable first-hand source material is in Cyrus Townsend Brady, *Indian Fights and Fighters* (New York, 1912), chaps. 5–7.

21. SW, *Annual Report* (1868), pp. 16–21; (1869), pp. 44–45. Senate Ex.

Docs., 40th Cong., 3d sess., No. 18, Pt. 1, pp. 2–3. Price, pp. 131–33. Berthrong, pp. 314–17. James T. King, *War Eagle: A Life of General Eugene A. Carr* (Lincoln, Neb., 1963), pp. 81–87. Brady, chaps. 8–9. Almost forty years later Generals Carr and Carpenter engaged in a public controversy over who commanded at Beaver Creek and who deserved the credit for the successful defense. See Brady. For Custer's court-martial, see p. 128, n. 26.

22. CIA, *Annual Report* (1869), p. 388. SW, *Annual Report* (1868), p. 19. Richardson, pp. 317–18. Hazen had to take a circuitous route via the settlements and did not reach Cobb until November 8. The Kiowas later explained that they had not returned to Larned because they feared treachery and disliked the idea of traveling with soldiers. Senate Ex. Docs., 40th Cong., 3d sess., No. 18, Pt. 1, pp. 6–8.

23. SW, *Annual Report* (1869), pp. 44–51. Sheridan, 2, 307–12. Sheridan, *Record of Engagements*, pp. 14–15. Custer, *Life on the Plains*, pp. 261–80. The characterization of Evans is from John F. Finerty, *War-Path and Bivouac* (Norman, Okla., 1961), p. 34. Another officer quoted Lt. Col. William B. Royall as characterizing Evans as "the most even-tempered man in the Army . . . always cross." William S. Bisbee, *Through Four American Wars* (Boston, 1931), p. 215.

24. Sheridan, 2, 311–12. SW, Annual Report (1869), pp. 45–56. E. S. Godfrey, "Some Reminiscences, Including the Washita Battle, November 25, 1868," *Cavalry Journal*, 37 (1928), 487, tells of the dispute over rank, which is delicately ignored by Sheridan and Custer in their official reports and personal reminiscences. Sheridan indicates merely that Sully left because the command was moving out of his district.

25. Principal sources for the Battle of the Washita (including official reports) are: Sheridan, 2, 310–22; Sheridan, *Record of Engagements*, pp. 15–17; Custer, chap. 10; Melbourne C. Chandler, *Of Garryowen in Glory: The History of the 7th U.S. Cavalry* (privately published, 1960), pp. 13–25; Keim, *Sheridan's Troopers on the Border*, chaps. 17–19; Berthrong, pp. 325–29; Godfrey, "Some Reminiscences, Including the Washita Battle, November 27, 1868," pp. 481–500; Grinnell, *Fighting Cheyennes*, chap. 22; Hyde, *Life of George Bent*, chap. 12; Nye, *Carbine and Lance*, pp. 60–70; Nye, *Plains Indian Raiders*, pp. 134–37.

26. Senate Ex. Docs., 40th Cong., 3d sess., No. 18, Pt. 1, pp. 24–25.

27. The Quaife edition of Custer's *My Life on the Plains*, pp. 353–55, contains a good analysis of the evidence of the number of Indians in the villages along the Washita. Quaife concludes that Custer could not have been surrounded by more than 1,500 warriors and probably by less. Moreover, at no time did they press him aggressively.

28. Cheyenne participants told Vincent Colyer in April 1869 that thirteen men, sixteen women, and nine children had been killed. CIA, *Annual Report* (1869), p. 83. George Bent, who was not present but had good Cheyenne connections, set the figures at eleven men, twelve women, and six children killed. Hyde, *Life of George Bent*, p. 322.

29. House Ex. Docs., 41st Cong., 2d sess., No. 240, pp. 4–5.

30. For the march to Fort Cobb see Sheridan, 2, chap. 14; Custer, chaps. 13 and 14; Sheridan's and Custer's reports in SW, *Annual Report* (1869), pp. 49–50, and House Ex. Docs., 41st Cong., 2d sess., No. 240, pp. 153–62; Nye, *Carbine and Lance*, pp. 70–75; Keim, chaps. 20–22; and Sheridan, *Record of Engagements*, pp. 16–17. The adventures of the Kansas Volunteers in the campaign are detailed in David L. Spotts and E. A. Brininstool, *Campaigning with Custer and the Nineteenth Kansas Volunteer Cavalry* (Los Angeles, 1928); and Lonnie J. White, "Winter Campaigning with Custer and Sheridan: The Expedition of the Nineteenth Kansas Volunteer Cavalry," *Journal of the West*, 6 (1967), 68–98. Custer states that he commanded the expedition and made all the decisions with the approval of

Sheridan, who merely accompanied. Sheridan's accounts portray him as exercising the command rather than Custer.

31. Senate Ex. Docs., 40th Cong., 3d sess., No. 18, Pt. 1, pp. 6–11, 13–18, 23–25, 30–31, 33, 35–38. *Ibid.*, No. 40, pp. 13–15. CIA, *Annual Report* (1869), pp. 391–92.

32. In *My Life on the Plains*, pp. 429–35, Custer charged Hazen with allowing himself to be victimized by the Kiowas and thus preventing their merited chastisement. Hazen, whose career no less than Custer's was marked by contention, published a rebuttal, *Some Corrections to My Life on the Plains* (St. Paul, Minn., 1875), reprinted in *Chronicles of Oklahoma, 3* (1925), 295–318.

33. This engagement has been overshadowed by the Battle of the Washita and has found few chroniclers. Nye, *Carbine and Lance*, pp. 78–83, gives a fairly good account, but much more detailed is Evans' unpublished report, Jan. 23, 1869, 6/1560M-AGO-1869, in Record Group 94, National Archives. The Indians say they suffered no casualties at Soldier Spring.

34. Nye, *Carbine and Lance*, pp. 75–77, 84–89.

35. Berthrong, pp. 334–35. Custer, chap. 15. Chandler, pp. 28–29.

36. Sheridan, 2, 345, 347.

37. Custer, chaps. 16 and 17. Spotts and Brininstool, pp. 135–99. Chandler, pp. 28–31. In the March operations the Nineteenth Kansas was commanded by Col. Horace L. Moore; Crawford had resigned in February to work to get his men paid. The women liberated by Custer were Mrs. Anna Morgan and Miss Sarah White. They had been captured in the Saline and Solomon raids of the previous August. The three chiefs—Big Head, Fat Bear, and Dull Knife—were placed in the prisoner compound at Fort Hays. Without an interpreter to explain his intentions, the commanding officer tried to move them to the guardhouse. Supposing they were to be executed, they resisted. Dull Knife and Big Head were killed and Fat Bear wounded.

38. Evans' report, cited in n. 33 above. Sheridan, unaware that Evans was not still on the Canadian, had ordered him to move eastward against the Cheyennes in concert with Custer's March expedition.

39. King, pp. 87–93. Don Russell, *The Lives and Legends of Buffalo Bill* (Norman, Okla., 1960), pp. 110–16. Armes, *Ups and Downs of an Army Officer*, pp. 278–96.

40. Berthrong, pp. 338–40. CIA, *Annual Report* (1869), pp. 82–83, 391–92. George Bent (Hyde, *Life of George Bent*, pp. 327–28) says the Dog Soldiers remained on the Republican throughout the winter of 1868–69. Some probably did, but it is clear, in light of Custer's encounter on the Sweetwater, that at least 200 lodges wintered in the South.

41. For the Republican River Expedition and the Battle of Summit Springs, see King, chap. 5; Price, *Across the Continent with the Fifth Cavalry*, pp. 135–41; Russell, chaps. 9 and 10; Sheridan, *Record of Engagements*, pp. 20–23; Berthrong, pp. 340–44; Hyde, *Life of George Bent*, chap. 13; Grinnell, *Fighting Cheyennes*, chap. 23; and Danker, ed., *Man of the Plains*, chap. 5.

42. For Sheridan's problems see his memoirs, 2, 340–42; for Carr see King, p. 92; for Evans, his report cited in n. 33 above.

43. Sheridan, 2, 340.

44. CIA, *Annual Report* (1869), p. 83.

45. Chandler, p. 29.

46. King, pp. 90–91. Evans report.

ELEVEN

Beyond the Plains, 1866-70

THE HEARTLAND of the Indian problem was the Great Plains. There the tribes were larger, more powerful, and better organized than elsewhere. There they threatened more sensitive national interests—the principal transcontinental arteries of travel and communication. The Great Plains were closer to the nation's population centers, more familiar to Americans, and more accessible to journalists and others who molded opinion. Relations with the Plains tribes, both military and diplomatic, featured an intensity, a drama, and a coherence lacking in more remote corners of the West, and easily overshadowed confused and sporadically reported events in distant Arizona or Oregon. Thus the assumptions, policies, and institutions that governed Indian relations for half a century or more emerged mainly from the Plains experience of 1866–70.

Yet during these years almost half the frontier army served elsewhere. Though dimmed in the public eye by their headline-winning colleagues on the Plains, the troops stationed in Texas, the Southwest, and the Pacific Northwest faced opponents no less challenging and conditions of climate and topography often far more physically demanding.

Before the Civil War Texas enjoyed the West's most comprehensive and strongly manned defense network. Two chains of forts extended nearly 400 miles from Red River to the Rio Grande, another down the Rio Grande to the Gulf of Mexico, and still another westward along the 600-mile emigrant and mail road from San Antonio to El Paso. In 1860 almost 3,000 soldiers, one-fifth of the Regular Army, held twenty-five Texas installations. They had contended valiantly but with doubtful results against Kiowa and Comanche raiders from north of the Red River who regularly ravaged frontier communities all the way into Mexico, and against Mescalero Apaches from New Mexico and Coahuila who struck repeatedly at trains on the El Paso Road. Texas forfeited the federal garrisons by joining the Confederacy. During the war frontier settlers who did not abandon their homes "forted up," organized "minuteman" militia companies, and looked for protection to the "Texas Frontier Regiment," which sought ineffectually to cover the whole line from the Red River to the Rio Grande.[1]

At war's end the Confederate frontier defense effort, little more than token at best, collapsed altogether. Indian raiders poured into the void. From north of Red River the Kiowas and Comanches came with mounting frequency. Whether at war or peace with Americans on the Arkansas, they had never relaxed their pressure on Texas. A generation of Indian agents had tried unsuccessfully to convince them that Texans were Americans; the Texan course in the Civil War hardly lent credibility to this effort. Now there was fresh incentive for raiding. Cattlemen edged westward to the frontier. The era of the long trail drives opened. Kiowas and Comanches took advantage of the new opportunities, for they, too, had a market—Comanchero traders from New Mexico who came regularly to rendezvous on the Staked Plains. The temptation easily overcame the promises so solemnly recorded in the Little Arkansas and Medicine Lodge treaties.[2]

In the south the principal menace came from another source—raiders from the mountains of Coahuila and Chihuahua, Mexico, beyond the international boundary. Mescalero Apaches had preyed on the western end of the El Paso Road since 1850, and Lipans had terrorized the Nueces settlements southwest of San Antonio even longer. With the postwar surge of travel to El Paso and the burgeoning of the cattle industry on the Nueces Plain, Mescalero and Lipan raids quickened. And now a third group joined in the pastime. Early in the century Mexico had enticed bands of Kickapoos to her northern frontier to serve as buffers against Comanche and Apache raiders. Unsettled by Civil War conditions in Kansas, some of their kinsmen decided to migrate, too. En route in Jan-

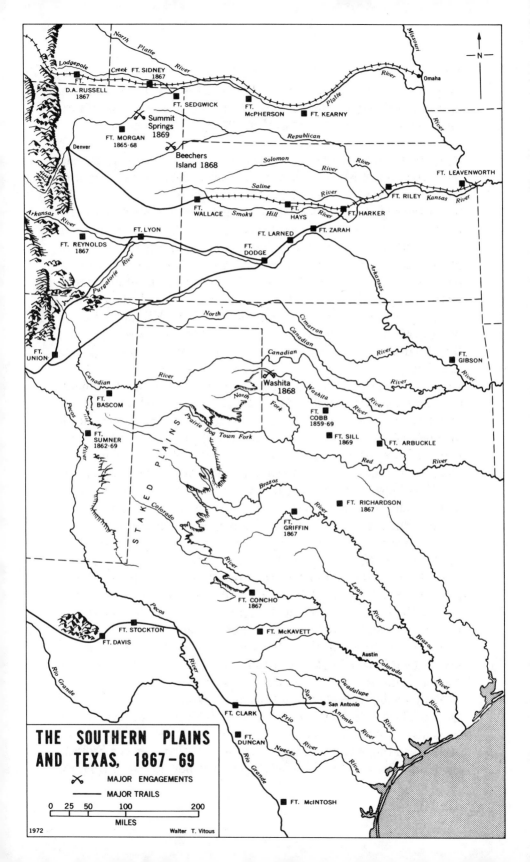

North Platte River
Lodgepole Creek
FT. SIDNEY 1867
FT. D.A. RUSSELL 1867
FT. SEDGWICK
Summit Springs 1869
FT. MORGAN 1865-68
Beechers Island 1868
Denver
FT. McPHERSON
FT. KEARNY
Platte River
Omaha
Missouri River
Republican River
Solomon River
Saline River
Smoky Hill River
FT. WALLACE
FT. HAYS
FT. HARKER
FT. RILEY
Kansas River
FT. LEAVENWORTH
Arkansas River
FT. REYNOLDS 1867
FT. LYON
FT. LARNED
FT. ZARAH
FT. DODGE
Purgatorie River
Arkansas River
North Canadian River
Cimarron River
FT. UNION
Canadian River
FT. GIBSON
FT. BASCOM
Washita 1868
North Fork
Washita River
FT. COBB 1859-69
FT. SILL 1869
FT. ARBUCKLE
FT. SUMNER 1862-69
Pecos River
S T A K E D P L A I N S
Prairie Dog Town Fork
Red River
Colorado River
Brazos River
FT. RICHARDSON 1867
FT. GRIFFIN 1867
FT. CONCHO 1867
Leon River
Brazos River
FT. McKAVETT
Austin
Colorado River
FT. STOCKTON
FT. DAVIS
Pecos River
Guadalupe River
San Antonio
Rio Grande
FT. CLARK
San Antonio River
FT. DUNCAN
Frio River
Nueces River
Brazos River
Rio Grande
FT. McINTOSH

THE SOUTHERN PLAINS AND TEXAS, 1867-69

✕ MAJOR ENGAGEMENTS

───── MAJOR TRAILS

0 25 50   100   200
MILES

1972   Walter T. Vitous

uary 1865, they were set upon at Dove Creek by Texas Rangers in a senseless attack that united all the Mexican Kickapoos in a remorseless guerrilla war against Texas border communities. Mexican authorities, preoccupied by revolutionary turmoil, made no effort to restrain the Mescaleros, Lipans, and Kickapoos, and the merchants of Mexican frontier towns encouraged them by providing a market for the fruits of the raids.[3]

Although federal troops returned to Texas in substantial numbers after the war, they were assigned at first wholly to interior stations and charged with policing a population lately in rebellion against the United States. Texas formed part of the Division of the Gulf, commanded by General Sheridan from headquarters in New Orleans. With passage of the Reconstruction Acts in March 1867, Texas fell, with Louisiana, into the Fifth Military District; a reorganization in 1868 contracted the district to Texas alone. The sole purpose of the military districts was to provide the organizational framework for military rule and "reconstruction" of the wayward South. This was the overriding concern of General Sheridan and his successor, General Hancock, as well as the series of lesser commanders who presided briefly over the Austin headquarters of the army in Texas. In both New Orleans and Austin the massive and complex exigencies of Reconstruction overwhelmed the appeals for help from the distant frontier settlements.

These appeals overflowed the desk of the Reconstruction governors, who implored Sheridan to respond to the frontier emergency.[4] But the general was preoccupied with fixing military rule on a resentful and sometimes violently resisting populace, with guaranteeing the safety of the freedmen, and with enforcing federal law. He believed that the governors and their petitioners deliberately exaggerated frontier conditions. "The mainspring of the whole movement is to get the United States troops from the interior of the State," he informed General Grant. "It is strange that over a white man killed by Indians on an extensive frontier the greatest excitement will take place, but over the killing of many freedmen in the settlements nothing is done."[5]

Prodded by President Johnson and by the prospect of state troops officered by ex-Confederates gathering at the call of the legislature, Sheridan at last relented. By mid-1867 Regulars had reoccupied the prewar posts of Stockton and Davis on the El Paso road, and Chadbourne and Belknap on the northwestern frontier.

They had also begun construction of a new post at Buffalo Springs, near Red River northeast of Fort Belknap. Fifteen hundred cavalrymen now patrolled the frontier; an equal number, mostly infantry, garrisoned interior stations; and 700 guarded the Mexican border.[6]

The Quartermaster Department began to rehabilitate the frontier forts in the spring of 1867. A quarantine prompted by a yellow fever epidemic slowed progress through the summer. By autumn post commanders, complaining of inadequate water supplies, had begun to urge new sites. Finally, in October, a board of officers was appointed to examine the whole question. As a result, in February 1868 General Hancock issued orders for the abandonment of Forts Chadbourne, Belknap, and the unfinished post at Buffalo Springs. They would be replaced by the new installations of Forts Burnham on Red River, Richardson at Jacksboro, Griffin on the Clear Fork of the Brazos, and Concho at the forks of the Concho. From here the line would extend to the Rio Grande by way of the reactivated prewar forts of McKavett, Terrett, Clark, and Duncan. Forts McIntosh, Ringgold, and Brown carried the line down the Rio Grande border to the Gulf. Forts Stockton, Davis, and Quitman would continue to guard the El Paso Road. Telegraph lines would connect the stations with one another and with headquarters. Fort Burnham was never built and the telegraph network remained some years in the future. The long delay in deciding the location of the forts and the money and labor wasted on Buffalo Springs, Belknap, and Chadbourne provoked severe criticism of the army. But by late 1868 a Texas frontier defense system had been fixed and manned that would endure without basic change for more than two decades.[7]

During 1867 and 1868 Texas' frontier defenders spent much of their time and energy building new posts and refurbishing old ones. But they also provided escort service for freight trains, stages, and cattle herds; patrolled the vast expanses of plain and desert that separated the forts; and searched out the trails of raiding parties that had struck and vanished. Such pursuits commonly turned out to be exhausting and profitless. Occasionally they ended in action—a brief exchange of gunfire, few casualties, and quick disengagement. Army records count 38 actions for 1867 through 1870, costing 16 troopers killed and 26 wounded. Estimates of Indian casualties, probably too generous, totaled

158 killed, 45 wounded, and 18 captured.[8] The duty was hard, inglorious, and frustrating, and it produced no demonstrable effect on the scale of Indian raiding.

Moreover, the seriousness of the situation remained unappreciated by top commanders. Sheridan relinquished the Fifth Military District in 1867 convinced that no more than a few depredations provoked by reckless frontiersmen lay behind the alarms that had forced him to reestablish the frontier forts,[9] and his attitude decisively influenced the thinking of Grant and Sherman. Though less suspicious, Hancock was also preoccupied with Reconstruction problems. So, for that matter, were the commanders in Austin —first Bvt. Maj. Gen. Charles Griffin (colonel of the Thirty-fifth Infantry); then, after his death in the autumn of 1867, Bvt. Maj. Gen. Joseph J. Reynolds (colonel of the Twenty-sixth Infantry). In his annual report for 1867, for example, Reynolds dramatized the continuing priority of Reconstruction duty by pointing out that during the year 384 citizens had been murdered by fellow citizens and only 26 by Indians.[10] This was small consolation to frontier settlers who knew that huge property losses and constant insecurity were part of the reckoning too. The emphasis began to shift in 1870, however, when the state at last qualified for readmission to the Union and the Fifth Military District gave way to the Department of Texas. Still, not until Sherman himself nearly lost his scalp on the Texas frontier did the realities begin to penetrate the thinking of top officials (see Chapter Twelve).

From 1862 to 1865, as U.S. commander in the Southwest, James Henry Carleton conducted one of the Civil War's noisiest sideshows. A contentious, arbitrary, domineering old dragoon, blessed with monumental certitude and inexhaustible energy, he tormented superiors and terrified subordinates, bullied civil officials and oppressed citizens. But he also warred on the Indians with a ruthlessness and persistence so far unrivaled in the Southwest. Mountain-man Kit Carson, commissioned a volunteer colonel, was his most effective weapon, made so chiefly by drive and direction supplied by Carleton. During the war years Carleton's California and New Mexico Volunteers conquered the Mescalero Apaches and corralled them on a reservation, Bosque Redondo, on the Pecos River in eastern New Mexico. They crushed the powerful Navajos, scourge of the Southwest for generations, and conducted 8,ooo of them from their homeland across the territory to the sterile flats of Bosque Redondo. They fought Kiowas and Comanches along the Sant Fe Trail, lifeline of the army in the Southwest. They campaigned diligently against Apaches and Yavapais of central and western Arizona, provoked to bitter hostility by a sudden influx of gold seekers to newly discovered diggings around Prescott and along the Colorado River.

But General Carleton failed to realize his grand design of purging the Southwest of Indians and tapping its mineral wealth. At Bosque Redondo the Navajos browbeat the Mescaleros. In December 1865 all 500 Mescaleros fled the reservation. Comanches from the plains in turn browbeat the Navajos, and disease swept their camps with fatal effect. Farming efforts failed. For four years, at enormous cost, the government subsisted them. "I think we could better send them to the Fifth Avenue Hotel to board," grumped General Sherman, who finally, as a member of the peace commission of 1867, negotiated a treaty that allowed the stricken people to go back home.[11]

So traumatic was the experience at Bosque Redondo that the Navajos never again challenged the whites. No similar trauma inhibited the Apaches. If anything, Carleton's vigorous and well-publicized campaigning stirred them up even more, and the Southwest continued to rock with Indian warfare into the postwar years. Mescaleros struck at the new farming settlements springing up in their old haunts in the Capitan Mountains, raided along the Rio Grande, and plagued the western stretches of the San Antonio–El Paso Road in Texas. West of the Rio Grande, Gila, Coyotero, Chiricahua, and Pinal Apaches interdicted the road from El Paso to Tucson and California, hit the settlements of the Santa Cruz Valley south of Tucson, and raided in Sonora and Chihuahua. North of the Gila River Yavapais struck back at the Prescott miners with bloody vengeance. Other Yavapais and Walapais menaced the Colorado River mines and made travel on the roads between Prescott and the Colorado a risky venture.[12]

The Apache problem thus spanned the Southwest from the Pecos to the Colorado and afflicted West Texas, New Mexico, and Arizona. Carleton, commanding the entire region, had been able to deal with the Apaches as a single problem. Postwar reorganization, however, carved Apacheria into three commands. The Texas forts in the Mescalero range—Stockton, Davis, and Quitman—fell into the Fifth Military District. New Mexico became a district in the Department of the Missouri. Arizona became a district in General McDowell's Department of California, which was, in turn, a unit of General Halleck's Division of the Pacific. Geography and distance decreed that, for logistical and communications purposes, Arizona look westward and New Mexico eastward. But the arrangement sacrificed unity of command, and for two decades the Apaches benefited.

In the postwar Regular Army Carleton received the lieutenant colonelcy of the Fourth Cavalry, but he continued to command the District of New Mexico in his brevet grade of major general until late in 1867, when Bvt. Maj. Gen. George W. Getty (colonel, Thirty-seventh Infantry) replaced him. Regulars of the Third Cavalry and Fifth Infantry relieved the California Volunteers, but for almost three years Carleton resisted Sherman's pressures to muster out all Volunteers. Until late 1867 a battalion of New Mexico Volunteers and a full regiment of black infantry, the 125th U.S. Colored Troops, supplemented the Regulars and kept the total strength between 1,000 and 1,500.[13]

Brig. Gen. John S. Mason, U.S.V., assumed command of the new District of Arizona in the summer of 1865. He made few basic changes in the rudimentary defense system sketched by Carleton in 1862–64. South of the Gila, to protect the California Road and the widely scattered settlements of southern Arizona, Carleton had established Fort Lowell at Tucson and Fort Bowie in Apache Pass of the Chiricahua Mountains. On the lower San Pedro Mason reactivated prewar Fort Breckinridge as Camp Grant, and on the upper San Pedro he laid out Camp Wallen. (It was abandoned in 1869, a year after Camp Crittenden had been built on a hill overlooking the malarial site of prewar Fort Buchanan.) North of the Gila, to guard the growing population of miners, Carleton had founded Fort Whipple at Prescott and Camp Lincoln (renamed Camp Verde in 1868) on the Verde River to the east. He had also planted Camp Goodwin on the middle Gila as a base for his abortive offensive against the Apaches and Yavapais in 1864. In 1865, to bring further pressure on the Indians threatening Prescott, Mason added Fort McDowell on the Verde near its confluence with the Salt. On the Colorado, Forts Yuma and Mojave dated from before the war. Although most of these posts endured, Arizona's defenses displayed neither the continuity nor the stability that marked New Mexico's. For the next twenty years posts were established, abandoned, moved, and renamed with bewildering rapidity as the Indian threat shifted or disease appeared or water gave out or supply problems grew critical.[14]

Manning these and other stations that came and went as expediency dictated were California and Arizona Volunteers left over from the war. Not until 1867 were they wholly replaced by Regulars—eight cavalry troops (First and Eighth) and twenty infantry companies (Ninth, Fourteenth, Thirty-second). This amounted to about 1,300 officers and men, but by 1869 the assignment of additional companies had raised the level to almost 2,000.[15]

Such unity of command as Mason could claim vanished in 1866 when Arizona was broken into four separate districts of the Department of California. General McDowell, the author of this measure, would now direct operations in Arizona from his San Francisco headquarters. Following an inspection tour in the spring of 1867, the division Inspector General, Maj. Roger Jones, turned in a report sharply critical of military dispositions in Arizona. He assailed the command structure, the proliferation of small posts, and the uncoordinated and sporadic scouting that seemed so futile. As remedies he urged a separate Department of Arizona, concentration of troops at a few strategic locations, and the conduct of comprehensive operations.[16]

McDowell disagreed on all three counts. In his opinion, the roots of the problem lay in other factors—in the character of Arizona's geography, in the character of the Apache and Yavapai enemy, and in the character of the troops assigned to fight them. In his rebuttal of Major Jones' criticism, McDowell stressed all three points. General Halleck concurred in their validity. In somewhat lesser degree, all three applied to New Mexico as well.[17]

No region of the American West presented more formidable geographical barriers to military operations than Arizona. The Mogollon Plateau, the San Francisco Peaks, and other high elevations contained inviting climate and scenery. But it was in the scorched, malarial bottoms of the Gila and its tributaries that most of the operations took place. Here were the vast deserts of sand and stone; the clusters of precipitous, rocky mountains webbed by treacherous canyons; the widely separated and uncertain sources of water; the profusion of vegetation armed with thorns; and the snakes, scorpions, centipedes, tarantulas, and Gila Monsters to be found in every habitation and camp site. Temperatures often reached 100 to 120 degrees. "I defy any one to make his way over this country without the aid of profanity," summed up an officer in 1868. "Many and many a time . . . I have come to some confounded cañon of piled-up rocks and slippery precipices, which would have been utterly impassable for myself and men if we had not literally cursed ourselves over."[18]

Furthermore, distance and terrain made logistics almost a full-time occupation for everyone. Supplies had to be shipped from San Francisco to Fort Yuma by steamer around the Baja California peninsula. Then they had to be hauled, under heavy escort, great distances to the far-flung posts. The troops, General Mason confessed, "can do little more than hold their posts, and escort their supply trains."[19] Aside from the drain on manpower, the process was enormously expensive. "The cost of the military establishment in Arizona," declared General Sherman in 1869, "is out of all proportion to its value as part of the public domain."[20]

The fighting traits of the Apaches and Yavapais accentuated the difficulties. No other Indians excelled them in cunning, stealth, endurance, perseverance, ruthlessness, fortitude, and fighting skill. They knew the geography of their homeland intimately and had mastered its harsh conditions perfectly. Moreover, one never knew which were hostile and which not. "It might be said of them at any time," remarked a lieutenant, "they have either just been hostile, are now, or soon will be."[21]

Only troops skilled in guerrilla warfare and as perfectly tuned to the natural environment as the Apaches could hope to master the conditions of enemy and terrain encountered in the Southwest. "It is not so much a large body, but an active one that is wanted," declared McDowell, "one moving without any baggage, and led by *active, zealous* officers, who really wish to accomplish something, and who are able to endure *fatigue*, and *willing* to undergo great *personal privations*." Generals Carleton and Mason had made the same point in similar language. The Regulars acquired such skills slowly or not at all, feared McDowell; worse, many made little effort to learn. Officers had just passed through a great war. Now, when they wanted rest and comfort, they wound up in exhausting, comfortless Arizona, many with newly acquired families. Too often they viewed their assignment as a punishment, to be endured until the blessed day of transfer to a more congenial clime.[22]

Although McDowell's complaint remained valid for many years, some did indeed meet his standards. One was Capt. George B. Sanford, at Fort McDowell. In November 1866 he led his troop of the First Cavalry high into the rugged recesses of the Sierra Ancha and demonstrated that a ranchería could be surprised and smashed.[23] Another was Capt. J. M. Williams of the Eighth Cavalry. In April 1867, with eighty-five troopers out of Fort Whipple, he maneuvered a band of Indians into two fights on the Verde, killed fifty and destroyed their ranchería.[24] During the summer of 1868 Maj. William R. Price and his subordinates, particularly Capt. S. B. M. Young and Maj. David R. Clendenin, campaigned tirelessly out of Fort Mojave and beat the Walapais into an uncertain peace.[25] At Fort Bowie in 1869–70 Capt. Reuben F. Bernard proved unusually adept at bringing Cochise's warriors to battle.[26] For the years 1866–70 the army recorded 137 small-unit actions with Indians in Arizona and claimed a kill of 649 at a cost of 26 killed and 58 wounded.[27] This record seemed to belie McDowell's pessimism. But the scale of depredations was a more accurate performance indicator than number killed, and year after year depredations continued without letup.

Friction between army and citizenry resulted. A populace tormented by murder, property loss, and constant insecurity savagely abused its defenders for their poor showing. At the same time, the army viewed the citizens with growing resentment. Too many were avowed exterminationists, and their insistence on classing all Indians as hostile sometimes added unnecessarily to the hostile ranks. The intensity, if not the origins, of both Yavapai and Walapai hostility could be traced to white treachery.[28] Furthermore, as the Indians kept the mines from full development, the major business of Arizona came to be the army. McDowell's successor, Gen. Edward O. C. Ord, put it bluntly in 1869: "Almost the only paying business the white inhabitants have in that Territory is supplying the troops. . . . If the paymasters and quartermasters of the army were to stop payment in Arizona, a great majority of the white settlers would be compelled to quit it. Hostilities are therefore kept up with a view to protecting inhabitants most of whom are supported by the hostilities."[29] Thus the populace damned the army for lethargy and ineffectiveness, and the army damned the populace for provoking war, then fattening on the soldiers who had to fight it.

In adjoining New Mexico General Carleton ceased to enjoy his wartime success—perhaps partly because of less experienced troops, partly because he spent so much time quarreling with critics of his Bosque Redondo program. General Getty, who replaced him in September 1867, did no better. Mescalero raids flashed along the eastern borders of settlement almost as far north as Taos. Gila Apaches continued to trouble the Rio Grande Valley settlements from Albuquerque south to El Paso. Both tribes infested the overland route—the Mescaleros in Texas, the Gilas in southwestern New Mexico. The destruction of mail coaches and slaughter of the passengers became a common tragedy.[30] Troops at Forts Stanton, McRae, Selden, Craig, Bayard, and Cummings mounted an occasional scout or pursuit, but with little energy and less effect. In the four years following the war, the army in New Mexico claimed only 33 combats (compared with 137 in Arizona) accounting for an estimated 92 Indian fatalities (compared with 649 in Arizona).[31]

In Arizona, junior officers like Sanford, Williams, Price, Bernard, and others had demonstrated that Regulars could surmount the geographical obstacles of the Southwest and occasionally even best the Apaches. Throughout Apacheria, however, it remained for better leadership and greater experience to give the army the energy, skill, and direction needed to overcome the Apaches.

Long known as a military intellectual, "Old Brains" Halleck marshalled some imposing statistics to demonstrate that the Division of the Pacific did not receive its fair allocation of the nation's military resources. The division embraced three states and four territories, he pointed out, 1,218,000 square miles, 12,750 miles of coastline, and a population of 700,000 whites and 130,000 Indians. That was one-third of the land area of the United States, more than one-third of the Indians, a coast three times the length of that fronting the Atlantic and Gulf of Mexico, but a population only one-sixtieth as strong for self-defense as the rest of the country. Yet he commanded only two cavalry regiments, an artillery regiment, and four infantry regiments—about 6,000 officers and enlisted men. That was only one-ninth of the U.S. Army.[32]

Understandably, Halleck did not stress that nearly half his

square miles and a considerable share of his coastline and Indian population fell in Alaska, purchased from Russia in 1867 and a military responsibility only at a few coastal points. Nor did he emphasize that only in Arizona and along the northwestern fringes of the Great Basin did his Indians require active campaigning. Nevertheless, he made a valid point. His division, counting Alaska, was bigger than Sherman's. Its distances were as vast and its mountain-and-desert terrain far more inhospitable to military operations. In addition, he struggled with logistical problems of greater magnitude than Sherman's. Although increasingly self-sufficient as California developed her agricultural and mineral potential, the division still drew heavily on eastern depots for many quartermaster and ordnance items. Whether shipped by the Atlantic-Gulf-Isthmus-Pacific route or, before 1869, by the uncompleted transcontinental railroad, the process was costly, time-consuming, and uncertain. Although many posts were accessible by coastal or river steamer, distance and terrain made distribution of supplies to interior posts a formidable operation. Finally, whether hostile or not, Halleck's Indians still had to be watched, and this, together with the coastal defenses, required about fifty posts, approximately the number that Sherman's division counted. Yet in 1867 Halleck commanded only one-half the manpower allotted to Sherman, and in 1868 the proportion dropped to one-fourth.[33]

The Department of California contained the States of California and Nevada and the Territory of Arizona. General McDowell commanded until 1868, when he was replaced by Bvt. Maj. Gen. (Brig. Gen.) Edward O. C. Ord. The Department of the Columbia embraced the State of Oregon and the Territories of Washington and Idaho. Bvt. Maj. Gen. Frederick Steele (colonel, Twentieth Infantry) commanded until late 1867, when he was succeeded by Bvt. Maj. Gen. (Brig. Gen.) Lovell H. Rousseau. Alaska was first attached as a district to the Department of California but in March 1868 was organized as a separate department, a status it held for two years until merged into the Department of the Columbia in July 1870. Bvt. Maj. Gen. Jefferson C. Davis (colonel, Twenty-third Infantry) commanded in Alaska.[34]

Halleck's network of posts underwent some major changes in the postwar period. Although the coastal defenses remained stable, shifting Indian troubles led to the abandonment of old posts and the founding of new ones. In the mountains of northern

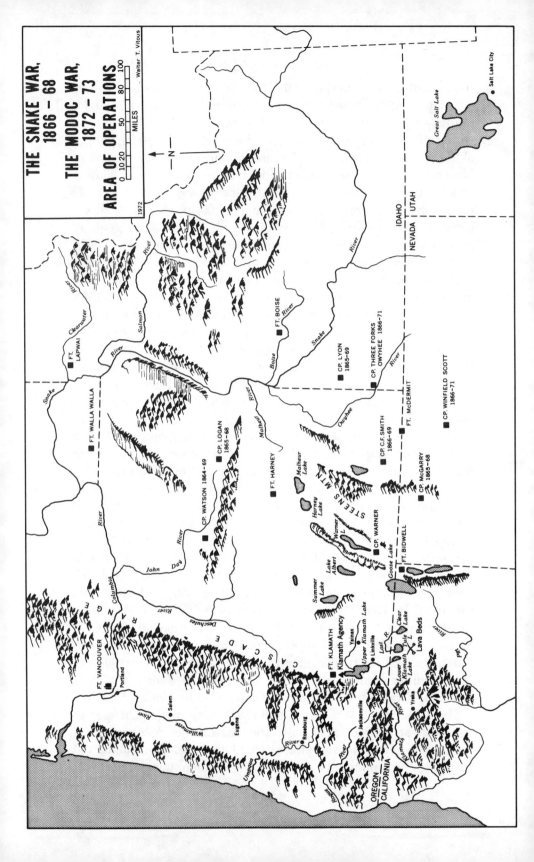

THE SNAKE WAR,
1866 – 68
THE MODOC WAR,
1872 – 73
AREA OF OPERATIONS

— Walter T. Vitous
1972

N

MILES
0 10 20   50   80   100

California the conquest of the Indians by Civil War Volunteers gave every indication of permanence, and the cluster of stations from which they had operated began to be phased out. Likewise in the Coast Range of Oregon and Washington, the forts that had figured in the Rogue River and Puget Sound wars of the middle 1850s proved no longer necessary. In California Fort Gaston remained until 1892, and in Washington Fort Vancouver continued to occupy a strategic stretch of the lower Columbia River.[35]

In Nevada the Paiutes had ceased to give much trouble. Fort Churchill was abandoned, but Camp Independence was retained in California's Owens River Valley, at the eastern foot of the Sierra Nevada, to intimidate Mono Paiutes upset over the continued intrusion of miners in this area.[36] Fort Halleck was planted near the upper Humboldt River in 1867 to give military support to the Central Pacific Railroad along its line across central Nevada. In the extreme northeastern reaches of the division, the Department of the Columbia maintained Forts Colville and Walla Walla, Washington, and Fort Lapwai, Idaho. These posts supported the Indian Bureau in its work with the formidable but at the moment complaisant Nez Percé tribe.

Next to Arizona, whose dozen or more forts were new, the most troubled area in Halleck's division lay in the plateau country drained by the Snake River and its tributaries. During the Civil War years the Northern Paiutes, commonly known as Snakes, had risen violently against prospectors pouring into the newly discovered gold regions of southwestern Idaho and southeastern Oregon. The campaigns of Oregon and Nevada Volunteers in 1864–66 had failed to bring these Indians under control, and the postwar Regulars inherited the task.[37] This combat zone fell in both the Department of California and the Department of the Columbia, and both had forts directed at the Paiutes. In the former were Forts Klamath and Harney and Camps Warner, Watson, Logan, Alvord, and C. F. Smith, Oregon; Fort Boise and Camps Lyon and Three Forks Owyhee, Idaho. In the latter were Fort Bidwell, California, and Fort McDermit and Camps McGarry and Winfield Scott, Nevada.[38]

For a time it seemed as though diplomacy might succeed in quieting the Paiutes. In October 1864 J. W. P. Huntington, Superintendent of Indian Affairs for Oregon, negotiated a treaty

with the Klamaths, Modocs, and Yahuskin Paiutes by which they
yielded 11.5 million acres in central and southern Oregon and
agreed to settle on the Klamath Lake Reservation, at the eastern
base of the Cascade Range just north of the California boundary.
Ten months later Pauline (or Paunina) and his fellow chiefs of
the Walpapi Paiutes subscribed to the treaty. Although other
Paiute bands occupied the lake-strewn plateaus of southeastern
Oregon and the deserts and mountains of northern Nevada, the
Yahuskins and Walpapis were the most powerful and warlike of
the Paiute groups. But the Walpapi commitment to peace proved
less than durable. Pauline and a few followers lived on the reservation during the winter of 1865–66, but in the spring they gave
way to the blandishments of the warring bands. From the Cas-
cades east to the Snake Valley and from the John Day River south
to the Humboldt, the Paiutes preyed on stagecoaches, freight
trains, and prospectors bound for the Idaho mines, and struck at
gold camps, ranches, farms, and stage stations in the mountains
drained by the upper John Day, Malheur, and Owyhee Rivers.[39]

Throughout 1865 and 1866, as the Oregon Volunteers phased
out, Regulars of the First Cavalry and Fourteenth Infantry tried to
come to grips with the Paiutes. They did succeed in fighting several
actions, but depredations continued to exact a terrible toll.[40] An
aroused citizenry excoriated the Army for want of energy and
determination. And in fact a newly assigned district commander
arriving at Fort Boise in December 1866 found cause for the
criticism of his predecessor. "The feeling against him and many
of his officers was very bitter," he recalled. "They were accused
of all manner of things. One thing was certain: they had not, nor
were they, making headway against the hostile Indians. There
was much dissipation amongst a good many officers, and there
seemed to be a general apathy amongst them, and indifference to
the proper discharge of duty."[41]

The new commander intended to change these conditions. He
was George Crook, lieutenant colonel of the Twenty-third Infantry (newly created out of the Second Battalion of the Fourteenth),
major general by brevet. The Paiute War would launch him on a
rapid rise to top rank among the army's Indian-fighting generals.
In 1866 Crook was two years short of forty, of spare, athletic
build, with close-cropped hair, a blond beard that parted at the
chin, and bright blue-gray eyes. In uniform he looked the soldier

to the very core. But he rarely wore a uniform, and he never indulged the military dash and ostentation that kept so many of his fellow generals in the public eye. Quiet to the the point of introspection, modest, unselfish, considerate, conscientious, Crook yet on occasion could pronounce savage judgment on the character, motives, and actions of associates. He also tended to be stubborn and independent beyond the limits usually tolerated by the military system. Of his outdoorsmanship the whole army stood in awe. Possessed of legendary stamina and endurance combined with an ability to meet the wilderness on its own terms, he was a deep student of nature, an avid huntsman and fisherman, a crack shot, and an accomplished horseman—although for hard work he preferred a mule.

Already, as the result of prewar experience in California and Oregon, Crook knew a great deal about Indians, and he would learn much more. He studied them as intensely as he studied the habits and psychology of birds and animals, so that, as an aide recalled, "he knew the Indian better than the Indian did." In war he was ruthless, in peace paternalistically humane and solicitous. His insistence on honest treatment of the Indian, on never making a promise he could not honor, amounted almost to an obsession. He subscribed to and consistently practiced the Carleton-McDowell injunction to get on the trail and stay on it despite all obstacles until the quarry was cornered. He went still further by giving new emphasis to techniques that were to become his hallmark—extensive use of Indians to fight Indians, and reliance on pack mules for field transportation. The former armed him with the Indian skill in guerrilla warfare and the psychological impact on the enemy of finding kinsmen arrayed against them. The latter gave him a mobility denied by wagon trains.[42]

One week after Crook's arrival at Fort Boise, a war party struck near the mouth of the Boise River. "I took Captain Perry's company of the First Cavalry," he recalled, "and left with one change of underclothes, toothbrush, etc., and went to investigate matters, intending to be gone a week. But I got interested after the Indians and did not return there again for over two years."[43] Throughout 1867 and into 1868 Crook stormed about the Paiute country. He galvanized lethargic garrisons, led them against the enemy, and set an example that stirred other officers to action. He fired incompetent guides and scouts and hired skilled trailers such as Archie McIntosh, who later went with him to Arizona. He enlisted bands of Shoshonis from Idaho and employed them with notable effect against the Paiutes. No less than the burning summer heat did the cold, snow, ice, and sleet of winter inhibit his movement. "Our beards were one mass of ice," he wrote of a late-winter scout. Pack mules, personally supervised, gave him wide-ranging freedom from supply bases.

Between December 1866 and August 1868 Crook personally led about a dozen extended scouts from Camps Warner, Lyon, C. F. Smith, and Fort McDermit and personally commanded in six engagements. Other officers caught his aggressive spirit. Together Crook and his subordinates kept the Paiutes constantly on the run for a year and a half and forced them into combat on some forty occasions. In fourteen engagements the enemy found himself hit by Shoshoni scouts as well as Regulars, and in four of these the scouts fought alone under the leadership of Chief Guide Archie McIntosh or one of his subordinates. In all, the troops reported Indian casualties of 329 killed, 20 wounded, and 225 captured.[44]

By mid-1868 the Paiutes had had enough of Crook's style of war. Pauline had been killed early in the conflict, in January 1867. Old Weawea had emerged as the most influential hostile leader. In June 1868 he sent word to Crook that he wanted to make peace, and with about 800 followers he came to Fort Harney on July 1 for a conference. Crook, arrayed in his seldom-used dress uniform, treated the chief as he would treat peace-seeking Indians the rest of his career—curtly, even rudely, and with a great show of reluctance to quit fighting. He was sorry to hear that the Indians desired peace, he told Old Weawea. "I was in hopes that you would continue the war." Every soldier killed could be replaced instantly. Every warrior killed could be replaced only as children grew up. "In this way it would not be very long before we would have you all killed off, and then the government would have no more trouble with you." At length, however, he allowed himself to be persuaded to let the Paiutes have peace. Old Weawea's people remained in the vicinity and drew rations from the army at Fort Harney. Ultimately, some settled on the Klamath Reservation and others on a reservation set aside in 1872 on the Malheur River. Many continued to live at large without any connection with an agency.[45]

That many took note of the unconventional techniques by which Crook has so expeditiously ended a seemingly hopeless Indian war may be doubted. That many took note of the result and marked Crook as a comer is certain. General Halleck and his successors, Gens. George H. Thomas and John M. Schofield, gave him high praise.[46] Nor was the achievement lost on a War Department plagued with an abundance of generals with creditable Civil War records but embarrassing Indian-fighting records. When General Rousseau left the Department of the Columbia in April 1868, Halleck made Crook the temporary department commander, a post he held, even though by lineal rank a junior lieutenant colonel, for two years. And then he was to receive rewards that still more dramatically violated the hallowed seniority tradition.

On the morning of October 9, 1867, the steamer *John L. Stevens* entered the harbor of Sitka, Alaska. Aboard were a company of the Ninth Infantry and one of the Second Artillery, come to establish U.S. authority in the vast new possession purchased from Russia the previous March. Aboard, too, was the improbably named general to whom Halleck had entrusted the mission— Jefferson C. Davis. (He had been one of Sherman's ablest wartime lieutenants, but was remembered chiefly as the hot-tempered, awesomely profane victor of a celebrated quarrel with a fellow general.) The troops were not allowed to go ashore until the official transfer party arrived, and that was another eight days. On October 18, in ceremonies in front of the Russian governor's palace, a seasick General Rousseau accepted Alaska from a Russian naval captain. Cannon saluted, the U.S. flag replaced the Russian, and the army found itself on a new Indian frontier.[47]

Alaska's principal value derived from furs—seal, otter, marten, mink, fox, bear—and her Indians played a key role in the harvest. Commercial activity and settlement concentrated in the Alexander Archipelago, where Sitka alone harbored 900 of Alaska's 2,000 white settlers. To the west, Kodiak Island and Cook Inlet also supported a handful of non-Indian residents. Military estimates placed the Indian population within reach of these centers at 60,000. They had a long history of dealing with the white man— with the Russians, resident in Alaska for more than a century; with "King Georges" of the Hudson's Bay Company, across the border in British Columbia; and with the "Bostons," U.S. traders who plied the inlets in search of profit. Thus the army's chief role was not to subjugate the Indians but to supervise a long-established trade relationship that now intensified as more and more "Bostons" arrived to seek fortunes in the Indian trade.[48]

During the ensuing year General Davis received three more companies of the Second Artillery, bringing his force to a total of 21 officers and 530 soldiers. Establishing his headquarters at Sitka, he sent detachments to found other posts at key centers of Indian-white contact—Fort Tongass, on Portland Channel facing Hudson's Bay Company territory in British Columbia; Fort Wrangel, on an island at the mouth of the Stikine River; Fort Kodiak, on Kodiak Island, strategic for relations with the Aleuts of the adjacent Alaska peninsula; Fort Kenay, near the head of Cook Inlet; and St. Paul, in the Pribilof Islands of the Bering Sea.[49]

Aside from building and maintaining their posts, the troops at these stations were charged mainly with preventing the manufacture and importation for Indian consumption of whiskey, on this frontier as on every other the prime tool of the fur trade. Despite a prohibition imposed by act of Congress, liquor of the vilest sort flowed freely into the territory. General Davis described it as "probably beyond chemical analysis; its effects upon the Indians are little better than strychnine."[50] The fitness of the army for this mission may be questioned. Far from suppressing the liquor traffic, soldiers appear to have been among the most energetic of its entrepreneurs. At every fort and at every nearby Indian village the evidence was dramatically and constantly apparent. "A greater mistake could not have been committed than stationing troops in their midst," concluded the department's medical director in 1869. "They mutually debauch each other, and sink into that degree of degradation in which it is utterly impossible to reach, either through moral or religious influences."[51]

Such friction as occasionally developed with the Alaskan Indians had its origin in the liquor problem. On New Year's Day 1869 a chief treated to a bottle by General Davis himself fell into an altercation with a sentry, apparently also drunk. Although the trouble was smoothed over, not everyone got the word. Several killings on both sides led finally, by order of Davis, to the shelling of a Kake village by the U.S.S. *Saginaw*.[52] More serious yet was an incident on Christmas Day 1869. A drunken Stikine Indian bit off the finger of the wife of the quartermaster sergeant at Fort Wrangel. The post commander sent a detachment to arrest the culprit, but he resisted and was killed. Another Indian retaliated by pumping fourteen bullets into the post trader. When the Indians declined to surrender this man, the garrison opened fire on the village with a six-pounder howitzer. For two days Indians and soldiers exchanged fire, until the Indians gave in. A hastily organized military court found the prisoner guilty of murder, and he was promptly hanged.[53]

The Fort Wrangel episode sparked congressional interest in Alaskan military affairs and developed testimony not only to the sorry condition of the troops there but also to the inefficiency of using soldiers in a nearly roadless land where virtually all travel was by water. Vessels manned by revenue officers or sailors would prove more effective, it was maintained.[54] The War Department had little inclination to contest the idea. Alaska was a costly and thankless responsibility and, for those assigned there, a station even more detestable than Arizona. In 1870, therefore, the Department of Alaska was reduced to a district and all posts except Sitka were abandoned. For the next seven years two artillery companies uneventfully garrisoned this post and then were quietly withdrawn altogether.[55]

NOTES

1. For prewar developments in Texas see Utley, *Frontiersmen in Blue*, pp. 70–77, 125–140. For wartime developments see W. C. Holden, "Frontier Defense in Texas during the Civil War," *West Texas Historical Association Year Book*, *4* (1928), 16–31; J. Evetts Haley, *Fort Concho and the Texas Frontier* (San Angelo, Tex., 1952), chap. 6; and Rupert N. Richardson, *The Frontier of Northwest Texas, 1846 to 1876* (Glendale, Calif., 1963), chap. 16.
2. Richardson, *Comanche Barrier to South Plains Settlement*, pp. 308–12. Richardson, *Frontier of Northwest Texas*, chap. 17. CIA, *Annual Report* (1869), p. 393.
3. The Kickapoo story is detailed in A. M. Gibson, *The Kickapoos: Lords of the Middle Border* (Norman, Okla., 1963), chaps. 15–16. Although dealing with a later period, the following sources provide background for this paragraph: House Reports, 45th Cong., 2d sess., No. 701; House Ex. Docs., 45th Cong., 1st sess., No. 13; House Misc. Docs., 45th Cong., 2d sess., No. 64.
4. For conditions in Texas, see James M. Day and Dorman Winfrey, eds., *Texas Indian Papers, 1860–1916* (Austin, Tex., 1961), pp. 103–04, 113, 155, 232–33.

5. Senate Ex. Docs., 45th Cong., 2d sess., No. 19, pp. 7–9. SW, *Annual Report* (1866), p. 48. Rister, *Border Command*, chap. 2.
6. SW, *Annual Report* (1867), pp. 378–80, 470–73. The 1867 returns showed 131 officers and 3,535 enlisted men present for duty in Texas. Serving at 37 posts, they consisted of three cavalry regiments (Fourth, Sixth, and Ninth) and parts of seven infantry regiments (First, Seventh, Twentieth, Twenty-sixth, Thirty-fifth, Thirty-ninth, and Forty-first). Eleven posts were Indian, twenty-two Reconstruction, and four border. All the Indian posts were garrisoned by cavalry: 45 officers and 1,453 enlisted men. Reconstruction posts, largely one-company stations in the towns, were held by 14 officers and 198 enlisted men of cavalry and 52 officers and 1,178 enlisted men of infantry. On the border were 20 officers and 706 enlisted men, mostly infantry.
7. SW, *Annual Report* (1867), pp. 378–79; (1868), pp. 211–12, 855–71. Reestablishment of frontier defenses is treated in C. C. Rister, *Fort Griffin on the Texas Frontier* (Norman, Okla., 1956), chap. 4; Haley, chap. 7; and Ernest Wallace, *Ranald S. Mackenzie on the Texas Frontier* (Lubbock, Tex., 1965), chap. 2. By mid-1868, 177 officers and 4,380 enlisted men garrisoned 31 Texas posts—1,522 on the Indian frontier, 1,600 on the Mexican border, and 1,435 in the interior. In contrast to 1867, most Indian posts now had some infantry as well as cavalry. SW, *Annual Report* (1868), pp. 766–68.
8. "Chronological List of Actions . . . with Indians from January 1, 1866, to January, 1891," in Peters, comp., *Indian Battles and Skirmishes*, pp. 4–25. SW, *Annual Report* (1868), pp. 711–16; (1869), pp. 143–45; (1870), pp. 41–42. See also Rister, *Fort Griffin*, chap. 4; Haley, chap. 9; W. H. Carter, *The Life of Lieutenant General Chaffee* (Chicago, 1917), chap. 9.
9. SW, *Annual Report* (1867), p. 379.
10. *Ibid.* (1869), p. 144.
11. I have treated Civil War New Mexico at greater length in *Frontiersmen in Blue*, chap. 12. The Sherman quotation, Sept. 21, 1866, is in House Ex. Docs., 39th Cong., 2d sess., No. 23, p. 15.
12. Apache organization and distribution tend to be complicated. I have relied heavily on mimeographed studies prepared for the Department of Justice for the Indian Land Claim cases, as follows: Albert H. Schroeder, *A Study of the Apache Indians* (5 vols., Santa Fe, N. Mex., 1960–63); Schroeder, *A Study of Yavapai History* (3 vols., Santa Fe, N. Mex., 1959); A. B. Bender, *A Study of the Mescalero Apache Indians, 1846–1880* (St. Louis, 1960). See also Ralph H. Ogle, *Federal Control of the Western Apaches, 1848–1886* (Albuquerque, N. Mex., 1940); C. L. Sonnichsen, *The Mescalero Apaches* (Norman, Okla., 1958); Frank C. Lockwood, *The Apache Indians* (New York, 1936); E. W. Gifford, *The Southeastern Yavapai*, University of California Publications in American Archaeology and Ethnology, *29* (Berkeley, Calif., 1932); Gifford, *The Northeastern and Western Yavapai*, ibid., *34* (Berkeley, Calif., 1936); Morris E. Opler, "An Outline of Chiricahua Apache Social Organization," in Fred Eggan, ed., *Social Anthropology of North American Tribes* (Chicago, 1955), pp. 173–242; and Grenville Goodwin, *The Social Organization of the Western Apache* (Tucson, Ariz., 1969).

   My accounts in this and subsequent chapters proceed from the following premises: Mescaleros ranged widely in New Mexico and Texas from bases in the Sierra Blanca, Guadalupe, and Sacramento Mountains of central and and southern New Mexico. Other Mescalero bands raided out of the Davis Mountains of West Texas, the Chisos Mountains of the Big Bend, and the Sierra del Carmen of Coahuila. In southwestern New Mexico, the Gila Apaches, loosely embracing the Mimbres, Copper Mine, Warm Spring, and Mogollon groups, a division of the Chiricahuas, ranged the continental divide from the Datil Mountains southward to Lake Guzman in Chihuahua. Adjoining them on the west, in eastern Arizona, were the Western Apaches, embracing the Coyotero (or White Mountain), Pinal, and Aravaipa Apaches on the middle Gila and upper Salt. In the Chiricahua Mountains to the south lived another band of Chiricahuas, and in the Sierra Madre of Mexico still another. All told, the Apaches probably numbered about 8,000. The Yavapai, numbering about 2,000, occupied the Tonto Basin and lower Salt and Verde Valleys and extended westward between the Gila and Bill Williams Rivers as far as the Colorado. These were Yuman rather than Apachean people, but were usually mistaken by the whites for Apaches. Accordingly, the three principal Yavapai divisions, Western, Southeastern, and Northeastern, are often erroneously called Apache-Mojave, Apache-Yuma, and Apache-Tonto. The Walapais, about 2,500 strong, ranged east of the Colorado northward from Bill Williams River. These were the hostile tribes. Peaceful tribes were the sedentary Yumas, Mojaves, and Chemehuevis of the Colorado River Valley; the Pimas, Papagoes, and Maricopas of the Santa Cruz Valley; and the Pueblos, Jicarilla Apaches, and Utes of the upper Rio Grande Valley.

13. House Ex. Docs., 39th Cong., 2d sess., No. 23, p. 15. SW, *Annual Report* (1867), pp. 40, 43, 440–41; (1868), pp. 732–33, 736–37.

14. See under appropriate headings in Prucha, *Military Posts of the United States;* Frazer, *Forts of the West;* and Ray Brandes, *Frontier Military Posts of Arizona* (Globe, Ariz., 1960). Early transitory posts were, in an arc around Prescott from east to north to west: Camps Reno (1868–70), Willow Grove (1867–69) and its successor Hualpai (1868–73), Date Creek (1867–73), El Dorado (1867), and Colorado (1868–71); in the upper Santa Cruz Valley south of Tucson: Camps Mason (1865–66) and Cameron (1866–67).

15. SW, *Annual Report* (1867), pp. 444–45; (1868), pp. 740–41; (1869), pp. 166–67.

16. *Ibid.* (1867), pp. 72–73, 82–84, 86–95; (1868), pp. 46–48; Carr, " 'The Days of the Empire,' " pp. 4, 19–21.

17. For McDowell's and Halleck's views, see SW, *Annual Report* (1867), pp. 82–83, 86–95; (1865), pp. 46–48.

18. *Army and Navy Journal,* 5 (June 6, 1868), 666. An excellent insight may be obtained from Bourke, *On the Border with Crook.*

19. Mason to Drum, April 29, 1866, RG 98, Dept. of the Pacific Letter Book 55, pp. 127–31, National Archives.

20. CIA, *Annual Report* (1869), p. 225.

21. Carr, p. 5.

22. For McDowell's views see SW, *Annual Report* (1866), pp. 34–36; (1867), pp. 89, 95. For Carleton, see Utley, p. 234; for Mason, see the document cited in n. 19 above.

23. SW, *Annual Report* (1867), pp. 116–19. Carr, p. 18. E. R. Hagemann, ed., *Fighting Rebels and Redskins: Experiences in Army Life of Colonel George B. Sanford, 1861–1892* (Norman, Okla., 1969), pp. 9–10.

24. SW, *Annual Report* (1867), pp. 130–31, 150–53.

25. Dan L. Thrapp, *The Conquest of Apacheria* (Norman, Okla., 1967), chap. 4.

26. Richard Y. Murray, *The History of Fort Bowie* (Unpublished Masters Thesis, Univ. of Arizona, 1951), pp. 119–23.

27. "Chronological List of Actions," in Peters, comp., pp. 4–25.

28. The Bloody Tanks affair of 1864, when Arizonans enticed a band of Yavapais into camp with food and tobacco, then slaughtered them, was but one of several episodes of like character that drove the Yavapais to hostility. Utley, p. 256. Another occurred in 1868, when teamsters invited some Yavapais to La Paz to make peace, then fell on them and killed a

dozen. The Walapais went to war in 1866 after a freighter murdered their principal chief on mere suspicion of complicity in the killing of a white man. A Prescott grand jury dismissed the case with a "unanimous vote of thanks" to the murderer. CIA, *Annual Report* (1869), pp. 216–18. Thrapp, pp. 39–40.

The army was not blameless in this regard. The terror in which Cochise and the Chiricahuas held southern Arizona resulted from military treachery at Apache Pass in 1861, and the Gilas could hardly forget the murder of Mangas Coloradas while he was held prisoner by Carleton's troops in 1863. Utley, pp. 161–63, 251–52. Also, in the spring of 1867 Col. John Irvin Gregg, commanding a district from Fort Whipple, solved the problem of whom to fight by declaring all Indians in his sector hostile and invalidating all safe-conduct passes issued by Indian agents. General McDowell cancelled the order and rebuked Gregg. "He certainly simplified the question as to what Indians were to be fought," conceded McDowell, "but at the same time greatly extended the military operations necessary to be carried out to fight them." McDowell noted that the order proved very popular with Arizonans and speculated that this was probably the motive that inspired it. SW, *Annual Report* (1867), pp. 105–6, 109–13, 121–22.

29. SW, *Annual Report* (1869), p. 124.
30. Apache hostilities are summarized in the annual reports of the Superintendent of Indian Affairs for the Territory: CIA, *Annual Report* (1867), pp. 192–93; (1868), pp. 160–61; (1869), pp. 244–49.
31. "Chronological List of Actions," in Peters, comp., pp. 4–25.
32. SW, *Annual Report* (1867), p. 69; (1868), p. 37. The regiments were the First and Eighth Cavalry, Second Artillery, and Ninth, Fourteenth, Twenty-third, and Thirty-second Infantry.
33. Comparison derived from troop distribution tables in SW, *Annual Report* (1867), pp. 436–39, 444–51; (1868), pp. 732–47. Sherman received reinforcements in 1868 to help fight the Cheyennes and their allies.
34. See pertinent sections of Raphael P. Thian, comp., *Notes Illustrating the Military Geography of the United States, 1813–1880* (Washington, D.C., 1881).
35. Abandoned between 1865 and 1868 were Forts Steilacoom, Wash.; Dalles, Yamhill, and Hoskins, Oreg.; Humboldt, Crook, Baker, Reading, and Camps Lincoln, Anderson, Jaqua, and Crook, Calif. Principal coastal fortifications were Fort Point, Point San José, Alcatraz Island, and Angel Island in San Francisco Bay and Forts Stevens and Cape Disappointment (later Canby) at the mouth of the Columbia. See appropriate headings in Prucha, *Guide to Military Posts of the United States*, and Frazer, *Forts of the West*.
36. Utley, p. 226. SW, *Annual Report* (1867), pp. 124–25.
37. Utley, pp. 225–27. "Snake" is a carelessly used term that has been applied to Shoshoni and Bannock as well as Northern Paiute. For identification of these bands and their leaders, see Omer S. Stewart, *The Northern Paiute Bands*, Anthropological Records, vol. 3, No. 2 (Berkeley, Calif., 1939).
38. See appropriate headings in Prucha and Frazer.
39. CIA, *Annual Report* (1866), pp. 5–6, 77–78, 89–91; (1867), pp. 71–73, 91–93, 95–103. The treaties are in Kappler, *Indian Affairs: Laws and Treaties*, 2, 865–68, 876–78.
40. Military engagements and depredations on citizens, 1865–67, are listed by Superintendent Huntington in CIA, *Annual Report* (1867), pp. 95–103.
41. *General George Crook: His Autobiography*, p. 143.
42. The quotation is by Maj. Cyrus Roberts in Finerty, *War-Path and Bivouac*, p. 321. Finerty, a newspaper correspondent with Crook in the 1876 Sioux campaign, also gives good sketches of Crook, pp. 6, 55–56, 317. The lengthiest and most appreciative evaluation is by his long-time aide, Capt.

John G. Bourke, in *On the Border with Crook, passim;* and "General Crook in the Indian Country," *Century Magazine, 41* (1891), 643–60. Some less attractive traits than described by Bourke emerge in Crook's autobiography, cited in note 41, above. A balanced assessment is James T. King, "George Crook: Indian Fighter and Humanitarian," *Arizona and the West, 9* (1967), 333–48. There is yet no biography of Crook, although King is currently writing one. See, finally, the obituary in *Army and Navy Journal,* 27 (March 29, 1890), 582–83.

43. Crook, p. 144. Subsequent operations are recounted by Crook on pp. 144–59 and in SW, *Annual Report* (1867), pp. 77–79, 124–25, 129–30, 140–41; (1868), pp. 68–72, 770–72. See also Oliver Knight, *Following the Indian Wars: The Story of the Newspaper Correspondents among the Indian Campaigners* (Norman, Okla., 1960), pp. 32–57, for the war as viewed by Joe Wasson, correspondent for the *Owyhee Avalanche* of Silver City, Idaho.

44. "Chronological List of Actions," in Peters, pp. 4–9.

45. The council is described by Crook's aide, A. H. Nickerson, in an appendix to Crook's autobiography, pp. 307–9. See also SW, *Annual Report* (1868), p. 72.

46. SW, *Annual Report* (1867), p. 70; (1868), p. 44; Crook, p. 160.

47. Joseph P. Peters, "Uncle Sam's Icebox Soldiers: The U.S. Army in Alaska, 1867–1877," *New York Westerners Brand Book, 9* (1962), 49–50. Lloyd Lewis, *Sherman: Fighting Prophet,* pp. 348–49, characterizes Davis as "a shaggy-bearded Hoosier who, as the son of Kentucky Indian-fighters, had run away from home at sixteen to fight Mexicans and to enjoy it so thoroughly that he refused a West Point nomination in order to remain on the frontier. Continuing in the army, he had earned a commission and had aimed the first gun that answered Charlestonians from Fort Sumter. He had fought in all the Cumberlanders' battles, was reputedly the most talented swearer in the whole Federal force, believed in slavery, and was half admired, half feared, as the killer of the bullying General William Nelson at Louisville in September, 1862. Nelson had insulted him, and in the midst of a dispute studded with God-damn-you-sirs had been shot by Davis's pistol."

48. A wealth of authoritative detail about the Indians of Alaska and their condition at the time of U.S. acquisition is in a report by General Halleck's aide, Bvt. Lt. Col. Robert N. Scott, Nov. 12, 1867, CIA, *Annual Report* (1868), pp. 308–17; and a report by U.S. Special Indian Commissioner Vincent Colyer, November 1869, *ibid.* (1869), pp. 533–616.

49. Peters, pp. 52–53. SW, *Annual Report* (1868), pp. 744–45.

50. Annual report for 1869, SW, *Annual Report* (1869), p. 136.

51. Quoted by Vincent Colyer, CIA, *Annual Report* (1869), p. 538. Colyer, a bitter critic of the army's demoralizing influence on Indians throughout the West, found ample support for his thesis in Alaska, and his report dwells at length on the liquor problem.

52. Peters, p. 56. CIA, *Annual Report* (1869), pp. 586–87, 589.

53. Senate Ex. Docs., 41st Cong., 2d sess., No. 67.

54. Senate Ex. Docs., 41st Cong., 2d sess., No. 68. Vincent Colyer mobilized this testimony.

55. Peters, p. 57.

☆ TWELVE ☆

Grant's Peace Policy, 1869-74

THE ELECTION OF GENERAL GRANT TO THE PRESIDENCY in
November 1868 gave the army cause for optimism. So far as
he had concerned himself with Indians at all amid the political
turbulence of the years since the Civil War, Grant had supported
Sherman and the other generals in their advocacy of a forceful
Indian policy. He had also defended their actions against the
strident attacks of the civilian authorities and their friends in the
humanitarian community.

Civil-military friction had attained new intensity by the end of
1868. The army, disgusted over the failure of the peace commission of 1867, grew increasingly militant. The proliferating humanitarian groups, horrified by the bloodshed on the Plains in
1868, grew increasingly vocal in demanding reform. The civilians
charged the army with usurping civilian authority, with de-
bauching and demoralizing any Indians that came within range
of military influences, with provoking unnecessary wars, with
failing to discriminate between peaceful and hostile Indians, and
with slaughtering women and children. Military officers, in turn,
ascribed Indian troubles to the ignorance, incompetence, corruption, mismanagement, and rapid turnover of Indian Bureau personnel and accused humanitarians of pontificating on a subject
with which they had no first-hand experience. Both charge and
countercharge contained enough substance to suggest credibility
and enough exaggeration and fabrication to fuel further
controversy.

Army leaders continued to advocate a simple solution to the

problem: transfer the Indian Bureau back to the War Department, its home before the creation of the Department of the Interior in 1849. Such a transfer, they argued, would end the uncertainty and contention over the respective roles, responsibilities, and jurisdictions of the civil and military arms of the government. It would promote efficiency by placing the Indians in the custody of capable, honest, educated officers committed to the well-being of their charges but also able, as Sherman emphasized, to apply force promptly, vigorously, and without the circumlocution ordained by the system of divided responsibility.[1] It would promote economy by eliminating corrupt agents, abolishing a sprawling bureaucracy, and assigning procurement of Indian goods to the Quartermaster and Commissary Departments.

Opponents of the army rejected this reasoning. They, too, abhorred conflict of authority, but that could easily be remedied by subordinating military commanders to Indian agents. Transfer would not bring greater efficiency or economy either, enemies of the proposal contended. Above all, they ridiculed the notion of entrusting the moral, intellectual, and material improvement of the Indians to men trained for war and distinguished for neither moral nor intellectual superiority. As the Secretary of the Interior declared in 1868, "Our experience during the period when the Indians were under military care and guardianship affords no ground for hope that any benefit to them or the treasury would be secured."[2]

A transfer measure had carried in the House of Representatives early in 1867, in the aftermath of the Fetterman disaster, but was drowned in the Senate by the movement that led to the creation of the peace commission. The commission at first advocated a separate, cabinet-level Department of Indian Affairs, but in October 1868, following the Cheyenne uprising on the southern Plains, came out in favor of transfer. Grant had participated in this meeting and applauded the proposal (see pp. 138–39). In response, as soon as Congress convened in December 1868, the House again passed a transfer bill.

As Grant took office in March 1869, therefore, the generals thought they had gained a powerful new ally in the battle with the civilians. But President Grant was not General Grant, and to the surprise of army officers his administration proved receptive to the reform impulses emanating from humanitarian circles.

Although scarcely the author of the collection of measures that came to be labeled "Grant's Peace Policy," the President fostered the official climate in which they took shape and gained official adoption.[3]

The Peace Policy emphasized peace—"conquest by kindness"— and clearly contemplated continued civilian supremacy in the conduct of Indian affairs. Among its more prominent features were the nomination of agents and superintendents by church groups, a Board of Indian Commissioners composed of philan-thropists serving without pay to oversee the disbursement of Indian appropriations, and an end to the treaty system by which Indian tribes were viewed as "domestic dependent nations" with which the United States must negotiate.[4] All Indians were to be concentrated on reservations and there educated, Christianized, and helped toward agricultural self-support.

Despite this pacific emphasis, the Peace Policy, as originally conceived, contained much that military men could approve. Only the Central and Southern Superintendencies, embracing certain of the Plains tribes, were manned by church-nominated officials— all Quakers. Virtually all the remaining superintendents and agents were army officers detailed to the Indian Bureau. Moreover, while reservation management focused on pursuits of peace, the army had sole responsibility for all Indians off the reservation. Here seemed to be an objective basis for separating hostile from peaceful Indians and civil from military responsibilities. Thus, while not the exclusively military approach officers had hoped for, the Peace Policy offered the prospect of a combined approach in which the military role was influential and fairly clearly defined.[5] And, as a further encouragement, the transfer issue by no means expired with the birth of the Peace Policy. Although the bill passed by the House in December 1868 failed in the Senate, another gained momentum in the next Congress.

In the glow of civil-military harmony fostered by Grant's un-folding Indian policy, army and Indian Bureau officials reached a "perfect understanding," as Commissioner Eli Parker termed it, of their respective roles. Indian agents and military command-ers received the resulting instructions in the summer of 1869. The Indian Bureau had "exclusive control and jurisdiction" of all Indians on their reservation, the army of all Indians off their reservation. The army would not interfere with any Indians on their reservation unless invited by the agent or his superiors. The army would treat all Indians off their reservation as hostile.[6]

As both military and civil personnel in the field quickly perceived, the new policy declaration left some basic questions unanswered. How, for example, did it apply to Indians such as the Apaches of Arizona for whom no reservation system had been developed? When civil authority asked the army to intervene on a reservation, who was in charge, the agent or the military commander? How could the Indian be prevented from using a reservation as a sanctuary from which to raid neighboring settlements? And if the army was summoned, how did it distinguish guilty from innocent?

Before a rational attack on these questions could be devised, the application if not the theory of the Peace Policy underwent a fundamental modification. On January 23, 1870, Maj. Eugene M. Baker and two squadrons of the Second Cavalry attacked and all but obliterated a Piegan village on Montana's Marias River. Humanitarians branded the affair a deliberate and unprovoked massacre of peaceful Indians, women and children as well as men. Sherman and Sheridan defended Baker, pointing out that these Piegans were demonstrably guilty of depredations and that the casualty figures belied the charge of massacre. Of 173 killed, 120 were men and 53 were women and children, while 140 women and children were taken captive and later released. The army's protestations, however, were overwhelmed by columns of sensationalism that filled eastern newspapers, and Baker stood convicted by public opinion of unspeakable barbarism.[7]

The furore set off by the Baker affair doomed the army's prospects of playing a significant role in the execution of the Peace Policy. The first casualty was the transfer measure, which seemed near passage as a provision of the army appropriation bill. The second casualty was the network of army officers serving as Indian agents, destroyed by a section of the appropriation act prohibiting military officers from holding civil posts.[8] Although the Baker incident provided the rationale for this ban, truer motives sprang from congressional annoyance at the President for eliminating the vast patronage reservoir of the Indian Bureau's field service. The President's response, extending the practice of church nomination to the posts vacated by the army officers and to other denominations in addition to the Quakers, frustrated the intent of the congressional action. But also, combined with the defensive stance in which the Baker issue had placed the army, church domination of Indian management inevitably gave the Peace Policy a strongly antimilitary complexion.[9]

The generals labored to restore balance to Indian management. Military force, they argued, was as essential to control and civilization of the Indian as education, self-support, and other techniques. Moral suasion could not alone bend "wild savages" to the will of the government. In three testing grounds of the early 1870s, application of Peace Policy precepts appeared to confirm the army point of view. In Arizona, in northern California, and in Indian Territory, the army saw its opinion prevail and the Peace Policy broadened to include the element of force that its framers had intended.

War Department orders of April 15, 1870, established Arizona as a full department in the Division of the Pacific. No longer would troops in Arizona receive direction from a general in San Francisco with whom it took three months to communicate. Although New Mexico remained a district in General Pope's Department of the Missouri, the army had at last acknowledged the magnitude of the Apache problem and taken a step essential to dealing with it effectively.[10] The first commanding general, Bvt. Maj. Gen. George Stoneman, colonel of the Twenty-first Infantry, threw away part of the organizational gain by establishing his headquarters at remote Drum Barracks on the southern California coast. He tried to adapt the Peace Policy to Arizona by instituting a network of "feeding stations" for Apaches who renounced raiding and by campaigning against those who did not. Stoneman's policies, however, accomplished little more than to set himself up as a target for the scurrilous abuse at which Arizona editors and political leaders were so proficient.[11]

One of Stoneman's feeding stations was at Camp Grant, a desolate post on the lower San Pedro River. Here Lt. Royal E. Whitman of the Third Cavalry earned the trust and affection of a growing band of Aravaipa and Pinal Apaches under Eskiminzin. But depredations continued, and nothing could convince Arizona's long-suffering populace that sanctuaries such as Camp Grant did not harbor the offenders. At dawn on April 30, 1871, a force of 148 Tucson citizens—Papago Indians, Mexicans, and white

Americans—fell on the sleeping Apache rancheria at Camp Grant. In a half-hour of savage slaughter, rape, and mutilation, they wiped out its inhabitants and carried off 29 children into slavery. Accounts differ on the number killed—as few as 86, or as many as 150. There is no disagreement that most were women and children.[12]

Applauded by frontiersmen, the Camp Grant Massacre appalled Easterners. President Grant threatened to clamp martial law on the Territory if the culprits were not tried. One result was to speed efforts to extend the Peace Policy to the Apaches. In July 1871 Vincent Colyer, secretary of the Board of Indian Commissioners and a humanitarian with impeccable credentials, set forth for the Southwest clothed with presidential authority to make peace with the Apaches and establish reservations for their control and civilization. Another result was the relief of General Stoneman. This was engineered by Arizona's Gov. Anson P. K. Safford, who also persuaded President Grant, over the objections of General Sherman and Secretary of War Belknap, to ignore the claims of forty colonels of the line and award the coveted departmental command to a mere lieutenant colonel. Thus did George Crook, fresh from his triumphs over the Paiutes, transfer from Oregon to Arizona.[13]

Reaching Arizona early in June 1871, Crook lost no time in touring his command and taking the measure of his adversary. The Apaches would have to be soundly thrashed, he concluded, before a lasting peace could be arranged. At this juncture, early in September, Vincent Colyer arrived in Arizona. Crook suspended operations as an enraged populace watched "Vincent the Good" try to "mesmerize the Apaches into peace." As a result of Colyer's labors, however, Apache and Yavapai bands began to gather on a series of temporary reservations he established at various military posts.[14]

Despite this rudimentary reservation system, murder and robbery continued. Crook gave the Indians until February 15, 1872, to report to an agency. But once more a peace emissary materialized. At the President's request, Brig. Gen. Oliver O. Howard, head of the Freedman's Bureau since 1866, turned his keen humanitarian instincts from black man to red. During April and May the one-armed, Bible-quoting general traced much the same steps as Colyer, made some revisions in Colyer's reservations, and induced more Indians to come to the agencies.[15] He failed, however, in a major purpose—to make peace with Cochise. This able Chiricahua leader had attained almost legendary stature in the decade since an army lieutenant with more zeal than judgment provoked him to a destructive and unremitting hostility.[16] No peace that failed to include Cochise could be successful.

In the autumn of 1872, therefore, Howard returned to complete his mission. He persuaded a white frontiersman, Thomas J. Jeffords, who had long been a friend of Cochise, to guide him to the elusive chieftain. Cochise had been signaling a desire to make peace for more than a year, and in fact he had spent the winter of 1871–72 on the Cañada Alamosa Reservation in New Mexico. Thus, Howard's daring in going all but unescorted into Cochise's Stronghold in the Dragoon Mountains assumes less importance than the negotiations—and concessions—that eventuated in peace. The journey and confrontation form an adventure of high drama which Howard fully exploited in his memoirs. His agreement with Cochise seems not to have been committed to writing. Apparently it was simply that the Chiricahuas could have a reservation in the familiar haunts of the Chiricahua Mountains, with Tom Jeffords as their agent. Imperfect and transitory as this settlement proved, the fact remains that Howard ended the Cochise wars.[17]

For more than a year, none too patiently, Crook had held his troops in check. Twice he had been forced to cancel offensive operations. Privately contemptuous of both Colyer and Howard, he had, nonetheless, treated them courteously and hospitably and had given them ample opportunity to test their methods.[18] Between them, Colyer and Howard had established a reservation system for the Apaches—Tularosa, New Mexico, for the Southern Apaches (Warm Springs, Mimbres, Mogollon, Copper Mine); the Chiricahua Reserve near Fort Bowie for Cohise's people; San Carlos, on the middle Gila River, replacing Camp Grant as a reservation for the Aravaipas, Pinals, and part of the Coyoteros; and reserves at Camps Verde and Date Creek for the Yavapais. More than 5,000 Apaches and Yavapais had professed peace and had begun to draw rations on these reservations.[19]

But the peace emissaries had not brought peace. Between September 1871 and September 1872, Apaches and Yavapais perpetrated 54 officially verified raids that took the lives of 44 people,

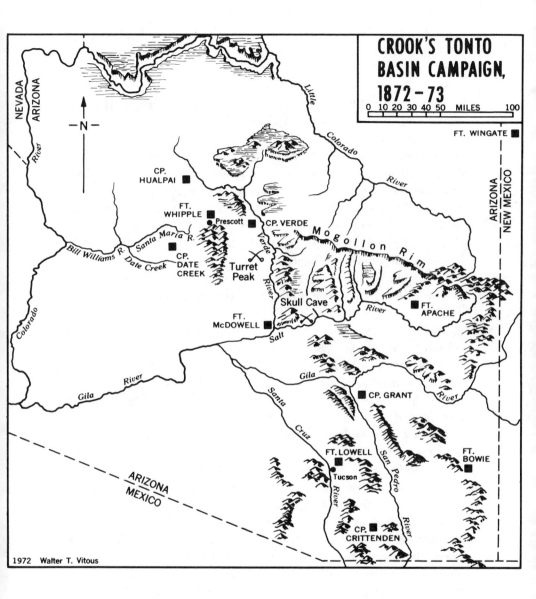

CROOK'S TONTO
BASIN CAMPAIGN,
1872-73

0 10 20 30 40 50 MILES   100

NEVADA
ARIZONA

— N —

Colorado River

FT. WINGATE

ARIZONA
NEW MEXICO

CP. HUALPAI

Little

Colorado River

FT. WHIPPLE

•Prescott

CP. VERDE

Mogollon Rim

Santa Maria R.

Bill Williams R.

Date Creek

CP. DATE CREEK

Turret Peak

Verde River

Skull Cave

FT. APACHE

Colorado

FT. McDOWELL

Salt

River

Gila River

Gila

River

CP. GRANT

Gila River

Santa Cruz

FT. LOWELL

•Tucson

San Pedro River

FT. BOWIE

ARIZONA
MEXICO

Santa Cruz River

CP. CRITTENDEN

1972   Walter T. Vitous

wounded 16, and recorded a loss of more than 500 head of stock. Although some of the newly settled reservation Indians acted in good faith and genuinely wanted peace, others participated in these raids. As usual, there was no effective way to distinguish between the two. Furious citizens excoriated Colyer and Howard, threatened the reservation Indians with another Camp Grant Massacre, and demanded that Crook be unleashed.[20] Even the Indian Bureau now admitted the need for force—not war, declared Commissioner of Indian Affairs Francis A. Walker, but discipline, as contemplated by the Peace Policy.[21] By whatever nomenclature, Crook's offensive of 1872–73 stands as one of the most brilliant and successful ever mounted against Indians.

Three factors, all tested in the Paiute operations in Oregon and Idaho, awarded Crook success. First, he made extensive use of Indian against Indian. Second, he developed his mule trains to peak efficiency, allowing him superlative mobility. And third, he gave the troops morale, confidence, energy, and determination unknown in Arizona under previous regimes. He inculcated in officers and men a precept fundamental to success: "The trail must be stuck to and never lost." As his aide recalled it, "No excuse was to be accepted for leaving a trail; if horses played out, the enemy must be followed on foot, and no sacrifice should be left untried to make the campaign short, sharp, and decisive."[22]

Crook's strategy called for a winter campaign. In winter food was harder to come by, and the enemy could choose between comfortless security in the cold, snowy high country or insecurity in the congenial lower elevations. Camps Verde, McDowell, Grant, and Apache defined a rough semicircle within which lay the precipitous Mogollon Rim and, falling away from the rim to the head of Tonto Creek, the rugged Tonto Basin. By fielding from these posts nine troop-strength commands of the First and Fifth Cavalry, each accompanied by a detachment of Indian scouts, Crook hoped to clear the country, along and outside the semicircle, of roving Apache and Yavapai bands, drive them into the Tonto Basin, then concentrate there for the kill.[23]

The campaign began on November 15. Led by the Indian scouts, the columns unerringly sought out the quarry and kept them moving. Often in their haste the Indians left food and other possessions to be destroyed. Sometimes they dropped their guard and let themselves be surprised. In some 20 actions during the winter, the troops killed almost 200 Indians. Accounting for 76 of the dead, the Battle of Skull Cave, on December 28, 1872, was the most spectacular and, for the Indians, the most demoralizing. A command under Capts. William H. Brown and James Burns trapped about 100 Yavapais in a shallow cave high on the wall of Salt River Canyon. Bullets ricocheted from the sloping roof and boulders dropped from above filled the cave with deadly missiles and all but annihilated the defenders.

Throughout the winter the scouting commands combed the Tonto Basin and its bordering mountains, the Mazatzals, the Sierra Ancha, and the Superstitions. It was the most punishing kind of soldiering, subjecting the troops to prolonged fatigue, hardships, and privations, and to extremes of climate and topography unmatched in the West. But it paid off in declining enemy morale. On March 27, 1873, a column led by Capt. George M. Randall, Twenty-third Infantry, surprised a rancheria on the top of Turret Peak, south of Camp Verde. Like the occupants of Skull Cave, those on Turret Peak considered themselves secure. Twenty-three died in Randall's charge.

Turret Peak broke Indian resistance. Groups of Apaches and Yavapais began to drift into the agencies to give up. On April 6, 1873, at Camp Verde, Crook met with Chalipun. He had 300 Yavapais with him and was said to represent 2,300. His speech of surrender, as summarized by Lt. John G. Bourke, explains why Crook won the Tonto Basin War:

. . . General Crook had too many cartridges of copper (*demasiadas cartuchos de cobre*). They had never been afraid of the Americans alone, but now that their own people were fighting against them they did not know what to do; they could not go to sleep at night, because they feared to be surrounded before daybreak; they could not hunt— the noise of their guns would attract the troops; they could not cook mescal or anything else, because the flame and smoke would draw down the soldiers; they could not live in the valley—there were too many soldiers; they had retreated to the mountain tops, thinking to hide in the snow until the soldiers went home, but the scouts found them out and the soldiers followed them. They wanted to make peace, and to be at terms of good-will with the whites.[24]

By the autumn of 1873 the Indian Bureau listed more than 6,000 Apaches and Yavapais enrolled at Camp Verde, Fort Apache, Fort

Bowie, and San Carlos in Arizona, and at Tularosa in New Mexico.[25]

In the Tonto Basin campaign, the militant aspects of the Peace Policy were decisively invoked, to the satisfaction of military and civil authorities alike. As an exercise in guerrilla operations against an unconventional foe, it had been classic in conception, almost flawless in execution, and decisive in results. For several years, under Crook's paternal eye and firm hand, the Apaches and Yavapais managed to live on the reservations in a condition of relative quiet that, however uncertain and potentially explosive, gave Arizona a period of unprecedented tranquility.

In October 1873 the military telegraph reached Prescott and Fort Whipple, Crooks' headquarters, from Fort Yuma, thus placing the Department of Arizona in close communication with higher headquarters. The first message clicked over the wire brought word of the promotion, in recognition of the Tonto Basin triumph, of Lieutenant Colonel Crook to brigadier general. In an era of rigid seniority, the President could pay no higher tribute or grant no greater reward than to jump an officer over so many seniors. The promotion outraged the officers thus ranked and left a legacy of rancor against Crook that persisted for years. But no officer deserved the honor more. None had studied and come to understand the nature of Indian warfare better. None had practiced it with greater skill.

The brigadier's billet awarded to Crook had been vacated the preceding spring by Edward R. S. Canby, commanding general of the Department of the Columbia. Assassinated by Modocs during a peace conference in California's lava beds, he became the first and only general officer of regular rank to lose his life in Indian warfare. A spare, beardless veteran of thirty-four years, Canby was well known to the public as a distinguished Civil War general and to the army as a kindly, courteous, accommodating gentleman with a wide circle of friends. His brutal murder, treacherously conceived and executed, electrified the nation and dealt a shattering blow to the Peace Policy.

Crook's victory over the Paiutes in 1867–68 had ended Indian hostilities in the lake-dotted, lava-scored plateaus of southern Oregon and northeastern California. Relations with the Modocs, however, continued ominous. Numbering between 400 and 800, these tough, warlike people claimed as their traditional homeland the country around Lost River and Lower Klamath, Tule, and Clear Lakes, along the California-Oregon boundary. In the 1850s and early 1860s the Modocs had frequently attacked travelers passing through their domain. But they had also cultivated close commercial relations with the miners at Yreka, some fifty miles to the west, who gave them the colorful names by which they are known in the white man's history. Thus did Kintpuash become Captain Jack. An able and ambitious young leader, Jack commanded the allegiance of the tribe's militant faction.

Captain Jack and his followers resisted the government's effort to bring the Modocs, Klamaths, and Snakes into treaty relations with the United States. Reluctantly he allowed himself to be pressed into signing the Treaty of 1864, by which these tribes ceded their lands and agreed to settle on a reservation in the Klamath country. Homesick, bullied by the more numerous Klamaths, the Modocs found no contentment on the reservation. Besides, the government delayed ratification of the treaty until 1869. In 1865 Captain Jack took his band back to Lost River. Here they remained while their homeland began to fill with settlers. In December 1869 Superintendent of Indian Affairs Alfred B. Meacham persuaded Jack to return to the reservation. But after a stormy three months, Jack and some sixty to seventy men with their families were back once more on Lost River, and his white neighbors grew more and more vocal in demanding his removal.

Both Meacham and his successor, Thomas B. Odeneal, favored forcible removal to the Klamath Reservation. The department commander, General Canby, refused to provide troops for such an undertaking while the permanent location of the Indians remained to be officially fixed.[26] In July 1872, however, the Indian Bureau accepted Odeneal's recommendation. Canby then authorized his subordinates at Camp Warner and Fort Klamath to help carry out the decision.[27]

These subordinates were Lt. Col. Frank Wheaton, Twenty-first Infantry, commanding the District of the Lakes at Camp Warner, and Maj. John ("Uncle Johnny") Green, First Cavalry, at Fort Klamath, the post closest to the Modoc camps on Lost River. Canby cautioned them that if troops had to be used "the force employed should be so large as to secure the result at once and

beyond peradventure." Not until November 1872 did Superintendent Odeneal decide to move against Jack. And then he acted
suddenly, requesting troops from Major Green "at once." Green
complied by ordering Capt. James Jackson and Troop B, First
Cavalry, three officers and forty enlisted men, to carry out the
superintendent's wishes.

Blame for what followed may be widely apportioned. Superintendent Odeneal promoted the decision to move Jack without
understanding the strength of his resolve not to move and without
giving serious enough consideration to alternative solutions that
might have proved feasible. Both Canby and Green accepted
Odeneal's judgments uncritically and surrendered the initiative to
him. A conspicuous characteristic of Canby was his reverence for
constituted authority. Always he strove to carry out the spirit as
well as the letter of decisions handed down from above. In his
mind Odeneal's July directive from the Commissioner of Indian
Affairs represented such a decision. Actually, it was only the Commissioner's ratification of Odeneal's decision. An officer more
jealous of his prerogatives or more sensitive to the historic rivalry
between the Indian Bureau and the army would not have acquiesced so easily. At least he would have taken the precaution
of arming himself with instructions from his own superiors. And
given the explosive potential of the situation, he would surely also
have kept closer control of his subordinates. Both General Schofield, Canby's immediate superior, and General Sherman later
implied as much.[28] Similarly, on the tactical level, Major Green
let himself be stampeded by Odeneal into acting without careful
planning, without consulting with Wheaton, without alerting
white settlers who might suffer from a misfire, and above all, without the force that might have "secured the result at once and
beyond peradventure."

At dawn on November 29 Jackson's command deployed at the
edge of Jack's camp, containing about seventeen families, on the
west bank of Lost River. The Indians met Jackson's demand for
their arms with animated derision. Firing erupted on both sides
at about the same time. After half an hour the Indians fled. Jackson reported killing "not less than sixteen" of "the worst men
among them." Actually, he killed only one and wounded another.
He lost one soldier killed and seven wounded, one of whom later
died. At the same time, across the river, a handful of ranchers

tried to seize Hooker Jim's people, about fourteen men and their families, but were thrown back and forced to take refuge in Dennis Crawley's cabin. Two of the civilians were killed and one wounded. The people from Captain Jack's village escaped by boat across Tule Lake. Those from Hooker Jim's village rode around the east side of the lake, slaughtering at least fourteen settlers along the way. South of the lake the two groups united in the natural fortress that would soon become known as "Captain Jack's Stronghold."[29]

Military officers likened the Stronghold to an ocean surf frozen into black rock. Wave after wave of jagged lava rolled over the plain south of Tule Lake. Nature had erected a gigantic fortress, complete with bastions, towers, breastworks, parapets, and bomb shelters. The Modocs knew every fissure, cavern, and passageway. They skillfully piled up rocks to give further strength to the defenses. Patches of grass afforded pasturage for the herd of cattle the defenders brought in. Sage brush and greasewood yielded fuel. Only water was lacking, and this the Modocs secured from Tule Lake.

Major Green took the field immediately after the Battle of Lost River. Colonel Wheaton came down from Camp Warner and assumed command on December 21. Reinforcements from Warner, Harney, Bidwell, and Vancouver brought the force to about 225 Regulars of the First Cavalry and Twenty-first Infantry. In addition, two companies of Oregon militia and one from California, slightly more than 100 men, joined the Regulars. Wheaton estimated enemy strength at 150 warriors. Actually, the lava beds never held more than 60 fighting men.[30]

On the night of January 16, 1873, concealed by darkness, Wheaton moved his men into the fringes of the lava flow, Major Green on the west, Capt. Reuben F. Bernard on the east. During the night a dense fog settled on the lava beds. At dawn the skirmish lines advanced through the murk as two twelve-pounder mountain howitzers dropped shells in front of them. The fog, shrouding the target area, made the artillery fire more dangerous to friend than foe, and it was silenced. Falling slowly back on both sides, the Modocs kept the troops under a heavy, accurate rifle fire. Both Green and Bernard came to chasms that their men considered suicidal to cross. The advance halted. The plan had been for the two attack groups to reach around the Stronghold on

the south, thus preventing the quarry from pulling off in that
direction. Thwarted in this intent, Green and Bernard tried to
unite their flanks on the north, along the boulder-strewn lake
shore. As this movement neared completion, in late afternoon, the
fog dissipated and placed the troops under the very muzzles of the
Modoc rifles. Pinned down among the rocks, the soldiers remained
there until darkness enabled them to withdraw.

The Battle of the Stronghold cost Wheaton seven Regulars
killed and nineteen wounded, two Volunteers killed and nine
wounded, two mortally. No Modoc had been hit by military fire;
none, indeed, had even been seen by the attackers. Worse than the
casualties, the day's ordeal had demoralized Wheaton's men. The
Volunteers went home. The Regulars settled down in cheerless
winter bivouacs, made the more uncomfortable by a late January
snowfall, while proponents of gentler methods had their day.

Former Indian Superintendent Alfred Meacham and other
prominent Oregonians had gone to the national capital in January
as members of the Electoral College to certify Grant's election to a
second term in the White House. While there they persuaded
Secretary of the Interior Columbus Delano that peace emissaries
might coax Jack out of the Stronghold more easily than the army
could blast him out. The President, the credibility of his Peace
Policy undermined by the stream of bad news from California
and elsewhere, approved, and named Meacham to head a Modoc
peace commission. During a month of inconclusive negotiations,
the commissioners demonstrated their unfitness for the mission.
Late in March, therefore, Secretary Delano gave General Canby
full authority over a reconstituted commission. "This actually de-
volves on you the entire management of the Modoc question," General Sherman advised his subordinate on March 24.

The Modocs had proved as elusive and frustrating in negotiations as in battle. One day they seemed willing to surrender; the
next they could not even be brought to talk. This reflected a confidence born of military victory, but also a rising dissension within
their ranks. Some wanted to surrender, others to fight on, still
others to seek favorable peace terms. Jack emerged as a moderate.
But an aggressive war faction led by Curley Headed Doctor, a
shaman, severely limited Jack's freedom to pursue negotiations
without imperiling his own authority. Factionalism verging on
violence split the Modoc leadership.

In hopes of fortifying the peace party and hastening meaningful negotiations, Canby stepped up the pace of military activity. Col. Alvin C. Gillem, First Cavalry, had succeeded Wheaton and had been heavily reinforced.[31] Bivouacs were pushed closer to the enemy and forward observation posts established. Patrols probed the edges of the lava beds. Colonel Gillem moved his headquarters and base camp to the southwestern shore of Tule Lake, scarcely three miles from the Stronghold. This pressure appeared to bring results, for early in April 1873 Jack and his lieutenants began direct discussions with the peace commission. The meetings took place at a point midway between the Stronghold and Gillem's camp. A lone tent was erected to provide shelter from sudden spring storms. Jack demanded a reservation on Lost River and amnesty for his people. Canby could only insist on unconditional surrender to the army as prisoners of war.

Canby's "compression" policy had still another effect. It agitated the factionalism among the Indians and made their temper and behavior all the more erractic and unpredictable. The militants began to discuss the possibility of killing the peace commissioners. Jack resisted this talk as far as he dared. But in a dramatic confrontation with the militants he was held up to a ridicule so humiliating that he agreed to take the lead in carrying out the plan.

Toby Riddle, Modoc wife of Canby's interpreter, learned of the plot and warned the commissioners of impending treachery. Canby could not believe the Modocs would attempt such a foolhardy act. Meacham and Commissioner L. S. Dyar thought otherwise. The remaining commissioner, Rev. Eleasar Thomas, a fundamentalist Methodist cleric, left the matter up to God, although Meacham wryly pointed out that God had not been in the Modoc camp all winter. On Good Friday, April 11, Canby donned his dress uniform and led the commission and its two interpreters to the council site. In the midst of the talks, Jack suddenly drew a pistol from beneath his coat and shot Canby full in the face. Other Indians attacked Meacham, Thomas, and Dyar. The Riddles and Dyar made good their escape. Shot, stabbed, and stripped, Canby, Meacham, and Thomas were left on the ground near the peace tent. Miraculously, Meacham still lived. Ultimately he recovered.

The death of the respected and well-liked Canby stunned the nation and enraged the army. "Any measure of severity to the savages will be sustained," Sherman wired General Schofield.[32]

War Department orders of April 14 named as Canby's successor hard-bitten Jefferson C. Davis, colonel of the Twenty-third Infantry and brevet major general. While he traveled from his Indiana home, Colonel Gillem took the offensive.

Gillem's assault plan almost duplicated Wheaton's. This time, however, the force was larger and no fog obscured vision. For three days, April 15 through 17, the two attacking formations worked their way slowly and undramatically into the heart of the lava beds. Indian and soldier exchanged sniping fire as the one fell back before the other's advance. At night the howitzers and four mortars bombarded the enemy positions. The third day's advance disclosed that the Modocs had abandoned the Stronghold, leaving behind the bodies of three men and eight women.

The Modocs had merely retreated into the lava beds farther south. On April 26 Gillem threw out a reconnaissance in force—five officers and fifty-nine enlisted men under Capt. Evan Thomas —to scout the new Modoc positions. Resting in the shadow of a sandy butte four miles to the south, they were ambushed by stealthy warriors. Half the command panicked. The rest stood with their officers in a valiant, disorganized defense. All five officers and twenty enlisted men perished; sixteen were wounded.[33]

Again disaster had struck. Again morale plummeted. Reaching Gillem's camp on May 2, General Davis discovered "a very perceptible feeling of despondency pervading the entire command." The Thomas disaster, he advised General Schofield, showed that "a great many of the enlisted men here are utterly unfit for Indian fighting of this kind, being only cowardly beef eaters."[34] By mid-May, however, Davis had been further strengthened and, according to the *Army and Navy Journal*, had "infused new life into a command demoralized by mismanagement."[35] On May 14 his battalions closed around the new Modoc defenses. They were empty. The war had suddenly become fluid; needed now were mobile cavalry columns to give pursuit.[36]

The Indians had abandoned the lava beds following another quarrel. Hooker Jim, Curley Headed Doctor, Bogus Charley, and others of the militants who had prodded Jack into assassinating the peace commissioners now began to lose heart. Water was scarce, and an attack on a military camp at Dry Lake on May 10 had gone badly. Hooker Jim and thirteen men, with their families, deserted Jack and headed west. On May 18, in the mountains south of Lower Klamath Lake, they ran into a mounted squadron under Capt. Henry C. Hasbrouck and sustained several casualties before scattering. Four days later they surrendered to General Davis.

Hooker Jim, characterized by Davis as "an unmitigated cutthroat" with "well-earned claims to the halter,"[37] volunteered to help catch Captain Jack. Such an opportunity was not to be scorned, and Davis authorized Hooker Jim, Bogus Charley, Steamboat Frank, and Shacknasty Jim to draw arms and rations and search out Jack. The defectors guessed correctly that the quarry would be found on Willow Creek, an affluent of Lost River east of Clear Lake. On May 28 Hooker Jim's party confronted Jack and urged him to surrender. Tired, hungry, and destitute, Jack's followers, thirty-seven men and their families, seemed willing. But Jack himself knew that surrender meant death. Angrily he ordered the traitors to go back and live with the white people. Meanwhile, Major Green pushed the cavalry forward in two squadrons under Hasbrouck and Jackson. On May 29 they surprised Jack's camp. The occupants scattered. For the next four days, Davis later wrote, "the pursuit . . . partook more of a chase after wild beasts than war."[38] Singly, in pairs, and in family groups, Jack's Modocs surrendered to the cavalry units scouring Willow Creek and the vicinity. On June 3 Capt. David Perry found Jack and his family hiding in a cave and persuaded him to give up. His "legs had given out," Jack explained.[39]

This outcome of the long and dismal Modoc War displeased General Sherman. "Davis should have killed every Modoc before taking him if possible," he wrote Sheridan on June 6; "then there would have been no complications."[40] Now he believed the proper course was to try Jack and the others involved in Canby's murder by military court, to turn over Hooker Jim and the men who killed the settlers after the Lost River fight to the state courts, and to send the rest east and distribute them among other reservations, "so that the name of Modoc should cease." He implored the Secretary of War for a swift decision, "before some Indian agent makes a fatal promise," and he directed Schofield to insure that the prisoners were held closely pending further orders.[41]

Ironically, these instructions reached Davis just in time to avert summary execution of Captain Jack and others. A scaffold had already been erected. Finally, a week later, Davis received authority

to bring the slayers of Canby and Thomas before a military commission. The panel of officers sat from July 1 to 9 taking evidence
against the six who were charged.[42] There was never much doubt
of the verdict or the sentence. President Grant commuted the sentence of two to life imprisonment. The other four were hanged at
Fort Klamath on October 3, 1873, and their heads shipped to the
Army Medical Museum in Washington. Because of their services
to the army, Hooker Jim and his cohorts escaped punishment for
the Tule Lake killings. During October the prisoners, 155 in number, were escorted to Indian Territory and settled on a small patch
of ground near the Quapaws. The name Modoc did not at once
cease to exist, but it no longer offered any obstacle to the settlement of the Modoc homeland.

The Modoc War bathed none of its participants in glory, or even
credit. The settlers who demanded Jack's removal could claim
little genuine provocation. The Indian Bureau, especially Superintendent Odeneal, displayed little insight into the problem and no
imagination in seeking alternatives to a confrontation over removal. General Canby and his subordinates allowed Odeneal to
lead them into a war they might have prevented. The army made
a mess of almost everything it attempted. Commanders quarreled
or simply did not cooperate; underestimated, then overestimated
the enemy; hesitated when they should have acted, acted when
they should have hesitated. Enlisted men proved too easily panicked, repulsed, and demoralized. In the end, Modoc defectors provided the key to military "victory." Even the Modocs, although
they battled with admirable courage, tenacity, and skill against
great odds, seemed driven to a treachery that doomed them.
Against the peace commission it was a blunder that destroyed all
hope of compromise; among themselves it was suicidal.

The Modoc War—more accurately, the slaying of Canby and
Thomas in the midst of a peace conference—did more to discredit
Grant's Peace Policy than any other influence before the Custer
disaster three years later. Newspapers across the land saw in it
spectacular evidence that Indians could not be trusted or reasoned
with. Whether editors called for extermination or moderation, all
judged Canby's death a grievous blow to the Peace Policy.[43] And
the saying made it so, even though the Modoc War actually taught
very few lessons about the efficacy of the Peace Policy. More rele-
vant to the debate, more sharply defining the real issues, were

events occurring simultaneously in Indian Territory. Here the "Fort Sill Sanctuary" had come to symbolize all that the army condemned in the Peace Policy. Here the army finally won a fundamental modification in its application.

As part of President Grant's program of purifying the Indian Service by enlisting the churches to nominate Indian agents, the Central Superintendency—Kansas and Indian Territory—fell to the Society of Friends. In the summer of 1869 Quaker agents, pacifists by religious conviction, took charge of some of the most warlike Indians on the continent. Lawrie Tatum, a balding, big-framed Iowa farmer of great courage and tenacity, was appointed to the Kiowas and Comanches. Elderly Brinton Darlington received the Cheyenne and Arapaho Agency, to be succeeded after his death in 1872 by John D. Miles, an energetic and able executive. Overseeing these agents from offices in Lawrence, Kansas, were Superintendent Enoch Hoag, a pious visionary, and his chief clerk, Cyrus Beede, whom General Sheridan characterized as "a little too simple for this earth."[44] Honesty, trust, generosity, forebearance, and persuasion were Quaker tools in the task of transforming the plains nomads into self-supporting Christian farmers.[45]

Except for the Kwahadi Comanches out on the Staked Plains, most of the Kiowa and Comanche bands regularly drew rations and other annuity goods at the Fort Sill agency. With almost equal regularity they scourged Texas frontier settlements all the way to the Rio Grande and even probed deep into Mexico. The Cheyennes and Arapahoes also preferred to roam unmolested. They too drew food and presents at their agency, relocated in 1870 from Camp Supply to a new site 100 miles down the North Canadian, but generally ranged to the west. A few Cheyennes joined in the Texas raids, but for the most part the tribe resisted the repeated invitations to make common cause with the Kiowas and Comanches against the whites. Instead, the Cheyennes fell tragic prey to impoverishment and debauchery, visited by whiskey sellers swarming across the Kansas border.

Under the Peace Policy, troops in Texas could attack raiders in Texas but could not cross Red River into the reservation. Likewise, the big garrison at Fort Sill could act only on application of the agent—one whose religious scruples enjoined nonviolence. Truly, as Texans charged, Fort Sill became a "city of refuge,"

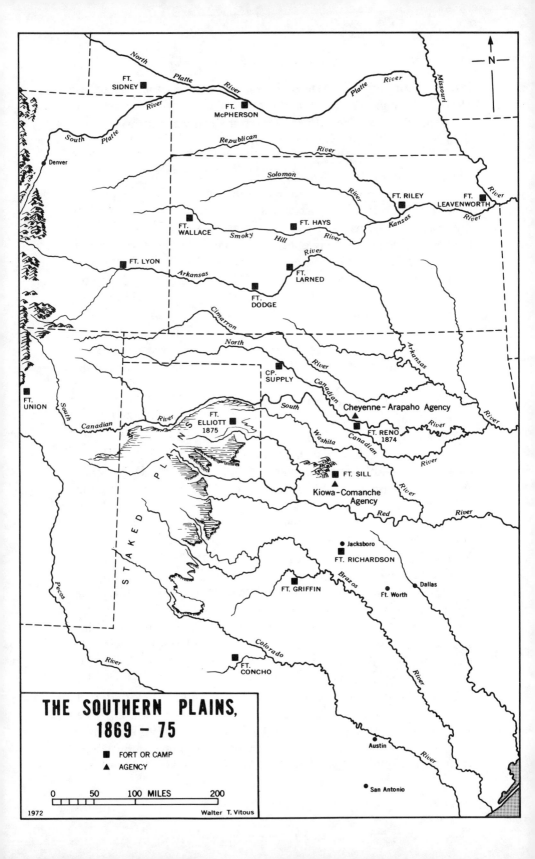

THE SOUTHERN PLAINS, 1869 – 75

■ FORT OR CAMP

▲ AGENCY

0   50   100 MILES   200

1972   Walter T. Vitous

where warriors received government supplies and protection while resting between raids. The pattern was clear, even to Tatum, but its dimensions were open to debate: Were Texans exaggerating the menace? Were the Staked Plains Kwahadis the principal culprits? Could the reservation Indians who were guilty be more effectively influenced by nonviolent techniques than by armed force?

Fort Sill's commander shared Tatum's optimism and gave him hearty support. Benjamin H. Grierson, the tall, heavily bearded colonel of the Tenth Cavalry, treated the Indians as kindly and as tolerantly as he did the black troopers of his regiment. He espoused the Peace Policy, and he worked closely with Tatum to make it succeed with the Kiowas and Comanches. Not surprisingly, many officers regarded Grierson as a traitor to the army; some even gave credence to the charges of Texas editors that he and Tatum were providing arms to the raiders and winking at their bloody forays into Texas.[46]

The year 1871 produced important changes in the Texas military system. The Fourth Cavalry replaced the lethargic Sixth, and its hard-hitting young colonel took station at Fort Richardson. Although only thirty-one in 1871, Ranald S. Mackenzie boasted a brilliant war record and qualities that led Grant to pronounce him "the most promising young officer in the army."[47] Tireless, highstrung, irascible from wounds and exposure, a harsh disciplinarian, Mackenzie whipped the Fourth into the best cavalry regiment in the army.[48] Sherman took further steps to bolster the defenses by assigning General Augur to command the Department of Texas and by making it part of Sheridan's Division of the Missouri and extending its authority over Fort Sill.[49]

Sherman took these actions following an eye-opening inspection of the Texas frontier forts in May 1871. He had never believed that Indian depredations were as bad as Texans portrayed them, and indeed he saw no evidence of their claims throughout most of the trip. On May 18, he and his small escort crossed Salt Creek Prairie, about eight miles west of Fort Richardson, under the very eyes of a big Kiowa raiding party lurking in ambush. The Indians numbered about 100, including such noted war leaders as Satanta, Satank, Big Tree, Eagle Heart, and Big Bow. Only the medicine man Mamanti's prediction of still richer prey saved Sherman and Insp. Gen. Randolph B. Marcy from death. That night a badly

wounded teamster staggered into Fort Richardson, where Sherman
and Mackenzie had spent the evening listening to the complaints
of a delegation of citizens from nearby Jacksboro. He told of the
massacre on Salt Creek Prairie of a train of ten wagons manned
by twelve teamsters. Four had escaped, but the rest had been
butchered, the wagons burned, and forty-one mules stolen. Now
convinced of the validity of the Texan appeals, Sherman launched
Mackenzie in pursuit of the raiders and himself grimly headed
for Fort Sill.

At Fort Sill Sherman found Tatum wavering in his dedication
to nonviolence. It gave way altogether on May 27, when the
Kiowas came in for rations. Satanta boasted to Tatum of his part
in the Salt Creek affair and demanded arms and ammunition for
further raids. At once the agent sent a note to Colonel Grierson
asking for the arrest of Satanta and others he had named. In a
tense confrontation on the porch of the commanding officer's quarters, Sherman and Grierson faced Satanta, Kicking Bird, Lone
Wolf, and other Kiowa chiefs. When Satanta repeated his boast,
Sherman ordered him, along with Satank and Big Tree, placed
under arrest for trial in the Texas state courts. Satanta threw off
his blanket and grasped his revolver. Others drew weapons. Sherman signaled. The shutters covering the front windows banged
open to reveal a phalanx of black troopers with carbines leveled.
The Indians subsided. Later in the conference, as tempers flared
again, Stumbling Bear fitted an arrow to his bow and let fly at
Sherman. Another Indian struck Stumbling Bear's arm and ruined
his aim. At the same time, Lone Wolf leveled his rifle at Sherman.
Grierson jumped on the chief and they sprawled on the floor. This
crisis also passed without bloodshed, and the three war leaders
were lodged in a cell to await deportation.

Sherman left Fort Sill on May 30. Mackenzie's column, worn
out in a fruitless chase through rain and mud, rode in on June 4.
Four days later they left for Fort Richardson, escorting the three
chiefs, heavily chained and closely guarded. Singing his death
song, old Satank managed to shuck off his manacles and attack
his guard. He was shot and killed. In Jacksboro a cowboy jury
duly pronounced the other two guilty of murder. In the belief that
they would exert more restraint on their people alive than dead,
Gov. Edmund J. Davis commuted their sentence from death to

life imprisonment. Satanta and Big Tree entered the state penitentiary at Huntsville.⁵⁰

Although widely heralded as a new dimension of the Peace Policy, the Jacksboro affair was actually an aberration brought about by an unusual combination of persons and circumstances. The Indians were not likely again to offer such indisputable proof of individual guilt as Satanta's boastful confession, nor place themselves in so vulnerable a position as Grierson's front porch. Jacksboro did not change the ground rules of army employment. It did not stop the raids in Texas. And it did not signal a new toughness in Indian management. To Superintendent Hoag, Tatum's call for military help was unforgivable heresy. In his mind, "influences irresistibly evil" emanating from Fort Sill explained the failure of the Indians to embrace the new way of life offered them.⁵¹ The Hoag mentality continued to dominate policy in Indian Territory.

The swift retribution visited on the three chiefs scared some Kiowas and infuriated others. The tribe polarized into a peace faction headed by Kicking Bird and a war faction headed by Lone Wolf. Both from the reservation sanctuary and the Staked Plains, Kiowa and Comanche war parties robbed, burned, and butchered the length of the Texas frontier. Occasionally they even harassed Fort Sill.

Barred from the reservation, Colonel Mackenzie turned to the Comanches of the Staked Plains. By keeping them occupied at home, he hoped to lessen their incursions against the settlements. Operations in the fall of 1871 featured a few skirmishes with warriors led by a rising young half-blood chieftain named Quanah Parker. In the summer of 1872 the Fourth returned to this area. Another command, under Lt. Col. William R. Shafter, also laced the vast table. Both expeditions were pioneering explorations in a little-known and hostile land. Mackenzie crossed the unmapped wilderness all the way to Fort Sumner, New Mexico. In the course of the march he exposed the pattern, magnitude, and participants of the *Comanchero* trade. For generations New Mexican traders, called *Comancheros*, had journeyed to the Staked Plains to trade whiskey, arms, and ammunition to the Kiowas and Comanches for the stock and other plunder of their raids on the Texas settlements. Henceforth the army would try to break up this commerce.⁵²

A second expedition rewarded Mackenzie's dogged search for

the enemy. On September 29, 1872, he surprised and attacked Mow-way's Kotsoteka Comanche village of 262 lodges on the North Fork of Red River, near McClellan Creek. The Indians were thoroughly routed and from thirty to sixty were killed, including some women and children. The troopers burned the village and seized 124 captives, mostly women and children, together with a huge pony herd. To the colonel's mortification, a party of warriors skillfully stampeded the ponies and won them back. The prisoners were confined in a stockade at Fort Concho.[53]

In Satanta and Big Tree at Huntsville and the captives at Fort Concho, the government possessed powerful levers in the effort to curb the Kiowas and Comanches. Quaker sentiment, however, favored the release of the prisoners. Such trust and generosity, it was hoped, would induce the Indians to call off their war against Texas. In October 1872 the Commissioner of Indian Affairs promised a delegation of chiefs visiting Washington that if the Kiowas behaved themselves, and if the governor of Texas agreed, Satanta and Big Tree would be freed in six months. Not surprisingly, the Kiowas remained comparatively quiet during the winter. The Interior Department and humanitarian groups pressed Governor Davis to honor the promise. The assassination of General Canby in April 1873 so inflamed public opinion as to alter the timetable, but in October 1873 Satanta and Big Tree were at last set free. The Fort Concho prisoners had already been released, in June.

The liberation of Satanta and Big Tree infuriated Sherman, and his fears proved well founded. Throughout the winter of 1873–74 Kiowa and Comanche war parties ravaged Texas. They returned to the reservation sanctuary without fear of retribution such as Tatum had called down upon the Jacksboro raiders. His authority undermined by the parole of the Kiowa chiefs, Tatum had resigned in the spring of 1873. James M. Haworth, his successor, shared Superintendent Hoag's rosy view of Indian management. At once the new agent removed the military guard from the agency. He seemed unlikely to emulate Tatum by asking the army to arrest Indians.

Influences propelling the southern Plains tribes toward a major uprising gathered force during the winter of 1873–74. For four years the Indians had endured mounting pressures and restraints of reservation life. They had also endured inadequate rations— sometimes no rations, when held back to compel the return of captives or stock taken in Texas—and varieties of food and other issue goods repugnant to their taste. They had watched with growing alarm the slaughter of the buffalo by white hide-hunters who left the carcasses to rot; 1,250,000 hides went east by rail in 1872–73.[54] Although these influences created serious unrest, the principal stimulus to war remained cultural values that exalted war and showered acclaim on the successful warrior. Still another influence gained increasing importance—revenge. Warriors killed in Texas raids had to be revenged by their kinsmen in more Texas raids. The death of Lone Wolf's son and nephew in a fight with a troop of the Fourth Cavalry near Fort Clark in December 1873 set the old war chief's mind to plotting revenge and placed him beyond all reach of Agent Haworth's conciliation.[55]

All these forces operated on the Cheyennes, too. In addition, whiskey continued to demoralize their camps, and white horse thieves from Kansas preyed on their herds. Retaliatory measures led to occasional conflicts in Kansas. Cheyenne warriors in mounting numbers participated in the Texas raids of Kiowas and Comanches.[56]

In the spring and early summer of 1874, Kiowa, Comanche, and Cheyenne warriors struck in all directions. On June 27 several hundred Comanches and Cheyennes attacked a rude village thrown up by hide-hunters on the North Canadian River at Adobe Walls, in the Texas Panhandle, scene of Kit Carson's battle with Comanches in 1864. A Comanche medicine man named Isatai led the attack, but once more Quanah Parker figured prominently in the fighting. Twenty-eight hunters wtih high-powered rifles beat off the Indians and inflicted serious losses. Angry and humiliated, the warriors scattered, bent on revenge. On July 12, at Lost Valley, near the site of the Salt Creek Prairie massacre of 1871, Lone Wolf exacted revenge for the death of his son and nephew by ambushing a party of Texas Rangers. Warriors fell on ranches and travelers in Kansas and Texas and boldly attacked army mail parties.[57]

Depredations had reached a level of intensity that only a Hoag or a Haworth could ignore or rationalize. Sherman pressed for permission to send troops after Indians on the reservation. "Defensively it will require ten thousand Cavalry to give [frontier settlers] a partial protection," he advised Secretary of War Belknap, "but offensively a thousand Cavalry can follow them and punish them as they surely merit." Both Secretary of the Interior Delano and Commissioner of Indian Affairs E. P. Smith proved receptive. Their acquiescence obtained, Belknap gave Sherman the desired authority. On July 20, 1874, Sherman wired Sheridan to turn loose the troops.[58]

Sherman's order gave official ratification to the existence of a state of war—the Red River War. The order also recorded the failure of the experiment of separating military and civil responsibility for the Indian at the reservation line. Nowhere were the fallacies of this simplistic approach more vividly demonstrated than in Indian Territory and Texas between 1869 and 1874. Quaker goodness had not kept the Indians on the reservation. The army had not been able to punish them off the reservation. Nor had the Jacksboro formula—arrest of individual Indians on the reservation for trial in civil courts off the reservation—provided a solution; after Jacksboro, Indians did not confess their depredations, and there was no other sure way to determine guilt. Opening the reservation to troops was the inevitable result. The wonder is that it was postponed so long after the "city of refuge" pattern became clear.

To the army, the order of July 20, 1874, marked a welcome, if belated, hardening of the Peace Policy. It eliminated the problem of how to catch raiders without following them home. But it resurrected an old, more familiar problem: how to distinguish between peaceful and hostile Indians. Separating the one class from the other was the army's first order of business in the Red River War.

NOTES

1. SW, *Annual Report* (1868), pp. 5–6.
2. CIA, *Annual Report* (1868), pp. iii–iv. The case for the opposition was stated in great detail by Commissioner of Indian Affairs N. G. Taylor in *ibid.*, pp. 7–15. The transfer question is treated in Donald J. D'Elia, "The Argument over Civilian or Military Indian Control, 1865–1880," *Historian*, 24 (1961–62), 207–25; Priest, *Uncle Sam's Stepchildren*, chap. 2; and Mardock, *The Reformers and the American Indian*, pp. 42–43 and *passim*.
3. For the Peace Policy, see Priest, chaps. 1–5; Mardock, chap. 4; and Fritz, *The Movement for Indian Assimilation*, chap. 3. A well-reasoned revisionist article is Henry G. Waltmann, "Circumstantial Reformer: President Grant & the Indian Problem," *Arizona and the West*, 13 (1971), 323–42.
4. Both the Board of Indian Commissioners and the abolition of the treaty system were the result of growing resentment in the House of Representatives over the Senate's paramount role in Indian policy. The House did not participate in the conclusion of treaties by the Executive or their ratifica-

tion by the Senate but had to appropriate the funds to carry them out. The House held up the Indian appropriation bill in 1869, and the Board of Indian Commissioners was the compromise that broke it loose. The House refused all compromise in 1871, and the Senate acceded to an act that abolished the treaty system—without, however, invalidating existing treaty obligations.

5. Mardock, pp. 53–54.
6. CIA, *Annual Report* (1869), pp. 5–6. Fritz, p. 81.
7. Official documents are printed in Senate Ex. Docs., 41st Cong., 2d sess., No. 49; House Ex. Docs., 41st Cong., 2d sess., No. 185; *ibid.*, No. 197; SW, *Annual Report* (1870), pp. 29–30; and CIA, *Annual Report* (1870), pp. 190–191. An analysis sympathetic to Baker is Robert J. Ege, *Tell Baker to Strike Them Hard: Incident on the Marias* (Bellevue, Neb., 1970). See also Athearn, *William Tecumseh Sherman and the Settlement of the West*, pp. 279–82; and Mardock, pp. 67–70.
8. 16 Stat. 319 (July 15, 1870).
9. Mardock, chap. 5. Fritz, pp. 73–76. Priest, chaps. 2–3. Waltmann, pp. 334–35. Athearn, p. 281.
10. Thian, *Notes Illustrating the Military Geography of the United States*, p. 52.
11. Ogle, *Federal Control of the Western Apaches, 1848–1886*, pp. 76–79.
12. CIA, *Annual Report* (1870), pp. 8, 137–40; (1871), pp. 69–76, 88. James R. Hastings, "The Tragedy at Camp Grant in 1871," *Arizona and the West*, *1* (1959), 146–60. Thrapp, *The Conquest of Apacheria*, chap. 7.
13. Ogle, pp. 81, 89. Crook, *Autobiography*, p. 160. CIA, *Annual Report* (1871), pp. 77–78. Most of the perpetrators of the massacre were brought to trial but easily acquitted. Colyer's mission was authorized by a clause in the Indian appropriation act that provided $70,000 for collecting the the Apaches on reservations, feeding them, and promoting civilization. 16 Stat. 546 (March 3, 1871).
14. Colyer's report, CIA, *Annual Report* (1871), pp. 41–95. Crook, pp. 162–68. Thrapp, pp. 95–106. Ogle, pp. 87–102. *Army and Navy Journal*, *9* (Aug. 5, 1871), 816.
15. Howard's report, June 1872, in CIA, *Annual Report* (1872), pp. 148–75. O. O. Howard, *My Life and Experiences among Our Hostile Indians* (Hartford, Conn., 1907), chaps. 7–10.
16. I have treated the Bascom Affair in *Frontiersmen in Blue*, pp. 162–63.
17. Howard's report, Nov. 7, 1872, CIA, *Annual Report* (1872), pp. 175–78. Howard, chaps. 12–14. See CIA, *Annual Report* (1872), p. 306, for Cochise's sojourn on the reservation. He left when Colyer moved the reservation to Tularosa.
18. Crook, pp. 168–73. SW, *Annual Report* (1872), pp. 78–79. See also Colyer's and Howard's reports cited in notes 14 and 15, above.
19. Reports of Colyer and Howard cited above.
20. See Colyer's and Howard's reports cited above for examples of citizen attacks on them. CIA, *Annual Report* (1871), pp. 78–81, details explicit threats of citizens of Silver City, N.M., to obliterate the Apaches of the Cañada Alamosa Reservation.
21. CIA, *Annual Report* (1872), pp. 5–6, 58, 94.
22. These factors are discussed by Crook in "The Apache Problem," 257–69; and *Autobiography*, p. 175; and by his aide, Lt. John G. Bourke, in *On the Border with Crook*, pp. 109–12, 138–39, 142, 149–57, 181–82. See also Thrapp, *Conquest of Apacheria*, chap. 8; and Gunther E. Rothenberg, "General George Crook and the Apaches, 1872–73," *Westerners Brand Book* (Chicago), *13* (Sept. 1956), 49–56. Also, late in 1871 Crook received fresh troops to work with as the Fifth Cavalry and Twenty-third Infantry replaced the Third Cavalry and the Twenty-first Infantry. Early in 1870

Sheridan had advised Sherman that it would be well to get the Third Cavalry out of the Southwest. "It was there before the war, and is I hear to some extent mixed up with the natives." Sheridan to Sherman, Jan. 3, 1870, Sherman Papers, vol. 27, LC.

23. My account of the 1872–73 campaign is drawn mainly from Bourke, chaps. 10 and 11; Bourke's journal in Bloom, "Bourke on the Southwest," *New Mexico Historical Review*, 9 (1934), 380–435; Thrapp, *Conquest of Apacheria*, chaps. 10 and 11; Thrapp, *Al Sieber, Chief of Scouts* (Norman, Okla., 1964), chaps. 7 and 8; Crook, pp. 175–86; Ogle, pp. 112–17; Rothenberg; and Price, *Across the Continent with the Fifth Cavalry*, chap. 15. See also Sidney B. Brinckerhoff, "Camp Date Creek, Arizona Territory, Infantry Outpost in the Yavapai Wars, 1867–73," *The Smoke Signal* (Tucson Corral of Westerners), No. 10 (Fall 1964), pp. 16–17.

24. Bourke, pp. 213–14.

25. CIA, *Annual Report* (1873), p. 342.

26. Canby's attitude emerges in letters of Feb. 5, 7, 17, 21, and April 13 and 17, 1872, House Ex. Docs., 43d Cong., 1st sess., No. 122, pp. 5–6, 9, 14–15, 17, 19–21.

27. *Ibid.*, pp. 26–28, 223–25, 237–38. The standard history of the Modoc War is Keith A. Murray, *The Modocs and Their War* (Norman, Okla., 1959). See also Erwin N. Thompson, *The Modoc War: Its History and Topography* (Sacramento, Calif., 1971); Verne F. Ray, *Primitive Pragmatists: The Modoc Indians of Northern California* (Seattle, Wash., 1963); and Ray H. Glassley, *Pacific Northwest Indian Wars* (Portland, Oreg., 1953). Important reminiscent accounts are Richard H. Dillon, ed., *William Henry Boyle's Personal Observations on the Conduct of the Modoc War* (Los Angeles, n.d.); Alfred B. Meacham, *Wigwam and War-Path* (Boston, 1875); Jeff C. Riddle, *The Indian History of the Modoc War and the Causes that Led to It* (n.p. 1914); and military accounts in Cyrus T. Brady, *Northwestern Fights and Fighters* (New York, 1913), Part 2. Official correspondence is in House Ex. Docs., 42d Cong., 3d sess., No. 201; Senate Ex. Docs., 42d Cong., 3d sess., No. 29; House Ex. Docs., 43d Cong., 1st sess., No. 122; *ibid.*, No. 185; House Ex Docs., 43d Cong., 2d sess., No. 131; Senate Ex. Docs., 44th Cong., Sp. Sess., No. 1.

28. Schofield, *Forty-Six Years in the Army*, p. 463. House Reports, 43d Cong., 1st sess., No. 384, p. 279. A competent biography of Canby (which, however, does not advance this thesis) is Max L. Heyman, Jr., *Prudent Soldier: A Biography of Major General E. R. S. Canby, 1817–1873* (Glendale, Calif., 1959).

29. Military orders and correspondence covering these events are in House Ex. Docs., 43d Cong., 1st sess., No. 122, pp. 32–36, 179–81.

30. In addition to the followers of Captain Jack and Hooker Jim, the lava beds sheltered the Hot Creek band of Shacknasty Jim. These people had sought to remain neutral. En route to the Klamath Reservation, however, they learned of a lynch party being organized by Linkville citizens inflamed by the Tule Lake killings and stampeded to the lava beds. Murray, pp. 97–100.

31. The military buildup involved three batteries of the Fourth Artillery serving as infantry, two companies of the Twelfth Infantry, another of the Twenty-first, and another of the First Cavalry.

32. April 13, 1873, in House Ex. Docs., 43d Cong., 1st sess., No. 122, p. 77.

33. For the army, the tragedy was magnified by the prominence of the officers. Captain Thomas was the son of Lorenzo Thomas, Adjutant General of the Army from 1861 to 1869. Lt. Thomas F. Wright was the son of Gen. George Wright, for a decade the army's most distinguished Indian fighter on the Pacific Coast, who had drowned in a shipwreck in 1865. Lt. Albion Howe's father, Bvt. Maj. Gen. Albion P. Howe, was currently major of his son's regiment, the Fourth Artillery.

34. May 4, 1873, House Ex. Docs., 43d Cong., 1st sess., No. 122, pp. 83–84.

35. June 7, 1873, p. 85.

36. Davis seized this occasion, with the scattering of the cavalry, to send Colonel Gillem back to San Francisco. At the same time, in a gesture of exoneration, he summoned Colonel Wheaton back to the front. The force now consisted of five troops of the First Cavalry, two companies of the Twelfth Infantry, five of the Twenty-first Infantry, and six batteries of the Fourth Artillery, for a total of 985 Regulars and 70 Warm Springs Indian scouts.

37. Annual report, Nov. 1, 1873, House Ex. Docs., 43d Cong., 1st sess., No. 122, p. 110.

38. *Ibid.*, p. 111.

39. *Ibid.* Perry recounts the surrender in Brady, p. 304. See also *Army and Navy Journal, 12* (Jan. 23, 1875), 375–79.

40. Sherman Papers, vol. 35, LC.

41. To Belknap, June 3; to Schofield, June 3. House Ex. Docs., 43d Cong., 1st sess., No. 122, pp. 84–86.

42. The six were Captain Jack, Schonchin John, Black Jim, Boston Charley, Barncho, and Slouck. The proceedings of the commission, including testimony by the defendents, are an important source document. *Ibid.*, pp. 133–83.

43. Athearn, *William Tecumseh Sherman and the Settlement of the West*, pp. 300–3. Fritz, *The Movement for Indian Assimilation*, pp. 170–71.

44. Quoted in Nye, *Carbine and Lance*, p. 157.

45. This phase of history is well documented and set forth in several excellent secondary works: Nye, *Carbine and Lance*, chaps. 6–9; Nye, *Plains Indian Raiders*, chaps. 16–17; Richardson, *The Comanche Barrier to South Plains Settlement*, pp. 323–71; Mooney, *Calendar History of the Kiowa*, pp. 188–210, 326–38; Leckie, *The Military Conquest of the Southern Plains*, chaps. 6–8; Berthrong, *The Southern Cheyennes*, chaps. 14–15; Wallace, *Ranald S. Mackenzie on the Texas Frontier*, chaps. 3–5. Important primary sources are Wallace, ed., *Ranald S. Mackenzie's Official Correspondence Relating to Texas, 1871–1873* (Lubbock, Tex., 1967); Carter, *On the Border with Mackenzie;* Lawrie Tatum, *Our Red Brothers and the Peace Policy of President Ulysses S. Grant* (Philadelphia, Pa., 1899); Thomas C. Battey, *The Life and Adventures of a Quaker among the Indians* (Boston, 1903); Richard H. Pratt, *Battlefield and Classroom: Four Decades with the American Indian, 1867–1904*, ed. Robert M. Utley (New Haven, Conn., 1964), chaps. 5–6.

46. Leckie, *Buffalo Soldiers*, p. 54. SW, *Annual Report* (1870), p. 9. See Leckie, pp. 7–8, for a sketch of Grierson. A music teacher in Illinois at the outbreak of the Civil War, Grierson rose rapidly in the volunteer service and won fame for "Grierson's Raid" through Mississippi in 1863. His volunteer origins, his lax habits of administration and discipline, and his association with a black regiment contributed to his unpopularity in the Regular Army.

47. Grant, *Memoirs*, p. 583.

48. Besides Wallace, Mackenzie's character emerges sharply in the following: Carter; Parker, *Old Army Memories;* Crane, *Colonel of Infantry;* J. H. Dorst, "Ranald Slidell Mackenzie," *Journal of the United States Cavalry Association, 10* (1897), 367–82.

49. Thian, *Military Geography of the United States*, pp. 99–100. GO 66, War Dept., Nov. 1, 1871, in Joe F. Taylor, ed., *The Indian Campaign on the Staked Plains, 1874–1875: Military Correspondence from War Department Adjutant General's Office File 2815–1874* (Canyon, Tex., 1962), pp. 7–8.

50. Principal sources for the Jacksboro affair are Nye, *Carbine and Lance*, pp. 123–47; Carter, pp. 75–104; Tatum, pp. 115–21; Pratt, pp. 42–48. Sher-

man's letters during his trip and extracts from Marcy's journal are in the Sherman Papers, LC. See also Sherman's account in House Reports, 43d Cong., 1st sess., No. 395, pp. 270–75. An assessment of the importance of this affair is C. C. Rister, "The Significance of the Jacksboro Indian Affair of 1871," *Southwestern Historical Quarterly*, 29 (1926), 181–200.

51. CIA, *Annual Report* (1872), p. 228.
52. J. Evetts Haley, "The Comanchero Trade," *Southwestern Historical Quarterly*, 38 (1934–35), 157–76. Charles L. Kenner, *A History of New Mexican-Plains Indian Relations* (Norman, Okla., 1969).
53. For Mackenzie's operations, see especially Wallace, *Ranald S. Mackenzie on the Texas Frontier*, chaps. 3–5; Wallace ed., *Ranald S. Mackenzie's Official Correspondence Relating to Texas, 1871–1873*, pp. 36–158; Carter; and W. A. Thompson, "Scouting with Mackenzie," *Journal of the United States Cavalry Association*, 10 (1897), 429–33.
54. E. Douglas Branch, *The Hunting of the Buffalo* (New York and London, 1929), p. 169.
55. These causes are summarized in Nye, *Carbine and Lance*, pp. 187–88.
56. Berthrong, p. 387, summarizes causes of Cheyenne hostility.
57. CIA, *Annual Report* (1874), pp. 214–15, 219–22, 232–34. SW, *Annual Report* (1874), pp. 30, 40. For Adobe Walls, see Rupert N. Richardson, "The Comanche Indians at the Adobe Walls Fight," *Panhandle-Plains Historical Review*, 4 (1931), 24–38; and Nye, *Bad Medicine and Good*, chap. 30. Lost Valley is ably chronicled in Nye, *Carbine and Lance*, pp. 192–200.
58. Taylor, ed., pp. 10–12. CIA, *Annual Report* (1874), pp. 9–10.

THIRTEEN

The Red River War, 1874-75

GENERAL SHERIDAN's strategy for meeting the Red River uprising closely paralleled his campaign plan of 1868–69, with
the important exception that operations were being launched in the
summer rather than the winter. Columns would converge from
several directions on the Indian haunts in the Texas Panhandle
and so wear down the fugitives that they would hasten back to
their agencies and submit. Sheridan is generally credited with
elaborating this concept into the comprehensive master plan by
which the southern Plains tribes were conquered for all time. Instead, it seems to have unfolded mainly under the direction of the
two department commanders whose jurisdictions were affected,
and without much coordination between them or guidance from
above. These were General Augur, commanding Texas and part
of Indian Territory, and General Pope, commanding Kansas, New
Mexico, and parts of Colorado and Indian Territory.

John Pope had commanded the Department of the Missouri
from his Fort Leavenworth headquarters for four years. In more
than a decade as a top frontier commander, he had shown himself
to be an able administrator and a thoughtful if prolix commentator
on the Indian problem in both its military and civil aspects. Yet
few officers got along well with Pope. The shattering humiliation
of Second Manassas in 1862 had tempered his bombast but not his
pomposity or vanity. Moreover, the bitter controversy set off by
that mismanaged battle, kept painfully alive by Gen. Fitz John
Porter's continuing effort to win vindication, made Pope belliger-

ently sensitive to the slightest implication of criticism. Friction with subordinates and superiors alike inevitably resulted.[1]

Command of Pope's main column fell to an even more temperamental officer. Young, handsome, the proud bearer of an extraordinary war record, happily teamed with an attractive wife whose uncles were General Sherman and Senator Sherman, Col. Nelson A. Miles was destined to become one of a small handful of successful Indian-fighting generals. He was no better liked than Pope. A powerful ambition almost unlimited in its ends as well as in its means spurred him time and again to solid achievement. It also drove him to disparage the achievements and abilities of others, to share laurels with bad grace, and to exploit every influence to advance his fortunes. Coloring the ambition was an acute defensiveness over his lack of formal military education; he had learned by self-study and experience and had risen by merit from the lowly status of Boston crockery clerk to major general and corps commander. The Red River War offered Miles, now colonel of the Fifth Infantry, his first postwar opportunity for distinction.[2]

Miles' command consisted of eight troops of the Sixth Cavalry and four companies of his own Fifth Infantry. Orders of July 27, 1874, from Pope's headquarters directed these units to rendezvous at Fort Dodge, Kansas, and to operate southward into Indian Territory as Custer had done in 1868. The same orders started a concentration of Eighth Cavalry units in New Mexico to operate eastward, down the Canadian, as had Major Evans in 1868. Ultimately, the New Mexico column consisted of four troops of the Eighth, about 225 officers and enlisted men, under Maj. William R. Price.[3]

With Miles and Price striking from north and west, General Augur planned to send three columns against the target area from the south and east. At Sheridan's suggestion, he moved Colonel Mackenzie and eight troops of the Fourth Cavalry from the Mexican border to Fort Concho. Mackenzie would maneuver from a supply base manned by infantry on the Freshwater Fork of the Brazos. A second column, led by Lt. Col. George P. Buell, Eleventh Infantry, would operate slightly to the north of Mackenzie. The third column would move directly west from Fort Sill under Lt. Col. John W. Davidson, Tenth Cavalry.[4] "Black Jack" Davidson had replaced Grierson as Fort Sill commander early in 1873. A tough old veteran of the prewar frontier, he applied a discipline

as harsh as Grierson's was lenient. Occasional fits of strange behavior were widely attributed to the lingering effects of sunstroke.[5]

In August 1874 Davidson had more immediate concerns than
preparing for a campaign on the Staked Plains. As usual on the
verge of an offensive, an effort had to be made to separate friendly
from hostile Indians. Friendlies were to be enrolled at the agencies
and accounted for often enough to ensure their continued neutrality. At Fort Sill the task fell to Davidson, at Darlington to Lt. Col.
Thomas H. Neill, Sixth Cavalry, whom Pope had sent with four
infantry companies and a cavalry troop to guard the agency. For
Neill and Agent Miles, enrollment presented no difficulty. Almost
all the Arapahoes submitted quietly, while almost all the Cheyennes remained defiantly absent. At Fort Sill, however, the enrollment was characterized by conflict between Davidson and Agent
Haworth, by great excitement among the Kiowas, and by a final
tally that included both Kiowas and Comanches of dubious neutrality.

A handful of Comanche chiefs, veterans of Adobe Walls, asked
to sign up after the rolls had been closed. Davidson refused. Big
Red Food then led his Nakoni Comanche band to Anadarko,
agency for the Wichita and confederated tribes on the Washita
River thirty miles north of Fort Sill. Lone Wolf and the Kiowa
war faction, most of whom had been enrolled, were camped near
here too. The agent saw trouble coming and sent to Fort Sill for
help. Davidson and four troops of the Tenth Cavalry arrived on
August 22. A demand for the Comanches to lay down their arms
and surrender as prisoners of war set off a wild melee in which
soldiers and Indians—Kiowas as well as Comanches—exchanged
long-range fire for two days. Neither side suffered much damage,
but a sizeable force of warriors marked themselves as hostiles.[6]

In military eyes, the Anadarko affair cleansed the rolls and produced a more satisfactory division between the combatant and noncombatant elements of the Kiowa and Comanche tribes. It also
stampeded some of the enrollees at Fort Sill, but many of these
did not flee to the hostile camps and drifted back to the agency
during September. By late August, then, the enemy consisted of
some 1,800 Cheyennes, 2,000 Comanches, and 1,000 Kiowas,
mounting in all perhaps 1,200 fighting men. They moved in large
encampments among the twisted breaks surrounding the headwaters of the Washita and the various forks of the Red, in the

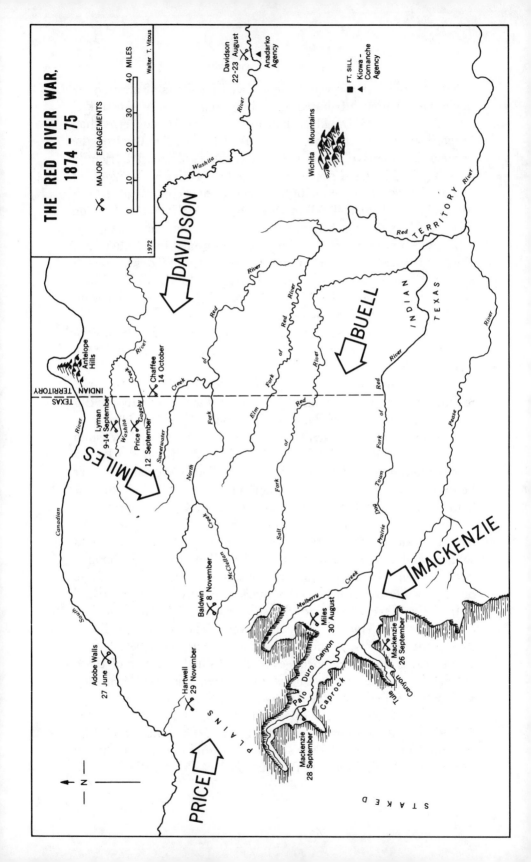

THE RED RIVER WAR, 1874 - 75

✗ MAJOR ENGAGEMENTS

MILES
0   10   20   30   40 MILES

Walter T. Vitous

1972

■ FT. SILL
▲ KIOWA - COMANCHE Agency

DAVIDSON

Davidson 22-23 August
Anadarko Agency

Wichita Mountains

Red   INDIAN   TERRITORY

BUELL

TEXAS

Washita River

Antelope Hills

Chaffee 14 October

INDIAN TERRITORY
TEXAS

Lyman 9-14 September
Cagehy
Price 12 September

MILES

Sweetwater Creek

North   Fork

Elm   Fork   of   Red   River

Salt   Fork

Town   Fork   of   Red   River

Prairie   Dog   Fork

Pease River

MACKENZIE

Canadian River

McClellan Creek

Baldwin 8 November

Mulberry Creek

Miles 30 August

Mackenzie 26 September
Tule Canyon

Caprock

Palo Duro Canyon

South

Adobe Walls 27 June

Hartwell 29 November

Mackenzie 28 September

PLAINS

PRICE

STAKED

Texas Panhandle. Toward this area the columns of Miles and Price marched during the final days of August 1874.

A drouth of unusual severity afflicted the southern Plains. Temperatures soared to 110 degrees and above. Water was scarce and bitterly alkaline. A devastating locust plague, darkening the skies and blanketing the prairies, laid the earth bare of vegetation. Soldiers, Indians, and their animals suffered acutely. At one point Miles' men opened the veins of their arms and moistened their lips with their own blood.

South from the Canadian the troops plodded, 744 strong.[7] On August 30, as they approached the Staked Plains escarpment, about 200 Cheyenne warriors burst from concealment at the base of the caprock and charged the advance guard. Miles deployed his infantry in the center and a cavalry squadron on each flank. ("Forward," shouted Capt. Adna R. Chaffee to his troop. "If any man is killed I will make him a corporal.") For five hours, over twelve miles, the troops drove the warrior force, swollen to nearly 600 by accessions of Comanches and Kiowas, from one line of hills to another. At each point of resistance, Gatling guns and howitzers opened fire and cavalry and infantry charged. Demoralized, the Indians fell back to new positions along the slopes of Tule Canyon. These, too, the troops carried, flushing the adversaries on to the Staked Plains beyond. Miles now had a large portion of the hostiles in his front, but he had exhausted his supplies and could go no farther. Destroying the villages and other property abandoned by the Indians, he turned back on his trail to replenish his provisions.

On September 7, while Miles tarried on the Prairie Dog Town Fork, the drouth ended abruptly. Storms swept the plains, dropping temperatures, filling streams, and turning the barren prairie into mud. Also on September 7 Miles connected with Major Price and his Eighth Cavalry squadron from New Mexico. Following separate routes, the two columns slogged painfully northward in search of desperately needed supplies. The Indians, also soaked by the storms, long remembered the next few weeks as "The Wrinkled-Hand Chase."

As Miles hastened northward to avert a supply crisis, he discovered his supply line suddenly infested with Indians. They were Kiowas and Comanches who had fled westward after the collision with Colonel Davidson at Anadarko and were now searching for the main body of hostiles on the Staked Plains. Among them were Lone Wolf, Mamanti, Satanta, Big Tree, and other noted war leaders. On September 9 about 250 warriors from these bands swooped down on Miles' supply train, 36 wagons escorted by a company of the Fifth Infantry and a detachment of the Sixth Cavalry under Capt. Wyllys Lyman. For three days, near the Washita, the warriors kept the train under close siege. A scout slipped out and rode to Camp Supply for help. On the twelfth, as a cold rain drenched the battlefield, the Indians drew off.

This movement was prompted by Major Price approaching from the south in search of his own supply train. As the rain clouds lifted about noon on the twelfth, Price discovered a large force of Indians moving westward across his front. About 150 warriors drew up on a ridge to cover the flight of the women and children. For three hours, over a distance of six or seven miles, the two sides skirmished before the warriors, their families now safe, scattered.

The next day, as Price's men paused for lunch, a lone white man made his way on foot into the lines. He was Billy Dixon, a scout for Miles. He told how he and Scout Amos Chapman, accompanied by four cavalrymen, had been carrying dispatches for Miles to Camp Supply. Approaching the Washita on the morning of the twelfth, they had been attacked by about 100 warriors (withdrawing from the Lyman fight) and had sought cover in a shallow buffalo wallow. Four of the six took severe wounds, but all day they held off the circling Indians. The day's rain, coupled with sinking temperatures, prompted the Indians to give up the contest. The battered defenders shivered through the night in their muddy, blood-tinted hole. One died. Price provided medical care and sent back to Miles' command for an ambulance, which arrived that night.[8]

The events of September 9–14 unsettled the Anadarko fugitives. If military estimates are accurate, they had lost twenty to thirty fighting men in the skirmishes with Lyman, Price, and the buffalo wallow defenders. Rain, cold, hunger, worn-out ponies, and swarming bluecoats dampened the war spirit. Woman's Heart led some of the Kiowas, thirty-five men with their families, back to the reservation. Apprehensive of Fort Sill, they gave up at the Darlington Agency early in October. Colonel Neill was astonished to find among them Satanta and Big Tree, who earnestly declared themselves guilty of no offense greater than a "momentary panic" triggered by the Anadarko affair.

The rest of the Kiowas and Comanches who had tangled with Lyman and Price safely evaded the troops and moved southwest in search of the main body of hostiles. Unable to pursue, Miles fumed over the supply problems that had pulled him back when almost upon the Indians and that now immobilized him on the Canadian. What especially galled him was a fear that one of the other columns advancing on the Staked Plains would find the Indians and reap the glory that logistical troubles had denied him after the action of August 30. Davidson posed no threat. Leaving Fort Sill on September 10, he had scouted Sweetwater and McClellan creeks and had probed the hills along the caprock; but on September 29, his supplies giving out, he turned back toward Fort Sill. Buell, too, seemed unlikely competition. Also organizing at Fort Sill, he did not take the field until September 24. Five days later, as Davidson marched for Sill, Buell laid out a base camp near the mouth of the Salt Fork of Red River.[9] By then, Miles' worst fears had been realized. The aggressive Mackenzie had struck.

Mackenzie had spent most of September stockpiling provisions on the Freshwater Fork of the Brazos at the mouth of Blanco Canyon.[10] Finally, on September 20, he led the column northward along the eastern edge of the Staked Plains. His eight cavalry troops numbered 21 officers and 450 enlisted men. Three companies of infantry guarded the supply base, while two escorted the expedition's wagon train. Chilling storms soaked the troopers and mired the wagons. Only the grim determination of Mackenzie's efficient quartermaster, Lt. Henry W. Lawton, kept the train in motion. Abundant signs testified to the proximity of Indians in large numbers.[11]

During the night of September 26, about 250 Comanches rushed Mackenzie's camp near Tule Canyon in an effort to stampede his horses. But Mackenzie had learned his lesson in 1872, when Mowway's men had recaptured the ponies lost in the Battle of McClellan Creek. The cavalry mounts had been staked, hobbled, cross side-lined, and ringed with pickets. Thwarted, the warriors sniped at the troops all night until, next morning, Mackenzie counterattacked and drove them off.

Already, Mackenzie's Tonkawa scouts had located an inviting

target in the upper reaches of Palo Duro Canyon, the broad
trough cut into the caprock by the Prairie Dog Town Fork of
Red River. Mamanti's Kiowas, Ohamatai's Comanches, and Iron
Shirt's Cheyennes had taken refuge here. Their lodges, several
hundred in number, extended down the canyon for three miles
from the mouth of a feeder canyon, Blanca Cita. At daybreak on
September 28 the Fourth Cavalry scrambled down the canyon wall
by way of a narrow, precipitous trail. Before the first cavalrymen
reached the bottom, the Indians began to flee. Each troop, upon
completing the descent, charged through the villages in pursuit.
Except for occasional skirmishing and long-range sniping, therefore, the Battle of Palo Duro Canyon was largely a rout. Only
three warriors were known to have been slain, and Mackenzie's
single casualty was a wounded trumpeter. But the encounter was
heartbreakingly costly to the Indians. Mackenzie burned all their
lodges, food stores, and camp equipment and left the canyon with
their entire pony herd, 1,424 head. The next day, at the head of
Tule Canyon, he cut out the finest ponies for his own men and had
the balance, more than 1,000, slaughtered.

The Indian country now fairly swarmed with soldiers. During
the first two weeks of October Mackenzie circled the head of Palo
Duro Canyon before turning back to his supply base. Buell pushed
up the Salt Fork of the Red from his supply base and found a
warm trail. On October 11 he burned a deserted camp of 75
lodges. The next day he found another, of 475 lodges, and destroyed it, too. The trail turned northward toward the head of
McClellan Creek to the Canadian. Discarded equipment and
worn-out ponies recorded the closeness of the pursuit. But at the
Canadian the quarry scattered, leaving Buell, with men and horses
exhausted, to turn back in search of badly needed supplies.[12]
Miles, at last resupplied, had also been active. Elements of his
command, now including Price's New Mexico troops, scouted the
valleys and plains south of the Canadian.

Late in October Miles launched another operation. Scouting reports indicated that large numbers of Indians had sought safety in
the western reaches of the Staked Plains. Miles hoped to get beyond them and flush them eastward, to be intercepted by Major
Price. The movement was partly successful. On November 8 a
detachment from Miles' command under Lt. Frank D. Baldwin
discovered Grey Beard's camp of more than 100 Cheyenne lodges

in the breaks of McClellan Creek. Baldwin placed his infantry
company in a string of 23 empty supply wagons he was escorting,
formed them in double column flanked by his mounted scouts and
a cavalry troop, and stormed into the village. The surprised occupants fled as Baldwin's unorthodox assault formation pursued
them vigorously over twelve miles of prairie.[13]

In Grey Beard's abandoned village, which was destroyed, the
troops found two young white girls, ages five and seven. They
were Adelaide and Julia German, two of four sisters seized in
western Kansas early in September when a war party waylaid the
emigrant family of John German and butchered the father,
mother, and eldest sister. The discovery of the two little girls
raised hopes of liberating their older sisters, Catherine and Sophia,
ages thirteen and eighteen.

Major Price, posted on the Washita to head off Indians retreating in front of Miles, fumbled a chance to strike Grey Beard. With
three troops of the Eighth Cavalry and two of the Tenth borrowed
from Colonel Davidson, back in the field once more after refitting
at Fort Sill, Price encountered the Cheyennes on November 8
moving across his front in headlong flight from Lieutenant Baldwin. "For some reason not yet satisfactorily explained," Miles later
reported, Price failed to attack. "After halting and grazing animals
for several hours, [he] moved in the opposite direction from the
scene of the engagement."[14]

As Grey Beard traveled northwest, toward the Canadian, Davidson took up the chase. At the edge of the Staked Plains he halted
while Capt. Charles D. Viele with 120 picked cavalrymen and Lt.
Richard H. Pratt's scouts continued the pursuit. In two days of
hard riding they wore out their horses without overtaking the
Cheyennes. Viele called off the pursuit and turned back.[15] Meanwhile, on November 12, Miles dispatched the Eighth Cavalry
squadron in the same direction. Capt. Charles A. Hartwell commanded instead of Price, relieved by Miles for failing to cut off
Grey Beard on the eighth.[16] On November 29 Hartwell attacked a
party of forty to fifty Cheyenne warriors, perhaps part of Grey
Beard's band, at the head of Muster Creek, a tributary of the
Canadian. The troops gave chase for twelve miles, but the
Cheyennes escaped safely into Palo Duro Canyon.[17]

Throughout November and December 1874, "northers"
pounded the Staked Plains. Soldiers and Indians alike found al-

most no relief from the torture of rain, sleet, snow, and freezing cold. At times the storms coated the prairie with ice, at other times buried it under drifted snow, at still other times left it a vast expanse of mud. Horses died by the score at the picket lines. Frostbite produced long casualty lists. Columns moved slowly and painfully, when they could move at all. Men lived in constant discomfort.

One after another of the army's striking forces yielded to winter blasts and logistical failures. Davidson returned to Fort Sill on November 29, Buell to Fort Griffin early in December. Mackenzie, after prowling the southern reaches of the Staked Plains, broke up his command shortly before Christmas. In December Miles sent the Eighth Cavalry squadron back to New Mexico. On January 2, 1875, with two companies of infantry and a troop of cavalry, he started a final swing around the headwaters of the branches of Red River. Swirling blizzards, bitter winds, and subzero temperatures plagued the march all the way to Fort Sill. But "the troops did not seem to suffer or complain," Miles wrote to his wife, "and it was quite amusing to hear them sing 'Marching Through Georgia' way out on these plains."[18] They reached their Washita base on February 3. Leaving Maj. James Biddle with four troops of the Sixth Cavalry and four companies of the Fifth Infantry to man a cantonment Sheridan had ordered established on the Sweetwater, Miles repaired to Camp Supply and disbanded his expedition. The cantonment became a permanent post, Fort Elliott, a year later.

Bad weather and military pressure had caused defections from the hostile camps as early as October. During November and December Kiowas and Cheyennes in small parties straggled in to give up at Sill and Darlington. Reports from the Staked Plains portrayed the hostiles as cold, destitute, afflicted with gnawing apprehension of attack by the bluecoats, and ripe for capitulation. Not until January and February, however, did significant numbers begin moving eastward. Late in February, through the good offices of Kicking Bird and Big Bow, Lone Wolf and almost 500 Kiowas were persuaded to surrender. Some of the Cheyennes, including Medicine Arrows and White Antelope, fled northward to join the Northern Cheyennes rather than place themselves at the army's mercy. But most of the balance of the tribe surrendered to Colonel Neill near Darlington during late February and early

March 1875. On March 6 alone, 820 Cheyennes laid down their
arms. Among the chiefs were Grey Beard, Stone Calf, Bull Bear,
Minimic, and Medicine Water. Stone Calf freed Catherine and
Sophia German, alive though badly used. The Comanches proved
more tardy, but emissaries from Fort Sill induced them to go to
the agency too. On April 18 Mow-way, White Horse, and almost
200 Kotsotekas and Kwahadis surrendered to Mackenzie, now
commanding Fort Sill, and on June 2 another 407 Kwahadis, including the elusive Quanah Parker, came in.

The surrender of Woman's Heart, Satanta, and other Kiowas at
Darlington Agency on October 7, 1874, raised the question of
what to do with offenders as they came into their agencies. As
General Sherman pointed out, "To turn them loose to renew the
same old game in the spring seems folly." About Satanta there
was little disagreement—except, predictably, from Superintendent
Hoag and Agent Haworth. He was speedily returned to the Texas
penitentiary, where on March 11, 1878, he took his own life by
throwing himself from an upper window. For all Indians who
could be charged with specific acts of murder or theft within the
past two years, General Sheridan favored trial by a military commission such as had disposed of Captain Jack and his Modoc
cohorts. Other "ringleaders" Sheridan would confine at a distant
military post such as Fort Snelling. For his part, Sherman would
colonize a small handful of the worst leaders among a distant tribe
such as the Chippewa of Lake Superior, where they could labor
for their subsistence. The rest he would place under military control on their own reservations. "If the Secy of the Interior will give
you half the usual appropriation you can safely undertake to maintain these tribes at peace," he telegraphed Secretary of War Belknap. "The other half," he observed, alluding to the imperatives of
Indian Bureau patronage, "would maintain the agencies comfortably in some Christian land, say Ohio."[19]

Anticipating the formation of a military commission, throughout the winter both Neill and Davidson seized from each party
that surrendered those warriors deemed guilty of murder, theft,
or other offenses. At Fort Sill, Lt. Richard H. Pratt, commander
of Davidson's Indian scouts, was charged with compiling a list of
offenders and gathering evidence against them. Both Pratt and
Neill relied heavily on informers among the Indians themselves.
Also, the German sisters pointed out Cheyenne warriors guilty of

depredations and of abusing them during their captivity. Those caught in the nets cast by Neill and Pratt were placed in irons and held in the guardhouses at Darlington and Fort Sill until their disposition could be decided.[20]

On April 6 a blacksmith at Darlington was placing leg irons on a Cheyenne named Black Horse when the taunts of some women prompted him to try to escape. Guards swiftly shot him down, but their bullets strayed into the main Cheyenne camps. After a brief exchange of fire, 100 to 150 men and a few women and children fled to a sand hill on the south side of the North Canadian River, where arms and ammunition had been secreted. Neill quickly surrounded them with three troops of cavalry. He raked the hilltop positions with deadly Gatling gunfire that killed six of the fugitives; but he could not get the cavalry to face the Cheyenne rifles in an attack. Even so, nineteen soldiers were wounded. That night, the Cheyennes slipped away and headed west.[21]

Many of these Indians subsequently drifted back to Darlington under the influence of an amnesty promised by General Pope. A party of about sixty, however, tried to reach the Northern Cheyennes. Lt. Austin Henely's troop of the Sixth Cavalry, out of Fort Wallace, found their trail and caught up with them on Sappa Creek, in northwestern Kansas, on April 23. About thirty escaped as the cavalry charged, but the rest were trapped in the depression of a dry stream bed. One by one Henely's men picked them off— nineteen men and eight women and children. Two soldiers were killed in the attack.[22]

Sappa Creek was the last of more than two dozen combat actions of the Red River hostilities. It took the lives of nearly as many Indians as all the others combined. Had success been measured in enemy casualties, the Red River offensive would be counted a dismal failure. But, as measured by the mass surrenders of early 1875, it was a resounding triumph. The hostiles had sustained damaging losses of food, shelter, stock, and other possessions. They had been kept constantly on the move, constantly in fear of surprise attack. They had suffered grievously from cold and hunger. Ultimately they had come to view the detested reservation as preferable to the terrible insecurity and discomfort of fugitive life in a frozen country swarming with soldiers. As in 1868–69, experience had validated Sheridan's total-war strategy.

Sheridan had conceived the overall strategy and spent most of

October 1874 in Indian Territory helping to put it into effect. Augur, while maintaining his headquarters at Fort Sill from August until almost Christmas, left the conduct of operations largely to Mackenzie, Davidson, and Buell. Pope gave closer supervision to his subordinates. This infuriated Miles, who believed that he should enjoy greater independence, especially when Pope went east late in September. "It required a peculiar kind of genius," he wrote to his wife, "to conduct an Indian campaign from West Point or Boston." All five columns ought to be under a single field commander, Miles thought, and he left little doubt which officer he judged best qualified for the assignment.[23] He was doubtless right, but in the end unity of command could have brought no more decisive results.

The successful conclusion of the campaign is all the more remarkable because from its beginning all the commands were beset by supply problems of the most extraordinary severity. They originated almost entirely in transportation deficiencies. Contractors responsible for moving supplies to Fort Griffin for Mackenzie, to Fort Sill for Davidson and Buell, and to Camp Supply for Miles failed repeatedly to meet their obligations. In addition, government transportation organic to the separate commands was inadequate to forward provisions from these forts to the field depots and to sustain columns away from their depots as long as desirable. As a result, all the commands suffered unexpected delays. More serious, forage shortages, combined with the scarcity of grass following the summer's drouth, hastened the breakdown of cavalry mounts.[24]

The main fault lay in the contract system itself. Supplies were carried by private train owners subcontracted by a prime contractor. He owned no wagons or mules himself, but he commanded the financial resources to assume the contract. Neither he nor the train owners came under military control, and they moved pretty much at their own pace. Pope favored government trains; but if that could not be allowed, the responsible commander, not a quartermaster officer beholden to Washington, should arrange contracts and regulate contractors. "It is the work we must have done," he declared, "and unless that *is* done, no amount of bonds or securities avail anything."[25]

Compounding these difficulties, the field commanders lacked enough government-owned teams and wagons to meet the transportation requirements that were not contracted. Miles, Davidson, and Buell were all forced back to their depots prematurely when supplies ran out—Miles early in September 1874 when in hot pursuit of Indians routed in the action of August 30. As Davidson remarked, "Expeditions with our limited transportation find themselves with only enough supplies to carry them back when they reach the present country of the Indians."[26] Miles protested vigorously that his sixty wagons could haul only enough rations and forage to supply his command for twenty-one days, and this was not enough. Pope, however, regarded this as simply one more of Miles' insatiable demands. "For anything like efficient service or rapid movement," Pope informed Sheridan, "Miles has all the transportation he can use advantageously, and to buy more mules and fit up wagons would be a long tedious and unnecessary labor and expense."[27] The complaint came not only from Miles, however, and Pope would have been well advised to go to the labor and expense, for in January 1875 winter immobilized the contract trains altogether. To supply the garrison of the Sweetwater cantonment for the rest of the winter, Pope virtually stripped his department of government trains and placed them on the road from Fort Dodge through Camp Supply to the cantonment. Even then, only Sheridan's prompt dispatch of fifty wagons and teams from the Department of Dakota saved Pope the necessity of withdrawing the command.[28]

Despite the cumbersome command arrangement and despite logistical deficiencies of the most chronic and exasperating character, Sheridan's "saturation strategy" paid off. It did so because Mackenzie, Davidson, Buell, and above all Miles persisted in the face of adversities that would have afforded many another commander plausibile justification for returning to home stations for the winter. The victory, moreover, proved permanent. The tribes of the southern Plains—Kiowa, Comanche, Cheyenne, Arapaho, Plains Apache—settled unhappily on their reservations and never again challenged the government with armed force.

The finality of the conquest may be attributed only in part to the vigor of military operations. The removal of leading men of the war factions was also significant, for it silenced the voices most likely to urge violence as a solution to reservation frustrations. The Attorney General ruled against Sheridan's proposed military commission, but on March 13, 1875, the President decided that the "ringleaders" and "such as have been guilty of crime" were to be imprisoned, without their families, in the East. A dubious justice attended the selection of the "ringleaders." The most noted chiefs were singled out and the balance capriciously chosen from among little-known warriors. On April 28, 1875, amid the wailing and weeping of Indian women, a train of eight wagons moved out of Fort Sill under charge of Lieutenant Pratt. Aboard, shackled to one another and to the wagons, were seventy-four Indians: thirty-three Cheyennes, including Grey Beard, Minimic, and Medicine Water; twenty-seven Kiowas, including Lone Wolf, Woman's Heart, and White Horse; eleven Comanches, of whom only Black Horse boasted any prominence; two Arapahoes; and one hapless Caddo. During the long journey by wagon and railroad, Grey Beard, after an unsuccessful suicide attempt, was shot and killed while trying to escape in Georgia.[29]

Under Pratt's supervision, the prisoners were confined in the damp recesses of the ancient Spanish fortress of Castillo de San Marcos at St. Augustine, Florida, which the U.S. Army maintained as Fort Marion. Some of the Indians quickly sickened and died. The rest Pratt treated with kindness and sympathy. They also afforded him the means of experimenting with concepts of Indian education that had begun to form in his mind even before leaving the frontier. When the prisoners were at last freed in 1878 to return to their homes, a handful remained to help carry forward Pratt's educational work. A year later he opened the Carlisle Indian School, the model for an expanding network of government boarding schools for Indians. Thus, from the wreckage of the Red River War sprang one of the most pervasive—and controversial—institutions of Indian policy during the generations in which its primary goal was extinction of Indian culture.[30]

NOTES

1. The Fitz John Porter case, at last resolved in Porter's favor in 1886, heavily influenced the army's internal politics, command relationships, and high-level promotions for two decades. The Sherman Papers, LC, abundantly document this judgment. A history of the controversy is Otto Eisenschiml, *The Celebrated Case of Fitz John Porter* (Indianapolis and New York, 1950). For Pope's handling of the Red River operations, see Ellis, *General Pope and U.S. Indian Policy*, chaps. 9–10.
2. There is no satisfactory biography of Miles. Virginia Johnson, *The Unregimented General: A Biography of Nelson A. Miles* (Boston, 1962), is

uncritical though valuable because it contains many extracts from Miles' voluminous correspondence. Miles wrote two autobiographies: *Personal Recollections and Observations* (Chicago, 1896); and *Serving the Republic* (New York, 1911).

3. Taylor, ed., *The Indian Campaign on the Staked Plains*, pp. 14–16.

4. Carter, *On the Border with Mackenzie*, pp. 474–78. Ernest Wallace, ed., *Ranald S. Mackenzie's Official Correspondence Relating to Texas, 1873–1879* (Lubbock, Tex., 1968), chap. 2.

5. Pratt, *Battlefield and Classroom*, p. 6.

6. The best account of this affair is Nye, *Carbine and Lance*, pp. 206–10. See also *Army and Navy Journal, 12* (Aug. 29, 1874), 38; (Sept. 5, 1874), 56.

7. Main sources for Miles' operations are *Personal Recollections and Observations*, chap. 11; Johnson chaps. 4–5; Baird, "General Miles's Indian Campaigns," pp. 351–53; and official reports in Taylor, ed., *passim*, but especially Miles to Asst. Adj. Gen. Dept. Mo., March 4, 1875, pp. 197–216. *Army and Navy Journal, 12* (Oct. 31, 1874), 186–87. Robert C. Carriker, ed., "Thompson McFadden's Diary of an Indian Campaign, 1874," *Southwestern Historical Quarterly, 75* (1971), 198–232.

8. Price's operations in the first phase of the campaign are covered in detail in Price to Williams, Sept. 23, 1874, in Taylor, ed., pp. 46–55.

9. Davidson to Asst. Adj. Gen. Dept. Tex., Oct. 10, 1874, in Taylor, ed., pp. 69–73. Davidson had six troops of the Tenth Cavalry and three companies of the Eleventh Infantry, together with forty-four Tonkawa scouts under Lt. Richard H. Pratt and a section of howitzers. Buell commanded four troops of the Ninth Cavalry and two of the Tenth. Two companies of the Eleventh Infantry guarded his train. Buell counted about 300, Davidson about 400 officers and men. For the organization of Davidson's command, see *Army and Navy Journal, 12* (Sept. 19, 1874), 85.

10. Known as "Anderson's Fort" in honor of the infantry commander Maj. Thomas M. Anderson, the supply base was on the site of Mackenzie's base camp in 1872. The Freshwater Fork of the Brazos is also known as Catfish Creek and White River.

11. Mackenzie was notorious for the infrequency and brevity of his official reports. Private correspondence is almost nonexistent. Most accounts of this expedition rest on Carter. See also Wallace, *Ranald S. Mackenzie on the Texas Frontier*, chap. 8; Wallace, ed., *Ranald S. Mackenzie's Correspondence Relating to Texas, 1873–1879*, chap. 2; Nye, *Carbine and Lance*, pp. 221–25; and Haley, *Fort Concho and the Texas Frontier*, pp. 213–26.

12. Buell's movements are detailed in Leckie, *The Buffalo Soldiers*, pp. 125–30. See also documents in Taylor, ed., pp. 79–83; and *Army and Navy Journal 12* (Oct. 31, 1874), 180.

13. W. C. Brown, "General Baldwin's Rescue of the Germain Sisters," in Alice Baldwin, *Memoirs of the Late Frank D. Baldwin*, pp. 70–78. *Army and Navy Journal, 12* (Nov. 21, 1874), 228.

14. Miles to Asst. Adj. Gen. Dept. Mo., March 4, 1875, in Taylor, ed., p. 203. See also pp. 102–6. *Army and Navy Journal, 12* (Nov. 14, 1874), 212–13. After resting and refitting for eleven days, Davidson had left Fort Sill for his second expedition on October 21.

15. Davidson's movements are detailed in Leckie, *The Buffalo Soldiers*, pp. 130–33; and by Pratt, chap. 8. See also Davidson's reports in Taylor, ed., pp. 108–9, 121–26, 139–40.

16. Johnson, pp. 66–67. "I have placed the little gentleman in arrest," Miles wrote his wife on Nov. 16, "ordered him to Camp Supply and shall prefer charges against him." Later, Pope wrote Miles a "beseeching letter" to drop the charges and let the matter die quietly. Miles to Shrman, Dec. 27, 1874, Sherman Papers, vol. 37, LC.

17. Miles' report in Taylor, ed., pp. 129, 204. Berthrong, p. 396.

18. Quoted in Johnson, p. 69. See also *Army and Navy Journal*, *12* (Feb. 27, 1875), 453–54; (March 20, 1875), 506.
19. The debate over this issue is contained in correspondence printed in Taylor, ed., pp. 90–102, 130–133, 178–79, 181–87. Sheridan's views, Oct. 5, Nov. 11, and Nov. 17, 1874, are on pp. 91, 102, 96; Sherman's, Feb. 26 and 27, March 1, 1875, on pp. 179, 183–84.
20. Pratt, chap. 9. Berthrong, pp. 396–403. Taylor, ed., pp. 194–96. Pratt discloses how he obtained the cooperation of Kicking Bird in this inglorious process by seeming to support the pretensions of a rival, Dangerous Eagle, to his chieftainship. On May 4, 1875, Kicking Bird died following a mysterious seizure. Poison was suspected, but never proved.
21. Berthrong, pp. 401–2. Leckie, *The Buffalo Soldiers*, pp. 135–40. Neill's report, April 7, 1875, in SW, *Annual Report* (1875), pp. 86–88. Neill's report gave high praise to the troop of the Sixth Cavalry but condemned the two troops of the Tenth, part of Davidson's command from Fort Sill. The report set off a long controversy in which the Tenth's officers plausibly defended the behavior of their men and criticised Neill. The dispute may be viewed against the backdrop of a feud between Neill and Davidson that Sherman settled in favor of Davidson. See Taylor, ed., pp. 144, 175–77.
22. Henely's report, April 26, 1875, in SW, *Annual Report* (1875), pp. 88–94. See also documents in Taylor, ed., pp. 221–33; and Homer W. Wheeler, *Buffalo Days: Forty Years in the Old West* (New York and Chicago, 1923), chap. 14.
23. Miles' letters to his wife, in Johnson, pp. 55–66. Miles to Sherman, Sept. 27, 1874, Sherman Papers, vol. 37, LC. At the request of the Secretary of War, Pope spent about ten days at West Point studying the curriculum. *Army and Navy Journal*, *12* (Oct. 10, 1874), 134.
24. For Mackenzie's complaints, see Wallace, ed., *Ranald S. Mackenzie's Official Correspondence Relating to Texas*, 1873–1879, pp. 105, 150–51, 157, 160. For Miles' complaints, see Johnson, pp. 59, 66; Taylor, ed., pp. 197–216.
25. Pope to Belknap, Jan. 23, 1875, Sherman Papers, vol. 90, pp. 409–17, LC. The supply problem is well treated in Robert C. Carriker, *Fort Supply, Indian Territory: Frontier Outpost on the Plains* (Norman, Okla., 1970), chap. 4.
26. Oct. 10, 1874, in Taylor, ed., p. 72.
27. Sept. 18, 1874, in *ibid.*, pp. 41–42.
28. Pope to Drum, Feb. 15, 1874, in *ibid.*, pp. 174–75. Sheridan to Augur, Dec. 1, 1874, in Wallace, ed., pp. 177–78.
29. Pratt, chap. 10. Mooney, *Calendar History of the Kiowa*, pp. 214–16.
30. Pratt, chaps. 11–20.

☆ FOURTEEN ☆

Sitting Bull, 1870-76

"HE HAD A BIG BRAIN and a good one, a strong heart and a generous one," recalled an old warrior of Sitting Bull. "No man in the Sioux nation was braver than Sitting Bull," said Frank Grouard, who lived with him for five years before becoming an army scout; and he added, "Sitting Bull's name was a 'tipi word' for all that was generous and great."[1] Of compelling countenance and commanding demeanor, quick of thought and emphatic in judgments, he enjoyed the rare distinction of exerting leadership not only as war and political chief but as religious functionary as well. His influence extended beyond his own tribe, the Hunkpapa Sioux, to the Blackfoot and other Sioux groups with which the Hunkpapas ranged the lower Yellowstone and up the Missouri to Fort Peck. Moreover, when these tribes came together with their Oglala, Brulé, Miniconjou, and Sans Arc kinsmen to the south, in the Powder and Bighorn country, Sitting Bull's counsel commanded still wider attention and respect. Even the Northern Cheyennes and Northern Arapahoes, who often traveled with the Sioux, responded to his leadership.

Hatred of white people and anger over their continued encroachment on Indian lands fueled a determination in Sitting Bull not to yield or compromise or even to negotiate. Whites had heard of him as early as 1865, when he prevented the Hunkpapas from talking peace with General Sully and led a vigorous assault on the Missouri River bastion of Fort Rice.[2] Ranging to the north and east of the Bozeman Trail, he had taken no part in Red Cloud's War of 1866–68 or in the far-reaching treaty that ended it. But after Red Cloud abandoned the warpath and made his mark on the Fort Laramie Treaty, Sitting Bull's name began to appear with growing frequency in the white man's newspapers as leader of the nontreaty Sioux. Other chiefs also figured prominently in the "hostile" leadership—Black Moon, No Neck, Black Twin, Four Horns—and, too, there were warriors of rising stature such as Crazy Horse of the Oglalas and Gall and Rain-in-the-Face of the Hunkpapas. But to the whites, Sitting Bull emerged in the early 1870s as the embodiment of Sioux hostility. And so far as the Indian political structure permitted such a distinction, it is probable that the Sioux themselves came close to viewing him in this role.

Sitting Bull's rise did not throw Red Cloud into eclipse. He remained the most powerful Oglala chief, in peace as in war seemingly possessed of infinite capacity for tormenting white officialdom. Mainly at issue was a fundamental objective of government policy toward the Sioux—to lure them onto a reservation and subserve them to the apparatus of Indian administration. The groundwork had been laid in the Treaty of 1868, which defined the Great Sioux Reservation—roughly present South Dakota west of the Missouri River—and promised free rations and other presents to those who would affiliate with an agency (see p. 135). Success of the reservation program, however, depended in large measure on firmly attaching Red Cloud's Oglalas and Spotted Tail's Brulés to an agency. As the government's best Indian negotiators discovered, these two chiefs were as formidable in diplomacy as in war.

A treaty stipulation of central importance to policy makers was that the Sioux agencies be built on the Missouri River. Supplies could then be forwarded quickly and cheaply by river steamer, and military surveillance would be facilitated. Because Congress had entrusted expenditure of the 1868 appropriation for feeding the Plains Indians to General Sherman (see pp. 136–37), the organization of the Great Sioux Reservation fell to the army. Sherman chose retired Gen. William S. Harney for the mission, and during the summer of 1868 he established the Missouri River agencies—Grand River Agency (moved and renamed Standing Rock Agency in 1875) for Hunkpapas, Blackfoot, and Yanktonais; Cheyenne River Agency for Miniconjous, Sans Arcs, Blackfeet, and Two Kettles; and Whetstone Agency for Brulés and Oglalas. Crow Creek and Lower Brulé Agencies served Lower Brulés, Yanktonais, and Two Kettles.[3]

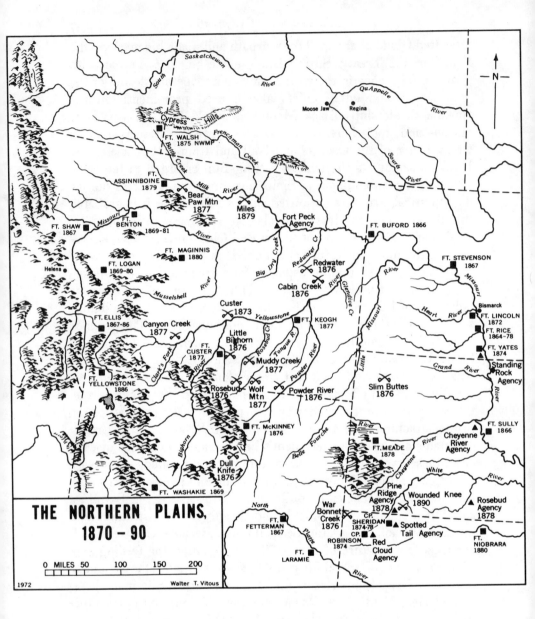

THE NORTHERN PLAINS, 1870–90

0 MILES 50 100 150 200

1972   Walter T. Vitous

Saskatchewan River
South
Qu'Appelle River
Moose Jaw   Regina
Cypress Hills
FT. WALSH 1875 NWMP
Frenchman Creek
Souris River
FT. ASSINNIBOINE 1879
Battle Creek
Milk River
Bear Paw Mtn 1877
Miles 1879
Fort Peck Agency
FT. BUFORD 1866
FT. SHAW 1867
FT. BENTON 1869–81
Missouri River
FT. STEVENSON 1867
FT. MAGINNIS 1880
Big Dry Creek
Redwater Cr.
Redwater 1876
Missouri River
Heart River
Bismarck
FT. LOGAN 1869–80
Helena
Musselshell River
Cabin Creek 1876
Glendive Cr.
FT. LINCOLN 1872
FT. RICE 1864–78
Custer 1873
Yellowstone
FT. KEOGH 1877
FT. YATES 1874
FT. ELLIS 1867–86
Little Bighorn 1876
Rosebud Cr.
Tongue R.
Powder River
Little Missouri River
Grand River
Standing Rock Agency
Canyon Creek 1877
FT. CUSTER 1877
Clark's Fork
Muddy Creek 1877
FT. YELLOWSTONE 1886
Rosebud 1876
Wolf Mtn 1877
Powder River 1876
Slim Buttes 1876
FT. SULLY 1866
Bighorn
FT. McKINNEY 1876
Belle Fourche River
FT. MEADE 1878
Cheyenne River
Cheyenne River Agency
Dull Knife 1876
White River
FT. WASHAKIE 1869
North Platte
War Bonnet Creek 1876
Pine Ridge Agency
Wounded Knee 1890
Rosebud Agency 1878
FT. FETTERMAN 1867
CP. SHERIDAN 1874–78
Spotted Tail Agency
CP. ROBINSON 1874
Red Cloud Agency
FT. NIOBRARA 1880
FT. LARAMIE
River

But Red Cloud and Spotted Tail had no desire to go to the Missouri River. They and their followers preferred more familiar and congenial haunts. For years they had hunted the Powder and upper Republican country and traded at Fort Laramie. They intended to continue this way of life. Despite the treaty, whose contents had been badly explained if not deliberately misrepresented to them, they insisted on picking up their rations and presents at an agency located somewhere near Fort Laramie.

For almost five years Red Cloud and his more polished rival, Spotted Tail, pursued a course of intransigence and obstructionism. They visited Washington, conferred with Great Father Grant and his lieutenants, and in turn received a procession of emissaries from the capital. To the disgust of the generals, step by step the government gave in. Finally, late in 1873, after several interim locations, agencies for the two tribes were fixed on the upper reaches of White River. The sites fell in Nebraska rather than the Great Sioux Reservation and were so distant from both the Missouri and the Platte as to make supply expensive and military oversight difficult. But by this time almost any location seemed preferable to further disputation.[4]

According to possibly inflated official figures, some 9,000 Oglalas, 2,000 Northern Cheyennes, and 1,500 Northern Arapahoes drew rations at Red Cloud Agency, and about 8,000 Brulés at nearby Spotted Tail Agency. On the Missouri River, about 7,000 Indians attached themselves to Grand River Agency and roughly the same number to Cheyenne River Agency. Some 3,000 were at Crow Creek and Lower Brulé. Whetstone never attracted more than 1,000 or 2,000, chiefly "Laramie Loafers," and was abandoned after establishment of the White River agencies.[5]

Agency Indians such as the Laramie Loafers felt the sting of Sitting Bull's taunt: "Look at me—see if I am poor, or my people either. . . . You are fools to make yourselves slaves to a piece of fat bacon, some hard-tack, and a little sugar and coffee."[6] And in fact only a small number of these thousands of Sioux and Cheyennes could be counted as confirmed "agency Indians." For most, the lure of the old hunting life proved as strong as the lure of the white man's hardtack and coffee. Nothing prevented them from sampling both. Back and forth they shuttled between the agencies and the camps of Sitting Bull and other nontreaty chiefs.

Not surprisingly, therefore, the agencies often played host to large numbers of Indians of volatile disposition. These people, observed Col. David S. Stanley, passed "half their time at these agencies and half in the hostile camps. They abuse the agents, threaten their lives, kill their cattle at night, and do anything they can to oppose the civilizing movement, but eat all the provisions they can get."[7] Because soldiers were regarded as a corrupting influence, the Sioux agencies were not located at the Missouri River posts: Grand River was 100 miles below Fort Rice, Cheyenne River 12 miles above Fort Sully, and Whetstone 30 miles above Fort Randall. But continuing disorders made military help imperative, and in the spring of 1870 General Hancock, Department of Dakota commander, stationed two infantry companies each at Grand River and Cheyenne River and one each at Crow Creek, Lower Brulé, and Whetstone. He judged this arrangement unsatisfactory because the troops were too few to compel respect for government authority, but his recommendation that the agencies be moved to the forts went unheeded.[8]

Five years of turmoil at the Missouri River agencies might have been taken as a hint of the fate in store for government personnel at Red Cloud and Spotted Tail Agencies, which were seventy-five miles from the nearest soldiers at Fort Laramie. As the winter of 1873–74 approached, thousands of turbulent Indians from the north descended on these agencies and made them nightmares of anarchy. There were several killings, including the chief clerk at Red Cloud and an army officer, Lt. Levi Robinson. Both agents, their lives constantly in jeopardy and all semblance of control lost, called urgently for help. Despite misgivings in the Indian Bureau, early in March 1874, on General Sherman's authority, Col. John E. Smith led a formidable expedition of nearly 1,000 cavalry and infantry from Fort Laramie in a punishing winter march to White River. The troublemakers stampeded back to the Powder River camps and the crisis passed. Near Red Cloud Agency Smith established a post that he named in honor of the slain Lieutenant Robinson. It was destined to become a key military base in the war shaping up with the Sioux. Camp Sheridan guarded Spotted Tail Agency.[9]

Not only the turmoil at the agencies prompted the confident military forecast of a general war with the Sioux. Friction with bands off the reservation grew yearly more ominous. They committed occasional depredations in Nebraska, harassed the Sweet-water mining camps around South Pass, and raided settlements in Montana's Gallatin Valley. Also, they tormented the Crows in their reservation homeland along the upper Yellowstone and the Shoshonis of Wind River.[10]

To those who suffered from these aggressions, white and Indian alike, the fluidity between agency and raiding Sioux added insult to injury. As General Hancock complained in 1872, the Sioux obtained arms and ammunition from traders at the Missouri River agencies and at private trading posts such as Forts Peck, Belknap, and Browning. Often leaving their women, children, and old people to be fed and cared for at the agency, they joined the nomads in raids, then came back to the agency to draw rations, boast openly of their deeds, and subject agency personnel to such abuse that troops had to be kept in residence for their protection.[11] Government policies that permitted such conditions aroused bitter protest in the West.

To meet the Sioux incursions, General Augur and his successor, General Ord, disposed most of the troops in the Department of the Platte to protect the Union Pacific Railroad and sent patrols each summer into threatened areas of western Nabraska. In 1870 Augur established Camp Stambaugh near South Pass to guard the Sweetwater miners and Camp Brown (renamed Fort Washakie in 1878) to keep the hostiles away from the Shoshoni Agency on Wind River. In the Department of Dakota, Fort Ellis gave a military presence to the exposed Gallatin Valley but failed to discourage Sioux raids. The Crows defended themselves as best they could while their agent complained of the ineptitude of the Fort Ellis garrison.[12]

The raids of the Sioux and their Cheyenne and Arapaho allies went considerably beyond the limits of the hunting grounds guaranteed them by the Treaty of 1868. The definition of the unceded territory was imprecise, but the Montana, Nebraska, and Sweetwater settlements fell unmistakably outside its most generous interpretation. In fact, the Indians no more than the whites respected treaty boundaries—even when clearly defined and understood—if contrary to their interests or inclinations. And to the Indians, quite apart from the usual raiding instinct, white violations of reservation and unceded lands furnished ample provocation and justification. Two provocations in particular made a test of arms almost inevitable.

In only two years, 1870–72, the rails of the Northern Pacific advanced across the Minnesota and Dakota prairie to the Missouri River. Their arrival at the Missouri brought forth the town of Bismarck on the east bank and, on the west bank three miles downstream, a new military post. First called Fort McKeen when it was established in the spring of 1872, it was renamed Fort Abraham Lincoln the following November. Far in front of the railhead, surveyors worked toward the Rockies. To the Sioux, watching their progress west of the Missouri, they were alarming harbingers of the iron horse.

Whether the projected route of the Northern Pacific up the Yellowstone Valley violated Sioux territory as described by the Treaty of 1868 might have been debated at some length—although, strangely, it was not. The definition of the unceded territory—east of the Bighorn Mountains and north of the North Platte River—left obscure whether it extended north of the Bighorns as far as the Yellowstone. There could be no debate, however, over the attitude of the Sioux. They had occupied the buffalo plains as far north as the Missouri for a couple of generations and regarded them as indisputably Sioux domain. The prospect of a railroad anywhere in this land was thoroughly obnoxious and sure to arouse angry opposition. They rightly saw in it a force that would bring about the destruction of the buffalo and an influx of whites, and that would consequently leave them little choice but to go to the reservation and live on the dole.[13]

General Sherman viewed the Northern Pacific in the same light, and he placed the army at the service of the railroad.[14] Formidable military escorts protected the surveyors in the summers of 1871, 1872, and 1873.[15] Sitting Bull's Sioux resisted, most vigorously the expedition of 1873. This expedition, commanded by Col. David S. Stanley, numbered almost 1,500 soldiers and 400 civilians, including ten troops of the Seventh Cavalry under Lt. Col. George A. Custer. A train of 275 wagons, supplemented by steamboats plying the Missouri and the Yellowstone, provided supplies.[16]

On August 4, 1873, near the mouth of Tongue River, about 300 warriors tried to draw Custer and two of his troops, reconnoitering in advance of the main column, into an ambush. Custer foiled the attempt and fought off the assailants for three hours, then mounted his command and charged with a vigor that scattered the Indians. A week later, on August 11, Custer and eight troops of the Seventh collided with swarming Sioux on the north bank of the Yellowstone below the mouth of the Bighorn. Custer expertly countered the Indian thrusts and, the band blaring "Garryowen," galloped in pursuit for ten miles.

Custer estimated that in the two actions his men had felled 40 warriors. He believed he had faced 800 to 1,000 warriors on August 11; Stanley's estimate of 500 is probably more accurate. In the first engagement one soldier had been wounded, in the second one killed and three wounded, including Lt. Charles Braden, down with a badly shattered leg that later forced his retirement for disability.

The Stanley expedition passed three months, June 20 to September 23, in the field, penetrating as far west as the Bighorn and examining the Musselshell Valley too. This expedition was bigger by far than its predecessors, stayed out longer, and stirred the Indians to greater fury, as evidenced by their tenacity in the two battles with Custer. Although the Panic of 1873 threw the Northern Pacific into bankruptcy and granted the Sioux several years' reprieve from the railroad, the surveys of 1871–73 added momentously to the accumulating Sioux grievances. And the white men had no sooner receded from the Yellowstone than they burst into the Black Hills.

Rumor had long endowed the Black Hills with great mineral wealth. Throughout the 1860s Dakota promoters had sought to verify the rumors, either through a government-sponsored geological survey or private gold-hunting expeditions. But this beautiful land of pine-clad mountains lay deep in Sioux country, and the army's help was indispensable. Before 1868, the army, fully occupied with the Union Pacific Railroad and the Bozeman Trail, had no wish to encourage new frontiers that would require military protection. After 1868, the army was bound to oppose any such venture, for the Fort Laramie Treaty placed the Black Hills plainly within the Great Sioux Reservation. Not even the uncertainties of the unceded territory clouded Sioux title to this part of their domain. Even so, public sentiment for opening the Hills grew steadily stronger. Indian rights seemed of minor consequence to men idled by the depression that gripped the nation in the wake of the Panic of 1873.[17]

By 1873 military interests also favored a penetration of the Black Hills. Pondering how best to counter Sioux raids in Ord's Department of the Platte, General Sheridan envisioned a large fort in the Black Hills, "so that by holding an interior point in the heart of the Indian country we could threaten the villages and stock of the Indians, if they made raids on our settlements." In the autumn of 1873 Sheridan discussed the matter with the President and the Secretaries of War and Interior and won their encouragement. The result was the Custer expedition of 1874. Its chief purpose was to locate a suitable site for a military post. The presence of two "practical miners" testified to other purposes as well.[18]

Numbering more than 1,000 men in ten troops of the Seventh Cavalry and two companies of infantry, the Black Hills Expedition left Fort Abraham Lincoln on July 2, 1874. The march was a grand picnic amid game-rich forests and lush meadows cut by clear streams abounding in fish. The engineers mapped the country, and Custer named the principal peaks for such military luminaries as Harney, Terry, and himself. Near Bear Butte, on the northeastern border of the Hills, Custer found a good location for a fort. The miners discovered traces of gold in the streams—enough to arouse warm interest but not enough to interfere with baseball games, glee club sings, and champagne suppers.

As the column turned back toward Fort Lincoln, Scout Charley Reynolds carried official reports and newspaper dispatches southwest to Fort Laramie for telegraphic transmission to the East. In these and subsequent reports Custer wrote glowingly of the rich farming, grazing, and lumbering potential of the Black Hills. Although one report contained a much-quoted reference to "gold among the roots of the grass," on the whole his assessment of mineral prospects was restrained. The expedition was back at Fort Lincoln by August 30. Already, based on the dispatches brought out by Reynolds, the press had whipped up a gold fever.

At once the President announced that the army would bar prospectors from Indian domain. But as the *New York Tribune* editorialized, "If there is gold in the Black Hills, no army on earth can keep the adventurous men of the west out of them."[19] The army tried, to the embarrassment and substantial loss of a number of parties intercepted en route or expelled after arrival. Through-

out the spring and summer of 1875, troops from the Missouri
River forts and from Camp Robinson and Fort Laramie performed
this service. General Crook, newly assigned to command the Department of the Platte after his dazzling Arizona successes, even
went into the Hills himself. Despite the efforts of the soldiers,
whose sympathies lay clearly with the intruders, some 800 miners
worked the streams of the Black Hills during the summer of
1875.[20]

Meanwhile, the government tried to solve the problem by pur-
chasing the Black Hills from the Sioux. In an effort to verify Custer's reports and fix a price, the geological survey long sought by
Dakotans was sent out from Fort Laramie in the summer of 1875.
Geologist Walter P. Jenny headed the expedition, and about 400
soldiers under Lt. Col. Richard I. Dodge went along as escort. The
very presence of more soldiers in the Hills further incensed the Indians, and Jenny's disclosure of rich mineral deposits compounded
the problem by stimulating still greater immigration.[21]

The question of ceding the Black Hills was broached to Red
Cloud and Spotted Tail during a visit to Washington in June
1875. Later, in September, a special commission headed by Sen.
William B. Allison went to Red Cloud Agency to continue the discussions. In a series of wild councils, the emissaries encountered
belligerence, intransigence, and what impressed them as an out-
rageously inflated conception of the worth of the Black Hills. Always a treasured part of the Plains Indians' hunting grounds, this
country had now become even more valuable to them simply because it had become so valuable to the white man. "Our Great
Father has a big safe, and so have we," declared Spotted Bear.
"This hill is our safe." It seemed worth much more than the paltry
$6 million the Great Father offered for it, or the $400,000 per
year for which he was willing to lease it. More skilfull negotiators
probably could have brought the agency chiefs to terms. But the
young men from the hunting bands in the north, although a minority, adamantly opposed any deal and stood ready to back up
this position by force if necessary. Mainly because of them, the
negotiations ended in stalemate.[22]

This outcome presented the government with an acute embarrassment. In every legal and moral sense the Black Hills belonged
to the Sioux, and no white man had a right to be there. Yet white
men already held effective possession, and the government could

not hope any longer to resist the public demand for an official opening of the coveted territory. The Allison commission had failed to throw a mantle of legal and moral rationalization over the seizure of the Black Hills. Another means had to be found.

The breakdown of negotiations for the Black Hills capped seven years of mounting frustration with the Sioux hunting bands. They raided all around the periphery of the unceded territory. They terrorized friendly tribes. They contested the advance of the Northern Pacific Railroad. They disrupted the management of the reservation Indians while obtaining recruits, supplies, and munitions at the agencies for these hostile activities. And now they interfered with the sale of the Black Hills. The right to roam outside the boundaries of the Great Sioux Reservation—on the upper Republican and in the unceded territory—made all this possible. In June 1875 Red Cloud and Spotted Tail were persuaded, for a monetary consideration, to relinquish the Republican River hunting rights. Three months later the failure of the Allison commission focused the attention of top government officials on the more crucial question of the unceded territory.

Almost from the ratification of the Treaty of 1868, military leaders had seen in the repeated aggressions of the hunting bands justification for extinguishing their right to range the unceded territory. "Inasmuch as the Sioux have not lived at peace," declared General Serman in 1873, "I think Congress has a perfect right to abrogate the whole of that treaty, or any part of it; . . . I would like to see the Sioux forced to live near the Missouri River, north of Nebraska, for that was the ultimate design and purpose of the Peace Commission of 1867–68."[23] Commissioner of Indian Affairs Francis Walker (1872–73) would tolerate any provocation to buy time for railroads and settlement to solve the problem, but his successor, Edward P. Smith, came to share Sherman's view. In a show of militance almost without precedent in the Indian Bureau, he urged in 1873 that a military command be stationed at every Sioux agency, that the Sioux be kept on the Great Sioux Reservation, and that the hunting bands be compelled, by military force if necessary, to quit the unceded territory and settle on the reservation.[24] The Black Hills crisis of 1875 won these views a wider acceptance than they had ever before attained.

On November 3, 1875, a meeting was held at the White House

that included President Grant, Secretary of War Belknap, Secretary of the Interior Zachariah Chandler, Commissioner of Indian Affairs Smith, and Generals Sheridan and Crook. Although the evidence is thin, almost certainly these discussions produced decisions, first, to withdraw troops from Black Hills duty, thereby allowing the mineral region to fill with prospectors; and second, to initiate immediate measures to force the hunting bands out of the unceded territory and onto the reservation, thereby ending their raiding activities and diminishing their power to obstruct a Black Hills settlement.[25]

As General Sherman understood the first decision, settlement would now be officially sanctioned all along the western boundary of the Great Sioux Reservation—i.e., in the unceded territory, which was now to be denied to the hunting bands—"and if some go over the Boundary into the Black Hills, I understand that the President and Interior Dept will wink at it for the present."[26] By the winter of 1875–76, the President and the Interior Department were winking at about 15,000 miners in the Black Hills.[27]

As for the second decision: On November 9, six days after the White House meeting, the Indian Bureau came up with some solid documentation for a forceful move against the Indians. Inspector E. C. Watkins, completing a tour of the Sioux country, penned a scathing indictment of "certain wild and hostile bands" under Sitting Bull and other chiefs who roamed the unceded territory. Describing their repeated offenses against settlers and other Indian tribes, he concluded: "The true policy, in my judgment, is to send troops against them in the winter, the sooner the better, and *whip* them into subjection." Both Commissioner Smith and Secretary Chandler instantly embraced this recommendation and commended it to the War Department. On December 6, in response to a directive from Secretary Chandler, Smith instructed the Sioux agents to send out runners to notify all Indians in the unceded territory to move onto the reservation by January 31, 1876. Otherwise, they would be certified as hostile and the army would come after them. Having thus made the Indian Bureau publicly responsible for a military offensive, Commissioner E. P. Smith resigned, and another Smith, J. Q., replaced him.

Runners carried the government's ultimatum to the winter camps on the Yellowstone and its tributaries. Even had the Indians been given ample time, and even had the season been congenial to travel, it is doubtful if many would have made an effort to comply. Not unexpectedly, January 31, 1876, came and went without measurable response. On February 1, therefore, Secretary Chandler notified Secretary Belknap that "Said Indians are hereby turned over to the War Department for such action on the part of the Army as you may deem proper under the circumstances"; and the army, "as requested by the Interior Department," promptly began organizing the winter campaign Inspector Watkins had called for in November.

The stage had been deftly set for a military solution to the long-festering Sioux problem. It is difficult to resist the conclusion that the sequence of events beginning with the Watkins report of November 9 and ending with Interior's action of February 1 certifying as hostile all Indians off the reservation proceeded according to a scenario carefully worked out at the White House on November 3. Thus began "Sitting Bull's War."[28]

General Sheridan saw success dependent on a quick move against the Indians while they lay vulnerable in their winter camps and before they received the usual spring reinforcements from the agencies. "Unless they are caught before early spring," he warned, "they cannot be caught at all."[29] Not until February 8, however, was Sheridan able to signal the advance to his subordinate generals, Terry in St. Paul and Crook in Omaha. Already Terry had learned that Sitting Bull was not on the Little Missouri, as reported, but about 200 miles farther west. This meant that the swift cavalry thrust Terry had hoped Custer might make from Fort Lincoln would have to be given up and an expedition involving considerably more preparation organized. Heavy snows slowed the concentration of the Seventh Cavalry at Fort Lincoln and stopped the flow of supplies over the Northern Pacific from St. Paul. Gradually, Terry's winter campaign came more and more to look like a spring or even a summer campaign.[30]

Meanwhile, General Crook was also discovering how powerful an antagonist a northern Plains winter could be. With his customary drive, he managed to have an expedition assembled at Fort Fetterman, Wyoming, by the end of February 1876. Consisting of five troops of the Second Cavalry, five troops of the Third, and two companies of the Fourth Infantry, it numbered almost 900 officers, enlisted men, and civilians. Crook had brought his pack trains from Arizona, and five trains of eighty mules each, supplemented by about eighty wagons, hauled forage and other provisions. Crook assigned command of the expedition to the affable and elderly colonel of the Third Cavalry, Joseph J. Reynolds, whose name had recently been tainted by contractor scandals in Texas. Crook went along himself, ostensibly as an observer but, except for one short, crucial period, actually in command. "Shrouded from head to foot in huge wrappings of wool and fur," according to Crook's aide, the men of the Bighorn expedition swung out of Fort Fetterman under clear skies on March 1 and headed up the old Bozeman Trail.[31]

The worst adversary turned out to be the weather. For four days, March 7–10, a "norther" pummeled the command, piling up snow and dropping the temperature below zero. The wagons had been left under infantry guard on Crazy Woman's Fork, and the troops suffered through tentless nights. Grimly they pushed on to the Tongue River and, following Indian signs, down that stream. Driving wind and bitter cold came in the wake of the storm. On three nights the mercury congealed in the thermometer. Ice and snow made marching treacherous and exhausting.

Crook turned east, toward the Powder. On March 16 the scouts spied a pair of Indians headed east. Possibly to afford Reynolds a chance to polish his tarnished reputation,[32] Crook gave him the mission of following them. Three of the two-troop squadrons into which the cavalry had been divided, about 300 men, moved out with Reynolds in the early evening. The remaining two squadrons and the pack trains stayed with Crook.

During the night the scouts discovered the Indian village, numbering about 100 lodges, in a cottonwood grove beside Powder River. At the time, the troops believed that it belonged to Crazy Horse. Subsequent evidence strongly indicates that it consisted mostly of Old Bear's Cheyennes and some visiting Oglala Sioux under He Dog, about 200 warriors and their families.[33] Reynolds' plan to strike the village from two directions miscarried because the scouts had not described its location or the topographical character of its approaches with sufficient exactitude. Nevertheless, one squadron managed to get into the village, drive its occupants into the bluffs bordering the valley, and begin the destruction of the lodges and their contents. Another squadron seized the pony herd, some 600 to 800 head. Then the warriors counterattacked. The leadership of Reynolds and two of the squadron commanders

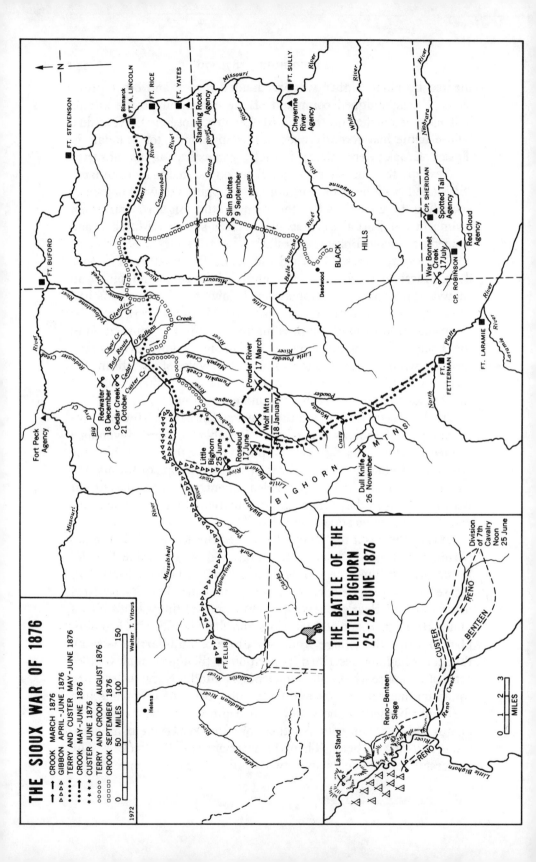

THE SIOUX WAR OF 1876

CROOK MARCH 1876
GIBBON APRIL - JUNE 1876
TERRY AND CUSTER MAY - JUNE 1876
CROOK MAY - JUNE 1876
CUSTER JUNE 1876
TERRY AND CROOK AUGUST 1876
CROOK SEPTEMBER 1876

0   50   100   150
MILES

Walter T. Vitous
1972

THE BATTLE OF THE LITTLE BIGHORN 25 - 26 JUNE 1876

0   1   2   3
MILES

Division of 7th Cavalry Noon 25 June

RENO
BENTEEN
CUSTER
Reno Creek
Little Bighorn
Reno-Benteen Siege
Last Stand
RENO
Little Bighorn River

proved unequal to the occasion, and the troops withdrew with more haste than dignity, leaving the bodies of two soldiers to the enemy. Compounding the humiliation, that night the Indians recaptured most of their pony herd.

Beyond the destruction of the village, Reynolds had not hurt the Indians too badly. He had inflicted few casualties and had let them take back their ponies. His own losses were four killed and six wounded. Crook and Reynolds rejoined, and, amid warm disputation and continued bitterly cold weather, the command limped back to Fort Fetterman. On the day of his arrival, Crook brought charges against Reynolds for mismanaging the Battle of Powder River. The implication was that his failure led to the failure of the campaign and the return to Fort Fetterman.[34] Actually, even Sheridan, the leading exponent of winter campaigns, recognized the true cause in "the severity of the weather."[35] As the disconsolate Reynolds complained to Sherman: "General, these winter campaigns in these latitudes should be prohibited. . . . The month of March has told on me more than any five years of my life."[36]

Defeating Crook and paralyzing Terry, winter had frustrated Sheridan's plan of forcing the hunting bands out of the unceded territory before spring. Thus winter had also made certain a summer campaign, for as the Commissioner of Indian Affairs correctly warned, "Nothing now could be so damaging as a failure to carry out the military threat thus made to them."[37] Actually, despite their statements for public consumption, Crook, Terry, and even Sheridan perceived from the first that more than a quick midwinter thrust would prove necessary. As early as February, all three foresaw a summer campaign.[38]

The strategy of the summer campaign evolved easily from the plans and movements already made. Crook would refit and again push northward. Once Custer's preparations were completed at Fort Abraham Lincoln, he would march westward. And Col. John Gibbon would move eastward from Fort Ellis, Montana. Since the Indians were mobile and their location indefinite, these columns would act independently, each searching for and, if possible, engaging the enemy. Although no concert of action was planned, hopefully Custer would sweep the hostiles westward toward the Bighorn River and Crook would drive them back on Custer. Gibbon, patrolling the north bank of the Yellowstone, would intercept any that tried to flee northward toward the Missouri. Thus the

Sioux campaign of 1876 was modeled after the successful Red River campaign of 1874–75—converging columns harassing and tiring the Indians and striving to bring some to battle. Also paralleling the Red River strategy, Sheridan proposed to place the agency Indians under military control and to build two forts in the hostile country, one at the mouth of the Tongue and the other at the mouth of the Bighorn.[39]

Gibbon was first in the field. Late in February Terry had instructed him to organize a command and march eastward to head off any Indians Crook might drive northward. Crook's withdrawal after the action of March 17 lessened the urgency. Even so, the "Montana Column" pushed off from Fort Ellis on March 30 and plowed through deep snow in the Bozeman Pass to the Yellowstone. The column consisted of six companies of the Seventh Infantry and four troops of the Second Cavalry—about 450 men in all. Maj. James Brisbin—"Grasshopper Jim"—commanded the cavalry despite crippling rheumatism. Pausing at the Crow Agency to enlist twenty-five Crow Indian scouts, Gibbon began fulfilling his assignment to patrol the north bank of the Yellowstone.[40]

Not until May 17 was the expedition from Fort Abraham Lincoln ready to march. Terry, not Custer, commanded. The flamboyant, yellow-haired cavalryman had allowed himself to be drawn into partisan political strife stirred up by the Belknap scandal. He had testified indiscreetly before a congressional committee hostile to the administration and had angered President Grant. For a time it seemed tht Custer would endure the humiliation of being left behind. But at last Grant yielded to his supplications and allowed him to go, but only as commander of his regiment.[41] The "Dakota Column" consisted of all twelve troops of the Seventh Cavalry under Custer, two companies of the Seventeenth Infantry and one of the Sixth to guard the supply train, a detachment of the Twentieth Infantry serving three Gatling guns, and about forty Arikara Indian scouts. Altogether the command numbered about 925 officers and enlisted men, of whom the Seventh Cavalry accounted for some 700. Provisions were hauled in 150 wagons and also were forwarded by steamer up the Missouri and the Yellowstone to the mouth of Glendive Creek, where three companies of the Sixth Infantry from Fort Buford converted "Stanley's Stockade," a relic of the Northern Pacific survey of 1873, into a supply base. Also, even though pack transportation had never been attempted in the Department of Dakota, the wagons carried 250 pack saddles that could be used on the wagon mules should the occasion arise. Throughout late May and early June the column made its sodden way across the rain-soaked prairies of western Dakota and eastern Montana.[42]

For the second time, on May 29, Crook cast off from Fort Fetterman and marched up the old Bozeman Trail, his command now composed of ten troops of the Third Cavalry and five of the Second, two companies of the Fourth Infantry and three of the Ninth —in all 47 officers and 1,000 enlisted men. Lt. Col. William B. Royall commanded the cavalry, Maj. Alexander Chambers the infantry. One hundred and twenty wagons and 1,000 pack mules carried supplies. On Goose Creek, an affluent of the Tongue where Sheridan, Wyoming, now stands, Crook established a base camp, and here, on June 14, he was joined by 176 Crow and 86 Shoshoni Indian auxiliaries.[43]

By June 1876, the area on which the three columns converged held many more Sioux and Cheyennes than in the winter. The Black Hills issue, worsening conditions at the agencies, and the government's attempt to take away the freedom to roam the unceded territory set off an unusually large spring migration of agency Indians to the camps of the hunting bands. How many can only be guessed, for both the Indian Bureau and the army had strong motives for playing a numbers game. It seems likely, however, that 500 lodges in March grew to as many as 2,000 in June.

Later the army, professing ignorance of the increase in enemy strength, blamed the failure of the campaign on the Indian Bureau's negligence in reporting the defections from the agencies. Pointing out that each of the converging columns was alone strong enough to cope with the 500 to 800 warriors the Indian Bureau had estimated to be absent from the reservation, General Sherman implied that knowledge of their true numbers would have altered military plans and dispositions and averted disaster.[44] All past experience, however, showed that agency Indians swelled the hunting bands every spring. Moreover, as early as April 27 the army knew that the young men of the Standing Rock Agency were heading west in large numbers,[45] and on May 30 Sheridan telegraphed Sherman that "information from Crook indicates that all the agency Indians capable of taking the field are now or soon will be on the warpath."[46] The truth is that the generals worried much

less about the enemy's strength than about his traditional reluctance to stand and fight. Campaigns usually failed because the Indians could not be caught and engaged in battle. Besides, chances
of encountering any significant portion of the warrior strength at
one time were remote. Grass and game could not long support
large gatherings of Indians.

But this year the Indians did travel together, and this year they
proved not averse to standing and fighting. After the Reynolds
battle, the destitute Cheyennes fled down Powder River and found
succor with Crazy Horse's Oglalas. With them they moved northeast and united with the Hunkpapas of Sitting Bull, Black Moon,
and Gall and the Miniconjous under Lame Deer and Hump. Incensed by the soldiers' attack on the Cheyennes, the chiefs resolved
to stay together for common defense. Westward they turned, to
the Powder, the Tongue, and finally the Rosebud. Two other Sioux
tribal circles, Sans Arc and Blackfoot, formed. The Cheyenne contingent grew with the accession of parties under Lame White
Man, Dirty Moccasins, and Charcoal Bear. Scatterings of Brulés,
Yanktonais, Northern Arapahoes, and Santees (Ikpaduta's Minnesota refugees) attached themselves to the larger bodies. Throughout April and May warriors and families, singly and in groups,
straggled in from the agencies to swell the village further. Organized in six separate tribal circles, five of Sioux and one of Cheyenne, ultimately it may have held as many as 15,000 people, 3,000
to 4,000 warriors. Or accepting more conservative evidence, it
may have numbered less than 10,000 with as few as 1,500 fighting
men. Even the lower figure, however, represented an unusually
large aggregation of Indians to stay together for so long. Every
few days, seeking fresh grass for the vast pony herd, the chiefs
moved camp. Hunters ranged far in all directions to keep the
camp kettles filled with meat.[47]

In mid-June, on the Rosebud, the Hunkpapas held a sun dance.
Sitting Bull experienced a vision of many soldiers "falling right
into our camp." All these dead soldiers, he said, would be gifts of
God. Immediately after the sun dance, the Indians moved across
the Wolf Mountains and laid out their camps on a stream flowing
into the Little Bighorn. Here, on June 16, hunters brought word
of many soldiers on the upper reaches of the Rosebud. Eager to
fulfill Sitting Bull's vision, warriors from all the camp circles assembled that night and rode back to the Rosebud.

On this same day, June 16, General Crook cut loose from his wagon train and crossed from the Tongue to the Rosebud. The next morning, as the column paused for coffee, the Sioux attacked. The Indian auxiliaries held the assailants at bay for twenty minutes until the troops got organized. After the initial confusion the soldiers acquitted themselves well. Cavalry charges cleared the critical heights commanding the valley on the north. Other units occupied the bluffs south of the valley. Fierce fighting raged as attack and counterattack rippled up and down a disjointed battle line some three miles in length. The broken terrain, a jumble of hills, ridges, and ravines, fragmented the action and prevented effective central direction.

Crook mistakenly thought Crazy Horse's village lay just to the north, beyond a gorge through which the Rosebud made its way after turning in that direction from an eastward sweep. He sent Capt. Anson Mills' squadron of the Third Cavalry to seize the village and began to disengage the rest of the command to follow in support. All portions of the line instantly came under heavy pressure. Attempting to withdraw from the extreme left, Lieutenant Colonel Royall and three troops of the Third were badly mauled and almost cut off before Crook sent two companies of the Ninth Infantry to their aid. During this action a bullet smashed Capt. Guy V. Henry's jaw and knocked him from his horse. Disconcerted, his troopers gave way. Sioux swarmed toward the fallen captain. Crows and Shoshonis raced to the rescue and in a hand-to-hand fight saved the wounded officer. Royall's experience persuaded Crook that he could not give Mills the promised support, and he dispatched an aide to cancel the offensive movement. Instead of marching back up the valley, Mills veered west and returned to the battlefield cross-country. This placed him opportunely behind the Sioux and Cheyennes. Thus pressed from the rear, they broke off the fight and abandoned the battlefield.

The engagement had lasted six hours and featured some of the hardest fighting of the Indian wars. Crook had been caught in unfavorable terrain. Although not outnumbered, he never gained the initiative. His one attempt to seize it, based on erroneous information, came close to disaster. Moreover, the Crows and Shoshonis had performed embarrassingly well and more than once had saved the troops from being overrun. In Crook's defense, it should be noted that the Sioux and Cheyennes fought with a wholly unexpected unity and tenacity. Together with unusually large numbers and a topography hostile to the soldiers, they enjoyed a combination of advantages extremely rare in Indian warfare. Custer encountered the same combination a week later, with consequences far more serious than Crook suffered.

Because he was left in possession of the battlefield, Crook ever after claimed the Battle of the Rosebud as a victory. In truth, he had been badly worsted. Controversy has clouded the casualty count, but it seems probable that Chief Scout Frank Grouard's statement of twenty-eight killed and fifty-six wounded is closer to the truth than Crook's officially reported ten and twenty-one.[48] And although he may have felled as many Sioux and Cheyennes as the thirty-six killed and sixty-three wounded later acknowledged by Crazy Horse, he limped back to his supply base on Goose Creek and refused to venture forth again until reinforced. In this retreat, rather than the casualties, lay the full measure of the defeat, for it neutralized him at the most critical juncture of the campaign.

Meanwhile, ignorant of the repulse of Crook and the combativeness of the Sioux, Terry prepared his offensive. He and Gibbon had met on June 9 aboard the supply steamer *Far West* on the Yellowstone and had agreed that the findings of Gibbon's Crow scouts made it unlikely that any Sioux would be found east of the Rosebud. Even so, Terry wanted to confirm this conclusion, and on June 10 he sent Maj. Marcus A. Reno and six troops of the Seventh Cavalry to scout the Powder and Tongue valleys. During Reno's absence, Gibbon concentrated his command on the Yellowstone opposite the mouth of the Rosebud, and Terry moved his supply base from Glendive Creek to the mouth of the Powder. The infantry and all the wagons stayed at this base while Custer, relying solely on pack transportation, advanced the other six troops of the Seventh to the mouth of the Tongue to await Reno's return.

Exceeding his instructions, Reno led his troops on westward from the Tongue to the Rosebud and there found the trail of Sitting Bull's village. On June 17, while Crook clashed with Crazy Horse near the head of the Rosebud, Reno's men were examining abandoned campsites forty miles downstream. Reno turned about here and descended the Rosebud to the Yellowstone. His unauthorized movement angered Terry when he learned about it by courier on the evening of June 19, for it added little to what he already knew and could have alerted the Sioux to his approach. A plan already formed in his mind, Terry moved at once to unite his cavalry at the mouth of the Rosebud and to start Gibbon's infantry back up the north side of the Yellowstone.

On the evening of June 21 Terry, Gibbon, Custer, and Brisbin gathered around a big map in the cabin of the *Far West* to work out final details of Terry's strategy. It focused not on how to defeat the enemy but on how to catch him. Its object, recalled Gibbon, was "to prevent the escape of the Indians, which was the idea pervading the minds of all of us."[49] Since the Crow scouts had discovered smoke in the direction of the Little Bighorn, the Sioux were assumed to be camped there. Custer and the Seventh Cavalry would march up the Rosebud and drive down the Little Bighorn from the south. Gibbon, after being ferried across the Yellowstone, would ascend the Bighorn and enter the Little Bighorn Valley from the north. Custer was expected to strike the blow, but not before Gibbon had moved into a position to block flight to the north. Since June 26 was the earliest Gibbon judged he could reach the mouth of the Little Bighorn, Custer's more mobile cavalry column was to ascend the Rosebud as far as its head, beyond the point where the Indian trail diverged westward, before crossing to the Little Bighorn. This would not only militate against premature contact but also relieve Terry's apprehension that the Sioux might escape to the south before his pincers closed from the north.

Terry's adjutant general reduced the understandings of the *Far West* conference to written orders handed Custer the next morning. This document explicitly stated Terry's intent that Custer and Gibbon so maneuver as to bottle up the Indians in the Little Bighorn Valley, his expectation that Custer not follow the Indian trail west from the Rosebud but continue to the head of this stream before turning to the Little Bighorn, and his anxiety that Custer constantly watch to his left so that the Indians might not slip off to the south. The orders were also, however, framed in courteous language reflecting Terry's feeling for his subordinate's injured pride and his awareness that unforeseen circumstances might require some other course of action. In thus connecting the explicit with the permissive, Terry laid the basis for endless controversy over whether Custer had disobeyed orders.

After staging an impressive review for Terry and Gibbon, the buckskin-bedecked Custer led the Seventh Cavalry up the Rosebud at noon on June 22. The regiment numbered between 600 and 700 horsemen. Among the scouts, since the Arikaras did not know the country, were six of Gibbon's Crows. Pack mules carried extra ammunition as well as rations and forage for fifteen days. Contrasting with the smart appearance of the cavalry, the train testified to the inexperience of its managers; Crook would have pronounced it disreputable. Not part of the column were Brisbin's four troops of the Second Cavalry or the Gatling gun platoon. Custer had declined Terry's offer of both—the Gatlings because they would hamper his mobility, the additional troops because they would not enable him to defeat any enemy that the Seventh could not handle alone.

Late on June 24 the Seventh Cavalry reached the point where the Indian trail diverged to the west. Terry's plan called for continuing up the Rosebud. Instead, Custer turned west on the trail. He would follow it to the divide between the Rosebud and Little Bighorn, he informed his officers, pass June 25 resting the men and reconnoitering the country beyond for the enemy village, then attack early on June 26, the day appointed for Gibbon to reach the mouth of the Little Bighorn. A night march of ten miles, in addition to the day's thirty, brought the regiment, exhausted and scattered, to within ten miles of the summit of the divide. At dawn, from a mountaintop to the front dubbed the "Crow's Nest," the scouts made out the Sioux village about fifteen miles in the distance. Custer ordered the regiment to the crest of the divide and went to the Crow's Nest himself. Although he could not see the village, he received reports of Indians observing his movements. Convinced that the Sioux had discovered him, and spurred by visions of escaping Indians, he made his fateful decision to move at once to the attack, even though his regiment was worn out and the location and strength of the village remained to be definitely fixed.

Topping the summit at noon on June 25, Custer sent three troops, 125 men, under the senior captain, Frederick W. Benteen, on a scout to the left, or south. As the exact position of the village was not known, this movement may have reflected the continuing apprehension that the Indians might get away to the south. Custer assigned another three troops to Major Reno, retained five under his personal command, and left one in the rear to escort the pack train. Reno and Custer followed the Indian trail down the valley of a creek toward the Little Bighorn. Ahead, dust rose from behind a line of bluffs hiding the Little Bighorn from view. Immediately in front, a party of about forty Sioux warriors, the rear guard of a small camp moving to join the parent village, came into view. To Custer, the dust and the retreating warriors probably signified escaping Indians. He ordered Reno to attack—as Reno recalled it, "to move forward at as rapid a gait as prudent, and to charge afterward, and that the whole outfit would support me."[50]

Although Custer had not seen it, the village lay just ahead, across the Little Bighorn River. Beginning with the Hunkpapa circle, it extended almost three miles downstream to the Cheyenne circle and occupied most of the half-mile width of the valley. However many warriors the village contained—the minimum 1,500 estimate, the 2,500 to 3,000 that most sources support, or the 4,000 to 6,000 of some authorities—there were a great many more than Custer had soldiers, even before the fragmentation of the regiment. Many of them boasted firearms, some the efficient Winchester repeater. If they had any warning of Custer's approach, it was not much—enough to paint and prepare themselves individually but not enough to make any battle plans or dispositions. But they reacted in the one way neither Custer nor his superiors expected. Instead of running, they fought.

After fording the Little Bighorn and advancing two miles down the valley, Reno charged the upper end of the village. When Sioux swarmed to confront him, he stopped the charge short of its objective, dismounted his 112 men, and spread them in a thin skirmish line. Flanked on his left, he withdrew to the shelter of a cottonwood grove on his right. Tangled brush in the timber inhibited control. Warriors infiltrated the position. Again Reno mounted his men—those who heard the command or saw others forming—and led them in a dash for better positions on the bluffs across the river. Sioux mingled with the fleeing troopers and took a heavy toll, especially at the river crossing, before the remnants of the command gained the top of the ravine-scored bluffs rising steeply from the right bank of the river. Reno's advance, battle, and retreat lasted about forty-five minutes. He lost, in killed, wounded, and missing, almost half his command, including four officers and Scout Charley Reynolds.

Reno had expected Custer's support from the rear. Instead, Custer veered to the north and rode parallel to the river, behind the

bluffs, toward the lower end of the village, a move probably
prompted by word from Reno that the Indians were not fleeing
but advancing to give battle. At one point Custer and his headquarters group rode to the top of the bluffs and for the first time
saw the immense encampment. Below, Reno was just advancing to
the attack. Sweeping his hat in encouragement, Custer rejoined
his command. He sent his trumpeter orderly with a note to Benteen to hasten forward and bring the ammunition packs. Glancing
back as he spurred his mount, Trumpeter Giovanni Martini
caught history's last glimpse of Custer and his 215 men in life.
Shortly afterward, warriors poured across the river at the center
of the village, where a large coulee parts the bluffs. The Hunkpapa chief Gall is credited with leading this movement. The troops
fell back to a high ridge farther downstream. More warriors, freed
by Reno's retreat, streamed to Gall's support. As this force pressed
from the south, another, under Crazy Horse, circled below the village and closed from the north. Trapped in broken terrain that
favored the Indian's style of warfare, the command fragmented
along and on both sides of the battle ridge. The fight was sharp
and short—probably no longer than an hour. Custer and a small
remnant—including two brothers and a nephew—gathered around
his personal pennant at the northern end of the ridge for the
memorable "last stand" that has become so cherished a part of
American history and folklore. No white man survived, at least
none who could prove his claim.

   Benteen's scout to the left had proved fruitless. Receiving
Custer's summons, he had hastened forward and united with
Reno's shattered command just as it completed the costly withdrawal from the valley. The sound of firing from downstream
gave notice that Custer was engaged. Some officers wanted to go
to his support and, despite Reno's refusal, rode off to the north.
Others followed with their units. They reached a hill from which
they could see the Custer battlefield, but smoke and dust obscured
the action there. Warriors riding from the Custer fight blocked
further advance and drove the troops precipitously back to the
original position. The pack train had arrived safely. Reno and
Benteen laid out a perimeter defense. The men dug rifle pits. For
the remaining daylight hours of that hot Sunday, they fought off
growing numbers of exultant Sioux and Cheyennes. Next morning, June 26, the Indians renewed the siege. Twice they formed

assault parties to attempt to breach the lines, but on both occasions counterattacks spoiled the effort. By early afternoon the firing had subsided. That evening, as the battered defenders of Reno Hill watched in silence, the great village moved off to the south.

The reason for the Indian exodus became apparent the next morning, June 27, when Terry and Gibbon marched up the valley from the north. Lt. James H. Bradley and the Crow scouts found the bodies of Custer's men, many stripped and mutilated, littering the battle ridge where they had fallen. In addition, Reno lost forty-seven killed and fifty-three wounded. An officer and sixteen enlisted men thought to have been slain in the valley turned up alive; they had been left in the timber but had remained hidden until the Indians departed. Altogether, half the Seventh Cavalry lay dead or wounded. How many Indians paid for this extraordinary victory with their lives is not known, for the dead were removed by the living. Estimates vary from 30 to 300.

The Battle of the Little Bighorn gave birth to one of history's enduring controversies. There are many intriguing "ifs." What if Custer had followed Terry's plan? What if Custer had attacked with his whole regiment instead of dividing it? What if Reno had stormed into the Sioux village instead of dismounting and then retreating? What if he and Benteen had moved promptly and aggressively downstream as soon as firing was heard? These and other questions fuel endless speculation.

Whatever may be said in mitigation, the ultimate responsibility for the disaster must rest with Custer. He departed from Terry's plan even though the circumstances on which it was premised turned out to be exactly as foreseen. He precipitated a battle a day early, with worn-out men and horses, and without knowing the strength and position of the enemy. He committed his regiment piecemeal, and at the critical time no component was in supporting range of the others. If all this adds up to an appalling violation of elementary military precepts, it must be borne in mind that Indian warfare was not conventional warfare. The conventional rules were not always pertinent. Moreover, both in conventional and Indian combat, Custer had achieved some of his most striking successes by boldly defying the rules. With a little of the legendary "Custer's luck," he might well have done the same at the Little Bighorn. But luck deserted him, and the imponderables in the complicated sequence of cause and effect that reached its bloody denouement on Custer Hill insure that men will ever find it a source of fascinating study and debate.[51]

History has indicted if not fully convicted Custer of responsibility for one of the most calamitous defeats in American military annals. General Crook, perhaps because of his superlative record before and after, has escaped serious criticism. In fact, however, he bears major blame for the fiasco on Powder River in March and shares the blame for the disaster to Custer. No militarily sound explanation has been given for his division of his command before the battle of March 17. The additional force would surely have enabled him to hold the gains that Reynolds lost and, with the supply train present, to have remained on the scene. Likewise, his withdrawal to his train after the battle of June 17 left the Indians free to meet Custer without distraction. Had he summoned his train and moved down the Rosebud, he would either have developed further action or have fallen in with Custer. In either case, the course of the campaign would have been very different. Privately, General Sherman believed Crook guilty of mismanagement on both occasions.[52]

Mistakes the generals made in abundance, and in probing them history has almost overlooked the assets the opposition brought to the contest. Never before or after were the northern Plains tribes better prepared for war. They were numerous, united, confident, superbly led, emotionally charged to defend their homeland and freedom, and able, through design or good fortune, to catch their adversary in unfavorable tactical situations. Even flawless generalship might not have prevailed over Sitting Bull's mighty coalition that summer. In large part the generals lost the war because the Indians won it.

NOTES

1. Wooden Leg in Thomas B. Marquis, *A Warrior Who Fought Custer* (Minneapolis, Minn., 1931), p. 383. See also pp. 180–81. This evaluation takes on added importance in that Wooden Leg was a Cheyenne. Grouard is quoted in Vestal, *Sitting Bull, Champion of the Sioux*, pp. 91, 113. Although the standard biography, this book must be used with great caution.
2. Utley, *Frontiersmen in Blue*, pp. 335–36.
3. Harney to Sherman, Nov. 23, 1868, Senate Ex. Docs., 40th Cong., 3d sess., No. 11, pp. 2–6.
4. In addition to annual reports of superintendent and agents in CIA, *Annual Report* (1869–74), see Olson, *Red Cloud and the Sioux Problem*, chaps.

6–9; Hyde, *Red Cloud's Folk*, chaps. 10–12; and Hyde, *Spotted Tail's Folk*, chaps. 6–7.

5. The number of agency Indians fluctuated from year to year, and even census counts were often wildly inaccurate. These figures are taken from statistical tables in CIA, *Annual Report* (1875), pp. 106–8.
6. Quoted in Mark H. Brown, *The Plainsmen of the Yellowstone: A History of the Yellowstone Basin* (New York, 1961), p. 229.
7. From Fort Sully, D. T., Aug. 24, 1869, CIA, *Annual Report* (1869), p. 331.
8. Hancock's annual reports for 1870 and 1872, in SW, *Annual Report* (1870), p. 26; (1872), p. 42. See also Athearn, *Forts of the Upper Missouri*, chap. 15.
9. SW, *Annual Report* (1874), pp. 32–34. Olson, pp. 166–67.
10. CIA, *Annual Report* (1869), pp. 271–76; (1870), pp. 176–80; (1871), pp. 416–17; (1875), pp. 302–3. SW, *Annual Report* (1869), p. 73; (1870), pp. 31–33; (1871), p. 27; (1874), pp. 25, 39; (1875), pp. 34, 62. House Misc. Docs., 43d Cong., 1st sess., No. 151. Senate Ex. Docs., 43d Cong., 1st sess., No. 46.
11. SW, *Annual Report* (1872), pp. 41–42. See also testimony of Lt. Col. Nelson H. Davis, House Reports, 43d Cong., 1st sess., No. 384, p. 172; and Capt. J. S. Poland, Standing Rock Agency, to AAG Dept. Dak., Dec. 30, 1875, Senate Ex. Docs., 44th Cong., 1st sess., No. 184, pp. 31–33.
12. SW, *Annual Report* (1870), pp. 31–32; (1871), p. 27; (1874), pp. 32–34, 39; (1875), pp. 62–63. CIA, *Annual Report* (1875), pp. 302–3.
13. CIA, *Annual Report* (1871), pp. 416–17; (1872), p. 262; (1873), pp. 166–67; (1874), p. 267. House Ex. Docs., 43d Cong., 3d sess., No. 96.
14. Sherman to Sheridan, Sept. 26, 1872, Sheridan Papers, LC.
15. For the expedition of 1871, see SW, *Annual Report* (1871), pp. 27–28; and Brown, pp. 196–97. For the 1872 expedition, see *ibid.*, pp. 197–203; SW, *Annual Report* (1872), pp. 39–41; and Vestal, chap. 18. A good account by a participant in this expedition is E. J. McClernand, "With the Indian and the Buffalo in Montana," *Cavalry Journal*, 35 (1926), 508–11. See also James H. Bradley's account in his diary of the Sioux campaign of 1876; Edgar I. Stewart, ed., *The March of the Montana Column: A Prelude to the Custer Disaster* (Norman, Okla., 1961), pp. 55–63.
16. SW, *Annual Report* (1873), pp. 40–41. Brown, pp. 207–10. George F. Howe, ed., "Expedition to the Yellowstone River in 1873: Letters of a Young Cavalry Officer [Lt. Charles W. Larned]," *Mississippi Valley Historical Review*, 39 (1952), 519–34. Charles Braden, "The Yellowstone Expedition of 1873," *Journal of the United States Cavalry Association*, 16 (1905), 218–41. Anon., "An Incident of the Yellowstone Expedition of 1873," *ibid.*, 15 (1904), 289–301. Stanley, *Personal Memoirs*, pp. 238–55. Chandler, *Of Garryowen in Glory*, pp. 38–41.
17. The Black Hills story is treated in the following sources: Watson Parker, *Gold in the Black Hills* (Norman, Okla., 1966). Harold E. Briggs, "The Black Hills Gold Rush," *North Dakota Historical Quarterly*, 5 (1930–31), 71–99. Arthur J. Larsen, ed., "The Black Hills Gold Rush," *ibid.*, 6 (1931–32), 302–18. Olson, chaps. 10–11. Hyde, *Red Cloud's Folk*, chaps. 12–13. Hyde, *Spotted Tail's Folk*, chap. 9.
18. SW, *Annual Report* (1873), p. 41; (1874), pp. 24–25. For details of the expedition, see Donald Jackson, *Custer's Gold: The United States Cavalry Expedition of 1874* (New Haven, Conn., 1966); *The Black Hills Engineer* (Custer Expedition Number), 17 (November, 1929); and W. M. Wemett, "Custer's Expedition to the Black Hills in 1874," *North Dakota Historical Quarterly*, 6 (1931–32), 292–301.
19. Quoted in *Army and Navy Journal*, 12 (April 10, 1875), 55. See also *ibid.* (March 20, 1875), 503.
20. Jackson, pp. 111–16. SW, *Annual Report* (1875), pp. 64–65, 69–70.

Herbert S. Schell, *History of South Dakota* (Lincoln, Neb., 1961), pp. 129–30.

21. Jenny's report, CIA, *Annual Report* (1875), pp. 181–83, SW, *Annual Report* (1875), p. 71.

22. The report of the Allison commission is in CIA, *Annual Report* (1875), pp. 184–200. The quotation is on p. 88. Good accounts of the negotiations are in Olson, chaps. 10–11; Hyde, *Red Cloud's Folk*, chap. 13; and Hyde, *Spotted Tail's Folk*, chap. 9.

23. Sherman to Sen. P. W. Hitchcock, Feb. 11, 1873, Sherman Papers, vol. 90, pp. 308–10, LC.

24. CIA, *Annual Report* (1873), p. 6.

25. Thus, although wishing for more evidence, I favor the Anderson side of the Brown-Anderson controversy over the origins of the Sioux War of 1876. Without diminishing the importance of the Sioux raids in Montana as a cause, I cannot accept the thesis that the Black Hills had little or nothing to do with the war. See Mark H. Brown, "Muddled Men Have Muddied the Yellowstone's True Colors," *Montana, the Magazine of Western History*, *11* (January, 1961), 28–37; and Harry H. Anderson, "A Challenge to Brown's Sioux Indian Wars Thesis," *ibid.*, *12* (January, 1962), 40–49.

26. Sherman to Sheridan, Nov. 20, 1875, Sheridan Papers, LC.

27. Briggs, p. 84.

28. Former Commissioner of Indian Affairs George W. Manypenny, a careful observer of the Washington scene and chairman of the second Black Hills commission, strongly hints at this explanation in *Our Indian Wards* (Cincinnati, Ohio, 1880), pp. 301–8. See also Parker, p. 71. The official correspondence is printed in House Ex. Docs., 44th Cong., 1st sess., No. 184.

29. House Ex. Docs., 44th Cong., 1st sess., No. 184, pp. 14–15. Sheridan's report in SW, *Annual Report* (1876), p. 400.

30. Sheridan's and Terry's annual reports, SW, *Annual Report* (1876), pp. 441, 459.

31. The definitive work on this expedition is J. W. Vaughn, *The Reynolds Campaign on Powder River* (Norman, Okla., 1966). See also Bourke, *On the Border with Crook*, chaps. 15–16. SW, *Annual Report* (1876), pp. 502–3.

32. So stated Lt. John G. Bourke, Crook's aide, in *On the Border with Crook*, p. 270.

33. The evidence is analyzed in Vaughn, chap. 7.

34. Crook's report, May 7, 1876, SW, *Annual Report* (1876), pp. 502–3.

35. Sheridan's annual report, Nov. 25, 1876, in *ibid.*, p. 441.

36. From Fort D. A. Russell, April 11, 1876, Sherman Papers, vol. 43, LC. The charges were tried in January 1877 at Cheyenne, Wyo., by a star-studded court presided over by Gen. John Pope. Reynolds defended himself aggressively, accusing Crook of seeking a scapegoat to cover his own mismanagement. But the court pronounced Reynolds guilty of most of the charges and sentenced him to suspension from rank and pay for one year. The President, citing Reynold's long and distinguished service, remitted the sentence. His reputation now ruined, he accepted disability retirement in June 1877. Vaughn's studies led him to conclude that, although Reynolds was guilty of some errors of judgment in the heat of combat, the court's findings were "cruelly unjust."

37. House Ex. Docs., 44th Cong., 1st sess., No. 184, p. 13.

38. Correspondence from all three is quoted in Robert P. Hughes, "The Campaign against the Sioux in 1876," *Journal of the Military Service Institution of the United States*, *18* (1896), 5–6. (Reprinted in Graham, *The Story of the Little Big Horn.*)

39. The strategy is most clearly detailed in Sheridan to Sherman, May 29, 1876, *ibid.*, pp. 53–54.

40. Principal accounts of Gibbon's movements are Gibbon's report, Oct. 17,

1876, SW, *Annual Report* (1876), pp. 471–76; Stewart, ed., *March of the Montana Column*; Gibbon, "Last Summer's Expedition against the Sioux," and "Hunting Sitting Bull," *American Catholic Quarterly Review*, 2 (1877), 271–304, 665–94, reprinted as *Gibbon on the Sioux Campaign of 1876* (Bellevue, Neb., 1969); Edward J. McClernand, "With the Indian and the Buffalo in Montana," *Cavalry Journal*, *36* (1927), 7–54; and John S. Gray, ed., "Captain Clifford's Story of the Sioux War of 1876," *Westerners Brand Book* (Chicago), 26 (1969–70), 73–79, 81–83, 86–88.

41. Monaghan, *Custer*, pp. 365–69. Whittaker, *Life of Custer*, pp. 553–60. Vol. 37 of the Sherman Papers, LC, contains illuminating data.

42. The literature of the march to the Little Bighorn and the historic battle that occurred there is the most voluminous of the Indian wars. I have written of these events in "The Battle of the Little Bighorn," Potomac Westerners, *Great Western Indian Fights* (New York, 1960), chap. 20; *Custer and the Great Controversy: Origin and Development of a Legend* (Los Angeles, 1962); and in *Custer Battlefield National Monument*, National Park Service Historical Handbook Series (Washington, D.C., 1969). My assessment of Custer is in "Custer: Hero or Butcher?" *American History Illustrated*, *5* (February 1971), 4–9, 43–48. A few standard works are W. A. Graham, *The Story of the Little Big Horn* (Harrisburg, Pa., 1945); Graham, *The Custer Myth: A Source Book of Custeriana* (Harrisburg, Pa., 1953); Graham, ed., *The Reno Court of Inquiry: Abstract of the Official Record of Proceedings* (Harrisburg, Pa., 1954); Edgar I. Stewart, *Custer's Luck* (Norman, Okla., 1955); Joseph Mills Hanson, *The Conquest of the Missouri* (New York, 1946); Edward S. Godfrey, "Custer's Last Battle," *Century Magazine*, *43* (1892), 358–87. Official reports are in SW, *Annual Report* (1876), pp. 443–44, 459–64, 476–80.

43. Principal sources for Crook's operations are J. W. Vaughn, *With Crook at the Rosebud* (Harrisburg, Pa., 1956); Vaughn, *Indian Fights*, chap. 4; Bourke, *On the Border with Crook*, chaps. 17–19; Anson Mills, *My Story* (Washington, D.C., 1918), pp. 394–412; Finerty, *War-Path and Bivouac*. Official reports are in SW, *Annual Report* (1876), pp. 442–43, 502–3.

44. SW, *Annual Report* (1876), pp. 30, 35. See also Sheridan in *ibid.*, pp. 441, 445, for the charge that Indian agents suppressed the number of absentees in order to continue drawing rations for them.

45. Maj. M. A. Reno (Fort Lincoln) to Asst. Adj. Gen. Dept. Dak., April 27, 1876, House Ex. Docs., 44th Cong., 1st sess., No. 184, p. 52. This telegram was forwarded from Terry's headquarters to Sheridan's and thence to the War Department.

46. Quoted in *ibid.*, p. 54. For further cogent evidence, see Hughes, pp. 15–17; and T. M. Coughlan, "The Battle of the Little Big Horn: A Tactical Study," *Cavalry Journal*, *43* (1934), 13.

47. The clearest account of Indian movements is Wooden Leg's in Marquis, *A Warrior Who Fought Custer*, chaps. 5–7. See also Peter J. Powell, *Sweet Medicine: The Continuing Role of the Sacred Arrows, the Sun Dance, and the Sacred Buffalo Hat in Northern Cheyenne History* (2 vols., Norman, Okla., 1969), *1*, chap. 7; Kate Big Head's story, "She Watched Custer's Last Battle," in Marquis, *Custer on the Little Bighorn* (p. p. 1967), Sec. 6; Grinnell, *The Fighting Cheyennes*, chap. 25; James McLaughlin, *My Friend the Indian* (Boston, 1910), chaps. 9–10; Godfrey, "Custer's Last Battle"; Vestal, chaps. 20–23; Mari Sandoz, *Crazy Horse, Strange Man of the Oglalas* (New York, 1942), pp. 302–334. For good indications that the hostile force was not as large as generally assumed, see Hughes, pp. 15–18; and Harry H. Anderson, "Cheyennes at the Little Big Horn—A Study of Statistics," *North Dakota Historical Quarterly*, 27 (1960), 81–94.

48. The controversy and evidence are discussed in Vaughn, *With Crook at the Rosebud*, pp. 65–67.

49. Gibbon, "Last Summer's Expedition," p. 22.

50. Reno's report, July 5, 1876, SW, *Annual Report* (1876), p. 477.
51. Custer's first biographer charged Reno with responsibility for the disaster, and Reno demanded a court of inquiry. The voluminous testimony taken by the court in 1879 is a prime source for study of the battle. It led the court to a finding that exonerated Reno while mildly criticising him. Personal scandal lost him his commission and pursued him to an early grave. See my *Custer and the Great Controversy*, chap. 3.
52. Sherman to Sheridan, Feb. 17, 1877, Sherman-Sheridan Letters, Sheridan Papers, LC.

FIFTEEN

The Conquest of the Sioux, 1876-81

O N JUNE 28, 1876, the Seventh Cavalry buried its dead on the
    battlefield of the Little Bighorn. Gibbon's men prepared
mule litters to move Major Reno's wounded troopers. A laborious
march brought them, in the predawn black of June 30, to the
mouth of the Little Bighorn. Capt. Grant Marsh had pushed the
Far West up the swollen Bighorn to this point. With the wounded
bedded down on the deck, Marsh piloted the steamer back down
the Bighorn. Gibbon's command and Reno's remnant of the
Seventh Cavalry followed by land. On July 3 Marsh ferried them
to the north bank of the Yellowstone, then cast off with his cargo
of wounded for the historic dash to the Fort Lincoln hospital.
Fifty-four hours and 710 miles later, draped in black and showing
her flag at half-mast, the *Far West* nosed into the Bismarck land-
ing. It was 11 P.M. on July 5. Before midnight the telegraph key
clicked out the first of 15,000 words: "Bismarck, D.T., July 5,
1876:—General Custer attacked the Indians June 25, and he, with
every officer and man in five companies, were killed. . . ."[1]
    The news from Bismarck stunned and horrified Americans en-
grossed in celebrating the centennial of the nation's birth and
squaring off for the contest to determine who would succeed
Ulysses S. Grant in the White House. Congress promptly voted
funds to build the two forts on the Yellowstone that Sheridan had
been promoting for three years.[2] Also, after acrimonious debate
over the comparative merits of Volunteers and Regulars, Congress
lifted the ceiling on army strength to permit the enlistment of an
additional 2,500 cavalry privates.[3] On July 26 the Secretary of the

Interior bowed to Sheridan's insistence on military control of the Sioux agencies.[4] By rail and river steamer, fresh troops hastened to the seat of war. Terry and Gibbon waited patiently on the Yellowstone. Crook and his officers rested beside streams teeming with trout and stalked deer, elk, and bear in the Bighorn Mountains.

Specifically, Crook awaited the Fifth Cavalry, which in June had been moved from Kansas, under Lt. Col. Eugene A. Carr, to the upper Cheyenne River to interrupt traffic between Red Cloud Agency and the hostile camps. After receiving news of the Custer disaster on July 10, Crook summoned the Fifth. A new colonel, youthful, baby-faced Wesley Merritt, had assumed command on July 1. He delayed the march to join Crook upon learning that 800 Cheyenne warriors were leaving Red Cloud Agency for the Powder River country. A forced march placed the Fifth across the main trail at War Bonnet, or Hat, Creek, twenty-five miles northwest of the agency. Here, on the morning of July 17, Merritt intercepted the vanguard of the Cheyenne force. The "Battle" of War Bonnett Creek consisted of the celebrated "duel" between "Buffalo Bill" Cody and Yellow Hand, or Yellow Hair, a subchief, and a bloodless chase of several dozen Cheyennes back toward Red Cloud Agency. However many Cheyennes may have been following, they gave up the plan of joining their brethren in the north. Even though the action on the War Bonnet was thus of considerable consequence, Merritt endured Crook's displeasure over the delay it caused. Not until August 3 did the regiment reach his base camp on Goose Creek.[5]

Once more, on August 5, Crook cut loose from his wagon train, which he sent back to Fort Fetterman, and aimed for the head of the Rosebud. His command now numbered a formidable 2,000—twenty-five troops of the Second, Third, and Fifth Cavalry organized in a brigade of five squadrons under Colonel Merritt; ten infantry companies of the Fourth, Ninth, and Fourteenth Regiments under Maj. Alexander Chambers; 213 Shoshoni warriors under Chief Washakie; and the ubiquitous pack train, organized in five divisions and carrying provisions for fifteen days. Before the expiration of this time, Crook expected to meet Terry and attach his command to the Yellowstone supply line.

Terry, meanwhile, had moved down river to the mouth of the Rosebud. Steamers brought reinforcements. On August 1 Lt. Col.

Elwell S. Otis landed with six companies of the Twenty-second Infantry. The next day six companies of the Fifth Infantry debarked under Col. Nelson A. Miles, who had urgently pressed his wife's uncle, General Sherman, for an opportunity to try his hand against the Sioux.[6]

Leaving his Rosebud supply depot defended by artillery and an infantry company, Terry marched up the Rosebud on August 8. Gibbon commanded a brigade of four infantry battalions formed from the Fifth, Sixth, Seventh, and Twenty-second Regiments. Major Brisbin led the cavalry, his own four troops of the Second and Reno's Seventh, now reorganized in eight troops. The column numbered about 1,700.

Surprised to confront each other, Crook and Terry met on August 10 in the Rosebud Valley at a point where the trail of the Indians turned eastward. The two generals decided to combine their commands and follow. Anxious to thwart any attempt at escape to the north, where Canada offered refuge, Terry dispatched Colonel Miles and his infantrymen to hold the main fording places of the Yellowstone and to patrol the river by steamer. The wagons were also returned to the Yellowstone. For a week the army toiled ponderously eastward to the Powder as cold rains and heavy mud tormented men and animals alike. At the mouth of the Powder, the expedition lay in a soggy, cheerless bivouac for another week while supplies were boated down from the Rosebud depot. Prospects of overtaking the quarry seemed so remote that the Shoshonis went home in disgust. "Buffalo Bill," pleading theatrical commitments, also took his departure. Lieutenant Colonel Carr, ever the carping critic, grumbled about continuing a futile campaign simply "because two fools do not know their business."[7] After some further fumbling, the two generals decided to part company, Terry to return to the Yellowstone, Crook to stay on the Indian trail.

In the opening days of September, therefore, Terry's army lay in camp at the mouth of Glendive Creek while the general pondered what to do next. He had received orders from Sheridan on August 26 to establish a temporary cantonment at the mouth of Tongue River and to leave Colonel Miles, with his entire regiment and Otis' six companies, to hold the Yellowstone Valley during the winter. Stockpiling enough supplies to last such a command all winter became an urgent task, especially since the Yellowstone was falling and three loaded steamers were already aground below Glendive Creek. Moreover, on September 3, word came from Crook, on Beaver Creek, a tributary of the Little Missouri, that the Indian trail had given out; the tribes had scattered. Terry's army could now hope to accomplish little more than use up supplies needed by Miles during the winter. On September 5, therefore, Terry disbanded the expedition, sending Gibbon's infantry and Brisbin's cavalry back to Forts Ellis and Shaw, Moore's infantry battalion to Fort Buford, and the Seventh Cavalry to Fort Lincoln. Under Colonel Miles, the remaining infantry labored to transport supplies upriver to the Tongue River cantonment.

After losing the Indian trail, Crook dropped into the Little Missouri valley and marched eastward to the head of Heart River on the trail made by Terry outbound the previous May. Rain and mud continued to plague the command, which Lieutenant Bourke characterized as the "brigade of drowned rats." Small parties of Indians testified to the proximity of at least some of the enemy. A comparatively fresh trail pointed south, toward the Black Hills. On September 5, with rations remaining for scarcely more than two days, and even though only about four days' march from Fort Lincoln, Crook decided to turn south on the trail. Scouts carried dispatches to Fort Lincoln asking Sheridan to have provisions rushed to meet the column at Custer City, in the Black Hills. The memorable trek that followed has come down in history as the "Mud March" and the "Horsemeat March." Constant rains drenched the column. Sodden prairie slowed the advance. Horses and mules dropped by the score. Rations gave out and the men subsisted on horsemeat. Although discovering abundant Indian signs, the troops were no longer able to pursue. The chase turned into a struggle for survival.

On September 7, on the north fork of Grand River, Crook ordered Capt. Anson Mills to push forward to the Black Hills mining town of Deadwood, more than 100 miles to the southwest, to procure food. Mills selected 150 Third Cavalrymen who still had serviceable mounts, 4 officers, and 61 pack mules. Frank Grouard went along as guide. In the rainy dawn light of September 9, near some rock formations known as Slim Buttes, Mills charged into a Sioux camp of thirty-seven lodges, drove the occupants into the hills, and promptly came under a harassing fire that lasted until Crook arrived with the main column shortly before noon. About

Charles Schreyvogel ranked second only to Frederic Remington as delineator of the Indian-fighting army. *A Sharp Encounter* (above) and *The Skirmish Line* (below) depict scenes typical of frontier combat. (Library of Congress)

I'd like to be a packer
And pack with George F. Crook
And dressed up in my canvas suit
To be for him mistook.
I'd braid my beard in two long tails,
And idle all the day
In whittling sticks and wondering
What the New York papers say.

This soldiers' doggerel made fun of Crook's inaction after the Battle of the Rosebud, 1876, but also captured something of the affection they felt for the reticent, unpretentious campaigner who more than any other general understood the special conditions and requirements of Indian warfare. This picture was taken at Fort Bowie, Arizona, in 1885. (Arizona Historical Society)

"The adult Apache is an embodiment of physical endurance—lean, well proportioned, medium sized, with sinews like steel, insensible to hunger, fatigue, or physical pains." So wrote General Crook of the typical warrior. This one is Mescalero. (Laboratory of Anthropology, Santa Fe, N.M.)

In fighting Apaches, said General Crook, "regular troops are as helpless as a whale attacked by a school of swordfish," and "the only hope of success lies in using their own methods." This meant pitting Apache against Apache. With Apache scouts, Crook, and later Miles, subjugated the "renegades." Above is a typical scout unit at Fort Grant, Arizona, in 1886. (Arizona Historical Society) Below is the adversary—Geronimo (*right*) and warriors photographed during the historic conference with Crook in the Sierra Madre in March 1886. (Smithsonian Institution)

An eccentric, hard-driving combat officer, Col. Ranald S. Mackenzie made the Fourth Cavalry the best of the ten mounted regiments. Insanity forced his early retirement in 1884. (National Archives)

Nelson A. Miles—"Bear's Coat" to the Sioux and Cheyennes. Insatiable ambition made him one of the frontier's most innovative, energetic, and successful commanders but also drove him to seek recognition and advancement by means that have left his reputation badly stained. He is shown here as colonel of the Fifth Infantry on the Yellowstone about 1877. (Montana Historical Society)

Military columns had to carry almost all supplies with them. The Indians, by contrast, lived off the country. Time and again logistical problems ruined an offensive movement. General Crook owed his success in large part to the mobility afforded by pack mules. Most officers, however, continued to rely on wagons. This is Custer's train in the Black Hills in 1874. (National Archives)

The Ninth and Tenth Cavalry and Twenty-fourth and Twenty-fifth Infantry were composed of black enlisted men and white officers. The black regiments consistently displayed low desertion and high reenlistment rates and also compiled notable combat records on the frontier. Above, in *Captain Dodge's Colored Troopers to the Rescue*, Frederic Remington depicts the relief of the besieged force on Milk Creek, Colorado, during the Ute uprising of 1879. (*Century Magazine*, October 1891) On the following page are the enlisted men of a company of the Twenty-fifth Infantry at Fort Snelling, Minnesota, about 1885. Service stripes mark most as veterans. (National Archives)

Before the Little Bighorn. Officers of the Seventh Cavalry and Sixth and Seventeenth Infantry pose with their ladies on the steps of the Custers' quarters at Fort Abraham Lincoln, D.T., 1875. (An asterisk indicates killed at the Little Bighorn.) Lt. Nelson Bronson, Lt. George D. Wallace, Lt. Col. George A. Custer,* Lt. Benjamin H. Hodgson,* Mrs. Custer, Mrs. McDougall, Lt. Thomas M. McDougall, Lt. William Badger, Mrs. Yates, Capt. George W. Yates,* Charles Thompson, Mrs. Calhoun (Margaret Custer), Miss Agnes Wellington, Capt. John S. Poland, Lt. Charles A. Varnum, Lt. Col. William P. Carlin, Mrs. Moylan, Capt. Thomas W. Custer,* Capt. William Thompson, Lt. James Calhoun,* Mrs. McIntosh, Capt. Myles Moylan, Lt. Donald McIntosh.* (National Park Service, Custer Battlefield National Monument)

Many great chiefs led the Sioux against the white man, but two stand out from all the others. Red Cloud won his fight for the Bozeman Trail in 1866–68, and Sitting Bull held together the powerful coalition that crushed Custer in 1876. These portraits are from oil paintings by Henry Raschen. (Collection of David Blumberg)

Artillery occasionally figured importantly in engagements against the Indians. The small-caliber, rapid-fire Hotchkiss mountain rifle was by all odds the favorite with commanders because of its mobility. Above is one of the guns that caused such havoc at Wounded Knee in 1890. Less satisfactory was the Gatling gun, forerunner of the machine gun. Below, pictured at Fort Lincoln, Dakota, is the battery that Custer declined to take with him to the Little Bighorn in 1876. (Library of Congress; Custer Battlefield National Monument)

Edward O. C. Ord. A vigorous old campaigner, his aggressive Mexican policies while holding the Texas command, 1875–81, lost him the confidence of Sherman and Sheridan. His forced retirement in 1881, however, to open a general's billet for Nelson A. Miles, scandalized many high-ranking officers. (National Archives)

One of the three major generals, John M. Schofield served ably as a division commander and succeeded Sheridan in 1888 as commanding general of the army. He possessed superior intellectual qualities and, more than other generals, sensed the needed organizational reforms. (National Archives)

The Ghost Dance outbreak and the Battle of Wounded Knee Creek in South Dakota in 1890 marked the close of the Indian Wars and the passing of the frontier. Above is the field of Wounded Knee after the fighting, with the medicine man Yellow Bird in the foreground. (Smithsonian Institution) On the following page, General Miles and his staff view the great Sioux encampment at Pine Ridge Agency on January 16, 1891, the day after the surrender. (Library of Congress)

fifteen men and women had been trapped in a gulch near the village. They inflicted several casualties on the troops and took heavy losses themselves before finally being persuaded to surrender. Among them, mortally wounded in the stomach, was Chief American Horse. Late in the afternoon more than 200 warriors, said by the captives to be from Crazy Horse's camp, attacked the command but were driven off. After appropriating a supply of dried meat for rations, the troops destroyed the village and its contents. Next morning, as they marched away, Sioux attacked the rear guard but were repulsed. Casualties in the Battle of Slim Buttes were three killed and twelve wounded. Among the latter was Lt. Adolphus H. von Leuttwitz, whose leg had to be amputated.[8]

After Slim Buttes, the regiments were dispersed and the summer campaign of 1876 came to an unheroic conclusion. Fortitude and uncommon endurance had marked the effort to avenge Custer. Shrewd, resolute leadership, however, had been conspicuously lacking. The catastrophies of June 17 and 25 had imbued Terry and Crook with great caution. As a result, they idled away a month awaiting reinforcements while the Indians removed themselves to the east, then scattered. When the armies resumed operations, they were so large as to have virtually no chance of bringing the quarry to battle. In pronouncing judgment, however, one must recognize how profoundly the Little Bighorn affected the minds not only of Crook and Terry but of most of their officers as well.[9] An enemy powerful enough to inflict so appalling a disaster seemed at the time to demand heavier armies than had yet been fielded. But once again the campaign demonstrated truths that so often eluded the frontier generals: heavy conventional columns rarely succeeded against the unconventional foe; the logistical requirements of provisioning so many men and horses so far from their bases usually turned such operations into exercises in self-preservation. "The fact of the case is," General Sheridan confided to Sherman, "the operations of Generals Terry and Crook will not bear criticism, and my only thought has been to let them sleep. I approved what was done, for the sake of the troops, but in doing so, I was not approving much, as you know."[10]

A few hundred Indians slipped back to the agencies during the autumn, but most remained out. Indeed, considerably more Indians left the agencies to join the hostiles than came in to surrender. The Interior Department had acquiesced in military control of the agencies. Hundreds of soldiers—the bulk of the reinforcements sent in from other departments after the Custer disaster—guarded every agency. Reports circulated that the guns and ponies of the agency Indians would be confiscated. To avoid such a calamity, many Sioux and Cheyennes who had spent the summer at the agencies now headed for the hostile camps.

Among the reinforcements forwarded to Camp Robinson were six troops of the Fourth Cavalry from Fort Sill under Col. Ranald S. Mackenzie. On October 23, as Crook watched, Mackenzie moved swiftly into positions around the camps of Red Cloud and Red Leaf, near Red Cloud Agency, and disarmed and dismounted the occupants. As the ultimate humiliation, Crook informed Red Cloud that the government now recognized Spotted Tail as chief of all the Sioux. At the same time, Terry dispatched Col. Samuel D. Sturgis and the Seventh Cavalry from Fort Lincoln to perform the same mission at the Missouri River agencies. At Standing Rock and Cheyenne River, Sturgis seized more than 2,000 ponies and assorted arms. The ponies were to be sold and cows bought for the Indians with the proceeds.[11]

The agency Indians had received other unwelcome visitors that autumn, too—another Black Hills commission. Reacting to the Custer slaughter, Congress decreed, in the annual Indian appropriation act signed on August 15, that no further appropriations would be made for subsisting the Sioux until they had relinquished all claim to the unceded territory and to the Black Hills. A commission headed by George W. Manypenny, former Commissioner of Indian Affairs, came west in September and October to deliver the ultimatum. This year the young men who had wrecked the efforts of the Allison commission of 1875 were absent in the north. Also, this commission settled for the signatures of a few chiefs instead of three-fourths of adult males, as specified in the Treaty of 1868. Amid great confusion and misunderstanding, chiefs at Red Cloud, Spotted Tail, and the Missouri River agencies placed their marks on the agreement. In exchange for continued issue of rations, the chiefs bound their tribes to give up the Black Hills and all hunting rights outside the newly defined Great Sioux Reservation.[12]

On the Yellowstone River at the mouth of the Tongue, Colonel Miles had been left with his entire regiment, the Fifth Infantry, and Lieutenant Colonel Otis' six companies of the Twenty-second Infantry. Also, two companies of the Seventeenth Infantry were to help stockpile supplies, then return to Dakota. Otis, with these two companies and four of his own regiment, occupied a camp on the north bank of the Yellowstone opposite the mouth of Glendive Creek. Through the autumn weeks Miles' men erected huts for the winter at the Tongue River Cantonment site while Otis forwarded supplies unloaded at his camp from steamers unable to reach the Tongue because of low water.[13]

Early in October, a large coalition of Hunkpapas, Miniconjous, and Sans Arcs under Sitting Bull, Gall, No Neck, Bull Eagle, Red Skirt, Pretty Bear, and others crossed the Yellowstone between Glendive Creek and Powder River. On October 11, and again on October 15 and 16, 400 to 600 warriors tried to block Otis' trains between Glendive and the Tongue. Following some sharp skirmishing, emissaries of Sitting Bull parleyed with Otis under a flag of truce. Otis gave them some hard bread and bacon, and shortly afterward the warriors called off the attack.[14]

Miles had learned of the Sioux movements and, concerned for the safety of the train, had moved down the Yellowstone with the entire Fifth Infantry, almost 500 strong. After meeting Otis on October 18, on Custer Creek, he marched swiftly to the northeast in search of Sitting Bull. Two days later the column overtook the Sioux near the head of Cedar Creek. An Indian appeared under a truce flag with word that Sitting Bull wanted to talk. On the twentieth and again on the twenty-first the two leaders, confronting each other between the lines, engaged in verbal sparring. Their respective demands—Sitting Bull that the whites get out of his country altogether, Miles that the Sioux give up and go to their agencies—admitted of no compromise. God Almighty had made him an Indian, declared Sitting Bull, and not an agency Indian either. Miles concluded, therefore, "that something more than talk would be required."

Breaking off negotiations, Miles drove the Indians from their camps and commenced a two-day running battle. The warriors fought back, firing the grass and counterattacking with a vigor that on one occasion forced their pursuers into a hollow square formation. But, even though outnumbered, the "walk-a-heaps" pushed the pursuit with a steady, well-disciplined persistence, while the artillery, skillfully served, kept the Sioux from pressing their forays too closely. The chase led down Bad Route Creek forty-two miles to the Yellowstone, which the fugitives crossed on October 24. In their flight they abandoned tons of meat, broken-down ponies and captured cavalry mounts, and camp equipage of all kinds.[15]

On October 27 a handful of Miniconjou and Sans Arc chiefs conferred with Miles and professed readiness to surrender their people, some 2,000 in number. Miles could not feed this many Indians, so he retained five chiefs as a guarantee that the bands would go to Cheyenne River and surrender. About forty lodges, the immediate following of the five hostages, turned themselves in at the agency on November 30. The rest, however, moved up the Powder and joined the large Oglala and Cheyenne village of Crazy Horse.

The Hunkpapas under Sitting Bull, Gall, and Pretty Bear had turned in the opposite direction, toward the Missouri, even before the "surrender" of the Miniconjous and Sans Arcs. Col. William B. Hazen and four companies of the Sixth Infantry steamed up the Missouri from Fort Buford to cut them off. At Fort Peck Agency, however, the resident Assinniboines and Yanktonais reported the hostiles, resting about twenty miles to the south, "on the last verge of destitution." Sure they must soon give up, Hazen left one company at the agency and returned to Fort Buford.[16]

Miles was less willing to leave the matter to Sioux discretion. He intended to keep his regiment in the field all winter if necessary to round up the hostiles. Winter clothing had been shipped up-river, and more was improvised. Pausing briefly at Tongue River Cantonment (held in his absence by two companies of the Twenty-second Infantry), Miles marched north again on November 5. For more than a month the Fifth Infantry, operating in three battalions, scoured the Missouri and its tributaries from the Musselshell to the Yellowstone. Blizzards pounded the columns. Temperatures dropped so low that the mercury froze in the thermometers. The battalions led by Miles and Capt. Simon Snyder marched 408 and 308 miles, respectively, before returning to the cantonment early in December. Lt. Frank Baldwin's battalion came in on December 23 after a march of 716 miles. Baldwin had picked up Sitting Bull's trail and skirmished with his warriors on December 7, then on the eighteenth had captured his camp of 122 lodges near the head of Redwater Creek and scattered the occupants.

While Miles and his little regiment—never as strong as 500—chased Sitting Bull back and forth across half of Montana, General Crook was at Fort Fetterman assembling another huge army: eleven troops of cavalry from the Second, Third, Fourth, and Fifth Regiments under Colonel Mackenzie and fifteen companies of infantry from the Fourth, Ninth, Fourteenth, and Twenty-fifth Regiments and the Fourth Artillery under Lt. Col. Richard I. Dodge. Four hundred Indian allies—Arapaho, Shoshoni, Bannock, Pawnee, and even Sioux and Cheyenne—went along. Almost 300 civilians manned 168 supply wagons and a pack train of 400 mules. Altogether, there were nearly 2,200 men.[17]

Departing Fort Fetterman on November 14, the expedition moved up the old Bozeman Trail to abandoned Fort Reno, which had been temporarily reactivated as a forward supply base. Pausing here four days to let a blizzard spend itself, Crook resumed the march on November 22. The objective, once again, was Crazy Horse, thought to be somewhere near the site of the Rosebud battle of June 17. But a scout brought word of a large Cheyenne village in the Bighorn Mountains not far to the west. Crook ordered Mackenzie with ten cavalry troops and all the Indian scouts to find and attack this camp.

In the misty dawn of November 25, Mackenzie's 1,100 horsemen burst into the Cheyenne village of Dull Knife and Little Wolf, about 200 lodges clustered in a canyon of the Red Fork of Powder River. Driven from their tepees with little more than rifles and ammunition belts, the Cheyenne warriors, about 400 in number, herded their families up the bluffs, then took positions among boulders and ravines on the slopes overlooking the camp. Some held one end of the village. A deadly fire kept the soldiers and Indian scouts off balance. In savage fighting, sometimes at point-blank range and even involving hand-to-hand combat, the two sides contended for the village. The Indian scouts fought fiercely and indeed bore the brunt of the battle. By mid-afternoon the village was secured and the battle lapsed into sporadic, long-range firing. Soldiers and Indian allies burned the tepees and their contents of meat, clothing, utensils, ammunition, arts and crafts and other finery, and herded 700 captured ponies. Military equipment bearing Seventh Cavalry markings, including a guidon made into a pillow case, testified to the Cheyenne role in the Little Bighorn.

Mackenzie had paid for his victory—an officer and five enlisted men killed and twenty-six wounded. The Cheyennes left thirty dead on the field and later admitted to a total loss of forty killed. But their real loss was the food, clothing, and shelter destroyed by Mackenzie. With only such possessions as they had carried from their beds when attacked, the Cheyennes trekked northward in search of Crazy Horse. The night after the battle, the temperature plunged to thirty degrees below zero. Eleven babies froze to death in their mothers' arms. After three weeks of the most intense suffering, the Cheyennes found succor with Crazy Horse on the upper Tongue River.[18]

Crook led his column eastward to the head of the Belle Fourche and down that stream to the head of the Little Missouri. Blizzards battered the troops, and temperatures dropping to forty and fifty degrees below zero made each day a struggle to prevent freezing. Soaring supply and transportation costs brought complaints from Sheridan. At last, late in December, Crook called off the campaign. By the end of the month the components of his command had been returned to their stations.[19]

As winter failed to bring a relaxation of military pressure, peace sentiment gained strength in the hostile camps. This was especially true in the Crazy Horse camp on Tongue River, for the wretched condition of the Cheyenne victims of Mackenzie's assault argued eloquently for peace. This village, swollen by the Miniconjous and Sans Arcs who "surrendered" to Miles on October 27 as well as by Dull Knife's Cheyennes, numbered 500 to 600 lodges containing about 3,500 people. Although Crazy Horse seems to have remained as uncompromising as ever, a delegation of chiefs set forth to open talks with Miles. On December 16, as they approched the Tongue River Cantonment, they were treacherously set upon by Miles' Crow scouts and five were slain. The rest escaped. Miles angrily dismounted the Crows and sent their ponies to the Sioux as an apology. But the damage had been done. The peace elements had been discredited.

The hostiles now began to harass the cantonment with minor raids designed to draw the soldiers up Tongue River into an ambush. Miles eagerly obliged, even though the Fifth Infantry was exhausted by the recent operations against Sitting Bull. With five companies of the Fifth and two of the Twenty-second, about 350 strong, he moved up the snow-drifted Tongue Valley during the last week of December. Artillery consisted of a Napoleon gun and a three-inch Rodman, disguised as supply wagons.

As so often happened when the Plains tribes attempted the decoy tactic, some warriors sprang the trap prematurely. On the afternoon of January 7, 1877, the scouts captured a small party of Cheyenne women and children, and that evening about 200 warriors vainly tried to recapture them. Then Miles was ready for a major action the next day.

Fresh snow accumulated during the night. Snow and ice covered the ground to a depth of one to three feet and a leaden sky threatened more as 500 Sioux and Cheyenne warriors, led by Crazy Horse and other chiefs, assailed Miles' command shortly after daybreak on January 8. Throughout the morning, as more snow fell, both sides energetically maneuvered for advantage and expended much ammunition. The artillery bombarded concentrations of warriors. Miles handled his units with great tactical skill. Around noon a blizzard set in and so hampered visibility that the Indians withdrew from the field. Casualties were light on both sides. After the Battle of Wolf Mountain, supply and transportation problems compelled Miles to turn back to Tongue River Cantonment, which he reached on January 18, 1877.[20]

Miles was jubilant over his achievements, and he boasted of them in long letters to General Sherman. "Enough has been done," he declared, "to demonstrate what can be accomplished by a perfect spy system, a properly organized command, and such energy & management used as enables us to *find*, *follow*, and *defeat* large bodies of these Indians every time and under all circumstances." He had done all this despite winter storms and supply deficiencies that amounted to "the worst management in the rear" he had ever known. His success was all the more remarkable, he believed, in comparison with General Crook's campaign, which "accomplished nothing but give the Indians renewed confidence."

Because of his triumphs, Miles averred, and because of a deliberate effort in Department of Dakota headquarters to undermine him, he wanted a department all his own. The District of the Yellowstone, created for him the previous autumn, was not enough. Pope could be packed off to New York and Terry sent to replace him at Fort Leavenworth. That would leave two colonels who ranked him—Hazen and Gibbon—"and they have been here so long they would doubtless welcome the opportunity to leave." "If you will give me this command and *one-half the troops now in it, I will end this Sioux war once and forever in four months.*"[21]

Although his official reports and private correspondence abounded in exaggerated claims, Miles had valid cause for self-congratulation. Mightily exasperated by his shameless self-promotion, Sherman and Sheridan nevertheless recognized the ability, energy, and tenacity with which he had carried out his mission, and by early February 1877 they were laying plans to grant him only slightly less than he had asked for. Sheridan's scheme was to enlarge the District of the Yellowstone to include the Powder River country from Crook's department and assign Miles to command it. He would be given two and one-half cavalry regiments, two and one-half infantry regiments, and the Pawnee Indian scouts, together with freedom to ignore all command boundaries in seeking out the hostiles. Mackenzie, meanwhile, would cover the Black Hills and Wyoming and Nebraska settlements and follow any bands that fled eastward from Miles. Significantly, Terry would remain in St. Paul and Crook in Omaha, ostensibly to keep supplies flowing.[22]

These elaborate plans could not be put into effect until spring opened the rivers. Meanwhile, the peace faction in the Crazy Horse village regained strength. The fiasco at Wolf Mountain was cited as evidence that the soldiers could not be beaten. Moreover, sometime in January, Sitting Bull visited the village and announced that he had decided to call off the war and take the Hunkpapas north to live in the country of the "Great Mother," Queen Victoria. Finally, runners from Cheyenne River and Red Cloud Agencies brought peace feelers from the government. Like Miles, however, they offered only unconditional surrender. This meant giving up guns and ponies. Also, it probably meant moving the Red Cloud and Spotted Tail Agencies back to the Missouri River, or even to Indian Territory. Such prospects fortified the war faction in its resistance. The growing difficulty of feeding so many people, however, led to a decision to break up the Tongue River village. Late in January, as Sitting Bull's people headed north, the Miniconjous and Sans Arcs scattered in small bands along the Little Missouri, while the Oglalas and Cheyennes went back to the Little Bighorn. A few groups slipped into Red Cloud and Spotted Tail Agencies to give up.[23]

Officers at Camp Robinson had attempted since early January to persuade the highly respected Brulé chieftain Spotted Tail to undertake a peace mission. Not until Crook softened the unconditional surrender terms did Spotted Tail consent. With 200 warriors he set forth in mid-February authorized to promise the hostiles that General Crook, friend and former commander of the new Great Father, Rutherford B. Hayes, would do all he could to help them stay in their home country, rather than move to the Missouri River. There would have to be a formal surrender of ponies and firearms, but it was understood that they would soon be quietly returned. When Miles learned of these attempts to lure away "his" hostiles, he framed similar terms and sent them with a mixed-blood scout, "Big Leggings" Johnny Brughier, to the camps on the Little Bighorn. One of the Cheyenne women captured on January 7 went along to tell her people how kindly she had been treated by the soldier chief—"Bear's Coat"—at Tongue River Cantonment.[24]

Spotted Tail's mission lasted almost two months. The new terms, coupled with the chief's great prestige, dissolved most of the opposition. Upon his return on April 5, he could report that virtually all the hostiles had agreed to surrender. Throughout the spring weeks of 1877, they came in large groups and small to surrender to the army and settle at the agencies. Altogether, more than 3,000 turned themselves in at Red Cloud, Spotted Tail, and Cheyenne River Agencies. Only 300, almost all Cheyennes, surrendered at Tongue River Cantonment—in Miles' mind another cause for resentment of Crook, since large numbers of Indians, having negotiated with Miles, were on their way to surrender to him when they learned of Spotted Tail's approach with possibly more generous terms. On May 6 the Oglalas came in to Red Cloud Agency led by Crazy Horse himself. He threw three Winchester rifles on the ground. With Sitting Bull in Canada, the great Sioux War seemed to be at an end.[25]

But not quite. Fifty-one lodges, mostly Miniconjous under Lame Deer, had separated from Crazy Horse on the Powder. Vowing never to surrender, these Sioux headed for the Rosebud to hunt buffalo. Miles learned of this movement from the Indians who surrendered to him on April 22. Five days later the Second Cavalry squadron from Fort Ellis, Capt. Edward Ball commanding, reported to him for duty. On May 1, with Ball's cavalry and six infantry companies (two of the Fifth and four of the Twenty-second), Miles started up the Tongue to look for Lame Deer. Some of the recent hostiles, most notably the Miniconjou Hump and the Cheyennes White Bull and Brave Wolf, went along as scouts.[26]

Sixty-three miles up the Tongue, Miles cut loose from his wagons. Leaving three infantry companies to guard the train and the other three to follow, he moved swiftly westward with the cavalry. The scouts found Lame Deer's camp on an eastern tributary of the Rosebud, Muddy Creek. At dawn on May 7 Miles led the four cavalry troops in a charge on the village. The surprised Sioux fled up the slopes beyond the tepees. One troop, assisted by the Indian scouts, seized the pony herd, 450 head.

Cut off from retreat, a small party of Sioux, including Lame Deer and the head warrior, Iron Star, were induced by Hump to surrender to Miles. Agitated and fearful, both laid their rifles on the ground. Lame Deer grasped Miles' hand and Iron Star the hand of Adj. George W. Baird. At this crucial moment a scout rode up and covered the Indians with his rifle. Instantly, both seized their rifles from the ground, and Lame Deer fired point-blank at Miles. Miles dodged and the bullet struck and killed a cavalryman behind him. The two Indians raced up a nearby hillside as Miles' party opened fire. Lame Deer was cut down. Iron Star tried to carry him but had to give up the attempt. Topping a hill, Iron Star ran head-on into the full troop of cavalry. The troop commander, Capt. James W. Wheelan, dropped the war leader with his pistol.

Fourteen Sioux had been left dead on the Muddy Creek battlefield. Miles lost four enlisted men killed and one officer and six enlisted men wounded. The cavalry pursued the fleeing Indians down the creek to the Rosebud, then returned to burn the village. More than half the captured ponies were slaughtered. The balance were taken back to Tongue River Cantonment and used to convert four companies of Miles' regiment into mounted infantry.

The fugitives from the Battle of Muddy Creek, some 225 people under Lame Deer's son, Fast Bull, kept Miles occupied most of the summer of 1877. Even though the mass surrenders of the spring made unnecessary the elaborate buildup envisioned by Sheridan, Miles received substantial reinforcements. Besides the Second Cavalry squadron, eleven troops of the Seventh Cavalry under Colonel Sturgis, four companies of the First Infantry and two of the Eleventh saw service under Miles. In various combinations, chiefly under Majs. Henry M. Lazelle and James Brisbin, Miles' troops scoured the Tongue, the Powder, and the Little Missouri in pursuit of Fast Bull. There were occasional skirmishes, but it was the constant harassment that finally broke the will to resist. In small groups, beginning in late July and ending in September, Fast Bull's people made their way to Camp Sheridan, near Spotted Tail Agency, and surrendered.[27]

Miles used part of his command to construct the two permanent posts for which Congress had appropriated funds the previous August, in the aftermath of the Custer disaster. He built one adjacent to the Tongue River Cantonment. The other occupied bluffs overlooking the confluence of the Bighorn and Little Bighorn Rivers, fifteen miles north of the Custer Battlefield. In November the former was named Fort Keogh, in honor of a captain slain at the Little Bighorn, and the latter Fort Custer.

On July 16, 1877, as the buildings of Fort Keogh rose from the valley at the mouth of Tongue River, the steamer *Rosebud* deposited Generals Sherman and Terry and their staffs on the Yellowstone shore. A round of inspections and evening socializing reached a climax two days later in a formal retreat ceremony. The General of the Army pinned medals to the tunics of thirty soldiers in recognition of combat heroism. To the accompaniment of the regimental band, the Fifth Infantry, two battalions afoot and one mounted on the Indian ponies seized at Muddy Creek, paraded for the dignitaries.[28]

The band, the flags, and the medals symbolized the dawn of a new day in the Yellowstone Valley. Scarcely a year earlier a white man entered this country at his peril. Now Forts Keogh and Custer planted the army in the very heart of the Sioux domain. Although Sitting Bull remained unbroken, General Sherman, visiting the site of Fort Custer, could truthfully declare: "The Sioux Indians can never again regain this country."

Throughout the summer of 1877, tension gripped the Indians of Red Cloud and Spotted Tail Agencies. The hope raised by Crook and Miles of agencies in their own country turned to disappointment and bitterness. The Northern Cheyennes left for distant places almost immediately after surrendering. As the Commissioner of Indian Affairs explained with a certain lack of candor, they "were suddenly seized by a desire to remove to Indian Territory," and on May 28, escorted by a troop of the Fourth Cavalry, 937 of them began a seventy-day trek to the agency of their southern kinsmen.[29] The Brulés and Oglalas unhappily contemplated a move, too—back to the Missouri River. The Indian appropriation act of August 15, 1876, had decreed that rations for the Sioux be issued at locations on the Missouri River. In signing the Black Hills treaty, the chiefs had consented.

But the source of greatest apprehension, to Indians as well as whites, was Crazy Horse. "This incorrigible wild man," as the agent described him, was "silent, sullen, lordly and dictatorial." He was also unpredictable, and the agency Indians feared he would set off an explosion that would hurt them all. Crazy Horse apparently believed that Crook had promised him an agency in the Powder River country, and the talk of going to the Missouri unsettled him. Also, the enlistment of Sioux scouts in August to help fight the Nez Percés angered the chief. He was sure they were to be used against Sitting Bull. The leading chiefs of the agency feared that Crazy Horse was preparing to bolt the reservation and go back to the Powder River country, and they drew back from him.[30]

The issue of the scouts threatened to precipitate a confrontation. The post commander at Camp Robinson, Lt. Col. Luther P. Bradley, summoned reinforcements from Fort Laramie. General Crook, en route for the corner of his department threatened by the Nez Percé War, detoured by way of Camp Robinson and, on September 2, ordered Bradley to arrest Crazy Horse. After a series of misadventures, the chief was finally taken into custody on September 5. Both Indians and soldiers were in the group that attempted to disarm him two days later. He fought back, and in the scuffle he received a mortal stab wound, whether from his own or another Indian's knife or an infantryman's bayonet has been debated ever since. When he died during the night, a Miniconjou chief voiced the sentiment of many saddened but greatly relieved Indians: "It is good, he has looked for death, and it has come."[31]

Late in September a delegation of chiefs headed by Red Cloud and Spotted Tail went to Washington to lay their grievances before the new Great Father. True to his promise, General Crook was there, too, urging that the Sioux not be forced to settle on the Missouri. President Hayes promised that if the Indians spent the winter on the Missouri, where their provisions had already been stockpiled, they could select new agency sites farther west in the spring. Even so, while the movement was in progress in late October, Crazy Horse's band and other "northern" Sioux, some 2,000 in number, broke free and headed back to the Powder. Ultimately, they joined Sitting Bull in Canada. The rest, after many tribulations, finally forced a reluctant government to make good the President's promise. In 1878 Spotted Tail and the Brulés settled on the south fork of White River, and Spotted Tail Agency became Rosebud Agency. Red Cloud and the Oglalas chose a location still farther west, on White Clay Creek, and Red Cloud Agency became Pine Ridge Agency.[32]

The Northern Cheyennes were less successful than the Sioux in asserting the right to live in their own country. Only after one of history's great tragedies dramatized the depth of their conviction did the remnants of this tribe win an agency in the north. The Northern Cheyennes arrived at the Cheyenne and Arapaho Agency in Indian Territory in August 1877. Unacclimated and greviously homesick, they died by the dozen during the winter of 1877–78. Finally, on September 7, 1878, Dull Knife and Little Wolf led 300 people in a desperate break for their northern homeland. Cavalry from Fort Reno and Camp Supply took up the chase and engaged them in a few inconclusive skirmishes. Troops also converged from posts in the Departments of the Platte and Dakota. Frightened Kansas citizens mobilized for self-defense. Violating a strict prohibition laid down by the chiefs, a few of the warriors killed some settlers. North of the Platte, in Nebraska, a dispute between Dull Knife and Little Wolf divided the fugitives. Part went with Dull Knife to surrender to the soldiers at Camp Robinson. The rest, under Little Wolf, continued northward in hopes of reaching the Yellowstone Valley.[33]

Dull Knife and his followers surrendered to a cavalry patrol near Camp Robinson on October 23, 1878. Domiciled in a barracks building at the post, for two months they resisted all appeals to return peacefully to Indian Territory. They had given up expecting to be allowed to live with the Sioux at Pine Ridge, and they would die before going south again. They meant it, as the post commander, Capt. Henry W. Wessells, Jr.,[34] discovered when he received orders to make them go. Early in January, after attempting unsuccessfully to persuade the women and children to leave the barracks, he cut off all food, water, and fuel. Nearly a week of hunger, thirst, and cold drove the prisoners to an almost suicidal break for freedom. On the bitterly cold night of January 9, 1879, with the ground covered by snow, they burst from the barracks windows, shot the guards with firearms the women had secreted at the time of surrender, and fled the post. The startled garrison turned out swiftly and gave chase, shooting down the escaping people as they were overtaken. Almost half—men, women, and children—fell before the army rifles, but the bloodbath earned such sympathy that the government relented. The survivors, including Dull Knife, settled at Pine Ridge.[35]

After parting with Dull Knife in October 1878, Little Wolf and his people eluded the army all winter. On March 27, 1879, on the Little Missouri River in the extreme southeastern tip of Montana, they surrendered to Lt. William Philo Clark and two troops of the Second Cavalry, out of Fort Keogh. Largely responsible for this result were the Two Moons Cheyennes, who had been serving Colonel Miles with great distinction ever since surrendering to him in April 1877. Little Wolf and his followers joined these Cheyennes at Fort Keogh, and the men signed on as scouts. In 1880, upon Miles' application, the Dull Knife people at Pine Ridge were also permitted to move to Fort Keogh. Gradually, as the need for the military services of the Indians diminished, they drifted up the Tongue and Rosebud Valleys to make their homes. In 1884 an Executive Order set aside the Tongue River Reservation for their permanent occupancy. Almost within sight of the Muddy Creek Battlefield of 1877, the Lame Deer Agency was established. At last the Northern Cheyennes, like the Sioux, had an agency in their homeland.[36]

For five years after the campaign of 1876, the specter of Sitting Bull loomed over the northern Plains. While he remained free, the Sioux War could not be regarded as conclusively ended. The first of the Hunkpapas had crossed the boundary into Canada in December 1876. Sitting Bull arrived in the spring of 1877. Including the Crazy Horse people who broke away from the southern agencies in October 1877, the refugee Sioux came to number more than 4,000 Indians in some 600 lodges. Hunkpapa, Oglala, Miniconjou, Sans Arc, and Blackfoot Sioux tribes were all represented. Besides Sitting Bull, prominent chiefs included Gall, Black Moon, No Neck, Iron Dog, Big Road, Low Dog, and Spotted Eagle.

Also, in October 1877 about 100 Nez Percé warriors and 50 women under White Bird joined the Sioux. They had slipped away from their people rather than surrender with Chief Joseph to Colonel Miles after the Battle of Bear Paw Mountain (see Chapter Seventeen). Following the buffalo, the refugee Indians scattered over the plains in the vicinity of Wood Mountain and the Cypress Hills.[37]

The North-West Mounted Police, scarcely four years old, maintained a post, Fort Walsh, on the southern edge of the Cypress Hills. The superintendent, Maj. J. M. Walsh, greeted the refugee bands and let them know exactly what was expected of them. They could stay in the country of the Great Mother only so long as they scrupulously obeyed her laws. Major Walsh and his scarlet-coated policemen treated the Sioux firmly, fairly, and above all consistently, and in return they were accorded not only obedience but respect bordering on reverence.

The influx of so many Sioux created grave dangers. The diminishing buffalo herds in Canada were insufficient to feed even the resident Blackfoot, Cree, Assinniboine, and other Indians, much less the newcomers. With the prospect of famine came the prospect of inter-tribal strife and of forays across the boundary in search of buffalo—forays certain to involve American lives and property. Both the Canadian and U.S. governments devoutly desired the Sioux back in the United States on a reservation.

In an attempt to bring about such a result, a commission headed by General Terry arrived at Fort Walsh in October 1877. Lt. Col. James F. Macleod, Commissioner of the North-West Mounted Police, came down from his headquarters to greet the American general and to help Major Walsh impress on the Sioux leaders the gravity of the question they must decide. The Canadian officers believed that Terry, so well known to the Sioux as their recent enemy, was an unwise choice for the mission of persuading them to give up their guns and ponies and go to a reservation. Indeed, Walsh barely succeeded in getting Sitting Bull and his fellow chiefs to meet the U.S. commissioners at all. On October 17, however, the conference took place in the officers' mess at Fort Walsh. As the police had feared, the chiefs truculently rejected Terry's overtures and dramatized their feelings by effusively embracing the redcoats while declining even to shake hands with the Americans. "You come here to tell us lies," Sitting Bull spat at Terry, "but we don't want to hear them. . . . Don't say two more words.

Go home where you came from." Under the circumstances, the commissioners heeded Sitting Bull's injunction and went home.[38]

Terry's failure aroused the scorn of Colonel Miles, who stepped up his campaign to have all of Montana and Dakota placed under his command. Given such a department, he wrote General Sherman early in 1878, and authority "to over-power and govern all these Indian tribes in this region," he would order the Third Infantry "from the Helena race track" to the mouth of the Musselshell, concentrate infantry from the Missouri River posts at Fort Peck Agency, mobilize the Crows, Arikaras, and Mandans, and in six weeks clear the country of hostile Indians. As Sherman well knew, the hostile Indians were in Canada. To allow the ambitious Miles anywhere near the border with a strong force seemed like a prescription for an international incident. "I cannot make you a Brigadier General," he wrote Miles on February 9, 1878, "nor can I advise a new department for your special command," and "most undoubtedly" a violation of British territory would land him in serious trouble. On the same day, Sherman issued orders barring military operations north of the Missouri River unless navigation were threatened or settlers molested.[39]

Miles would not relent. He gathered political support in Montana, and he pressed his own case while in Washington serving on an equipment board in the winter of 1878–79. "I have told him plainly," an exasperated Sherman exploded to Sheridan, "that I know no way to satisfy his ambitions but to surrender to him absolute power over the whole Army, with President & Congress thrown in. . . . He wants to remain on the Equipment Board, and at the same time to command all of Terry's troops, to advance north of the British line, drive back Sitting Bull & Co., and if necessary follow them across the Border as Mackenzie did on the Mexican Border." Indeed, confirming Sherman's fears, Miles had solicited his private blessing of a foray into Canada to smash the Sioux such as Mackenzie had led into Mexico against the Kickapoos in 1873 (see Chapter Eighteen). "Because as you explained Generals Sheridan and Mackenzie once consented to act unlawfully in defiance of my authority in a certain political contingency," Sherman informed Miles, "is no reason why I should imitate so bad an example."[40]

Sherman had no desire to let Miles get near the border, but in the spring and summer of 1879 the Sioux themselves afforded him the opportunity. Famine threatened them in Canada. In fact, about 200 lodges gave up the struggle and returned to their reservations in the United States. Small parties of those not yet ready for such a drastic solution dropped into Montana to hunt buffalo. The As- sinniboine agent at Fort Peck, which had been moved down the Missouri to the mouth of Poplar River in 1877, complained of their encroachment on the game resources of his reservation. Miles, therefore, won authority to organize an expedition to drive the Sioux back across the border. Noting that "Genl Miles is too apt to mistake the dictates of his personal ambition for wisdom," Sherman cautioned Sheridan to insure that he did not precipitate a boundary incident. Sheridan, who regarded the Sioux threat as much exaggerated ("gotten up by traders and Montana interests, helped along by Miles' scouts"), replied that he would "gradually circumscribe his opportunities north of the Missouri River."[41]

Miles' command consisted of seven troops of the Second Cavalry and seven mounted companies of the Fifth Infantry—in all 33 offi- cers, 643 enlisted men, and 143 Crow and Cheyenne scouts. As the column moved up the south bank of Milk River on July 17, Lt. William Philo Clark and the Indian auxiliaries, scouting a southern tributary of the Milk, Beaver Creek, came unexpectedly upon a hunting party under Sitting Bull himself. In a running fight, the Sioux fell back to Milk River and crossed their women and children, then counterattacked. Outnumbered, the scouts were hard-pressed until Miles came up and dispersed the Sioux with two Hotchkiss rapid-fire cannon. The troops followed Sitting Bull's trail to the boundary and halted. On July 23 Major Walsh visited the military camp and exchanged views with Miles. Their differ- ing assessments of the actions and attitudes of the Sioux were barely concealed by official courtesy. Next Miles rounded up sev- eral hundred "Red River half-breeds," from whom the Sioux ob- tained ammunition, and expelled them from U.S. territory. Then, in obedience to orders originating with a President anxious to avoid any offense to the Canadian government, he withdrew to the Missouri and in September broke up the expedition.[42]

Terry heaped fulsome praise on Miles, and Sherman and Sheri- dan, doubtless relieved that no diplomatic trouble had been pro- voked, added their compliments. The Mounted Police, however, believed that the U.S. Army's attack on Sitting Bull had simply deferred the day when he would surrender. "So long as there remains a gopher to eat," he vowed to Major Walsh, "I will not go back." But the disappearance of the buffalo placed even the gopher in peril, and throughout 1879 and 1880 the Sioux camps dwindled as, one after another, the chiefs took their hungry people across the boundary to surrender. At last, on July 19, 1881, Sitting Bull and forty-five men, sixty-seven women, and seventy-three children rode into Fort Buford, the final vestige of the mighty alliance that had crushed Custer five years earlier. Sitting Bull handed his Winchester to his eight-year-old son and told him to present it to the post commander, Maj. David H. Brotherton. "I wish it to be remembered that I was the last man of my tribe to surrender my rifle," the chief declared, "and this day have given it to you."[43]

In May and June 1881 a procession of chartered steamers transported almost 3,000 Sioux down the Missouri River to Fort Yates, the military post guarding Standing Rock Agency, for assignment to appropriate agencies. On July 29 the *General Sherman* cast off from Fort Buford with Sitting Bull and those who had surrendered with him. Although it paused at Fort Yates, the vessel continued downstream and debarked its passengers at Fort Randall. The government was not quite ready to set the old chief free among the reservation Sioux. For two years he would live under the rifles of the soldiers at Fort Randall.

Nelson A. Miles was not present at the surrender of Sitting Bull to savor the triumph and garner the laurels. In December 1880 his long-prosecuted offensive on the political front had yielded him the star of a brigadier general,[44] and he left the Yellowstone to assume command of the Department of the Columbia. Nevertheless, more than any other officer, Miles deserved the laurels for converting the disasters of the summer of 1876 into the succession of achievements that culminated at Fort Buford on July 19, 1881.

In part his success stemmed from the establishment of a permanent post on the Yellowstone. Tongue River Cantonment and its successor, Fort Keogh, afforded Miles the invaluable asset of a fixed base in the heart of the Indian country. It domiciled his troops within comparatively easy striking range of the enemy. It greatly simplified the logistical problem that had so plagued Crook and Terry. And it helped undermine the morale and resilience of the Indians.

A larger part of the explanation, however, lay in the abilities of Colonel Miles. He was an excellent regimental commander. John F. Finerty, the *Chicago Times* correspondent who observed him in 1876 and went with him to Milk River in 1879, described him as "a splendid field soldier, prompt, bold, and magnetic. He was always in high spirits, which is a good thing in a commanding officer."[45] He was also energetic, innovative, imaginative, flexible in strategy and tactics, and inflexible in pursuit of objectives. Together with less attractive traits rooted in vanity and ambition, Miles displayed all these qualities in Montana between 1876 and 1880.

Neither weather nor fatigue turned Miles from his course, nor did the tendency to overestimate enemy capabilities that afflicted so many officers after the Custer battle. He went to Montana determined to keep after the Sioux until he crushed them or forced them to surrender. This is pretty much what he did. The army contained few top officers so little deterred by obstacles.

Ignoring the conventional wisdom that cavalry was necessary for offensive operations, Miles employed his infantry aggressively. His campaign of October 1876 to January 1877 seemed to justify his declaration to a congressional committee a year later that "a body of infantry troops can walk down any band of Indians in the country in four months."[46] The achievements of the "walk-a-heaps" against Sitting Bull, Crazy Horse, and Chief Joseph's Nez Percés, contrasting dramatically with the performance of the cavalry at the Little Bighorn, touched off an extended discussion in Congress and the army over whether infantry was not, after all, superior to cavalry for Indian warfare. Although in fact most of Miles' successes were won with conventional cavalry and mounted infantry, he demonstrated new uses for the infantry on the frontier and in the process gave this arm renewed pride and a sense of accomplishment.

Like Crook, Miles appreciated the benefits of Indian allies, and he made extensive use of them. The Cheyennes and Sioux who surrendered to him in April 1877 remained at Fort Keogh until 1881, nominally as prisoners of war but actually as auxiliaries to the troops. Together with Crow allies, they participated significantly in all of Miles' operations as scouts and, in battle, as combatants. They were responsible for his remarkable record of finding enemy camps. In almost every engagement they figured tacti-

290] FRONTIER REGULARS

cally in important, sometimes decisive ways. Also, functioning as spies, they kept Miles informed of sentiment and plans in the hostile camps. Miles paid high tribute to this spy system, but regrettably he left almost no explanation of how it operated. Crook, too, owed a large debt to his Indians; as has been noted, they led Mackenzie to Dull Knife's village in November 1876 and then took prominent part in the action. Crook also maintained an efficient network of spies who fomented discord among the hostiles and reported on their temper and intentions.

Spotted Tail is usually assigned generous credit for the midwinter peace mission that eventuated in the surrender of most of the hostiles in the spring of 1877. The achievement was substantial, and it is not diminished by recognition of the army's vital role in keeping them so stirred up during a long, hard winter that they were receptive to Spotted Tail's inducements. Crook and Mackenzie participated in this process: the action of November 26, 1876, impoverished the Cheyennes and disheartened the Sioux. But Crook's subsequent operations did not threaten the hostiles. It was Miles, campaigning relentlessly in winter storms, who so wore down his adversaries that they either surrendered with Crazy Horse or sought safety with Sitting Bull in Canada. And it was Miles, too—although here the effect is less clear—whose aggressive presence on the international boundary served notice on the Sioux refugees in Canada that they could return to the United States only if they submitted unconditionally and went to a reservation.

As Sioux hostility faltered, and even after it ended, the army continued to expand the northern Plains defense system. Forts Keogh and Custer had been constructed in 1877. Responding to the threat posed by Sitting Bull, Congress appropriated money for Fort Assinniboine, which was established on Milk River in May 1879 by Col. Thomas H. Ruger and the Eighteenth Infantry. Fort Maginnis followed in August 1880, blocking the Judith Basin route by which war parties from Canada slipped down to the Yellowstone. To the south, at the eastern base of the Bighorn Mountains, Fort McKinney was established in 1877 and named in honor of a lieutenant killed on the nearby Dull Knife battlefield. Sheridan himself picked the site for Fort Meade, established in August 1878 near Bear Butte on the northeastern edge of the Black Hills. Fort Robinson continued to watch over the Oglalas at Pine Ridge, while

Fort Niobrara was built in 1880 on the Niobrara River to the east to watch over the Brulés at Rosebud Agency.[47]

As usual, the military presence invited settlement. The Northern Pacific Railroad, reenergized in 1879 and completed in 1883, was an even more persuasive attraction. Cattlemen, sheepmen, and dirt farmers spread up the valleys of Montana and Wyoming. "Prosperous farms and cattle ranches exist where ten years ago no man could venture," wrote General Sherman in his annual report for 1880. "This is largely due to the soldier, but in equal, if not greater measure, to the adventurous pioneers themselves, and to that new and greatest of civilizers, the railroad."[48] The surrender of Sitting Bull signified the passing of the northern Plains from the Indian to the soldier, the pioneer, and the railroad.

NOTES

1. The story is vividly told in Hanson, *The Conquest of the Missouri*, chap. 38. This is a biography of Marsh.
2. 19 Stat. 95–96 (July 22, 1876).
3. 19 Stat. 204 (Aug. 15, 1876). See also Richardson, *Messages and Papers of the Presidents*, 7, 376; and *Cong. Rec.*, 44th Cong., 1st sess., pp. 5674–75, 5694–96 (Aug. 15, 1876).
4. CIA, *Annual Report* (1877), p. 14.
5. Cody's contest with Yellow Hand, a close-range exchange of gunfire in which Cody proved a better shot than his adversary, was greatly embellished by press-agentry and dime-novel sensationalism. It has been one of the frontier's enduring legends, dramatized in Cody's Wild West shows and, more recently, in several motion pictures. For Merritt's movements, see King, *Campaigning with Crook*, chap. 3; and "The Story of a March," *Journal of the Military Service Institution of the United States*, 3 (1890), 121–29; James T. King, *War Eagle*, chap. 7; Price, *Across the Continent with the Fifth Cavalry*, chap. 16; and Russell, *The Lives and Legends of Buffalo Bill*, chap. 17. For Crook's delay here, see James T. King, "General Crook at Camp Cloud Peak: 'I am at a Loss What to Do,'" *Journal of the West*, *11* (1972), 114–27.
6. From Fort Leavenworth, June 15, 1876, Sherman Papers, vol. 44, LC.
7. King, *War Eagle*, p. 172. For this phase of the campaign, see Finerty, *War-Path and Bivouac*, chaps. 17–18; King, *Campaigning with Crook*, chaps. 6–7; Gibbon, pp. 50–64; Bourke, *On the Border with Crook*, chap. 20; and SW, *Annual Report* (1876), pp. 466–71, 475–76, 504–9.
8. Official reports are in SW, *Annual Report* (1876), pp. 506–13. Good accounts are in Mills, *My Story*, pp. 170–74; King, *Campaigning with Crook*, chap. 9; Finerty, chap. 20; and Bourke, pp. 369–76. The village contained many trophies of the Little Bighorn, including a Seventh Cavalry guidon and Capt. Myles W. Keogh's gauntlets.
9. Maj. Alfred L. Hough, arriving on the Yellowstone in October, found a consensus among veterans of the campaign that the annihilation of Custer's command had so demoralized the troops and their leaders—"in fact they were afraid of the Indians"—that "everything went wild, there appeared to be no settled plans." Robert G. Athearn, ed., "A Winter Campaign

against the Sioux," *Mississippi Valley Historical Review*, *35* (1948–49), 279.

10. Feb. 10, 1877, Sherman Papers, vol. 45, LC. For a critical assessment of Crook's management of the campaign, see James T. King, "Needed: A Re-evaluation of General George Crook," *Nebraska History*, *45* (1964), 223–35.

Seeking to learn what had gone wrong, Major Hough, quoted in the preceding note, found that "At General Sheridan's Head Quarters nothing was said, and if I attempted to turn the conversation on the subject, it was avoided. At Genl. Terry's Head Quarters the whole tone of the talk was apologetic; giving reasons for this and for that, everybody seemed to feel that they had done something for which they had to find an excuse. At Bismarck I met censure and criticism. At Buford it was ridicule of the most censorious nature." Hough traveled from St. Paul to Bismarck in a special railroad car with Sheridan and Terry. "I was impressed with the opinion that both of them felt that the campaign against the Sioux . . . was a failure for which they would be held responsible by the people. Especially was this the case with General Terry who was nervous, excited, and depressed in spirits; he had changed much since I had last seen him in 1869." Athearn, ed., pp. 274, 279.

11. Olson, *Red Cloud and the Sioux Problem*, pp. 230–235. *Nebraska History*, *15* (1934), 277–95. SW, *Annual Report* (1876), pp. 469–70; (1877), pp. 533–34, 537–40.

12. 19 Stat. 191–92 (Aug. 15, 1876). Kappler, *Indian Affairs*, *1*, 168–72. Olson, pp. 224–30.

13. Principal sources for Miles' operations from autumn 1876 to spring 1877 are official reports in SW, *Annual Report* (1876), pp. 469–71, 482–87; (1877), pp. 487–500, 523–29, 540–47. Miles, *Personal Recollections and Observations*, chaps 17–19. Johnson, *Unregimented General*, chap. 10. Luther S. Kelly, *"Yellowstone Kelly": Memoirs of Luther S. Kelly*, ed. M. M. Quaife (New Haven, Conn., 1926), chaps. 9–10. Kelly was Miles' chief scout. Important to an understanding of these events are two excellent articles by Harry H. Anderson: "Nelson A. Miles and the Sioux War of 1876–77," *Westerners Brand Book* (Chicago), *16* (1959), 25–27, 32; and "Indian Peace-Talkers and the Conclusion of the Sioux War of 1876," *Nebraska History*, *44* (1963), 233–54.

14. Miner's and Otis' reports, Oct. 12 and 27, in SW, *Annual Report* (1876), pp. 485–87, 485–87, 515–18. John S. Gray, "Sitting Bull Strikes the Glendive Supply Trains," *Westerners Brand Book* (Chicago), *28* (1971), 25–27, 31–32.

15. In addition to sources cited in note 13 above, see *Army and Navy Journal*, *14* (Feb. 10, 1877), 431.

16. Hazen's reports, Nov. 2 (2) and 9, 1876, in SW, *Annual Report* (1876), pp. 471, 481–82. Hazen had been kept at Fort Buford since 1872 and, despite seniority, systematically denied a part in any of the operations of 1872–77 in the Department of Dakota. During the trial of Secretary of War Belknap in 1876, it was alleged that this exile "in the Arctic regions" resulted from Hazen's testimony before the House Comimttee on Military Affairs in 1872 accusing Belknap of profiting from the sale of the Fort Sill post tradership. Prickett, "The Malfeasance of William Worth Belknap," p. 109. Hazen himself, however, attributed his eclipse to the animosity of General Sheridan. Sheridan and Hazen, it will be recalled (p. 153), clashed at Fort Cobb in 1868 when Hazen prevented Sheridan from treating the Kiowas as hostile. Hazen to Sherman, May 5, 1877, Sherman Papers, vol. 46, LC. Hazen finally won appointment as Chief Signal Officer in 1880. His seven-year tenure was stormy. "No one in the service," the *Army and Navy Journal* marveled in an obituary, "had a more unfortunate faculty

for involving himself in controversies." *24* (Jan. 22, 1887), 520. Major Hough, quoted in notes 9 and 10 above, wrote to his wife from Fort Buford in October 1876: "I have a difficult place to fill, midway between two ambitious men, Hazen and Miles, who are making plans to effect their own advancement." Athearn, ed., pp. 277–78. Hough was relieving Otis at the Glendive supply depot.

17. The most detailed account of Crook's expedition and the Dull Knife fight is Bourke, "Mackenzie's Last Fight with the Cheyennes." See also Lessing H. Nohl, Jr., "Mackenzie against Dull Knife: Breaking the Northern Cheyennes in 1876," in K. Ross Toole *et. al.*, eds., *Probing the American West: Papers from the Santa Fe Conference* (Santa Fe, N.M., 1962), pp. 86–92. The Indian side of the story is in Grinnell, *The Fighting Cheyennes*, chap. 27; and Powell, *Sweet Medicine, 1*, chaps. 11–12.

18. There appears to be no sound basis for the story that Crazy Horse refused the Cheyennes his hospitality. Its origins were in factional quarrels that developed in the village later and that prompted the Cheyennes, after their surrender, to criticise Crazy Horse. Anderson, "Indian Peace-Talkers," p. 246, n. 24.

19. Bourke vividly remembered Christmas Day 1876: "Beards, moustaches, eyelashes and eye-brows were frozen masses of ice. The keen air was filled with minute crystals, each cutting the tender skin like a razor, while feet and hands ached as if beaten with clubs. Horses and mules shivered while they stood in column, their flanks white with crystals of perspiration congealed on their bodies, and their nostrils bristling with icicles." "Mackenzie's Last Fight," p. 218.

20. In addition to sources cited in note 13 above, see Don Rickey, Jr., "The Battle of Wolf Mountain," *Montana, the Magazine of Western History, 13* (Spring, 1963), 44–54.

21. Miles to Sherman, Nov. 18, 1876; Jan. 20, Feb. 1 and 2, March 14 and 29, April 8 and 30, 1877, Sherman Papers, vols. 45 and 46, LC. See also Miles' letters to his wife during this period in Johnson, pp. 150–70.

At the same time, Miles launched a campaign to win promotion to the next vacancy of brigadier general that fell open. He sought testimonials from all over the army and enlisted political influence wherever he could find it. Urging Sherman to advance his cause, he confided that the post he really wanted was Secretary of War.

In a letter to his wife, Miles names those in the rear he blames for not properly supporting him: General Terry and his quartermaster, Maj. Benjamin Card, at St. Paul, Colonel Hazen at Ford Buford, and Colonel Otis at the Glendive depot.

22. Sheridan to Sherman (confidential), Feb. 10, 1877, Sherman Papers, vol. 45, LC.

23. Anderson, "Indian Peace-Talkers," pp. 238–39.

24. The negotiations are well treated in *ibid.*, pp. 239–54; in Hyde, *Spotted Tail's Folk*, pp. 237–46; and Olson, pp. 230–38. See also Crook's annual report in SW, *Annual Report* (1877), pp. 84–86.

25. The surrender scene as described by the *New York Herald* is printed in *Army and Navy Journal, 14* (May 12, 1877), 637. See also Olson, p. 239.

26. For this expedition, see SW, *Annual Report* (1877), pp. 497–98, 524–26; John F. McBlain, "The Last Fight of the Sioux War of 1876–77," *Journal of the United States Cavalry Association, 10* (1897), 122–27; *Army and Navy Journal, 14* (June 16, 1877), 723; Miles, chap. 19; Johnson, pp. 173–76; and Grinnell, pp. 387–97.

27. SW, *Annual Report* (1877), pp. 55–56, 542–45, 574–75

28. *Ibid.*, p. 545. Generals Sheridan and Crook, with their staffs and Insp. Gen. Delos B. Sackett, visited the post on July 24. *Ibid.*

29. CIA, *Annual Report* (1877), p. 19. As Grinnell (p. 400) describes it, the

Cheyennes, confused and uncertain, were half persuaded, half forced to go south. The story of these people is told in Mari Sandoz, *Cheyenne Autumn* (New York, 1953). See also Verne Dusenberry, *The Northern Cheyenne* (Helena, Mont., 1955). This eighteen-page brochure is an excellent source of information about the Northern Cheyennes.

30. CIA, *Annual Report* (1878), pp. 36–38. Olson, pp. 235–46. Hyde, *Spotted Tail's Folk*, pp. 248–53. Hyde, *Red Cloud's Folk*, pp. 294–98.

31. Bradley's report quoted by Olson, p. 245. In addition to sources cited in note 30 above, see first-hand accounts in E. A. Brininstool, *Crazy Horse* (Los Angeles, 1949). See also Sandoz, *Crazy Horse*.

32. See the two books by Hyde cited above plus a third: *A Sioux Chronicle* (Norman, Okla., 1956), chap. 1. See also Olson, chap. 13.

33. Sandoz, *Cheyenne Autumn*. Dusenberry. Grinnell, chaps. 29 and 30. Powell, *Sweet Medicine*, *1*, chaps. 15–17. Official reports are in SW, *Annual Report* (1878), pp. 39–50; (1879), pp. 77–78; CIA, *Annual Report* (1878), pp. xxii–xxiv, 56–57; (1879), pp. xvi–xvii, 58–59. Indian Bureau reports persuasively counter the stories that the Northern Cheyennes were starving in Indian Territory. The people who went with Dull Knife numbered 124 (40 men, 47 women, 37 children); those who followed Little Wolf 149 (46 men, 61 women, 42 children).

34. The son of the Henry W. Wessells who relieved Colonel Carrington after the Fetterman disaster.

35. According to Grinnell (p. 426), sixty-four were killed, twenty were sent south to face trial for depredations in Kansas, fifty-eight went to Pine Ridge, and eight or ten were missing and presumed dead. Wessells probably misjudged the depth of the Indians' feeling, but having resorted to extreme measures felt he could not relent. General Crook excused Wessells, blaming instead the orders from Washington that prompted his course of action. SW, *Annual Report* (1879), p. 77. A board of officers convened by Crook mildly censured Wessells but concluded that the tragedy was unavoidable and that no blame attached to anyone in the military service. *Army and Navy Journal*, *16* (March 15, 1879), 571.

36. Little Chief's Northern Cheyennes had been sent to Indian Territory in the autumn of 1878, just as Dull Knife and Little Wolf were fleeing northward. Discontented here, this band was allowed to return to Pine Ridge in 1881. Not until 1891, however, in the aftermath of the Ghost Dance disturbance at Pine Ridge (see Chapter 21), were these people allowed to go to Tongue River. Appropriately, this move was engineered, over the opposition of the Indian Bureau, by Maj. Gen. Nelson A. Miles.

37. An excellent account of the Sioux in Canada is Turner, *The North-West Mounted Police*, *1*, chaps. 6–11. For location of various bands, see also *Army and Navy Journal*, *16* (Aug. 24, 1878), 43.

38. Turner, *1*, 357–73. For the report of the Terry commission, see House Ex. Docs., 45th Cong., 2d sess., No. 1, Part 5, Vol. 8, pp. 719–28.

39. Miles to Sherman, Jan. 8, 1878, vol. 47; Sherman to Miles, Feb. 9, 1878, vol. 90, pp. 518–19. Sherman Papers, LC. SW, *Annual Report* (1878), p. 66. Sherman favored a command structure tailored to the number of line generals, which meant there should be one less department instead of one more. "If we make Depts for Colonels," he wrote Sheridan, "there will be no peace or harmony." Nov. 4, 1878, Sherman-Sheridan Letters, vol. 2, Sheridan Papers, LC.

40. Exchange of letters between Sherman and Miles, March 9 and 10, 1879, in vol. 91, pp. 119–22, Sherman Papers, LC. Sherman to Sheridan, March 9, 1879, Sherman-Sheridan Letters, Sheridan Papers, LC. Besides frustrating Miles' campaign for a department, Sherman posted the Eighteenth Infantry to Montana. Its colonel, Thomas H. Ruger, ranked Miles. With Hazen and Gibbon, this made three colonels in the Department of Dakota who

were Miles' senior. He wrote Sherman that this was "the severest injury that has been done me by any official or friend."

41. SW, *Annual Report* (1879) pp. 59–61. Sherman to Sheridan, July 19, 1879, Sherman-Sheridan Letters, vol. 2, Sheridan Papers, LC. Sheridan to Sherman, July 21, 1879, Sherman Papers, vol. 50, LC.
42. Miles' report, Sept. 1879, in SW, *Annual Report* (1879), pp. 61–64. See also pp. 4–5, 43. Turner, *1*, 461–74. Finerty, *War-Path and Bivouac*, Part 2, chaps. 1–10. Johnson, pp. 217–21. Miles, pp. 306–10. *Army and Navy Journal*, *16* (Aug. 2, 1879), 954.
43. Turner, *1*, chaps. 9–10. CIA, *Annual Report* (1880), pp. xxvii–xxix, 113, 116; SW, *Annual Report* (1881), pp. 92–107. Vestal, chaps. 29–30.
44. At the expense of the forcible retirement of General Ord. See p. 356.
45. Finerty, p. 249.
46. Dec. 13, 1877, House Misc. Docs., 45th Cong., 2d sess., No. 56, p. 237. For further discussion of this question, see p. 49.
47. See under appropriate headings in Prucha, *Military Posts of the United States;* and Frazer, *Forts of the West.*
48. SW, *Annual Report* (1880), p. 4.

SIXTEEN

Nez Percé Bid for Freedom, 1877

IN SEPTEMBER 1874 Brig. Gen. Oliver Otis Howard arrived in Portland, Oregon, to take command of the Department of the Columbia. Aside from a sleeve emptied at Seven Pines in 1862, he was widely noted for two conspicuous characteristics—an all-pervading religion and a well-developed social consciousness. During the Civil War, in which he rose to command the Army of the Tennessee under Sherman, the nation knew him as "the Christian general." After the war he devoted himself to the elevation of the former slaves as head of the Freedmen's Bureau of the War Department and as a founder and president of Howard University for blacks in Washington, D.C. The assignment to make peace with the Apaches in 1872 afforded him an opportunity to apply his humanitarian instincts to Indians (see Chapter Twelve).[1]

Sherman frowned on his lieutenant's somewhat ostentatiously displayed social and religious activities. He believed that soldiers should stick to soldiering and leave "education, charity, and religion" to civilian philanthropists. When unworthy subordinates and the vicious cross-currents of Reconstruction politics plunged Howard's administration of the Freedman's Bureau into scandal, he was glad enough to heed his chief's advice. Sherman expressed satisfaction "that you have come to the manly conclusion to assume your appropriate place among the officers of our army," and recommended him for the post vacated by Canby's assassination, held in the interim by Col. Jefferson C. Davis.[2]

Lavishing his humanitarianism on the Indians of the Northwest, Howard viewed himself as their true friend and convinced himself that they viewed him in the same light. Actually, his powerful brand of religion, clouding his understanding of the equally strong and pervasive spiritual motivation of the Indians, inhibited genuine communication. A cultural gulf, the more dangerous because unrecognized, separated him from the chiefs with whom he dealt. Against this background, he thrust himself into the festering problem of the "nontreaty" Nez Percés.

The "nontreaty" Nez Percés acquired this label by refusing to subscribe to the Treaty of 1863. This treaty, forced on the Nez Percés when parts of their mountain homeland were found to contain rich gold deposits, greatly contracted the reservation originally set aside for them in 1855. Most of the tribe settled within the new boundaries, mainly along Idaho's Clearwater River. But the nontreaties did not. Among them were bands of White Bird and Toohoolhoolzote, on the lower Salmon River to the south. Across the Snake River to the west, in Oregon, another band resided in the Wallowa Valley, shadowed on the south and west by the Wallowa and Blue Mountains and bounded on the north by the Grande Ronde River. These Nez Percés followed the venerated Chief Joseph—Old Joseph. When he died in 1871, his mantle passed to his son, Young Joseph, who swiftly displayed the statesmanlike characteristics for which his father was noted.[3]

As the Grande Ronde country began to attract settlers in the early 1870s, pressure mounted for the removal of Joseph and his band to the reservation in Idaho. The Nez Percés argued eloquently that Old Joseph had refused to sign the Treaty of 1863 and thus had never sold the Wallowa. Acknowledging the truth of this stand, the government in 1873 caused part of the Wallowa Valley to be set aside, by executive order of President Grant, as a reservation for Joseph's band. But the vociferous protest of Oregon citizens and officials led to a reconsideration of the matter, and in 1875 the order was rescinded and the Wallowa officially opened to settlement. This breach of faith infuriated all the nontreaties. Eagle from the Light, White Bird, Looking Glass, Toohoolhoolzote, and other chiefs conferred with Joseph and, after heated debate over whether to take up arms, decided to try to live in amity with the whites. Despite the best intentions, however, coexistence was bound to be shattered sooner or later by an aggressive settler or any angry young Indian.

General Howard began to concern himself with the Wallowa

problem in 1875. His sympathies, shaped by reports from officers at Forts Lapwai and Walla Walla, lay with Joseph. An investigation in 1876 by his own adjutant general, Maj. H. Clay Wood, strengthened his conviction that the Nez Percés had been wronged. His solution, however, was not to confirm them in the possession of their homeland but to compensate them fully for it and persuade them—if necessary, force them—to go to the reservation in Idaho. Although the issue remained primarily the responsibility of the Indian Bureau, Howard took the initiative in promoting this solution. The murder of an Indian by a settler in the Wallowa Valley helped him win the creation of a commission to settle the matter. In October 1876, the Secretary of the Interior appointed Howard one of five commissioners to treat with the Nez Percés. Also named to the commission were Major Wood and three easterners who knew nothing about the Nez Percés or their problem. Although not titular chairman of the commission, Howard led and the others followed.

The two-day council with Chief Joseph and other nontreaty leaders began on November 13, 1876, in the church at the Lapwai Agency, headquarters of the Nez Percé Reservation. The resolve of the Wallowa people not to part with their land at any price quickly became apparent. The commissioners were impressed with the sincerity and conviction of the Indians but also increasingly irritated by their stubborn refusal to bow to the wishes of the Great Father. The religious character of the ties that bound the Nez Percés to their homeland escaped Howard. Joseph's repeated allusion to the earth as his mother struck the general as nonsense. Moreover, he tended to confuse Joseph's spiritual attachment to the land of his father with the unsettling "Dreamer" cult sweeping the Columbia River tribes. This religion, the creation of a prophet named Smohalla, was understood to call for the destruction of all white people and was consequently causing government authorities serious concern. Joseph became the victim of a growing tendency of the whites to equate any form of Indian dissent with this incendiary new doctrine. The Lapwai conference ended in stalemate. The commission—i.e., Howard—recommended that, if further persuasion failed to move Joseph to the Lapwai Reservation "within a reasonable time," force should then be used. The commission's report won quick approval in Washington.[4]

Force, of course, meant the army. Indeed, the commission had also recommended that troops be stationed temporarily in the Wallowa Valley, and on March 7, 1877, the Interior Department requested their help in effecting Joseph's removal. Secretary of War Cameron, General Sherman, and Howard's immediate superior in San Francisco, General McDowell, all took great pains to stress that the role of the army in general, and of these troops in particular, was simply to aid the Indian Bureau. As with the Sioux a year earlier, the Indian Bureau, not the army, must stand responsible to the public if war broke out with the Néz Percés. Hence, McDowell cautioned Howard, "the paramount importance that none of the responsibility of any step which may lead to hostilities shall be initiated by the military authorities."[5]

Howard's leading part in the dispute with Chief Joseph had already in some degree compromised this objective. Even so, despite McDowell's warnings, he continued to figure prominently in the affair. Agent J. B. Montieth's efforts to persuade Joseph to move gave little hope of succeeding, and again, early in May 1877, Howard met with Joseph at Lapwai. This time the council took place in a tent on the parade ground of the fort instead of at the agency. Other nontreaty leaders appeared in support of Joseph, among them White Bird and Toohoolhoolzote from Salmon River and Looking Glass from the south fork of the Clearwater. In three days of often fiery debate, Howard rejected the Indians' explanations and arguments and insisted that they move within the reservation boundaries. His intransigence, coupled with news that cavalry from Fort Walla Walla had occupied the Wallowa Valley, convinced the chiefs that no course remained to them but acquiescence or war. They acquiesced.[6]

Howard gave the nontreaties thirty days to move. Joseph's people hurriedly gathered their stock and began the journey, enduring great hardship and property loss in crossing the rushing waters of the Snake River during the spring runoff. They joined the Salmon River bands of Toohoolhoolzote and White Bird and, on Camas Prairie south of the reservation boundary, paused to dig camas roots and wait out the time of freedom remaining to them. Grief, resentment, and anger stirred tempers. Again the chiefs debated the question of whether to go to the reservation or take up arms. On June 13 and 14 three young men of White Bird's band settled this question by deeds instead of words. Fired by whiskey, they killed four whites especially noted for bad treatment of Indians.

Ignoring the counsel of Joseph and his brother Ollokot, who wanted to try to explain to General Howard that the raid was unsanctioned by the tribal leadership, the nontreaties made their way south toward White Bird's Salmon River homeland.

Reports of the killings reached Fort Lapwai by courier from Mount Idaho, a village on the eastern edge of Camas Prairie, on the afternoon of June 15. General Howard, desiring to be present when the nontreaties came in, had arrived at the fort the day before. The Fort Lapwai garrison consisted of two troops of the First Cavalry and one company of the Twenty-first Infantry. Ordering a concentration of units from elsewhere in the department, Howard promptly dispatched Capt. David Perry with all the cavalry, slightly more than 100 troopers, to the relief of the Camas Prairie and Salmon River settlers. Perry marched through a rainy night and all the following day. At Grangeville the next evening he learned of more atrocities. (That morning, seventeen warriors had primed themselves with firewater and embarked on a two-day killing spree that took the lives of about fifteen more settlers.) The local citizenry persuaded Perry and his officers to make a night march and try to cut off the Nez Percés before they could cross the Salmon River and lose themselves in the mountains beyond. After a few hours' rest the cavalry pushed on to Mount Idaho, picked up eleven volunteers, and headed for the Salmon. At daybreak on June 17, exhausted by a ride of seventy miles and the better part of two nights and a day in the saddle, Perry started down White Bird Creek toward the Salmon.

The previous afternoon the Nez Percés had erected their lodges close to the Salmon at the mouth of White Bird Canyon, the gorge by which White Bird Creek dropped almost 3,000 feet to the river. Joseph later testified that they intended to gather their stock and, in an effort to avoid war, journey eastward across the Rocky Mountains to the buffalo plains, a trek Nez Percé hunting parties had made regularly for generations.[7] After dark an Indian picket brought word of Perry's approach. The chiefs conferred most of the night and at length decided to try to talk peace with the soldiers, but if that failed, to fight. The village contained about 135 fighting men, but many of these, sodden with whisky, could not be roused. Some sixty to seventy warriors took station among the rolling hills and ravines that masked the village from the trail down the steep, grassy slope of White Bird Hill.

The Mount Idaho volunteers and a small advance guard under Lt. Edward R. Theller (an infantry officer on detail) preceded the blue column as it descended White Bird Hill. The Nez Percé truce party, displaying a white flag, appeared in front of the volunteers. They opened fire and the battle was on. Perry brought his command into line to charge. Against the front and both flanks the warriors, on foot, pressed aggressively and with deadly marksmanship. The volunteers, occupying a key knoll on the extreme left, stampeded when hit with a determined attack, thus exposing Perry's line to enfilading fire. His troopers, many fresh from recruiting stations, gave way. Singly and in clusters, they fled back up the canyon. The officers could only follow, rallying some for organized defense wherever possible. Trapped in a ravine, Lieutenant Theller and eighteen men were wiped out. With about fourteen men, Lt. William R. Parnell fought a disciplined withdrawal to the top of White Bird Hill, where he joined with Perry and a remnant of his troop. Less than thirty strong, this force made a succession of defensive stands all the way back to Mount Idaho. Not until the command was reassembled and the missing accounted for could the price of the defeat be reckoned: one officer and thirty-three enlisted men slain. Three Indians had been wounded, none killed.

White Bird Canyon shook the army badly. The Nez Percés had demonstrated a leadership, discipline, and tactical skill that, added to the fighting qualities of the individual warriors, routed a superior force of regular soldiers. Howard's commendation of Captain Perry and attempt to rationalize the disaster eased the humiliation no more than it concealed the military deficiencies that had contributed to the defeat—overconfidence, weak leadership, and poor marksmanship, horsemanship, and discipline. Although exhaustion of men and horses afforded some measure of explanation, White Bird Canyon was only the first of several episodes of the Nez Percé War that reinforced the First Cavalry's reputation for mediocrity.

As soon as he learned of the White Bird fiasco, Howard ordered still more troops to the front and asked General McDowell to obtain reinforcements from other departments. On June 22, five days after Perry's defeat, Howard had assembled enough troops to march from Fort Lapwai to the scene of hostilities. On June 29, at the mouth of White Bird Canyon, another contingent joined.

Howard now had more than 400 men in four troops of the First Cavalry (including Perry's decimated squadron), six companies of the Twenty-first Infantry, and five companies of the Fourth Artillery serving as infantry. (Part of the Fourth, ending the military occupation of Alaska, had come directly to the seat of war.) Other units, rendezvousing at Fort Boise, were to maneuver so as to prevent the Nez Percés from escaping to the south.

The Nez Percés crossed the Salmon River and plunged into the narrow belt of mountains separating it from the Snake. As Howard made preparations to follow, some of the local citizens convinced him that Looking Glass, whose village lay forty miles to the northeast, near the forks of the Clearwater, planned to join the hostiles. Actually, Looking Glass urged neutrality on his people, but on June 29 Howard sent Capt. Stephen G. Whipple with two cavalry troops and two Gatling guns to "surprise and capture this chief and all that belonged to him." Accompanied by a contingent of Mount Idaho volunteers, Whipple reached the Nez Percé village on the morning of July 1. He intended to parley with Looking Glass, but weakly he let the civilians control the preliminaries and provoke a conflict. The Indians, some forty men with their families, fled as the whites sprayed the village with bullets, then destroyed it. Furious, Looking Glass abandoned his neutral stance and threw in with the hostiles.[8]

Howard had no sooner gotten his men to the west side of the Salmon than his quarry, on July 2, slipped back to the east side at a ford beyond the mountains and some fifty miles downstream. Moving eastward across Camas Prairie, the Indians skirmished with Whipple's cavalry and roughly handled several contingents of citizen volunteers. On July 3 warriors fell on a reconnoitering detachment of ten troopers under Lt. Sevier M. Rains and wiped out the entire party. On the south fork of the Clearwater, these Indians united with Looking Glass and set up camp on the west side at the mouth of Cottonwood Creek. They now numbered about 300 fighting men and 500 women and children. Scouts kept on the alert for the soldiers' next move.

On July 5 Howard had reached the ford by which the Nez Percés had returned to the east bank of the Salmon. In vain he tried to cross his column, then disconsolately turned it back on the mountainous trial to the White Bird Crossing. Not until July 10, at last free of the twisted Salmon country, did he succeed in uniting all his

command, including the cavalry from Camas Prairie, on the south
fork of the Clearwater. For two days, July 9 and 10, a force of
volunteers had been under siege on a hilltop west of the Clearwater that they dubbed Mount Misery. Howard hoped they would
continue to distract the Nez Percés while he slipped up on their
village from the south. Although this engagement ended on the
tenth, it did indeed preoccupy the Indians while Howard closed on
their rear.

The route on march on July 11 lay northward across an open
plateau east of and about 1,000 feet above the narrow valley of
the Clearwater. Steep, timbered bluffs, cut deeply by a succession
of ravines choked with trees and boulders, rose precipitously from
the valley. To head the ravines, the troops kept so far from the
edge of the bluffs that they could not see into the valley. The
column therefore passed the unsuspecting village before discovering it shortly after noon. Then Howard announced his presence by
firing the howitzers from too great a range to do any damage.
While he reversed his march to attack the village, warriors
swarmed into blocking positions. Posted at the edge of the bluffs
and in two ravines, they ringed Howard on three sides and forced
him to deploy on the open prairie in an elliptical perimeter defense
some two and one-half miles in circumference, with the pack train
in the center. For the next seven hours, until nightfall, the howitzers and Gatlings raked the Nez Percé positions, the two sides
exchanged desultory small-arms fire, and parties of warriors thrust
at the army lines probing for weak points and trying to silence
the artillery. Both Indians and soldiers fought with a sustained
desperation uncommon in Indian combat.

The next morning the battle was resumed, although the Nez
Percés, beginning to argue over strategy, pressed less energetically.
Howard withdrew Capt. Marcus P. Miller's Fourth Artillery battalion from the line for use as an assault force against the ravine
on the south. Before it could be launched, however, another force
wandered onto the battlefield from the south. This was Capt.
James B. Jackson's troop of the First Cavalry from Fort Klamath,
Oregon, under orders to search out and join Howard. Trailing
Jackson was a 120-mule pack train with supplies from Fort Lapwai. Howard dispatched Miller's battalion to escort the newcomers
to the safety of the defenses. On the way in, as he passed the head
of the offending ravine, Miller suddenly wheeled by the left flank

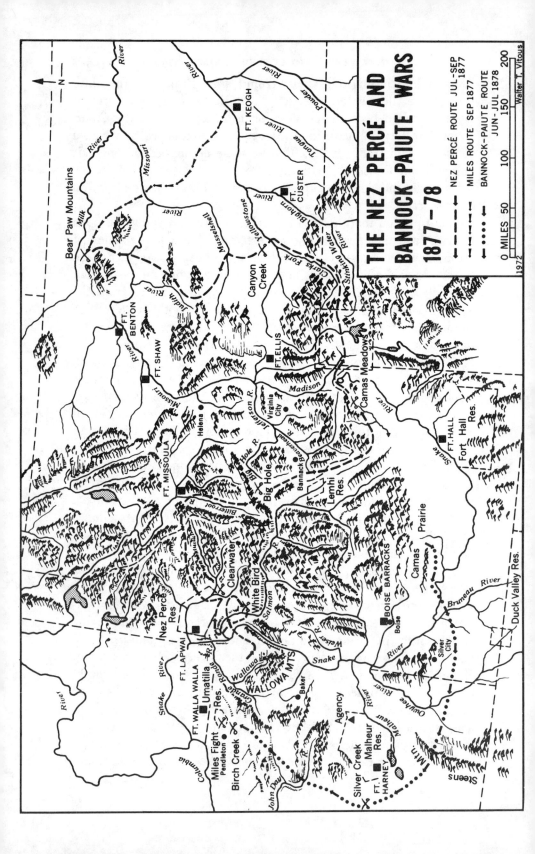

THE NEZ PERCÉ AND
BANNOCK-PAIUTE WARS
1877-78

Walter T. Vitous
1972

NEZ PERCÉ ROUTE JUL-SEP 1877
MILES ROUTE SEP 1877
BANNOCK-PAIUTE ROUTE JUN-JUL 1878

0 MILES 50 100 150 200

and charged. This move flushed the ravine of Indians. Instantly the main body of soldiers rushed to the attack. The warriors fell back across the Clearwater to the village, where all the Indians hastily abandoned their lodges and fled to the north. While the troops tumbled down the slope in pursuit, the artillery, advanced to the edge of the bluffs, opened fire and hastened the exodus.

In the Battle of the Clearwater, army casualties totaled thirteen dead and twenty-seven wounded, two fatally. Howard claimed twenty-three Indians slain, although the Nez Percés later admitted to only four killed and six wounded. Again, as at White Bird Canyon, the Nez Percés had shown a surprising talent for fighting the white soldiers on their own terms. "They fought as well as any troops I ever saw," marveled Howard. This time, however, they had been driven from the field, and Howard might well have ended the war had he pursued and rounded them up that day. Instead, after crossing the Clearwater to the abandoned village, he tarried until next morning. This enabled the Indians to cross the river near Kamiah and, after an exchange of gunfire with Howard's advance guard at the ford, to put themselves comfortably beyond his reach.

On the night of July 15, at a camp on the camas grounds of Weippe Prairie, the Nez Percé leaders discussed the next move. With forceful certitude, Looking Glass advocated a trek across the rugged Bitterroot Mountains to the buffalo plains of Montana. Here, he contended, the Nez Percés would find haven with the Crows or, if that proved illusory, perhaps even with Sitting Bull in Canada. Some day the trouble would blow over and they could return. There is a suggestion that Joseph and his brother Ollokot had grave reservations about this course, but whether they spoke in opposition is not known. White Bird, Toohoolhoolzote, and other headmen could propose no better move, and so it was decided. The next morning the calvalcade began the climb to the tortuous Lolo Trail by which, for generations, their people had surmounted the Bitterroots to reach the buffalo ranges beyond.

The eastward movement of the Nez Percés, Howard later wrote, "really ended the campaign within the limits of my department." One suspects that he would have been greatly relieved had responsibility for the Nez Percés passed to General Terry now that they were about to enter his department. But Howard had a command assembled, and Sherman had made it plain that he was to finish the job without regard to department boundaries. Also, newspaper criticism, intensifying ever since White Bird Canyon, was deeply mortifying, the more so when the press reported that the President was being urged to replace Howard with Crook. Even so, Howard delayed two weeks considering various plans of action and awaiting reinforcements with which to bolster the pursuing column and police the Indians in his rear.

Finally, on July 30, the reorganized command broke camp on the Clearwater and, in a downpour of cold rain, headed for the Lolo Trail. Perry's cavalry squadron remained behind, now under Maj. John Green, to patrol the Nez Percé Reservation. Replacing it was another squadron of four troops of the First, commanded by Maj. George B. Sanford, which had arrived from Fort Boise. The infantry, augmented by four companies, now consisted of a battalion of six companies of the Twenty-first, one of the Eighth, and one of the Twelfth under Capt. Evan Miles and a seven-company battalion of the Fourth Artillery under Captain Miller. The howitzer and Gatling guns, dismantled and packed on mules, were commanded by Lt. H. G. Otis. A 350-mule pack train hauled supplies. In all, Howard had about 200 cavalrymen, 360 infantrymen, 25 Bannock Indian scouts, and 150 packers and other civilians.

The Indians, meanwhile, had reached the Montana end of the Lolo Trail, slipped easily around a military strongpoint settlers derisively labeled "Fort Fizzle,"[9] and headed up the Bitterroot Valley. Citizens traded amicably, if nervously, with the unwelcome travelers. Veering to the southeast, the Nez Percés climbed from the Bitterroot Valley and on August 6 crossed the Continental Divide. The next day they descended to a pleasant camp site in the valley of the Big Hole River. Here, over the protest of the other chiefs, Looking Glass demanded that they pause to rest and cut lodge poles. The people were tired and without proper shelter since the Battle of the Clearwater. Moreover, the friendly attitude of the Bitterroot settlers seemed reassuring.

The delay proved disastrous. Col. John Gibbon, commanding the District of Montana at Fort Shaw, had concentrated elements of his regiment, the Seventh Infantry, at Missoula. On August 4 he set forth up the Bitterroot Valley with six undermanned companies—15 officers and 146 enlisted men—riding in wagons. Later, 45 volunteers joined.

At dawn on August 9 Gibbon led his men in a surprise attack

on the Indian camp. From the very edge of the village they raked the newly erected tepees with rifle fire and, as the startled occupants tumbled from their robes and dashed for safety, exacted a heavy toll. Within twenty minutes he held possession of the village. But White Bird and Looking Glass rallied the warriors. Inflamed by the loss of so many tribesmen, they directed a deadly fire at the soldiers from covered positions on all sides. "At almost every crack of a rifle from the distant hills some member of the command was sure to fall," recalled Gibbon, who himself caught a bullet in the thigh. So accurate was the Nez Percé marksmanship that Gibbon soon had to abandon the village and fall back to a patch of timber on the slope from which the attack had been launched. For the rest of that day and all the next, the warriors held the troops under close siege while their families resumed the trek to the south and east. By the night of August 10 the Indians had disappeared.

The Nez Percés left Gibbon's command badly shot up. Two officers (Capt. William Logan and Lt. James H. Bradley), twenty-two enlisted men, and six civilians had been killed, while five officers, thirty enlisted men, and four civilians had been wounded. One officer (Lt. William L. English) and one enlisted man died later. But the Indians had suffered even more grievously, almost entirely in the opening moments of the fight. Gibbon's burial details counted eighty-nine bodies, many of women and children, on the battlefield. The Nez Percés had again outfought the army, but they had paid dearly for the victory—and also for Looking Glass' intransigence in insisting on the halt that turned out so fatally. Thereafter the chief temporarily lost his preeminent position in the Nez Percé leadership.[10]

As the Seventh Infantrymen set about burying their dead on the morning of August 11, General Howard and a small advance guard rode into Gibbon's bivouac. The cavalry arrived the next day. On the thirteenth, as Gibbon headed for Deer Lodge with his battered command, Howard once more took up the pursuit. Already, however, even though burdened by wounded, the Nez Percés had traveled almost 100 miles. Turning west, they had again crossed the Continental Divide to descend to Idaho's Lemhi River Valley. Frightened settlers gathered in the towns for self-defense, and militia companies formed to combat the invaders. Giving substance to the alarm, Nez Percé warriors killed four whites and seized 250 horses on Montana's Horse Prairie Creek, and on Birch Creek, in Idaho, they plundered a train of freight wagons and killed another five whites.

Howard's Nez Percé guides assured him that the fugitives were following a favored route and would soon turn east, skirt the northern edge of the Snake River Plain, and cross Yellowstone National Park to the plains beyond. Howard saw an opportunity, by taking a shorter route by way of Red Rock River and Henry's Lake, to intercept them at Targhee Pass, gateway to the Madison River corridor into the park. Having made a sound decision, he then wavered as ignorance of the country raised doubts and volunteer officers urged conflicting advice on him. (These volunteers, swarming about the command in undisciplined confusion, caused a great deal more trouble than they were worth. A newspaper correspondent scored the typical volunteer as "an undoubted fraud, having almost as little pluck as principle and as meagre a conception of discipline as a backwoods schoolmaster."[11]) In the end, heeding the appeals of stage company officials whose line to the south was threatened, Howard crossed the Continental Divide at Monida Pass and found himself on the trail of the Indians—now, as predicted, traveling east again—one day's march in their rear.

On August 19 Howard pushed forward with as much haste as his tired command could muster and bivouacked at a camp site abandoned that morning by the Nez Percés. It lay on still another camas ground, Camas Meadows, south of Henry's Lake. During the night some 200 Nez Percé warriors returned to Camas Meadows and precipitated a lively skirmish by trying to run off the stock. The cavalry horses had been picketed, but the Indians escaped with 150 mules. At daybreak Major Sanford and three cavalry troops gave chase. They had succeeded in recovering part of the mules when the warriors counterattacked so vigorously that Sanford ordered a retreat. One of the troops failed to fall back and, surrounded, fought off the Indians until rescued by Howard.[12]

In addition to the stolen stock, Camas Meadows cost Howard one killed and seven wounded. Since he declined to press the fight —much to the disgust of the Bannock scouts—it also allowed the Nez Percés to escape once again. Compounding this humiliation, a command sent to block Targhee Pass and hold the Indians until Howard could fall on their rear concluded that they had taken another route and abandoned the position. Three days later, on

August 22, the Nez Percés crossed Targhee Pass and entered Yellowstone National Park.

Howard's infantry finally caught up with him at Camas Meadows, and on August 22 they moved on to Henry's Lake, at the western end of Targhee Pass. Here unit commanders and medical officers joined in pronouncing the men unfit to continue the chase. They were exhausted, clothed in rags, plagued with sickness, short on all classes of supplies, and above all discouraged over their continuing failure to overtake the Nez Percés. Most of the officers wanted to call off the campaign. Howard, faced with confessing failure and thus confirming increasingly strident newspaper criticism or pressing pursuit that appeared altogether futile, agonized in indecision. As the Nez Percés crossed Yellowstone National Park, frightening and scattering tourists and killing two, the troops rested four days beside Henry's Lake, and the general and a few aides rode to Virginia City to buy provisions and communicate by telegraph with higher authority.

A recent tourist in the national park had been none other than General Sherman, who had left shortly before the Nez Percés arrived. Now in Helena, he received a telegram from Howard, at Virginia City, on August 24. After reporting recent movements and present conditions, Howard stated that, if troops from the east could intercept the Nez Percés, "I think I may stop near where I am, and in a few days work my way back to Fort Boise slowly." Sherman answered promptly and bluntly: "That force of yours should pursue the Nez Percés to the death, lead where they may. . . . If you are tired, give the command to some young energetic officer." From McDowell's adjutant general came language only slightly less biting: "The general in all kindness asks me to suggest to you to be less dependent on what others at a distance may or may not do, and rely more on your own forces and your own plans." No other troops were closer to the Nez Percés than Howard's, and it seemed to the division commander that Howard "will certainly be expected by the General of the Army, the War Department and the country, to use them in carrying on the most active and persistent operations practicable, to the very end." Stung but also re-energized, Howard fired off a wire to Sherman: "I never flag. . . . Neither you nor General McDowell can doubt my pluck or energy." On August 28 his command resumed the pursuit of the Nez Percés.[13]

Generals Terry and Crook were in the East, quelling labor riots, but General Sheridan had already taken steps to provide the hoped-for help from his division. It centered, as August gave way to September, on the towering, incredibly tangled Absaroka Range guarding the eastern flank of Yellowstone National Park. Two rivers offered pathways from the summit to the plains below— Clark Fork, flowing northeast to the Yellowstone; and the Stinking Water (now the Shoshone), flowing eastward to the Bighorn River Basin. Col. Samuel D. Sturgis and six troops of the Seventh Cavalry, a detachment from Col. Nelson A. Miles' command operating against the Sioux from the Tongue River Cantonment, took station on August 31 near the canyon by which Clark Fork issues from the mountains. Two days earlier Sheridan had ordered a concentration of the Fifth Cavalry, under Col. Wesley Merritt, on the lower reaches of the Stinking Water.

Until Merritt could reach his assigned position, Sturgis had to worry about both outlets. On September 8 a patrol sighted the Nez Percés striking southward, toward the Stinking Water outlet, and Sturgis moved swiftly to cut them off. Two days later, having ascended the Stinking Water expecting momentarily to meet them, he came on trails that disclosed a disheartening truth. Descending Clark Fork with Howard close in their rear, the Nez Percés had discovered cavalry blocking their escape route. Feinting south far enough to deceive Sturgis, they had doubled back to Clark Fork and safely gained the open plains. Not only had the Indians slipped by Sturgis, but so had Howard. On September 11 Sturgis caught up with Howard on Clark Fork east of the mountains.[14]

Smarting with humiliation, Sturgis informed Howard of his desire to try by a forced march to overhaul the Nez Percés. Howard assented, and next morning the Seventh Cavalry, its horses fresh in comparison with Sanford's, trotted down Clark Fork Valley toward the Yellowstone. The Nez Percés slowed, meanwhile, as parties of warriors raided settlements and killed a scattering of whites. On September 13, after tearing up the village of Coulson—now Billings—they waylaid a stagecoach and were playfully cavorting about on it when Sturgis' column, having forded the Yellowstone, deployed to attack. The Indians ascended Canyon Creek, which here cuts a gap in the rimrock bordering the north side of the Yellowstone. Warriors fell back and skillfully fought off the cavalry while their families got away. Sturgis tried several maneuvers, all of which failed, and the Battle of Canyon Creek ended, once again, in the escape of the Nez Percés. Sturgis lost three men killed and eleven (including one officer) wounded. In addition, he suffered wide criticism for the timid—some intimated cowardly—way in which he managed the battle.[15]

As the Seventh Cavalry splashed across the Yellowstone to engage the Nez Percés at Canyon Creek, a courier veered to the east. He bore a dispatch from Howard to Colonel Miles. Explaining how the Nez Percés had slipped around Sturgis and were now headed north, toward the Musselshell River, it asked if Miles could try to intercept or overtake them. For a month and a half Miles had closely watched the unfolding epic of the Nez Percés, hesitant to move against them because of uncertainty over the intentions of Sitting Bull, now in Canada. Howard's dispatch, reaching Tongue River Cantonment on the evening of September 17, gave the energetic colonel all the invitation he needed. Before daybreak next morning he had ferried all his available force, five companies of infantry and two troops of cavalry, to the north bank of the Yellowstone.

Miles' column moved swiftly to the northwest, en route overtaking and absorbing four troops of cavalry under orders to meet and escort General Terry to Canada for conferences with Sitting Bull (see p. 285). The command now consisted of a battalion of four companies of the Fifth Infantry mounted on Indian ponies seized at the Battle of Muddy Creek (see p. 280), Capt. Simon Snyder commanding; a squadron of three troops of the Second Cavalry under Capt. George H. Tyler; a squadron of three troops of the Seventh Cavalry under Capt. Owen Hale; and about thirty Sioux and Cheyenne scouts. A breech-loading Hotchkiss gun, a Napoleon gun, and a supply train of two strings of pack mules and forty wagons guarded by another company of the Fifth Infantry completed the column, which numbered between 350 and 400 men. At the mouth of the Musselshell on September 25 Miles received word that the Nez Percés had crossed the Missouri upstream, at Cow Island, two days earlier. After attacking a lightly held military supply dump, they had moved on northward. Commandeering a passing steamer, Miles ferried his troops across the Missouri and raced to cut off the fugitives before they could reach the Canadian boundary.

The Nez Percés had slackened their pace. Once more, as on

the eve of the Big Hole, Looking Glass argued that the people needed rest and that the soldiers had been left far enough in the rear to permit a less rigorous pace. In fact, Howard had deliberately fallen behind in hopes of slowing the Indians and giving Miles time to get in front of them.[16] Again Looking Glass prevailed. For five days, after crossing the Missouri, the Nez Percés halted early each afternoon. On September 29, having passed between the Bear Paw and Little Rocky Mountains, they laid out their camp in the valley of Snake Creek, a tributary of Milk River on the northern flank of the Bear Paws, about forty miles from the international border. A cold rain fell intermittently and clouds hung low on the barren prairie. They helped to conceal Miles' soldiers as they emerged from behind the Little Rockies and marched across the open gap separating them from the Bear Paws.

September 30 opened clear and cold, with ice on the streams. Moving west, the column cut the trail of the Nez Percés and turned north on it. Shortly afterward the Indian scouts found the village. About midmorning the tepees came into view. At Miles' direction, the two cavalry squadrons moved left front into line and broke into a gallop. Hale's squadron of the Seventh charged directly at the camp, while Tyler's squadron of the Second, accompanied by the Sioux and Cheyenne allies, veered to the left and made for the pony herd pastured on the benchland west of the valley. Synders' mounted infantry followed the Seventh as reserve.

After a sharp fight Tyler succeeded in gathering up most of the pony herd. Hale, however, promptly ran into trouble. Remnants of ancient streambanks, cut by deep coulees, rose steeply from the valley on the south and east of the village. Upon discovering the approach of the soldiers, warriors had rushed up the cutbank and taken well-covered positions on the crest. At a range of 200 yards they opened on the charging troopers with the deadly fire for which they had become so noted. The cavalry faltered, then dismounted and barely held their own until Snyder's battalion of the Fifth came up and helped secure the crest. The Nez Percés fell back to new positions closer to the village.

The attack on the village cost Miles heavily, especially in the Seventh Cavalry. He had lost twenty-two enlisted men killed and thirty-eight wounded. Shrewdly, the Indian marksmen had concentrated on officers and noncommissioned officers. Their fire had felled Captains Hale, Myles Moylan, and Edward S. Godfrey, and Lt. Jonathan W. Biddle of the Seventh, Lt. Henry Romeyn of the Fifth, and Miles' adjutant, Lt. George W. Baird. Hale and Biddle were dead, the others severely wounded. In the Seventh, only one officer remained unhit. Seven sergeants of the Seventh, including all three first sergeants, were dead, while three sergeants and two corporals had been wounded. Unhappily but prudently, Miles decided to suspend the assault and place the Nez Percé camp under siege.[17]

"Excepting the fieldpiece that occasionally mouthed a shell into that seemingly deserted hollow," recalled Scout "Yellowstone" Kelly, "the battle had degenerated into a duel between sharp-shooters on either side."[18] Well protected among hills and ravines bordering the village, the Indians easily held the troops at a respectable distance. Even the Napoleon gun, converted into a howitzer by digging in its trail, failed to blast them from their shelters. But their prospects gave no cause for optimism. Several dozen more people lay dead or wounded. Among the dead were Toohoolhoolzote, Ollokot, and Poker Joe, the last a mixed blood who had served as guide ever since the Bitterroot Valley and whose influence had grown steadily. Surrounded, their ponies gone, their misery worsened by a storm that dumped five inches of snow, they clung to one bleak hope—that messengers who had slipped out under cover of night would find Sitting Bull in Canada and persuade him to come to their relief.

This possibility worried Miles, too, as did the prospect of General Howard's arrival to assume command and with it a share of the credit for the capture of the Nez Percés. On October 1, therefore, Miles displayed a white flag and invited a parley. White Bird and Looking Glass wanted no part of negotiations, but Joseph went forth to meet Miles. The talks were unproductive, and Miles, violating his own truce flag, refused to let Joseph return to his people. At the same time, however, Lt. Lovell H. Jerome, apparently believing the Indians were about to surrender, strayed into their lines and was likewise seized. Furious that Jerome had cancelled his advantage, Miles released Joseph the next day, and the Nez Percés in turn released Jerome.

For five days, October 1 to 5, the siege continued as both sides exchanged desultory fire and suffered increasingly from the damp cold and snow. Howard and his aides arrived with a small escort on the fourth. To Miles' joy, the general generously declined to take command until after the Indians had surrendered. To the Nez Percés, Howard's appearance signaled the approach of more soldiers. Help from the Sioux seemed remote, as in fact it was. On October 5 the chiefs again argued over whether to reopen talks, Joseph favoring this course and Looking Glass and White Bird opposing it. The debate ended with Joseph preparing to meet Miles and the other two determined to lead their people in a desperate flight toward the Canadian sanctuary. Immediately after this council a bullet struck Looking Glass in the forehead, killing him instantly. Joseph met with Miles and Howard. If the Nez Percés gave up, Miles promised, they could spend the winter at his post on the Yellowstone, then in the spring go back to the Lapwai Reservation in Idaho. Joseph returned to the village. His mind made up, in the afternoon he enacted the final ceremony. Confronting Miles as Howard looked on, Joseph uttered the moving, often quoted words that ended: "Hear me, my chiefs! I am tired. My heart is sick and sad. From where the sun now stands I will fight no more forever."

A little more than 400 people surrendered with Joseph—and less than one-fourth of these were warriors. The rest of those in the village escaped either during Miles' initial assault on September 30 or with White Bird on the night of October 5, after Joseph's surrender. According to the North-West Mounted Police, 98 warriors and about 200 women and children ultimately reached Sitting Bull's camp.[19]

The Nez Percé War had originated in the resistance of Joseph's band to the government order to move to the Lapwai Reservation. Understandably, therefore, Howard and Miles had treated with Joseph on the basis of his return to that reservation. Without such a guarantee, he later declared, he would not have surrendered. But Sherman and Sheridan did not want the Nez Percés sent back, and neither did the people of Idaho. Accordingly, in November, over the vociferous protests of Miles, the prisoners were shipped down the Missouri and detained at Fort Leavenworth until they were placed on a small reserve in Kansas the following spring. Here, unacclimated, many sickened and died. A new location in Indian Territory brought no improvement. Tirelessly, Joseph worked for justice. With the powerful aid of Miles and others, he gradually touched the conscience of Americans and at last, in 1884, won permission to go back to the Northwest—but not to Idaho, for he and his immediate band still were held responsible for the Camas Prairie murders that set off the war. In May 1885, with about 150 followers, he was placed on the Colville Reservation in Washington, while the Looking Glass and White Bird people, 118 in number, were admitted to the Lapwai Reservation. Here they joined a scattering of other veterans of the war who had made their way back from the Canadian refuge. Their leader there, White Bird, had died in 1882.

Joseph refused to give up hope of returning to his beloved Wal-lowa Valley in Oregon, and for years he agitated the question. In 1897 he journeyed to Washington and urged his cause on President McKinley and the general-in-chief of the army, Nelson A. Miles. Both Miles and Howard helped, and for a time the prospects seemed encouraging. But the whites of the Wallowa refused to part with any land for Indian occupancy. His hopes finally crushed, Joseph died on the Colville Reservation on September 21, 1904.

The trek of the Nez Percés is one of history's great epics—and great tragedies. In three months approximately 800 people—men, women, and children—traveled 1,700 miles across some of the most difficult terrain in North America. They outmarched, outwitted, and outfought all that the U. S. Army could throw against them. They left about 120 of their people dead on the trail, almost half of them women and children. They killed about 180 white men, mostly soldiers, and wounded another 150. Their just cause, their unity of purpose and action, their seemingly bottomless reservoirs of courage, endurance, and tenacity, their sheer achievement and final heartbreaking failure when on the very threshold of success, have evoked sympathy and admiration for almost a century.

Such sentiments gained wide acceptance even before the flight ended at Bear Paw Mountains. Americans especially marveled at the humanity and military proficiency that characterized the retreat. As General Sherman wrote: "The Indians throughout displayed a courage and skill that elicited universal praise; they abstained from scalping, let captive women go free, did not commit indiscriminate murder of peaceful families which is usual, and fought with almost scientific skill, using advance and rear guards, skirmish-lines and field fortifications."[20] And Colonel Miles added:

"The Nez Percés are the boldest men and best marksmen of any Indians I have ever encountered, and Chief Joseph is a man of more sagacity and intelligence than any Indian I have ever met; he counseled against the war, and against the usual cruelties practiced by the Indians, and is far more humane than such Indians as Crazy Horse and Sitting Bull."[21]

In appraisals like this by the men who fought the Nez Percés may be glimpsed the origins of a Chief Joseph legend that, despite the recent works of Alvin Josephy, Mark Brown, and Merrill Beal,[22] continues to dominate the literature of the Nez Percé War. As chief of the Wallowa band and spokesman for the nontreaty Nez Percés, Joseph early emerged in the public view as *the* leader of the nontreaty Nez Percés. Later, when the fugitives repeatedly evaded and fought off their military pursuers, the officers thus humiliated portrayed Joseph as a strategic and tactical genius, a veritable "red Napoleon." This image made their own failures more plausible, to themselves as well as the public. Howard was the main author of the legend, his prolific pen producing books and articles alike for more than a quarter of a century. Miles contributed, too, for the "red Napoleon" thesis enhanced his victory at Bear Paw. The death or escape of the other chiefs, Joseph's powerful and widely quoted surrender speech, and his long and highly conspicuous life after the war served to reinforce the legend.

In reality, Joseph was more a political than a military leader, and anyway, as in most tribal political systems, the important decisions came from a council of chiefs. In the Nez Percé War Joseph shared the leadership with Looking Glass, White Bird, Toohoolhoolzote, and others, including most notably, beginning in the Bitterroot Valley, Poker Joe. Except after the Big Hole, Looking Glass seems to have dominated the council fairly constantly. Joseph, in fact, did not assert significant influence until Bear Paw convinced him of the hopelessness of further resistance. Great and good man that he assuredly was, Joseph was not the principal Nez Percé leader, still less a "red Napoleon."

Although Joseph cannot be credited with brilliant generalship, the Nez Percés did display a collective military capability, as distinguished from individual prowess and skill, that amazed the professionals and made them look foolish. For army leaders the

Nez Percé War afforded precious little glory. Almost immediately, however, they fell to quarreling over the division of honors. Miles, ignoring Howard's long pursuit of the Indians and his generosity in letting Miles accept the surrender at Bear Paw, tried to claim all the credit for himself and his command. Howard, reacting to the slight, committed some indiscretions that angered Sheridan. Terry and, later, Gibbon became embroiled in the dispute, too, and at last Sherman had to indicate in emphatic tones that it had gone far enough.

If the Nez Percé War produced any hero outside the Indian camp, Miles bears the distinction. He reacted instantly to Howard's appeal for help, marched rapidly to cut off the Nez Percés, and attacked promptly and aggressively once he had discovered them. Although favored in several instances with unusual good luck, he displayed an energy and determination that proved decisive. But for Miles, the Nez Percés would have made good their escape to Canada.

The bitterness of Howard and his men toward Miles is understandable. His arrogant assumption of full credit ignored three months of exhausting and frustrating campaigning. It also ignored the possibility that the pursuit so slowed the Indians that Miles was able to overtake them and so disheartened them that he was able to defeat them. Or, as expressed in the erroneous attribution to General Sheridan that got Howard into trouble, "General Miles pounced upon and captured a game which had been chased to death by Howard and Sturgis."[23]

Allowing Howard due credit for a long and wearing chase, he still may be charged with faulty generalship on several occasions. His attempt to neutralize Looking Glass, who was already neutral, added strength to the fugitive bands and gave them their most forceful leader; without him, it is doubtful that they would have held out so long or, indeed, even tried to leave Idaho. Howard's overnight delay in pursuing the Indians after his victory at the Clearwater permitted the Indians to get across the river and regroup, thus losing him his best chance of ending hostilities. Finally, his long pause on the Clearwater awaiting Major Green's arrival from Fort Boise gave the Indians a lead in their flight to Montana that Howard never overcame.

General McDowell, whose aide had arrived on the Clearwater

battlefield in the final stages of the action, perceived these mistakes almost at once. Writing confidentially to General Sherman on July 31, he stated:

Professionally and playing the easy part of the critic, it seems to me Howard erred in counting on the immediate cooperation of Green's command from Boise. He does not seem to have known of the time it took for Green to get his orders and for the troops to get to, and from Boise. . . .

In the second place Howard seems to have made a capital mistake in giving up the direct pursuit of Joseph after defeating him. I understand from my aide-de-camp that he did this on the theory 'that it was useless to attempt to follow a flying Indian! and that the only effective way was to try to head him off, and for this he laid back and waited for the 2d Infantry and Green's force to arrive to make his combined movement. . . .[24]

Almost from the beginning, newspapers throughout the country scored Howard for the slowness of his march. On several occasions, an extra burst of effort seemed all that was needed to close on the quarry. This was especially true in the third week of August, just before and after the Camas Meadows action, near Henry's Lake. However, the evidence is persuasive that, once he started up the Lolo Trail, Howard pushed his men to the limits of endurance. Surgeons and unit commanders united in declaring the four-day rest at Henry's Lake imperative to prevent the command from collapsing altogether. Howard's troops lacked the drive, stamina, and leadership of, for example, Miles' troops, who had been fighting the Sioux for more than a year. Even so, it is easy to believe that at one point or another along the trail an energetic thrust would have won for Howard the distinction that finally went to Miles.

Colonel Gibbon's failure lay less in tactical error than in weakness of numbers. He had enough men to take the Nez Percé camp by surprise but not enough to press the advantage or even hold his gain. The Big Hole defeat was widely cited to show the sad condition into which the infantry regiments had been allowed to lapse. General Terry found it painful to contemplate that six companies could field no more than 146 men and to behold its colonel fighting, rifle in hand, like a private. Had the Seventh Infantry been maintained at even the minimum authorized strength, Terry felt, probably rightly, Gibbon could have whipped the Nez Percés at the Big Hole and ended the war.[25]

Colonel Sturgis appears in many accounts as a comic bumbler. Unfortunate victim of a clever strategem would be a fairer appraisal; to be deceived by the Nez Percés was not proof of incompetence. Moreover, the blunders of others diverted units that were to have reported to Sturgis and that would have enabled him to cover both the Clark Fork and Stinking Water exits from Yellowstone National Park. His performance at Canyon Creek is more vulnerable to criticism, although even here it is unlikely that greater energy or different tactics would have materially changed the outcome.

Of all the army participants, therefore, only Miles emerged from the Nez Percé War with enhanced reputation. And his honors were tarnished by his treacherous seizure of Chief Joseph in violation of a truce flag and by his selfish grab for all the glory. Rather, it is the Nez Percés—the chiefs, the warriors, the old men, the women and children—who excite the admiration, respect, and sympathy of posterity. Truly have they been called "The Patriots."[26]

NOTES

1. A good biography of Howard is John A. Carpenter, *Sword and Olive Branch: Oliver Otis Howard* (Pittsburgh, Pa., 1964).
2. Sherman to Howard, Nov. 29, 1873, Sherman Papers, vol. 90, pp. 301-2. See also *ibid.*, Nov. 12, 1872, p. 220.
3. The literature of the Nez Percé War and its antecedents is voluminous. I have relied mainly on three recent works: Alvin M. Josephy, Jr., *The Nez Percé Indians and the Opening of the Northwest* (New Haven, Conn., 1965); Merrill D. Beal, *"I Will Fight No More Forever": Chief Joseph and the Nez Percé War* (Seattle, Wash., 1963); and Mark H. Brown, *The Flight of the Nez Percé: A History of the Nez Percé War* (New York, 1967).
4. Major Wood refused to subscribe to such peremptory action and filed a dissenting report. The commission's report is in CIA, *Annual Report* (1877), pp. 211-17. Excellent commentary on the commission and council appears in letters of the wife of the Fort Lapwai surgeon: Abe Laufe, ed., *An Army Doctor's Wife on the Frontier: Letters from Alaska and the Far West, 1874-1878* (Pittsburgh, Pa., 1962), pp. 216-24.
5. SW, *Annual Report* (1877), pp. 116-17.
6. Howard's official report of the conference, May 22, 1877, is in *ibid.*, pp. 589-97. His version of his dealings with the Nez Percés was later set forth in *Nez Percé Joseph* (Boston, 1881) and *My Life and Experiences among Our Hostile Indians*, chap. 17. Principal Indian accounts are Chief Joseph, "An Indian's View of Indian Affairs," *North American Review, 128* (1879), 412-33; Lucullus V. McWhorter, *Yellow Wolf: His Own Story* (Caldwell,

Ida., 1948); and McWhorter, *Hear Me, My Chiefs!* (Caldwell, Ida., 1952).

7. "Chief Joseph's Own Story," in Brady, *Northwestern Fights and Fighters*, p. 64. For the Battle of White Bird Canyon, in addition to works already cited in this chapter, see first-hand accounts in *ibid.* by Captains Perry and Parnell, chaps. 4 and 5. I have also relied heavily on John D. McDermott, *Forlorn Hope: A Study of the Battle of White Bird Canyon* (MS. report, National Park Service, 1968).

8. The origins, purposes, and progress of Whipple's mission have been confused by conflicting evidence. The most satisfactory analysis is Brown, *Flight of the Nez Percé*, pp. 164–69.

9. The official report of this affair is in SW, *Annual Report* (1877), pp. 500–1. The evidence is confused and contradictory. See Josephy, p. 569, note 27, for an analysis.

10. Gibbon's report is in SW, *Annual Report* (1877), pp. 68–72. In addition to the books cited in notes 3 and 6 above, see Gibbon's later account, "The Battle of the Big Hole," *Harpers Weekly, 39* (1895), 1215–16, 1235–36; and G. O. Shields, "The Battle of the Big Hole," in Brady, *Northwestern Fights and Fighters*, chap. 10.

11. Quoted in Brown, p. 289.

12. The dilatory troop was L, Second Cavalry, under Capt. Randolph Norwood. The troop had been escorting General Sherman on a tour of Montana forts, and Sherman had sent it to help Howard. Regimental rivalry apparently explains in large part the isolation of Norwood's troop at Camas Meadows, but who should be faulted, Norwood or Sanford, is not clear.

13. The text of the exchange with Sherman is in SW, *Annual Report* (1877), pp. 12–14. McDowell's telegram is quoted in Brown, pp. 302–3. Brown, chap. 19, has the clearest analysis of this stage of the campaign. While at Henry's Lake, Howard wrote a lengthy report dated August 27 detailing his operations from the outbreak of hostilities to the Camas Meadows engagement. This appears twice in SW, *Annual Report* (1877), pp. 119–31 and 601–13. Later he submitted a complete report, with map, covering the entire campaign. Dated Dec. 26, 1877, it is printed in *ibid.*, pp. 585–660.

14. The confused topography makes these movements difficult to reconstruct. The clearest description is in Brown, chap. 21. Sturgis' report, a labored self-defense, is in SW, *Annual Report* (1877), pp. 507–11.

15. Sturgis' official report is in SW, *Annual Report* (1877), pp. 511–12. The reports of his squadron commanders, Maj. Lewis Merrill and Capt. Frederick W. Benteen, are in *ibid.*, pp. 569–72. See also Theodore W. Goldin, "The Seventh Cavalry at Cañon Creek," in Brady, *Northwestern Fights and Fighters*, chap. 13.

16. Miles later ridiculed this contention, but Brown, p. 366, cites persuasive supporting evidence.

17. Casualties are detailed in SW, *Annual Report* (1877), p. 75. For the Battle of Bear Paw Mountains (or Snake Creek, or Eagle Creek), in addition to sources already cited, see Miles' reports in *ibid.*, pp. 74–76, 514–16, and 527–29; and Captain Moylan's report in Chandler, *Of Garryowen in Glory*, pp. 74–76. See also Johnson, *Unregimented General*, chaps. 15–16; Quaife, ed., *"Yellowstone Kelly,"* chap. 11; and Miles, *Personal Recollections*, chap. 20–21. Other accounts by participants are Ami F. Mulford, *Fighting Indians in the Seventh United States Cavalry* (p.p., Corning, N.Y., 1879), chaps. 27–30; McClernand, "With the Indian and the Buffalo in Montana," pp. 198–206; and Henry Romeyn, "The Capture of Chief Joseph and the Nez Percé Indians," Montana Historical Society *Contributions*, 2 (1896), 283–91.

18. Kelly, p. 193.

19. Turner, *North-West Mounted Police, 1*, 342.

20. SW, *Annual Report* (1877), p. 15.

21. *Ibid.*, p. 529.
22. See especially Josephy, pp. 519, 531–32, 542–43, 598; and Beal, pp. 247–49.
23. *Chicago Times*, Oct. 25, 1877, quoted in Brown, p. 422.
24. Sherman Papers, vol. 46, LC. Col. Frank Wheaton and the Second Infantry had been ordered from Georgia. Howard planned to have Wheaton lead a second expedition to Montana farther north while his own went up the Lolo Trail. This movement was overtaken by events and never materialized.
    Three weeks later McDowell again wrote Sherman, this time in reference to Colonel Miles: "I have many times wished that he could have had Howard's right column [i.e., the one Wheaton was to have led], or, his [Howard's] command immediately after Joseph's defeat [at Clearwater], as I am sure the whole affair would have been closed up a month ago." Aug. 24, 1877, *ibid.*
25. SW, *Annual Report* (1877), p. 505.
26. Josephy, title of chap. 13.

Bannock, Paiute, Sheepeater, and Ute, 1878-79

THE NEZ PERCÉ BID FOR FREEDOM has excited popular fascina-
tion ever since 1877. Less well remembered, in part because
overshadowed by the more memorable conflict with the Nez
Percés, are hostilities that broke out in 1878 and 1879 with some
of their neighbors—Bannocks, Paiutes, Sheepeaters, and Utes.

In 1877 almost 600 Bannocks were enrolled at the Ross Fork,
or Fort Hall, Agency on the upper Snake River in southeastern
Idaho. This agency also supervised almost 1,000 Shoshonis. About
150 miles to the north, Bannocks and Shoshonis shared the tiny
Lemhi Reservation with Sheepeaters. Numbering about 900,
these "Lemhis" acknowledged the leadership of Bannock Chief
Tendoy. The Fort Hall Bannocks boasted no leader of comparable stature; none had emerged to replace the respected Taghee,
dead since 1871. By the end of 1877, however, a chief named
Buffalo Horn had attracted a strong following. He had proved his
mettle as a scout for the army in the Sioux campaigns of 1876–77
and in the Nez Percé War. Crook, Howard, and Miles all spoke
highly of him.[1]

The Bannocks enjoyed a close friendship with the Paiutes and
affiliated Western Shoshonis who ranged over much of southern
Idaho, eastern Oregon, and northern Nevada. Four reservations—
Pyramid Lake, Walker River, and Duck Valley in Nevada and
Malheur in Oregon—claimed only tenuous allegiance from these
Indians. Mostly they drifted about their homeland hunting small
game, fishing the lakes and rivers, and gathering camas roots and
pine nuts. In 1878 the Paiute agents counted almost 8,000 Paiutes

and Western Shoshonis, only 1,100 of whom were listed as "habitually on reserves."[2] The best-known Paiute leader was Winnemucca, whose band usually lived on the upper Owyhee River. Among the Malheurs, the leading chief was Egan, although a sinister shaman named Oytes enjoyed considerable prominence too.

For five years in the middle 1860s the Yahuskin and Walpapi Paiutes, usually called Snakes, had ravaged Oregon settlements and travel routes until badly whipped by General Crook in 1866–68 (see Chapter Eleven). Since then, neither Paiutes nor Bannocks had caused any serious trouble. But by the middle 1870s mounting white pressures spread unrest through both tribes. Game grew scarce and unhindered pursuit of it more difficult. Yet the agents could not provide sufficient rations to subsitute for the declining yield of traditional food-gathering practices. Later, asked what sparked the Bannock-Paiute uprising, General Crook replied: "Hunger. Nothing but hunger."[3]

Other causes contributed. The Nez Percé War had an unsettling effect. At Fort Hall Agency further unrest attended the wounding of two white men by a drunken Bannock in August 1877 and the slaying of another white in November. Efforts to track down the murderer so excited the Indians that the agent called for military help. Three companies of the Fourteenth Infantry from Camp Douglas, Utah, arrived at the agency early in December. The arrest of the culprit in January 1878 created such alarm that Col. John E. Smith seized fifty-three Bannock warriors and confiscated their arms and ponies, thus adding still more to their resentment. General Crook visited the agency early in April and pronounced the trouble subsiding. Actually, Bannock emissaries were already among the Paiutes stirring up a war sentiment. The bands on the Malheur Reservation seemed especially receptive. The agent sought to dampen their combativeness by threatening to invite Crook to visit Malheur Agency, too. "No name is better known or more dreaded by them," he reported. Subsequent events showed the specter of Crook less frightening than the agent supposed.[4]

The episode that finally touched off warfare occurred on Camas Prairie, a favored root-digging area about ninety miles southeast of Boise, Idaho, where Bannocks, "Lemhis," and even some Paiutes and Umatillas from Oregon congregated in the spring of 1878.

Long a source of food, Camas Prairie had been confirmed to the Bannocks in the Treaty of 1868. But the clerk who wrote out the treaty rendered the term as "Kansas Prairie," and as a result it had never been formally reserved for the Indians. They regarded it as theirs all the same, and for several seasons they shared it amicably with white stockmen. But increasingly the destruction of the camas roots, especially by hogs, angered the tribesmen. Already belligerent when they arrived in the spring of 1878, the Bannocks talked threateningly of expelling the whites altogether. Against this background, on May 30 a Bannock shot and wounded two white men.

The assault, apparently perpetrated without specific provocation, brought the smoldering discontent to a climax. The Lemhi and part of the Fort Hall Indians hastened back to their agencies, but Buffalo Horn and his followers, sure they would be punished anyway, decided to launch a grand plundering raid. Counting Paiutes and Umatillas, the warrior force numbered about 200. Tearing up a road station and ferry, they crossed Snake River and rode westward across southern Idaho, killing ten whites along the way. A skirmish with volunteers from Silver City on June 8 took the life of Buffalo Horn and left the raiders leaderless. They continued west to Steens Mountain, in Oregon. Here they united with Egan, Oytes, and the Malheur Paiutes, who had quietly slipped off their reservation on June 5. Altogether, the Indians at Steens Mountain numbered about 700, with some 450 fighting men.

Although Fort Hall lay within Crook's Department of the Platte, the Bannock-Paiute uprising took place in General Howard's Department of the Columbia. To him, for a second summer, fell the task of mobilizing troops and organizing a campaign. Capt. Reuben F. Bernard and his troop of the First Cavalry at Boise Barracks had taken the field on May 31, the day after the violence on Camas Prairie. A big-framed, heavy-bearded veteran of many battles, Bernard pressed the fugitives closely across Idaho and into Oregon, pausing finally at a place called Sheep Ranch, on Jordan River a few miles above its confluence with the Owyhee. By this time, June 12, Howard had reached Boise and asserted personal control of operations.[5]

Howard had been braced for an outbreak for more than a month. Dispatches from Col. Frank Wheaton at Fort Lapwai had warned of unusual restlessness and activity among the "Columbia River renegades" of Washington and the Umatillas and Paiutes of Oregon. Troops at all the posts in the department had received standby orders. When the blowup came, it was unexpected only in location. Ordering a concentration on Boise of elements of the First Cavalry, Twenty-first Infantry, and Fourth Artillery, Howard instructed Wheaton to move to Fort Walla Walla and deploy the Second Infantry to watch the Columbia River Indians. General McDowell ordered units of the Eighth and Twelfth Infantry from other parts of the division to the war zone. After conferring with Wheaton at Fort Walla Walla, Howard and his aides traveled by stagecoach to Boise, arriving on June 12.

Because the Bannock rights to Camas Prairie were widely conceded, even by the governor of Idaho, General McDowell wanted Howard to explore the possibilities of an amicable settlement before resorting to arms. In Sarah Winnemucca, daughter of the Paiute chief, Captain Bernard found a means of communicating with the Indians. The Paiute "princess" volunteered for the mission and Howard authorized it. In the Steens Mountain camp Sarah found the war fervor so strong that she barely succeeded in escaping with her father and a handful of peaceably disposed followers. Oytes' preachings kept excitement high, and Egan, the Paiute war chief, reluctantly agreed to take the place of the fallen Buffalo Horn as hostile leader. On June 15 at Sheep Ranch Sarah described her ordeal and observations to General Howard.

As Howard moved on Steens Mountain in three columns, the hostiles broke camp and traveled northwest across the desert to Silver Creek, forty-five miles west of Camp Harney. Here, at daybreak on June 23, Captain Bernard and three troops of cavalry pounced on them. In three successive waves, his squadron swept through the village and drove its surprised occupants across the creek and to the top of some steep bluffs on the other side, where they took strong defensive positions. Bernard refused to pay the price of an assault, and the two sides exchanged long-range fire the rest of the day. The Indians stole away in the night. Although casualties were light on both sides, the Bannock-Paiute coalition suffered a crippling blow in the loss of the camp and all its contents.

At Malheur Agency, deserted by the agent and sacked and

badly damaged, Howard gathered a command of about 480 men in seven companies of foot and four troops of horse. Bits of intelligence from various sources convinced him that the hostiles, now traveling north toward the populated John Day Valley, had been reinforced by Klamaths and planned a union with the Umatillas, Cayuses, and perhaps even the Columbia River groups. Alerting units to the north under Colonels Wheaton and Cuvier Grover to prevent such a junction, Howard took up the pursuit.

Over the tortuous topography surrounding the branches of the John Day River the troops toiled grimly along the trial, "The country over which we have marched," the general reported from the mouth of the south fork on July 2, "is the most broken and rugged I have ever seen." The Indians, skirmishing with militia and pillaging ranches, pushed hard to stay ahead of Bernard's cavalry, ranging far in front of the infantry. Northeastward to the slopes of the Blue Mountains and the edge of the Umatilla Reservation the chase continued. On July 7 troops dispatched southward by Wheaton joined at Pilot Rock, about twenty miles south of Pendleton. Additional units of the First Cavalry brought Bernard's force to seven troops—a formidable command for a captain. But Bernard was a superlative field soldier, who enjoyed the full confidence of the department commander, and it is probably not entirely coincidental that Colonel Grover left the campaign for an eastern recruiting detail or that Major Sanford, the other field officer of the regiment in the area, never managed to play more than a supporting role.

On July 8 scouts discovered the hostiles strongly posted atop rocky bluffs on Birch Creek near Pilot Butte. Howard watched as Bernard led the attack with his entire cavalry command. "The advance was made along several approaches in a handsome manner, not a man falling out of ranks," Howard reported. "The different sides of the hill were steeper than Missionary Ridge [site of a famous Civil War battle], still the troops, though encountering a severe fire that emptied some saddles and killed many horses, did not waver, but skirmished to the very top." The warriors fell back to new and higher positions, from which the troopers drove them in still another assault. A third time, now in a stand of timber, the Indians formed, only to be flanked, struck frontally, and driven in disorder from the field. Their horses exhausted, the cavalry could not pursue. "Captain Bernard is entitled to special credit for this engagement," declared General Howard, "as indeed for the entire campaign."[6]

After Birch Creek the hostiles went south. Howard suspected that they intended to cross into the Nez Percé country of Idaho. Capt. Evan Miles and a large infantry force were moving north from the John Day while Major Sanford and another command held positions on the Grande Ronde. Ordering these officers to try to spoil the Indian plans, Howard took Bernard's cavalry and headed for Idaho by way of Fort Walla Walla.

With Howard and the cavalry leaving the vicinity, the Bannocks and Piautes suddenly turned north again and descended on the Umatilla Reservation. Throughout, the attitude and intentions of the Umatillas had been ambiguous. When Captain Miles arrived at the agency on July 12, however, they gathered under a white flag to watch the action. Miles had a large force—seven companies of the Twenty-first Infantry, two of the Fourth Artillery, and a troop of cavalry. On the morning of July 13 he deployed these units in a sweeping arc to inclose the agency buildings. For about six hours a large warrior force probed cautiously at Miles' lines and kept up a desultory long-range fire. Finally, in mid-afternoon, Miles ordered a general advance and drove the Indians eastward into the mountains.[7]

Two days later a party of Umatillas caught up with the Bannocks and Paiutes. By pretending to join the hostiles, they lured Chief Egan, already suffering from wounds sustained at Silver Creek, away from his warriors and killed him. His bloody scalp, presented to Captain Miles, failed to establish positive identification, but doubt vanished when the surgeon went out—"on an errand for the Medical Museum," as he wrote his wife—and obtained Egan's head.[8]

On July 14, the day after Captain Miles' fight, Colonel Wheaton arrived at the Umatilla Agency. With him were Bernard's six cavalry troops, whose march to Idaho had been stopped at Fort Walla Walla. James W. Forsyth, newly promoted to lieutenant colonel of the First Cavalry, had assumed command from Bernard. Wheaton launched Forsyth on the trial of the hostiles. On July 20 his advance skirmished briefly with a rear-guard party, but the rugged wilderness surrounding the head of the John Day's north fork thwarted effective pursuit. Howard, meanwhile, had left Wheaton to patrol the stage road up the Snake to Boise and had hurried up the Grande Ronde with Major Sanford's squadron to join Forsyth. The general caught up on the twenty-third, and four days later the column limped into the Malheur Agency.

By now, as Howard divined, the Bannock-Paiute coalition had dissolved, the Paiutes scattering in small bands over southeastern Oregon and the Bannocks working their way back toward Idaho. Dividing his army into battalion-size components, Howard advanced on a broad front, probing the deserts and valleys south into Nevada and east into Idaho. Although the fight had gone out of the Paiutes, the Bannocks left a trail of bloodshed and destruction. One band, emulating the Nez Percés, attempted to gain the buffalo plains and seek a haven with Sitting Bull in Canada. Troops from General Sheridan's division, however, notably a small command under Col. Nelson A. Miles, cut them off in the mountains east of Yellowstone National Park and in several skirmishes drove them back to their home country.[9]

The war had ended in Oregon, the Paiutes now giving up in large numbers at Malheur Agency and Fort McDermit, Nevada. The surrender on August 12 of Oytes, the principal Paiute leader after Egan's death, signified the collapse of Paiute resistance. As Bannock operations shifted eastward, Howard turned over field command to Colonel Forsyth and started back to his headquarters at Fort Vancouver, Washington. An engagement in Wyoming on September 12 with Bannocks brought the war to a close.

Altogether 131 Bannocks surrendered to or were captured by troops as the hostilities petered out. Held as prisoners through the winter at Camp Brown and Forts Keogh and Hall, they were released the following summer to return to their reservation. The Paiute prisoners, about 600 in number, were placed under guard at Camp Harney and ultimately moved to the Yakima Reservation in Washington. The Malheur Reservation was officially closed.

The Bannock-Paiute uprising invites comparison with the Nez Percé bid for freedom. Approximately the same number of Indians led their pursuers in a long-distance chase through exceedingly difficult country and at last, worn out and decimated, succumbed to superior force. The distance of the chase was less by about half and there were considerably fewer casualties on both sides—nine soldiers killed and fifteen wounded, thirty-one citizens slain, and seventy-eight Indians reported dead. More than 1,000 soldiers were pitted against the Bannocks and Paiutes—slightly less than those against the Nez Percés if the commands of Gibbon, Sturgis, and Miles are reckoned along with Howard's. The army achieved battlefield successes in 1878 that eluded it in 1877. In some ways, however, the campaign against the Bannocks and Paiutes raised greater challenges than the Nez Percé operations. The lava-strewn deserts of southeastern Oregon, almost bereft of grass and water, rapidly used up both men and animals and immensely complicated the supply problem. So, too, did the jumble of mountains and canyons farther north. Summer heat aggravated the demands of rugged terrain. Rightly did General Howard conclude: "The campaign has been a hard, long, and expensive one. Many of the troops have marched greater distances than during the Nez Percé war, and in all the services I have been called upon to render the government I have never known officers and soldiers to encounter and overcome greater obstacles."[10]

Howard himself turned in a better performance in 1878 than in 1877. That the Bannocks and Paiutes did not equal the Nez Percés in military skills detracts only slightly from Howard's record of tenacious pursuit and effective maneuver of supporting and blocking elements. Captain Bernard shares considerable credit for the tenacity; he could get more out of horses and horsemen than the other senior officers of the First Cavalry. But Howard almost alone deserves praise for the manipulation of many commands over a large and rugged expanse of territory in such manner as to box the quarry and leave no alternative but to fight or scatter. Walled in when they reached the Umatilla country, the hostiles fought twice, then scattered. The mop-up operation, too, was organized in a comprehensive fashion that, except for the Canada-bound Bannocks, led to the prompt surrender of most of the fugitives. Thus did the Bannock-Paiute War enable the one-armed "praying general" to gloss over the stains left on his reputation by the Nez Percé War.

Some of the Bannocks Howard chased back to Idaho took refuge in the Salmon River Mountains, which give rise to the middle and south forks of the Salmon River. A scattering of Sheepeaters—Indians whose origins are obscure but who were locally regarded as "renegade" Bannocks and Shoshonis—had led a marginal existence in these mountains for years. Although sometimes mildly troublesome, usually they did not bother the handful of whites in the area. With them the Bannocks spent the winter of 1878–79. Early in May 1879 word reached General Howard from the Lemhi agent that in February Indians had killed five Chinese prospectors on Loon Creek, a tributary of the Salmon's middle fork. Howard at once issued instructions for Captain Bernard to lead his troop of the First Cavalry from Boise Barracks to search out the murderers, and for an equal force, about fifty mounted Second Infantrymen under Lt. Henry Catley, to strike southwest from Camp Howard, a temporary post near Grangeville, Idaho. Later, the general dispatched a force of twenty Indian scouts enlisted at the Umatilla Agency by Lts. Edward S. Farrow and William · C. Brown. Whether Bannocks or Sheepeaters committed the Loon Creek murders, the operations of 1879 have become known as the Sheepeater War.[11]

It was a war less against Indians—they probably mustered no more than thirty fighting men—than against one of the most rugged wildernesses in North America. Towering mountains loom over canyons so deep and narrow that the sun lights the bottom only at midday. Winter comes early and lingers late. Although Bernard and Catley took the field in June, not until mid-July did snowpacks melt enough to open a way to the heart of the Sheepeater domain. Fallen timber obstructed the march through the mountains, and cliffs and boulders made streams almost impossible to follow. Stock gave out by the dozen. Bernard wrote of "pack-mules being carried down-stream, rolling down mountains, causing the loss of many rations and other supplies." "The country is no doubt as rough as any in the United States," he reported on July 15, "and to get at the Indians will be a work of great difficulty."[12]

Bernard failed to find the Indians, but they found Lieutenant Catley. In late July he picked up an Indian trail leading down the canyon of Big Creek, a stream flowing east into the middle fork of the Salmon. Ambushed by about fifteen warriors on July 29, Catley retreated to his pack train. The next day he tried to climb out of the canyon. The Indians, however, surrounded him on an eminence called Vinegar Hill and attempted to burn him out. Back-fires barely averted disaster. Abandoning most of their baggage, Catley and his fifty men slipped out of the trap during the night and headed for home. Learning of this reverse, Colonel Wheaton, at Fort Lapwai, dispatched an officer to face Catley back toward the Indians and ordered Capt. Albert G. Forse, with twenty-five

First Cavalrymen, to take over Catley's command. The lieutenant's "precipitate retreat before inferior numbers is astounding," stormed General Howard.[13] A court-martial later convicted him of misconduct, but the President set aside the sentence of dismissal from the service.

On the south fork of the Salmon, at the mouth of Elk Creek, Bernard united his troop with Farrow's scouts and Forse's infantry and cavalry. On August 13 they set forth for the area in which Catley had found the Indians. Six days later, in Big Creek Canyon near the scene of the Vinegar Hill fight, the Umatilla scouts captured a Sheepeater camp with all its contents, including some of Catley's baggage, but the inhabitants escaped. Next morning the Indians attacked the supply train, which was still forming, under light escort, after the columns had begun the day's march. Driven off, they scattered through the mountains. With no trail to follow, the troops, badly worn and short on rations, won permission from General Howard to call off the campaign and return to their posts.

Lieutenant Farrow secured Howard's blessing for one last try at rounding up the enemy. After obtaining fresh supplies, on September 16 he and Brown with their Umatillas once more plunged into the Sheepeaters' wilderness homeland. Frigid nights warned of winter's approach. On the twenty-first, the scouts picked up a trail and captured two women, a boy, and an infant. At daybreak next morning, in the Salmon canyon below the mouth of the middle fork, they charged into a Sheepeater camp, only to find that once more the occupants had escaped. But the constant pursuit was wearing them down, and communication established with them through the captured women raised the hope of surrender. For more than a week Farrow patiently worked on the hostiles while his supplies dwindled dangerously and, beginning on the twenty-eighth, a four-day storm drenched the antagonists alternately with rain, snow, and sleet. At last, on October 1 and 2, a total of fifty-one Indians—men, women, and children—straggled into Farrow's camp and gave up. Most were Sheepeaters. Their Bannock friends, who were largely responsible for getting them into trouble in the first place, had slipped away and doubtless later lost themselves among their brethren on the Lemhi Reservation. After spending the winter at Fort Vancouver, the Sheepeater prisoners were placed on the Fort Hall Reservation.

In the Sheepeater conflict the soldiers of Bernard, Catley, and

Forse performed a minor miracle in even surviving through three months of campaigning in the forbidding Salmon River Range. In such country, even an experienced leader like Bernard could not bring to bay a handful of natives well adapted to their alpine environment. As he complained, "Should they discover us before we do them, they can hide in the timbered rocky mountains for a long time and go from point to point much faster than we can, even if we knew where to go."[14] As so often happened, Indian allies furnished the Regulars with the key to success. Bernard, Forse, and Catley helped wear out the Sheepeaters. But Farrow, Brown, and the Umatillas twice seized their camp and finally, after the others had left the field, ran them down and convinced them to surrender. The scouts and their officers, Howard concluded, "deserve special mention for gallantry, energy, and perseverance, resulting in success."[15]

Friendly neighbors of the Bannocks and Paiutes, and also linguistically related, the Utes occupied the basin of the upper Colorado River between the Rocky Mountains and the Wasatch Range in Utah and extended south and east across the San Luis Valley into northern New Mexico. A powerful, warlike people, superlative horsemen, skilled huntsmen, they regularly followed the buffalo on the Plains east of the mountains and carried on intermittent warfare with the Plains tribes. Also, like their Navajo enemies to the south, they tended herds of cattle and sheep. The Utes began to associate regularly with whites along the eastern and southern edges of their domain in the 1850s and 1860s. Occasionally they fought with the interlopers—most notably in a war of 1855—but more often joined them as auxiliaries in campaigns against the Navajos and the Plains tribes.[16]

In 1868 a treaty commission, that included the Utes' long-time friend and one-time agent Kit Carson, worked out an arrangement with the seven Colorado bands by which they accepted a generous slice of western Colorado as their reservation and relinquished claim to all other territory. Two bands (Yampa and Grand River) affiliated with an agency established on White River, in the remote northern part of the reservation, and the others (Tabeguache, Uncompahgre, Moache, Capote, and Wiminuche) with two agencies in the southern part of the reservation. The affiliation was largely nominal, the Indians continuing to roam much as they always had, but by 1878 the agents reported 800 people enrolled at White River, 2,000 at Los Pinos, and 934 at Southern Ute. The Uintah Valley Agency, in northeastern Utah, claimed another 430 Utes of the Uintah band.[17]

The most powerful Ute chieftain was Ouray, a wise and articulate statesman with a ready wit and a penetrating ability to expose the pretenses by which white officials sought to mask their acquisitive enterprises. Ouray, an Uncompahgre, lived in the south, was associated with Los Pinos Agency. Principal chiefs at White River were Douglas and Jack. Neither exerted more than local influence.

In the 1870s new mineral strikes in Colorado subjected the Utes to severe stress. The silver boom gave rise to mining camps all over the Rockies and spilled prospectors down the western slope toward Ute territory. Silver strikes in the San Juan Mountains led to the San Juan Cession of 1873, by which Ouray, acknowledging the inevitable, yielded four million acres, one-fourth of the reservation, to the miners. Disputes over the boundaries of the cession, and over the eastern boundary of the reservation, kept Ute relations with their white neighbors in constant turmoil. Moreover, the San Juan discoveries inspired visions of similar riches hidden elsewhere on the reservation. Winning statehood and thus voting representation in Congress in 1876, Coloradans mounted a strident campaign to have the tribe removed to Indian Territory and the reservation opened. To bolster the demand, they charged the Utes with almost every unsolved murder and robbery in the state and some, too, that had never happened. The forest fires that raged over the drouth-stricken mountains in the summer of 1879 were also blamed on the Utes. Ouray, weakened by illness soon to prove fatal, with difficulty restrained his people.[18]

Colorado's war of nerves against the Utes formed the backdrop for the explosion at White River Agency in the autumn of 1879. But the immediate cause was personalized in the agent who took over at White River in the spring of 1878. This was Nathan C. Meeker, an elderly eccentric who had dabbled in several of the unorthodox intellectual and social movements of the period. His latest project, a utopian colony north of Denver named for his friend and backer, Horace Greeley, had not met expectations. At White River Meeker looked forward not only to reviving his finances but also to indulging his fondness for social experimentation by leading his charges swiftly to a state of civilization and

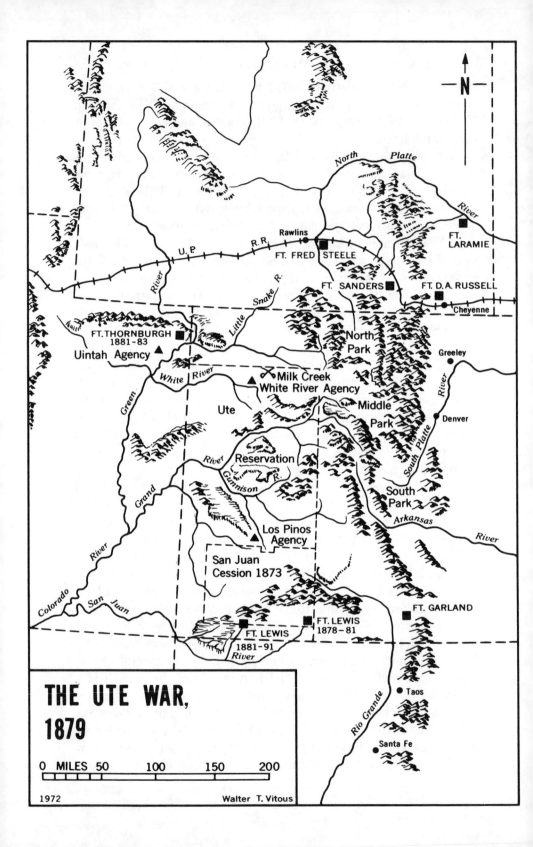

N

FT. LARAMIE

North Platte River

Rawlins
U.P R.R.
FT. FRED STEELE

FT. SANDERS
FT. D.A. RUSSELL
Cheyenne

River

Little Snake R.

FT. THORNBURGH
1881-83
Uintah Agency

North Park

Greeley

White River

Milk Creek
White River Agency

Ute

Green River

Middle Park

Denver

South Platte River

Reservation

Gunnison R.

South Park

Los Pinos
Agency

Grand River

Arkansas River

San Juan
Cession 1873

Colorado River

San Juan

FT. GARLAND

FT. LEWIS
1878-81

FT. LEWIS
1881-91

River

Rio Grande

Taos

Santa Fe

THE UTE WAR, 1879

0 MILES 50   100   150   200

1972   Walter T. Vitous

agricultural self-sufficiency. His uncompromising demand that the Utes abandon their customs and instantly become farmers and his persistence in plowing the grassy meadows on which their ponies grazed brought the White River Utes, already upset by years of stormy relations with the whites, to the brink of revolt.[19]

All that summer Meeker called for military help in restraining his charges and forcing them to do his bidding. In late July he journeyed to Denver and discussed conditions at White River Agency with General Pope, whose department embraced the Ute Reservation. Pope pointed out that he had sent Capt. Francis S. Dodge's troop of the Ninth Cavalry to Middle Park to investigate the reports of Utes setting forest fires. If needed, Dodge could hasten to Meeker's aid. The agent also discussed his problem with Maj. Thomas T. Thornburgh, whom he met on the train en route back to Rawlins, Wyoming, rail depot for the White River Agency. Thornburgh commanded Fort Fred Steele, near Rawlins. Although in Crook's department rather than Pope's and 175 miles from White River, this was still the post nearest the agency. Thornburgh explained that he could not give much assistance from so great a distance and could not march to the agency without orders from superior authority. Not until Chief Douglas roughed up Meeker on September 10 and prompted him to declare the lives of agency personnel in danger did the army show much interest in his appeals for help. Then, after an exchange of correspondence between Secretaries McCrary and Schurz and Generals Sherman and Sheridan, followed by the misdirection of orders to Pope instead of Crook, Thornburgh received telegraphic instructions on September 16 to lead a relief column to Meeker's agency.[20]

"Tip" Thornburgh, youthful major of the Fourth Infantry, enjoyed family connections that had advanced him rapidly to field grade—from first lieutenant to major and paymaster in one step. Although many resented his good fortune, he stood high in the favor of General Crook, who had helped him return to the line when staff routine palled. On September 21 Thornburgh led a troop of the Third Cavalry and a company of the Fourth Infantry out of Fort Steele. The next morning, in Rawlins, he picked up a troop and a half of the Fifth Cavalry, under Capt. J. Scott Payne, rushed by rail from Fort D. A. Russell, near Cheyenne, Wyoming. Altogether, the column counted 153 officers and enlisted men, 25 civilians, and 33 supply wagons.

No act of Meeker's so infuriated the Utes as his summons of soldiers. Word spread that they came at his request to put them in chains and move them to Indian Territory. Thornburgh took the measure of their anger on September 26, when the expedition reached the crossing of Bear River (now the Yampa), about sixty miles from White River Agency. Jack and about ten other prominent Utes visited him and, complaining bitterly of Meeker, asked over and over why the soldiers were coming to White River. Meeker, too, grew alarmed and quickly embraced an Indian proposal to ask Thornburgh to halt his command and, accompanied by no more than five soldiers, ride to the agency for talks with the chiefs. The danger of an armed collision ran high, as both Meeker and Thornburgh clearly recognized. Although Thornburgh agreed to Meeker's proposal, further reflection prompted him to modify the plan so far as to advance the troops to a camp site within supporting distance of the agency. Understanding that the major had agreed to leave his men behind, the Utes predictably interpreted their further advance as evidence of bad faith.[21]

Shortly before noon on September 29 the cavalry column splashed across Milk Creek, a stream that marked the northern border of the Ute Reservation some fifteen miles north of White River Agency. Thornburgh now had with him only the cavalry, about 120 troopers. The infantry and eight wagons had remained at the camp site of September 25 on Fortification Creek to establish a depot for forwarding supplies from Fort Steele. On a ridge beyond Milk Creek, Jack, with about 100 well-armed warriors, commanded the trail. As soon as Thornburgh saw them, he deployed his horsemen to the right and left but also sent his adjutant, Lt. Samuel A. Cherry, to try to open conversations. Jack later declared that the Indians wanted to talk, too, but "I was with General Crook the year before fighting the Sioux, and I knew in a minute that as soon as this officer deployed his men out in that way it meant a fight; so I told my men to deploy too." Approaching the Ute lines, Cherry "took off my hat and waved it in a friendly way." Then someone—Cherry said an Indian—fired a shot and the battle was on.[22]

The Utes pressed aggressively on the front and flanks of the cavalry and threatened to get between them and the train, which had begun to corral in the valley on the other side of Milk Creek. As Thornburgh rode back toward the creek to look after the train, a Ute sharpshooter took aim and sent a bullet into his brain. Command devolved on Captain Payne, who drew the troopers back to the train. It had been awkwardly positioned, separated from the creek by 150 yards of open valley and exposed to fire from bluffs on two sides. Throughout the afternoon the Utes raked the corral with bullets. They also fired the prairie grass and sagebrush and very nearly burned the defenders from their positions. Backfires helped lessen the impact of the flames when they struck the corral. By nightfall, in addition to Major Thornburgh, ten men lay dead and another twenty-three (including Payne, another officer, and the surgeon) wounded. Three-fourths of the horses and mules had been hit. The Utes later conceded twenty-three warriors killed in the fighting on this day.[23]

Having shed soldiers' blood, the Utes had little to lose by turning their fury on the cause of their troubles. On the afternoon of September 29, as fighting raged on Milk Creek, warriors methodically slaughtered Meeker and nine of his employees at White River Agency. They spared Mrs. Meeker and daughter Josephine, carrying them and another woman and her two children into captivity.

That night, Captain Payne started couriers northward with word of his situation, and in the predawn hours of October 1 news of Milk Creek sped over the telegraph wires from Rawlins. By the morning of October 2, Union Pacific trains had deposited the first elements of a relief force at Rawlins. Under Col. Wesley Merritt, four troops of the Fifth Cavalry and five companies of the Fourth Infantry hurried south on the road to Milk Creek. Also on October 2 Captain Dodge and his black troopers from Middle Park rode into Payne's lines. Dodge had learned of Milk Creek from settlers and had made a twenty-three-hour forced march to the battlefield. He found Payne still pinned down by long-range fire and now with forty-two wounded. Within a short time all of Dodge's horses had fallen victim to Indian marksmen.[24] The Utes maintained the siege until Merritt's arrival on the morning of October 5, then, after a brief skirmish, drew off to the south.

That afternoon a messenger reached Merritt from the south. He had copies of a letter from Ouray to the White River chiefs commanding them to stop fighting, and he reported that Jack and his associates had consented to obey Ouray's injunction. The messenger also gave his opinion, based on inferences drawn from Jack, that Meeker had been killed and the agency women made prisoners. On October 11, having arranged for Payne and his men to return to Rawlins, Merritt marched to White River Agency. He found the buildings burned and the bodies of Meeker and his employees lying where they had fallen.

News of the Milk Creek disaster and the slayings at White River electrified the nation, and suspense over the fate of the captive women sustained public interest in the army's response. Sheridan poured reinforcements into the Ute country. Union Pacific officials, Crook's aide recalled, "turned over their track to General Williams and Colonel Ludington, the two staff officers charged with aiding the Merritt expedition."[25] By October 11, when he reached the agency, Merritt commanded more than 700 soldiers, and as many more, elements of the Third Cavalry and Fourth, Seventh, Ninth, and Fourteenth Infantry, were hurrying to join him. General Pope placed other forces south and east of the Ute Reservation. Col. Edward Hatch concentrated about 500 men of the Ninth Cavalry and Fifteenth, Nineteenth, and Twenty-second Infantry at Fort Lewis, a new post at Pagosa Springs, on the upper San Juan River.[26] Col. Ranald S. Mackenzie brought six troops of the Fourth Cavalry from Texas and took station at Fort Garland, in the San Luis Valley. Infantry units swelled his command to 1,500.

Although Sherman and Sheridan favored prompt and severe punishment of the Utes, Interior Secretary Carl Schurz stepped in to blunt their response. He feared that a large-scale offensive would involve all the Utes in war and signal the death of the Meeker women. Through Ouray, Schurz believed, the release of the captives and a peaceful settlement of the conflict might be arranged. For this mission he selected former Ute agent Charles Adams, then a postal inspector in Colorado, and commissioned him a special agent of the Interior Department. With the fate of the captive women in the balance, Sherman could hardly turn down Schurz's request on October 13 to call off the offensive while Adams pursued his assignment.

The order caught Merritt already in motion southward toward Grand River in search of the White River Utes. Returning to the agency, he expressed his wonder at "being equipped for a campaign by one arm of the government and halted in its execution by another arm of the same government, on the verge of winter in a country where all campaigning very shortly will be beyond human execution." Sheridan put it more strongly. He had fifteen to sixteen hundred men at White River Agency, dependent for supplies on a long and difficult road to railhead that would soon be closed by winter snow. "We went to the agency at the solicitation of the Indian Bureau, whose agent was murdered and our men killed and wounded, and now we are left in the heart of the mountains with our hands tied and the danger of being snowed in staring us in the face. I am not easily discouraged, but it looks as though we had been pretty badly sold out in this business."[27]

But the complaints of the generals subsided when Adams succeeded in freeing the women. Accompanied by a delegation of Utes, including a chief specially commissioned by the ailing Ouray to speak for him, Adams sought out the camps of the White River Utes atop Grand Mesa. In a stormy conference on October 21 he persuaded their leaders to yield the women—although only after Ouray's emissary threatened to mobilize the rest of the Utes in a war against the rebels and Adams promised to stop the advance of Merritt's soldiers. Adams journeyed on north to Merritt's camp and gave his news to the world in a dispatch telegraphed from Rawlins.

The big commands assembled at White River and Forts Lewis and Garland served mainly as stage dressing for the remaining scenes of the Ute drama. Colonel Hatch sat with Adams and Ouray on a commission named by Secretary Schurz to examine witnesses and single out Indians deserving punishment. After a series of tedious and confusing meetings at Los Pinos Agency during November and December, the commission finally decided that the Utes had not intended to fight Thornburgh and that none should be judged culpable. At the same time two of the commissioners— Ouray dissenting—listed twelve Indians for further trial for the murder of the agency personnel and the "outrages" visited on the women during their captivity.[28]

The question of punishment was overshadowed by the larger question of opening the Ute Reservation. Coloradoans seized upon the uprising to demand expulsion of the Indians. During a visit to Washington early in 1880, Ouray and a delegation of chiefs acceded to an agreement drawn up by the Indian Bureau. In consideration of cash payments and the creation of a trust fund, the White River Utes were to move to Utah and settle on the Uintah

Reservation, while the rest of the tribesmen were to take farming lands in severalty in the Gunnison and La Plata River valleys of southwestern Colorado. Also, Ute leaders were to use their influence to apprehend the twelve Indians charged with crime by the Hatch Commission. Approving the agreement on June 15, 1880, Congress added provisos that blocked the White River share of the money until the twelve Indians had been surrendered and also that tapped this money for annual payments to the Meeker women and other relatives of the men slain at the agency on September 29, 1879. A commission headed by that perennial commission chairman, George W. Manypenny, went to Colorado in the summer of 1880 and, in accordance with the Treaty of 1868, obtained the signatures on this agreement of three-fourths of the tribe's adult males. On August 24, 1880, while assisting the commission in this task, Ouray finally succumbed to Bright's Disease at the age of forty-seven.[29]

Colonel Merritt returned to his station in November 1879, but a large portion of his command passed a comfortless winter in makeshift shelters at White River Agency. In July 1880 these troops were replaced by six companies of the Sixth Infantry, which occupied the site, under less trying conditions, through the winter of 1880–81. Colonel Mackenzie, after wintering at Fort Garland, pushed his force across the mountains to Los Pinos Agency in May 1880 and used them to keep peace between the Indians and whites anticipating the opening of Ute lands.

By the summer of 1881 most of the White River Utes had moved to the Uintah Reservation, lured by annuity payments that tacitly acknowledged the impossibility of further prosecution of the twelve "criminals."[30] Also, another reservation had been established adjacent to the Uintah Reservation for the Uncompahgre and Tabaguache Utes of Los Pinos. They had been unable to find enough farming lands along the Gunnison and at length had agreed to move to Utah too. At the last moment they balked, but Colonel Mackenzie staged an impressive display of force, and they went.

In September 1881 the infantry at the old White River Agency site moved downstream to the Green River and established Fort Thornburgh to guard the Indians now collected on the two Utah reservations. The post was moved northward to a new location in the spring of 1882 and abandoned in 1883. The Southern Utes—

Moache, Capote, and Wiminuche—remained in southwestern Colorado, occupying a narrow strip of territory along the New Mexico border. In 1881 Fort Lewis was moved from Pagosa Springs seventy-five miles westward to La Plata River to watch over these Indians.

The troubles at White River Agency grew out of Agent Meeker's stubborn attempt at instant acculturation. "I don't think that Mr. Meeker understood those Indians," testified the perceptive Charles Adams. "He was a great agriculturist, and he thought he could succeed in forcing the Indians to work and to accept the situation as farmers, but he did not take into consideration that it is almost impossible to force Indians into that sort of labor all at once."[31] But Meeker's policy did not ordain the violence of September 29, 1879. That occurred, probably without premeditation, because the Utes believed Thornburgh and Meeker guilty of bad faith. Considerable evidence fortifies Adams' initial opinion that "if Major Thornburgh had gone to the agency with escort simply, the whole trouble would have been averted; that the party of young men under Jack went out to fight unknown to the older chiefs, and that the loss of so many young men excited the others so that the killing at the agency could not be averted."[32] Yet this conclusion does not necessarily convict Thornburgh of faulty decisions. He knew the Indians to be exceedingly agitated and threatening violence momentarily. Prudence demanded that he not place himself so far from the support of his command as to be wholly at their mercy. Crossing Milk Creek onto the reservation, however, he unwittingly set off the explosion of which he and Meeker became the most prominent casualties.

The Ute War opened as a military show but quickly turned into a civilian show. The finale came as the product of diplomacy rather than force, with no military role beyond Colonel Hatch's membership on the peace commission and the influence on Ute decisions of almost 4,000 soldiers massed menacingly in the background. After violence removed Meeker and Thornburgh, the central figures were Schurz, Adams, and Ouray. Schurz, despite some eccentricities one of the ablest administrators ever to head the Interior Department, took personal command of the diplomatic effort and steered it skillfully through the tortuous politics of the situation. Adams carried out his assignment with sensitivity and political acumen. Ouray demonstrated that, despite declining powers, he still possessed an almost bicultural grasp of the Indian and white social, political, and economic orders and in a showdown could still impose his will on other Ute leaders. Together, Schurz, Adams, and Ouray produced a settlement that avoided further bloodshed.

NOTES

1. Population statistics are from CIA, *Annual Report* (1877), p. 292. For a history of the Bannocks, see Brigham D. Madsen, *The Bannock of Idaho* (Caldwell, Ida., 1958). Although seriously flawed, the standard history of the Bannock War is George F. Brimlow, *The Bannock Indian War of 1878* (Caldwell, Ida., 1938).
2. CIA, *Annual Report* (1878), pp. 290–92. Stewart, *The Northern Paiute Bands*, deals with the organization and distribution of these Indians.
3. *Army and Navy Journal*, 15 (Aug. 10, 1878), 5. See also Crook's annual report in SW, *Annual Report* (1878), p. 90. The Bannocks drew rations, according to Crook, sufficient for four out of seven days.
4. Madsen, pp. 202–7. Brimlow, chaps. 4–5. CIA, *Annual Report* (1878), pp. xii–xx, 49–50, 118–19. SW, *Annual Report* (1878), p. 90.
5. For these operations, in addition to sources already cited, see Howard's annual report and a compendium of official correspondence annexed to General McDowell's annual report in SW, *Annual Report* (1878), pp. 127–92, 208–36. See also Don Russell, *One Hundred and Three Fights and Scrimmages: The Story of General Reuben F. Bernard* (Washington, D.C., 1936), chap. 8; Howard, *My Life and Experiences among Our Hostile Indians*, chaps. 27–31; R. Ross Arnold, *The Indian Wars of Idaho* (Caldwell, Ida., 1932), chaps. 10–12; George F. Brimlow, ed., "Two Cavalrymen's Diaries of the Bannock War, 1878 [Lt. William C. Brown and Pvt. Frederick W. Mayer]," *Oregon Historical Quarterly*, 68 (1967), 221–58, 293–316; and Chandler B. Watson, "Recollections of the Bannock War," *ibid.*, 317–29. Stanley R. Davison, ed., "The Bannock-Paiute War of 1878: Letters of Major Edwin C. Mason," *Journal of the West*, 11 (1972), 128–42. The reports of the Malheur and Umatilla agents are also illuminating: CIA, *Annual Report* (1878), pp. 119–20, 122–23.
6. Howard's report in SW, *Annual Report* (1878), pp. 170, 222. See also Russell, pp. 129–30.
7. Miles' report in SW, *Annual Report* (1878), pp. 224–26.
8. Laufe, ed., *An Army Doctor's Wife on the Frontier*, p. 346. See Brimlow, pp. 150–54, for other details of this episode.
9. For these operations, see SW, *Annual Report* (1878), p. 67; Brimlow, chap. 16 and pp. 224–25; and Miles, *Personal Recollections*, chap. 13.
10. SW, *Annual Report* (1878), p. 235.
11. See W. C. Brown, *The Sheepeater Campaign* (Caldwell, Ida., 1926); Howard, chap. 32; Arnold, chap. 13; Russell, chap. 9; C. B. Hardin, "The Sheepeater Campaign," *Journal of the Military Service Institution of the United States*, 47 (1910), 25–40; SW. *Annual Report* (1879), pp. 155–60. For speculation on Sheepeater antecedents, see Ake Hultkrantz, "The Source Literature on the 'Tukudika' Indians in Wyoming: Facts and Fancies," in Earl H. Swanson, Jr., ed., *Languages and Cultures of Western North America: Essays in Honor of Sven S. Liljeblad* (Caldwell, Ida., 1970), pp. 246–64.

12. SW, *Annual Report* (1879), p. 157.
13. *Ibid.*, p. 159. Catley's report is on p. 158.
14. *Ibid.*, p. 157.
15. *Ibid.*, p. 163.
16. Standard histories are Robert Emmitt, *The Last War Trail: The Utes and the Settlement of Colorado* (Norman, Okla., 1955); and Wilson Rockwell, *The Utes, A Forgotten People* (Denver, Colo., 1956).
17. CIA, *Annual Report* (1878), pp. 282–83, 294–95. For the 1868 treaty see Kappler, *Indian Affairs: Laws and Treaties*, 2, 990–93.
18. This background is set forth in the standard history of the Ute outbreak of 1879: Marshall Sprague, *Massacre: The Tragedy at White River* (Boston and Toronto, 1957). See also the account in J. P. Dunn, *Massacres of the Mountains: A History of the Indian Wars of the Far West, 1815–1875* (New York, 1886), chap. 20. Correspondence concerning Ute affairs, 1873–79, is in Senate Ex. Docs., 46th Cong., 2d sess., Nos. 29 and 30.
19. Nearly all of Meeker's correspondence and reports are in Senate Ex. Docs., 46th Cong., 2d sess., No. 31. Revealing insights appear in testimony taken by the House Committee on Indian Affairs in January 1880: House Misc. Docs., 46th Cong., 2d sess., No. 38; and by the Ute Commission of 1879: House Ex. Docs., 46th Cong., 2d sess., No. 83.
20. These events emerge from correspondence printed in extraordinary disorder in Senate Ex. Docs., 46th Cong., 2d sess., No. 30. See also SW, *Annual Report* (1879), pp. 8–9.
21. For the exchange of letters between Meeker and Thornburgh, see SW, *Annual Report* (1879), pp. 9–10. For the meeting between Jack and Thornburgh and other events of the march, see especially testimony of former agent Charles Adams, Captain Payne, Lt. Samuel A. Cherry, and Jack himself in House Misc. Docs., 46th Cong., 2d sess., No. 38.
22. See Cherry's testimony in House Misc. Docs., 46th Cong., 2d sess., No. 38, pp. 64–66. Jack's words are quoted by Agent Charles Adams in testimony in *ibid.*, p. 14. This conforms well with Jack's own testimony, p. 196.
23. The best sources for this action are in the testimony of Cherry, Payne, and Jack in *ibid.* The figure thirty-seven is commonly agreed by Indian sources as total Ute casualties, the other fourteen falling in action with agency employees and a civilian freight train en route to the agency. See especially Adams to Schurz, Oct. 24, 1879, in Senate Ex. Docs., 46th Cong., 2d sess., No. 31, p. 13.
24. Dodge's detailed report, Oct. 27, 1879, is in Senate Ex. Docs., 46th Cong., 2d sess., No. 31, pp. 105–8.
25. Bourke, *On the Border with Crook*, p. 426. Lt. Col. Robert Williams was Crook's adjutant general, Maj. M. I. Ludington his quartermaster. See also Wesley Merritt, "Three Indian Campaigns," reprinted from *Harper's New Monthly Magazine* (April 1890) as *Merritt and the Indian Wars*, ed. Barry C. Johnson (London, 1972); and SW, *Annual Report* (1879), p. 12.
26. Fort Lewis was established at this site in October 1878. Prucha, *Guide to Military Posts*, p. 85. For events with this command see Robert G. Athearn, ed., "Major Hough's March into Southern Ute Country, 1879," *Colorado Magazine*, 25 (1948), 97–109.
27. Senate Ex. Docs., 46th Cong., 2d sess., No. 30, pp. 89, 96.
28. The commission's report is in House Ex. Docs., 46th Cong., 2d sess., No. 83.
29. CIA, *Annual Report* (1880), pp. xxiv–xxv, 14–18, 193–98.
30. Douglas, who "had connection with" Mrs. Meeker, was lodged in the Fort Leavenworth prison to await trial, but a year later was quietly released. None other of the twelve was taken into custody.
31. House Misc. Docs., 46th Cong., 2d sess., No. 38, p. 13.
32. To Schurz, Oct. 24, 1879, Senate Ex. Docs., 46th Cong., 2d sess., No. 30, p. 14.

EIGHTEEN

Mexican Border Conflicts, 1870-81

THE INTERNATIONAL BOUNDARY between the United States and Mexico raised no barriers to the passage of Indian raiders. For generations, war parties of Kiowas, Comanches, and occasionally Cheyennes and Arapahoes from the Great Plains regularly stabbed deep into Coahuila and Durango and returned with stock and other plunder, scalps, and captives. Mescalero Apaches from New Mexico and Chiricahua and Western Apaches from Arizona scourged Chihuahua and Sonora. Likewise, Americans from Texas to Arizona suffered constantly from raiders based south of the border. Kickapoos, Lipans, and Apaches, these Indians were refugees from the United States who had found new homes in the mountains of northern Mexico. The incursions of Indians from one nation into the other disturbed relations between the United States and Mexico for years and, in the 1870s and 1880s, presented the U.S. Army with one of its severest challenges.

Other conditions aggravated the Indian problem along the border. Vast expanses of waterless desert and rough, barren mountains favored the Indians and speedily incapacitated conventional troops. Smugglers, rustlers, bandits, and assorted scoundrels of both countries infected the border with a pervasive spirit of lawlessness. Revolution in Mexico and Reconstruction in Texas added to the disorder. Finally, mutual suspicion and distrust, born of the Texas Revolution and the Mexican War and fed by loud talk in the United States of further territorial gain at Mexico's expense, inhibited a cooperative approach to border problems.[1]

A large share of the U.S. Army occupied the border region. In

1873, for example, more than 800 soldiers garrisoned five posts in the border zone of Arizona and New Mexico, while 2,500 held eight stations along Texas' Rio Grande frontier.² For fifteen years most of the latter were black, a circumstance that, exciting the prejudices of Texans and Mexicans alike, heightened tensions. Confusing the racial amalgam still more, a company of Seminole-Negroes helped police the Rio Grande. Originally from Florida, where the blend resulted from the union between Indians and runaway slaves, and more recently refugees from their later home in Indian Territory, the Seminole-Negroes proved highly effective auxiliaries. They owed much of their success to Lt. John L. Bullis, a tough, desert-wise officer detached from the Twenty-fourth Infantry to lead them.³ Despite their strength, U.S. units but rarely apprehended raiding parties from either side of the boundary. Fewer in numbers and often preoccupied with revolutionary concerns, Mexican troops achieved even less success.

On the American side of the border, the worst destruction centered in the Texas ranch country south and west of San Antonio. The perpetrators of these raids were Lipans, Mescalero Apaches, and Kickapoos. The Lipans, rarely mustering more than thirty warriors under the wily Washa Lobo, usually lived in a village within a dozen miles of Zaragosa. The Mescaleros, about 225 fighting men in four bands, roamed the mountains farther west, south of the Big Bend of the Rio Grande. The Kickapoos, numbering some 1,300, inhabited villages in Nacimiento Canyon of the Sabinas River, near Santa Rosa.⁴

From their desert and mountain lairs, the raiders slipped across the Rio Grande in parties of five to twenty-five. Circling north of Forts Duncan and Clark, they awaited a full moon before sweeping through the abundant cattle and horse herds along the upper Nueces and its tributaries. Any luckless cowboy or traveler who got in the way was left butchered. By hard riding, the warriors could be safely back across the river with their stolen stock before the troops could intervene.

Between 1865 and 1873 the Kickapoos were the principal culprits. With land grants and other inducements, the Mexican government had encouraged them to migrate from Kansas and help defend the frontier settlements against Kiowa and Comanche marauders. In 1862, and again in 1865, Texans had attacked emigrating bands. In retaliation, the Kickapoos had declared open

war on Texas and year after year had prosecuted it with deadly
effect. With the connivance of Mexican officialdom, the Indians
disposed of thousands of stolen cattle, horses, and other loot to
traders in Santa Rosa and other Mexican towns.

Moved by the protests and appeals of the victims of these raids,
in 1870 the State Department sought Mexico's permission for U.S.
troops to cross the boundary in pursuit of Indians. Constitutionally,
only the Mexican Congress could grant this concession, and political disaster awaited the Mexican President who asked for it. Trying another approach, in 1871 the Indian Bureau, with Mexican
aid that was more apparent than real, launched an effort to induce
the Kickapoos to return to their American reservation. Before
these negotiations could bear fruit, however, President Grant, in
January 1873, announced a more aggressive policy.[5]

To carry out this policy, the President directed the transfer of
Col. Ranald S. Mackenzie and the Fourth Cavalry to the border.
The energetic Mackenzie, who already stood high in Grant's favor,
had earned wide recognition for his recent operations against the
Comanches (see p. 211). The regiment began to rendezvous at
Fort Clark in March 1873. On April 11 Mackenzie appeared, ac-
companied by Secretary of War Belknap and General Sheridan.
In San Antonio they had met with the department commander,
General Augur. In further secret sessions at Fort Clark, Mackenzie received his instructions. No record seems to have been made,
and the only source is Mackenzie's adjutant, Lt. Robert G. Carter,
who was not present but whom the colonel took into his confidence.
Sheridan, according to Carter, directed Mackenzie to plan and execute a "campaign of annihilation, obliteration and complete destruction." Pressed for more explicit orders, he is said to have
pounded the table and declared vehemently: "Damn the orders!
Damn the authority! You are to go ahead on your own plan of
action, and your authority and backing shall be Gen. Grant and
myself. With us behind you in whatever you do to clean up this
situation, you can rest assured of the fullest support. You must
assume the risk. We will assume the final responsibility should
any result."[6]

There can be little question that Sheridan intended, as Mackenzie understood him to intend, a strike into Mexico to destroy the
raiders in their homes. Dispatching three trusted scouts to recon-
noiter the Kickapoo villages, Mackenzie imposed a harsh regimen

of drill and target practice on his troops. Besides the spies in Mexico, only Mackenzie and Carter knew that the preparations looked to a campaign across the border. Carter recalled the colonel's temperament, never very stable, as one of acute nervousness and irritability during this trying period.

Mackenzie's spies reported to him on the night of May 16, 1873. They had found three villages on the upper San Rodrigo River about forty miles west of Piedras Negras. Numbering fifty to sixty lodges each, one was Kickapoo, one Lipan, and one Mescalero. Moreover, most of the Kickapoo fighting men had left their homes that morning. Mackenzie issued marching orders at once. Rendezvousing the next day between Fort Clark and the Rio Grande, the cavalrymen crossed the river at nightfall. The expedition consisted of six troops of the Fourth Cavalry, about 400 strong, and a heavily laden mule train. Also, Lieutenant Bullis and twenty-five Seminole-Negro scouts from Fort Duncan rode with the command.

Next morning, May 18, Mackenzie reached his objective. Wave after wave of troopers swept through he Kickapoo village near Remolino with carbines blazing. The last wave dismounted to fire the grass lodges. With the warriors absent, the women, children, and old men fought desperately but ineffectively. Nineteen died in the defense and forty were taken captive. One soldier was killed, two wounded. Destroying the other two villages, whose occupants had fled, the troops and their prisoners hurried back to the river. Not until safely on the U.S. side of the border on the nineteenth, exhausted by almost sixty hours of sleepless activity, did they dare pause for rest.[7]

Mackenzie's Kickapoo expedition was a bold and daring maneuver. A collision with Mexicans would almost certainly have brought on a rupture in relations between Mexico and the United States. Only swift movement prevented such a collision, and this proved possible only because the Battle of Remolino burdened Mackenzie with so few wounded men to impede his withdrawal from Mexican soil. Although public opinion in Mexico reacted with predictable outrage, the precarious new regime of President Sebastián Lerdo de Tejada rode out the storm and confined its action to a belated and surprisingly mild protest.

The vagueness of Mackenzie's authority made his invasion of Mexico all the more daring. He seems to have acted entirely on Sheridan's implication, orally conveyed, that President Grant

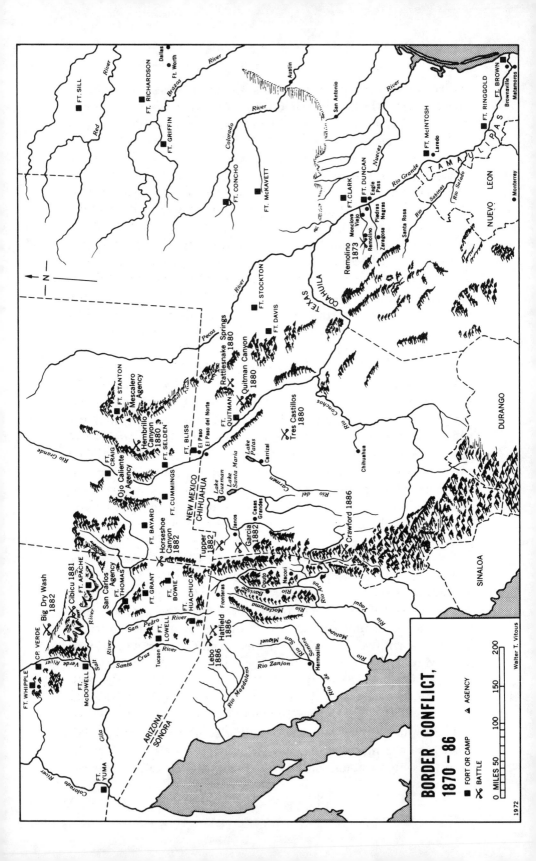

BORDER CONFLICT, 1870-86

■ FORT OR CAMP   ▲ AGENCY
✕ BATTLE

0 MILES 50 100 150 200

Walter T. Vitous

1972

favored this course. How accurately Sheridan understood and represented the President's desires is speculative. General Sherman, if he shared in the secret at all, disapproved. "McKenzie [*sic*] will of course be sustained," he wrote Sheridan on June 3, "but for the sake of history, I would like to have to him report clearly the facts that induced him to know that the Indians he attacked and captured were the identical Indians that engaged in raiding Texas. Had he followed a fresh trail there would be law to back him." The new Mexican President seemed friendly to the United States and deserved support, but he "will find it hard to preserve his popularity if he submits to positive insult from us, the 'Gringoes.' " Sheridan's reply, innocent of any understanding of diplomatic requirements, was that of course Mackenzie had struck guilty Indians, for "there is none of them guiltless."[8] One wonders how firmly the United States would have backed Mackenzie had his adventure provoked a major diplomatic confrontation.

Pitting half a cavalry regiment against a handful of women, old men, and children, the Battle of Remolino can hardly be classed a great feat of arms. It is even less creditable because Mackenzie knew the fighting men had departed and hastened to strike before they returned. Indeed, Remolino is one of the rare instances in which the Regular Army stands convicted of warring purposely, rather than incidentally or accidentally, on women and children; and the boastful writings of Beaumont, Carter, and other veterans conceal the true character of the opposition. Nevertheless, Remolino produced results. For the first time, the Kickapoos began to negotiate seriously with U.S. commissioners for a return to the United States. Three months after Remolino, 317 began the trek to Indian Territory, and two years later another 115 made the journey. Also, fearful of further punishment, those who remained in Mexico dramatically scaled down their Texas raids.[9]

For three years after Mackenzie's blow fell on the Kickapoos, Texas enjoyed a respite from incursions of Indians based in Mexico. Grateful Texans heaped praise on the Fourth Cavalry and its hard-hitting young colonel. Coahuila, too, at last gained relief from Kiowa and Comanche depredators. Their conquest in the Red River War of 1874–75 (see Chapter Thirteen) broke the deadly pattern of raids from which Mexicans had suffered for a century and a half. By 1876, however, the lesson of Remolino had dimmed, and once more violence came to the Rio Grande border. Kickapoos participated occasionally, but now the principal offenders were Lipans and Mescalero Apaches.

The raiders stirred up commanders even less respectful of diplomatic amenities than Mackenzie. Brig. Gen. Edward O. C. Ord commanded the Department of Texas. Of somewhat disorderly and imprecise mind, he was a vigorous old campaigner with a reputation for physical prowess. "I'll bet today he can ride that frontier with any corporal," General Sherman told a congressional committee. Sherman added that as a young subaltern Ord "would swim rivers with ice floating in them when he might have bridged them, and he would go over the tops of mountains when he might have gone around."[10] Sherman thus unwittingly revealed why Ord, temperamentally, was not the most appropriate commander for a troubled international frontier. The officer charged with the upriver border defenses seemed an unlikely choice for any field assignment. But despite a mountainous frame that would have immobilized most men, Lt. Col. William R. Shafter, Twenty-fourth Infantry, had led his black soldiers in punishing campaigns all over Texas for almost a decade. Coarse, profane, a harsh disciplinarian, "Pecos Bill" had proved himself an effective leader.[11]

Ord and Shafter shared the belief that the best way of dealing with the new wave of marauding was to root out the marauders in their homes, as Mackenzie had done, even though it violated the territory of a friendly neighbor. After a particularly bloody raid in the spring of 1876, Ord instructed Shafter to go after the offenders in their Mexican villages. In June Shafter began to probe the mountains and deserts of Coahuila for the Indians. On July 30 a detachment from his command—Lieutenant Bullis with twenty Seminole-Negro scouts and twenty black cavalrymen —smashed a Lipan village of twenty-three lodges near Zaragosa. For the rest of 1876 and into 1877, Ord and Shafter played fast and loose with the doctrine of "hot pursuit" by which they justified their incursions. Although a rough correlation could be demonstrated between Indian raids in Texas and the U.S. response in Coahuila, Shafter's columns rarely crossed the border in hot pursuit or even on an enemy trail. But time and again Bullis' scouts and the Tenth Cavalrymen at Forts Duncan and Clark, always under orders from Shafter, thrust into Mexico.[12]

The 1876 crossings aroused little response from the Mexican government. For one thing, except for the march that ended in the fight near Zaragosa on July 30, Shafter's columns kept west of the settlements, in almost uninhabited deserts and mountains imperfectly known even to the Mexicans. For another, Mexican officials gave tacit consent to the operations—or at least so Shafter claimed. Finally, the revolution launched in 1876 by Porfirio Díaz wholly occupied President Lerdo's state governments in a struggle for self-preservation. By early 1877 Díaz had triumphed, in part by exploiting Mexican hostility toward the United States. The kind of "consent" underlying Shafter's Mexican adventures, if indeed it ever existed, could no longer be expected.

An international incident occurred almost at once. The new governor of Coahuila proclaimed aid to U.S. forces operating on Mexican soil a treasonable offense, and officials at Piedras Negras imprisoned two Mexicans who had guided Shafter to Zargosa the previous July. When word reached General Ord that they would be shot as traitors, he ordered Shafter to liberate them. At dawn on April 3, 1877, citizens of Piedras Negras awoke to find three troops of the Tenth Cavalry ringing the town, two companies of the Twenty-fourth Infantry drawn up on the plaza, and a determined Shafter demanding release of the prisoners. But Mexican authorities had been wakeful enough to spirit them into the interior before Shafter could spring his trap, and he withdrew as gracefully as possible. Mexico loudly protested this indignity to her sovereignty.[13]

A sort of war of nerves developed between the new Mexican President and the new U.S. President, Rutherford B. Hayes. Hayes used Díaz' need for U.S. recognition as a lever to force Mexico to remedy the border situation, and Díaz used the U.S. demand for such a remedy, particularly for a treaty permitting border crossings in hot pursuit, as a lever to pry loose recognition. Although the two governments remained in "unofficial" diplomatic communication in Washington and Mexico City, neither president showed any disposition to give in first.[14]

On June 1, Hayes opened still further the gulf between the two countries. Colonel Shafter had reported on May 10 that the Indians were now taking refuge in Mexican towns, and in an endorsement General Ord had asked "how far in such cases I can authorize the troops to go." The answer came out of a meeting of

the President with his Cabinet. Ord was free, Secretary of War
McCrary advised General Sherman on June 1, "when in pursuit of
a band of the marauders, and when his troops are either in sight
of them or upon a fresh trail, to follow them across the Rio
Grande, and to overtake and punish them."

Actually, the order of June 1 announced a policy much more
restrictive than Ord and Shafter had followed in practice, but it
was the announcement more than the practice that incensed Mexicans. Indignation swept Mexico. The United States had treated
Mexicans "as savages, as Kaffirs of Africa," complained the foreign minister; a declaration of war would have been less offensive
to the national honor. President Díaz had only recently sent a
trusted lieutenant, Gen. Gerónimo Treviño, to the northern frontier to cooperate with the Americans in calming border tensions.
Now, even as Treviño amiably socialized with Ord and Shafter
at Fort Clark, new instructions sped to him: "Repel force with
force."[15]

Ord liked the Mexican general and wanted to avoid such a confrontation. Even so, one very nearly occurred in September 1877,
when Shafter tried to repeat his successful strategy of July 1876.
Sending Bullis and nearly 100 cavalrymen and scouts against
a Lipan camp reported 20 miles west of Zaragosa, Shafter followed with six troops of cavalry, almost 300 men. After attacking
and destroying the village, Bullis rode for an appointed rendezvous—but with the Zaragosa garrison of about 100 cavalrymen
on his trail. Discovery of Shafter's formidable command, however, inspired a fortunate caution in the Mexican leader, Col. Ino-
cente Rodriguez. The two forces maneuvered at each other for a
time, but no encounter developed. Shafter, also suddenly seized
by a prudence born of the explosive potential of the situation, got
out of Mexico so precipitately that his officers grumbled about
turning tail before "a handful of Mexicans." The incident intensified the anti-American fever in Mexico and further impeded a
settlement of the differences between the two nations.[16]

In Washington, the administration's belligerent Mexican policy
came under mounting attack. Democrats accused the President of
trying to drum up a foreign war to divert public attention from
the questionable credentials with which he had entered the White
House after the disputed election of 1876. Merchants and finan-
ciers with Mexican interests fretted over the delay in resuming

normal relations. When Congress convened in special session in October 1877, both the foreign affairs and military affairs committees of the House looked into the border controversy. High officials of the State and War Departments testified, as did Ord, Shafter, and Bullis. Shafter in particular came under heavy fire from Democratic interrogators, who forced him to admit that he sought opportunities to cross the border and did not adhere to the limitations of hot pursuit. He even confessed his opinion that the best solution was to demand that Mexico stop the raids, and if she failed, to declare war.[17]

Such uncomplicated and extreme solutions disturbed General Sherman, especially since he knew that Ord privately entertained similar views.[18] In fact, Sherman had come increasingly to share Sheridan's assessment that a large measure of the border turmoil would subside if Ord were withdrawn. "I have lost confidence in his motives," Sheridan complained to his superior late in 1877, "and his management of his department is a confusion which is demoralizing to his subordinates." "I am more than convinced," Sherman confessed in reply, "that a cooler & less spasmodic man in Texas would do more to compose matters on that border than the mere increase of the Cavalry." But to remove Ord now would seriously damage his reputation, and Sherman was not prepared to do that to his West Point classmate and long-time friend.[19]

Also, Ord's removal would almost certainly be unfavorably received in Texas, and during the winter of 1877–78 Sherman found himself virtually a hostage to the Texas congressional delegation. In the special legislative session that began in October 1877, the Democrats resumed their effort to emasculate the army (see Chapter Four), and Texas' Democratic representatives held the key. "The Texas members claim that we of the Army owe them a debt of gratitude for saving the Army Bill this Extra Session," Sherman wrote to Sheridan on November 29, 1877, "which is true for the Democrats had the power and were resolved to cut us down to 20,000 this Session and to 17,000 in the Regular Term. There is some force to this claim, and unless we can reconcile the Texas Democrats in the House, we will be slaughtered this winter." Sherman urged his subordinate to do everything possible to reduce border irritations, "as well as to quiet the clamor of the Texas people, and of the *Texas Representatives*."[20] One move sure to help still the clamor could be made at once. On December 3, 1877,

Sheridan ordered the return to Texas of Mackenzie and the Fourth Cavalry.[21]

Threatened with embarrassing congressional action, President Hayes at length relented, and in April 1878 extended recognition to the Díaz government. But Mexico still refused to treat seriously for a resolution of border problems so long as the offensive order of June 1, 1877, to General Ord remained in force. And Ord, dramatizing the administration's determination to let the order stand, saw to it that the U.S. flag again appeared south of the Rio Grande—this time in a parade surpassing all others in ostentation. Mackenzie commanded.

The Mackenzie expedition consisted of eight troops of cavalry, three battalions of infantry under Colonel Shafter, three batteries of artillery (including one of Gatling guns), Bullis' scouts, and a train of forty wagons—more than one thousand men. Seizing the first opportunity to cross on a fresh trail, Mackenzie and advance elements of the command forded the Rio Grande above the mouth of Devil's River on June 12, 1878, leaving the main force to follow under Shafter. They reunited on the upper Rio San Diego five days later. From here, the column marched to the head of the San Rodrigo and down that stream toward the Rio Grande. At Remolino on June 19 and again at Monclova Viejo on June 21, Mexican troops drew up to block the advance. Each time Mackenzie sent word that he was coming through; then, as the cavalry maneuvered, Shafter marched the infantry directly at the Mexican line. Each time, the Mexican force gave way rather than contend with the overwhelmingly superior aggressors. After twice humiliating the Mexicans, Mackenzie recrossed the Rio Grande.[22]

Blatantly violating Mexican territory, the Mackenzie expedition still further inflamed public opinion in Mexico. Rumors of impending war with the United States swept the capital. The Díaz government protested forcefully, pointing out that expeditions of this size and composition obviously had purposes other than chasing a handful of Indians. The Foreign Office made clear that the invasion had severely imperiled the progress of treaty negotiations on the border issue. But Díaz kept the crisis in hand.[23]

Although relations between the United States and Mexico remained tense for another two years, forces were at work that would resolve the problem. Díaz steadily consolidated his regime and gave undoubted evidence of its stability. Of compelling influence in Washington, he manifested a receptivity to American investment in Mexico that lined up American capitalists on the side of amicable relations. And on the border, raiding activity declined markedly, owing in part to the vigor of U.S. operations in Mexico under the order of June 1, 1877, and also in part to a series of campaigns prosecuted by General Treviño in 1878—the latter, American officers believed, motivated largely by humiliation at the repeated border crossings by U.S. troops. Díaz continued to insist on revocation of the June 1 order as the price of a reciprocal crossing treaty. With the conditions that had prompted it much alleviated, President Hayes finally, in 1880, paid the price. And in 1882, following consent by the Mexican senate, Díaz at last agreed to a treaty.[24]

Viewed as a purely military enterprise, the operations of Shafter and, later, Mackenzie attract admiration. They visited enough punishment on the offending Indians to discourage them from raiding in Texas and prompted Mexico, once the Díaz revolution had been consolidated, to make more than perfunctory efforts to restrain them. Lieutenant Bullis deserves major credit for this success, for he served as the main striking arm, first of Shafter, then of Mackenzie. He proved himself one of the frontier army's ablest junior officers, and his Seminole-Negroes compiled a record that marked them as perhaps the most consistently effective Indian auxiliaries the army employed.

Viewed in a larger perspective than the purely military, the Mexican adventures of Ord, Mackenzie, and Shafter appear in less creditable light, at least to posterity. At best, they revealed the United States taking advantage of the domestic distractions of a less-powerful neighbor to bully her into compliance with difficult demands. At worst, they partook of scarcely veiled projects for the seizure of still more Mexican territory. Such imperial aspirations, loudly articulated by Texas editors and politicians, strongly appealed to both Ord and Shafter. How far they abetted this "clamor," as Sherman and Sheridan termed it, and how far in turn the clamor exaggerated the magnitude of border lawlessness, is not clear. The belief of Sherman and Sheridan that Ord's departure would calm matters is at least suggestive.

Ord continued to give dissatisfaction to Sheridan, who resented his habit of writing personal letters to Sherman on official subjects and who complained on December 12, 1879:

356] FRONTIER REGULARS

General Ord's eccentricity of character and the devious methods he employs to accomplish his ends, some time since forced me to doubt his motives in some of his official actions and so much has this impression gained on me that for a long time I have reluctantly avoided any personal correspondence with him. I have doubted his motives in some of his recommendations for expenditures of public money and even in his calls for and disposition of troops; and the facility with which revolutions, raids, murders and thefts are generated on the Rio Grande border whenever an emergency demands the temporary withdrawal of troops or even a special officer from the Department of Texas is somewhat remarkable.[25]

With border troubles subsiding, Sherman probably would have found a way to transfer Ord gracefully to another assignment. But late in 1880, in a move that outraged Sherman and sent shock waves through the army, President Hayes forcibly retired Ord in order to give his star to Nelson A. Miles. Easing the blow somewhat, a grateful Texas congressional delegation secured passage of an act elevating Ord to full major general on the retired list.[26]

If Texans could complain of Indian incursions from Coahuila, so with equal bitterness could Chihuahuans and Sonorans complain of Indian incursions from New Mexico and Arizona. Military pressure on the Mescalero Apaches in 1870–71, General Howard's pact with Cochise and the Chiricahua Apaches in 1872, and General Crook's Apache and Yavapai campaigns of 1872–73 gave New Mexico and Arizona an interval of near peace. But Mexicans did not share in it. Mescaleros based on the Fort Stanton Reservation, New Mexico, continued to raid in Chihuahua. More devastating were plundering expeditions launched into both Chihuahua and Sonora from the Chiricahua Reservation, whose southern boundary conveniently coincided with the border between Sonora and Arizona. Moreover, although clouded with uncertainty, the Howard-Cochise agreement seems to have included a promise that the army would stay away from the Chiricahua Reservation, and Cochise, at least, understood further that continued marauding in Mexico would not be regarded in the United States as a breach of the peace. Mexican officials, viewing both ends of the border, could be forgiven an inability to reconcile United States policies on the Arizona frontier with those pursued so intransigently on the Texas frontier.[27]

Actually, United States policies were aimed at controlling the Apaches—not so much to end the raiding in Mexico as to prevent its resumption in the United States. How best to insure this control sorely plagued—and badly divided—civil and military officials. Army officers insisted that only military force could guarantee control, and General Crook, enjoying high prestige among both Arizonans and Indians as a result of his victorious campaigns of 1872–73, ruled the Apache reservations in fact, if not in form. Incensed civil officials contested his dictatorial methods, and the resulting friction kept the reservations in turmoil. Not until 1875, after Crook had transferred to the Department of the Platte, was civil authority successfully asserted.

Leading the challenge was John P. Clum, a pugnacious, bombastic, and utterly uninhibited youth of twenty-three who became agent at San Carlos Reservation in 1874. Through a combination of honesty, trust, courage, and shrewd judgment, backed by an Indian police force to supply coercion when needed, Clum succeeded simply by managing the Apaches without military help. At the same time, he confounded his military detractors with an unceasing barrage of charges, threats, and denunciations. An especially favored target was Crook's successor, August V. Kautz, colonel of the Eighth Infantry but assigned to departmental command in his brevet grade of major general—as Sherman explained it, through President Grant's "natural and proper predilection to his old comrades." Although something of a controversialist himself, Kautz met his match in Clum.[28]

The civil-military conflict sounded a dominant theme throughout a series of moves that, although not initially conceived as a comprehensive policy, still in sum added up to one. Designed to promote both control and economy, these moves brought about the concentration of the scattered Apache groups on the furnace-like patch of rocky desert at San Carlos, on the upper Gila River. Fifteen hundred Aravaipas and Pinals moved there from Camp Grant in 1873. In March 1875 the Indian Bureau closed out the Camp Verde Reservation and sent its residents, some 1,400 Yavapai and associated peoples, to San Carlos. Four months later, about 1,800 Coyoteros moved down from the high country around Fort Apache.[29]

Next to go were the troublesome Chiricahuas, whose reservation had continued to provide a base for raids into Mexico not

only by Chiricahuas but by visiting Apaches from other reservations. Agent Tom Jeffords' influence on the Chiricahuas had diminished after the death of Cochise in June 1874. Taza and
Nachez lacked their father's strength, and the tribe began to
break into factions. Jeffords, never popular with the Indian
Bureau, came under mounting attack both from Arizona officials
and from his own superiors. Finally, early in 1876, Clum received
orders to move the Chiricahuas to San Carlos. They feuded bitterly over whether to go peacefully. General Kautz concentrated
the entire Sixth Cavalry to help them make up their minds. After
the peace and war factions had fought out the issue, with eight
killed, the tribe acquiesced. On June 12, 1876, Clum led 325
Chiricahuas northward to new homes.[30]

Abolition of the Chiricahua Reservation not only failed to bring
relief to Mexican frontier settlements, but also precipitated a
revival of hostilities in Arizona and New Mexico. Clum had removed less than half the Chiricahuas to San Carlos. The balance,
about 400, went to New Mexico or faded into the Sierra Madre,
the massive, towering mountain range dominating western Mexico
that offered Apaches a fortress and a refuge. These Chiricahuas,
aided by friends from the Ojo Caliente Reservation in southwestern New Mexico, murdered and plundered on both sides of
the border. Their principal leaders were Juh, Noglee, and a cunning, vicious fighter whose squat, thick-set figure would soon become the terror of the Southwest—Geronimo.

General Kautz believed that the seriousness of the depredations
was exaggerated, part of an effort to force him to move department headquarters from Prescott to Tucson. This campaign he
attributed to the "Tucson Ring," that sinister combination of
contractors and their political friends that the army blamed for
many of its Arizona frustrations. Whether or not such a "ring"
really existed, Kautz, like his predecessors and successors, fulmi-
nated against it. Rancorous feuds with Governor Safford, Agent
Clum, and other public figures preoccupied Kautz and led to
demands for his removal.[31]

But the renewed border violence compelled attention. Kautz
energized his garrisons and established two new posts—Camp
Thomas on the Gila River upstream from San Carlos Agency and
Camp Huachuca, close to the border southeast of Tucson. Working out of Fort Bowie, Lts. Austin Heneley and John A. Rucker

of the Sixth Cavalry performed especially notable service during the winter of 1876–77.[32] Col. Edward Hatch, commanding the District of New Mexico, set troops from Forts Bayard, Cummings, Selden, and McRae to policing the border. But it remained to the brash young San Carlos agent to neutralize, however temporarily, the menace of Geronimo and the Chiracahuas.

Clum's feat, of which he boasted loudly the rest of his long life, resulted from a growing understanding of the role of the Ojo Caliente Reservation in fostering hostilities. The Indians on this reservation—about 400 Southern or "Warm Springs" Apaches, representing a mix of the Mimbres, Gila, and Mogollon groups— had long been close friends and allies of the Chiricahuas. Some of the Chiracahuas had settled here after the removal of their kins- men to San Carlos in June 1876. Also, Geronimo and the Chirica- huas from Mexico made Ojo Caliente a rest, supply, and recruiting depot for raiding expeditions. Ordered to abolish the reservation and take its occupants to San Carlos, Clum arrived at Ojo Caliente Agency on April 20, 1877. The eight troops of the Ninth Cavalry sent by Colonel Hatch to assist had not appeared yet, but the presence of Geronimo and his band made it imperative to act at once. In a tense and perilous confrontation, Clum and his Indian policeman faced down the Apache leader. When Maj. James F. Wade and his column marched in on April 22, they found Geronimo and sixteen other hostile leaders shackled in the agency jail. Rounding up all the Indians who could be located, 343 Warm Springs Apaches and 110 Chiricahuas, Clum headed them west on the trail to San Carlos.[33]

The Warm Springs Apaches did not remain long at San Carlos. They had not wanted to leave their New Mexico homeland, and indeed, rather than do so, many of the men had simply slipped away to the mountains. For those who went, San Carlos proved every bit as uncongenial as expected. The military-civil conflict, which caused Clum's resignation in July 1877, and a growing antipathy among the diverse tribes now collected there contributed to the unrest. The principal Warm Springs chief was not one to tolerate a disagreeable situation. A worthy successor of the great Mangas Coloradas, Victorio was a dynamic, aggressive leader, impatient of any form of restraint, highly skilled in the methods of Apache warfare. On September 2, 1877, he led his people and some Chiricahuas, 310 in all, in a break from San Carlos.

For two years, 1877–79, Victorio traced a bewildering course around New Mexico trying to find a home satisfactory both to him and to the government. The break from San Carlos quickly collapsed as troops and Indian police harried the fugitives into surrendering at Fort Wingate, New Mexico. The army held them at Ojo Caliente, their old home, while the Indian Bureau pondered the problem and finally, almost a year later, decided to return them to San Carlos. Victorio refused to go and with about eighty men took to the mountains while the women, children, and old men journeyed back to the hated Arizona reservation. Early in 1879 Victorio again attempted to settle at Ojo Caliente, then in June appeared at the Tularosa Agency of the Mescalero Apaches, east of the Rio Grande, to investigate the possibility of living there. Cordially welcomed by the agent, who promised to try to have the Warm Springs families transferred from San Carlos, the chief at last seemed to have found a home. On September 4, 1879, however, suddenly persuaded that he was to be arrested and sent to Silver City for trial, he decamped once again. His own people, some Chiricahuas, and a few restless Mescaleros accompanied him. Two days later a war party of about sixty Apaches wiped out the eight-man herd guard of Troop E, Ninth Cavalry, at Ojo Caliente, and made off with forty-six horses. Victorio had declared war.[34]

During September and October 1879 Victorio's warriors spread over their mountain homeland in southwestern New Mexico, killing an occasional sheepherder or rancher who came within reach. Colonel Hatch deployed most of the Ninth Cavalry to the scene of action. After several skirmishes with the black troopers, Victorio gathered his men and headed for Mexico. Maj. A. P. Morrow followed across the border with a command so badly diminished and exhausted by hard service that Victorio easily held his own when overtaken near the Corralitos River on October 27. Morrow limped back across the line to Fort Bayard.[35]

The hostiles rested in the Candelaria Mountains of northern Chihuahua. More warriors joined them—chiefly Mescaleros from the Tularosa Reservation and from the bands in the Sierra del Carmen against which Shafter and Bullis had campaigned in 1876–78. From 60 men, Victorio's following grew to between 125 and 150. He showed his strength by ambushing and virtually annihilating two parties of Mexicans from Carrizal. This atrocity, taking the lives of twenty-six men in all, aroused General Treviño, who organized an expedition against the Apaches late in December. Almost at once, in January 1880, they slipped back across the border into the United States. Three times they clashed indecisively with Morrow's troopers in the San Andres Mountains, then disappeared.[36]

Late in February 1880 Colonel Hatch came south to take personal charge. Convinced that the hostiles drew supplies and recruits from the Tularosa Reservation, he won permission to disarm and dismount the agency Indians. To bolster his undermanned and worn-out regiment, two troops of the Sixth Cavalry and two Indian scout companies came from Arizona, and Col. Benjamin H. Grierson was to march from Texas with five troops of the Tenth Cavalry. Hatch intended to converge on the agency from the west and meet Grierson, moving from the east.

The timing was arranged to allow Hatch's command to probe the San Andres Mountains. Intelligence reports placed Victorio in Hembrillo Canyon, and Hatch planned to meet a column from Fort Stanton there on April 7. A broken water pump at Aleman Well delayed the colonel, and he pushed forward Capt. Curwen B. McLellan with 125 Sixth Cavalrymen and Indian scouts to keep the appointment. Reaching the canyon on the morning of April 8, McLellan found the Fort Stanton squadron, 100 black troopers under Capt. Henry Carroll, pinned down and closely pressed by Victorio's warriors. McLellan attacked at once and, joining with Carroll's men, drove the Apaches out of the canyon. They made good their escape by quietly stealing around Hatch, who was coming up with the balance of the command under Morrow. Captain Carroll and seven enlisted men had been wounded in the fight. Carroll claimed three Apaches killed, but only one body was found on the battlefield. Bad luck had cost Hatch a rare opportunity to destroy Victorio.[37]

The disarming of the Mescaleros went badly. Hatch and Grierson met at the Tularosa Agency on April 12. By the sixteenth they had succeeded in assembling about 320 Indians. The disarming had barely begun when firing broke out and the Indians stampeded up a mountainside. Grierson's cavalry charged in pursuit. A few Mescaleros fell victim to the carbine fire, between thirty and fifty escaped to join Victorio, and the rest returned quietly to their homes that night. Although Hatch and Grierson seized few arms, the sobering effect of this experience on the Mescaleros, reinforced by the presence of a strong guard left behind by Hatch, virtually eliminated the Tularosa Agency as a haven and supply base for Victorio.[38]

After Hembrillo Canyon, Victorio and his followers had gone back to their mountain homeland west of the Rio Grande. Throughout May 1880 they killed and pillaged in the Black and Mogollon ranges, around Silver City, and even as far west as San Carlos, in Arizona, where their families still resided. (That the Indian Bureau fed the women and children while the army fought the men enraged Sherman. "Does not this magnanimity verge on the borders of folly?" he asked.[39]) Trying to bring the raiders to bay, Hatch and Morrow wore out and all but dismounted the Ninth Cavalry. At length, on May 23, an Indian scout company under H. K. Parker struck Victorio in the Black Range near the head of the Palomas River, a tributary of the Rio Grande. In a desperate fight, the scouts killed thirty hostiles and reportedly wounded Victorio in the leg before withdrawing because of depleted water and ammunition. After this setback, Victorio once again headed for Mexico. Major Morrow's squadron of the Ninth twice intercepted the fugitives, but failed to prevent their escape across the boundary.[40]

Certain that Victorio would return as soon as he had rested, Hatch asked to have Colonel Grierson again sent up from Texas to help. Grierson protested. Instead, he wished to distribute his command, eight troops of the Tenth Cavalry and four companies of the Twenty-fourth Infantry, along the Rio Grande west of Fort Davis and thus transfer the battleground from New Mexico to Texas. This would avoid the need to leave Texas unprotected and, if successful, keep the hostiles away from the Mescalero Reservation and nearby settlements. General Ord backed Grierson, and on June 28 General Sheridan consented.[41]

Grierson had won a rare opportunity. A mild-mannered, big-hearted man, he had not fared well in the postwar army. He owed his Tenth Cavalry commission to the famed "Grierson's Raid" through Mississippi in 1863. But lack of West Point credentials, identification with black troops, and the active personal enmity of General Sheridan helped make his frontier career frustrating and undistinguished. He now made the most of his chance. Rather than breaking down his troops in fruitless pursuit, as Hatch had done, he posted them at key water holes at which the enemy was likely to stop. His judgment that Victorio would reenter the United States through Texas rather than New Mexico proved correct. Hounded by nearly 500 Mexican troops under Col. Adolph Valle, the elusive Apache crossed the Rio Grande late in July 1880. He promptly became enmeshed in Grierson's web of sub-posts.

Grierson himself held the position that turned out to be crucial —a water hole named Tinaja de las Palmas in parched Quitman Canyon. With two officers, twenty-one cavalrymen, and his teen-age son Robert, the colonel had fortified the position upon learning of Victorio's approach up the canyon at the head of 150 warriors. On the morning of July 30, the little force of black cavalrymen held off the attacking Indians until relief columns, previously summoned, charged onto the battlefield from both east and west, "& golly," wrote young Robert in his diary, "you ought to've seen 'em turn tail & strike for the hills."[42] Thwarted in several attempts to pass, the Apaches pulled back into Mexico.

Again on August 2 Victorio crossed into Texas and, after two days of maneuvering, slipped through the screen of soldiers and rode northward on the west side of the forbidding Sierra Diablo Range, aiming for the Mescalero Reservation. With two troops of cavalry, Grierson raced northward, marching sixty-five miles in twenty-one hours. Bolstered by two more troops, he took posses-sion of strategic Rattlesnake Springs and on the afternoon of August 6, in a sharp but bloodless exchange of fire, kept the Apaches away from the water hole. Later in the day, eight miles to the east, the warriors jumped a provision train en route from Fort Davis. The escorting infantrymen held their own while Grier-son's cavalry rode to the rescue and drove off the attackers. Baffled, Victorio once again turned back to Mexico.

Victorio next became the objective of combined Mexican-Ameri-can operations. In February 1880 President Hayes had revoked the objectionable order of June 1, 1877, authorizing U.S. troops to cross the border without Mexican permission, and President Díaz, in turn, proved receptive to proposals for cooperative action against Victorio. In September 1880, while Grierson guarded the Rio Grande frontier, Col. George P. Buell crossed into Chihuahua with a large expedition of infantry and cavalry from New Mexico, and Col. Eugene A. Carr marched from Arizona with nearly all of the Sixth Cavalry to join him. They were to unite with Col. Joaquin Terrazas and about 1,000 Mexican troops for a sweep through Victorio's favorite haunts in the Candelaria Mountains.

These plans went awry when it became apparent that Victorio had gone farther south. The prospect of so many American soldiers plunging so deep into Chihuahua was disquieting to Mexicans. There is also more than a suggestion that Colonel Terrazas, a prominent political figure, felt confident of destroying Victorio without foreign help and did not intend to share any credit with Americans. Citing Buell's Apache scouts as objectionable, he therefore ordered the U.S. commanders to leave Mexico at once. Five days later, as the American troops made their way back toward the border, Terrazas trapped Victorio in a canyon of the Tres Castillos Mountains and next morning, October 15, 1880, attacked. Sixty warriors and eighteen women and children died in the slaughter. This time Victorio's legendary cunning failed him. A bullet from the rifle of a Tarahumari Indian auxiliary ended his extraordinary career.[43]

The remnant of Victorio's following, those who escaped the battle and those who were absent from camp on that fatal day, gave allegiance to wrinkled, battle-scarred old Nana, whose remarkable powers had been diminished only slightly by an age approaching, if not exceeding, seventy years. In July and August 1881 Nana and fifteen warriors swept through southwestern New Mexico in a memorable raid that led Colonel Hatch and his Ninth Cavalry in an exhausting chase featuring no less than a dozen small-unit combat actions.[44] Then suddenly the area of Apache hostilities shifted westward, to Arizona and Sonora, and Nana turned up as a lieutenant to a leader fully as able as Victorio and even more difficult and costly to run down—Geronimo.

The services of Hatch and Grierson and the Ninth and Tenth Cavalry in the Victorio War of 1879–80 earned the bitter denunciation of frontier editors in the areas afflicted by Victorio's incursions and have ever since been overshadowed by the scarcely more dramatic campaigns against Geronimo. One respected authority ascribes this to a tendency, then and later, to underrate or even ridicule the achievements of the black regiments.[45] In truth, as both Generals Ord and Pope acknowledged, the black soldiers who pursued Victorio had endured some of the most punishing ordeals in the history of the Indian wars. The deserts and mountains of southern New Mexico and western Texas quickly broke down conventional troops. Of the Black Range and San Mateo Mountains, Hatch wrote: "The well known Modoc lava beds are a lawn compared with them." Yet despite a condition of almost constant exhaustion, the black soldiers kept at the task, four times prompting Victorio to drop into Mexico to rest and refit. Hatch and Morrow did as well as could be expected considering the hostility of the land and the skills of their adversary. Grierson conducted a masterly campaign that turned the land's hostile features back on the enemy. Victorio at last met his match in Chihuahua, but in Texas and New Mexico he met some worthy foes.

NOTES

1. Excellent analyses of border problems are in J. Fred Rippy, *The United States and Mexico* (New York, 1926), chaps. 9, 16, 17; and Robert D. Gregg, *The Influence of Border Troubles on Relations between the United States and Mexico, 1876–1910* (Baltimore, Md., 1937). See also Clarence C. Clendenen, *Blood on the Border: The United States Army and the Mexican Irregulars* (New York, 1969), chap. 4.
2. SW, *Annual Report* (1873), pp. 62–63, 68–69.
3. Kenneth W. Porter, "The Seminole-Negro Indian Scouts, 1870–1881," *Southwestern Historical Quarterly*, 55 (1951–52), 358–77. Kenneth W. Porter and Edward S. Wallace, "Thunderbolt of the Frontier," *The Westerners New York Posse Brand Book*, 8 (1961), 73–75, 82–86.
4. The clearest and most detailed description of these Indians and their habits was by William Schurchardt, U.S. consul at Piedras Negras, in annex to House Reports, 45th Cong., 2d sess., No. 701, pp. 40–45. See also Lieutenant Bullis' testimony in House Misc. Docs., 45th Cong., 2d sess., No. 64, pp. 190–91.
5. The Kickapoo problem is well presented in A. M. Gibson, *The Kickapoos, Lords of the Middle Border* (Norman, Okla., 1963), chaps. 15–18. See also Wallace, *Ranald S. Mackenzie on the Texas Frontier*, chap. 6; and Wallace and Adrian S. Anderson, "R. S. Mackenzie and the Kickapoos: The Raid into Mexico in 1873," *Arizona and the West*, 7 (1965), 105–26.
6. Carter, *On the Border with Mackenzie*, pp. 422–23.
7. For the Battle of Remolino, see sources cited in notes 5 and 6 above. Official correspondence is in Wallace, ed., *Ranald S. Mackenzie's Official Correspondence Relating to Texas, 1871–1873*, Part III. See also E. B. Beaumont, "Over the Border with Mackenzie," *United Service*, 12 (1885), 281–88.
8. Sherman to Sheridan, June 3, 1873, Sherman-Sheridan Letters, Sheridan Papers; Sheridan to Sherman, June 6, 1873, Sherman Papers, Vol. 35. LC.
9. Gibson, chaps. 18–19.
10. House Misc. Docs., 45th Cong., 2d sess., No. 64, p. 26.
11. Shafter is well characterized in Parker, *The Old Army*, pp. 100–1; and in Crane, *Experiences of a Colonel of Infantry*, pp. 64, 82, 85, 256. I have written of Shafter in "Pecos Bill on the Texas Frontier," *The American West*, 6 (1969), 4–13, 61–62, upon which portions of this chapter are based.

12. House Misc. Docs., 45th Cong., 2d sess., No. 64, pp. 158–59, 168, 188. The Shafter Papers at Stanford University contain a few documents bearing on border crossings, which I have used through the courtesy of Erwin N. Thompson. See also Porter, "The Seminole-Negro Scouts," p. 370.

13. House Ex. Docs., 45th Cong., 1st sess., No. 13, pp. 9, 11, 56–59. House Misc. Docs., 45th Cong., 2d sess., No. 64, pp. 179–80.

14. This story is well developed in Rippy, chap. 17; Gregg, chap. 2; and, from the Mexican viewpoint, Daniel Cosío Villegas, *The United States Versus Porfirio Díaz*, Nettie Lee Benson, trans. (Lincoln, Neb., 1963).

15. House Ex. Docs., 45th Cong., 1st sess., No. 13, pp. 14–15, 18, 59–61, 71–72, 145–47, 159. House Misc. Docs., 45th Cong., 2d sess., No. 64, pp. 7, 33, 94. House Reports, 45th Cong., 2d sess., No. 701, pp. 448–50. Gregg, chap. 2.

16. House Ex. Docs., 45th Cong., 1st sess., No. 13, pp. 53–54, 240–41. House Misc. Docs., 45th Cong., 2d sess., No 64, pp. 169, 191–93, 268–69. House Ex. Docs., 45th Cong., 3d sess., Vol. 1, "Foreign Relations," pp. 532–33. Bullis to Dodt, Oct. 12, 1877, Shafter Papers, Stanford, University.

17. House Misc. Docs., 45th Cong., 2d sess., No. 64. House Reports, 45th Cong., 2d sess., No. 701. See also House Ex. Docs., 45th Cong., 1st sess., No. 13.

18. Sherman to Ord, Nov. 2, 1876, Sherman Papers, vol. 90, pp. 451–53. Ord to Sherman, April 2, 1877, *ibid.*, vol. 46, LC.

19. Sheridan to Sherman, Nov. 24, 1877, Sherman Papers, vol. 47. Sherman to Sheridan, Nov. 29, 1877, Sherman-Sheridan Letters, Sheridan Papers, LC.

20. Sherman-Sheridan Letters, Sheridan Papers, LC.

21. Wallace, ed., *Ranald S. Mackenzie's Official Correspondence Relating to Texas, 1873–79*, p. 201.

22. For this expedition see *ibid.*, Pt. III; Wallace, *Ranald S. Mackenzie on the Texas Frontier*, chap. 10; Crane, pp. 73–77; Parker, pp. 104–12; and the following documents in RG 94, National Archives: Mackenzie to Vincent, May 28, 1878; Ord to Mackenzie, May 30, 1878; Sheridan to Townsend, June 4, 1878; and Mackenzie's report, June 23, 1878.

23. House Ex. Docs., 45th Cong., 3d sess., "Foreign Affairs," pp. 557–57, 570–74.

24. Gregg, chap. 3. Rippy, chaps. 7–8. SW, *Annual Report* (1879), pp. 6–7, 44–45, 85–86, 89–93.

25. Sheridan to Sherman (confidential), Dec. 12, 1879, Sherman Papers, vol. 51, LC.

26. In Sherman's observation, President Hayes was easily moved by personal appeals, and he had bowed to the continued imprecations of Miles' many friends and promised to promote him to brigadier general. He could do this before leaving office on March 4, 1881, only by forcibly retiring a general who had reached the age of sixty-two. Major General McDowell and Brigadier General Ord were the two who qualified. Of the two, McDowell was older, more senior, and by far wealthier. But he also enjoyed the friendship of Hayes and President-elect Garfield.

After returning from a trip to San Francisco, McDowell's headquarters, with Hayes, Sherman wrote to Terry: "McDowell entertained us in San Francisco in the sumptuous manner for which he is distinguished, and for which he is abundantly able. He also came east with a flourish to vote for Garfield in New York, where votes were wanted. Nevertheless, the moment I heard that the President had called Miles here I saw that Ord's commission was in danger. I was Ord's chum at West Point, served with him side by side ten years in Florida, the South, and California, and am familiar with his career since. He is a rough diamond, always at work on the most distant frontier; has a far better war record, and is a hardier, stronger soldier than McDowell [in] every way; he is as poor as a rat, having been all his life taxed with the care of parents and a large family. I was, therefore, bound as a man to go to his rescue, when I feared that neglect would result in an act of palpable, gross injustice. I put it in writing that if the President would retire McDowell and Ord, I and all would say amen, but if Ord alone would be forced out, I believed the Army and the world [would] cry shame!" Sherman to Terry, Dec. 5, 1880, Sherman Papers, vol. 91, pp. 541–44, LC.

Later in December Sherman wrote to President-elect Garfield: "I entertain for General McDowell the same friendly feeling, which I know you do, but I then believed, and now believe that [his retirement] would have saved you in time the delicacy of action in McDowell's case which must arise in your administration, for I have such faith in your sense of manly justice, that you cannot go on sparing McDowell, to retire others equally or more meritorious to give places to the young vigorous Colonels, who are moving heaven and earth to secure promotion, among whom I will name Getty, Mackenzie, Hatch, Grierson, Merritt, Gibbon, Willcox, &c, &c, who commanded corps and Divisions during the war, and who properly claim recognition. My judgment was and is that the passing over McDowell to reach Ord was a terrible discrimination, calculated to shake the faith of the Army in what is construed Justice, without which no officer or soldier will strive for excellence, or be disposed to serve his country in distant stations with fidelity and zeal, preferring to seek promotion by intrigue and favor." Dec. 20, 1880, vol. 91, pp. 571–73. See also Ord to Sherman, Nov. 11, 1880, vol. 53; Sherman to Ord, Nov. 19, 1880, vol. 91, pp. 524–25; Sherman to Sen. S. B. Maxey, Dec. 17, 1880, vol. 91, 562–63, all in Sehrman Papers, LC. See also Sherman to Sheridan, Nov. 13 and 19, 1880, Sherman Sheridan Letters, vol. 2, Sheridan Papers, LC.

27. For affairs on the Chiricahua Reservation, see Ogle, *Federal Control of the Western Apaches*, pp. 133 passim.

28. The Sherman quote is in Sherman to Kautz, Feb. 26, 1876, Sherman Papers, vol. 90, pp. 540–41, LC. The Clum story is told in Ogle, chap. 6, and Thrapp, *The Conquest of Apacheria*, chap. 14. Clum's version is in a series of polemics in the *New Mexico Historical Review:* "Apache Misrule," *5* (1930), 138–53, 221–39; "Geronimo," *3* (1928), 1–40, 121–44, 217–64; "The San Carlos Apache Police," *4* (1929), 203–19, *5* (1930), 67–92; "Victorio," *4* (1929), 107–27. See also Woodworth Clum, *Apache Agent: The Story of John P. Clum* (New York, 1936). An excellent history of Kautz' regime is Andrew Wallace, *Gen. August V. Kautz and the Southwestern Frontier* (Unpublished Ph.D. dissertation, University of Arizona, 1967).

29. CIA, *Annual Report* (1873), pp. 289–90; (1875). pp. 42–43, 215–20.

30. SW, *Annual Report* (1876), pp. 98–99. CIA, *Annual Report* (1876), pp. 3–4, 10–12. Ogle, pp. 162–70. Thrapp, pp. 169–70.

31. SW, *Annual Report* (1877), pp. 138–47. *Army and Navy Journal, 14* (April 7, 1877), 563. Kautz to Sherman, April 9, 1877, Sherman Papers, vol. 46, LC. Wallace, *Gen. August V. Kautz*, chap. 10.

32. Kautz' operations are detailed in SW, *Annual Report* (1877), pp. 133–37.

33. Ogle, pp. 172–75. Thrapp, pp. 171–76. Clum, "Geronimo." CIA, *Annual Report* (1877), pp. 20–21; (1879), pp. xxxviii–xxxix.

34. Thrapp, pp. 179–81. CIA, *Annual Report* (1879), pp. xxxviii–xl, 114; (1880), pp. xliv, 120.

35. SW, *Annual Report* (1880), p. 86. Sheridan, *Record of Engagements*, p. 92. Leckie, *The Buffalo Soldiers*, pp. 210–14. Thrapp, pp. 182–88.

36. Leckie, pp. 214–15. Thrapp, pp. 189–93. James B. Gillett, *Six Years with the Texas Rangers* (New Haven, Conn., 1925), chap. 13.

37. SW, *Annual Report* (1880), pp. 94–95. Leckie, pp. 215–16. Thrapp, pp. 194–97. Thomas Cruse, *Apache Days and After* (Caldwell, Ida., 1941), chap. 6.

38. SW, *Annual Report* (1880), pp. 93–98, 154–57. CIA, *Annual Report*

(1880), pp. 129–30. Cruse, pp. 77–80. Thrapp, pp. 197–98. Leckie, pp. 217–19.

39. *Army and Navy Journal, 17* (March 27, 1880), 693.
40. SW, *Annual Report* (1880), pp. 96–110. Thrapp, pp. 198–203. Leckie, pp. 219–22.
41. For Grierson's operations, see his unusually complete report in SW, *Annual Report* (1880), pp. 158–63; Thrapp, 203–7; and Leckie, pp. 223–28. I have written events in *Fort Davis National Historic Site, Texas* (National Park Service Historical Handbook, Washington, D.C., 1965), pp. 42–45.
42. Robert Grierson Diary, Fort Davis National Historic Site, Texas.
43. Thrapp, pp. 207–10. Leckie, pp. 227–29. Cruse, chap. 7. Gillett, chap. 15. King, *War Eagle*, pp. 192–94. Martin L. Crimmins, ed., "Colonel Buell's Expedition into Mexico in 1880," *New Mexico Historical Review, 10* (1935), 133–42.
44. Sheridan, *Record of Engagements*, pp. 99–100.
45. Leckie, pp. 224–25.

☆ NINETEEN ☆

Geronimo, 1881-86

AMONG APACHE LEADERS at the beginning of the 1880s, many boasted larger stature than Geronimo. Aged Nana, Victorio's successor, combined the roles of elder statesman and vigorous war chief. Corpulent, mischievous Juh led the Nednhi band—Chiricahuas and others who made their home in Mexico's Sierra Madre and their living by raiding settlements. Able, intelligent Chihuahua headed a Chiricahua band. Nachez, second son of Cochise but a weak leader, had succeeded to the chieftainship of the reservation Chiricahuas following his brother's death during a trip to Washington, D.C., in 1876. Kaytennae (Nana's heir apparent), Loco, Benito, Zele, Noglee, Chato, Mangas, and others enjoyed notable reputations.[1]

But it was Geronimo who finally emerged, in the middle 1880s, as the preeminent war leader of the Apaches. Of all the leaders, recalled a warrior who rode with him, "Geronimo seemed to be the most intelligent and resourceful as well as the most vigorous and farsighted. In times of danger he was a man to be relied upon."[2] Although not a chief, and despised by many of his own people, he compiled a record of intransigence in peace and skill in war that made him the terror of two nations. Mexican peasants regarded him as a devil sent to punish them for their sins.[3] To Americans, he personified all the merciless brutality of Apache warfare.

In 1880–81, as Victorio and Nana ravaged New Mexico and Chihuahua, Geronimo resided in comparative quiet at San Carlos. Following his seizure by Agent Clum at Ojo Caliente in April

1877 (see p. 359), he had remained at San Carlos for a year before riding off to the Sierra Madre to join Juh's Nednhis in plundering Mexican settlements. Mexican military pressures at length, in January 1880, prompted Geronimo, Juh, and 105 followers to return to the San Carlos Reservation.[4] Conditions there made it fairly predictable that these stubbornly independent spirits would not remain long.

A variety of factors kept the reservation Indians constantly agitated. Despite a rudimentary irrigation system, farming efforts went largely unrewarded. Ration issues that might have compensated never reached adequate levels, the result of paltry appropriations compounded by contract profiteering and simple theft. Military inspection of issues dramatized but failed to eliminate fraud. After Clum, patronage politics visited a series of incompetent or corrupt agents on the Apaches. The "stench in the nostrils of honest men," as the head of the Board of Indian Commissioners branded San Carlos' administration, permeated even the Washington office of the Indian Bureau and moved Interior Secretary Carl Schurz to order Commissioner of Indian Affairs Ezra Hayt to clear his desk and depart within one hour. A year's interlude, 1879–80, gave the Apaches an efficient and honest military administration by Capt. Adna R. Chaffee, but his civilian successor returned conditions to normal.[5]

The reservation festered with factional intrigue. It flourished both within and between the white and Indian communities, the currents overlapping and merging and intersecting in confused ebb and flow. Indian, white, and Indian-white alliances formed and dissolved in bewildering complexity. In addition, the concentration at San Carlos of Chiricahua, Warm Springs, Coyotero (White Mountain), Aravaipa, and Pinal Apaches, Apache-Yumas, Apache-Mojaves (Yavapais), and even a handful of Yumas and Mojaves, revived historic antipathies and heightened tensions. Boredom born of idleness, mixed with liberal doses of the potent native drink, *tizwin*, enlarged still more the potential for trouble.

White settlers, encircling the reservation in growing numbers, contributed to discontent. Arizona's population doubled between 1880 and 1882, from 40,000 to 80,000. Mining and agricultural communities sprang up around the reservation. Miners intruded on the west. On the east Mormon farmers diverted waters of the

Gila, on which the precarious crops of the Indians depended. Coal was found in the south. Although the Apaches had no great attachment to the malarial bottoms of the Gila, they viewed with alarm the increasing encroachment of settlers on the reservation.

Conditions at San Carlos would have severely tried the most docile and obedient Indians. The Apaches were neither docile nor obedient. "These tigers of the human race," General Crook later wrote, "resented anything like an attempt to regulate their conduct, or in any way to interfere with their mode of life"[6]—which of course was what the reservation was all about. It may well be doubted that even an ideal reservation could have contained a people so warlike and so contemptuous of restraint.

No Apaches were more independent or warlike than the Chiricahuas and Warm Springs. Those who were not in Mexico lived near the Camp Goodwin subagency about fifteen miles up the Gila from San Carlos. Juh and Geronimo were here with the people who had surrendered early in 1880. Other prominent leaders were Nachez and Loco. Principally from these Chiricahua and Warm Springs bands came the Indians who, between 1881 and 1886, fought the last of the Apache wars. White called them "renegades," connoting, somewhat inaccurately, outlaws from their parent tribes on the reservation.

The trouble that set off the Chiricahua and Warm Springs outbreak of 1881 originated, paradoxically, with the White Mountain Apaches. Occupying forested, game-rich mountains in the northern part of the reservation, they endured few of the hardships and privations of their kinsmen in the burning deserts of the Gila. But during the summer of 1881 many of them fell under the influence of a shaman named Nakaidoklini, who preached a heady doctrine that offered the prospect of raising the dead and ridding the earth of the white interlopers. Featuring a special dance, the religion recalled similar creeds embraced by native groups in the past and anticipated the Ghost Dance movement that swept the Plains tribes eight years later. Nakaidoklini's preachments greatly excited the White Mountain bands and even affected the White Mountain scouts at Fort Apache.[7]

The commandant of Fort Apache, Col. Eugene A. Carr, Sixth Cavalry, did not view Nakaidoklini's activities as particularly ominous. San Carlos Agent J. C. Tiffany, however, saw deadly peril in a doctrine that called for the abrupt departure of all white people. He wanted the medicine man arrested at once and, if necessary, killed. The department commander seemed chiefly concerned with insuring that responsibility for any trouble rested with the Indian Bureau. Bvt. Maj. Gen. Orlando B. Willcox, colonel of the Twelfth Infantry, had succeeded General Kautz in March 1878. Since then, he had demonstrated scant aptitude for the difficult task of managing a department full of Apaches. Also, Willcox and Carr disliked each other and communicated with cold formality. In August 1881, a three-way conversation over the telegraph uncertainly linking Fort Apache, San Carlos Agency, and Whipple Barracks gained Tiffany the backing of Willcox and presented Carr with orders to arrest Nakaidoklini—an assignment the colonel regarded as heavy with the risk of unnecessary violence.

Carr's apprehension proved justified. On August 30 he marched into Nakaidoklini's village on Cibicu Creek, about thirty miles northwest of Fort Apache, with two troops of cavalry, eighty-five men, and a detachment of twenty-three White Mountain scouts. In a tense confrontation, the mystic submitted and, placed in the custody of Sgt. John MacDonald, was warned that if he tried to escape he would be killed. His angry followers, about one hundred strong, dogged Carr's march down the valley. As the command bivouacked for the night, they suddenly attacked. At the same moment the scouts mutinied. Their first volley caught Capt. Edmund C. Hentig in the back and cut down six soldiers. Nakaidoklini tried to crawl to safety, but Sergeant MacDonald, down with a bullet in his leg, and a trumpeter shot and killed him. A hastily formed skirmish line swept the assailants across the creek, and the two sides exchanged fire until nightfall. The encounter had cost Carr Captain Hentig and four men killed and another four wounded, two mortally. He was surrounded by a growing body of warriors and had lost most of his horses. Under cover of darkness, therefore, he led his command in a stealthy withdrawal from the battlefield that undoubtedly averted a disaster on the morrow.

Held by only a handful of infantry, Fort Apache lay under threat of retaliation by outraged Apaches. Several killings in the vicinity warned of an attack on the fort itself—a tactic to which Indians almost never resorted. The arrival of Carr's battered column on the afternoon of August 31 lessened the danger. Even so, on September 1 warriors opened fire on the fort, wounding an infantry officer and shooting Carr's horse from beneath him. Assault parties pressed in on two sides and gained some of the outlying buildings. They were driven off, however, and the effort to take the fort collapsed.

Garbled reports reaching San Carlos told of the massacre of Carr and his entire command at Cibicu. Eastern newspapers spread the word with sensational headlines reminiscent of those that proclaimed the Custer disaster. With the telegraph cut and the post surrounded, not until September 4 did Carr get a courier through with a report of the Battle of Cibicu and the attack on Fort Apache.

Relief over Carr's safety did not temper General Sherman's determination to see the offenders severely punished. "I want this annual Apache stampede to end right now," he wired General McDowell, "and to effect that result will send every available man in the whole Army if necessary."[8] General Pope, visiting in Santa Fe when the news of Cibicu burst, hastened a relief force from Fort Wingate and recalled Mackenzie and six troops of the Fourth Cavalry from Ute duty in Colorado. McDowell sent reinforcements from California. Sherman, incensed over Willcox's delay and indecision, designated Mackenzie as field commander charged with rounding up the Apaches who had attacked Carr.

During the balance of September, Carr raced about the reservation in response to a barrage of confusing and contradictory orders from Willcox. His movements, however, combined with the heavy buildup of troops on the reservation, frightened most of the fugitives into surrendering. By the time Mackenzie assumed command at Fort Apache late in September, few organized groups remained at large. Five of the mutinous scouts who had surrendered were brought before a court-martial, which sentenced three to death by hanging and two to imprisonment at Alcatraz. Despite some sentiment for harsh punishment, no action was ever taken against the other Apache participants in the Cibicu affair.

Given the history of antipathy between Willcox and Carr, a dispute over Cibicu was predictable. Agent Tiffany, of course, bore prime responsibility for insisting on the arrest. But Willcox promptly placed interpretations on the confused exchange of telegrams preceding the arrest that threw on Carr the responsibility for doing the agent's bidding. The controversy might have re-

mained a local matter but for other quarrels between the two officers that at length provoked Willcox into preferring charges
against Carr for exceeding orders in attempting to seize Nakaidoklini and for mismanaging the Battle of Cibicu. A court of inquiry
in the summer of 1882, however, gave Carr an almost total vindication, noting only certain errors of judgment in his dispositions at
Cibicu.[9]

Even this gentle stigma infuriated Carr and motivated years of
unsuccessful attempts to purge it from his record. Without injustice, however, the court might have been considerably more critical. During the confrontation with Nakaidoklini and the subsequent march to the night's bivouac, Carr seemed to ignore highly
visible evidence of the volatile disposition of the Apaches and to
treat the whole affair with deliberate indifference. He took no precautions to meet the violence that was obviously possible, if not
probable. Also, even though he knew the scouts to be under
Nakaidoklini's spell, he failed to guard against their disaffection.
He should have been ready for battle, yet the eruption of gunfire
caught his command dispersed and unprepared. The court displayed remarkable charity in characterizing such negligence as
"only" errors of judgment.

But the worst errors are chargeable to Willcox. He succumbed
to Agent Tiffany's alarm and overrode Carr's judgment. The order
to arrest Nakaidoklini was unwise, as General McDowell later
stated.[10] That the medicine man's followers escaped punishment
conceded as much. And Willcox's effort to make it appear as
though his orders were merely a response to Carr's assessment of
the danger posed by Nakaidoklini was a petty maneuver to evade
responsibility that the record plainly shows to have been his. Willcox's role in Cibicu and its aftermath marked him, in the eyes of
Generals McDowell and Sherman, as unsuited for departmental
command.

The most serious and lasting consequence of Cibicu was to re-
kindle Chiricahua hostilities, for in suppressing one uprising the
army accidentally touched off another. Throughout the White
Mountain disturbances, the Chiricahuas had remained quietly at
the Camp Goodwin subagency, but the swarming of troops on the
reservation filled them with apprehension that they were to be
punished for depredations in Mexico. On September 25, 1881,
General Willcox, who had established himself at Fort Thomas, ac-

cepted the surrender of two White Mountain bands and paroled them to the subagency, seven miles down the Gila. On September 30, however, Maj. James Biddle led a squadron of cavalry down from the fort to take them back into custody. The White Mountains fled to the Chiricahua camps. That night, fearing an attack by the soldiers, seventy-four Chiricahuas under Juh, Nachez, Geronimo, and Chato cut out for Mexico. Willcox himself gave chase with a hastily assembled command of cavalry, infantry, and scouts. On October 2, at Cedar Springs on the west flank of the Pinaleño Mountains, the warriors fell back and fought off their pursuers for the better part of the day while the women and children made good their escape. In the Sierra Madre the Chiricahuas united with Nana and what remained of Victorio's following, resting after their devastating raids in New Mexico (see p. 364). Once more the Apache threat hung over the Southwest.[11]

In January 1882 word reached San Carlos that the Apaches in Mexico intended to force Loco and his Warm Springs band to join them in the Sierra Madre. General Willcox alerted his border posts, and Colonel Mackenzie, now commanding the District of New Mexico, placed Lt. Col. George A. Forsyth on the line of the Southern Pacific Railroad with six troops of the Fourth Cavalry. Nevertheless, on April 19, 1882, a war party under Juh, Nachez, Geronimo, Chihuahua, and Chato burst upon the Camp Goodwin subagency and, killing police chief Albert D. Sterling, made off with Loco and several hundred people. Killing and looting their way up the Gila Valley, the Apaches turned southeast to the Peloncillo (or Stein's Peak) Range, which hugs the Arizona-New Mexico border. Between thirty and fifty dead white people littered the trail behind them.

The army went into action instantly, though for the most part ineffectually. However, on April 23 one of Forsyth's patrols uncovered the hostiles in Horseshoe Canyon of the Peloncillos. With five troops of the Fourth Cavalry and a scout company, he rushed into a hard-fought action that cost him five dead and seven wounded but failed to destroy the enemy. Another command, two troops of the Sixth Cavalry and some scouts under Capt. Tullius C. Tupper, took up the pursuit and followed the trail into Chihuahua. On April 28, about twenty miles south of the border, Tupper caught up with the fugitives and attacked, but withdrew after using up most of his ammunition without dislodging them from defensive positions. Forsyth, too, pursued into Mexico and, absorbing Tupper, pushed south on the Apache trail. On April 30, however, the column met up with a large force of Mexican infantry under Col. Lorenzo Garcia, who told of a disaster he and his 250 soldiers had inflicted on the Apaches the day before. Preoccupied with Tupper in their rear, they had walked into an ambush prepared by Garcia. In a furious contest they had killed twenty-two Mexicans and wounded sixteen but had lost seventy-eight of their own people killed, mostly women and children, and another thirty-three women and children captured. The rest of the Indians had fled into the Sierra Madre. Ordered out of Mexico by Garcia, Forsyth called off the chase and returned to the United States.[12]

The alarm created by the Loco outbreak had scarcely died down when trouble again erupted at San Carlos. A White Mountain warrior named Natiotish had established leadership of a small band of men who, refusing to surrender after Cibicu, had been in hiding ever since. On July 6, 1882, some of them ambushed and killed J. L. "Cibicu Charley" Colvig, Sterling's successor as San Carlos police chief, and three policemen. Gathering strength until they numbered about sixty, the warriors raided northwest into the Tonto Basin. From Verde, Whipple, McDowell, Thomas, and Apache, fourteen troops of cavalry took the field. Ascending Cherry Creek, the fugitives climbed the escarpment of the Mogollon Rim to General Springs, a favored watering place on the "Crook Trail" between Forts Apache and Verde. Following him below, Natiotish spotted Captain Chaffee's troop of the Sixth Cavalry and decided to set a trap. A deep, narrow canyon gashed the pine-covered plateau seven miles north of General Springs. On the far edge Natiotish concealed his warriors.

Veteran guide Al Sieber led Chaffee's column. The next day, July 17, Sieber unmasked the trap. Moreover, undetected by Natiotish, Chaffee had been reinforced during the night by Maj. A. W. Evans' squadron of two troops of the Third Cavalry and two of the Sixth, out of Fort Apache. Evans generously let Chaffee manage the battle. While occupying the Indians with fire across the canyon from one rim to the other, Chaffee skillfully slipped two parties, each consisting of two cavalry troops and some Indian scouts, across the canyon to strike on both enemy flanks. The attacks were vigorous and conclusive. Between sixteen and twenty-seven warriors died, and virtually none escaped unhit. The remnants scattered back to the reservation.

The Battle of Big Dry Wash—a misnomer, since it occurred on a branch of East Clear Creek—marked the end of hostilities with all Apaches except the Chiricahuas and Warm Springs in Mexico. It was also one of the few instances in which regular troops bested Apaches in conventional battle—principally because it was one of the few instances in which Apaches allowed themselves to be drawn into conventional battle.[13]

The Natiotish uprising provided further confirmation of the need for a change in the management of Arizona military affairs. Cibicu, the breakout of Juh, Geronimo, and others, and the raid that sucked Loco and his people into the hostile ranks aroused strong sentiment in Arizona for General Willcox's replacement. Sherman, who had sharply criticized Willcox for his handling of the Nakaidoklini affair, toured Arizona in the spring of 1882 and, in fact, almost got caught up in the Loco outbreak. Probably the decision to replace Willcox was reached shortly after his return. But not until July 14, a week after Natiotish and his warriors began their raid, did War Department orders reassign George Crook to the Arizona command.

The new commanding general, taking command at Whipple Barracks on September 4, 1882, defined his task in terms of three major objectives: to bring the reservation Indians under control, to give protection to the lives and property of citizens, and to subjugate the hostiles operating out of the Sierra Madre.[14] In large measure, the second depended on the other two.

First on the agenda were the reservation Indians. Crook went to San Carlos to guage their temper and to take the measure of the new agent, P. P. Wilcox. The Indians proved sullen, suspicious, and frustrated to the brink of revolt. The agent, more encouragingly, proved willing to let the army establish itself on the reservation and take on responsibility for management and discipline of the Indians.[15]

To establish military authority, Crook selected four officers he thought possessed special aptitude for dealing with Indians. Modest, efficient Capt. Emmet Crawford headed the group. Lt. Britton Davis aided him at San Carlos Agency. Lts. Charles B. Gatewood and Hamilton Roach worked with the White Mountain bands out of Fort Apache. These officers applied methods tested in Crook's previous Apache experience—scout companies whose men lived with their people when not on assignment, a system of identification tags keyed to census records, a network of "Confidential Indians" reporting attitudes and intentions in the scattered camps, and, above all, the judicious exercise of firmness tempered by honesty, justice, tact, and patience. These techniques broke down the unity of bands, fostered factions sympathetic to Crook's aims, and gave military authorities warning of impending trouble.[16]

Crook next turned his attention to the Chiricahuas and Warm Springs in Mexico. President Díaz had finally acquiesced in a reciprocal crossing treaty, signed on July 29, 1882, and Crook prepared to campaign in Mexico if necessary.[17] Again he would employ tested methods—Indian scouts as the chief tactical arm and pack trains for logistical support. "The nearer an Indian approaches to the savage state the more likely he will prove valuable as a soldier," Crook believed. The scouts, therefore, were "the wildest I could get."[18] At San Carlos and Fort Apache Crawford and Gatewood recruited about 250 such warriors and organized them in five companies.

While Chihuahua rocked with depredations throughout the winter of 1882–83, Arizona remained ominously untouched. The hostiles had withdrawn far to the south, amid the great gorges containing the head streams of the Yaqui River, and from here they sniped at the villages along the eastern flank of the Sierra Madre. Crook himself went to the border and sent Apache emissaries southward to try to open communication with them. Three of Crawford's scout companies patrolled the border and probed quietly into Mexico in an unsuccessful attempt to discover their whereabouts. In March 1883, however, the Apaches organized two major raiding parties. One, under Geronimo and Chihuahua, thrust west and south into Sonora in search of stock. The other, under Chato and Benito, headed north to replenish ammunition supplies in the United States.[19]

Chato's foray electrified the Southwest. With twenty-five warriors, he entered Arizona on March 21 near Fort Huachuca. In the next week, riding night and day, the raiders shot and plundered their way eastward into New Mexico, then slipped back into Chihuahua without once having even been glimpsed by the hundreds of soldiers and citizen volunteers racing frantically about trying to intercept them. They killed at least eleven people. From Washington General Sherman fired off a telegram ordering Crook to pursue and destroy the hostile Apaches without regard to department or national boundaries.[20]

Crook reacted promptly and energetically. At Willcox, a station on the newly completed Southern Pacific Railroad, he stockpiled supplies and concentrated both Regulars and scouts. He journeyed by rail to Albuquerque to coordinate his strategy with the New Mexican commander, Ranald Mackenzie. Crook then traveled by train to the capitals of Sonora and Chihuahua to clear his proposed movements with Mexican officials. By the end of April he was ready. While elements of the Third and Sixth Cavalry under Colonel Carr guarded strategic border points, Crook would lead a compact, carefully balanced column into the Apache haunts. It consisted of 193 scouts under Crawford and Gatewood, Adna Chaffee's troop of the Sixth Cavalry (forty-five strong), and of course the ubiquitous pack train, 350 mules carrying ammunition and rations for sixty days. Of crucial importance, by a stroke of good fortune Crook had the services of an expert guide. One of Chato's raiders who had put in at San Carlos, he had promptly fallen into the toils of Lieutenant Davis and readily agreed to take Crook to the hostile camps. His name was Tzoe, but the troops dubbed him "Peaches."[21]

Crossing the Mexican boundary at San Bernardino Springs on May 1, the expedition followed the San Bernardino River to the Bavispe, then up that stream to the mountains. "The whole Sierra Madre is a natural fortress," marveled Crook as his column penetrated an incredible tangle of towering, pine-capped ridges and plunging, rocky canyons that Mexican troops had never dared to enter. Pack mules slipped from the trails and fell to their death below. Each summit revealed a still higher one beyond. Apache signs abounded. On May 15 Crawford's scouts stormed into the camps of Chato and Benito, and in several hours of fighting killed nine warriors and destroyed the thirty lodges composing the rancheria.

Crook knew that, thus alerted, the quarry could not again be engaged. But a captive girl told him that some, if not most, of the hostiles could be persuaded to surrender, especially when they learned of Crook's presence in the very heart of their stronghold, guided by one of their own people, and hunting them with kinsmen from San Carlos. Crook freed the girl to act as an emissary, and within two days the Chiricahua and Warm Springs people began to filter in. They included, in the final tally, Geronimo, Chihuahua, Chato, Benito, Loco, Nachez, Nana, and Kaytennae. Only Juh remained obdurate, and few of his followers were said to have survived recent encounters with Mexicans.[22]

For a week Crook sparred with the Apache leaders—chiefly Geronimo, whose example, all sensed, would guide the others. He obviously wanted to return to San Carlos and give reservation life another try. Crook contrived an elaborate show of reluctance, explaining that the white people would condemn him for allowing the Apaches to escape the punishment they so richly merited. Only when Geronimo "begged"—or so Crook and his officers described it—did the general accede. But Geronimo now declared that he must tarry in Mexico long enough to gather in some of his scattered people, and Crook, his rations dwindling alarmingly, could no longer delay his departure. He recrossed the border on June 10 with 52 men and 273 women and children, mainly Warm Springs followers of Loco and old Nana, and the promise of Geronimo and his associates that the Chiricahuas would follow as soon as possible.

The fullness of Crook's victory thus remained to be demonstrated. As the months passed with no sign of the Chiricahuas, he became increasingly a target of ridicule. Indeed, one story that gained wide currency pictured Crook as Geronimo's captive in the Sierra Madre. Late in 1883, however, the Chiricahuas began to straggle northward into the United States. Nachez arrived first, with ninety-three people, followed in February 1884 by Chato and Mangas with sixty. At last, early in March, Geronimo and eighty followers, trailing a herd of stolen Mexican cattle, reached the border. Lieutenant Davis and his scouts—now almost wholly Chiricahua and Warm Springs warriors—met their kinsmen at the boundary and escorted them to San Carlos.[23] With Juh now dead (he either drowned or fell to his death from a bluff while drunk), the Sierra Madre no longer harbored any significant number of Apaches.

Geronimo's surrender, although belated, stamped Crook's campaign into Mexico a complete success. An operation bold in conception and daring in execution had put to the test the unorthodox methods he had long championed. Pack transportation afforded maximum mobility. Indian scouts, supported by a small regular contingent, ferreted out the adversary. No obstacle, no matter how seemingly insurmountable, was allowed to deflect the expedition from its course. Crook won not by rounding up the fugitives or besting them in combat. Had they wished, they could have escaped at any time or even turned on him and inflicted severe damage. Rather, he won by demonstrating that he could mobilize Apache against Apache in a determined offensive and could penetrate the inner recesses of bastions always thought impregnable. Also, he knew Indian thought patterns well enough to exploit the demoralization this knowledge created once negotiations began. The Sierra Madre campaign of 1883 seemed to validate all the theories of Indian fighting Crook had formulated.

The surrender of the hostiles precipitated the question of how to manage them. Agent Wilcox resisted their return to San Carlos and enlisted (or manufactured, Crook charged) strong support for his viewpoint among the reservation Indians. Secretary of War Robert T. Lincoln summoned Crook to Washington for conferences with Interior Secretary Henry M. Teller and Indian Commissioner Hiram Price. An agreement signed by the two cabinet officers on July 7, 1883, gave Crook full responsibility for the recent hostiles and "entire police control of all the Indians on the San Carlos Reservation." To Captain Crawford fell the assignment of carrying out the army's part of the agreement.[24]

The Chiricahua program, the exclusive property of the army, unfolded with surprising smoothness. Lieutenants Gatewood and Davis took the late hostiles to the high country around Fort Apache, scattered them along the streams draining south into Black River, and launched them on an agrarian life that they pursued with somewhat less than total devotion. Geronimo, Nachez, Chihuahua, and others remained distant and restless; but with scouts, spies, and the help of leaders such as Chato, Lieutenant Davis kept his charges in a generally satisfactory state of order and contentment. Most of what trouble occurred sprang from Crook's ban on wife-beating and *tizwin*-making. Kaytennae, a youthful leader receiving his first taste of reservation life, built on the discontent engendered by these proscriptions to mount a serious challenge to military authority. But in June 1884 Davis reacted decisively. Backed by loyal scouts and four troops of cavalry, he arrested Kaytennae and sent him down to San Carlos, where Crawford had him tried by an Indian jury and packed off to Alcatraz prison—"for safe keeping," as Crook phrased it.[25]

The army's experience with its other function at San Carlos proved less satisfactory. The wording of the agreement of 1883 vesting in Crook "entire police control" of the reservation contained ominous potential for controversy over where the line ran separating his responsibilities from those of the agent. Quarrels between Captain Crawford and Agent Wilcox and his successor, C. D. Ford, confused and distressed reservation management and prompted Crawford, early in 1885, to request a transfer. Crook delivered virtually an "all-or-nothing" ultimatum in which he urged an expansion of military powers or relief from all responsibility for reservation Indians. General Pope, now McDowell's successor as division commander in San Francisco and the proud bearer of two stars, vigorously seconded Crook. In Washington, however, Crook and his theories found less favor with Sheridan than they had with Sherman. Also, the Arthur administration was about to give way to that of Grover Cleveland. Thus, the issue was allowed to lie unresolved for several months.[26] Meanwhile, the Chiricahua peace blew up.

The 1885 outbreak grew out of a challenge to military rule such as Kaytennae had organized a year earlier. This time, however, the conspiracy commanded broader support and involved nearly all the principal Chiricahua and Warm Springs leaders except Chato. Their discontent centered, as usual, on the regulations governing *tizwin* and treatment of women. On the morning of May 15, 1885, the chiefs came in a body to Lieutenant Davis' tent, confessed to a *tizwin* drunk the night before, and dared him to do something about it. Davis played for time by explaining that so serious a matter would have to be submitted to General Crook for a decision. But the telegram had to pass through San Carlos, where Capt. Francis E. Pierce had replaced Crawford. Lacking his predecessor's experience, Pierce relied on Al Sieber for advice. Sieber, sleeping off a hangover, minimized the importance of the message and Pierce pigeonholed it. Two days later, acutely agitated over the continuing failure to hear from Crook, forty-two men and ninety-two women and children fled the reservation. Among them were Geronimo, Nachez, Chihuahua, Nana, and Mangas. Geronimo headed directly for Mexico. Chihuahua and his following, skillfully dodging some twenty troops of cavalry and more than

100 Indian scouts, raided in southwestern New Mexico and south-eastern Arizona for almost three weeks before slipping across the international boundary.[27]

Even before Chihuahua crossed into Mexico, Crook had organized his response. Essentially it repeated familiar strategy. The reciprocal crossing agreement with Mexico had been renewed for one year on October 31, 1884,[28] and Crook dispatched two highly mobile forces into Mexico to scour the Sierra Madre and try to flush out the Apaches. One, under Captain Crawford (recalled from his new Texas assignment) and Lieutenant Davis, consisted of a troop of the Sixth Cavalry and ninety-two scouts and crossed the border on June 11. The other, under Capt. Wirt Davis and Lt. Matthias W. Day, consisted of a troop of the Fourth Cavalry and 100 scouts and crossed the border on July 13. To keep the Indians from returning to the United States, Crook stationed a troop of cavalry and a scout detachment at every watering place on the boundary from the Rio Grande west to the Santa Cruz Valley, and backed them with a second line of reserves posted at key points along the Southern Pacific Railroad. Altogether, some 3,000 soldiers, three-fourths of them cavalry, patrolled the border country. Crook established his headquarters at Fort Bowie, in strategic Apache Pass at the northern end of the Chiricahua Mountains.[29]

The Sierra Madre campaign of 1885 was an exhausting and largely profitless struggle against heat, insects, hunger, thirst, and fatigue. Crawford's scouts struck a hostile camp once, on June 23, and Wirt Davis' scouts three times, on July 28, August 7, and September 22. But in each instance the occupants escaped with slight loss. Late in September the fugitives even mounted a counterattack that sent twenty warriors on a swift horse-stealing foray into southeastern Arizona. Crook's elaborate border defenses proved no more successful at intercepting Apaches than his offensive forces in Mexico. In October, at Crook's summons, Crawford and Wirt Davis put in at Fort Bowie to refit and prepare for another assault on the Sierra Madre.

As if to point up the failure of the campaign, early in November Chihuahua's brother Josanie led about a dozen warriors in a raid across New Mexico and Arizona that in sheer magnitude of achievement surpassed all raids that had gone before. As summarized by Crook, within four weeks Josanie and his party rode no less than 1,200 miles, killed 38 people, captured and wore out

250 animals, and escaped back into Mexico without encountering any of the scores of army patrols that tried desperately to cut them off.

While Josanie rampaged across the Southwest, Crook fended off a threat from still another quarter. On November 29, as Wirt Davis took the field once more and Crawford made final preparations, Lieutenant General Sheridan appeared at Fort Bowie. He came at the behest of Secretary of War William C. Endicott to discuss with Crook a growing conviction in Washington that a satisfactory resolution of the Apache problem depended on removing all the Chiricahua and Warm Springs people to a location distant from the Southwest. Crook, backed by Crawford, opposed the measure, explaining that the newly reconstituted scout companies contained many Chiricahuas, whose performance could not fail to be affected by a removal scheme. The discussion also touched on undefined "kindred matters" that can only be guessed at. In light of later developments, it is not unlikely that Sheridan expressed or implied skepticism of Crook's heavy reliance on Indian scouts. For the moment, however, with a new campaign just beginning, he could not well challenge Crook's opinions or methods openly.[30]

In fact, Crook's second expedition departed even further from orthodoxy than his first. Crawford's scout battalion, two fifty-man companies under Lt. Marion P. Maus and William E. Shipp, had been recruited mainly from White Mountain and Chiricahua bands around Fort Apache—the latter tribesmen of the very people being hunted—and this time no regular unit went along. Regulars were supposed to provide rallying points for the scouts and protection for the pack trains, but Crawford had discovered that they also severely inhibited the scouts' mobility, and he was willing to forego these advantages. Wirt Davis declined the risk of treachery; his scouts came from the San Carlos tribes, and a cavalry troop accompanied them.

While Davis and Crawford worked deeper and deeper into Mexico, Crook sipped Christmas eggnog at Fort Bowie and ignored Sheridan's anxious telegraphic requests for information. At last, on January 9, 1886, Crawford found the main Apache camp in a tangled and frigid wilderness near the head of the Aros River, some 200 miles south of the international boundary. A braying mule gave warning of his presence, and the attack the next morning fell on a hastily vacated camp. But, their sense of security shattered once more, the leaders—Geronimo, Nachez, Chihuahua, and Nana—sent a woman to tell Crawford that they wanted to talk. The scouts rested in the abandoned Apache camp while awaiting a conference to be held on January 11.

Tragedy intervened. Unknown to Crawford, a force of 150 Mexican militiamen had also trailed Geronimo to this camp, and on the morning of January 11 they attacked. Crawford hastily mounted a large rock in full view of the Mexicans to expose his blue uniform and brown beard. A bullet fired at close range drove itself into his brain. While Geronimo and his people watched from surrounding heights, the scouts and the Mexicans exchanged fire for two hours before Lieutenant Maus managed to persuade the Mexican commander of his error—if indeed it was an error.[31] Deep in unfriendly country, faced by hostile Apaches and suspicious Mexicans, ammunition and food almost gone, Maus saw little choice but to retrace the path to Fort Bowie.

But the hostile leaders, their haven violated by both American and Mexican pursuers, still wanted to talk. They opened communication through two women, and on January 13, 1886, Maus sat down with Geronimo, Nachez, Chihuahua, and Nana. Geronimo said that he wanted to discuss the possibility of surrender with General Crook personally, and for that purpose would meet with him near San Bernardino in "two moons." As earnest of good faith, he yielded nine people, including his own and Nachez's wife and old Nana, to act as hostages. Leaving Crawford's body in the care of the *presidente* of Nacori, Maus hurried north to report to Crook.[32]

On March 25, 1886, Crook and his staff seated themselves with Geronimo and his lieutenants in a wooded ravine at Cañon de los Embudos, twelve miles south of the border. The Apaches were "as fierce as so many tigers," Crook wrote that night, and very independent and distrustful. He sought unconditional surrender. "If you stay out," he warned, "I'll keep after you and kill the last one, if it takes fifty years." But he was bluffing, as Geronimo doubtless divined, and at last offered terms—confinement in the East with their families for two years, followed by return to the reservation. At night and between formal meetings trusted scouts worked on the hostiles; among the most effective was Kaytennae, "thoroughly reconstructed" by his two-year imprisonment at Alcatraz. At a second meeting, on March 27, Chihuahua, Nachez, and finally Geron-

imo made surrender speeches. Leaving Lieutenant Maus to escort
the Indians, the general hastened to Fort Bowie to wire the good
news to Sheridan. He was premature. With mescal obtained from
an itinerant trader, the Apaches drank themselves into a frenzy,
and on the night of March 28 Geronimo and Nachez, with twenty
men and thirteen women, scattered into the mountains. Chihuahua
and Nana, with about a dozen men and forty-seven women and
children, accompanied Maus to Fort Bowie.[33]

In Washington, Crook's reputation plummeted. Even before
word arrived of Geronimo's escape, Crook's terms were repudiated.
President Cleveland refused to approve any arrangement short of
unconditional surrender, and Sheridan wired Crook to go back
and obtain it. "Take every precaution against the escape of the
hostiles," read the orders, and "insure against further hostilities
by completing the destruction of the hostiles unless these terms
are accepted." Indians who had already surrendered on certain
conditions were now to surrender without condition or be slaughtered—a proposition utterly repugnant to one who regarded honesty as the first principle of Indian relations. Then Sheridan
learned of Geronimo's flight. His answering dispatches, petulantly
conveying his displeasure, questioned both the reliability and
loyalty of the Chiricahua scouts and suggested the propriety of
abandoning offensive operations altogether. With forty-six companies of infantry and forty troops of cavalry, Sheridan thought,
Crook ought to be able to erect effective defenses against raids
from Mexico. From hard experience, Crook knew that to be a vain
hope. On April 1 he asked to be relieved from command. Sheridan
reacted instantly. The next day orders sped to Fort Leavenworth,
Kansas, assigning Brig. Gen. Nelson A. Miles to command the
Department of Arizona.[34]

Sheridan's orders to Miles implicitly but emphatically discredited Crook's basic approach to Apache warfare. After the death of
Crawford, the lieutenant general wrote in his annual report, he
concluded "that the Indian scouts could not be wholly depended
upon to fight and kill their own people."[35] Thus, in charging Miles
to mount a vigorous campaign to destroy or capture the hostiles,
Sheridan advised "making active and prominent use of the Regular troops of your command."[36] Relieving a "very much worried
and disappointed" Crook at Fort Bowie on April 12, 1886,[37] Miles
at once began plotting the new strategy.

The new features were less real than apparent. As in Crook's time, mobile striking forces would probe the mountains of Mexico and try to dig out or wear down the hostiles. Although composed mainly of Regulars, they enjoyed the services of Apache scouts. Miles also reorganized the border defenses. The high mountains, bright sunlight, and clear atmosphere invited use of the heliograph. Manipulating mirrors mounted on a tripod, trained operators could flash messages as far as twenty-five or thirty miles. Establishing a series of "districts of observation," he covered southern Arizona and New Mexico with a network of heliograph stations. In all, there were twenty-seven, connecting virtually all the high peaks of the region. To each district Miles assigned well-equipped mobile columns to intercept any marauding Indians sighted by observers at the heliograph stations.[38]

How effective this system might have proved is speculative, for the hostiles struck before it could be fully developed. Rampaging down the Santa Cruz Valley on April 27, they scattered in small raiding parties to the north and east. One party, tenaciously pursued by Capt. Thomas C. Lebo's troop of the Tenth Cavalry, veered back into Mexico and, in the Pinito Mountains thirty miles south of the boundary, fought a brisk skirmish on May 3 with the black troopers. Another ran afoul of Capt. Charles A. P. Hatfield's troop of the Fourth Cavalry near Santa Cruz, Sonora, on May 15 and lost their stock, only to regain it a few days later in an ambush of Hatfield's command. After this foray, the Apaches dropped deep into Mexico and Miles' elaborate defenses went untested.[39]

To conduct the operations in Mexico, Miles had turned to Capt. Henry W. Lawton, a big-framed, hard-bitten (and hard-drinking) veteran of Mackenzie's campaigns. His medical officer was an equally athletic young surgeon with line-officer aspirations named Leonard Wood. Miles selected them because they believed, with him, that picked white troops could prevail over Apaches. The expedition, formed at Fort Huachuca, consisted of Lawton's troop of the Fourth Cavalry, 35 strong, 20 picked infantrymen from the Eighth Regiment, 100 pack mules with 30 packers, and 20 White Mountain and San Carlos Apache scouts.[40] On May 5 Lawton led his command into Mexico.[41]

For four months Lawton pursued the quarry from one mountain range to the next. The 2,000-mile trek took the command far southward, to the Sonora and Yaqui Rivers, and forms a record of hardship and perserverance notable in U.S. military annals. As Leonard Wood recalled the ordeal:

One who does not know this country cannot realize what this kind of service means—marching every day in the intense heat, the rocks and earth being so torrid that the feet are blistered and rifle-barrels and everything metallic being so hot that the hand cannot touch them without getting burnt. It is a country rough beyond description, covered everywhere with cactus and full of rattlesnakes and other undesirable companions of that sort. The rain, when it does come, comes as a tropical tempest, transforming the dry cañons into raging torrents in an instant. . . . We had no tents and little or no baggage of any kind except rations and ammunition. Suits of underclothing formed our uniform and moccasins covered our feet.[42]

They all walked; the horses broke down the first week. Lawton lost forty pounds, Wood thirty. Only one-third of the enlisted men made it to the end; the rest were replacements added during the march. Three sets of officers served. And for all the effort, only once did the expedition corner any Apaches. The Indian scouts discovered the camp and led the Regulars to it, but as they moved into position on July 14 the enemy took alarm and fled.

While Lawton's men struggled in the Mexican wilds, General Miles pursued two other measures destined to prove consequential. One was the removal of all Chiricahua and Warm Springs Apaches from Arizona. Sooner or later, he believed, they would furnish ammunition and reinforcements to their kindred on the warpath. Already, Chihuahua, Nana, Josanie, and the people who had surrendered to Crook in March had been packed off to Fort Marion, Florida. On August 29, 1886, the reservation Chiricahuas were summoned to Fort Apache for a routine roll call, swiftly surrounded by an overwhelming force of cavalry, and marched off to the railroad at Holbrook. There, 382 Indians, including most of the scouts who had served Crook, boarded a train for Florida.[43]

The other measure was a peace overture—essentially a replay of the stratagem that had twice awarded success to Crook, and also an acknowledgment of the failure of offensive operations. At Fort Apache Miles selected two Chiricahuas, Kayitah and Martine, known to have influence with Geronimo and Nachez. With Crawford dead and Britton Davis out of the army, Lt. Charles B.

Gatewood was the only remaining officer known and respected by Geronimo. Although in ill health, he heeded Miles' summons and led the peace party into Mexico. After two weeks of fatiguing travel, Gatewood joined up with a disconsolate Lawton on the Aros River. Reports now placed the hostiles 200 miles to the north, not far from the Arizona border, directing peace feelers at Mexican authorities in Fronteras. Lawton and Gatewood hastened northward. Other U.S. commands converged on Fronteras.

The hostiles had let the Mexicans believe that a surrender might be arranged, but only to gain time to rest and reprovision. Through Kayitah and Martine, however, Gatewood secured an audience with Geronimo. On August 24, five days before the Chiricahua removal from Fort Apache, the meeting took place in a bed of the Bavispe River. Gatewood delivered Miles' ultimatum: "Surrender, and you will be sent with your families to Florida, there to await the decision of the President as to your final disposition." Geronimo was willing to surrender if he could return to the reservation, but not if he had to go to Florida. Only after Gatewood dropped the disconcerting news that all the other Chiricahuas were even then being moved to Florida did Geronimo weaken. He would surrender—but only to General Miles in person.

Preoccupied with the seizure of the reservation Indians, Miles tried to avoid such a meeting. His insistence that the Apaches surrender to Lawton almost wrecked the shaky accord Gatewood had arranged. Retaining their arms—and Gatewood—they moved nervously northward as Lawton and other units trailed at a respectful distance. The slightest threat, real or imagined, would have stampeded them, as the approach of a Mexican force almost did. At last, the reservation Indians securely en route to the railroad, Miles gave in. The surrender took place at Skeleton Canyon, sixty-five miles southeast of Fort Bowie, on September 4, 1886. Four days later the prisoners were assembled on the parade ground at Fort Bowie and, as the Fourth Cavalry band played "Auld Lang Syne," were escorted to Bowie Station and loaded on a train for Florida.[44]

Elated, President Cleveland wired Miles to hold the Apaches at Fort Bowie until they could be turned over to Territorial officials for criminal trial. Like Crook, however, Miles had accepted a surrender that was not wholly without conditions. The Indians had been promised that their lives would be spared and that they would be held in Florida with their families as prisoners of war until the President decided what to do with them. Gatewood had promised this on Miles' authority in Mexico, and Miles himself had repeated it at Skeleton Canyon. To hand them over to civil authority would certainly violate the latter condition and almost certainly the former. Moreover, the prisoners had already been entrained for Florida. The President ordered them stopped in Texas until he could learn just what terms had been granted. Miles evaded the issue and wrote wordy dispatches that explained little. After a month of voluminous correspondence, the President decided that the terms were such that the prisoners could not honorably be relinquished to civil authority and directed that they resume the journey to Florida.[45]

The surrender of Geronimo and the exile of the Chiricahuas ended for all time the Apache threat to Arizona and New Mexico and their Mexican neighbors. A bloody warfare that began when the first European set foot on Apache domain came to a bloodless close—but not in Skeleton Canyon or even in the Bavispe cane-brakes where Gatewood conferred with Geronimo. The Apaches had capitulated in such surroundings before. Rather, the Apache wars ended in the railroad coaches rattling across Texas en route to Florida. It was the removal of the Chiricahuas, hostile and neutral alike, that brought peace to the Southwest.

The morality of the removal precipitated a heated controversy, especially as the victims, lifted from their natural environment and set down in a hostile one, began to die in disconcerting numbers. The exile of the men who had loyally served Crook as scouts, and even Kayitah and Martine, who had led Gatewood into Geronimo's lair, struck many as particularly reprehensible, although it is unlikely that they cared to stay in Arizona when all their people had gone to Florida. Also, despite Miles' promise, the men were confined at Fort Marion and their families at Fort Pickens. Generals Crook and Howard joined the Indian Rights Association in a crusade for justice to the Apaches. Miles, supported by vocal western interests, resisted. The battle abated only slightly when Crook died in 1890. The effort on behalf of the Indians brought the reunion of the men with their families in 1887 and their removal, a year later, to a more healthful location in Alabama. In 1894, again over Miles' opposition, they were sent to Fort Sill, Oklahoma, where Geronimo died in 1909. In 1913, 187 Chiricahuas were allowed to transfer to the Mescalero Reservation in New Mexico. The rest remained at Fort Sill.[46]

The dispute over the Chiricahua removal was part of a larger controversy that marked the aftermath of Geronimo's surrender and that troubled the army well into the twentieth century. Even in the final stages of the campaign, after the change of command, tension between a Crook faction and a Miles faction sprang up in the Department of Arizona, the product both of the long personal rivalry between the two generals and of genuine differences of opinion over method. After the surrender the controversy intensified and broadened to embrace, besides the removal issue, an unseemly quarrel over who deserved the credit for ending hostilities.

The official reports of Miles and Lawton, and Miles' subsequent autobiographical publications, described success in terms of Lawton's tenacious pursuit and Miles' own persuasiveness at Skeleton Canyon. Gatewood, a Crook protégé, received scant recognition. As Miles advanced, so too did Lawton and Wood, both of whom possessed undoubted abilities. Lawton rose to brigadier and was killed in the Philippines in 1899. Wood, colonel of the regiment Theodore Roosevelt led up San Juan Hill in 1898, reached the top of the army ladder in 1910. By contrast, Gatewood sank into obscurity. His health broken by the rigors of the Sierra Madre, and injured in a dynamite explosion, he died in 1896, still a first lieutenant. But there were many in the army who believed Gatewood was the victim of grave injustice and some, indeed, who conceived Geronimo's surrender as due exclusively to Gatewood's peace mission. These officers inspired a still-growing body of literature that challenges Miles' version and asserts Gatewood's claims.

Both versions contain elements of truth. Lawton's persistent campaigning almost certainly helped put Geronimo in a frame of mind conducive to peace talks. So, most assuredly, did Miles' removal of the reservation Indians, which badly discouraged the hostiles when they learned of it from Gatewood. Moreover, a wrong attitude or demeanor in Miles at Skeleton Canyon could easily have provoked another stampede back to the Sierra Madre. But to Gatewood belongs a large credit that has come to him only posthumously. At enormous risk of life, he went into the hostile camp and talked Geronimo into giving up. Probably no other officer available to Miles could have done this. No other was known and trusted by the hostiles. No other better knew the mind of these

particular Indians. Miles and his adherents are to be faulted less
for their significant part in ending the Geronimo hostilities than
for excluding Gatewood from the fruits of victory.

Although widely cited as discrediting Crook's methods, Miles'
strategy did not differ fundamentally from his predecessor's. The
final surrender was brought about in the same way as those of
March 1883 and March 1886—by wearing down the quarry and
then inducing him to give up. Miles gave greater public visibility
to Regulars than had Crook, as indeed his orders and Sheridan's
expectations required, but Apache auxiliaries went along. Lawton
demonstrated that white troops could endure and persevere in the
Sierra Madre, but in this he merely confirmed what Adna Chaffee,
Wirt Davis, and others had already shown with less ostentation.
Lawton did not demonstrate that Regulars could compete with
Apaches in tracking down and ferreting out other Apaches; Gatewood's peace mission tacitly acknowledged the emptiness of this
hope. Miles thus differed from Crook only in emphasis. He used
fewer Indian scouts, drew them from tribes other than Chiricahua,
and made sure that public attention did not stray from the Regulars to the scouts.

In truth, Miles' conduct of the Geronimo campaign deserves a
better judgment than history has rendered. He undertook an extremely difficult assignment in unfamiliar territory against an unfamiliar enemy under unfavorable circumstances. That he succeeded with methods similar to Crook's is less a reason for criticism than for tribute to his perception of reality and his versatility
in making his superiors think he was following other methods.
His removal of the reservation Chiricahuas, cruel and unjust
though it was, proved to be the vital factor in assuring the finality
of Apache warfare. Miles' selfish bid for glory at the expense of
others, though perhaps rich in immediate benefits, left him highly
vulnerable to adverse judgment by posterity and thus, in the long
view, obscured his genuine achievements.

But the real hero of the army's Apache campaigns remains
George Crook. He devised and carried out the only military techniques that ever seriously challenged Apaches in warfare, and he
articulated principles of dealing with Apaches and managing their
reservations that, if consistently applied, could not have failed to
give a brighter aspect to the dismal record of relations with these
tribes in the final decades of the nineteenth century. With only

slight exaggeration, correspondent Charles F. Lummis wrote prophetically from Fort Bowie upon Crook's departure in April 1886:

. . . When the doings of this decade have been refined from prejudice into history, when the mongrel pack which has barked at the heels of this patient commander has rotted a hundred years forgotten—then, if not before, Crook will get his due. In all the line of Indian fighters from Daniel Boone to date, one figure will easily rank all others—a wise, large-hearted, large-minded, strong-handed, broad-gauge man— George Crook.[47]

NOTES

1. For characterizations of the Apache leaders see especially Lockwood, *The Apache Indians;* Betzinez, *I Fought with Geronimo;* Britton Davis, *The Truth about Geronimo* (New Haven, Conn., 1929); and Eve Ball, "The Apache Scouts: A Chiricahua Appraisal," *Arizona and the West,* 7 (1965), 315–28. A recent and creditable biography of Geronimo is Alexander B. Adams, *Geronimo: A Biography* (New York, 1971).
2. Betzinez, p. 58.
3. John G. Bourke, *An Apache Campaign in the Sierra Madre* (2d ed., New York, 1958), p. 108.
4. Ogle, *Federal Control of the Western Apaches*, p. 198 n. SW, *Annual Report* (1880), pp. 206–7.
5. *Ibid.*, chap. 7. Chaffee's experiences are recounted in Carter, *The Life of Lieutenant General Chaffee,* chap. 12.
6. George Crook, *Resumé of Operations against Apache Indians, 1882 to 1886* (p.p., 1886; reprint with notes and introduction by Barry C. Johnson, London, 1971), p. 10.
7. For Nakaidoklini and the Battle of Cibicu, see SW, *Annual Report* (1881), pp. 121, 140–45, 153–55; (1882), pp. 144–46; Thrapp, *The Conquest of Apacheria,* chap. 17; Ogle, pp. 203–6; Cruse, *Apache Days and After,* chaps. 9–14; King, *War Eagle,* chaps. 8–9; Dan L. Thrapp, *General Crook and the Sierra Madre Adventure* (Norman, Okla., 1972), chaps. 1 and 2; and Carter, *From Yorktown to Santiago with the Sixth U.S. Cavalry,* pp. 210–21. Nakaidoklini's religion is briefly described and compared with others in James Mooney, *The Ghost Dance Religion and the Sioux Outbreak of 1890,* 14th Annual Report of the Bureau of American Ethnology (Washington, D.C., 1896), pp. 704–5.
8. Sept. 16, 1881, in SW, *Annual Report* (1881), p. 144.
9. The controversy is treated in King, pp. 220–26.
10. SW, *Annual Report* (1881), pp. 140–41. King, p. 224.
11. CIA, *Annual Report* (1881), pp. ix–x. Ogle, pp. 208–10. Lockwood, pp. 243–47. Thrapp, *Conquest of Apacheria,* pp. 231–34. The Battle of Cedar Springs is described by a participant in Anton Mazzanovich, *Trailing Geronimo* (3d ed., p.p., 1931), chaps. 9–10. See also SW, *Annual Report* (1881), pp. 146–47.
12. Thrapp, *The Conquest of Apacheria,* chap. 18; *General Crook and the Sierra Madre Adventure,* chaps. 6–8; and *Al Sieber,* chap. 14, contain the most detailed accounts. See also Ogle, pp. 213–15; Clendenen, *Blood on the Border,* chap. 5; Lockwood, pp. 246–48; SW, *Annual Report* (1882), p. 72; and Sheridan, *Record of Engagements,* p. 101. Forsyth relates his experiences in *Thrilling Days of Army Life* (New York, 1902), pp. 79–121;

and Indian movements are detailed by Betzinez, who participated, in chaps. 7–8. Although the evidence is conflicting, probably 700 people, including 175 fighting men, made this dash from San Carlos back to Mexico. A captured woman told Forsyth that thirteen warriors had died at Horseshoe Canyon and six more in the Tupper fight, but General Crook's Indian informants reported only one killed by Forsyth and fourteen by Tupper.

13. Davis, *The Truth about Geronimo*, pp. 10–28; Will C. Barnes, "The Apaches' Last Stand in Arizona, The Battle of Big Dry Wash," *Arizona Historical Review, 3* (1931), 36–59; Carter, chap. 13; Cruse, chaps. 16–17; Thrapp, *Al Sieber*, chap. 15; Lockwood, pp. 248–55 & map opp. p. 247; and SW, *Annual Report* (1882), pp. 72, 150–51.

14. Crook, *Résumé of Operations*, p. 8.

15. Crook's annual report, Sept. 9, 1885, SW, *Annual Report* (1885), p. 169. Willcox's annual report, Aug. 9, 1883, CIA, *Annual Report* (1883), p. 8. Ogle, pp. 217–18.

16. SW, *Annual Report* (1883), pp. 160–61. Crook, *Résumé of Operations*, pp. 10–11. Davis' *Truth about Geronimo* gives a fascinating account of this process.

17. It was to remain in effect for two years—reduced to one year by a supplementary agreement of Sept. 21, 1882—and applied only when a unit was in "close pursuit" and in "unpopulated or desert parts" of the boundary. The pursuers were to give notice of their presence to local authorities and and retire as soon as they had fought the enemy or lost the trail. 22 Stat. 934–36 (July 29, 1882). Gregg, *The Influence of Border Troubles on Relations between the United States and Mexico*, pp. 152–53.

18. Crook, "The Apache Problem," p. 263.

19. SW, *Annual Report* (1883), pp. 161–62. Thrapp, *The Conquest of Apacheria*, pp. 262–66. Hostile movements that winter are recounted by Betzinez, who was there, chaps. 9–11.

20. SW, *Annual Report* (1883), pp. 141–42, 162, 173. Bourke, *An Apache Campaign*, pp. 26–27. Thrapp, *The Conquest of Apacheria*, pp. 267–71. Lockwood, p. 264. Most sources, repeating Crook, say Chato rode 400 miles in six days, but about 200 miles in seven or eight is more accurate. Sources also conflict on the number of victims; there may have been as many as twenty-six.

21. For Crook's Mexican expedition, see Bourke, *An Apache Campaign;* SW, *Annual Report* (1883), pp. 162–63; 173–78; Thrapp, *The Conquest of Apacheria*, pp. 272–94; Thrapp, *Al Sieber*, chap. 17; Thrapp, *General Crook and the Sierra Madre Adventure*, chaps. 11–14; Betzinez, chaps. 12–13; and Lockwood, chap. 13.

22. The fight with Colonel Garcia on April 29, 1882, had been devastating. See p. 376. Also, in the summer of 1882 citizens of Casas Grandes had lured Apaches into town to make peace, plied them with liquor, and slaughtered a large number—Bourke (*Apache Campaign*, p. 23) says ten or twelve were killed and twenty-five or thirty women were captured, but Betzinez (pp. 77–78) implies considerably heavier losses.

23. Davis, pp. 79–101.

24. SW, *Annual Report* (1885), pp. 184–85. Ogle, pp. 221–22.

25. Davis, chaps. 7–8, gives an excellent account of Chiricahua affairs in 1884–85. See also Thrapp, *The Conquest of Apacheria*, chap. 23; and SW, *Annual Report* (1884), pp. 131–36; (1885), pp. 169–79.

26. Ogle, pp. 222–31. SW, *Annual Report* (1884), pp. 128–29; (1885), pp. 171–75, 180–84.

27. Again Davis, chap. 9, is the best source, but see also both Thrapp books and Crook's report, April 10, 1886, SW, *Annual Report* (1886), pp. 147–48. Crook later wrote: "I am firmly convinced that had I known of

the occurrences reported in Lieutenant Davis' telegram of May 15, 1885, which I did not see until months afterward, the outbreak of Mangus and Geronimo, a few days later, would not have occurred." Crook, *Résumé of Operations*, p. 11.

28. Gregg, p. 159.

29. For Crook's campaign of 1885-86, see SW, *Annual Report* (1886), pp. 1-12, 72-73, 147-64; Crook, *Résumé of Operations;* Davis, chaps. 11-13; Crook, *Autobiography*, pp. 254-66; Thrapp, *The Conquest of Apacheria*, chaps. 24-25, and *Al Sieber*, chap. 19; Odie B. Faulk, *The Geronimo Campaign* (New York, 1969), chaps. 4-5; Betzinez, chap. 14; H. W. Daly, "The Geronimo Campaign," *Journal of the United States Cavalry Association, 19* (1908), 247-62; Charles P. Elliott, "The Geronimo Campaign of 1885-86," *ibid., 21* (1910), 211-36; W. E. Shipp, "Captain Crawford's Last Expedition," *ibid., 5* (1892), 343-61; Lummis, chap. 9; and Marion P. Maus, "A Campaign against the Apaches," in Miles, *Personal Recollections*, pp. 450-71.

30. SW, *Annual Report* (1886), pp. 7, 71.

31. U.S. participants persuasively contended that the Mexicans knew they were attacking a U.S. military force and persisted in the attack even after the fact had been repeatedly demonstrated. (See especially SW, *Annual Report* [1886], pp. 152-53, 155-75; Shipp, pp. 355-56, 358-59; and Maus, pp. 457-64.) Mexican investigators so confused the affair that the United States at length accepted their finding that it had been an accident. (Gregg, pp. 160-65.) In any case, the Mexican irregulars were not inclined to distinguish between Chiricahua scouts and Chiricahua hostiles. Villagers in Sonora and Chihuahua believed the scouts guilty of depredations, and official complaints had been lodged with Crook even before Crawford's death.

32. Crawford lingered unconscious for seven days before dying. His body, buried at Nacori, was recovered two months later and shipped to his Nebraska home. Still later it was reburied in Arlington National Cemetery.

33. The transcript of the conference, recorded by Captain Bourke, together with related correspondence, is published in Senate Docs., 51st Cong., 1st sess., No. 88. Davis, chaps. 12-13, reproduces much of it. See also *Bourke, On the Border with Crook*, pp. 478-79.

34. This correspondence is reproduced by Davis, Miles, and in Crook, *Résumé of Operations*. The command shakeup incident to the death of General Hancock and the retirement of General Pope facilitated the transfer. Howard, promoted to major general, replaced Pope as commander of the Division of the Pacific (thus becoming the immediate superior of Miles, his old rival for Nez Percé honors). Crook took Howard's place as commander of the Department of the Platte. Schofield relinquished the Division of the Missouri to Terry, also newly promoted to major general, and followed Hancock in the Division of the Atlantic.

35. SW, *Annual Report* (1886), p. 72.

36. Drum to Miles, April 3, 1886, *ibid.*, pp. 72-73.

37. Miles to Mrs. Miles, April 12, 1886, in Johnson, *Unregimented General*, p. 231.

38. SW, *Annual Report* (1886), pp. 164-67. Miles, *Personal Recollections*, pp. 481-84.

39. SW, *Annual Report* (1886), p. 167. Thrapp, *The Conquest of Apacheria*, pp. 351-52. Leckie, *The Buffalo Soldiers*, pp. 243-44. *Army and Navy Journal, 46* (July 3, 1909), 1240-41.

40. The various Apache tribes that lived around the San Carlos Agency had become known as San Carlos Indians to distinguish them from the Chiricahua and White Mountain Apaches around Fort Apache.

41. For Lawton's operations, see his report, Sept. 9, 1886, in SW, *Annual*

Report (1886), pp. 176–81; Wood's narrative in Miles, *Personal Recollections*, pp. 505–17; Wood's diary in Jack C. Lane, ed., *Chasing Geronimo: The Journal of Leonard Wood, May–September 1886* (Albuquerque, N.M., 1970); H. C. Benson in *Army and Navy Journal*, *46* (July 3, 1909), 1240–41; and Lawrence Vinton (Lawrence Jerome), "The Geronimo Campaign: As Told by a Trooper of 'B' Troop of the 4th U.S. Cavalry," *Journal of the West*, *11* (1972), 157–69. See also Hermann Hagedorn, *Leonard Wood: A Biography* (2 vols., New York, 1931), *1*, 67–103.

42. Wood in Miles, p. 517.
43. SW, *Annual Report* (1886), pp. 14–15, 73–74, 170–71. Johnson, *Unregimented General*, pp. 239–44. Miles, pp. 495–505.
44. For Gatewood's mission and the surrender of Geronimo, see Senate Ex. Docs., 49th Cong., 2d sess., No. 117; SW, *Annual Report* (1886), pp. 172–75, 179–80; Charles B. Gatewood, "The Surrender of Geronimo," *Proceedings of the Annual Meeting and Dinner of the Order of Indian Wars of the United States* (Washington, D.C., 1929); Faulk, pp. 111–31; Parker, *The Old Army Memories*, chap. 8; Lane, ed., part 3; Miles, chap. 40; Davis, chap. 13; and Thrapp, *The Conquest of Apacheria*, pp. 354–67.
45. SW, *Annual Report* (1886), pp. 12–15, 144–46. Miles contended that a misunderstanding had arisen through the failure of General Howard to relay the full report of the surrender, in which the terms were set forth. Johnson, p. 253.
46. House Ex. Docs., 49th Cong., 2d sess., No. 117. Herbert Welsh, *The Apache Prisoners at Fort Marion, St. Augustine, Florida* (Indian Rights Association, 1887). CIA, *Annual Report* (1913), p. 34; (1914), pp. 56–57. The story is well summarized by Schmitt in Crook, *Autobiography*, pp. 289–300.
47. Lummis, pp. 56–57.

TWENTY

Ghost Dance, 1890-91

THE SURRENDER OF GERONIMO and his handful of followers marked the collapse of the last significant Indian group ranging free of reservation restraints. In the short span of two decades, the final surge of the westward movement had overwhelmed all the tribes of the trans-Mississippi West. Their territory appropriated, their traditional food sources destroyed, they had yielded to military coercion and diplomatic persuasion and accepted the proffered substitute—reservations and government dole.

Ever since the inauguration of Grant's Peace Policy, the army had played a fairly well-defined role in the reservation program— to make war on all Indians off the reservation and, upon application of the agent, to put down disorders on the reservation. Most of the large-scale military operations of the 1870s had, in fact, been mounted against reservation Indians forcefully resisting or fleeing from the reservation process. The Modoc, Nez Percé, Paiute, Bannock, and Ute wars all grew out of reservation troubles. Even the Red River War of 1874–75 and the Sioux War of 1876– 81 involved relatively few Indians who had never been on a reservation. And the Apache hostilities of the 1880s occurred with people who had tried and rejected reservation life.

Officers bitterly objected to their exclusion from reservation affairs until after violence had erupted. In their view, this gave them the unenviable task of fighting a war they had been denied any part in preventing. Col. Orlando B. Willcox expressed the army's resentment in these words: "After depriving the Indian of his lands and proper means of subsistence, at what point in his subse-

quent career of starvation, misery, and desperation shall you regard him as a public enemy? For it is only at some such point that
the military can come in without being regarded as an intruder."[1]
Not with complete consistency, Sherman identified the same problem: "The Indian Bureau keeps feeding and clothing the Indians,
regardless of their behavior, till they get fat and saucy, and then
we are only notified that the Indians are troublesome, and are
going to war, after it is too late to provide a remedy."[2]

The Little Bighorn catastrophe of 1876 gave point to such complaints and dealt the death blow to Grant's already thoroughly discredited Peace Policy. But the label, more than the substance, was
destroyed. The basic aims of the reservation program endured
through succeeding administrations, Democratic as well as Republican. These were, first, to control the Indian and keep him from
disturbing settlers, and second, to indoctrinate him in the white
man's civilization and care for him while teaching him to care for
himself. The army's mission, too, remained basically unchanged.
However, with the increasing effectiveness of the reservation as a
means of control, if not of civilization, the army's Indian service
focused less on chasing Indians off the reservation and more on
guarding them on the reservation.

This changing orientation intensified the historic rivalry and
discord between the army and the Indian Bureau. Army officers
charged agents with corruption and mismanagement. Agents replied with complaints of military meddling in reservation affairs
and immoral use of Indian women by soldiers. The army and its
friends continued to urge the transfer of the Indian Bureau to the
War Department as the solution to the Indian problem. As in the
past, advocates emphasized the obvious truth that the army, rather
than the Indian Bureau, possessed the power needed to control the
Indians, although the congressional authorization in 1878 of Indian police forces, over the vociferous opposition of the army,
somewhat weakened this argument. With the growing importance
of the reservation, proponents also contended that the army could
more efficiently administer the reservations and more successfully
"civilize" the Indians. The controversy reached a peak in 1876–79,
when transfer became one of the several issues involved in the congressional movement to reorganize and reform the army (see
Chapter Four). The Banning committee, the Cameron commission,
and the Burnside committee all grappled with the question. Twice,

in 1876 and again in 1878, the House of Representatives passed a transfer measure, only to see it killed in the Senate. Although not again a serious proposal in Congress, transfer remained a much-debated issue well into the 1890s.[3]

Underlining its claim to superiority in managing and civilizing Indians, the army took on an increasingly humanitarian image. Repeatedly in the late 1870s and the 1880s, officers appeared as articulate and forceful defenders of the Indian. A well-publicized example was the battle of Generals Howard and Crook against the deportation of the Chiricahua Apaches to Florida at the time of the surrender of Geronimo in 1886. Another was Colonel Miles' advocacy of Chief Joseph's cause after the Nez Percé surrender in 1877. General Pope eloquently, if verbosely, assailed the inequities of federal Indian policy for more than three decades. Such actions partially offset the familiar picture of cavalry storming through a village cutting down fleeing Indians.[4]

Further contributing to the humanitarian stance, some treaties and executive agreements with Indian tribes required an army officer to oversee the issuance of Indian goods and rations. The conspicuous presence of a military observer in such transactions dramatized the historic reputation of the Indian Bureau and drew a contrast between civilian dishonesty and military integrity highly favorable to the army's image.

Finally, despite the statutory ban on military appointees to civil posts, local circumstances frequently compelled the Indian Bureau to accept army officers temporarily as "acting" Indian agents. The performance as agents of such officers as Adna R. Chaffee, Ezra P. Ewers, and George M. Randall cast the army in a notably humanitarian character. "Oh, where is my friend Randall—the captain with the big mustache which he always pulled?" an Apache chief asked about a former agent. "When he promised a thing he did it."[5] Such tributes were common and reinforced the army's contention that Indians preferred military to civilian agents.

The army's changing role in the West brought with it amenities of daily life unknown in earlier years. "The period of 'temporary huts' for the troops is passed," General Schofield declared in 1884.[6] The reservation system, fixing Indian tribes to specific locations, enabled concentration to get underway (see p. 47), and posts selected for retention were given comfortable, substantial buildings. Plumbing and sewage systems were installed in many.

The spreading network of railroads vastly eased frontier life, affording rapid travel anywhere and bringing food and consumer goods in greater abundance and variety. With the telegraph, the railroad permitted timely communication, both personal and official, with the outside world. Also, as settlement spread, the Regulars on the frontier enjoyed an increasing social intercourse with nearby civilian communities almost wholly absent in the past.

Another change of significance in the 1880s occurred in the composition of the top command. The generation that had guided the army through the Indian conflicts of the 1870s at last began to pass into retirement. Sherman stepped down in 1883, handing his post, but not his four-star rank, to Sheridan. Congress gave Sheridan four stars in 1888, three months before death ended his brief and unhappy tenure. His successor, the able Schofield, had to content himself with only two stars. These changes, together with the retirement of McDowell and the death of Hancock, gave the brigadiers of the 1870s their long-awaited promotions. After comparatively brief service, Pope, Terry, Crook, and Howard retired or died. In turn, the aspiring young colonels who had so tormented Sherman—Miles, Mackenzie, Gibbon, Merritt, Ruger, Stanley— finally became brigadiers. Miles ultimately made it to the top—the army's last commanding general. Mackenzie, his closest rival as an Indian-fighter, went insane less than two years after earning his star.[7]

"I now regard the Indians as substantially eliminated from the problem of the Army," Sherman wrote in 1883, on the eve of his retirement. "There may be spasmodic and temporary alarms, but such Indian wars as have hitherto disturbed the public peace and tranquillity are not probable."[8] All the tribes had been corraled on reservations. Almost no place remained to which Indians might flee when discontent boiled over. Herds of longhorns grazed the Staked Plains, last bastion of the southern Plains tribes. Stockmen occupied the Powder, Bighorn, and Yellowstone country, long the Sioux and Cheyenne hunting grounds. Mining communities sprouted all over the Oregon and Idaho mountains where once Nez Percé, Paiute, and Bannock would have sought refuge. Although Mexico's Sierra Madre still held forth a fading alternative for the Apaches, Sherman's forecast was essentially correct. The Indians had been conquered. They had no realistic choice but to accommodate to reservation life.

The reservation process struck the tribes with stunning impact. All the customs and institutions of the old way of life—social, political, economic, military, and religious—came under incessant attack from reservation officials. Agents, schoolteachers, missionaries, farmers, blacksmiths, and others strove to make the Indian over in the white man's image. They promoted factionalism that split the tribes into "progressives" and "nonprogressives." They withheld rations and freely employed the Indian police in campaigns to neutralize the chiefs, break up the tribal relationship, suppress "barbarous" practices, educate the children, and make farmers and Christians of all. At the same time, the spoils system continued to burden the reservations with incompetent or corrupt officials. Hunger and want often stalked the reservations as rations and other supplies, inadequate to begin with, passed through various levels of fraudulent shrinkage before reaching the Indians, and as attempts at agricultural self-support repeatedly encountered the realities of western soil and climate.[9]

Also, continued pressures on the reservations from land-hungry whites raised fears of further losses of land. The Dawes Act of 1887 gave substance to these fears. It provided for the division of the reservations into individual allotments—a measure long championed by reformers as essential to civilization and self-support—and for the opening of remaining reservation land to white settlement. Most Indians resisted allotment. They were chagrined to find the government seeking to throw open "surplus" land anyway, in advance of allotments and even, in many instances, before surveys had been undertaken. As an old Sioux expressed it, "They made us many promises, more than I can remember, but they never kept but one; they promised to take our land and they took it."[10]

A decade of intensive and unrelieved civilization programs threw the Indians into a state of shock. The old ways had been purged, or corrupted, or rendered meaningless by the new environment. No satisfactory new ways had been substituted. Anger, bitterness, frustration, resentment, and, above all, a pervasive sense of helplessness and futility settled over the reservations. The people were no longer Indians but not yet whites; indeed, they did not know who they were.

Throughout history, people subjected to cultural disaster of this magnitude have sought solutions in religion. Often a messiah has come forth to guide the afflicted to the promised land. In

North America such was Popé, who led the Pueblo rebellion of
1680 against the Spanish in New Mexico; such was Pontiac, who
threw the English back from the Appalachian frontier in 1763;
and such was the Prophet, the spiritual power of Tecumseh's
bloody crusade against the Americans of the Old Northwest in the
first decade of the nineteenth century.

The stresses of the reservation program brought forth similar
mystics. Smohalla agitated the Columbia River groups in the
1870s. Nakaidoklini gave the Apaches visions of a new order
before he was cut down by Carr's troopers at Cibicu in 1881.
Even the Crows, historically friendly to the whites, had their
prophet in Sword Bearer, whose exhortations swept their Montana
reservation with religious frenzy in 1887. Sword Bearer died in a
collision with troops from Fort Custer and the movement collapsed. Surpassing all in the power of his teachings and the
response of his followers was a gentle Paiute shaman named
Wovoka. His Ghost Dance religion precipitated the final important confrontation between soldiers and Indians.[11]

Paradoxically, Wovoka preached a peaceful doctrine, blending
elements of Christianity with the old native religion. To the
emissaries from tribes all over the West who gathered at his
Nevada home in 1889 and 1890, he foretold a new world, in
which Indians would be reunited with dead friends and relatives
in a blissful and eternal life, free of pain, sickness, want, and
death, free, above all, of white people. By praying, dancing the
prescribed Ghost Dance, and singing Ghost Dance songs, Indians
could "die" and be permitted brief glimpses of the world to come.
In the meantime, they must embrace a rigid moral code strongly
suggestive of Christianity's Ten Commandments. Especially, enjoined Wovoka, "Do no harm to anyone. You must not fight."

The Ghost Dance gripped most of the western tribes without
losing this peaceful focus. Among the Teton Sioux, however, it
took on militant overtones. The Sioux had been shaken with
particular ferocity by the civilization program. They had recently
been stampeded by smooth-talking government commissioners
into parting with half the Great Sioux Reservation—the "surplus"
that would remain after allotments—and accepting six separate
reservations. A ration cut brought hunger and worse. Disease
carried off large numbers of people. In their bitterness and despair,
the Sioux let the Ghost Dance apostles, Short Bull and Kicking

Bear, persuade them that the millennium prophesied by Wovoka might be facilitated by destroying the white people. Wearing "ghost shirts" that the priests assured them would turn the white man's bullets, the Sioux threw themselves wholeheartedly into a badly perverted version of the Ghost Dance.[12]

Military leaders pondered the prospects of war. The key commander was no stranger to the Sioux. Maj. Gen. Nelson A. Miles had inherited the Division of the Missouri when General Crook died suddenly in March 1890. Miles discounted the fashionable view that the progress of settlement made Indian warfare no longer possible. On the contrary, he pointed out, most Indians now possessed repeating rifles and abundant ammunition. If they broke out, the cattle herds of white stockmen afforded a commissary and their horse herds a source of fresh mounts. But the army enjoyed assets too. Forts ringed the Sioux country—Lincoln, Yates, Bennett, Sully, and Randall along the Missouri River on the east; Niobrara, Robinson, and Laramie on the south; and Meade on the west. Telegraph lines connected these posts with one another and with department headquarters in Omaha and St. Paul. Railroads made it possible to speed troops to trouble spots in a matter of hours. Veterans of campaigns against the Sioux scarcely more than a decade in the past marveled at such radically changed military conditions.

By November 1890 the Ghost Dance had brought at least two of the Sioux reservations to the edge of anarchy. The Oglalas of Pine Ridge and the Brulés of Rosebud defied their agents and danced themselves to pitches of excitement that raised fears for the lives of government employees. Daniel F. Royer, the inept Pine Ridge agent, emitted frantic cries for military help. Citizens of nearby Dakota and Nebraska communities took alarm and stirred up their representatives in Washington. At last a reluctant Indian Bureau conceded loss of control, and on November 13 President Benjamin Harrison directed the Secretary of War to take action. On November 20 elements of the Second and Eighth Infantry and Ninth Cavalry, 600 strong, occupied Pine Ridge and Rosebud Agencies. Other units boarded trains at posts all across the nation for the journey to the Sioux country. Brig. Gen. John R. Brooke, commander of the Department of the Platte, stationed himself at Pine Ridge Agency.[13]

The appearance of troops separated the Indians into two groups that the whites called "friendlies" and "hostiles." Those who wanted no part of a test of arms with the soldiers gathered at the agencies. Those intent on further defiance withdrew to remote points of the reservation and continued to dance. By early December the Oglala and Brulé "hostiles" had united and taken refuge on an elevated plateau rising several hundred feet above the prairie between White and Cheyenne rivers, in the northwest corner of the Pine Ridge Reservation. Their village contained about 600 lodges—some 600 men with their families. Short Bull and Kicking Bear conducted the dances. The most prominent chiefs were Little Wound of the Oglalas and Two Strike of the Brulés.[14]

While General Brooke made peace overtures to the Indians in the "Stronghold," Miles tried to head off trouble on the other reservations. At Standing Rock dwelled Sitting Bull, still the mightiest of Sioux chiefs, still uncompromisingly opposed to the white man's ways. The Ghost Dance had taken hold in his camps on Grand River, and he had seized upon it as a powerful weapon in his long contest with the government for the allegiance of the Hunkpapas. At Cheyenne River, the Miniconjou reservation, the leaders of disaffection were Hump and Big Foot. One of Miles' officers succeeded in pacifying Hump, and Big Foot retired to his village near the forks of Cheyenne River. Miles issued orders for the arrest of both Sitting Bull and Big Foot.

The veteran agent at Standing Rock, James McLaughlin, had been urging Sitting Bull's arrest for several weeks, but preferred to accomplish it with Indian police rather than soldiers. Lt. Col. William F. Drum, commander of Fort Yates, agreed. Defying Miles' expectations, they worked out a plan for using police while Drum's soldiers stood by within supporting distance. At dawn on December 15, forty-three "metal breasts" surrounded Sitting Bull's cabin and quickly seized the chief. His followers rushed to the rescue, and a furious fight broke out at close range. By the time Capt. Edmond G. Fechet's squadron of the Eighth Cavalry reached the battle site, six policemen and as many dancers lay dead or dying. Among them was Sitting Bull. The chief who more than any other personified the spirit of Indian resistance, whose death more than any other event symbolized the end of resistance, had died at the hands of his own people, shot down by his captors at the first outbreak.[15]

News of the slaying of Sitting Bull reverberated across the nation and revived public interest in an Indian war that so far had produced no warfare. It also touched off a controversy between the War and Interior Departments over which was to blame for the old chief's death. Finally, it sent some 400 Hunkpapa dancers flying southward to the reservation of the Miniconjous. Aided by Hump, military authorities persuaded most of the Hunkpapas to go to Fort Bennett and surrender. The rest, thirty-eight, took refuge with Big Foot's people.

The assignment to arrest Big Foot fell to Lt. Col. Edwin V. Sumner, who commanded a "camp of observation" at the forks of Cheyenne River. Big Foot's commitment to the Ghost Dance had weakened, and Sumner judged his arrest unnecessary and certain to provoke a fight. Since his orders left the timing to him, he delayed in carrying them out. But, unknown to him, Big Foot, a noted peacemaker, had received an invitation from the Oglala chiefs to come to Pine Ridge and restore harmony. His people, distrustful of Sumner and frightened by the approach of the entire Seventh Infantry up Cheyenne River, insisted that he go. On the night of December 23 the Miniconjous and their Hunkpapa guests, some 350 people in all, quietly slipped out of their village and headed south.

Big Foot's escape infuriated General Miles, who had assumed personal command of field operations, with headquarters at Rapid City, on December 17.[16] In his view, the appearance of the Miniconjous on the Pine Ridge Reservation could have explosive consequences. Peace emmissaries from General Brooke had succeeded in detaching Little Wound's Oglalas and Two Strike's Brulés from the dancers in the Stronghold and were making one last concerted effort to persuade the rest to come in and give up. Determined to prevent Big Foot from getting into the Stronghold, Miles threw Col. Eugene A. Carr's Sixth Cavalry and Maj. Guy V. Henry's squadron of the Ninth into blocking positions. But Big Foot was not trying to reach the Stronghold. He slipped around these troops on the east, through the tangled topography of the Badlands, and pointed his march toward Pine Ridge Agency. On White River pneumonia struck the chief, and, desperately ill, he traveled swathed in blankets in the bed of his wagon.

To Custer's old regiment fell the distinction of intercepting Big

Foot. On December 28 Maj. Samuel M. Whitside and four troops of the Seventh Cavalry, scouting eastward from Pine Ridge Agency, came face to face with the Miniconjous. After a few apprehensive moments, the Indians consented to a military escort. Together the soldiers and the Sioux camped in the valley of Wounded Knee Creek, twenty miles east of the agency. That night Col. James W. Forsyth arrived on the scene with the rest of the Seventh, Light Battery E of the First Artillery, and some Oglala scouts. Forsyth carried orders from General Brooke to disarm Big Foot's people and march them to the railroad in Nebraska for movement to Omaha.

The Indians awoke on the morning of December 29, 1890, to find themselves closely surrounded by 500 soldiers. From a low hill to the north four Hotchkiss cannon pointed threateningly at the village. Forsyth assembled the Indian men, 120 in all, in front of a large heated army tent in which the sick Big Foot had been placed. The women and children, 230 in number, began packing for the day's march. Forsyth's demand for their guns upset the Indians. But they were so plainly outnumbered, out-gunned, and boxed in on all sides that no one, soldier or Indian, seems to have regarded a fight as possible.

The process of disarmament, however, stirred emotions on both sides. The Indians refused to produce the Winchester repeaters so much in evidence the day before, and the soldiers had to search for them in the lodges and beneath the blankets of both men and women. As tempers rose, a medicine man named Yellow Bird pranced about performing incantations and calling for resistance. In a scuffle between a soldier and an Indian, a rifle went off. Instantly the young men threw off their blankets, leveled their rifles, and sent a volley crashing into the nearest formation of soldiers.

In a murderous, face-to-face melee, Indians and soldiers shot, stabbed, and clubbed one another. Women and children scattered in panic as bullets laced the tepees. The close-range action ended abruptly, and the combatants broke from the council square. On the hilltop the artillerymen jerked their lanyards. A storm of ex-ploding shells leveled the village, sought out fleeing knots of Sioux, and filled a ravine where many took shelter with deadly flying shrapnel. Gradually the fighting subsided as the surviving Indians fled the battlefield. They left it a scene of frightful carnage: more than 150 Indians dead, including Big Foot and Yellow Bird, and another 50 wounded; 25 officers and soldiers killed and 39 wounded.[17] Wagons bore the injured to improvised hospitals at Pine Ridge Agency. A snowstorm made white mounds of the bodies left scattered around the battlefield. On New Year's Day of 1891 burial parties gathered the Indian dead and interred them in a mass grave on the hill from which the Hotchkiss guns had wrought their devastation.

General Miles viewed Wounded Knee as an outrageous blunder. He relieved Forsyth of command and convened a court of inquiry to probe the killing of women and children and the deployment of the regiment in such fatal proximity to the Indians. The testimony showed conclusively that the troops, with several exceptions, had made every possible effort to avoid harming noncombatants. The testimony also supported Forsyth's placement of his units for the task of disarming the Indians, although here the judgments were less persuasive, especially in light of Miles' repeated injunctions to his subordinates never to let their units mix with Indians, friendly or not. Despite the conclusions of the court, Miles branded Forsyth guilty of incompetence, inexperience, and irresponsibility, and of disobeying orders. The Secretary of War and General Schofield disagreed, however, and ordered the colonel restored to his command.

Although Miles judged too harshly, Forsyth's dispositions do invite criticism. He deployed his units to disarm the Indians, not to fight a battle. But the possibility of a battle, no matter how remote, should have been considered and his troops kept at a greater distance from the Indians. At it was, he exposed some of his men to deadly close-range fire not only from the Indians but from one another as well. Moreover, the presence of so many soldiers in the very midst of the Indians doubtless contributed to their nervousness and helped provoke the conflict. But a more fundamental error, chargeable to Miles and Brooke, was the order to disarm the Indians. This stemmed from a misapprehension, by all the military chieftains save Sumner, of the true temper of Big Foot. Had he and his people simply been escorted to Pine Ridge, bloodshed would have been avoided and, it may well be, a helpful, or at least not a harmful, influence injected into the situation there.

Because so many Indians perished, because at least sixty-two of the dead were women and children, Wounded Knee has come down in the national conscience as a massacre. But massacre implies deliberate and indiscriminate slaughter, such as Chivington perpetrated at Sand Creek in 1864. Wounded Knee was not deliberate; overcharged emotions touched off a bloodbath that neither side intended or foresaw. Nor was it indiscriminate; the troops tried to spare women and children, and did spare many, but they were mixed up with the men and often impossible to identify in the smoke and confusion. "Tragedy" is a label that more accurately suggests the causes and progress of this most regrettable of frontier encounters. Even so, the vivid memory of shattered corpses and maimed survivors makes the Indians' preference for "massacre" wholly understandable.

The consequences of Wounded Knee proved far more disastrous than any Big Foot could possibly have wrought by appearing at Pine Ridge in good health with rifle in hand. Brooke's latest peace effort had succeeded. The dancers, under Short Bull and Kicking Bear, had abandoned the Stronghold on December 27 and were making their way slowly and apprehensively toward the agency. Wounded Knee halted the march. It also stampeded Two Strike's Brulés, who had surrendered on December 15, and some of the Oglalas under Little Wound, Big Road, and No Water. Dragging a protesting Red Cloud with them, these Indians fled the agency and joined with the people from the Stronghold in an immense camp laid out along White Clay Creek about fifteen miles north of Pine Ridge Agency.

On the day after Wounded Knee, December 30, warriors from this camp fired some sheds near the Drexel Mission church four miles north of the agency. Brooke sent the Seventh Cavalry to investigate. Forsyth failed to secure the ridges on both sides of the valley and allowed himself to be drawn into a trap, with one squadron pinned down by enemy fire and the other prevented by Indians on the ridges from going to its support. Major Henry's squadron of the Ninth Cavalry joined the fray. They had just completed an all-night march of fifty miles from White River, but they urged their exhausted mounts to the rescue, drove the Sioux from their dominating positions, and extricated the Seventh from its embarrassing predicament. Drexel Mission reflected no credit on Forsyth and cost him one man killed, an officer mortally wounded, and five enlisted men wounded.

Now based at Pine Ridge, General Miles undertook the task

of neutralizing the "hostile" village. It contained about 4,000
people, some 800 to 1,000 fighting men. But Miles had it ringed,
at cautious distances, with 3,500 soldiers. Another 2,000 stood by
at still greater distances. During the early days of January 1891,
he slowly contracted the ring while making peace overtures
through Indian emissaries. Confused, frightened, alternately de-
fiant and submissive, quarreling among themselves, pressed gently
by troops who drew in a little closer each day, the chiefs moved
slowly and hesitantly toward the agency. Gradually the great
village dissolved, and the people streamed into the agency. The
final surrender took place on January 15 when Kicking Bear
yielded his rifle to General Miles.

In scarcely more than two weeks Miles had ended the Ghost
Dance uprising without the further violence that, in the aftermath
of Wounded Knee, appeared certain. He succeeded because he
understood Indian psychology. He foresaw that, given the divided
leadership in the Sioux village, a careful mix of diplomacy and the
threat of force could bring about the desired result without more
bloodshed. With great patience and skill, he had pursued this
course to a successful conclusion.

Six days after the surrender Miles' army staged a final grand
review. A stiff gale shrouded Pine Ridge Agency in clouds of dust
as regiment after regiment paraded before the general and his
staff. In compact ranks the First Infantry marched behind its
colonel, "Pecos Bill" Shafter. Eugene Carr's saber flashed from
his spurs to his fur cap as the Sixth Cavalry trotted by. "Henry's
Brunettes," black faces grim behind carbines at the salute, followed their gaunt major, buried deep in a buffalo overcoat.
Massed trumpets shrilled as the troopers of the Seventh Cavalry
approached. The storm whipped the bright yellow linings of their
capes, and Shafter's regimental band swung into "Garryowen,"
the rollicking air that had spurred Custer's charge at the Washita
twenty-two years earlier. Miles gave way to a rising excitement,
waved his hat vigorously, then hung it on the pommel of his
saddle while the wind tore at his graying hair. On the hillsides,
however, hundreds of blanket-swathed Sioux watched impassively.
As the artillery clattered off the parade field, emptying the valley
of all save the blasting dust, they witnessed the curtain fall on the
four-century drama of the Indian wars.[18]

The Ghost Dance was the Indian's last hope. Accommodation

had failed. Retreat had failed. War had failed. And now Wounded Knee made it plain that religion had failed. No choice remained but to submit to the dictates of the government. Whether coincidentally or not, in this very year of 1890 the statisticians of the Census Bureau discovered that they could no longer trace a distinct frontier of settlement on the map of the United States. Only three years later a young historian named Frederick Jackson Turner appeared before the convention of the American Historical Association in Chicago to present a paper entitled "The Significance of the Frontier in American History."

In the movement that Turner traced and that he perceived as a central determinant of American history, the frontier Regulars of 1866–90 had figured prominently. Their part is recorded in more than 1,000 combat actions, involving 2,000 military casualties and almost 6,000 Indian casualties.[19] But other statistics are revealing too. In the year of Wounded Knee four transcontinental railroads spanned the West, where in 1866 there had been none. In 1890, 8.5 million settlers occupied the Indian's former hunting grounds, where in 1866 there had been less than 2 million. The buffalo herds that blackened the Great Plains with perhaps 13 million animals in 1866 had vanished by 1880 before the rifles of professional hide hunters.[20] These figures tell more about the means by which the Indian was subjugated than do battle statistics.

No one perceived the true military role more clearly than Sherman himself, who could have been pardoned had he claimed full credit for his beloved Regulars. Reflecting upon the tranquility that lay on the frontier at the time of his retirement in 1883, he concluded: "The Army has been a large factor in producing this result, but it is not the only one. Immigration and the occupation by industrious farmers and miners of lands vacated by the aborigines have been largely instrumental to that end, but the *railroad* which used to follow in the rear now goes forward with the picketline in the great battle of civilization with barbarism, and has become the *greater* cause."[21]

Turner himself, taking an imaginary station at historic South Pass, failed even to see the soldiers among that procession of conquerors that passed before his mind's eye. The army deserved his mention, but only as one of many groups that pushed the frontier westward and doomed the Indian. Other frontiersmen—trappers, traders, miners, stockmen, farmers, railroad builders, merchants—

share largely in the process. They, rather than the soldiers, deprived the Indian of the land and the sustenance that left him no alternative but to submit. The army's particular contribution was to precipitate a final collapse that had been ordained by other forces. In this perspective the frontier army finds its true significance.

Thus the frontier army was not, as many of its leaders saw it, the heroic vanguard of civilization, crushing the savages and opening the West to settlers. Still less was it the barbaric band of butchers, eternally waging unjust war against unoffending Indians, that is depicted in the humanitarian literature of the nineteenth century and the atonement literature of the twentieth. Rather, the frontier army was a conventional military force trying to control, by conventional military methods, a people that did not behave like a conventional enemy and, indeed, quite often was not an enemy at all. This is the most difficult of all military assignments, whether in Africa, Asia, or the American West. The bluecoats carried it out as well as could be expected in the absence of a later generation's perspective and hindsight. In the process they wrote a dramatic and stirring chapter of American history, one that need not be diminished by today's recognition of the montrous wrong it inflicted on the Indian.

NOTES

1. SW, *Annual Report* (1878), p. 194.
2. Testimony before House military committee, Jan. 31, 1874, House Reports, 43d Cong., 1st sess., No. 384, p. 276.
3. Fritz, *The Movement for Indian Assimilation*, chap. 7. Priest, *Uncle Sam's Stepchildren*, chap. 2. Mardock, *The Reformers and the American Indian*, pp. 159–67. D'Elia, "The Argument over Civilian or Military Indian Control." For subsequent indications of controversy, see John Gibbon, "Transfer of Indian Bureau to War Department," *American Catholic Quarterly Review*, *19* (1894), 244–59; and L. D. Green, "The Army and the Indian," *Harper's Weekly*, *38* (May 19, 1894), 471.
4. See especially Richard N. Ellis, "The Humanitarian Generals," *Western Historical Quarterly*, *3* (1972), 169–78; and Ellis, "The Humanitarian Soldiers," *Journal of Arizona History*, *10* (1969), 55–62.
5. Bourke, *On the Border with Crook*, p. 436.
6. SW, *Annual Report* (1884), p. 103.
7. The three major generalcies in the 1880s were occupied as follows: (1) McDowell, 1872–82 (ret.); Pope, 1882 (ret.); Terry, 1886–88 (ret.); Crook, 1888–90 (died). (2) Schofield, 1869–95 (prom.). (3) Hancock, 1866–86 (died); Howard, 1886–94 (ret.). The six brigadier generalcies were occupied as follows: (1) Pope, 1866–82 (prom.); Mackenzie, 1882–84 (disability ret.); Stanley, 1884–92 (ret.). (2) Augur, 1869–85 (ret.);

Gibbon, 1885–96 (died). (3) Howard, 1866–86 (prom.); Ruger, 1886–96 (prom.). (4) Terry, 1866–86 (prom.); Potter, 1886 (ret.); Willcox, 1886–87 (ret.); Merritt, 1887–95 (prom.). (5) Ord, 1866–80 (ret.); Miles, 1880–90 (prom.); Grierson, 1890 (ret.). (6) Crook, 1873–88 prom.); Brooke, 1888–97 (prom.). For the forcible retirement of Ord and the elevation of Miles, see p. 356.

8. SW, *Annual Report* (1883), p. 45.
9. I have written of this process in *The Last Days of the Sioux Nation*, chaps. 2–3. It emerges clearly in the annual reports of the Commissioners of Indian Affairs throughout the 1880s. For other glimpses, see Mc-Laughlin, *My Friend the Indian;* Hyde, *A Sioux Chronicle;* Julia B. McGillycuddy, *McGillycuddy, Agent* (Palo Alto, Calif., 1941); and Clark Wissler, *Indian Cavalcade, or Life on the Old-Time Indian Reservations* (New York, 1938).
10. Indian Rights Association, *Ninth Annual Report* (1891), p. 29.
11. The most authoritative account of the content and spread of the religion, as well as its antecedents, is Mooney, *The Ghost Dance Religion and the Sioux Outbreak of 1890.* For a biography of the prophet, see Paul Bailey, *Wovoka, the Indian Messiah* (Los Angeles, Calif., 1957).
12. My account of the Ghost Dance among the Sioux is taken essentially from my earlier work on this subject, *The Last Days of the Sioux Nation.*
13. Awkwardly, the Sioux reservations lay in the Department of the Dakota, Brig. Gen. Thomas H. Ruger commanding, but were more accessible to Brooke's Department of the Platte. Miles therefore chose to carry out his mission under Brooke's leadership. Until he assumed personal command in the field, Miles directed affairs from his Chicago office.
14. Red Cloud, old and with failing eyesight, remained at Pine Ridge Agency pursuing a course of studied neutrality. The Brulés' great leader, Spotted Tail, had been assassinated in an intratribal feud in 1881. His people had drifted without strong leadership ever since.
15. Principal sources for this episode are McLaughlin, chaps. 11–12; E. G. Fechet, "The True Story of the Death of Sitting Bull," *Proceedings and Collections of the Nebraska State Historical Society*, 2d ser., 2 (1898), 179–89; Stanley Vestal, ed., *New Sources of Indian History, 1850–1891* (Norman, Okla., 1934), *passim;* SW, *Annual Report* (1891), pp. 194–99.
16. Miles had his inspector general assemble evidence to bring Sumner before a court of inquiry, but the findings did not support such proceedings. Although Sumner had orders to arrest Big Foot, their language permitted discretion. Not until December 24, only hours after Big Foot's flight, did Sumner receive a direct order to make the arrest at once.
17. Indian casualties cannot be exactly counted. The burial detail found 146 dead on the battlefield—84 men and boys, 44 women, and 18 children. The Pine Ridge hospital received 51 wounded, of whom at least 7 died. To this may be added a probable 20 to 30 not discovered on the field who either died or recovered from wounds. Military casualties were 1 officer, 6 NCOs, and 18 privates killed; 4 officers, 11 NCOs, 22 privates, and 2 civilians wounded.
18. The scene is graphically described in Charles G. Seymour, "The Sioux Rebellion, The Final Review," *Harper's Weekly, 35* (Feb. 7, 1891), 106.
19. These figures are for 1866–90 as computed from the AG "Chronological List" printed in Peters, comp., *Indian Battles and Skirmishes.* Casualties break down into 69 officers killed and 68 wounded and 879 enlisted men killed and 990 wounded. Indian casualties, extracted from military records and therefore somewhat suspect, total 4,371 killed, 1,279 wounded, and 10,318 captured.
20. The army is frequently charged with pursuing an official policy of exterminating the buffalo. There was never any such policy. None, indeed,

was necessary, for the hide hunters needed no encouragement to carry on their profitable and wholly legal business. However, both civil and military officials concerned with the Indian problem applauded the slaughter, for they correctly perceived it a crucial factor that would force the Indian onto the reservation. Secretary of the Interior Columbus Delano stated this view in 1874: "The buffalo are disappearing rapidly, but not faster than I desire. I regard the destruction of such game . . . as facilitating the policy of the Government, of destroying their hunting habits, coercing them on reservations, and compelling them to begin to adopt the habits of civilization," House Reports, 43d Cong., 1st sess., No. 384, p. 99. General Sheridan often expressed similar opinions, and in 1874 suggested that the Texas legislature strike medals of gratitude for award to the buffalo hunters. "These men have done more in the last two years, and will do more in the next year, to settle the vexed Indian question than the entire regular army has done in the last thirty years," he declared. "They are destroying the Indian's commissary." Mari Sandoz, *The Buffalo Hunters* (New York, 1954), p. 173.

21. SW, *Annual Report* (1883), pp. 45–46.

☆ BIBLIOGRAPHY ☆

Like *Frontiersmen in Blue*, this work assumes that printed original sources and monographic literature were together adequate to support a history such as I envisioned. Certain portions of the text, however, rest in large part on manuscript sources. These documents are principally in the William T. Sherman and Philip H. Sheridan Papers in the Library of Congress and in official records in the National Archives and Record Service, Washington, D.C., in Record Groups 75 (Bureau of Indian Affairs), 94 (Adjutant General's Office), 98 (U.S. Army Commands), and 107 (Secretary of War). I have also carefully examined the files of the *Army and Navy Journal*, 1866–1885.

GOVERNMENT DOCUMENTS

U.S. Army. *Regulations of the Army of the United States and General Orders in Force on the 17th of February 1881.* Washington, D.C., 1881.

U.S. Commissioner of Indian Affairs. *Annual Reports*, 1866–91. Also in U.S. Serials as follows:

1866: House Ex. Doc. No. 1, 39th Cong., 2d sess., Vol. 2 (Serial 1284).
1867:   "   "   "   " ", 40th Cong., 2d sess., Vol. 3 (Serial 1326).
1868:   "   "   "   " ", 40th Cong., 3d sess., Vol. 2 (Serial 1366).
1869:   "   "   "   " ", 41th Cong., 2d sess., Vol. 3 (Serial 1414).
1870:   "   "   "   " ", Pt. 1, 41st Cong., 3d sess., Vol. 4 (Serial 1449).
1871: House Ex. Doc. No. 1, Pt. 1, 42d Cong., 2d sess., Vol. 3 (Serial 1505).
1872: House Ex. Doc. No. 1, Pt. 1, 42d Cong., 3d sess., Vol. 3 (Serial 1560).
1873: House Ex. Doc. No. 1, Pt. 5, 43d Cong., 1st sess., Vol. 4 (Serial 1601).
1874: House Ex. Doc. No. 1, Pt. 5, 43d Cong., 2d sess., Vol. 6 (Serial 1639).
1875: House Ex. Doc. No. 1, Pt. 5, 44th Cong., 1st sess., Vol. 4, Pt. 1 (Serial 1680).
1876: House Ex. Doc. No. 1, Pt. 5, 44th Cong., 2d sess., Vol. 4, Pt. 1 (Serial 1749).
1877: House Ex. Doc. No. 1, Pt. 5, 45th Cong., 2d sess., Vol. 8 (Serial 1800).

1878: House Ex. Doc. No. 1, Pt. 5, 45th Cong., 3d sess., Vol. 9, Pt. 1 (Serial 1850).
1879: House Ex. Doc. No. 1, Pt. 5, 46th Cong., 2d sess., Vol. 9, Pt. 1 (Serial 1910).
1880: House Ex. Doc. No. 1, Pt. 5, 46th Cong., 3d sess., Vol. 9, Pt. 1 (Serial 1959).
1881: House Ex. Doc. No. 1, Pt. 5, 47th Cong., 1st sess., Vol. 10 (Serial 2018).
1882: House Ex. Doc. No. 1, Pt. 5, 47th Cong., 2d sess., Vol. 11, Pt. 1 (Serial 2100).
1883: House Ex. Doc. No. 1, Pt. 5, 48th Cong., 1st sess., Vol. 11, Pt. 1 (Serial 2191).
1884: House Ex. Doc. No. 1, Pt. 5, 48th Cong., 2d sess., Vol. 12, Pt. 1 (Serial 2287).
1885: House Ex. Doc. No. 1, Pt. 5, 49th Cong., 1st sess., Vol. 12 (Serial 2379).
1886: House Ex. Doc. No. 1, Pt. 5, 49th Cong., 2d sess., Vol. 8 (Serial 2467).
1887: House Ex. Doc. No. 1, Pt. 5, 50th Cong., 1st sess., Vol. 11 (Serial 2542).
1888: House Ex. Doc. No. 1, Pt. 5, 50th Cong., 2d sess., Vol. 11 (Serial 2637).
1889: House Ex. Doc. No. 1, Pt. 5, 51st Cong., 1st sess., Vol. 12 (Serial 2725).
1890: House Ex. Doc. No. 1, Pt. 5, 51st Cong., 2d sess., Vol. 12 (Serial 2841).
1891: House Ex. Doc. No. 1, Pt. 5, 52d Cong., 1st sess., Vol. 15 (Serial 2934).

U.S. Congress. *Congressional Globe*, 39th–42nd Cong. (1866–73).
Congressional Record, 43d–51st Cong. (1873–91).
U.S. Congress. House of Representatives.
House Ex. Doc. No. 113, 39th Cong., 1st sess., Vol.12, 1866, Serial 1263. Organization of the Army.
House Ex. Doc. No. 20, 39th Cong., 2d sess., Vol. 6, 1866, Serial 1288. Inspection of military posts.
House Ex. Doc. No. 23, 39th Cong., 2d sess., Vol. 6, 1866, Serial 1288. Protection across the continent.
House Ex. Doc. No. 45, 39th Cong., 2d sess., Vol. 7, 1866, Serial 1289. Inspection by Generals Rusling and Hazen.
House Ex. Doc., No. 71, 39th Cong., 2d sess., Vol. 11, 1866, Serial 1293. Massacre of troops near Fort Phil Kearny.
House Ex. Doc. No. 88, 39th Cong., 2d sess., Vol. 11, 1866, Serial 1293. Commissioners to Indian tribes.
House Ex. Doc. No. 111, 39th Cong., 2d sess., Vol. 11, 1866, Serial 1293. General Ingalls' inspection report.
House Ex. Doc. No. 97, 40th Cong., 2d sess., Vol. 11, 1867, Serial 1337. Report of Indian peace commissioners.

House Ex. Doc. No. 239, 40th Cong., 2d sess. ,Vol. 15, 1867, Serial 1341. Subsistence of Indian tribes.

House Report No. 33, 40th Cong., 3d sess., Vol. 1, 1868, Serial 1388. Army organization.

House Miscellaneous Document No. 35, 41st Cong., 2d sess., Vol. 3, 1869, Serial 1433. Management of Indians in British North America.

House Misc. Doc. No. 95, 41st Cong., 2d sess., Vol. 3, 1869, Serial 1433. Cavalry for New Mexico.

House Misc. Doc. No. 139, 41st Cong., 2d sess., Vol. 3, 1869, Serial 1433. Outrages committed by Indians.

House Misc. Doc. No. 142, 41st Cong., 2d sess., Vol. 3, 1869, Serial 1433. Indian depredations in Texas.

House Ex. Doc. No. 146, 41st Cong., 2d sess., Vol. 7, 1869, Serial 1418. Indian affairs in Oregon.

House Ex. Doc. No. 158, 41st Cong., 2d sess., Vol. 7, 1869, Serial 1418. Number of Indians in various tribes.

House Ex. Doc. No. 185, 41st Cong., 2d sess., Vol. 7, 1869, Serial 1418. Expedition against Piegan Indians.

House Ex. Doc. No. 197, 41st Cong., 2d sess., Vol. 7, 1869, Serial 1418. Expedition against Piegan Indians.

House Ex. Doc. No. 228, 41st Cong., 2d sess., Vol. 7, 1870, Serial 1418. Sites of military posts in Texas.

House Ex. Doc. No. 240, 41st Cong., 2d sess., Vol. 7, 1870, Serial 1418. Difficulties with Indian tribes.

House Ex. Doc. No. 201, 42d Cong., 3d sess., Vol. 9, 1873, Serial 1567. Difficulties with Modoc Indians.

House Report No. 74, 42d Cong., 3d sess., Vol. 1, 1872, Serial 1576. Army and staff organization.

House Report No. 85, 42d Cong., 3d sess., Vol. 1, 1872, Serial 1576. Revised army regulations.

House Report No. 87, 42d Cong., 3d sess., Vol. 1, 1872, Serial 1576. Expenditures in the War Department.

House Ex. Doc. No. 80, 43d Cong., 1st sess., Vol. 9, 1874, Serial 1607. Apache Indians in Arizona and New Mexico.

House Ex. Doc. No. 108, 43d Cong., 1st sess., Vol. 9, 1874, Serial 1607. Intercourse with Indian tribes.

House Ex. Doc. No. 122, 43d Cong., 1st sess., Vol. 9, 1874, Serial 1607. Modoc War.

House Ex. Doc. No. 185, 43d Cong., 1st sess., Vol. 12, 1874, Serial 1610. Cost of Modoc War.

House Misc. Doc. No. 151, 43d Cong., 1st sess., Vol. 3, 1874, Serial 1619. Protection of citizens of Montana.

House Ex. Doc. No. 275, 43d Cong., 1st sess., Vol. 17, 1874, Serial 1624. Reduction of the military establishment.

House Report No. 395, 43d Cong., 1st sess., Vol. 2, 1874, Serial 1624. Depredations on the Texas frontier.

House Ex. Doc. No. 131, 43d Cong., 2d Sess., 1874, Serial 1648. Expenses of the Modoc War.

House Ex. Doc. No. 96, 43d Cong., 3d sess., Vol. 8, 1874, Serial 1566. Teton Sioux Indians.

House Ex. Doc. No. 103, 44th Cong., 1st sess., Vol. 12, 1875, Serial 1689. Supplies for Indians at Red Cloud Agency.

House Ex. Doc. No. 135, 44th Cong., 1st sess., Vol. 12, 1875, Serial 1689. War Department jurisdiction over Alaska.

House Ex. Doc. No. 145, 44th Cong., 1st sess., Vol. 12, 1875, Serial 1689. Sioux Indians.

House Ex. Doc. No. 184, 44th Cong., 1st sess., Vol. 14, 1876, Serial 1691. Expedition against the Sioux Indians.

House Report No. 240, 44th Cong., 1st sess., Vol. 1, 1876, Serial 1708. Transfer of Indian Bureau.

House Report No. 354, 44th Cong., 1st sess., Vol. 2, 1876, Serial 1760. Reduction of officers' pay, reorganization of the Army, and transfer of the Indian Bureau.

House Ex. Doc. No. 13, 45th Cong., 1st sess., Vol. 1, 1877, Serial 1773. Mexican Border troubles.

House Misc. Doc. No. 56, 45th Cong., 2d sess., Vol. 4, 1877, Serial 1818. Reorganization of the Army.

House Misc. Doc. No. 64, 45th Cong., 2d sess., Vol. 6, 1878, Serial 1820. Texas border troubles.

House Report No. 701, 45th Cong., 2d sess., Vol. 3, 1878, Serial 1824. U.S. Relations with Mexico.

House Report No. 241, 45th Cong., 2d sess., Vol. 1, 1878, Serial 1822. Transfer of Indian Bureau to War Department.

House Ex. Doc. No. 83, 46th Cong., 2d sess., Vol. 24, 1879, Serial 1925. Ute Commission.

House Misc. Doc. No. 38, 46th Cong., 2d sess., Vol. 4, 1880, Serial 1931. Ute Indian outbreak.

House Report No. 1084, 63d Cong., 2d sess., Vol. 3, 1913, Serial 6560. Pensions for Indian War veterans. Contains "Historical Resume of Certain Indian Campaigns," by Capt. S. V. B. Schindel.

U.S. Congress. Senate.

Senate Ex. Doc. No. 41, 39th Cong., 1st sess., Vol. 2, 1866, Serial 1238. Brevet appointments in the Army.

Senate Ex. Doc. No. 15, 39th Cong., 2d sess., Vol. 2, 1867, Serial 1277. Fort Phil Kearny massacre.

Senate Ex. Doc. No. 16, 39th Cong., 2d sess., Vol. 2, 1867, Serial 1277. Fort Phil Kearny massacre.

Senate Report No. 156, 39th Cong., 2d sess., 1867, Serial 1279. Condition of the Indian Tribes.

Senate Ex. Doc. No. 2, 40th Cong., 1st sess., 1867, Serial 1308. Protection to trains on the Overland Route.

Senate Ex. Doc. No. 13, 40th Cong., 1st sess., 1867, Serial 1308. Indian hostilities.

Senate Ex. Doc. No. 7, 40th Cong., 1st sess., 1867, Serial 1308. Expeditions against the Indians.

Senate Ex. Doc. No. 7, 40th Cong., 3d sess., 1868, Serial 1360. Troops protecting the Missouri River and Union Pacific Railroad.

Senate Ex. Doc. No. 11, 40th Cong., 3d sess., 1868, Serial 1360. Report of General Harney on Sioux of Upper Missouri.

Senate Ex. Doc. No. 13, 40th Cong., 3d sess., 1869, Serial 1360. Battle of the Washita.

Senate Ex. Doc. No. 18, Pts. 1, 2, and 3, 40th Cong., 3d sess., 1869, Serial 1360. Battle of the Washita.

Senate Ex. Doc. No. 27, 40th Cong., 3d sess., 1869, Serial 1360. Brevet rank.

Senate Ex. Doc. No. 36, 40th Cong., 3d sess., 1869, Serial 1360. Indians killed by General Custer.

Senate Ex. Doc. No. 40, 40th Cong., 3d sess., 1869, Serial 1360. Indian affairs in Military Division of the Missouri.

Senate Ex. Doc. No. 5, 41st Cong., 2d sess., Vol. 1, 1869, Serial 1405. Disbursement for Indian tribes.

Senate Ex. Doc. No. 49, 41st Cong., 2d sess., Vol. 2, 1870, Serial 1406. Engagement of Colonel Baker with Piegan Indians.

Senate Ex. Doc. No. 67, 41st Cong., 2d sess., Vol. 2, 1870, Serial 1406. Bombardment of Indian village of Wrangel, Alaska.

Senate Ex. Doc. No. 68, 41st Cong., 2d sess., Vol. 2, 1870, Serial 1406. Wrangel, Alaska, previous to bombardment.

Senate Ex. Doc. No. 84, 41st Cong., 2d sess., Vol. 2, 1870, Serial 1406. Indians of southeastern Oregon.

Senate Ex. Doc. No. 89, 41st Cong., 2d sess., Vol. 2, 1870, Serial 1406. Encroachments on Indians in Wyoming.

Senate Ex. Doc. No. 29, 42d Cong., 3d sess., 1873, Serial 1545. Modoc and other Indian tribes.

Senate Ex. Doc. No. 46, 43d Cong., 1st sess., Vol. 2, 1874, Serial 1581. Depredations of Indians in Montana.

Senate Ex. Doc. No. 2, 43d Cong., sp. sess., 1874, Serial 1629. Invasion of the Black Hills.

Senate Ex. Doc. No. 9, 43d Cong., 2d sess., 1875, Serial 1629. Promotion in the staff corps.

Senate Ex. Doc. No. 22, 43d Cong., 2d sess., 1875, Serial 1629. Indians killed by U.S. troops.

Senate Ex. Doc. No. 1, 44th Cong., sp. sess., 1877, Serial 1719. Operations of troops in Modoc country.

Senate Ex. Doc. No. 14, 45th Cong., 2d sess., Vol. 1, 1878, Serial 1780. Cost of the Nez Percé War.

Senate Ex. Doc. No. 19, 45th Cong., 2d sess., Vol. 1, 1878, Serial 1780. Claims of Texas.

Senate Ex. Doc. No. 33, Pts. 1 and 2, 45th Cong., 2d sess., Vol. 1, 1878, Serial 1780. Cost of the Sioux War.

Senate Ex. Doc. No. 47, 45th Cong., 2d sess., Vol. 2, 1878, Serial 1781. Company cooks in the Army.

Senate Ex. Doc. No. 62, 45th Cong., 2d sess., Vol. 2, 1878, Serial 1781. Certificates of merit in the military service.

Senate Report No. 555, 45th Cong., 3d sess., Vol. 1, 1879, Serial 1837. Burnside Report on reorganization of the Army.

Senate Ex. Doc. No. 29, 46th Cong., 2d sess., Vol. 1, 1880, Serial 1882. Mining camps on the Ute Reservation.

Senate Ex. Doc. No. 31, 46th Cong., 2d sess., 1880, Serial 1882. Ute Indians in Colorado.

Senate Report No. 740, 46th Cong., 3d sess., Vol. 1, 1881, Serial 1948. Relief of General Ord.

Senate Ex. Doc. No. 97, 49th Cong., 2d sess., Vol. 2, 1887, Serial 2448. Massacre of troops near Fort Phil Kearny.

Senate Ex. Doc. No. 117, 49th Cong., 2d sess., Vol. 2, 1887, Serial 2449. Surrender of Geronimo.

Senate Ex. Doc. No. 33, 50th Cong., 1st sess., Vol. 1, 1888, Serial 2504.
Indian operations on the Plains; defense of Colonel Carrington.
Senate Ex. Doc. No. 83, 51st Cong., 1st sess., Vol. 9, 1890, Serial 2686.
Treatment of Apache Indians.
Senate Ex. Doc. No. 88, 51st Cong., 1st sess., Vol. 9, 1890, Serial 2686.
Apache Indians.

U.S. Secretary of War. *Annual Reports*, 1866–91:

1866: House Ex. Doc. No. 1, 39th Cong., 2d sess., Vol. 3 (Serial 1285).
1867: House Ex. Doc. No. 1, 40th Cong., 2d sess., Vol. 2, Pts. 1 and 2
(Serial 1324 and 1325).
1868: House Ex. Doc. No. 1, 40th Cong., 3d sess., Vol. 3 (Serial 1367).
1869: House Ex. Doc. No. 1, Pt. 2, 41st Cong., 2d sess., Vol. 2, Pt. 1
(Serial 1412).
1870: House Ex. Doc. No. 1, Pt. 2, 41st Cong., 3d sess., Vol. 2, Pt. 1
(Serial 1446).
1871: House Ex. Doc. No. 1, Pt. 2, 42d Cong., 2d sess., Vol. 2, Pt. 1
(Serial 1503).
1872: House Ex. Doc. No. 1, Pt. 2, 42d Cong., 3d sess., Vol. 2, Pt. 1
(Serial 1558).
1873: House Ex. Doc. No. 1, Pt. 2, 43d Cong., 1st sess., Vol. 2, Pt. 1
(Serial 1597).
1874: House Ex. Doc. No. 1, Pt. 2, 43d Cong., 2d sess., Vol. 1 (Serial
1635).
1875: House Ex. Doc. No. 1, Pt. 2, 44th Cong., 1st sess., Vol. 1 (Serial
1674).
1876: House Ex. Doc. No. 1, Pt. 2, 44th Cong., 2d sess., Vol. 2, Pt. 1
(Serial 1742).
1877: House Ex. Doc. No. 1, Pt. 2, 45th Cong., 2d sess., Vol. 2 (Serial
1794).
1878: House Ex. Doc. No. 1, Pt. 2, 45th Cong., 3d sess., Vol. 1 (Serial
1843).
1879: House Ex. Doc. No. 1, Pt. 2, 46th Cong., 2d sess., Vol. 1 (Serial
1903).
1880: House Ex. Doc. No. 1, Pt. 2, 46th Cong., 3d sess., Vol. 2 (Serial
1952).
1881: House Ex. Doc. No. 1, Pt. 2, 47th Cong., 1st sess., Vol. 2 (Serial
2010).
1882: House Ex. Doc. No. 1, Pt. 2, 47th Cong., 2d sess., Vol. 1 (Serial
2091).
1883: House Ex. Doc. No. 1, Pt. 2, 48th Cong., 1st sess., Vol. 1 (Serial
2182).
1884: House Ex. Doc. No. 1, Pt. 2, 48th Cong., 2d sess., Vol. 1 (Serial
2136).
1885: House Ex. Doc. No. 1, Pt. 2, 49th Cong., 1st sess., Vol. 1 (Serial
2369).
1886: House Ex. Doc. No. 1, Pt. 2, 49th Cong., 2d sess., Vol. 1 (Serial
2461).
1887: House Ex. Doc. No. 1, Pt. 2, 50th Cong., 1st sess., Vol. 1 (Serial
2533).
1888: House Ex. Doc. No. 1, Pt. 2, 50th Cong., 2d sess., Vol. 1 (Serial
2628).

1889: House Ex. Doc. No. 1, Pt. 2, 51st Cong., 1st sess., Vol. 1 (Serial 2715).
1890: House Ex. Doc. No. 1, Pt. 2, 51st Cong., 2d sess., Vol. 1 (Serial 2831).
1891: House Ex. Doc. No. 1, Pt. 2, 52nd Cong., 1st sess., Vol. 1 (Serial 2921).

U.S. Statutes at Large, Vols. 14–26 (1866–91).

ARTICLES

Anderson, Harry H. "A Challenge to Brown's Indian Wars Thesis." *Montana, the Magazine of Western History*, *12* (January 1962), 40–49.
———. "Cheyennes at the Little Big Horn—A Study of Statistics." *North Dakota Historical Quarterly*, *27* (1960), 81–94.
———. "Indian Peace-Talkers and the Conclusion of the Sioux War of 1876." *Nebraska History*, *44* (1963), 233–54.
———. "Nelson A. Miles and the Sioux War of 1876–77. *Westerners Brand Book* (Chicago), *16* (1959), 25–27, 32.
Anon. "Incident of the Yellowstone Expedition of 1873." *Journal of the U.S. Cavalry Association*, *15* (1904), 289–301.
Athearn, Robert G., ed. "A Winter Campaign against the Sioux." *Mississippi Valley Historical Review*, *35* (1948–49), 272–84.
———. "Major Hough's March into Southern Ute Country, 1879." *Colorado Magazine*, *25* (1948), 97–109.
Baird, G. W. "General Miles's Indian Campaigns." *Century Magazine*, *42* (1891), 351–70.
Ball, Eve. "The Apache Scouts: A Chiricahua Appraisal." *Arizona and the West*, *7* (1965), 315–28.
Barnes, Will C. "The Apaches' Last Stand in Arizona: The Battle of Big Dry Wash." *Arizona Historical Review*, *3* (1931), 36–59.
Beaumont, E. B. "Over the Border with Mackenzie." *United Service*, *12* (1885), 281–88.
Bloom, Lansing B., ed. "Bourke on the Southwest." *New Mexico Historical Review*, 8 (1933), 1–30; 9 (1934), 33–77, 159–83, 273–89, 375–437; *10* (1935), 1–35, 271–322; *11* (1936), 77–122, 188–207, 217–82; *12* (1937), 41–77, 337–52; *13* (1938), 192–238.
Bourke, John G. "General Crook in the Indian Country." *Century Magazine*, *41* (1891), 643–60.
———. "Mackenzie's Last Fight with the Cheyennes: A Winter Campaign in Wyoming and Montana." *Journal of the Military Service Institution of the United States*, *11* (1890), reprint, Bellevue, Neb., 1970.
Boylan, Bernard L. "The Forty-Fifth Congress and Army Reform." *Mid-America*, *61* (1959), 173–86
Braden, Charles. "The Yellowstone Expedition of 1873." *Journal of the Military Service Institution of the United States*, *16* (1905), 218–41.
Briggs, Harold E. "The Black Hills Gold Rush." *North Dakota Historical Quarterly*, *5* (1930–31), 71–99.
Brimlow, George F., ed. "Two Cavalrymen's Diaries of the Bannock

War, 1878." *Oregon Historical Quarterly*, *68* (1967), 221–58, 293–316.

Brinckerhoff, Sidney B. "Camp Date Creek, Arizona Territory, Infantry Outpost in the Yavapai Wars, 1867–73." *Smoke Signal* (Tucson Westerners), No. 10 (Fall 1964).

———. "Frontier Soldiers in Arizona." *Journal of Arizona History*, *12* (1971), 168–82.

———, and Pierce Chamberlain. "The Army's Search for a Repeating Rifle, 1873–1903." *Military Affairs*, *32* (1968), 20–30.

Brown, Mark H. "Muddled Men Have Muddied the Yellowstone's True Colors." *Montana, the Magazine of Western History*, *11* (January 1961), 28–37.

Brown, W. C. "General Baldwin's Rescue of the Germain Sisters." In Alice C. Baldwin, *Memoirs of the Late Frank D. Baldwin* (Los Angeles, 1929).

Cabannis, A. A. "Troop and Company Pack-Trains." *Journal of the U.S. Cavalry Association*, *3* (1890), 248–52.

Carpenter, L. H. "The Story of a Rescue." *Journal of the U.S. Cavalry Association*, *17* (1896), 267–76.

Carr, C. C. C. " 'The Days of the Empire'—Arizona, 1866–69." *Journal of the U.S. Cavalry Association*, 2 (1889), 3–22.

Carriker, Robert C., ed. "Thompson McFadden's Diary of an Indian Campaign, 1874." *Southwestern Historical Quarterly*, *75* (1971), 198–232.

Clary, David A. "The Role of the Army Surgeon in the West: Daniel Weisel at Fort Davis, Texas, 1868–1872." *Western Historical Quarterly*, *3* (1972), 53–66.

Clum, John P. "Apache Misrule." *New Mexico Historical Review*, *5* (1930), 138–53, 221–39.

———. "Geronimo." *New Mexico Historical Review*, *3* (1928), 1–40, 121–44, 217–64.

———. "The San Carlos Apache Police." *New Mexico Historical Review*, *4* (1929), 203–19; 5 (1930), 67–92.

———. "Victorio." *New Mexico Historical Review*, *4* (1929), 107–27.

Coughlan, T. M. "The Battle of the Little Big Horn: A Tactical Study." *Cavalry Journal*, *43* (1934), 13–21.

Crimmins, Martin L., ed. "Colonel Buell's Expedition into Mexico in 1880." *New Mexico Historical Review*, *10* (1935), 133–42.

Crook, George. "The Apache Problem." *Journal of the Military Service Institution of the United States*, *27* (1886), 257–69.

Daly, H. W. "The Geronimo Campaign." *Journal of the U.S. Cavalry Association*, *19* (1908), 247–62.

Davis, Theodore. "A Summer on the Plains." *Harper's New Monthly Magazine*, *36* (February 1868), 292–307.

Davison, Stanley R., ed. "The Bannock-Piute War of 1878: Letters of Major Edwin C. Mason." *Journal of the West*, *11* (1972), 128–42.

D'Elia, Donald J. "The Argument over Civilian or Military Indian Control, 1865–1880." *Historian*, *24* (1961–62), 207–25.

Dorst, J. H. "Ranald Slidell Mackenzie." *Journal of the U.S. Cavalry Association*, *10* (1897), 367–82.

Elliott, Charles P. "The Geronimo Campaign of 1885–86." *Journal of the U.S. Cavalry Association*, *21* (1910), 211–36.

Ellis, Richard N. "Copper-Skinned Soldiers: The Apache Scouts." *Great
Plains Journal, *5* (1966), 51–67.
———. "The Humanitarian Generals." *Western Historical Quarterly*, *3*
(1972), 169–78.
———. "The Humanitarian Soldiers." *Journal of Arizona History*, *10*
(1969), 55–62.
Essin, Emmett M., III. "Mules, Packs, and Packtrains." *Southwestern*
Historical Quarterly, *74* (1970), 52–63.
Fechet, E. G. "The True Story of the Death of Sitting Bull." *Proceedings*
and Collections of the Nebraska State Historical Society, 2d ser., 2
(1898), 179–89.
Forbes, Archibald. "The United States Army." *North American Review*,
135 (1882), 127–45.
Forsyth, George A. "A Frontier Fight." *Harper's New Monthly Magazine*,
91 (1895), 42–62.
Garfield, James A. "The Army of the United States." *North American*
Review, *136* (1878), 193–216, 442–66.
Garfield, Marvin H. "Defense of the Kansas Frontier, 1866–67." *Kansas*
Historical Quarterly, *1* (1931–32), 326–45.
Gatewood, Charles B. "The Surrender of Geronimo." *Proceedings of the*
Annual Meeting and Dinner of the Order of Indian Wars of the
United States. Washington, D.C., 1929.
Gibbon, John. "Hunting Sitting Bull." *American Catholic Quarterly Re-*
view, *2* (1877), 665–94.
———. "Last Summer's Expedition against the Sioux." *American Cath-*
olic Quarterly Review, *2* (1877), 271–304.
———. "The Battle of the Big Hole." *Harper's Weekly*, *39* (1895),
1215–16, 1235–36.
———. "Transfer of the Indian Bureau to War Department." *American*
Catholic Quarterly Review, *19* (1894), 244–59.
Godfrey, Edward S. "Cavalry Fire Discipline." *Journal of the Military*
Service Institution of the United States, *19* (1896), 252–59.
———. "Custer's Last Battle." *Century Magazine*, *43* (1892), 358–87.
———. "Some Reminiscences, Including an Account of General Sully's
Expedition against the Southern Plains Indians, 1868." *Cavalry*
Journal, *36* (1927), 417–25.
———. "Some Reminiscences, Including the Washita Battle, November
25, 1868." *Cavalry Journal*, *37* (1928), 481–50.
Gray, John S., ed. "Captain Clifford's Story of the Sioux War of 1876."
Westerners Brand Book (Chicago), *26* (1969–70), 73–79, 81–83,
86–88.
———. "Sitting Bull Strikes the Glendive Supply Trains." *Westerners*
Brand Book (Chicago), *28* (1971), 25–27, 31–32.
Green, L. D. "The Army and the Indian." *Harper's Weekly*, *38* (1894),
471.
Haley, J. Evetts. "The Comanchero Trade." *Southwestern Historical*
Quarterly, *38* (1934–35), 157–76.
Hall, W. P. "The Use of Arms, Mounted." *Journal of the U.S. Cavalry*
Association, *1* (1888), 34–37.
Hardin, C. B. "The Sheepeater Campaign." *Journal of the Military Service*
Institution of the United States, *47* (1910), 25–40.

Hastings, James R. "The Tragedy at Camp Grant in 1871." *Arizona and the West, 1* (1959), 146–60.

Hickok, H. R. "Our Cavalry Organization as Viewed in the Light of Its History and of Legislation." *Journal of the U.S. Cavalry Association, 22* (1912), 995–1009.

Holabird, S. B. "Army Wagon Transportation." *Ordnance Notes—No. 189.* Washington, D.C., April 15, 1882.

Holden, W. C. "Frontier Defense in Texas During the Civil War." *West Texas Historical Association Year Book, 4* (1928), 16–31.

Howe, George F., ed., "Expedition to the Yellowstone River in 1873: Letters of a Young Cavalry Officer." *Mississippi Valley Historical Review, 39* (1952), 519–34.

Hughes, Robert P. "The Campaign against the Sioux in 1876." *Journal of the Military Service Institution of the United States, 18* (1896), reprinted in W. A. Graham, *Story of the Little Big Horn* (Harrisburg, Pa., 1945).

Hutchins, James S. "Boots and Saddles on the Frontier." *Westerners Brand Book* (Chicago), *12* (March 1966), 1–3, 6–8.

———. "Mounted Riflemen: The Real Role of Cavalry in the Indian Wars." In K. Ross Toole *et al.*, eds., *Probing the American West: Papers from the Santa Fe Conference.* Santa Fe, N.M., 1962, pp. 79–85.

———. "The Army Campaign Hat of 1872." *Military Collector and Historian, 16* (1964), 65–73.

———. "The Cavalry Campaign Outfit at the Little Big Horn." *Military Collector and Historian, 7* (1956), 91–101.

Jenness, George B. "The Battle of Beaver Creek." *Transactions of the Kansas State Historical Society, 9* (1905–6), 443–52.

Joseph, Chief. "An Indian's View of Indian Affairs." *North American Review, 128* (1879), 412–33.

King, Charles. "The Story of a March." *Journal of the Military Service Institution of the United States, 3* (1890), 121–29.

King, James T. "General Crook at Camp Cloud Peak: 'I Am at a Loss What to Do.'" *Journal of the West, 11* (1972), 114–27.

———. "George Crook: Indian Fighter and Humanitarian." *Arizona and the West; 9* (1967), 333–48.

———. "Needed: A Reevaluation of General George Crook." *Nebraska History, 45* (1964), 223–35.

Kloster, Donald E. "Uniforms of the Army Prior and Subsequent to 1872." *Military Collector and Historian, 14* (1962), 103–12.

Larsen, Arthur J., ed. "The Black Hills Gold Rush." *North Dakota Historical Quarterly, 6* (1931–32), 302–18.

McBlain, John F. "The Last Fight of the Sioux War of 1876–77." *Journal of the U.S. Cavalry Association, 10* (1897), 122–27.

McClernand, E. J. "With the Indian and the Buffalo in Montana." *Cavalry Journal, 25* (1926), 500–11; *26* (1927), 7–54, 191–207.

Mattison, Ray H. "The Army Post on the Northern Plains, 1865–1885." *Nebraska History, 35* (1954), 1–27.

———. "The Indian Reservation System on the Upper Missouri, 1865–1890." *Nebraska History, 36* (1955), 141–72.

————. "The Military Frontier on the Upper Missouri." *Nebraska History, 37* (1956).

Millbrook, Minnie Dubbs. "The West Breaks in General Custer." *Kansas Historical Quarterly, 36* (1970), 113–48.

Montgomery, Mrs. Frank. "Fort Wallace and Its Relation to the Frontier." *Kansas Historical Collections, 17* (1926–28), 189–282.

Murray, Robert A. "Commentaries on the Col. Henry B. Carrington Image." *Denver Westerners Roundup, 24* (March 1968), 3–12.

Nohl, Lessing H., Jr. "Mackenzie against Dull Knife: Breaking the Northern Cheyennes in 1876." In K. Ross Toole, *et al.*, eds. *Probing the American West: Papers from the Santa Fe Conference* (Santa Fe, N.M., 1962), pp. 86–92.

Peters, Joseph P. "Uncle Sam's Icebox Soldiers: The U.S. Army in Alaska, 1867–1877." *New York Westerners Brand Book, 9* (1962), 49–50.

Porter, Kenneth W. "The Seminole-Negro Indian Scouts, 1870–1881." *Southwestern Historical Quarterly, 55* (1951–52), 358–77.

————, and Edward S. Wallace. "Thunderbolt of the Frontier." *New York Westerners Brand Book, 8* (1961), 73–75, 82–86.

Prickett, Robert C. "The Malfeasance of William Worth Belknap." *North Dakota History, 17* (1950), 5–52, 97–134.

Reeve, Frank D., ed. "Frederick E. Phelps: A Soldier's Memoirs." *New Mexico Historical Review, 25* (1950), 37–56, 109–35, 187–221.

Richardson, Rupert N. "The Comanche Indians at the Adobe Walls Fight." *Panhandle-Plains Historical Review, 4* (1931), 24–38.

Rickey, Don, Jr. "The Battle of Wolf Mountain." *Montana, the Magazine of Western History, 13* (Spring 1963), 44–54.

Rister, C. C. "The Significance of the Jacksboro Indian Affair of 1871." *Southwestern Historical Quarterly, 29* (1926), 181–200.

Romeyn, Henry. "The Capture of Chief Joseph and the Nez Percé Indians." Montana Historical Society *Contributions*, 2 (1896), 283–91.

Rothenberg, Gunther E. "General George Crook and the Apaches, 1872–73." *Westerners Brand Book* (Chicago), *13* (September 1955), 49–56.

Russell, Don. "Captain Charles King, Chronicler of the Frontier." *Westerners Brand Book* (Chicago), *9* (March 1952), 1–3, 7–8.

————. "The Army of the Frontier, 1865–1891." *Westerners Brand Book* (Chicago), *6* (July 1949), 33–35, 38–40.

Seymour, Charles G. "The Sioux Rebellion, the Final Review." *Harper's Weekly, 35* (1891), 106.

Shipp, W. E. "Captain Crawford's Last Expedition." *Journal of the U.S. Cavalry Association, 5* (1892), 343–61.

————. "Mounted Infantry." *Journal of the U.S. Cavalry Association, 5* (1892), 76–80.

Sprague, Marshall. "The Dude from Limerick." *The American West, 3* (Fall 1966), 53–61, 91–93.

Stacey, C. P. "The Military Aspect of Canada's Winning of the West, 1870–1885." *Canadian Historical Review, 21* (1940), 1–24.

Straight, Michael. "Carrington: The Valor of Defeat." *Corral Dust* (Potomac Westerners), *4* (December 1959), 25–27.

Thane, James L., Jr. "The Montana 'Indian War' of 1867." *Arizona and the West, 10* (1968), 153–70.

Thompson, W. A. "Scouting with Mackenzie." *Journal of the U.S. Cavalry Association, 10* (1897), 429–33.

Utley, Robert M. "Custer: Hero or Butcher?" *American History Illustrated, 5* (February 1971), 4–9, 43–48.

———. "Pecos Bill on the Texas Frontier." *The American West, 6* (1969), 4–13, 61–62.

———. "The Battle of the Little Bighorn." In Potomac Westerners, *Great Western Indian Fights* (New York, 1960), chap. 20.

Vinton, Lawrence. "The Geronimo Campaign: As told by a Trooper of 'B' Troop of the 4th U.S. Cavalry." *Journal of the West, 11* (1972), 157–69.

Wallace, Ernest, and Adrian S. Anderson. "R. S. Mackenzie and the Kickapoos: The Raid into Mexico in 1873." *Arizona and the West, 7* (1965), 105–26.

Waltmann, Henry G. "Circumstantial Reformer: President Grant & the Indian Problem." *Arizona and the West, 13* (1971), 323–42.

Watson, Chandler B. "Recollections of the Bannock War." *Oregon Historical Quarterly, 68* (1967), 317–29.

White, Lonnie J. "General Sully's Expedition to the North Canadian, 1868," *Journal of the West, 11* (1972), 75–98.

———. "Winter Campaigning with Custer and Sheridan: The Expedition of the Nineteenth Kansas Volunteer Cavalry." *Journal of the West, 6* (1967), 68–98.

BOOKS

Adams, Alexander B. *Geronimo: A Biography.* New York, 1971.

Ambrose, Stephen E. *Upton and the Army.* Baton Rouge, La., 1964.

Armes, George A. *Ups and Downs of an Army Officer.* Washington, D.C., 1900.

Arnold, R. Ross. *The Indian Wars of Idaho.* Caldwell, Ida., 1932.

Ashburn, P. M. *A History of the Medical Department of the United States Army.* Boston, 1929.

Athearn, Robert G. *Forts of the Upper Missouri.* Englewood Cliffs, N.J., 1967.

———. *William Tecumseh Sherman and the Settlement of the West.* Norman, Okla., 1956.

Bailey, Paul. *Wovoka, the Indian Messiah.* Los Angeles, Calif., 1957.

Baldwin, Alice Blackwood. *Memoirs of the Late Frank D. Baldwin, Major General, U.S.A.* Los Angeles, Calif., 1929.

Battey, Thomas C. *The Life and Adventures of a Quaker among the Indians.* Boston, 1903.

Beal, Merrill D. *"I Will Fight No More Forever": Chief Joseph and the Nez Percé War.* New York, 1967.

Bender, A. B. *A Study of the Mescalero Apache Indians, 1846–1880.* St. Louis, Mo., 1960 (multilith).

Bernardo, C. Joseph, and Eugene H. Bacon. *American Military Policy: Its Development Since 1775.* Harrisburg, Pa., 1957.

Berthrong, Donald J. *The Southern Cheyennes. Norman, Okla.*, 1963.
Betzinez, Jason, with W. S. Nye. *I Fought with Geronimo*. Harrisburg, Pa., 1959.
Biddle, Ellen McG. *Reminiscences of a Soldier's Wife*. Philadelphia, Pa., 1907.
Bigelow, Donald N. *William Conant Church and the Army and Navy Journal*. New York, 1952.
Bisbee, William S. *Through Four American Wars*. Boston, 1931.
Black Hills Engineer. Custer Expedition Number, *17* (1929).
Bourke, John G. *An Apache Campaign in the Sierra Madre*. 2d ed., New York, 1958.
———. *On the Border with Crook*. Chicago, 1891.
Boyd, Mrs. Orsemus B. *Cavalry Life in Tent and Field*. New York, 1894.
Bradley, James H. *The March of the Montana Column: A Prelude to the Custer Disaster*, ed. Edgar I. Stewart. Norman, Okla., 1961.
Brady, Cyrus T. *Indian Fights and Fighters*. New York, 1912.
———. *Northwestern Fights and Fighters*. New York, 1913.
Branch, E. Douglas. *The Hunting of the Buffalo*. New York & London, 1929.
Brandes, Ray. *Frontier Military Posts of Arizona*. Globe, Ariz., 1960.
———, ed. *Troopers West: Military and Indian Affairs on the American Frontier*. San Diego, Calif., 1970.
Brimlow, George F. *The Bannock Indian War of 1878*. Caldwell, Ida., 1938.
Brinckerhoff, Sidney B. *Metal Uniform Insignia of the Frontier U.S. Army, 1846–1902*. Museum Monograph No. 3, Arizona Historical Society. Tucson, Ariz., 1972.
———. *Military Headgear in the Southwest, 1846–1890*. Museum Monograph No. 1, Arizona Historical Society. Tucson, Ariz., 1963.
Brininstool, E. A., and Grace R. Hebard. *The Bozeman Trail*. 2 vols., Cleveland, Ohio, 1922.
———. *Crazy Horse*. Los Angeles, Calif., 1949.
Brown, Dee. *Fort Phil Kearny, An American Saga*. New York, 1962.
Brown, Mark H. *The Flight of the Nez Percé: A History of the Nez Percé War*. New York, 1967.
———. *The Plainsmen of the Yellowstone: A History of the Yellowstone Basin*. New York, 1961.
Brown, W. C. *The Sheepeater Campaign*. Caldwell, Ida., 1926.
Bruce, Robert. *The Fighting Norths and Pawnee Scouts*. New York, 1932.
Carpenter, John A. *Sword and Olive Branch: Oliver Otis Howard*. Pittsburgh, Pa., 1964.
Carriker, Robert C. *Fort Supply, Indian Territory: Frontier Outpost on the Plains*. Norman, Okla., 1970.
Carrington, Frances C. *Army Life on the Plains*. Philadelphia, Pa., 1910.
Carrington, Margaret I. *Absaraka, Home of the Crows*, ed. Milo M. Quaife. Chicago, 1950.
Carter, Robert G. *On the Border with Mackenzie, or Winning West Texas from the Comanches*. New York, 1961.
Carter, William H. *From Yorktown to Santiago with the Sixth U.S. Cavalry*. Baltimore, 1900.
———. *The Life of Lieutenant General Chaffee*. Chicago, 1917.

Chandler, Melbourne C. *Of Garryowen in Glory: The History of the 7th U.S. Cavalry.* p.p., 1960.

Chappell, Gordon. *Brass Spikes and Horsehair Plumes: A Study of U.S. Army Dress Helmets, 1872–1903.* Museum Monograph No. 4, Arizona Pioneers Historical Society, Tucson, Ariz., 1966.

———. *The Search for the Well-Dressed Soldier, 1865–1890.* Museum Monograph No. 5, Arizona Historical Society, Tucson, Ariz., 1972.

———. *Summer Helmets of the U.S. Army, 1875–1910.* Wyoming State Museum Monograph No. 1, Cheyenne, Wyo., 1967.

Clendenen, Clarence C. *Blood on the Border: The United States Army and the Mexican Irregulars.* New York, 1969.

Clum, Woodworth, *Apache Agent: The Story of John P. Clum.* New York, 1936.

Cochran, Mrs. M. A. *Posey; or, From Reveille to Retreat, An Army Story.* Cincinnati, 1896.

Crane, Charles J. *Experiences of a Colonel of Infantry.* New York, 1922.

Crawford, Samuel J. *Kansas in the Sixties.* Chicago, 1911.

Crook, George. *General George Crook: His Autobiography,* ed. Martin F. Schmitt. Norman, Okla., 1946.

———. *Résumé of Operations against Apache Indians, 1882 to 1886.* p.p., 1886. Reprint with notes and introduction by Barry C. Johnson. London, 1971.

Cruse, Thomas. *Apache Days and After.* Caldwell, Ida., 1941.

Custer, Elizabeth B. *Boots and Saddles, or Life in Dakota with General Custer.* New York, 1885.

———. *Following the Guidon.* New York, 1890.

———. *Tenting on the Plains, or Gen'l Custer in Kansas and Texas.* New York, 1893.

Custer, George A. *My Life on the Plains,* ed., Milo M. Quaife, Chicago, 1952.

Danker, Donald F., ed. *Man of the Plains: Recollections of Luther North, 1856–1882.* Lincoln, Neb., 1961.

Davis, Britton. *The Truth about Geronimo.* New Haven, Conn., 1929.

Day, James M., and Dorman Winfrey, eds. *Texas Indian Papers, 1860–1916.* Austin, Texas, 1961.

Dillon, Richard H., ed. *William Henry Boyd's Personal Observations on the Conduct of the Modoc War.* Los Angeles, Calif., n.d.

Downey, Fairfax. *Indian-Fighting Army.* New York, 1941.

Dunn, J. P. *Massacres of the Mountains: A History of the Indian Wars of the Far West, 1815–1875.* New York, 1886.

Dusenberry, Verne. *The Northern Cheyennes.* Helena, Mont., 1955.

Ege, Robert J. *Tell Baker to Strike Them Hard: Incident on the Marias.* Bellevue, Neb., 1970.

Eggan, Fred., ed. *The Social Anthropology of North American Tribes.* Chicago, 1955.

Eisenschiml, Otto. *The Celebrated Case of Fitz John Porter.* Indianapolis and New York, 1950.

Ellis, Richard N. *General Pope and U.S. Indian Policy.* Albuquerque, N.M., 1970.

Emmitt, Robert. *The Last War Trail: The Utes and the Settlement of Colorado.* Norman, Okla., 1955.

Faulk, Odie B. *The Geronimo Campaign.* New York, 1969.

Finerty, John F. *War-Path and Bivouac, or, The Conquest of the Sioux.* Norman, Okla., 1961.

Foner, Jack D. *The United States Soldier Between Two Wars, 1865–1898.* New York, 1970.

Forsyth, George A. *The Story of the Soldier.* New York, 1900.

———. *Thrilling Days of Army Life.* New York, 1902.

Fowler, Arlen L. *The Black Infantry in the West, 1869–1891.* Westport, Conn., 1971.

Frazer, Robert W. *Forts of the West.* Norman, Okla., 1965.

Fritz, Henry. *The Movement for Indian Assimilation, 1860–1890.* Philadelphia, 1963.

Frost, Lawrence A. *The Court-Martial of General George Armstrong Custer.* Norman, Okla., 1968.

———. *The Custer Album: A Pictorial Biography of General George A. Custer.* Seattle, 1964.

Fry, James B. *The History and Legal Effect of Brevets in the Armies of Great Britain and the United States.* New York, 1877.

Ganoe, William A. *The History of the United States Army.* New York, 1924.

Gibbon, John. *Gibbon on the Sioux Campaign of 1876.* Bellevue, Neb., 1969.

Gibson, A. M. *The Kickapoos: Lords of the Middle Border.* Norman, Okla., 1963.

Gifford, E. W. *The Northeastern and Western Yavapai.* University of California Publications in American Archaeology and Ethnology, *34.* Berkeley, Calif., 1936.

———. *The Southeastern Yavapai.* University of California Publications in American Archaeology and Ethnology, *29.* Berkeley, Calif., 1932.

Gillett, James B. *Six Years with the Texas Rangers.* New Haven, Conn., 1925.

Glassley, Ray H. *Pacific Northwest Indian Wars.* Portland, Oreg., 1953.

Gluckman, Aracadi. *United States Martial Pistols and Revolvers.* Buffalo, N.Y., 1939.

———. *United States Muskets, Rifles, and Carbines.* Buffalo, N.Y., 1948.

Goodwin, Grenville. *The Social Organization of the Western Apache.* Tucson, Ariz., 1969.

Graham, W. A., ed. *The Reno Court of Inquiry: Abstract of the Official Record of Proceedings..* Harrisburg, Pa., 1954.

———. *The Custer Myth: A Source Book of Custeriana.* Harrisburg, Pa., 1953.

———. *The Story of the Little Big Horn.* Harrisburg, Pa., 1945.

Grant, Ulysses S. *Personal Memoirs of U. S. Grant,* ed. E. B. Long. Cleveland and New York, 1952.

Greene, Duane N. *Ladies and Officers of the United States Army; or, American Aristocracy, A Sketch of the Social Life and Character of the Army.* Chicago, 1880.

Gregg, Robert D. *The Influence of Border Troubles on Relations between the United States and Mexico, 1876–1910.* Baltimore, Md., 1937.

Grinnell, George B. *The Fighting Cheyennes.* 2d ed., Norman, Okla., 1956.

————. *Two Great Scouts and Their Pawnee Battalion*. Cleveland, Ohio, 1928.

Hagan, William T. *Indian Police and Judges*. New Haven, Conn., 1966.

Hagemann, E. R., ed. *Fighting Rebels and Redskins: Experiences in Army Life of Colonel George B. Sanford, 1861–1892*. Norman, Okla., 1969.

Haley, J. Evetts. *Fort Concho and the Texas Frontier*. San Angelo, Tex., 1952.

Hammer, Kenneth M. *The Springfield Carbine on the Western Frontier*. Bellevue, Neb., 1970.

Hanson, Joseph Mills. *The Conquest of the Missouri*. 2d ed., New York, 1946.

Hazen, W. B. *Some Corrections to My Life on the Plains*. St. Paul, Minn., 1875. Reprinted in *Chronicles of Oklahoma, 3* (1925), 295–318.

Heitman, Francis B., comp. *Historical Register and Dictionary of the United States Army*. 2 vols., Washington, D.C., 1903.

Heyman, Max L. *Prudent Soldier: A Biography of Major General E. R. S. Canby, 1817–1873*. Glendale, Calif., 1959.

Hill, Douglas. *The Opening of the Canadian West*. New York, 1967.

Howard, Oliver O. *My Life and Experiences among Our Hostile Indians*. Hartford, Conn., 1907.

————. *Nez Percé Joseph*. Boston, 1881.

Huntington, Samuel P. *The Soldier and the State: The Theory and Politics of Civil-Military Relations*. Cambridge, Mass., 1957.

Hutchins, James S. Introduction to *Ordnance Memoranda No. 29: Horse Equipments and Cavalry Accoutrements as Prescribed by G.O. 73, A.G.O. 1885*. Pasadena, Calif., 1970.

Hyde, George E. *Life of George Bent, Written from His Letters*, ed. Savoie Lottinville. Norman, Okla., 1967.

————. *Red Cloud's Folk: A History of the Oglala Sioux Indians*. Norman, Okla., 1937.

————. *A Sioux Chronicle*. Norman, Okla., 1956.

————. *Spotted Tail's Folk: A History of the Brulé Sioux*. Norman, Okla., 1961.

Ingersoll, L. D. *A History of the War Department of the United States*. Washington, D.C., 1879.

Jackson, Donald. *Custer's Gold: The United States Cavalry Expedition of 1874*. New Haven, Conn., 1966.

Johnson, Virginia, *The Unregimented General: A Biography of Nelson A. Miles*. Boston, 1962.

Jones, Douglas C. *The Treaty of Medicine Lodge: The Story of the Great Treaty Council as Told by Eyewitnesses*. Norman, Okla., 1966.

Josephy, Alvin M., Jr. *The Nez Percé Indians and the Opening of the Northwest*. New Haven, Conn., 1965.

Kane, Lucille M., trans. and ed. *Military Life in Dakota: The Journal of Philippe Régis de Trobriand*. St. Paul, Minn., 1951.

Kappler, Charles J., comp. *Indian Affairs: Laws and Treaties*. 2 vols. Washington, D.C., 1904.

Keim, DeB. Randolph. *Sheridan's Troopers on the Border: A Winter Campaign on the Plains*. Philadelphia, 1891.

Kelly, Luther S. *"Yellowstone Kelly": Memoirs of Luther S. Kelly*, ed. Milo M. Quaife. New Haven, Conn., 1926.

Kenner, Charles L. *A History of New Mexican-Plains Indian Relations.* Norman, Okla., 1969.

King, Charles. *Campaigning with Crook.* Norman, Okla., 1964.

King, James T. *War Eagle: A Life of General Eugene A. Carr.* Lincoln, Neb., 1963.

Knight, Oliver. *Following the Indian Wars: The Story of the Newspaper Correspondents among the Indian Campaigners.* Norman, Okla., 1960.

Lane, Jack C., ed. *Chasing Geronimo: The Journal of Leonard Wood, May–September 1886.* Albuquerque, N.M., 1970.

Lane, Lydia Spencer. *I Married a Soldier.* Philadelphia, Pa., 1893.

Laufe, Abe, ed. *An Army Doctor's Wife on the Frontier: Letters from Alaska and the Far West, 1874–1878.* Pittsburgh, Pa., 1962.

Leckie, William F. *The Buffalo Soldiers: A Narrative of Negro Cavalry in the West.* Norman, Okla., 1967.

————. *The Military Conquest of the Southern Plains.* Norman, Okla., 1963.

Lewis, Lloyd. *Sherman: Fighting Prophet.* New York, 1932.

Lockwood, Frank C. *The Apache Indians.* New York, 1936.

Luddington, M. I., comp. *Uniforms of the Army of the United States from 1774–1889.* Washington, D.C., 1889.

Lummis, Charles F. *General Crook and the Apache Wars.* Flagstaff, Ariz., 1966.

McCracken, Harold, ed. *Frederic Remington's Own West.* New York, 1960.

McDermott, John D. *Forlorn Hope: A Study of the Battle of White Bird Canyon.* Washington, D.C., 1968 (multilith).

McGillycuddy, Julia B. *McGillycuddy, Agent.* Palo Alto, Calif., 1941.

McLaughlin, James. *My Friend the Indian.* Boston, 1910.

McWhorter, Lucullus V. *Hear Me, My Chiefs!* Caldwell, Ida., 1952.

————. *Yellow Wolf: His Own Story.* Caldwell, Ida., 1948.

Madsden, Brigham D. *The Bannock of Idaho.* Caldwell, Ida., 1958.

Manypenny, George W. *Our Indian Wards.* Cincinnati, Ohio, 1880.

Mardock, Robert W. *The Reformers and the American Indian.* Columbia, Mo., 1971.

Marquis, Thomas B. *Custer on the Little Bighorn.* p.p., 1967.

————. *A Warrior Who Fought Custer.* Minneapolis, Minn., 1931.

Mattes, Merrill J. *Indians, Infants, and Infantry: Andrew and Elizabeth Burt on the Frontier.* Denver, Colo., 1960.

Mazzanovich, Anton. *Trailing Geronimo.* 3d ed., Los Angeles, Calif., 1931.

Meacham, Alfred B. *Wigwam and War-Path.* Boston, 1875.

Merritt, Wesley. "Three Indian Campaigns." Reprinted from *Harper's New Monthly Magazine* (April 1890) as *Merritt and the Indian Wars*, ed. Barry C. Johnson. London, 1972.

Miles, Nelson A. *Personal Recollections and Observations.* Chicago, 1896.

————. *Serving the Republic.* New York, 1911.

Mills, Anson. *My Story.* p.p., Washington, D.C., 1918.

Monaghan, Jay. *Custer: Life of General George Armstrong Custer.* Boston, 1959.

Mooney, James. *Calendar History of the Kiowa Indians.* 17th Annual Report of the Bureau of American Ethnology. Washington, D.C., 1898.

——. *The Ghost Dance Religion and the Sioux Outbreak of 1890.* 14th Annual Report of the Bureau of American Ethnology. Washington, D.C., 1896.

Mulford, Ami F. *Fighting Indians in the Seventh United States Cavalry.* Corning, N.Y., 1879.

Murray, Keith A. *The Modocs and Their War.* Norman, Okla., 1959.

Murray, Richard Y. *The History of Fort Bowie.* MA Thesis, Univ. of Ariz., Tucson, 1951.

Murray, Robert A. *The Army on Powder River.* Bellevue, Neb., 1969.

——. *Military Posts in the Powder River Country of Wyoming, 1865–1894.* Lincoln, Neb., 1968.

Nye, W. S. *Bad Medicine and Good: Tales of the Kiowas.* Norman, Okla., 1962.

——. *Carbine and Lance: The Story of Old Fort Sill,* Norman, Okla., 1937.

——. *Plains Indian Raiders: The Final Phases of Warfare from the Arkansas to the Red River.* Norman, Okla., 1968.

Ogle, Ralph H. *Federal Control of the Western Apaches, 1848–1886.* Albuquerque, N.M., 1940.

Oliva, Leo E. *Soldiers on the Santa Fe Trail.* Norman, Okla., 1967.

Olson, James C. *Red Cloud and the Sioux Problem.* Lincoln, Neb., 1965.

Ostrander, Alson B. *An Army Boy of the Sixties.* Chicago, 1924.

Parker, James. *The Old Army Memories.* Philadelphia, Pa., 1929.

Parker, Watson. *Gold in the Black Hills.* Norman, Okla., 1966.

Parsons, John E., and John S. du Mont. *Firearms in the Custer Battle.* Harrisburg, Pa., 1953.

Peters, Joseph P., comp. *Indian Battles and Skirmishes on the American Frontier.* New York, 1966.

Potomac Westerners. *Great Western Indian Fights.* New York, 1960.

Powell, Peter J. *Sweet Medicine: The Continuing Role of the Sacred Arrows, the Sun Dance, and the Sacred Buffalo Hat in Northern Cheyenne History.* 2 vols., Norman, Okla., 1969.

Pratt, Richard H. *Battlefield and Classroom: Four Decades with the American Indian, 1867–1904,* ed. Robert M. Utley. New Haven, Conn., 1964.

Price, George F. *Across the Continent with the Fifth Cavalry.* 2d ed., New York, 1959.

Priest, Loring B. *Uncle Sam's Stepchildren: The Reformation of United States Indian Policy, 1865–1887.* New Brunswick, N.J., 1942.

Prucha, Francis Paul. *Guide to the Military Posts of the United States.* Madison, Wis., 1964.

Randall, James G., ed. *The Diary of Orville Hickman Browning.* 2 vols., Springfield, Ill., 1933.

Ray, Verne F. *Primitive Pragmatists: The Modoc Indians of Northern California.* Seattle, Wash., 1963.

Richardson, James D., comp. *A Compilation of Messages and Papers of the Presidents, 1789–1897.* 10 vols., Washington, D.C. 1897.

Richardson, Rupert N. *The Comanche Barrier to South Plains Settlement.* Glendale, Calif., 1933.

————. *The Frontier of Northwest Texas, 1846 to 1876*. Glendale, Calif., 1963.

Rickey, Don, Jr. *Forty Miles a Day on Beans and Hay: The Enlisted Soldier Fighting the Indian Wars*. Norman, Okla., 1963.

Riddle, Jeff C. *The Indian History of the Modoc War and the Causes That Led to It*. n.p., 1914.

Rippy, J. Fred. *The United States and Mexico*. New York, 1926.

Risch, Erna. *Quartermaster Support of the Army: A History of the Corps, 1775–1939*. Washington, D.C., 1962.

Rister, C. C. *Border Command: General Phil Sheridan in the West*. Norman, Okla., 1944.

————. *Fort Griffin on the Texas Frontier*. Norman, Okla., 1956.

Rockwell, Wilson. *The Utes, A Forgotten People*, Denver, Colo., 1956.

Rodenbough, Theo. F. *From Everglade to Cañon with the Second Dragoons*. New York, 1875.

————, and William F. Haskin. *The Army of the United States: Historical Sketches of Staff and Line*. New York, 1896.

Roe, Frances M. A. *Army Letters from an Officer's Wife*. New York, 1909.

Russell, Don. *The Lives and Legends of Buffalo Bill*. Norman, Okla., 1960.

————. *One Hundred and Three Fights and Scrimmages: The Story of General Reuben F. Bernard*. Washington, D.C., 1936.

Sabin, Edwin L. *Building the Pacific Railway*. Philadelphia and London, 1919.

Sandoz, Mari. *The Buffalo Hunters*. New York, 1954.

————. *Cheyenne Autumn*. New York, 1953.

————. *Crazy Horse, Strange Man of the Oglalas*. New York, 1942.

Schell, Herbert S. *History of South Dakota*. Lincoln, Neb., 1961.

Schmitt, Martin F., and Dee Brown. *Fighting Indians of the West*. New York, 1948.

Schofield, John M. *Forty-Six Years in the Army*. New York, 1897.

Schroeder, Albert H. *A Study of the Apache Indians*. 5 vols., Santa Fe, N.M., 1960–63 (multilith).

————. *A Study of Yavapai History*. 3 vols., Santa Fe, N.M., 1959 (multilith).

Sheridan, Philip H. *Outline Descriptions of the Posts in the Military Division of the Missouri*. Chicago, 1876.

————. *Personal Memoirs*. 2 vols., New York, 1888.

————. *Record of Engagements with Hostile Indians within the Military Division of the Missouri from 1868 to 1882*. Washington, D.C., 1882.

Sonnichsen, C. L. *The Mescalero Apaches*. Norman, Okla., 1958.

Spotts, David L., and E. A. Brininstool. *Campaigning with Custer and the Nineteenth Kansas Volunteer Cavalry*. Los Angeles, 1928.

Sprague, Marshall. *Massacre: The Tragedy at White River*. Boston and Toronto, 1957.

Stanley, David S. *Personal Memoirs of Major General D. S. Stanley, U.S.A.* Cambridge, Mass., 1917.

Stanley, Henry M. *My Early Travels and Adventures in America and Asia*. 2 vols., New York, 1905.

Stewart, Edgar I. *Custer's Luck*. Norman, Okla., 1955.

Stewart, Omer C. *The Northern Paiute Bands*. Anthropological Records, vol. 13, no. 2. Berkeley, Calif., 1939.

Summerhayes, Martha. *Vanished Arizona: Recollections of My Army Life*, 1908; Lippincott ed., Philadelphia, 1963.

Swanson, Earl H., Jr., ed. *Languages and Cultures of Western North America: Essays in Honor of Sven S. Liljeblad*. Caldwell, Ida., 1970.

Tatum, Lawrie. *Our Red Brothers and the Peace Policy of President Ulysses S. Grant*. Philadelphia, Pa., 1899.

Taylor, Joe F., ed. *The Indian Campaign on the Staked Plains, 1874–1875: Military Correspondence from War Department Adjutant General's Office File 2815–1874*. Canyon, Tex., 1962.

Thian, Raphael P., comp. *Legislative History of the General Staff of the Army of the United States . . . from 1775 to 1901*. Washington, D.C., 1901.

———. *Notes Illustrating the Military Geography of the United States, 1813–1880*. Washington, D.C., 1881.

Thompson, Erwin N. *Modoc War: Its Military History and Topography*. Sacramento, Calif., 1971.

Thorndike, Rachel Sherman, ed. *The Sherman Letters: Correspondence between General and Senator Sherman from 1837 to 1891*. New York, 1894.

Thrapp, Dan L. *Al Sieber, Chief of Scouts*. Norman, Okla., 1964.

———. *The Conquest of Apacheria*. Norman, Okla., 1967.

———. *General Crook and the Sierra Madre Adventure*. Norman, Okla., 1972.

Trobriand, Philippe Régis de. *See* Kane, Lucille M.

Turner, John P. *The North-West Mounted Police, 1873–1893*. 2 vols., Ottawa, 1950.

Upton, Emory. *The Military Policy of the United States*. Washington, D.C., 1917.

Utley, Robert M. *Custer Battlefield National Monument*. National Park Service Historical Handbook, Washington, D.C., 1969.

———. *Fort Davis National Historic Site*. National Park Service Historical Handbook, Washington, D.C., 1965.

———. *Frontiersmen in Blue: The United States Army and the Indian, 1848–1865*. New York, 1967.

———. *The Last Days of the Sioux Nation*. New Haven, Conn., 1963.

Van de Water, Frederick F. *Glory Hunter: A Life of General Custer*. Indianapolis, Ind., 1934.

Vaughn, J. W., *Indian Fights: New Facts on Seven Encounters*. Norman, Okla., 1966.

———. *The Reynolds Campaign on Powder River*. Norman, Okla., 1966.

———. *With Crook at the Rosebud*. Norman, Okla., 1956.

Vestal, Stanley, ed. *New Sources of Indian History, 1850–1891*. Norman, Okla., 1934.

———. *Sitting Bull, Champion of the Sioux*. 2d ed., Norman, Okla., 1957.

Villegas, Daniel Cosío. *The United States Versus Porfiro Díaz*, trans. Nettie Lee Benson. Lincoln, Neb., 1963.

Wallace, Andrew. *Gen. August V. Kautz and the Southwestern Frontier*. Ph.D. Dissertation, Univ. of Ariz., Tucson, 1967.

Wallace, Ernest. *Ranald S. Mackenzie on the Texas Frontier*. Lubbock, Tex., 1965.
———, ed. *Ranald S. Mackenzie's Official Correspondence Relating to Texas, 1871–1873*. Lubbock, Tex., 1967.
———. *Ranald S. Mackenzie's Official Correspondence Relating to Texas, 1873–1879*. Lubbock, Tex., 1968.
Weigley, Russell F. *History of the United States Army*. New York, 1967.
———. *Towards an American Army: Military Thought from Washington to Marshall*. New York and London, 1962.
Wellman, Paul. *Death on Horseback: Seventy Years of War for the American West*. Philadelphia, Pa., 1947.
Welsh, Herbert. *The Apache Prisoners at Fort Marion, St. Augustine, Florida*. Indian Rights Association, 1887.
Wheeler, Homer W. *Buffalo Days: Forty Years in the Old West*. New York and Chicago, 1923.
White, Leonard D. *The Republican Era, 1869–1901: A Study in Administrative History*. New York, 1958.
Whitman, S. E. *The Troopers: An Informal History of the Plains Cavalry*. New York, 1962.
Whittaker, Frederick. *Complete Life of Gen. George A. Custer*. New York, 1876.
Wissler, Clark. *Indian Cavalcade, or Life on the Old-Time Indian Reservations*. New York, 1938.
Young, Otis E. *The West of Philip St. George Cooke, 1809–1895*. Glendale, Calif., 1955.

INDEX

Index

Arthur, Pres. Chester A., 382
Articles of War, 63, 84, 85
Artillery, 11, 15–6, 24, 36 n8, 149, 183, 223, 230; described, 72–3; at Hayfield Fight, 124; in Modoc War, 201, 204; in Nez Percé War, 302–3, 311, 313, 354; in Sioux War of 1876, 252, 258, 273–4, 276–7; at Soldier Spring, 154; at Wagon Box Fight, 129; at Wounded Knee, 406–7
Artillery School, 44
Assinniboine Indians, 274, 285
Augur, Gen. Christopher C., 19, 34, 35, 106, 113–4, 120–3, 132–8, 148, 156, 209, 219–20, 241, 346, 411 n7
Austin, Tex., 166, 168

Babcock, Lt. Col. Orville E., 125 n4
Bad Route Creek (Mont.), 274
Baird, Lt. George W., 280, 313
Baja California (Mex.), 172
Baker, Maj. Eugene M., xiv, 191
Baldwin, Lt. Frank D., 226–7, 274
Ball, Capt. Edward, 279
Bands (military), 88
Banning, Rep. Henry B., 19, 61 *passim*, 398
Bannock Indians, 4, 5, 275, 308, 330–1, 332, 400; war with, 322–9, 397
Barncho (Modoc), 217 n42
Battles: Adobe Walls (Tex.), 213, 221; Bear Paw Mountain (Mont.), 285, 312–7; Beaver Creek (Kan.), 120, 149, 160 n21; Beechers Island (Colo.), 53, 147–8; Big Dry Wash (Ariz.), 376–7; Big Hole (Mont.), 16, 24, 50, 306–7, 316, 318; Birch Creek (Oreg.), 326–7; Camas Meadows (Ida.), 308–9, 318, 320 n12; Canyon Creek (Mont.), 310–11, 319; Cedar Springs (Ariz.), 375; Cibicu (Ariz.), 54, 372–4, 376, 377, 402; Clearwater (Ida.), 303–5, 306, 317; Dove Creek (Tex.), 166; Drexel Mission (S.D.), 408; Fetterman Disaster, 104–7, 109 n31, 111–5, 123, 189; Hat Creek (Neb.). *See* War Bonnet Creek; Hayfield Fight (Mont.), 71, 124, 128 n41; Hembrillo Canyon (N.M.), 361–2;

Horseshoe Canyon (N.M.), 375; Lava Beds (Calif.), 201–4; Little Bighorn (Mont.), 16, 17, 24, 25, 61, 67 n11, 70, 72, 116, 206, 258–62, 267, 271, 275, 281, 289, 291 n9, 398; Lost River (Calif.), 200–1; Lost Valley (Tex.), 213; McClellan Creek (Tex.), 212, 225; Marias (Mont.), xiv, 191; Milk Creek (Colo.), 336–8, 341; Muddy Creek (Mont.), 280, 281, 311; Palo Duro Canyon (Tex.), 226; Powder River (Mont.), 249–51, 262; Rattlesnake Springs (Tex.), 363; Remolino (Mex.), 347–50; Rosebud (Mont.), 255–6, 262, 275; Sand Creek (Colo.), 97, 111, 113, 114, 150, 152, 408; Sappa Creek (Kan.), 230; Silver Creek (Oreg.), 325, 327; Skull Cave (Ariz.), 197; Slim Buttes (S.D.), 270–1; Soldier Spring (Okla.), 154, 156, 158; Summit Springs (Colo.), 156–7; Thomas Disaster (Calif.), 204; Tinaja de las Palmas (Tex.), 363; Tres Castillos (Mex.), 364; Turret Peak (Ariz.), 197; Vinegar Hill (Ida.), 330–1; Wagon Box (Mont.), 71, 124–5, 129 n42; War Bonnet Creek (Neb.), 268; Washita (Okla.), 70, 150–3, 154, 156, 157, 409; White Bird Canyon (Ida.), 300–2, 305, 306; Wolf Mountains (Mont.), 276–7, 278; Wounded Knee Creek (S.D.), xiii, 25, 41 n79, 51, 406–8, 412 n17.
Bavispe River (Mex.), 379, 389–90
Beal, Merrill, 316
Bear Butte (S.D.), 244
Bear Paw Mountain (Mont.). *See* Battles
Bear River (Colo.), 336
Beaumont, Col. Eugene B., 349
Beauregard, Gen. P.G.T., 61
Beauvais, G.P., 126 n12
Beaver Creek (Kan.). *See* Battles
Beaver Creek (Mont.-N.D.), 287
Beecher, Lt. Frederick, 148
Beechers Island (Colo.). *See* Battles
Beede, Cyrus, 207
Belknap, Sec. War William W., 74, 193, 213, 229, 247–8, 346; im-

Jackson, Capt. James B., 200–1, 205, 303
Jefferson Barracks, Mo., 24
Jeffords, Thomas J., 194, 358
Jenness, Lt. John C., 124
Jenny, Walter P., 245
Jerome, Lt. Lovell H., 313
Jicarilla Apache Indians, 184 n12. *See also* Apache Indians
John Day River (Oreg.), 178, 326–7
John L. Stevens (steamer), 181
Johnson, Pres. Andrew, 10, 11, 113, 134, 136, 139 n5, 140 n14, 142, 167
Jones, Maj. Roger, 171
Jordan River (Oreg.), 324
Josanie (Apache), 383–4, 388
Joseph. *See* Chief Joseph
Josephy, Alvin, 316
Judge Advocate General, 36 n9
Judge Advocate General's Department, 11
Judith Basin (Mont.), 290
Juh (Apache), 358, 369–70, 375, 377, 380

Kake Indians, 182
Kamiah, Ida., 305
Kansas (State), 2, 3, 13, 53, 95, 97, 130, 131, 164, 207, 213, 219–20, 283, 314, 345; operations of 1867 in, 115–20; war of 1868–69 in, 143 *passim*
Kansas Pacific Railroad, 3
Kautz, Gen. August V., 25, 357–8, 372
Kaw Indians, 138
Kayitah (Apache), 388–90
Kaytennae (Apache), 369, 380–2, 385
Keim, DeB. Randolph, 82
Kelly, Luther F., 50, 313
Keogh, Capt. Myles W., 284, 291
Kickapoo Indians, 166, 286, 344–9
Kicking Bear (Sioux), 402–4, 408, 409
Kicking Bird (Kiowa), 115, 140 n16, 210, 211, 228, 235 n20
King, Capt. Charles, xiii, 66–7
King, Col. John H., 41 n89
King cartridge box, 75
Kinney, J.F., 126 n12
Kinney, Capt. Nathaniel C., 100
Kintpuash (Modoc). *See* Captain Jack
Kiowa Indians, 4, 5, 95, 160 n13, 169;

and Hancock campaign of 1867, 114 *passim*; and Medicine Lodge treaties, 133; Mexican raids, 344, 345, 349; in Plains warfare (1868–69), 141 *passim*; in Red River War, 221 *passim*; Texas raids, 35, 97, 115, 127 n18, 137, 144, 164, 207–14
Kiowa-Apache Indians, 94, 133, 160 n13
Kiowa-Comanche Agency and Reservation, 144, 207 *passim*
Klamath Indians, 178, 199, 326
Klamath Lake Indian Reservation, 178, 180, 199, 216 n30
Kodiak Island (Alaska), 181–2
Kotsoteka Comanche Indians, 144, 160 n13, 212, 229. *See also* Comanche Indians
Krag-Jorgensen rifle, 72
Kwahadi Comanche Indians, 154, 160 n13, 207, 209, 229. *See also* Comanche Indians

La Plata River (Colo.), 340, 341
Lake Guzman (Mex.), 184 n12
Lame Deer (Sioux), 254, 279–80
Lame Deer Agency (Mont.), 284
Lame White Man (Cheyenne), 254
Lane, Sen. Henry, 10
Lapwai Agency (Ida.), 298–9. *See also* Nez Percé Reservation
Lava Beds (Calif.). *See* Battles
Lawrence, Kan., 207
Lawton, Gen. Henry W., 18, 76, 225, 387–92
Lay, Capt. Richard C., 39 n55
Lazelle, Maj. Henry M., 281
Leavenworth, Kan., 1, 94. *See also* Fort Leavenworth
Leavenworth, Agent Jesse H., 115 *passim*, 144
Lebo, Capt. Thomas C., 387
Lemhi Reservation (Ida.), 322, 330–1
Lemhi River (Ida.), 307
Lerdo de Tejada, Pres. Sebastián, 347, 349, 351
Leuttwitz, Lt. Adolphus H. von, 271
Lincoln, Sec. War Robert T., 381
Linkville, Oreg., 216 n30
Lipan Indians, 164–6, 344, 347, 350 *passim*
Little Arkansas Treaties (1865), 95–7, 140 n11, 164

Medicine Arrows (Cheyenne), 155, 228

Medicine Lodge Creek (Kan.), 133–4, 148

Medicine Lodge Treaties, 133 *passim*, 143, 144, 164

Medicine Water (Cheyenne), 229, 233

Meeker, Josephine, 337–9

Meeker, Nathan C., 333–7, 341

Meeker, Mrs. Nathan C., 337–9, 343 n30

Meigs, Quartermaster Gen. Montgomery C., 73, 76

Merritt, Gen. Wesley, 17, 25, 268, 310, 337–9, 366 n26, 400, 411 n7

Mescalero Apache Indians, 356; flee reservation, 169; raids, 164–6, 174, 344–5, 347, 350; range, 184 n12; in Victorio War, 360–5. *See also* Apache Indians

Mexico, 76, 184 n12, 286; border friction with U.S., 344–56; Indian raids from, 164–6, 344 *passim*, 356 *passim*, 374 *passim*; Indian raids in, 164, 207, 344, 345–6. *See also* specific Mexican states

Miles, Capt. Evan, 306, 327

Miles, Agent John D., 207, 221

Miles, Gen. Nelson A., xiii, 18, 25, 34, 72–3, 322, 328–9, 400, 411 n7, 412 n13; and Apache campaign (1886), 386–93; characterized, 220, 289; evaluation of Sioux command, 288–90; in Ghost Dance troubles, 403–9; in Nez Percé War, 310–9, 321 n24; on Pope, 231; in Red River War, 220 *passim*; seeks preferment, 277–8, 286–7, 293 n21; and Sioux expedition of 1879, 287; in Sioux War of 1876, 54, 269–70, 272–81

Military Service Institution of the U.S., 44

Militia. *See* Volunteers

Milk Creek (Colo.). *See* Battles

Milk River (Mont.), 287, 289, 290, 312

Miller, Capt. Marcus P., 303–4, 306

Mills, Maj. Anson, 20, 75, 90, 255, 270

Milner, Moses, 50

Mimbres Apache Indians, 184 n12, 194, 359. *See also* Gila Apache Indians; Apache Indians

Miniconjou Sioux Indians, 95, 122, 123, 135, 236–7, 404 *passim*; in war of 1866, 100 *passim*; in Sioux War of 1876, 254 *passim*, 273 *passim*. *See also* Sioux Indians; Teton Sioux Indians

Minimic (Cheyenne), 229, 233

Minnesota (State), 94, 119, 121, 242

Mississippi River, 1, 93

Missoula, Mont., 306

Missouri (State), 13, 131

Missouri River, 2, 3, 93, 94, 97, 120–2, 132, 135, 236 *passim*, 272, 274 *passim*, 282, 286–8, 311–2, 314, 403

Moache Ute Indians, 332, 341. *See also* Ute Indians

Modoc Indians, 5, 34, 178, 229; war with, 198–207, 397

Mogollon Apache Indians, 184 n12, 194, 359. *See also* Apache; Gila Apache; Chiricahua Apache Indians

Mogollon Mountains (N.M.), 362

Mogollon Plateau (Ariz.), 171

Mogollon Rim (Ariz.), 196, 376

Mojave Indians, 184 n12, 370

Monclova Viejo, Mex., 354

Monida Pass (Ida.), 308

Montana (Territory), 2, 4, 14, 33, 40 n63, 46, 54, 65, 94, 95, 98, 100, 119–20, 126, 241, 402; defenses, 121–2; Nez Percé War in, 305–15; Sioux Wars in, 251 *passim*, 267 *passim*, 286–8

Montieth, Agent J.B., 299

Mooers, Surgeon John H., 148

Moore, Col. Horace L., 162 n37

Morgan, Mrs. Anna, 162 n37

Morrill, Sen. Lot, 4

Morrow, Maj. A.P., 360–1, 362, 365

Morton, Surgeon Samuel M., 109 n25

Mount Idaho, Ida., 300, 302

Mow-way (Comanche), 212, 225, 229

Moylan, Capt. Myles, 313

Muddy Creek (Mont.). *See* Battles

Mules (supply), with Crook, 48–9, 248–9, 268, 378 *passim*; with Custer, 258